THE BHAGAVAD-GĪTĀ

Mahabharata. Bhagavadgita. English.

THE BHAGAVAD-GĪTĀ

WITH A COMMENTARY
BASED ON THE ORIGINAL SOURCES

R. C. ZAEHNER

OXFORD UNIVERSITY PRESS
LONDON OXFORD NEW YORK

OXFORD UNIVERSITY PRESS

London Oxford New York
Glasgow Toronto Melbourne Wellington
Cape Town Ibadan Nairobi Dar es Salaam Lusaka Addis Ababa
Delhi Bombay Calcutta Madras Karachi Lahore Dacca
Kuala Lumpur Singapore Hong Kong Tokyo

First published by the Clarendon Press, 1969
First issued as an Oxford University Press paperback, 1973

This reprint, 1975

Printed in the United States of America

CONTENTS

ABBREVIATIONS

A.	*Aṅguttara Nikāya.*
BhG.	*Bhagavad-Gītā.*
BU.	*Bṛhadāraṇyaka* Upanishad.
ChU.	*Chāndogya* Upanishad.
D.	(i) *Dīgha Nikāya* (ii) (Paul) Deussen's translation of the Bhagavad-Gītā in *Vier philosophische Texte des Mahâbhâratam*, Leipzig, 1906.
Dhp.	*Dhammapada.*
E.	(Franklin) Edgerton, *The Bhagavad Gītā*, Harvard University Press, third printing, 1952.
H.	(W. Douglas P.) Hill, *The Bhagavadgītā*, Oxford University Press, 1953.
Iti.	*Itivuttaka.*
KaU.	*Kaṭha* Upanishad.
KauU.	*Kauṣītakī* Upanishad.
M.	*Majjhima Nikāya.*
MāU.	*Māṇḍūkya* Upanishad.
MaiU.	*Maitrī* Upanishad.
MBh.	*Mahābhārata.*
MuU.	*Muṇḍaka* Upanishad.
PU.	*Praśna* Upanishad.
R.	Rāmānuja.
Rām.	*Rāmāyaṇa.*
Rk.	(S.) Radhakrishnan, *The Bhagavadgītā*, London, 1948.
RV.	*Rig-Veda.*
S.	(i) *Saṁyutta Nikāya*, (ii) (Emile) Senart, *La Bhagavadgītā*, Paris, 1922.
Ś.	Śankara.
Sn.	*Suttanipāta.*
ŚU.	*Śvetāśvatara* Upanishad.
Ud.	*Udāna.*
Up.	Upanishad.

INTRODUCTION

DURING the last war we used to see notices everywhere asking if our journey was really necessary. In conscience we had often to admit that it was not. Today publishers might well ask authors: 'Is your *book* really necessary?' In the case of a new edition of the *Bhagavad-Gītā* they would seem to be doubly justified in asking such a question. What, then, is the justification of the present work?

As recently as 1944 the Harvard University Press published an edition of the Gītā by the late Professor Franklin Edgerton in two volumes[1] which some might think was all that was needed for the student and the general reader, for it contains the original Sanskrit with a literal translation on the opposite page, notes, an 'interpretation', and, for good measure, a reprint of Sir Edwin Arnold's well-known poetical rendering. This surely should be enough for anyone. Also in English there is W. Douglas P. Hill's admirable annotated translation (republished in 1953) with an even fuller introduction originally published by the Oxford University Press in 1928. Hill's translation, moreover, is very much more readable than Edgerton's which is so literal as sometimes to be barely comprehensible, and his notes again are fuller. In French there is an excellent, scholarly, and lucidly objective study by Etienne Lamotte (*Notes sur la Gītā*, Paris, Geuthner, 1929) who has indeed anticipated much that I have to say in this book.

These authors, unlike most commentators on the Gītā, were primarily interested in the actual content of the Gītā, not in what they thought that content ought to be. In this they seem to have been reacting both against the Indian tradition (both ancient and modern)[2] in which the individual commentator seeks to impose his own views on to the text, and against the German tendency initiated by Garbe and continued notably by Rudolf Otto which sought to establish an *Ur-Gītā*, an original Gītā, from which they

[1] This has now appeared as a paperback without the Sanskrit.

[2] The best-known modern translation of this sort is that of Sir Sarvapalli Radhakrishnan, London, Allen and Unwin, 1948. The Gītā has also been commented on by such illustrious figures as Mahatma Gandhi, Aurobindo Ghose, and Vinoba Bhave.

eliminated whatever they considered to be alien to the matter in hand as they (each in his own individual way) understood it. Hill, Edgerton, and Lamotte, on the other hand, were primarily interested in what the Gītā actually said, not in what others said it said or what they said it had in pristine times *not* said. This is very much my own approach too; but I have tried to go a little further. It was once fashionable to emphasize the various strands that go to make up the Gītā as we now have it, and to classify them as Sāṁkhya, Vedānta, or Bhakti as the case might be, thereby emphasizing the apparent incoherence of the poem. It therefore seemed to me that the only sound way of tackling the Gītā might be 'by putting as little as possible of oneself into it . . . to consider it as a whole that should be explained by itself and by the *milieu* out of which it grows',[1] to interpret from the parallel passages within itself and from similar passages to be found in the Upanishads which the author of the Gītā certainly knew. Further, the didactic portions of India's Great Epic, the *Mahābhārata* (though probably all of them are later than the Gītā) can sometimes be usefully adduced in clarification of its thought.

It was only after teaching the Gītā for a number of years that it appeared to me, with each re-reading, to be a far more unitary work than most modern scholars had been prepared to concede; and it was this realization that impelled me to write an edition of my own.

Since my election to the Spalding Professorship of Eastern Religions and Ethics at the University of Oxford in 1952, my principal interest (apart from the study of the great religions as such) has been in the phenomenon of mysticism. In my *Mysticim Sacred and Profane* (Clarendon Press, 1957) I tried to show that there are varieties of mystical experience just as there are varieties of religious experience in general. The great divide seemed to be between those types of mysticism which regarded love as being the central phenomenon of the whole experience and those which, disregarding love altogether, expressed themselves exclusively in terms either of unity or of the escape or 'liberation' from time, the phenomenal world, and all that conditions it. Very rarely, it seemed, did the two combine, for very few people among the mystics themselves apparently had had both experiences and witnessed to the distinction between the two. In that book I was

[1] Lamotte, op. cit., p. 127.

able to cite the Flemish mystic of the fourteenth century, Ruysbroeck, almost alone. Subsequently I discovered that the same distinction had been made by the Muslim mystics, Al-Junayd of Baghdad, Ibn Ṭufayl of Andalusia, and the Iranian, Najm al-Dīn Rāzī,[1] and, on the Hindu side, pre-eminently in the Bhagavad-Gītā. As I grew increasingly familiar with the text of this wonderful work, it became ever more insistently clear to me that here was a text the whole purpose of which seemed to me to demonstrate that love of a personal God, so far from being *only* a convenient preparation for the grand unitary experience of spiritual 'liberation' (the *mokṣa* or *mukti* of the Upanishads and the *vimutti* of the Buddhists), was also the crown of this experience itself which, without it, must remain imperfect. This point the modern commentators seemed almost entirely to have missed because, often unconsciously, they were conditioned by the most ancient and the most authoritative of the medieval commentaries, that of the founder of the extreme school of Vedāntin non-dualism, Śankara. Meanwhile the commentaries of the 'modified non-dualist' Rāmānuja, so much nearer in spirit to the Gītā, and of the dualist Madhva and his successors had largely fallen into neglect. The exception is Lamotte who writes: 'Contrary to what one might suppose, the return of the soul into *brahman* is not yet the final stage (*terme définitif*) or at least the exact expression of perfect deliverance. Krishna who has supplanted the *brahman* both in theodicy and in cosmology now surpasses it in eschatology too: it is union with Krishna, the Bhagavat, which is the ultimate and final stage of deliverance.'[2] Unfortunately, Lamotte's book is little read in the Anglo-Saxon world, and the publication of this edition is, then, designed to rectify the balance.

This, however, does not mean that I am simply trying to read my own interpretation of the mystical phenomenon into the Gītā as critics will doubtless not be slow to assert. Hence I have not followed the method of even so impartial and objective a scholar as Edgerton who reduced his notes to a minimum and offered his own 'interpretation' of the Gītā by rearranging it according to topic without unduly obtruding his own views. This I have done too, though I have tried to be as brief as I can in the introductory section.

[1] R. C. Zaehner, *Hindu and Muslim Mysticism*, London, Athlone Press, 1960.
[2] Lamotte, op. cit., p. 81.

In 'interpreting' the Gītā, as in interpreting any sacred text (or indeed any text) the danger is that the interpreter will quote all that is grist to his mill while failing to draw attention to what embarasses him in other parts of the text. The only complete answer to this is to produce an accurate translation, leaving it to the reader to interpret the book as best he can. This, however, is easier said than done for two reasons. First, many of the keywords of the Gītā are so ambivalent in meaning as to make such an 'accurate' translation impossible without either misrepresenting the original or failing to bring out the multiplicity of meaning these keywords may contain in any single instance. Secondly, most recent translations of the Gītā (particularly the more popular ones) have not been accurate at all, and by being both inaccurate and theologically biased, a very false view of what the Gītā actually says has been passed off on an unsuspecting public. In other words the public cannot actually know if the translation is accurate unless the author provides it with what seem to him to be sound reasons for thinking it is accurate. This being so, it seemed to be best to present the Gītā in three forms.

First, I offer what seems to me an accurate and (I hope) readable translation of the Gītā without the apparatus of notes. This is intended for such as wish to read it through in its 'raw' state without being reminded the whole time of the interconnexions between the parts or the origin of the various doctrines it propounds. This translation is substantially the same as I made in the new edition of the Everyman's Library *Hindu Scriptures*.

Secondly, there is the same text accompanied by the Sanskrit original in transliteration and very full notes; and this forms the bulk of the book. It has not been my concern in these notes to list the views and interpretations of either the ancient or the modern commentators (both Hill and Edgerton are adequate in this respect). As far as the ancient commentators (Śankara and Rāmānuja) are concerned, I have confined myself on the whole to their interpretation of individual words and phrases, since in their philosophical commentaries they almost invariably read their own philosophical and theological views into the text, however forced and incongruous this may turn out to be. The bulk of the commentary is rather drawn from the Gītā itself, from the Upanishads, and other relative texts like the *Sāṁkhya-kārikā*, the *Yoga-sūtras*, and the doctrinal portions of the *Mahābhārata*. In this way I have tried to illuminate one part of the Gītā by another. As a result it seems to show a coherence within the general frame of Hindu thinking that has not always been obvious before. Again, to judge from my own experience and that of others, I know full well that simply to quote a reference in order to elucidate a point is futile. In nine cases out of ten the reader cannot be bothered to look the reference up and the point is simply not made. Hence, when a point has seemed to me of sufficient importance, I have inserted the relevant quotation in full. This has the advantage for the reader of fixing any given passage into the general context in which it belongs. For a proper understanding of the Gītā this is essential.

Even so convinced a believer in the essential unity of the Gītā as myself, however, must concede that transitions from one topic to another are often disconcertingly abrupt.

Hence, *thirdly*, I have thought it worth while to add an appendix in which the main topics dealt with have been brought together. This will enable the critic who may think that in my theological introduction I have slurred over parts that are at variance with what I conceive to be the general trend of the Gītā, to spot the contradictions (if such they are) right away. Moreover, the grouping of cognate texts together in the appendix is intended to bring out the Gītā's teaching on the main subjects of which it treats.

THE GĪTĀ IN CONTEXT

As everyone knows, the Bhagavad-Gītā is an episode in India's Great Epic, the *Mahābhārata.* The main story of the *Mahābhārata* is the war between two branches of the Kaurava family—the Kauravas proper, that is, the hundred sons of Dhritarāshtra, led by the eldest brother, Duryodhana, on the one hand, and, on the other hand, their cousins, the Pāndavas or sons of Pāndu led by *their* eldest brother, Yudhishthira. Yudhishthira had been cheated out of his kingdom in a game of dice to which he had been challenged. He lost, and was thereby condemned to cede his share of the kingdom to Duryodhana while he and his four brothers had to go into exile for thirteen years, the last of which they had to spend in concealment. All this they did, but when Yudhishthira asked for his kingdom back, Duryodhana bluntly refused. Yudhishthira who was by nature a pacifist and had an instinctive loathing for war, reduced his demands to a mere five villages: still Duryodhana refused. As a final gesture Yudhishthira sent his friend, Krishna, son of Vasudeva, and head of a neighbouring clan, the Vrishnis, on an embassy in which Krishna was to make a final bid for peace.

Krishna, however, was not merely a local prince of no very great importance: he was God incarnate—the great God Vishnu who had taken on human flesh and blood 'for the protection of the good, for the destruction of evil-doers, for the setting up of the law of righteousness' (4. 8). This Duryodhana and everyone else knew, but even so when it came to choosing between Krishna's person and his army, Duryodhana chose the army, while Arjuna, Yudhishthira's younger brother and Krishna's bosom friend, chose Krishna alone. Duryodhana then, knowing full well that Krishna was God, rejected for the last time Yudhishthira's offer, thereby defying God Himself. Yudhishthira, having gone to the utmost limit to avoid war, now reluctantly gives in and the scene is now set for a battle that was to prove ferociously destructive. There is, however, a last-minute hitch: Arjuna's nerve fails him.

Arjuna had hitherto been of the war party, and Krishna who had volunteered to act as his charioteer is dumbfounded at his sudden volte-face. Of all people Arjuna, his boon-companion and comrade in arms, the hero who had wrestled with the great God Śiva as Jacob had wrestled with the angel of the Lord, the bravest of the brave and the soul of generosity—Arjuna flatly refuses to fight. This is the starting-point of the Bhagavad-Gītā, the 'Lord's Song', and the ostensible purpose of the Gītā is to persuade Arjuna to fight. True, throughout the poem this is never wholly lost sight of; but the bulk of the poem is not concerned with the respective merits of war and peace, but with the deepest things of man and God. No wonder, then, that German scholars have sought to dig out an original Gītā from under what they considered to be a mass of strictly irrelevant metaphysics. No wonder that others have tried to treat the Gītā as a separate poem that somehow or other got itself inserted into the fabric of the Great Epic from which for some reason it has never been extricated. And yet the very improbability of its setting should give us pause for reflection.

There is plenty of didactic matter in the *Mahābhārata*—almost the whole of books twelve and thirteen and much of books three and five, but in none of these is Krishna the teacher. Only in book fourteen does he condescend to teach Arjuna again—in the so-called *Anugītā* or 'Gītā Recapitulated' which, in fact, is no recapitulation at all for it omits all that teaching in the Gītā which, because it was new, was described by Krishna as being 'most mysterious'—the revelation of the love of God. This is no accident, for Arjuna had proved himself unworthy of receiving the divine mystery: in the heat of battle he had forgotten every word Krishna had said! In the *Anugītā* he is merely treated to a rehash of what his far more religious-minded brother had been told by the dying 'grandsire', Bhīshma, at enormous and wearisome length throughout those mammoth books twelve and thirteen of by far the longest epic in the world. Hence, it is fair to conclude that the Gītā was originally conceived of as an integral part of the Epic. It is spoken by the Lord incarnate at the most solemn moment of the whole enormous story, the moment to which everything else has been working up—the moment when a just retribution will overwhelm God's enemies.

Arjuna refuses to obey the divine command—and for the best of reasons: he will not fight a fratricidal war simply for love of power; he will not slay his own kith and kin among whom are many of his benefactors including his own beloved teacher, Drona. To convince him that he must Krishna is not content merely to use arguments already familiar to him—his caste-duty as a warrior for instance; he sees fit rather to reveal to him the structure of the universe as it really is and in which Arjuna is merely a pawn moved by the hand of an all-powerful God whose will no man or god can resist or thwart.

THE PHILOSOPHICAL BACKGROUND

As with almost every major religious text in India no firm date can be assigned to the Gītā. It seems certain, however, that it was written later than the 'classical' Upanishads with the possible exception of the *Maitrī* and that it is post-Buddhistic. One would probably not be going far wrong if one dated it at some time between the fifth and second centuries B.C. From the contents of the Gītā itself it is clear that both the principal teachings of the Upanishads and of early Buddhism were familiar as was the dualistic teaching commonly called *Sāṁkhya* which was later to receive its definitive form in the *Sāṁkhya-kārikā* of Iśvarakrishna.

Of the native commentators on the Gītā it is Rāmānuja who probably comes nearest to the mind of the author of the Gītā. His philosophy is known as *viśiṣṭādvaita* usually translated as 'qualified monism'. In his commentary on the Gītā as elsewhere he is concerned with establishing the absolute supremacy of the personal God (Krishna) not only over the phenomenal world but also over the impersonal Absolute, Brahman. In this he reacts against the absolute monism of Śankara for whom Reality, Brahman, was unfractionably One, all diversity and multiplicity being ultimately an illusory appearance. This world of illusory appearance (*māyā* or *prakṛti*) includes everything that is in any way conditioned by time, space, or causation: its characteristic feature is 'action' (*karma*) which is the principle of change. It must then follow that God Himself, in so far as he is an agent and involved in the affairs of this world, is *from the point of view of absolute reality*, not fully real. Real is Brahman only, and Brahman is One. This, according to Śankara, is not just a metaphysical statement but a fact, or rather *the* fact of mystical experience. When the mystic says, 'I am Brahman' (BU. 1. 4. 10), he is speaking the literal and only truth: the source and ground of the whole universe of appearance is *identical* with the inmost essence of man: there *is* nothing else. All that appears to be 'other' is ultimately a distortion of the truth. As the *Chāndogya* Upanishad (6. 1. 4) puts it: 'Just as all that is made up of clay can be known by one lump of clay—its modifications are verbalizations, [mere] names—the reality is just "clayness",' so is what IS, as opposed to what appears, just Brahman, and 'that you [and I] are' (ibid. 6. 8. 7 ff.). There is an absolute identity, then, between the human soul in its timeless depth and the 'godhead', Brahman, which is the One Real beneath all appearance including the personal God.

This is Śankara's interpretation of the teaching of the Upanishads, and in many passages in those not very consistent books it is quite legitimate. If such an interpretation is true, then it must mean the death-blow to theism of any sort. This Rāmānuja saw very clearly and, in his philosophy which owes more to the Gītā than to any other sacred text, he tries to turn the tables on his adversary and to rehabilitate God even above the Absolute.

According to Rāmānuja the universe can be divided into two segments (and in this he follows the Sāṁkhya): matter and spirit. Matter or material Nature is dynamic (as in Marx) and includes everything that is subject to change; and this comprises not only what we normally understand by matter but also the senses, mind, ego, and what we in the West would call soul, that is the responsible element in man which reaps the consequences of his good and evil deeds. Spirit (*puruṣa*) is not, as in the non-dualist Vedānta, just one world-soul, one 'Self' that is identical in all contingent beings; it is a plurality of 'spiritual monads' or 'selves' which attach themselves to psychosomatic organisms, indwell them for so long as they are 'bound' in the process of transmigration, but which are ultimately 'released' or 'liberated' from matter to resume their separate eternal existence in an *ambiance* that is conditioned by neither space nor time nor change. These two, the world of change and the world of changeless eternal beings, constitute the 'body' of the Lord. The Lord—God—is the 'soul' or 'self' of this body just as the embodied 'self' is the 'soul' of each human individual: but whereas the embodied self is the eternal and changeless centre of a changing psychosomatic organism, God is the eternal centre of both the active universe of matter *and* the totality of immortal and timeless 'spirits' or 'selves': he is 'the divine Person who is beyond the beyond', as the *Mundaka* Upanishad (3. 2. 8) puts it. If, as most of the Upanishads teach, Brahman is the 'All'—both the sum-total of eternal beings and the source and ground of all that comes to be and passes away, then God, the divine 'Person', is not only the 'All' but beyond the All: He is an eternity beyond both the manifold eternals (individual selves) and of course far beyond the ever-changing world of matter. In the words of the *Śvetāśvatara* Upanishad (5. 1) which of all the Upanishads stands nearest to the Gītā:

> In the imperishable, infinite city of Brahman[1]
> Two things there are—
> Wisdom and unwisdom, hidden, established there:
> Perishable is unwisdom, but wisdom is immortal:
> Who over wisdom and unwisdom rules, He is Another.

This, according to Rāmānuja, is the principal theme of the Gītā, and in this, I think, he is absolutely right.

It is now time to consider the main concepts of the Gītā in some detail.

[1] Or in the better attested reading: 'In the imperishable, infinite supreme Brahman . . .'.

THE TEACHING OF THE GĪTĀ

A. THE HUMAN BEING

1. *The Individual Self*

As befits its context within the Great Epic the first topic that Krishna broaches in his dialogue with Arjuna is the nature of the 'embodied self', a topic that is immediately relevant since Arjuna, if he is to fight at all, will not only be risking his own life but will also inevitably be depriving others of theirs. The first thing, then, that Krishna establishes is the immortality of the embodied self. This self is immortal in two senses: as a timeless monad, a 'minute part' of God Himself (15. 7) 'it is never born nor dies, ... nor will it ever come to be again: unborn, eternal, everlasting is it—primeval' (2. 20). Since it has its being outside time, to speak of its birth or death is meaningless. And yet in so far as it does in fact become linked with an individual psychosomatic organism 'it is constantly [re-]born and constantly [re-]dies' (2. 26). In itself it is static, timeless, eternal: in its transmigrations from body to body it is indissolubly connected with a given human personality. Salvation, then, consists in the final dissociation of the eternal monad from the ultimately material personality to which it is bound: it is the 'unlinking of the link with suffering and pain' (6. 23). This phrase has a notably Buddhistic ring, and the first descriptions of the process of liberation of the self from matter which appear at the end of Chapter II are thoroughly Buddhistic. All trace of being an ego, all trace of possessing anything at all must be ruthlessly swept away if the true self is to return to its spiritual home—'Nirvāna which is Brahman too' (2. 72). Here the Buddhist idea of the 'liberation' of the self is accepted, and Buddhist terminology is used.

The Buddhists, however, were so careful not to define what the self was that it has often been maintained that they denied the existence of a self altogether. The Gītā certainly does not do this. On the contrary the 'self-in-itself' is a 'minute part' of God, yet while involved in the transmigratory process it is so closely identified with a given personality that it can be 'fooled' (3. 40) and 'doubt' (4. 40). The self can only be realized in its timeless immortality by intense concentration, by a process of 'integration' (*yoga*), and by complete detachment from the outside world. This state of complete detachment in which the self returns to its natural state where birth and death are a sheer impossibility and which is the 'fixed, still state of Brahman' (2. 72) and in which 'one sees the self in self and finds content therein' (6. 20)—this state of still, static, timeless bliss is felt to be the 'utmost joy' (6. 21) because it is beyond time and presumably beyond death and all suffering since it means actually to *be* the timeless Brahman (5. 24). Before the Gītā, particularly in Buddhist circles, this state was generally regarded as being something permanent, but in the Gītā even this 'inmost self', the deepest root of the human personality, can be 'shaken' when confronted with the vision of the personal God (11. 24). This is something quite new and needs to be pointed out.

In itself the self is both static and passive: it cannot act nor can it initiate action. Action is the sphere of material Nature, and the self can only be said to act in so far as it is still conjoined to a psychosomatic organism (5. 13–15); its sole independent function is to experience (13. 20), and it is because it 'attaches itself to these (psychosomatic elements) [that] it comes to birth in good and evil wombs' (13. 21). Yet it would be a mistake to suppose that there is an *absolute* distinction between the self and the psychosomatic organism to which it is attached, for the self is the centre of the whole personality, its principle of unity. Though inactive itself it acts as a magnet to the principal faculties of the whole human personality. It exercises its magnetism most strongly on what is most akin to it, the 'soul' or contemplative intellect (*buddhi*), whereas its power of attraction is much less powerful in the mind or discursive intellect (*manas*) and weakest of all in the senses in which 'passion and hate are seated', those 'brigands on the road' (3. 34).

In the Gītā self-realization which means the felt experience of the self as a timeless monad and particle of God, is the result of the absorption of all the powers of the human personality into the self: they are not destroyed but fused into a unity. This process is called *yoga* which, in these contexts, I have translated as 'integration'. That this is what it means rather than 'discipline', any attentive reader of Chapters V and VI will readily understand. Here we must be content to mention two similes used very early in the work to illustrate that 'detachment' is to be interpreted as the detachment of the senses from their proper objects only to be absorbed into the centre of the personality—the self: the process is one of concentration, not destruction. 'When [a man] draws in on every side his senses from their proper objects as a tortoise [might draw in] its limbs—firm-stablished is the wisdom of such a man' (2. 58). And again: 'As the waters flow into the sea, full-filled, whose ground remains unmoved, so too do all desires flow into [the heart of] man: and such a man wins peace—not the desirer of desires' (2. 70). Such peace which is achieved by the fusion of all the faculties of the human personality into the timeless self is the culminating point of the process of integration. In it one reaches Brahman (5. 6), 'becomes Brahman and draws nigh to the Nirvāna that is Brahman too' (5. 24); and because Brahman is changeless being in all things, 'devoid of imperfection and ever the same' (5. 19), so does the self, because it has absorbed into itself all the multiplicity of its single personality, now see itself expanded into what seems to be a state of being that comprises the whole universe both in its unity and its multiplicity. 'Well versed in spiritual exercise (*yoga*), his self made pure, his self and senses quelled, his self become the [very] self of every contingent being, though working still he is not defiled' (5. 7), for 'he sees the self in all beings standing, all beings in the self' (6. 29). This means that the integrated man experiences a quite indescribable freedom of the spirit where there is no more time or space, no causation, and no action. Out of the body he feels as free as the wind, or a cloud, or thunder and lightning (ChU. 8. 12. 2): 'in all the worlds (and in every state of being) freedom of movement is his' (ibid. 7. 25. 2).

Such is the state of the integrated self. While yet conditioned by the phenomenal world, however, the self is at war with itself, that is to say, if the timeless self and its ally soul (*buddhi*) fail to restrain the discursive intellect, and that in its turn fails to curb the senses, then there is bound to be a regression: and so it can be said:

> Raise self by self, let not the self droop down; for self's friend is self indeed, so too is self self's enemy. Self is the friend to the self of him whose self is by the self subdued; but for the man bereft of self self will act as an enemy indeed (6. 5–6).

Hence the self must be not only integrated but purified of all sense of being a responsible ego: though the whole human personality is now centred on it, it must recognize that in itself it is merely a spectator at a play enacted by the body, mind, soul, and senses. This means spiritual freedom, the reverse is bondage:

With body, mind, soul, and senses alone and isolated [from the self] do integrated men engage in action renouncing attachment for the cleansing of the self. The integrated man, renouncing the fruit of works, gains an abiding peace: the man not integrated, whose works are prompted by desire, being attached to fruits, is bound (5. 11–12).

And this brings us to the bondage which matter or material Nature brings upon the self.

11. *Material Nature: the Bondage of the Spirit*

(*a*) *The Unmanifest*

As we have seen, in the Sāṁkhya system matter and spirit are totally distinct and independent principles. In the Gītā this is not true, for God is the source of both. 'Spirits' or 'selves' are said to be 'minute parts' of Him (15. 7) and, like Him, have their essential being in eternity, not in time. Matter or material Nature (*prakṛti*, *svabhāva*) is no more independent of Him than are individual selves. Nature, not the self, is the source of all change: 'Neither agency nor worldly works does [the body's] lord engender, nor yet the bond that work to fruit conjoins: it is inherent Nature that initiates the action' (5. 14). Of its very nature it is a flux that throws up individuals only to destroy them and reabsorb them again: '[A world of] moving and unmoving things material Nature brings to birth while I (Krishna) look on and supervise: this is the cause [and this the means] by which the world revolves' (9. 10). Nature has no beginning and no end: it is characterized by change and quality; it is 'the cause of cause, effect, and agency' (13. 19–20). It combines with 'selves' to form the world as we know it (13. 26); but in this combination it is Nature alone 'which in every way does work and acts' (13. 29).

The action of Nature is cyclic. When at rest it is called the 'Unmanifest'. When it starts to move, diversity appears—the whole process being likened to a day and night of the creator-god, Brahmā:

At the day's dawning all things manifest spring forth from the Unmanifest; and then at nightfall they dissolve [again] in that same thing called 'Unmanifest'. Yes, this whole host of beings comes ever anew to be; at fall of night it dissolves away all helpless; at dawn of day it rises up again (8. 18–19).

When Nature moves from the 'Unmanifest' into a 'manifest' state of being, it differentiates itself into the five gross elements, the senses and their objects, mind, soul (*buddhi*), and ego (7. 4: 13. 5–6). But in the Gītā Nature is not independent: it belongs to Krishna, the personal God. Moreover, 'Nature' as defined above and which corresponds more or less exactly to the Sāṁkhya categories, is only Krishna's *lower* Nature. There is a higher Nature 'developed into life by which this world is kept in being' (7. 5). This would seem to refer to what Teilhard de Chardin calls the 'biosphere', the world of conscious beings which are composites, as we have seen, of spirit and matter—the individual human selves 'bound' in the material world. This union of spirit and matter is not fortuitous but willed by God Himself: 'Subduing my own material Nature ever again I emanate this whole mighty host of beings—powerless themselves, from Nature comes the power' (9. 8). Nature is the female principle, Krishna the male. 'Great Brahman (i.e. Nature) is to Me a womb, in it I plant the seed: from this derives the origin of all contingent beings. In whatever womb whatever form arises and grows together, of [all] those [forms] great Brahman is the womb, I the father, giver of the seed' (14. 3–4).

The use of the words 'great Brahman' to mean material Nature cannot detain us here: they will be discussed under the heading 'Brahman' (below, p. 37). This passage, however, explains how individual selves can be said to be 'minute parts' of God. They are quite literally the σπερματικοὶ λόγοι of the Neo-Platonists, 'seminal words' made flesh in the womb of Nature, spiritual monads caught up in matter. But matter binds; and, like any mother, is unwilling to let her son go free: hence she does all she can to deceive him: as such she is *māyā* which, at this stage of the language, means both 'creative power' and 'deceit'. *Māyā is* Nature, and Nature is *māyā*: 'for [all] this [Nature] is my creative power (*māyā*) . . . hard to transcend. Whoso shall put his trust in Me alone', says Krishna, 'shall pass beyond this [my] uncanny power (*māyā*)' (7. 14–15). Material Nature blinds the self to its own true origin and home, but it is none the less part and parcel of God Himself, his female side which is none the less inseparably his, for as in the *Śvetāśvatara* Upanishad (6. 16) God is the 'cause of the round of birth and death, [cause of] deliverance, [cause of our] sojourn here and [our] imprisonment'.

In the individual human being too it is Nature, not the self, that acts throughout the whole transmigratory process. So, one's character in the present life is conditioned by all one has done in lives lived long ago. 'As is a man's own nature, so must he act, however wise he be. [All] creatures follow Nature: what will repression do?' (3. 33). What indeed, for 'it is inherent Nature that initiates the action' (5. 14). Man is not really a free agent, for whatever you may resolve to do, your nature which is not inherited from your parents but from your former lives, 'will constrain you. You are bound by your own works which spring from your own nature; [for] what, deluded, you would not do, you will do perforce' (18. 59–60).

(*b*) *The Three Constituents of Nature*

'Every man is powerless and made to work by the constituents born of Nature' (3. 5). Thus are we warned at the beginning of the third chapter. What are these constituents? The word I have translated 'constituent' literally means 'strand', and the three constituents are the three strands that combine to make up the rope which is material Nature: they are the very stuff of which matter or Nature is made, and 'there is no existent thing in heaven or earth nor yet among the gods which is or ever could be free from these three constituents from Nature sprung' (18. 40). In Sanskrit these three constituents are called *sattva*, *rajas*, and *tamas*; 'goodness' or 'purity', 'passion' or 'energy', and 'darkness', 'dullness', or 'sloth'. These 'constituents' are quite basic to the Sāṁkhya system, but their nature and the mode of their manifestation are more clearly, more exhaustively, and more illuminatingly described in the Gītā than almost anywhere else. We first hear of these strange strands in one of the most enigmatic hymns of the *Atharva-Veda* (10. 8. 43):

> A lotus with nine gates[1] enveloped by three strands,—
> In it is a being strange, possessed of self:
> That [it is that] knowers of Brahman know.

The idea again seems to be present in *Chāndogya* Upanishad 6. 4. 1 ff. where all contingent being is apportioned between fire, water, and food (solid matter) which represent respectively the colours red, white, and black. Everything in the phenomenal world

[1] i.e. the body.

is reducible to these three basic qualities. The 'red' of the *Chāndogya* corresponds to the 'passion' or 'energy' of the Gītā and the Sāṁkhya, the white to 'goodness' or 'purity', and the black to 'darkness', 'dullness', or 'sloth'. Goodness tends to the release of the self from matter, Passion is instinct with purposeful activity, whereas Darkness induces torpor, sloth, and deadly inactivity. How the three work in all the spheres of life the Gītā tells at length in 14. 5–19, 17. 1–22, and 18. 7–39. Their salient characteristics, however, are listed in 14. 5–9:

Goodness—Passion—Darkness: these are the constituents from Nature sprung that bind the embodied [self] in the body though [the self itself] is changeless. Among these Goodness, being immaculate, knowing no sickness, dispenses light, [and yet] it binds by [causing the self] to cling to wisdom and to joy. Passion is instinct with desire, this know. From craving and attachment it wells up. It binds the embodied [self] by [causing it] to cling to works. But from ignorance is Darkness born: mark this well. All embodied [selves] it leads astray. With fecklessness and sloth and sleepiness it binds. Goodness causes [a man] to cling to joy, Passion to works; but Darkness, stifling wisdom, attaches to fecklessness.

Since the three constituents are the very stuff of Nature which is at the same time God's uncanny power so quick to deceive, they must in the last analysis (like everything else) derive from God. And so Krishna says: 'Know too that [all] states of being whether they be of Goodness, Passion, or Darkness proceed from Me; but I am not in them, they are in Me. By these three states of being inhering in the constituents this whole universe is led astray and does not understand that I am far beyond them and that I neither change nor pass away. For [all] this is my creative (and deceptive) power (*māyā*), composed of the constituents, divine, hard to transcend' (7. 12–14). Once again God's creative activity is seen primarily as a veil between the individual self and the divine essence.

(*c*) (i) Karma—*Works—Action*

'By these three states of being inhering in the constituents this whole universe is led astray': and God is the source of the constituents. The constituents are, however, the source of all activity. This point is made very clear as early as 3. 27–28:

It is material Nature's [three] constituents that do all works wherever [works are done]; [but] he whose self is by the ego fooled thinks, 'It is I who do.' But he who knows how constituents and works are parcelled out in categories, seeing things as they are, thinks thus: 'Constituents on constituents act,' [and thus thinking] remains unattached.

Yet so long as a man is in this world he is swayed by the constituents and is therefore bound to act if only for the purpose of maintaining life (3. 8), and as he acts so will he affect his future births. 'As is a man's own nature, so must he act, however wise he be. [All] creatures follow Nature: what will repression do?' (3. 33.) Since, then, a man is bound to act, and since all action 'binds'—since 'this world [itself] is bound by bonds of work' (3. 9)—how is he ever to win liberation from the bonds of work and therefore from rebirth—how is he to win that spiritual freedom which both the Buddhists and the Upanishads regarded as being the highest goal? The short and sufficient answer is: 'By detachment.' Man must be like God not only in his eternal rest but also in his selfless activity. God established human society and laid down the rules by which man should live (4. 13), and He therefore expects man to co-operate with Him in promoting the welfare of the world (3. 25). God has set the wheel of phenomenal existence in motion and 'whoso fails to match his turning [with the turning of the wheel], living an evil life, the senses his pleasure-ground, lives out his life in vain' (3. 16). 'There is nothing that [God] need do nor anything unattained that [He] need gain, yet work [is the element] in which [He] moves' (3. 22); but works can never affect Him nor has He any yearning for their fruits (4. 14). If a man really understands this, he will imitate God in this and do his duty in a totally detached spirit (3. 25). The perfected man takes pleasure in self alone—he has reached that 'fixed, still state of Brahman' (2. 72) which is beyond all temporal things, beyond all works, whether they be good or evil (2. 50)—hence there is nothing he *needs* to do, just as God needs to do nothing. 'He has no interest in works done or works undone on earth—no [interest] in all contingent beings: on such interest he does not depend' (3. 17–18). But how many such perfected men are to be found in this 'impermanent and joyless world' (9. 33)? Precious few. Hence, since the vast majority of mankind act out of self-interest and would only lapse into a brutish inactivity if their betters were seen to opt out of the world, the enlightened man should set an example of virtuous action, though always remaining inwardly detached from what he is doing. As Krishna tartly says: 'Let not a wise man split the soul of witless men attached to work: let him encourage all [manner of] works, himself though busy, acting as an integrated man' (3. 26).

To contrast action and inactivity, the performance of work and its renunciation, is to create an unreal dilemma; for if you act without having any interest or care for the result of what you do, you have already renounced. It is not the deed itself, but the ultimately selfish motive behind the deed that must be renounced. As the *Íśā* Upanishad succinctly puts it: 'Abandon, and then enjoy.' Work should be done *as if* you were doing nothing at all. 'The man who sees worklessness in work [itself], and work in worklessness, is wise among his fellows, integrated, performing every work' (4. 18). In other words the active life even of a warrior is no bar to sustained contemplation so long as all interest in the results has been suppressed. 'Stand fast in Yoga, surrendering attachment', Krishna tells his friend: 'in success and failure be the same and then get busy with your works. Yoga means "sameness and indifference"' (2. 48). But it also means 'skill in [performing] works' (2. 50). There is no contradiction here, for the truly perfected man resembles God both in his unutterable tranquillity and in his spontaneous activity. Through the constituents God alone is the real agent; and so 'by dedicating the work that is proper [to his caste] to Him who is the source of the activity of all beings, by whom this whole universe was spun, a man attains perfection and success' (18. 46). Not to do this is to court disaster, for 'you are bound by your own works which spring from your own nature, [and] what, deluded, you would not do, you will do perforce' (18. 60).

Karma (works, action) is constantly contrasted with *jñāna* (wisdom, knowledge), the latter word meaning, like the Greek *gnosis* and the Arabic *maʿrifa*, not knowledge as normally understood but the intuitive apperception of ultimate Reality beyond space and time. Wisdom is thus both the ultimate goal of works and at the same time abolishes them. 'When all a man's emprises are free from desire [for fruit] and motive, his works burnt up in wisdom's fire, then wise men call him learned (4. 19). . . . He works for sacrifice [alone], and all the work [he ever did] entirely melts away' (4. 23). Work should be regarded as essentially a sacrifice, but unlike the routine sacrifices to the gods which are designed to produce material benefits, this sacrifice is a true sacrifice of the human will and the goal of it is to have done once for all with the *bondage* that purposeful work entails. Hence all works performed in sacrifice 'in wisdom find their consummation' (4. 33). It is said that 'as a kindled fire reduces its fuel to ashes, so does the fire of wisdom reduce all works to ashes' (4. 37)—this because wisdom supersedes works performed as sacrifice, the latter being the means, the former the end. 'For the silent sage who would climb [the ladder of] spiritual exercise works are said to be the means; but for that same [sage] who has reached the state of integration they say quiescence is the means' (6. 3).

To sum up then: action of its very nature binds. Therefore detach yourself from it. Go on doing what is God's will for you to do, but accept failure as gladly as you would welcome success, indifferent always to the result. Works are only yours on loan: they in no sense belong to you. Perform them, then, in a spirit of sacrifice: return them to God to whom they really belong. Only so will you achieve that state from which, being beyond time, there is no return. In this state you will have passed beyond good and evil, for 'a man who has reached a state where there is no sense of "I", whose soul is undefiled—were he to slaughter [all] these worlds—slays nothing. He is not bound' (18. 17).

(*c*) (ii) *Sacrifice*

The Vedic sacrifices to the gods were designed to bring their own reward. Man sustains the gods so that they may sustain him in return (3. 11). This, as the *Muṇḍaka* Upanishad (1. 2. 7–10) had already seen, was a rather sordid commerce and did not in any case lead to immortality. The practitioners of *this* sacrifice were 'self-wise, puffed up with learning, passing their days in the midst of ignorance. They wander round, the fools, doing themselves much hurt, like blind men guided by the blind' (ibid. 1. 2. 8).

In a very special sense the sacrifice *is* Brahman: 'the offering is Brahman, Brahman the [sacrificial] ghee offered by Brahman in Brahman's fire: who sinks himself in this [sacrificial] act which is Brahman, to Brahman must he thereby go' (4. 24). Brahman, then, is the sacrifice, the oblation, and the priest who offers up the oblation: but It is not the *object* of sacrifice. This is the personal

God, Krishna alone who is 'recipient and Lord of all sacrifices' (9. 24), though like Brahman all of whose attributes He takes on, He is also the sacrifice itself, the sacred formula, the fire, and the sacrificial ghee offered in the fire (9. 16).

Sacrifice itself is said to derive from works (3. 14), and works, as we have seen, should be performed as sacrifice: only so can the bondage inherent in them be destroyed. Moreover, sacrifice understood in this sense is a sure way to release. There are a great many 'interior' sacrifices too (4. 26 ff.) all 'spread out athwart the mouth of Brahman' and the man who performs them 'comes to primeval Brahman' (4. 31–32). The 'mouth of Brahman', probably meaning the sacrificial fire, is, it seems, the gateway which both joins and separates Brahman conceived of as the materials of the sacrifice and the 'fixed, still state of Brahman' which is synonymous with liberation. As with works in general sacrifice can only lead to liberation if it is done in a spirit of complete detachment and because it has been ordained by God:

> The sacrifice approved by [sacred] ordinance and offered up by men who would not taste its fruits, who concentrate their minds on this [alone]: 'In sacrifice lies duty:' [such sacrifice] belongs to Goodness (17. 11).

Once again the message is: 'Detach yourself from all you do whether sacred or profane even if it is prescribed by religion and very good.'

Along with sacrifice works of penance and the giving of alms are duties incumbent on all. '[Works of] sacrifice, the gift of alms, and works of penance are not to be surrendered; these must certainly be done: it is sacrifice, alms-giving, and ascetic practice that purify the wise. But even these works should be done [in a spirit of self-surrender], for [all] attachment [to what you do] and [all] the fruits [of what you do] must be surrendered' (18. 5–6). This, Krishna says, is his 'last decisive word'.

(*c*) (iii) *Works appropriate to the Four Social Classes*

Krishna claims to be author of the moral law (14. 27), and an integral part of this is the system of the four social classes—Brāhmans, princely warriors, peasants and artisans, and serfs. This fourfold ordering of society He claims to have 'generated'

Himself (4. 13). In his moral teaching, then, the incarnate God innovates nothing: He merely conserves what had been corrupted by time (4. 7). One of the reasons advanced for Arjuna's going to war with his cousins is his duty as a member of the warrior class (2. 31): to stray from class or caste duty is deadly. 'Better one's own duty [to perform], though void of merit, than to do another's well: better to die within [the sphere of] one's own duty: perilous is the duty of other men' (3. 35: cf. 18. 47). 'Never should a man give up the work to which he is born, defective though it be: for every enterprise is choked by defects, as fire by smoke' (18. 48).

Certain virtues inhere in the four classes: they are there by nature. That they frequently are not was a matter that caused Arjuna's elder brother, the righteous Yudhishthira, much heart-searching. The Gītā, however, ignores this issue. Thus the Brāhman is characterized by calm, self-restraint, ascetic practice, purity, long-suffering, uprightness, wisdom, and religious faith; the warrior by courage, ardour, endurance, skill, unwillingness to flee in battle, generosity, and a noble pride. The peasants and artisans must engage in agriculture, animal husbandry, and trade, while the serfs have no other duty than to serve others (18. 42–44). Man must do his caste duty and enjoy it, but even so he must detach himself from it by dedicating it to God 'who is the source of the activity of all beings' (18. 46); only so can he win perfection. The social system itself, then, is ordained by God; and man, in following the rules laid down by Him, acknowledges Him as their author and offers them back to Him in sacrifice.

(*d*) *The Human Psyche*

(i) *Mind and Senses*

The human psyche consists of 'soul', mind, ego, and the five senses. All these are evolutes from material Nature: they are not the self. *Yoga* or 'integration' means bringing all the faculties of the psyche under the control of the self. Curiously enough the Gītā has very little to say about the 'ego' except that it must be eliminated. It is a false centre of the personality in so far as it thinks it acts (3. 27: 18. 59): it does nothing of the sort, as we have seen, for it is the constituents of Nature which are alone responsible for action under God's supervision (above, pp. 15–17).

Of the other components of the human psyche it is the soul which stands nearest to the self: by nature it looks towards the self. At the other end stand the senses which look outward to their proper objects—sight to visual forms, hearing to sound, and so on. In the middle stands the mind—*sensus communis* and discursive thought—which is ambivalent, looking in whichever direction exerts the more powerful attraction. The beginning of the process of integration, then, is to detach the senses from their proper objects, for 'hither and thither the senses rove, and when the mind is attuned to them, it sweeps away [whatever of] wisdom a man may possess, as the wind [sweeps away] a ship on the water' (2. 67). So the senses must be curbed (2. 61), 'subdued to self and disjoined from passion and hate' (2. 64), that ubiquitous pair of opposites which indwells them as its natural habitat (3. 34). It is the mind that should control the senses (3. 7: 6. 24), for the mind is more exalted than they (3. 42); yet the mind itself is fickle and difficult to curb as the wind (6. 34); so it too must be controlled by the soul and brought into subjection to the self (6. 25), for integration means the subjection of all the factors of the human personality to the self—of senses to mind, mind to soul, and soul to self.

(*d*) (ii) *The Soul* (Buddhi)

Buddhi is the highest faculty in man's material nature, for in the Gītā as in Marxism man's psychological faculties, even the highest of them, are rooted in matter. Yet there is something ambivalent about *buddhi* in the Gītā: it seems to stand on the brink between the world of pure spirit (the self) and man's physical and psychic nature. According to the Gītā's own definition *buddhi* corresponds more or less exactly to what we in the West call 'soul', since it is not only intellect but also will. 'The essence of the soul is will and it is really single, but many-branched and infinite are the souls of men devoid of will' (2. 41). Unlike the self the soul, exalted though it is, is not exempt from the onslaught of the passions, and if it is corrupted the self will itself be fooled (3. 40). So too the soul is not of its nature unconcerned with works (5. 11) because it is subject to the play of the three constituents of material Nature, and it can even be 'destroyed' (2. 63). In the Sāṁkhya system and in much of the didactic portions of the *Mahābhārata* there is a preponderance of the constituent 'Goodness' in the soul, and the two are sometimes identified, but this does not seem to be so in the Gītā. The soul is *naturally* unitive—it is single and its function is to integrate the whole personality into the immortal self, but it can be corrupted and dissipated by the senses acting through the mind, and this is perdition (2. 63). Hence any one of the three constituents may predominate in the soul. If Goodness predominates, then the soul, because it discriminates correctly between spirit and matter and because it sees that liberation into spirit, into the self, is the only true salvation, remains unitive; but if either of the other constituents predominates, then it will be led astray by wrong views (18. 30–32).

The soul, whether integrated or not, represents the whole personality and it is the subject that transmigrates (6. 43), but of all the faculties it is the only one that is capable of grasping and apprehending the self in its timeless glory. 'When thought by spiritual exercise is checked and comes to rest, and when of [one]self one sees the self in self and finds content therein, that is the utmost joy which transcends [all things of] sense and which soul [alone] can grasp' (6. 20–21). Soul too must control the mind as the mind controls the senses (6. 25–26), for it is the organ of integration (2. 39 ff.), and by integration a man becomes Brahman and, having become Brahman, he comes to God Himself (18. 49–54).

The soul, then, as the organ of integration, is that which brings the whole human personality into subjection to the self: its true function is to spiritualize matter, for it is ideally the bridge between spirit and matter rather like the sacrificial fire, the mouth of Brahman, which is the bridge between Brahman understood as the sacrifice and Brahman understood as timeless being.

III. *Heaven and Hell*

Heaven and hell are temporary states and heaven therefore never appears as man's final goal: it can only be a prelude to a better incarnation which will bring a man nearer to final liberation (6. 41). Vedic religion was, according to the Gītā, only concerned with securing for man the temporary joys of paradise (2. 45: 9. 20–21): hence its inadequacy.

It is usually alleged that hell in Hinduism is, like heaven, a temporary state, and yet in the sixteenth chapter of the Gītā Krishna describes the state of those men who inherit a 'devilish destiny' in terms so strong as to make one wonder how salvation can be possible for them. Liberation, the final release from the round of birth and death, is frequently referred to as the 'highest way': it is final and definitive. Similarly in 16. 20 Krishna speaks of the 'lowest way', and if we read this passage without any preconceptions we can scarcely avoid the conclusion that this too is final: such men have reached a point of no return. They have deliberately chosen enmity to God, and for such, Krishna makes abundantly clear, divine grace is not available.

> Selfishness, force, and pride, desire and anger—[these do] they rely on, envying and hating Me who dwell in their bodies as I dwell in all. Birth after birth in this revolving round, these vilest among men, strangers to [all] good, obsessed with hate and cruel, I ever hurl into devilish wombs. Caught up in devilish wombs, birth after birth deluded, they never attain to Me: and so they tread the lowest way. Desire—Anger—Greed: this is the triple gate of hell, destruction of the self: therefore avoid these three (16. 18–21).

This would seem to be final.

IV. *Liberation, Spiritual Freedom, and How to Win it*

(*a*) *Integration* (Yoga)

The word *yoga* is used in a vast number of senses in the Bhagavad-Gītā. When it is first used it means the 'integration' of the personality for which *buddhi*, the 'soul', is the responsible agent. It entails complete detachment from all outside interests (2. 48), but it also implies activity, for the basic meanings of the root *yuj-* are first 'to yoke or join' (hence 'integration'), and 'to prepare for, to make efforts for'. Hence I have translated it as 'spiritual exercise' in very many contexts. In Chapter II we already run into two definitions of *yoga* which at first sight seem to contradict each other. These are 'sameness-and-indifference' (2. 48) and 'skill in [performing] works' (2. 50). The two, however, complement each other, for just as God 'tirelessly busies Himself with works' (3. 23), yet in his essence remains 'the Changeless One who does not do [or act]' (4. 13), 'the same in all contingent beings' (9. 29: 13. 27), indifferent to them in that He neither hates them nor loves them (9. 29), so too must man engage in works in a spirit of 'sameness and indifference': this is *Yoga*, 'integration' and 'spiritual exercise'. Yoga is, then, both the *process* which results in integration and the goal, 'integration' itself, both the process of training the character in the one great virtue of detachment and the result of that training—'sameness and indifference'. Hence there is no contradiction between *yoga* as spiritual *exercise* and *saṁnyāsa*, 'renunciation [of works]': the one is the means, the other the end (6. 3–4). Yet even the fully integrated man continues to act but in a spirit of complete detachment from all that he does (5. 7). For him clods of earth, stones, and gold are all the same (6. 8): 'in Brahman integrated by spiritual exercise he finds unfailing joy' (5. 21), for Brahman, as changeless being, is by definition 'devoid of imperfection and ever the same' (5. 19).

The fullest description of Yoga as 'integration' and 'spiritual exercise' culminating in 'sameness and indifference' and (yet another definition!) 'the unlinking of the link with suffering and pain' is to be found in 6. 18–29. Since this passage not only illustrates the protean ambivalence of the word *yoga* but also throws into relief the complex of ideas resumed in this word, we reproduce the passage in full:

When thought, held well in check, is stilled in self alone, then is a man from longing freed though all desires assail him: then do men call him 'integrated' (*yukta*). As a lamp might stand in a windless place, unflickering—this likeness has been heard of such men of integration (*yogin*) who control their thought and practise integration (*yoga*) of the self. When thought by spiritual exercise (*yoga*) is checked and comes to rest, and when of [one]self one sees the self in self and finds content therein, that is the utmost joy which transcends [all things of] sense and which soul [alone] can grasp. When he knows this and [knowing it] stands still, moving not an inch from the reality [he sees], he wins a prize beyond all others—or so he thinks. Therein he [firmly] stands, unmoved by any suffering, however grievous it may be. This he should know is what is meant by 'spiritual exercise' (*yoga*),—the unlinking of the link with suffering and pain. This is the act of integration (*yoga*) that must be brought about with [firm] resolve and mind all undismayed. . . . For upon this athlete of the spirit (*yogin*) whose mind is stilled the highest joy descends: [all] passion laid to rest, free from [all] stain, Brahman he becomes. [And] thus [all] flaws transcending, the athlete of the spirit (*yogin*), constant in integrating (*yuj-*), self with ease attains unbounded joy, Brahman's [saving] touch. With self integrated by spiritual exercise (*yoga-yukt'ātmā*), [now] he sees the self in all beings standing, all beings in the self: the same in everything he sees.

This is the supreme goal of 'integration'—to see all beings in the self, and the self in all beings, to see 'the same' in everything because the integrated man has *become* Brahman which is changeless, 'ever the same'; and so he can even go so far as to say that he has 'become the [very] self of every contingent being' (5. 7), because, since he has become Brahman, and Brahman 'penetrates everywhere' (3. 15), he too feels himself to be omnipresent because he has not only transcended time but also *space*. This is the 'prize beyond all others—or so he thinks'. It is indeed the highest state to which the spiritual exercise of Yoga, 'integration', can take you.

This is a state that can be reached by a man's own efforts provided, of course, that his character has been sufficiently purified from the passions in previous births. It can only be achieved by detachment and renunciation which means 'sameness and indifference' to all the pairs of opposites (see Appendix pp. 435–7). This is essential. There are, however, two other powerful aids which man can use to assist him on his laborious journey from this world of time and space to that freedom of the spirit from all that is conditioned by time and space and which the Hindus call *mokṣa*, 'liberation' or 'release'. These are the purely physical techniques which have come to be specifically associated with the word *yoga* in the West on the one hand and meditation and devotion to God on the other. All that the Gītā has to say about Yogic techniques will be found in the Appendix pp. 433–4, and there would seem little point in repeating this here. We must, however, say a few words about *bhakti*, 'loving devotion' to God.

(*b*) Bhakti, *Devotion, Loyalty, and Love*

The word *bhakti* means a variety of things (see p. 181), but in the Gītā it means devotion and loyalty to Krishna, the personal God, trust in Him and love of Him. It also means God's love for man (4. 11) and the original meaning of the word which is 'participation' is never wholly lost. In the Great Epic the root *bhaj-* is frequently used of sexual love and this, of course, played an important part in the Krishna cult of later days. In the Gītā there is no trace of this and the past participle of the same root, *bhakta*, is best translated as 'loyal, devoted, and devout', for it has all these meanings.

As we have seen, the Gītā starts from Buddhist and Sāṁkhya premisses in which God plays no part at all, whereas in the Upanishads no clear distinction is made between the personal God seen as King and Lord and the impersonal Absolute, Brahman, though the latter is clearly subordinated to the former in *Śvetāśvatara* Upanishad 5. 1. In that Upanishad, moreover, God is to be known by meditation, and by 'knowing' Him a man is 'from all fetters freed' (2. 15 etc.): God is not yet an object of love, and we therefore hear little or nothing of 'union with God'. So too in the *Yoga-sūtras* the theoretical background of which is almost identical with that of the Sāṁkhya, the existence of God is admitted (which it is not in the Sāṁkhya), but only as a fit subject for meditation. Meditation on God as the only spiritual entity which is never bound to material Nature leads not to union with Him but (ultimately) to the realization by the individual spirit or self of itself as a timeless and independent spiritual monad. This is the background against which the earlier chapters of the Gītā are written.

Thus Chapters II and V which deal primarily with the integration of the personality and the liberating experience that this brings about, do not in any way connect this experience with God. In 2. 61 concentration on the personal God is mentioned in passing as being at the most a concomitant of the experience of integration, but in Chapter V which is devoted almost entirely to this experience God is only mentioned in the last paragraph, and then apparently as an afterthought. All this, however, changes abruptly at 6. 30 which is the turning-point and as it were the watershed of the whole book; for it is here that for the first time the integration of the self, 'becoming Brahman', is brought into relationship with the love of Krishna, the personal God.

What no commentator who has in any way been influenced by Śankara seems to realize is that devotion to God is not only one of the means that will lead to the vision of the self which is also liberation, but that this devotion and love, now raised to a higher power, gives content and purpose to liberation itself. There is a lower and a higher *bhakti* (18. 54): the one is little more than conventional piety directed to God, the other is the completion and fruition that the self enjoys *after* its final emancipation from the bonds of the phenomenal world and its experience of the Timeless—the experience of 'Nirvāna which is Brahman too' (2. 72). This we shall return to after discussing the many ways in which the Gītā describes liberation. Yet the earlier stage is seldom wholly separated from the later, for God aids his devotees by his grace, raising them out of the phenomenal world into the domain of liberation where, though all things seem to cohere in One, distinctions yet remain; and so 'for him I am not lost, nor is he lost for Me' (6. 30).

Bhakti in its initial stages means both trustful faith and love; and this God rewards by bringing his devotee near to Him (4. 11: 7. 23: 8. 10, 15: 9. 25, 28, 34: 10. 10: 11. 55: 18. 65, 68) or, after raising him out of this world of coming to be and passing away (12. 7), causes him to enter into his very being (8. 5: 11. 54: 13. 18: 18. 55) and to abide in Him (6. 31: 12. 8). Perhaps the clearest account of how God's grace is said to work is to be found in 12. 6–8:

> Those who cast off all their works on Me, solely intent on Me, and meditate on Me in spiritual exercise, leaving no room for others, [and so really] do Me honour, these will I lift up on high out of the ocean of recurring death, and that right soon, for their thoughts are fixed on Me. On Me alone let your mind dwell, stir up your soul to enter Me; thenceforth in very truth in Me you will find your home.

Yet even the humblest offering of a flower or fruit or water God will accept as a gift of love. Let a man but offer up all he does to God, and he will be freed from all the bonds that actions bring in their wake: God will grant him integration and spiritual freedom so that he can come near to Him and abide in Him even as God abides in him. Devout love effaces all sin because the intention is right, and none who practise it, even if they are women or serfs who have no right to avail themselves of the Vedic rites, would fail to win eternal rest (9. 26–32).

(*c*) Mokṣa, *Liberation or Spiritual Freedom*

'Liberation' is the spiritual goal of both Hindus and Buddhists: in the Gītā it is the 'fruit' of the whole process of spiritual integration around the self. The Buddhists were extremely wary of describing it in any but negative terms:

> There is [they said][1] a state of being where there is neither earth nor water, fire nor air . . . neither this world nor the next nor both together,

[1] *Udāna*, p. 80.

neither sun nor moon. There, I say, there is neither coming nor going nor standing still, neither falling nor arising: it is not based on anything, does not develop, and does not depend on anything. That is the end of suffering.

There is . . . an unborn, unbecome, unmade, uncompounded; and were there not an unborn, unbecome, unmade, uncompounded, then no escape could be discerned from what is born, becomes, is made, and compounded. But since there is an unborn, unbecome, unmade, uncompounded, a way of escape can be discerned from what is born, becomes, is made, and compounded.

This is perhaps the minimal description of what is meant by 'liberation', and it is the premiss from which the Gītā starts. For the Buddhists the state which they called Nirvāna was synonymous with immortality, and so too for the Gītā (2. 15) wise men are 'conformed to immortality': 'freed from the bondage of [re-]birth they fare on to that region that knows no ill' (2. 51). They draw near to 'calm serenity' (2. 64) and win peace (2. 70: cf. 4. 39: 5. 12, 29: 6. 15). And so 'the man who puts away all desires and roams around from longing freed, who does not even think, "This I am", or "This is mine", *draws near to peace*. This is the *fixed, still state of Brahman*: . . . standing therein at the time of death *to the Nirvāna that is Brahman too he goes*' (2. 71–72).

Liberation means release from the bondage of works (2. 39: 9. 28), from old age and death (7. 29), and from material Nature itself 'to which [all] contingent beings are subject' (13. 34): it is the way by which one approaches Brahman (2. 72: 5. 6, 24) and becomes Brahman (5. 24: 6. 27: 14. 26: 18. 53), itself the highest way and home from which 'there is no returning' (8. 21: cf. 5. 17). Liberation means never to be born again (8. 16), and once a man has reached this beatific state he draws near to God Himself (4. 9: 7. 23: 8. 7, 10, 15: 9. 25, 28, 34: 10. 10: 11. 55), participates in his mode of being (8. 5: 13. 18), and enters into Him (11. 54: 12. 8: 18. 55).

As we have seen (pp. 10–11) the phrase *brahma-bhūta*, 'become Brahman', seems to have been borrowed from Buddhism. How should it be understood in the Gītā? The key seems to be found in 5. 21 where we read: '[His] self detached from contacts with the outside world, in [him]self he finds his joy, [his] self in Brahman integrated by spiritual exercise (*brahma-yoga-yukt'ātmā*), he finds unfailing joy.' This means that the liberated man sees no distinction between 'within' and 'without', between 'knower' and 'known', between subject and object because Brahman is 'ever the same' (5. 19), the unvarying principle which sustains and illuminates all things from within, everywhere present, and immanent in all things. Hence the perfected man sees his self as having 'become the very self of every contingent being' (5. 7); and seeing himself thus infinitely expanded he 'takes pleasure in self alone . . . in self alone content' (3. 17), because he 'sees all beings in [him]self' (4. 35). Knowing the self to be of this nature he bathes in the atmosphere of Nirvāna which is also Brahman (5. 26): he sees 'the self in all beings standing, all beings in the self: the same in everything he sees' (6. 29). This is the 'prize beyond all others—or so he thinks. Therein he [firmly] stands, unmoved by any suffering, however grievous it may be' (6. 22).

The liberated man has passed clean out of the phenomenal world: he has passed from the sphere of *karma*, 'action', into the sphere of transcendent wisdom (*jñāna*) which is synonymous with perfect peace (4. 39). Works can never affect him again nor bind him, for he is wholly detached from them; 'burnt up in wisdom's fire' (4. 19) they 'entirely melt away' (4. 23): for it is said of wisdom that not only does its fire 'reduce all works to ashes' (4. 37) but also that 'all works without exception in wisdom find their consummation' (4. 33). Thus works beside wisdom are as nothing except in so far as they reflect it and lead to it. And the definition of wisdom is this: it is 'that [kind of] knowledge by which one sees one mode of being, changeless, undivided in all contingent beings, divided [as they are]' (18. 20). This is the basic dogma of the Gītā, and according to it both the self and Brahman and God *are* in some sense that one mode of being, changeless and undivided. Does this mean that the self as it is in itself is therefore *identical* with Brahman and therefore with God? Were this literally so, then there could be no question of love or devotion to God at least once this identity was realized. Is, then, the way of loving devotion merely a preparation for the final goal of liberation?

(*d*) *The Higher* Bhakti, *Love in Freedom*

The true nature of the self is defined right at the beginning of the Gītā (2. 20): 'Never is it born nor dies; never did it come to be, nor will it ever come to be again: unborn, eternal, everlasting is this—primeval. It is not slain when the body is slain.' The self, then, has its natural habitat outside time. Once liberated and once it has integrated the whole of its material substratum into the oneness of itself, it is 'the [very] self of every contingent being' (5. 7). It is, then, omnipresent, beyond space: it is Brahman (5. 24: 6. 27: 14. 26: 18. 53: cf. 2. 72); and Brahman, in purely pantheistic terms, *is* God (below, p. 37). Does this imply, then, that the self too *is* God? In a sense 'yes', since it shares in his mode of being (4. 10: 8. 5: 13. 18: 14. 19): and then again 'no', since it is only a 'minute part' of God (15. 7) which on its descent into the phenomenal world 'becomes a living [self], drawing to itself the five senses and the mind which have their roots in Nature' (ibid.).

In the Sāṁkhya-Yoga system liberation means the definitive detachment of the self or spiritual monad from its material envelope and the total *isolation* of itself within itself both from matter and from all other spiritual monads. This is because in that system these monads are of their very nature autarchic and detached. In the Gītā this is not so, for the self is a 'part' of God: its nature is pure wisdom which, in its embodied state, is overcast by desire as fire is by smoke (3. 38–39). Liberation is achieved by the integration of matter into spirit, by purification of the total self, and by achieving that original oneness which is characteristic of the self-in-itself as it is of Brahman. This is the 'rebirth' of the 'minute part' of God into eternity, identical with God in its eternal essence as a spark is with the fire from which it proceeds (BU. 2. 1. 20: MuU. 2. 1. 1: MaiU. 6. 26, 31), but still isolated from God in so far as it has been individualized by its assumption of a material envelope though this has now itself been so integrated and purified as to be indistinguishable from the self.

In the Gītā there are two stages in the process of liberation: first, there is the realization of the self as eternal, and secondly, there is the discovery of God as identical in eternal essence but as distinct in power and personality. In the first two accounts of liberation (in Chapters II and V) God plays no significant part at all. Only in Chapter VI does He assert his supremacy and priority, and from that point on it is not so much liberation (now taken for granted) that is emphasized; it is rather the relationship of selfless love (*bhakti*) that develops (in eternity!) between God, the whole, and the self, the part. The revelation of the totality of God is very gradual, but for anyone who will but take the trouble to read the

Gītā from beginning to end—that is, in the order in which it was presumably written—the emergence of a loving God out of an impersonal Brahman in and out of the experience of liberation cannot fail to stand out. The only way to make this clear is to quote the relevant passages *in the order in which they occur*. These are:

2. 71–72: The man who puts away all desires and roams around from longing freed, who does not think, 'This I am,' or 'This is mine,' draws near to peace. *Ths is the fixed, still state of Brahman*; he who wins through to this is nevermore perplexed. Standing therein at the time of death, *to the Nirvāna that is Brahman too he goes*.

5. 16 ff.: But some there are whose ignorance of the self by wisdom is destroyed. Their wisdom, like the sun, illumines that [all-]highest. Souls [bent on] that, selves [bent on] that, with that their aim and that their aspiration, they stride [along the path] from which there is no return, [all] taints by wisdom washed away. . . . While yet in this world they have overcome [the process of] emanation [and decay], for *their minds are stilled in that which is ever the same: for devoid of imperfection and ever the same is Brahman; therefore in Brahman [stilled] they stand.* Winning some pleasant thing [the sage] will not rejoice, nor shrink disquietened when the unpleasant comes his way: *steadfast and still* his soul, [all] unconfused, he will know Brahman, *in Brahman [stilled] he'll stand.* [His] self detached from contacts with the outside world, in [him]self he finds his joy, [his] *self in Brahman integrated by spiritual exercise*, he finds unfailing joy. . . . His joy within, his bliss within, his light within, the man who is integrated in spiritual exercise *becomes Brahman* and *draws nigh to Nirvāna that is Brahman too.*

Nirvāna that is Brahman too win seers in whom [all] taint of imperfection is destroyed; their doubts dispelled, with self controlled, they take their pleasure in the weal of all contingent beings. Around these holy men whose thoughts are [fast] controlled, estranged from anger and desire, *knowing [at last] the self*, fares Nirvāna that is Brahman too. . . With senses, mind, and soul restrained, the silent sage, on deliverance intent, who has forever banished fear, anger, and desire, *is truly liberated.* Knowing Me to be the proper object of sacrifice and mortification, great Lord of all the worlds, friend of all contingent beings, he reaches peace.

The last stanza scarcely fits in with what has gone before but refers back to 4. 24 where Brahman is identified with the sacrifice and looks forward to 9. 24 where Krishna describes himself as 'of all sacrifices the recipient and Lord'. There are thus two ways of liberation, (i) by 'wisdom' through which a man 'becomes

Brahman' and (ii) by sacrifice by which, because it *is* Brahman, one reaches peace (cf. 4. 24). Krishna, irrelevantly in the context, merely asserts here that He alone is the proper object of sacrifice: that is, He is that Wisdom in which 'all works without exception find their consummation' (4. 33).

The third passage is 6. 8–47, and it is critical:

With self content in wisdom learnt from holy books and wisdom learnt from life, with sense subdued, sublime, aloof, [this] athlete of the spirit (*yogin*) [stands]: 'Integrated', so is he called; the same to him are clods of earth, stones, gold. . . . Let the athlete of the spirit ever *integrate* [*him*]*self*, standing in a place apart, alone, his thoughts and self restrained, devoid of [earthly] hope, possessing nothing. . . . [There] let him sit, [*his*] *self all stilled*, his fear all gone, firm in his vow of chastity, his mind controlled, his thoughts on Me, *integrated*, [*yet*] *intent on Me*. Thus let the athlete of the spirit be *constant in integrating self*, his mind restrained; *then will he approach that peace which has Nirvāna as its end and which subsists in Me*. . . .

When thought, held well in check, is *stilled in self alone*, then is a man from longing freed though all desires assail him: *then do men call him 'integrated'*. As a lamp might stand in a windless place, unflickering—this likeness has been heard of such athletes of the spirit who control their thought and practise integration of the self.

When thought by spiritual exercise is checked and *comes to rest*, and when of [one]self *one sees the self in self* and finds content therein, that is the *utmost joy which transcends* [*all things of*] *sense* and which soul [alone] can grasp. When he knows this, and [knowing it] *stands still*, moving not an inch from the reality [he sees], *he wins a prize beyond all others—or so he thinks*. Therein he [firmly] stands, unmoved by any suffering, however grievous it may be. This he should know is what is meant by 'spiritual exercise' (*yoga*)—*the unlinking of the link with suffering and pain*. This is the act of integration that must be brought about with [firm] resolve and mind all undismayed. . . . For upon this athlete of the spirit whose mind is stilled *the highest joy descends*: [all] passion laid to rest, free from [all] stain, *Brahman he becomes*. [And] thus [all] flaws transcending, the man of integration (*yogin*), *constant in integrating self*, with ease attains unbounded joy, *Brahman's* [*saving*] *touch*. With self integrated by spiritual exercise [now] *he sees the self in all beings standing, all beings in the self: the same in everything he sees*.

Who sees Me everywhere, who sees the All in Me, for him I am not lost, nor is he lost to Me. Who standing firm on unity communes in love (*bhaj-*) *with Me as abiding in all beings, in whatever state he be, that athlete of the spirit abides in Me*. By analogy with self who sees the same

(Brahman) everywhere, be it as pleasure or as pain, he is the highest athlete of the spirit, *or so men think*. . . .

Higher than the [mere] ascetic is the athlete of the spirit held to be, yes, *higher than the man of wisdom*, higher than the man of works: be, then, a spiritual athlete, Arjuna! But of all athletes of the spirit the man of faith who loves and honours (*bhaj-*) Me, his *inmost self absorbed in Me—he is the most fully integrated* (*yuktatama-*): this do I believe.

This passage reaffirms what we had already been told in Chapters II and V. The integrated man is, like Brahman Itself, 'sublime, aloof' (*kūṭastha-*, 6. 8: cf. 12. 3), 'his self all stilled': he has achieved the 'fixed, still state of Brahman' which is Nirvāna. This we had already been told in 2. 72. But we are now told that Nirvāna itself 'subsists in' Krishna, the personal God: it is not, as it had seemed at first, a completely unconditioned form of existence, but is what it is because it subsists in God. The self now 'becomes Brahman' and experiences the 'utmost joy which transcends [all things of] sense': this is a 'prize beyond all others—*or so he thinks*'.

This qualification is important for, from the Buddhist point of view, Nirvāna is by definition the highest state of bliss one can achieve since it is eternal and exempt from the vicissitudes of time. Moreover, in this state the mystic 'sees the self in all beings standing, all beings in the self'. He seems to be conterminous with the whole wide universe just as God is. This should mean, one would have thought, that the mystic must realize himself as the One Eternal—as God. And so 'by analogy with self' he next sees God everywhere, he sees the All in God: *but*—and this is the vital sentence —'for him I am not lost', Krishna says, 'nor is he lost to Me'. To make it quite clear that this is not identity but participation in a timeless mode of existence, Krishna goes on to say: 'Who standing firm on unity communes in love with Me as abiding in all beings, in whatever state he be, that athlete of the spirit abides in Me.' This is the higher *bhakti*, that love of God which had only been dimly sensed before but which is here brought to perfection because it is an eternal love and can only be fully savoured when a man is fully 'integrated', is fully himself, liberated from all the bonds of matter and space and time which condition matter, in short when a man is free.

Detachment from all things connected with the world is the

necessary precondition for entry into the 'fixed, still state' of Nirvāna, but in Nirvāna itself love is not abolished, as it is in the Buddhist scheme of things—rather it is rekindled by God's grace. And so it is quite natural that the next chapter should start with the words: '*Attach* your mind to Me.' With these words the Gītā breaks totally new ground: the achievement of liberation and Nirvāna does *not* mean that God simply disappears as a Person as He does in the Sāṁkhya-Yoga system: rather He is present in the timeless just as much as He is in time. This is from now on drummed in time and time again. So in 7. 28 we read: 'Released [at last] from the confusion of duality . . . they love and worship Me': 'devoted in their love and integrated ever [in themselves] they pay Me worship' (9. 14): '[your]self [now] integrated by renunciation and spiritual exercise, set free, you will draw nigh to Me' (9. 28): 'now that you have thus integrated self, your striving bent on Me, to Me you will [surely] come' (9. 34): 'to these men who are ever integrated and commune with Me in love I give that integration of the soul by which they may draw nigh to Me' (10. 10).

'Wisdom' means to 'become Brahman', to 'know all' and so in a sense to *be* all. But God is more than the All and so 'whoever knows Me, unconfused, as the Person [All-]Sublime, knows all and [knowing all] communes with Me with all his being, all his love' (15. 19), because God is the *foundation* of the All, both of time and of eternity: and so He can say:

> And as to those who do Me honour with spiritual exercise, in loyalty and love undeviating, passed [clean] beyond these constituents, to becoming Brahman they are conformed. For I am the base supporting Brahman—immortal [Brahman] which knows no change—[supporting] too the eternal law of righteousness and absolute beatitude (14. 26–7).

Liberation itself depends on God; and God can, if He is so minded, shatter it. Even man's 'inmost self', particle of God though it may be and therefore timeless and immortal, can be shaken out of its very beatitude if such is God's pleasure. So in the tremendous theophany of Chapter XI when Arjuna asks if he may be vouchsafed the sight of Krishna's universal form, the vision shakes his whole being to its foundation. 'I see You', he cries out in terror, 'and *my inmost self is shaken*: I cannot bear it, I find no peace, O Vishnu' (11. 24). This is a very far cry from the 'fixed, still state of Brahman' with which we began.

This is the real message of the Gītā: the immortal state of Brahman which is Nirvāna is still imperfect unless and until it is filled out with the love of God. And so it is only fitting that the book should end with a yet clearer restatement of its main theme:

Let a man give up all thought of 'I', force, pride, desire and anger and possessiveness, let him not think of anything as 'mine', at peace;—[if he does this,] to becoming Brahman is he conformed. Brahman become, with self serene, he grieves not nor desires; the same to all contingent beings *he gains the highest love and loyalty to Me.* By love and loyalty he comes to know Me as I really am, how great I am and who; and once he knows Me as I am, he enters [Me] forthwith (18. 53–55).... And now again give ear to this my highest Word, of all the most mysterious: 'I love you well.' Therefore will I tell you your salvation. Bear Me in mind, love Me and worship Me, sacrifice, prostrate yourself to Me: so will you come to Me, I promise you truly, for you are dear to Me.

This is the message of the Gītā—the union of man (with whom this introduction started) with God (with whom it will end). What follows is necessarily an anticlimax.

v. *The Perfect Man*

The ideal man is described five times in the Gītā (see the Appendix, IV). In Chapter II he is the 'man of steadied wisdom', the man who is perfectly detached; but in Chapter XII, in accordance with the enlargement of the idea of liberation and its fulfilment in the love of God, the perfect man must in addition be *bhakta*, 'loyal, devoted, and devout'. As all the essential passages form a compact whole and will be found collected together in the Appendix, there is no need to repeat here what has been said there. The relevant passages will be found on pp. 442–3, 448–9.

B. BRAHMAN

During the Upanishadic period Brahman had come to mean the Absolute—the eternal ground from which the universe proceeds. In the *Iśā* and *Śvetāśvatara* Upanishads, however, Brahman had come to mean the totality of existence, both the eternal world of changeless being and the phenomenal world of coming to be and passing away. Brahman, then, is the 'All': but in these two

Upanishads a personal God appears, and He is greater and 'other' than the All. And so we read (*Iśā*, 9–10):

Blind darkness enter they
Who revere the uncompounded:
Into a darkness blinder yet
[Go they] who delight in the compounded.

Other, they say, than what becomes,
Other, they say, than what does not become:
So from wise men have we heard
Who instructed us therein.

This 'other', this 'Lord' 'encompasses' even this unmoving One which is yet swifter than thought (ibid. 4): 'He, the wise Sage, all-conquering, self-existent, encompassed that which is resplendent, incorporeal, invulnerable, devoid of sinews, pure, unpierced by evil: [all] things He ordered each according to its nature for years unending' (ibid. 8).

So too in the *Śvetāśvatara* (5. 1) we read:

In the imperishable, infinite city[1] of Brahman
Two things there are—
Wisdom and unwisdom, hidden, established there:
Perishable is unwisdom, but wisdom is immortal:
Who over wisdom and unwisdom rules, He is Another.

This, in the main, seems to be the position of the Gītā. Brahman is not only the 'fixed, still state' which is the natural habitat of the liberated self, it is also material Nature, the womb into which the personal God plants his seed (14. 3). It is the sacrifice (4. 24) too of which God alone is the 'recipient and Lord' (9. 24: 5. 29). It is, if you like, the whole kingdom of time and eternity of which God is king. Hence God is the 'base supporting Brahman' as He is the base of 'the eternal law of righteousness and absolute beatitude' (14. 27).

In 13. 12–17 the 'highest Brahman' seems to be identical with Krishna Himself, though even here there is a variant reading which would make even this 'highest Brahman' dependent on God. In that passage Brahman receives attributes which elsewhere in the Gītā fall to Krishna. If It is not fully identical with the personal God, It is at least his 'body' as Rāmānuja understood that body to be, that is to say, it is *both* the All which comprises both

[1] Reading *pure* for *pare*. See n. 1, p. 9.

the material Nature and the individual spiritual monads or selves of the Sāṁkhya system *and* the 'fixed, still state of Brahman', the 'Nirvāna that is Brahman too'. As such It is 'established in the heart of all' just as Krishna is in 18. 61 and 16. 18. There would indeed seem to be no point in drawing a distinction between the *highest* Brahman and Krishna because Krishna is also the *highest* Self (13. 31) and the *highest* Person (13. 22) and as such distinct from all other selves and persons. So too He is the *highest* Brahman (10. 12) and therefore distinct from and higher than the Brahman of the *Iśā* and *Śvetāśvatara* Upanishads. In 17. 23–8 Brahman is identified with pure Being, and this appears to contradict 13. 12 where It is neither Being nor Not-being. The contradiction, however, becomes less offensive when we remember that in the Gītā Brahman is both Being, becoming, and the sacrifice in which the two meet. To sum up, it can be said that in the Gītā Brahman is the 'All', both temporal and eternal, while the 'highest' Brahman is identical with the personal God, Krishna, who transcends both.

C. GOD

I. *The Absolutely Supreme*

Krishna is God, the Supreme Being, 'highest Brahman' (10. 12), 'highest Self' (13. 22: 15. 17), the 'Person [All-]Sublime' (13. 22: 15. 17). He is the base supporting Brahman (14. 27) and in Him Nirvāna subsists (6. 15). He is, then, as much the source of the eternal world, Brahman, as He is of the phenomenal world. In the great theophany of Chapter XI, however, He reveals Himself not as the eternally at rest but as the eternally active—creator, preserver, and destroyer. 'Time am I', He declares, 'wreaker of the world's destruction, matured—[grimly] resolved here to swallow up the worlds' (11. 32). Like Śiva He is as terrible as He is kind.

II. *The Unmoved Mover*

In Himself God is changeless (4. 6, 13: 7. 13, 24: 11. 18: 13. 27), but through material Nature and its three constituents He is in reality the sole agent. Unlike man who is 'bound' by the constituents of Nature unless and until he can win liberation, God acts in perfect freedom: He is never nor can He ever be bound. 'In the three worlds there is nothing that I need do, nor anything unattained that I need to gain, yet work [is the element] in which I move. For if I were not tirelessly to busy Myself with works, then would men everywhere follow in my footsteps. If I were not to do my work, these worlds would fall to ruin, and I should be a worker of confusion, destroying these [my] creatures' (3. 22–24).

From this passage it is clear that the maintenance of the world is willed by God. How or why this should be so is not revealed since the world-process is cyclical and endless—emanated ever anew only to be re-absorbed. Yet so long as it exists and is 'manifest' it follows or should follow the laws laid down for it by God.

The four-caste system did I generate with categories of constituents and works; of this I am the doer,—this know—[and yet I am] the Changeless One who does not do [or act]. Works can never affect Me. I have no yearning for their fruits (4. 13–14).

Yet though the world is willed by God, it nevertheless conceals Him as He is in his changeless essence. In this sense material Nature is seen as an 'uncanny power' (*māyā*).

Know too that [all] states of being whether they be of [Nature's constituent] Goodness, Passion, or Darkness proceed from Me; but I am not in them, they are in Me. By these three states of being inhering in the constituents this whole universe is led astray and does not understand that I am far beyond them and that I neither change nor pass away. For [all] this is my creative power (*māyā*), . . . hard to transcend. Whoso shall put his trust in Me alone, shall pass beyond this [my] uncanny power (*māyā*) (7. 12–14).

For it is this *māyā* and the way God uses it that conceals Him as He is in his essence. Nevertheless, the whole process is willed by Him for He surveys and approves its good working (9. 10).

God, as we have seen, transcends both the phenomenal and the eternal, the perishable and the 'Imperishable'. He is both wholly immanent and wholly transcendent. Beyond both perishable and Imperishable He is the '[All-]Highest Self: the three worlds He enters and pervades, sustaining them—the Lord who passes not away. Since', He goes on to say, 'I transcend the perishable and am more exalted than the Imperishable itself, so am I extolled in Vedic as in common speech as the 'Person [All-]Sublime' (15. 17–18).

God is the One: but He is not a One who obliterates and nullifies the manifold: rather He binds the many together in a coherent whole since the whole is his body and a body is an organism in which all the parts are interdependent. And so it is that in the great theophany of Chapter XI Arjuna sees 'the whole [wide] universe in One converged, there in the body of the God of gods, yet divided out in multiplicity' (11. 13, cf. 11. 7: 13. 16: 18. 20). In a very real sense the material world and the individual selves that inhabit it, whether 'bound' or 'released', form the 'body' of God: in this at least Rāmānuja is faithful to the central insight of the Gītā.

Krishna is also a God of grace, always ready to save those who are devoted to Him (9. 26 ff. etc.) yet implacable to those who wilfully turn their back on Him (16. 7–20). Man's ultimate end is to be united to God, to 'enter into' Him as the Gītā puts it; but at the end of each world-cycle all must willy-nilly enter Him. How great, however, is the difference between those who have prepared for the meeting with the divine fire and those who have not! Some enter in with songs of praise, while others go in against their will and are ground to powder by the divine wrath (11. 21, 26–9). The fire is the same, but for the pure it has no terrors, it can only purify them further; but for the wicked it is the very torment of hell:

> As many swelling, seething streams rush headlong into the [one] great sea, so do these heroes of this world of men enter into your blazing mouths. As moths, in bursting, hurtling haste rush into a lighted blaze to [their own] destruction, so do the worlds, well-trained in hasty violence, pour into your mouths to [their own] undoing (11. 28–9).

This is the dark side of the picture, and a sinister note is again struck in 18. 61 just before God makes his final revelation, that He loves man well.

> In the region of the heart of all contingent beings dwells the Lord, twirling them hither and thither . . . [like puppets] mounted on a machine. In Him alone seek refuge with all your being, all your love; and by his grace you will attain an eternal state, the highest peace. . . . And now again give ear to this my highest Word, of all the most mysterious: 'I love you well.' Therefore will I tell you your salvation. Bear Me in mind, love Me and worship Me, sacrifice, prostrate yourself to Me: so will you come to Me, I promise you truly, for you are dear to Me. Give up all things of law, turn to Me, your only refuge, [for] I will deliver you from all evils; have no care (18. 61–6).

Such, then, are the main doctrines of the Gītā. There are also many other miscellaneous topics in it—the fate of the soul at death, the standing of traditional religion and the values of worship directed to other gods, and the nature of a 'person'. All this will be found under the appropriate headings in the Appendix and needs no elaboration by this or any other editor.

TRANSLATION

CHAPTER I

The Setting

Dhritarāshtra said:

(1) On the field of justice, the Kuru-field, my men and the sons of Pāndu too [stand] massed together ready for the fight. What, Sanjaya, did they do?

Sanjaya said:

(2) Then did Duryodhana, the king, seeing the ranks of Pāndu's sons drawn up [for battle], approach the teacher, [Drona,] with these words:

(3) 'Teacher, behold this mighty host of Pāndu's sons drawn up [in ranks] by (Dhrishtadyumna,) the son of Drupada, your own wise pupil. (4) Here are brave men, great archers, the equal of Bhīma and Arjuna in battle—Yuyudhāna, Virāta, and Drupada, the mighty charioteer, (5) Dhrishtaketu, Cekitāna, the Kāśis' valiant king, Purujit, Kuntibhoja, and the king of the Śibis, foremost of fighting men, (6) brave Yudhāmanyu and valiant Uttamaujas, Subhadrā's son, and the sons of Draupadī, all of them mighty charioteers. (7) Listen too, great Brāhman, to [the list of] those outstanding on our side, the captains of my army; I will enumerate them so that you may be kept informed. (8) Yourself, Bhīshma, Karna, and Kripa, victorious in battle, Aśvatthāman, Vikarna, and Somadatta's son as well, (9) and many another fighting man will lay down his life for me. Various are their arms and weapons, and all are skilled in war. (10) Imperfect are those our forces, though Bhīshma [himself] protects them, but perfect are these their forces which Bhīma guards. (11) So stand firm in all your goings, each in his appointed place. Guard Bhīshma above all others, every one of you.'

(12) To give him cheer, [Bhīshma,] the aged grandsire of the Kuru clan, roared like a lion, loud [and strong], and undaunted blew his conch. (13) Then conchs, drums, cymbals, trumpets, and kettledrums burst into sudden sound: tumultuous was the din. (14) Then too did [Krishna,] Madhu's scion and [Arjuna,] son of Pāndu, standing [erect] on their great chariot yoked to

white steeds, their godly conchs blow. (15) [The conch called] Pāncajanya did Krishna blow, [that called] Devadatta Arjuna; the mighty conch [called] Paundra blew wolf-bellied [Bhīma,] doer of dreadful deeds. (16) [The conch called] Anantavijaya blew Kuntī's son, Yudhishthira, the king: Sughosha and Manipushpaka [blew] Nakula and Sahadeva: (17) and the Kāśis' king, archer supreme, and Śikhandin, the great charioteer, and Dhrishtadyumna, Virāta, and unconquered Sātyaki, (18) Drupada and the sons of Draupadī and Subhadrā's strong-armed son, each blew his conch [resounding] from every side. (19) The tumultuous din [they made] rent the hearts of Dhritarāshtra's sons, making heaven and earth resound.

(20) Then Pāndu's son, whose banner is an ape, scanning [the ranks of] Dhritarāshtra's men drawn up, took up his bow: the clash of arms was on. (21) Then between the two armies, Sire, he addressed Krishna in these words:

'Halt the chariot, unfallen [Lord], (22) that I may scan these men drawn up, spoiling for the fight, [that I may see] with whom I must do battle in this enterprise of war. (23) I see them here assembled, ready to fight, seeking to please Dhritarāshtra's baleful son, by waging war.'

(24) Thus addressed by Arjuna, Krishna brought that splendid chariot to a halt between the two armies (25) in front of Bhīshma and Drona and all the rulers of the earth.

Said he: 'Son of Prithā, behold these Kurus assembled [here].'

(26) There as they stood the son of Prithā saw fathers, grandsires, teachers, uncles, brothers, sons, grandsons, and comrades, (27) fathers-in-law and friends in both armies; and seeing them, all his kinsmen, [thus] arrayed, the son of Kuntī (28) was filled with deep compassion and, desponding, spoke these [words]:

'Krishna, when I see these mine own folk standing [before me], spoiling for the fight, (29) my limbs give way, my mouth dries up, trembling seizes upon my body, and my [body's] hairs stand up in dread. (30) [My bow,] Gāndīva, slips from my hand, my very skin is all ablaze; I cannot stand and my mind seems to wander. (31) Krishna, adverse omens too I see, nor can I discern aught good in striking down in battle mine own folk. (32) Krishna, I do not long for victory nor for the kingdom nor yet for things of pleasure. What should I do with a kingdom? What with enjoyments or [even] with life? (33) Those for whose sake we covet kingdom, enjoyments, things of pleasure, stand [here arrayed] for battle, surrendering life and wealth—(34) teachers, fathers, sons, and grandsires too; uncles, fathers-in-law, grandsons, brothers-in-law—kinsmen all. (35) Krishna, though they should slay [me], yet would not I slay them, not for the dominion over the three worlds, how much less for the earth [alone]! (36) Should we slaughter Dhritarāshtra's sons, Krishna, what sweetness then is ours? Evil, and only evil, would come to dwell with us, should we slay them, hate us as they may. (37) Therefore we have no right to kill the sons of Dhritarāshtra and their kin. For, Krishna, were we to lay low our own folk, how could we be happy? (38) And even if, bereft of sense by greed, they cannot see that to ruin a family is wickedness and to break one's word a crime, (39) how should we not be wise enough to shun this evil thing, for we clearly see that to ruin a family is wickedness. (40) Once the family is ruined, the primeval family laws collapse. Once law is destroyed, then lawlessness overwhelms all [that is known as] family. (41) With lawlessness triumphant, Krishna, the family's women are debauched; once the women are debauched, there will be a mixing of caste. (42) The mixing of caste leads to hell—[the hell prepared] for those who wreck the family and for the family [so wrecked]. So too their ancestors fall down [to hell], cheated of their offerings of food and drink. (43) These evil ways of men who wreck the family, [these evil ways] that cause the mixing of caste, [these evil ways] bring caste-law to naught and the eternal family laws. (44) A sure abode in hell there is for men who bring to naught the family laws: so, Krishna, have we heard. (45) Ah! Ah! so are we [really] bent on committing a monstrous evil deed? intent as we are on slaughtering our own folk because we lust for the sweets of sovereignty. (46) O let the sons of Dhritarāshtra, arms in hand, slay me in battle though I, unarmed myself, will offer no defence; therein were greater happiness for me.'

(47) So saying Arjuna sat down upon the chariot-seat [though] battle [had begun], let slip his bow and arrows, his mind distraught with grief.

CHAPTER II

Krishna Protests

Sanjaya said:

(1) To him thus in compassion plunged, his eyes distraught and filled with tears, [to him] desponding Krishna spoke these words:

The Blessed Lord said:

(2) Whence comes this faintness on you [now] at this crisis-hour? This ill beseems a noble, wins none a heavenly state, [but] brings dishonour, Arjuna. (3) Play not the eunuch, son of Prithā, for this ill beseems you: give up this vile faint-heartedness. Stand up, chastiser of your foes!

'I will not Fight'

Arjuna said:

(4) Krishna, how can I fight Bhīshma and Drona in battle, [how assail them] with [my] arrows? for they are worthy of respect. (5) For better were it here on earth to eat a beggar's food than to slay [our] teachers of great dignity. Were I to slay [my] teachers, ambitious though they be, then should I be eating blood-sullied food. (6) Besides we do not know which is for us the better part, whether that we should win the victory or that they should conquer us. There facing us stand Dhritarāshtra's sons. Should we kill them, we should hardly wish to live. (7) My very being is oppressed with compassion's harmful taint. With mind perplexed concerning right [and wrong] I ask you which is the better course? Tell me [and let your words be] definite [and clear]. I am your pupil and put all my trust in you. So teach me. (8) For I cannot see what could dispel my grief, [this] parching of the senses, not though on earth I were to win a prosperous, unrivalled empire or sovereignty over the gods themselves.

Sanjaya said:

(9) These [were the words that] Arjuna addressed to Krishna, and then he said to him: 'I will not fight!' And having spoken held his peace.

(10) [Standing] between the two armies, Krishna, faintly smiling, spoke these words to Arjuna in his [deep] despondency.

The Blessed Lord said:

(11) You sorrow for men who do not need your sorrow and [yet] speak words that [in part] are wise. Wise men do not sorrow for the living or the dead.

The Undying Self

(12) Never was there a time when I was not, nor you, nor yet these princes, nor will there be a time when we shall cease to be—all of us hereafter. (13) Just as in this body the embodied [self] must pass through childhood, youth, and old age, so too [at death] will it assume another body: in this a thoughtful man is not perplexed. (14) But contacts with the objects of sense give rise to heat and cold, pleasure and pain: they come and go, impermanent. Put up with them [then], Arjuna. (15) For wise men there are, the same in pleasure as in pain, whom these [contacts] leave undaunted: such are conformed to immortality.

(16) Of what is not there is no becoming; of what is there is no ceasing to be: for the boundary-line between these two is seen by men who see things as they really are. (17) Yes, indestructible [alone] is That—know this—by which this whole universe was spun: no one can bring destruction on That which does not pass away. (18) Finite, they say, are these [our] bodies [indwelt] by an eternal embodied [self],—[for this self is] indestructible, incommensurable. Fight then, scion of Bharata. (19) Who thinks this [self] can be a slayer, who thinks that it can be slain, both these have no [right] knowledge: it does not slay nor is it slain. (20) Never is it born nor dies; never did it come to be nor will it ever come to be again: unborn, eternal, everlasting is this [self],—primeval. It is not slain when the body is slain. (21) If a man knows it as indestructible, eternal, unborn, never to pass away, how and whom can he cause to be slain or slay? (22) As a man casts off his worn-out clothes and takes on other new ones, so does the embodied [self] cast off its worn-out bodies and enters other new ones. (23) Weapons do not cut it nor does fire burn it, the waters do not wet it nor does the wind dry it. (24) Uncuttable, unburnable, unwettable, undryable it is—eternal, roving everywhere, firm-set, unmoved, primeval. (25) Unmanifest, unthinkable, immutable is it called: then realize it thus and do not grieve [about it].

(26) And even if you think that it is constantly [re-]born and constantly [re-]dies, even so you grieve for it in vain. (27) For sure is the death of all that is born, sure is the birth of all that dies: so in a matter that no one can prevent you have no cause to grieve.

(28) Unmanifest are the beginnings of contingent beings, manifest their middle course, unmanifest again their ends: what cause for mourning here?

(29) By a rare privilege may someone behold it, and by a rare privilege indeed may another tell of it, and by a rare privilege may such another hear it, yet even having heard there is none that knows it. (30) Never can this embodied [self] be slain in the body of anyone [at all]: and so you have no need to grieve for any contingent being.

Caste Duty and Honour

(31) Likewise consider your own [caste-]duty, then too you have no cause to quail; for better than a fight prescribed by law is nothing for a man of the princely class. (32) Happy the warriors indeed who become involved in such a war as this, presented by pure chance and opening the doors of paradise. (33) But if you will not wage this war prescribed by [your caste-]duty, then, by casting off both duty and honour, you will bring evil on yourself. (34) And [all] creatures will recount your dishonour which will never pass away; and dishonour in a man well trained [to honour is an evil] surpassing death. (35) 'From fear he fled the battlefield'—so will they think of you, the mighty charioteers. Greatly esteemed by them before, you will bring contempt upon yourself. (36) And many a word that is better left unsaid will such men say who wish you ill, disputing your capacity. What could cause [you] greater pain than this? (37) If you are slain, paradise is yours, and if you gain the victory, yours is the earth to enjoy. Stand up, then, son of Kuntī, resolute for the fight.

Be the Same in All Things

(38) Hold pleasure and pain, profit and loss, victory and defeat to be the same: then brace yourself for the fight. So will you bring no evil on yourself.

The Soul's Practice of Contemplation

(39) This wisdom (*buddhi*) has [now] been revealed to you in theory; listen now to how it should be practised. If you are

controlled by the soul (*buddhyāyukto*), you will put away the bondage that is inherent in [all] works. (40) Herein no effort goes to seed nor is there any slipping back: even a very little of this discipline (*dharma*) will protect [you] from great peril.

(41) The essence of the soul is will and it is really single, but many-branched and infinite are the souls of men devoid of will.

Vedic Religion

(42–44) The essence of the soul is will—[but the souls] of men who cling to pleasure and to power, their minds seduced by flowery words, are not attuned to enstasy. Such men give vent to flowery words, lacking discernment, delighting in the Veda's lore, saying there is naught else. Desire is their essence, paradise their goal—their words preach [re-]birth as the fruit of works and expatiate about the niceties of ritual by which pleasure and power can be achieved. (45) [All Nature is made up of] the three 'constituents': these are the Veda's goal. Have done with them, Arjuna: have done with [all] dualities, stand ever firm on Goodness. Think not of gain or keeping the thing gained, but be yourself! (46) As much use as there is in a water-tank flooded with water on every side, so much is there in all the Vedas for the Brāhman who discerns.

Action is Arjuna's Duty

(47) [But] work alone is *your* proper business, never the fruits [it may produce]: let not your motive be the fruit of works nor your attachment to [mere] worklessness. (48) Stand fast in Yoga, surrendering attachment; in success and failure be the same and then get busy with your works. Yoga means 'sameness-and-indifference'.

The Soul's Practice of Contemplation again

(49) For lower far is [the path of] active work [for its own sake] than the spiritual exercise of the soul (*buddhi-yoga*). Seek refuge in the soul! How pitiful are they whose motive is the fruit [of works]! (50) Whoso performs spiritual exercise with the soul (*buddhi-yukta*) discards here [and now] both good and evil works: brace yourself then for [this] Yoga; for Yoga is [also] skill in [performing] works. (51) For those wise men who are integrated by the soul (*buddhi-yukta*), who have renounced the fruit that is born of

works, these will be freed from the bondage of [re-]birth and fare to that region that knows no ill. (52) When your soul passes beyond delusion's turbid quicksands, then will you learn disgust for what has been heard [ere now] and for what may yet be heard. (53) When your soul, by scripture once bewildered, stands motionless and still, immovable in enstasy, then will you attain to sameness-and-indifference (*yoga*).

The Man of Steady Wisdom

Arjuna said:

(54) What is the mark of the man of steady wisdom immersed in enstasy? How does he speak, this man of steadied thought? How sit? How walk?

The Blessed Lord said:

(55) When a man puts from him all desires that prey upon the mind, himself contented in self alone, then is he called a man of steady wisdom. (56) Whose mind is undismayed [though beset] by many a sorrow, who for pleasures has no further longing, from whom all passion, fear, and wrath have fled, such a man is called a man of steadied thought, a silent sage. (57) Who has no love for any thing, who rejoices not at whatever good befalls him nor hates the bad that comes his way—firm-stablished is the wisdom of such a man. (58) And when he draws in on every side his senses from their proper objects as a tortoise [might draw in] its limbs—firm-stablished is the wisdom of such a man.

(59) For the embodied [self] who eats no more objects of sense must disappear—save only the [recollected] flavour—and that too must vanish at the vision of the highest. (60) And yet however much a wise man strive, the senses' tearing violence may seduce his mind by force.

(61) Let him sit, curbing them all, integrated (*yukta*), intent on Me: for firmly established is that man's wisdom whose senses are subdued.

(62) Let a man [but] think of the objects of sense—attachment to them is born: from attachment springs desire, from desire is anger born. (63) From anger comes bewilderment, from bewilderment wandering of the mind, from wandering of the mind destruction of the soul: once the soul is destroyed the man is lost.

(64) But he who roves among the objects of sense, his senses

subdued to self and disjoined from passion and hate, and who is self-possessed [himself], draws nigh to calm serenity. (65) And from him thus becalmed all sorrows flee away: for once his thoughts are calmed, his soul stands firmly [in its ground].

(66) The man who is not integrated has no soul, in him there is no development: for the man who does not develop there is no peace. Whence should there be joy to a peaceless man? (67) Hither and thither the senses rove, and when the mind is attuned to them, it sweeps away [whatever of] wisdom a man may possess, as the wind [sweeps away] a ship on the water. (68) And so whose senses are withheld from the objects proper to them, wherever he may be, firm-stablished is the wisdom of such a man.

(69) In what for all [other] folk is night, therein is the man of self-restraint [wide-]awake. When all [other] folk are awake, that is night for the sage who sees. (70) As the waters flow into the sea, full filled, whose ground remains unmoved, so too do all desires flow into [the heart of] man: and such a man wins peace—not the desirer of desires. (71) The man who puts away all desires and roams around from longing freed, who does not think, 'This I am', or 'This is mine', draws near to peace. (72) This is the fixed, still state of Brahman; he who wins through to this is nevermore perplexed. Standing therein at the time of death, to Nirvāna that is Brahman too he goes.

CHAPTER III

Why?

Arjuna said:

(1) If you think that [the contemplative life of] the soul is a loftier [course] than [the mere performance of] acts, then why do you command me to do a cruel deed? (2) You confuse my soul [and intellect], or so it seems, with distinctly muddled words: so tell me with authority the one [simple way] whereby I can attain the better part.

Work and Bodily Life are Inseparable

The Blessed Lord said:

(3) Of old did I proclaim the twofold law [that holds sway] in this world—for men of theory the spiritual exercise (*yoga*) of wisdom, for men of action the spiritual exercise through works.

(4) Not by leaving works undone does a man win freedom from [the bond of] works, nor by renunciation alone can he win perfection's prize. (5) For not for a moment can a man stand still and do no work, for every man is powerless and made to work by the constituents born of Nature. (6) Whoso controls his limbs through which he acts but sits remembering in his mind sense-objects, deludes [him]self: he is called a hypocrite. (7) But more excellent is he who with the mind controls those limbs (or senses) and through these limbs [themselves] by which he acts embarks on the spiritual exercise of works, remaining detached the while.

(8) Do the work that is prescribed [for you], for to work is better than to do no work at all; for without working you will not succeed even in keeping your body in good repair. (9) This world is bound by bonds of work save where that work is done for sacrifice. Work to this end then, Arjuna, from [all] attachment freed.

Sacrifice

(10) Of old the Lord of Creatures said, emitting creatures and with them sacrifice: 'By this shall ye prolong your lineage, let this be to you the cow that yields the milk of all that ye desire.

(11) With this shall ye sustain the gods so that the gods may sustain you [in return]. Sustaining one another [thus] ye shall achieve the highest good. (12) For, [so] sustained by sacrifice the gods will give you the food of your desire. Whoso enjoys their gift yet gives them nothing [in return] is a thief, no more nor less.'

(13) Good men who eat the leavings of the sacrifice are freed from every taint, but evil are they and evil do they eat who cook [only] for their own sakes.

(14) From food do [all] contingent beings derive and food derives from rain; rain derives from sacrifice and sacrifice from works. (15) From Brahman work arises, know this, and Brahman is born from the Imperishable; therefore is Brahman, penetrating everywhere, forever based on sacrifice. (16) So was the wheel in motion set: and whoso here fails to match his turning [with the turning of the wheel], living an evil life, the senses his pleasure-ground, lives out his life in vain.

Satisfaction in Self alone

(17) Nay, let a man take pleasure in self alone, in self his satisfaction find, in self alone content: [for then] there is naught he needs to do. (18) In works done and works undone on earth he has no interest—no [interest] in all contingent beings: on such interest he does not depend.

Act without Attachment as God does

(19) Therefore detached, perform unceasingly the works that must be done, for the man detached who labours on to the highest must win through. (20) For only by working on did Janaka and his like attain perfection's prize. Or if again you consider the welfare [and coherence] of the world, then you should work [and act].

(21) Whatever the noblest does, that too will others do: the standard that he sets all the world will follow. (22) In the three worlds there is nothing that I need do, nor anything unattained that I need to gain, yet work [is the element] in which I move. (23) For if I were not tirelessly to busy Myself with works, then would men everywhere follow in my footsteps. (24) If I were not to do my work, these worlds would fall to ruin, and I should be a worker of confusion, destroying these [my] creatures.

(25) As witless [fools] perform their works attached to the work [they do], so, unattached, should the wise man do, longing to bring

about the welfare [and coherence] of the world. (26) Let not a wise man split the soul of witless men attached to work: let him encourage all [manner of] works, himself though busy, acting as an integrated (*yukta*) man.

Material Nature is the sole Real Agent

(27) It is material Nature's [three] constituents that do all works wherever [works are done]; [but] he whose self is by the ego fooled thinks, 'It is I who do'. (28) But he who knows how constituents and works are parcelled out in categories, seeing things as they are, thinks thus: 'Constituents on constituents act', [and thus thinking] remains unattached. (29) By the constituents of Nature fooled are men attached to the constituents' works. Such men, dull-witted, only know in part. Let not the knower of the whole upset [the knower of the part].

(30) Cast all your works on Me, your thoughts [withdrawn] in what appertains to self; have neither hope nor thought that 'This is mine': cast off this fever! Fight!

(31) Whatever men shall practise constantly this my doctrine, firm in faith, not envying, [not cavilling,] they too will find release from works. (32) But whoso refuses to perform this my doctrine, envious [yet and cavilling], of every [form of] wisdom fooled, is lost, the witless [dunce]! Be sure of that. (33) As is a man's own nature, so must he act, however wise he be. [All] creatures follow Nature: what will repression do?

(34) In [all] the senses passion and hate are seated, [turned] to their proper objects: let none fall victim to their power, for these are brigands on the road.

(35) Better one's own duty [to perform], though void of merit, than to do another's well: better to die within [the sphere of] one's own duty: perilous is the duty of other men.

Our Enemy Desire

Arjuna said:

(36) Then by what impelled does [mortal] man do evil unwilling though he be? He is driven to it by force, or so it seems to me.

The Blessed Lord said:

(37) Desire it is: Anger it is—arising from the constituent of Passion—all devouring, mightily wicked, know that this is [your]

enemy on earth. (38) As fire is swathed in smoke, as a mirror is [fouled] by grime, as an embryo is all covered up by the membrane envelope, so is this [world] obscured by that. (39) This is the wise man's eternal foe; by this is wisdom overcast, whatever form it takes, a fire insatiable. (40) Sense, mind, and soul, they say, are the places where it lurks; through these it smothers wisdom, fooling the embodied [self]. (41) Therefore restrain the senses first: strike down this evil thing!—destroyer alike of what we learn from holy books and what we learn from life.

(42) Exalted are the senses, or so they say; higher than the senses is the mind; yet higher than the mind the soul: what is beyond the soul is he. (43) So know him who is yet higher than the soul, and make firm [this] self yourself. Vanquish the enemy, Arjuna! [Swift is he] to change his form, and hard is he to conquer.

CHAPTER IV

The Divine Incarnations

The Blessed Lord said:

(1) This changeless mode of life (*yoga*) I to Vivasvat [once] proclaimed; to Manu Vivasvat told it, and Manu to Ikshvāku told it [again]. (2) Thus was the tradition from one to another handed on, the royal seers came to know it; [but] in the long course of time this mode of life here was lost. (3) This is the same primeval mode of life that I preach to you today; for you are loyal, devoted (*bhakta*), and my comrade, and this is the highest mystery.

Arjuna said:

(4) Later is your birth, earlier Vivasvat's: how should I understand your words that in the beginning You did proclaim it?

The Blessed Lord said:

(5) Many a birth have I passed through, and [many a birth] have you: I know them all but you do not. (6) Unborn am I, changeless is my Self, of [all] contingent beings I am the Lord! Yet by my creative energy (*māyā*) I consort with Nature—which is mine—and come to be [in time].

(7) For whenever the law of righteousness withers away and lawlessness arises, then do I generate myself [on earth]. (8) For the protection of the good, for the destruction of evil-doers, for the setting up of the law of righteousness I come into being age after age.

To know God is to share in His Mode of Being

(9) Who knows my godly birth and mode of operation (*karma*) thus as they really are, he, his body left behind, is never born again: he comes to Me. (10) Many are they who, passion, fear, and anger spent, inhere in Me, making Me their sanctuary; made pure by wisdom and hard penances, they come to [share in] my own mode of being. (11) In whatsoever way [devoted] men approach Me, in that same way do I return their love. [Whatever their occupation and] wherever they may be, men follow in my footsteps.

Action and Inaction—Human and Divine

(12) Desiring success in their (ritual) acts men worship here the gods; for swiftly in the world of men comes success engendered by the act [itself].

(13) The four-caste system did I generate with categories of 'constituents' and works; of this I am the doer, [the agent,]—this know—[and yet I am] the Changeless One who does not do [or act]. (14) Works can never affect Me. I have no yearning for their fruits. Whoso should know that this is how I am will never be bound by works. (15) Knowing this the ancients too did work though seeking [all the while] release [from temporal life]: so do you work [and act] as the ancients did in days of old.

(16) What is work? What worklessness? Herein even sages are perplexed. So shall I preach to you concerning work; and once you have understood my words, you will find release from ill. (17) For a man must understand [the nature] of work, of work ill done, and worklessness [all three]: profound [indeed] are the ways of work.

(18) The man who sees worklessness in work [itself], and work in worklessness, is wise among his fellows, integrated, performing every work. (19) When all a man's emprises are free from desire [for fruit] and motive, his works burnt up in wisdom's fire, then wise men call him learned. (20) When he has cast off [all] attachment to the fruits of works, ever content, on none dependent, though he embarks on work [himself], in fact he does no work at all. (21) Nothing hoping, his thought and self controlled, giving up all possessions, he only does such work as is needed for his body's maintenance, and so he avoids defilement. (22) Content to take whatever chance may bring his way, surmounting [all] dualities, knowing no envy, the same in success and failure, though working [still] he is not bound. (23) Attachment gone, deliverance won, his thoughts are fixed on wisdom: he works for sacrifice [alone], and all the work [he ever did] entirely melts away.

Works as Sacrifice

(24) The offering is Brahman, Brahman the [sacrificial] ghee offered by Brahman in Brahman's fire: who sinks himself in this [sacrificial] act which is Brahman, to Brahman must he thereby go. (25) Some adepts offer sacrifice to the gods as their sole object;

in the fire of Brahman others offer sacrifice as sacrifice [which has merit in itself]. (26) Yet others offer the senses—hearing and the rest—in the fires of self-restraint; others the senses' proper objects—sounds and the like—in the fires of the senses. (27) Others offer up all works of sense and works of vital breath in the fire of the spiritual exercise of self-control kindled by wisdom. (28) Some offer up their wealth, some their hard penances, some spiritual exercise, and some again make study and knowledge [of scripture] their sacrifice—religious men whose vows are strict. (29) Some offer the in-breath in the out-breath, likewise the out-breath in the in-breath, checking the flow of both, on breath-control intent. (30) Others restrict their food and offer up breaths in breaths. All these know the [meaning of] sacrifice, and by sacrifice [all] their defilements are made away. (31) Eating of the leavings of the sacrifice, the food of immortality, they come to primeval Brahman. This world is not for him who performs no sacrifice—much less the other [world].

(32) So, many and various are the sacrifices spread out athwart the mouth of Brahman. They spring from work, all of them: be sure of this; for once you know this, you will win release. (33) Better than the sacrifice of wealth is the sacrifice of wisdom. All works without exception in wisdom find their consummation.

Transcendent Wisdom

(34) Learn to know this by humble reverence [of the wise], by questioning, by service, [for] the wise who see things as they really are will teach you wisdom. (35) Once you have known this you will never again be perplexed as you are now: by [knowing] this you will behold [all] beings in [your]self—every one of them—and then in Me.

(36) Even though you were the very worst among all evil-doers, [yet once you have boarded] wisdom's bark, you will surmount all [this] tortuous [stream of life]. (37) As a kindled fire reduces its fuel to ashes, so does the fire of wisdom reduce all works to ashes. (38) For nothing on earth resembles wisdom in its power to purify; and this in time a man himself may find within [him]self—a man perfected in spiritual exercise. (39) A man of faith, intent on wisdom, his senses [all] restrained, wins wisdom; and, wisdom won, he will come right soon to perfect peace.

(40) The man, unwise, devoid of faith, of doubting self, must perish: this world is not for the man of doubting self, nor the next [world] nor yet happiness.

(41) Let a man in spiritual exercise [all] works renounce, let him by wisdom [all] doubts dispel, let him be himself, and then [whatever] his works [may be, they] will never bind him [more]. (42) And so [take up] the sword of wisdom and with it cut this doubt of yours (*ātmanaḥ*), unwisdom's child, still lurking in your heart: prepare for action (*yoga*) now, stand up!

CHAPTER V

The Unity of Theory and Practice—Renunciation and Action

Arjuna said:

(1) 'Renounce [all] works': [such is the course] you recommend: and then again [you say]: 'Perform them.' Which *one* is the better of the two? Tell me this [in clear,] decisive [words].

The Blessed Lord said:

(2) Renouncing works—performing them [as spiritual exercise]—both lead to the highest goal; but of the two to engage in works is more excellent than to renounce them.

(3) This is the mark of the man whose renunciation is abiding: he hates not nor desires, for, devoid of all dualities, how easily is he released from bondage.

(4) 'There must be a difference between theory and practice', so say the simple-minded, not the wise. Apply yourself to only one whole-heartedly and win the fruit of both. (5) [True,] the men of [contemplative] theory attain a [high] estate, but that [same state] achieve the men of practice (*yoga*) too; for theory and practice are all one: who sees [that this is true], he sees [indeed].

Transcending Works by purifying the Self

(6) But hard to attain is [true] renunciation without [the practice of some] spiritual exercise: the sage well versed in spiritual exercise (*yoga-yukta*) right soon to Brahman comes. (7) Well versed in spiritual exercise, his self made pure, his self and senses quelled, his self become the [very] self of every contingent being, though working still, he is not defiled.

(8) 'Lo, nothing do I do': so thinks the integrated man (*yukta*) who knows things as they really are, seeing the while and hearing, touching, smelling, eating, walking, sleeping, breathing, (9) talking, evacuating, grasping, opening and shutting the eyes. 'The senses are busied with their proper objects: [what has that to do with me?' This is the way] he thinks.

(10) And on he works though he has [long] renounced attachment, ascribing his works to Brahman; [yet] is he not stained by evil as a lotus-petal [is not stained] by water. (11) With body, mind, soul, and senses alone-and-isolated [from the self] do men engaged in spiritual exercise (*yogin*) engage in action renouncing attachment for the cleansing of the self. (12) The integrated man, renouncing the fruit of works, gains an abiding peace: the man not integrated, whose works are prompted by desire, being attached to fruits, is bound.

No Agent is the Self

(13) [And so,] all works renouncing with the mind, quietly he sits in full control—the embodied [self] within the city with nine gates: he neither works nor makes another work. (14) Neither agency nor worldly works does [the body's] lord engender, nor yet the bond that work to fruit conjoins: it is inherent Nature that initiates the action. (15) He takes not on the good and evil works of anyone at all—[that] all-pervading lord. By ignorance is wisdom overspread; thereby are creatures fooled.

The Light of Wisdom

(16) But some there are whose ignorance of self by wisdom is destroyed. Their wisdom, like the sun, illumines that [all-]highest. (17) Souls [bent on] that, selves [bent on] that, with that their aim and that their aspiration, they stride [along the path] from which there is no return, [all] taints by wisdom washed away.

Brahman and Nirvāna

(18) [These] wise ones see the self same thing in a Brāhman wise and courteous as in a cow or an elephant, nay, as in a dog or outcaste. (19) While yet in this world they have overcome [the process of] emanation [and decay], for their minds are stilled in that-which-is-ever-the-same: for devoid of imperfection and ever-the-same is Brahman: therefore in Brahman [stilled] they stand. (20) Winning some pleasant thing [the sage] will not rejoice, nor shrink disquietened when the unpleasant comes his way: steadfast-and-still his soul, [all] unconfused, he will know Brahman, in Brahman [stilled] he'll stand. (21) [His] self detached from contacts with

the outside world, in [him]self he finds his joy, [his] self in Brahman integrated by spiritual exercise (*brahma-yoga-yukt'ātmā*), he finds unfailing joy. (22) For the pleasures men derive from contacts assuredly give rise to pain, having a beginning and an end. In these a wise man takes no delight. (23) Only the man who [remains] in this world and, before he is released from the body, can stand fast against the onset of desire and anger, is [truly] integrated, [truly] happy. (24) His joy within, his bliss within, his light within, the man who-is-integrated-in-spiritual-exercise (*yogin*) becomes Brahman and draws nigh to Nirvāna that is Brahman too. (25) Nirvāna that is Brahman too win seers in whom [all] taint-of-imperfection is destroyed; their doubts dispelled, with self controlled, they take their pleasure in the weal of all contingent beings. (26) Around these holy men whose thoughts are [fast] controlled, estranged from anger and desire, knowing [at last] the self, fares Nirvāna that is Brahman too. (27) [All] contact with things outside he puts away, fixing his gaze between the eyebrows; inward and outward breaths he makes the same as they pass up and down the nostrils. (28) With senses, mind, and soul restrained, the silent sage, on deliverance intent, who has forever banished fear, anger, and desire, is truly liberated.

(29) Knowing Me to be the proper object of sacrifice and mortification, great Lord of all the worlds, friend of all contingent beings, he reaches peace.

CHAPTER VI

The Unity of Renunciation and Spiritual Exercise

The Blessed Lord said:

(1) The man who does the work that is his to do, yet covets not its fruits, he it is who at once renounces and yet works on (*yogin*), not the man who builds no sacrificial fire and does not work. (2) What men call renunciation is also spiritual exercise (*yoga*): you must know this. For without renouncing [all set] purpose no one can engage in spiritual exercise. (3) For the silent sage who would climb [the ladder of] spiritual exercise works are said to be the means; but for that same [sage] who has reached the state of integration (*yoga*) they say quiescence is the means. (4) For when a man knows no attachment to objects of sense or to the deeds [he does], when he has renounced all purpose, then has he reached the state of integration, or so they say.

The Two Selves in Man

(5) Raise self by self, let not the self droop down; for self's friend is self indeed, so too is self self's enemy. (6) Self is the friend to the self of him whose self is by the self subdued; but for the man bereft of self self will act as an enemy indeed.

The Spiritual Self

(7) The higher self of the self-subdued, quietened, is rapt in enstasy—in cold as in heat, in pleasure as in pain, likewise in honour and disgrace. (8) With self content in wisdom learnt from holy books and wisdom learnt from life, with sense subdued, sublime, aloof (*kūṭastha*), [this] athlete of the spirit (*yogin*) [stands]: 'Integrated (*yukta*)', so is he called; the same to him are clods of earth, stones, gold. (9) Outstanding is he whose soul views in the selfsame way friends, comrades, enemies, those indifferent, neutrals, men who are hateful and those who are his kin—the good and the evil too.

Spiritual Exercise and its Physical Conditions

(10) Let the athlete of the spirit ever integrate [him]self standing in a place apart, alone, his thoughts and self restrained, devoid of [earthly] hope, possessing nothing. (11) Let him set up for [him]self a steady seat in a clean place, neither too high nor yet too low, bestrewn with cloth or hide or grass. (12) There let him sit and make his mind a single point, let him restrain the operations of his thought and senses and practise integration (*yuñjyād yogam*) to purify the self. (13) [Remaining] still, let him keep body, head, and neck in a straight line, unmoving; let him fix his eye on the tip of his nose, not looking round about him. (14) [There] let him sit, [his] self all stilled, his fear all gone, firm in his vow of chastity, his mind controlled, his thoughts on Me, integrated, [yet] intent on Me. (15) Thus let the athlete of the spirit (*yogin*) be constant in integrating [him]self, his mind restrained; then will he approach that peace which has Nirvāna as its end and which subsists in Me.

(16) But [this] spiritual exercise is not for him who eats too much, nor yet for him who does not eat at all, nor for him who is all too prone to sleep, nor yet for him who [always] stays awake. (17) [Rather] is [this] way of integration (*yoga*) for him who knows-the-mean (*yukta*) in food and recreation, who knows-the-mean in his deeds and gestures, who knows-the-mean in sleeping as in waking; [this] practice-of-the-mean (*yoga*) [it is] that slaughters pain.

(18) When thought, held well in check, is stilled in self alone, then is a man from longing freed though all desires assail him: then do men call him 'integrated'. (19) As a lamp might stand in a windless place, unflickering—this likeness has been heard of such athletes of the spirit (*yogin*) who control their thought and practise integration of the self.

The Goal of Spiritual Exercise

(20) When thought by spiritual exercise is checked and comes to rest, and when of [one]self one sees the self in self and finds content therein, (21) that is the utmost joy which transcends [all things of] sense and which soul [alone] can grasp. When he knows this and [knowing it] stands still, moving not an inch from the reality [he sees], (22) he wins a prize beyond all others—or so he thinks. Therein he [firmly] stands, unmoved by any suffering,

however grievous it may be. (23) This he should know is what is meant by 'spiritual exercise' (*yoga*),—the unlinking of the link with suffering-and-pain. This is the act-of-integration (*yoga*) that must be brought about with [firm] resolve and mind all undismayed. (24) Let him renounce all desires whose origin lies in the will—all of them without remainder; let him restrain in every way by mind alone the senses' busy throng. (25) By soul held fast in steadfastness he must make the mind [too] subsist in the self; then little by little will he come to rest; he must think of nothing at all. (26) Wherever the fickle mind unsteady roves around, from thence [the soul, *buddhi*] will bring it back and subject it to the self. (27) For upon this athlete of the spirit whose mind is stilled the highest joy descends: [all] passion laid to rest, free from [all] stain, Brahman he becomes. (28) [And] thus [all] flaws transcending, the athlete of the spirit, constant in integrating [him]self, with ease attains unbounded joy, Brahman's [saving] touch. (29) With self integrated by spiritual exercise (*yoga-yukt'ātmā*) [now] he sees the self in all beings standing, all beings in the self: the same in everything he sees.

(30) Who sees Me everywhere, who sees the All in Me, for him I am not lost, nor is he lost to Me. (31) Who standing firm on unity communes-in-love (*bhaj-*) with Me as abiding in all beings, in whatever state he be, that athlete of the spirit abides in Me. (32) By analogy with self who sees the same [Brahman] everywhere, be it as pleasure or as pain, he is the highest athlete of the spirit, or so men think.

Arjuna's Inadequacy

Arjuna said:

(33) So fickle [is my mind] that I cannot descry this still, firm-stablished state of this spiritual exercise which You have preached as 'being the same [in everything]'. (34) For fickle is the mind, impetuous, exceeding strong: how difficult to curb it! As difficult as to curb the wind, I would say.

The Blessed Lord said:

(35) Herein there is no doubt, hard is the mind to curb and fickle, but by untiring effort and by transcending passion it can be held in check. (36) Hard to come by is this integrated state (*yoga*) by one whose self is not restrained; this [too] I think; but

a man who strives, his self controlled, can win it if he but use [the appropriate] means.

Justification by Faith

Arjuna said:

(37) [Suppose] a man of faith should strive in vain, his restless mind shying away from spiritual exercise (*yoga*): he fails to win the perfect prize of integration (*yoga*)—what path does he tread [then]? (38) Does he, both objects unachieved, come crashing down and perish like a riven cloud, his [firm] foundation gone, bemused on Brahman's path? (39) Krishna, this doubt You can dispel for me so that none of it remains, for there seems to be no other who can dispel this doubt [of mine].

The Blessed Lord said:

(40) Not in this world nor in the next is such a man destroyed-or-lost: for no doer of fair works will tread an evil path, my friend, no, none whatever. (41) The worlds of doers of good works he'll win and dwell there countless years: and then will he be born again, this man who failed in spiritual exercise, in the house of holy men by fortune blest. (42) Or else he will be born in a family of men well-advanced-in-spiritual-exercise (*yogin*), possessed of insight; but such a birth as this on earth is yet harder to obtain. (43) There is he united with the soul as it had matured in his former body; and once again he strives to win perfection's prize. (44) By [the force of] that same struggle he had waged in former times he is carried away though helpless [of himself]; for even he who only wants to know what integration is, transcends that 'Brahman' which is [no more than] wordy rites. (45) But cleansed of taint [that] athlete of the spirit strives on with utmost zeal, through many, many births [at last] perfected; and then the highest path he treads. (46) Higher than the [mere] ascetic is the athlete of the spirit held to be, yes, higher than the man of wisdom, higher than the man of works: be, then, a spiritual athlete, Arjuna! (47) But of all athletes of the spirit the man of faith who loves-and-honours (*bhaj-*) Me, his inmost self absorbed in Me—he is the most fully integrated: this do I believe.

CHAPTER VII

The Two Natures of God

The Blessed Lord said:

(1) Attach your mind to Me: engaging [still] in spiritual exercise put your trust in Me: [this doing] listen how you may come to know Me in my entirety, all doubt dispelled. (2) This wisdom [derived from sacred writ] and the wisdom [of experience] I shall proclaim to you, leaving nothing unsaid. This known, never again will any other thing that needs to be known here remain. (3) Among thousands of men but one, maybe, will strive for [self-]perfection, and even among [these] athletes who have won perfection['s crown] but one, maybe, will come to know Me as I really am.

(4) Eightfold divided is my Nature—thus: earth, water, fire and air, space, mind and also soul—and the ego. (5) This is the lower: but other than this I have a higher Nature; this too must you know. [And this is Nature] developed into life by which this world is kept in being. (6) To all beings these [two Natures] are [as] a womb; be very sure of this. Of this whole universe the origin and the dissolution too am I. (7) Higher than I there is nothing whatsoever: on Me this universe is strung like clustered pearls upon a thread.

Some Essential Attributes of God

(8) In water I am the flavour, in sun and moon the light, in all the Vedas [the sacred syllable] Oṁ, in space [I am] sound, in men [their] manliness am I. (9) Pure fragrance in the earth am I, flame's onset in the fire: [and] life am I in all contingent beings, in ascetics [their] fierce austerity. (10) Know that I am the primeval seed of all contingent beings: insight (*buddhi*) in men of insight, glory in the glorious am I. (11) Power in the powerful am I—[such power] as knows neither desire nor passion: desire am I in contingent beings, [but such desire as] does not conflict with righteousness.

God and the Constituents of Nature

(12) Know too that [all] states of being whether they be of [Nature's constituent] Goodness, Passion, or Darkness proceed

from Me; but I am not in them, they are in Me. (13) By these three states of being inhering in the constituents this whole universe is led astray and does not understand that I am far beyond them and that I neither change-nor-pass-away. (14) For [all] this is my creative power (*māyā*), composed of the constituents, divine, hard to transcend. Whoso shall put his trust in Me alone, shall pass beyond this [my] uncanny power (*māyā*). (15) Doers of evil, deluded, base, put not their trust in Me; their wisdom swept away by [this] uncanny power, they cleave to a devilish mode of existence.

Different Types of Devotee

(16) Fourfold are the doers of good who love-and-worship Me—the afflicted, the man who seeks wisdom, the man who strives for gain, and the man who wisdom knows. (17) Of these the man of wisdom, ever integrated, who loves-and-worships One alone excels: for to the man of wisdom I am exceeding dear and he is dear to Me. (18) All these are noble-and-exalted, but the man of wisdom is [my] very self, so do I hold, for with self [already] integrated he puts his trust in Me, the one all-highest Way. (19) At the end of many a birth the man of wisdom gives himself up to Me, [knowing that Krishna,] Vasudeva's son, is All: so great a self is exceeding hard to find.

Worship of Other Gods

(20) [All] wisdom swept away by manifold desires, men put their trust in other gods, relying on diverse rules-and-precepts: for their own nature forces them thereto. (21) Whatever form, [whatever god,] a devotee with faith desires to honour, that very faith do I confirm in him [making it] unswerving-and-secure. (22) Firm-stablished in that faith he seeks to reverence that [god] and thence he gains his desires, though it is I who am the true dispenser. (23) But finite is the reward of such men of little wit: whoso worships the gods, to the gods will [surely] go, but whoso loves-and-worships Me, to Me will come indeed.

The Unknown God

(24) Fools think of Me as one unmanifest [before] who has reached [the stage of] manifestation: they know nothing of my

higher state, the Changeless, All-Highest. (25) Since [my] creative power (*māyā*) and the way I use it (*yoga*) conceal Me, I am not revealed to all; this world, deluded, knows Me not—[Me,] the Unborn and Changeless. (26) [All] beings past and present and yet to come I know: but there is no one at all that knows Me. (27) By dualities are men confused, and these arise from desire and hate; thereby are all contingent beings bewildered the moment they are born. (28) But some there are for whom [all] ill is ended, doers of what is good-and-pure: released [at last] from the confusion of duality, steady in their vows, they love-and-worship Me. (29) Whoso shall strive to win release from old age and death, putting his trust in Me, will come to know that Brahman in its wholeness—as it appertains to self, the whole [mystery] of works, (30) as it appertains to contingent beings, and to the divine—and Me [too] as I appertain to sacrifice. And whoso shall know Me [thus] even at the time of passing on, will know [Me] with an integrated mind.

CHAPTER VIII

Some Definitions

Arjuna said:

(1) What is That Brahman? What that which appertains to self? [And] what, O best of men, are works? What is that called which appertains to contingent beings? What that which appertains to the divine? (2) Who and in what manner is He who appertains to the sacrifice here in this body? And how, at the time of passing on, can You be known by men of self-restraint?

The Blessed Lord said:

(3) The Imperishable is the highest Brahman; it is called 'inherent nature' in so far as it appertains to [an individual] self,—as the creative force (*visarga*) known as 'works' which gives rise to the [separate] natures of contingent beings. (4) In so far as it appertains to [all] contingent beings, it is [their] perishable nature, and in so far as it appertains to the gods, [it is] 'person (spirit)'. In so far as it appertains to sacrifice [it is] I here in this body, O best of men who bodies bear.

Where to direct your Thoughts at Death

(5) Whoso at the hour of death, abandoning his mortal frame, bears Me in mind and passes on, accedes to my own mode of being: there is no doubt of this. (6) Whatever state a man may bear in mind when in the end he casts his mortal frame aside, even to that state does he accede, for ever does that state make him grow into itself. (7) Then muse upon Me always and fight; for if you fix your mind and soul on Me, you will, nothing doubting, come to Me. (8) Let a man's thoughts be integrated by spiritual exercise (*yoga-yukta*) and constant striving: let them not stray to anything else at all; so by meditating on the divine exalted Person, [that man to that Person] goes. (9) The Ancient Seer, Governor [of all things, yet] smaller than the small, Ordainer of all, in form unthinkable, sun-coloured beyond the darkness—let a man meditate on Him [as such]. (10) With mind unmoving at the time of passing

on, by love-and-devotion integrated and by the power of spiritual exercise too, forcing the breath between the eyebrows duly, so will that man draw nigh to that divine exalted Person.

(11) The imperishable state of which the Vedic scholars speak, which sages enter, their passion spent, desiring which men lead a life of chastity, that state will I proclaim to you in brief. (12) Let a man close up all [the body's] gates, stem his mind within the heart, fix his breath within the head, engrossed in Yogic concentration, (13) let him utter [the word] Oṁ, Brahman in one syllable, keeping Me in mind; then, when he departs, leaving aside the body, he will tread the highest way.

(14) How easily am I won by him who bears Me in mind unceasingly, thinking of nothing else at all—an athlete of the spirit ever integrated [in himself] (*nitya-yuktasya yoginaḥ*). (15) Coming right nigh to Me these great of self are never born again, [for rebirth is] the abode of suffering, knows nothing that abides: [free from it now] they attain the highest prize. (16) The worlds right up to Brahmā's realm [dissolve and] evolve again; but he who comes right nigh to Me shall never be born again.

The Day and Night of Brahmā

(17) For a thousand ages lasts [one] day of Brahmā, and for a thousand ages [one such] night: this knowing, men will know [what is meant by] day and night. (18) At the day's dawning all things manifest spring forth from the Unmanifest; and then at nightfall they dissolve [again] in that same thing called 'Unmanifest'. (19) Yes, this whole host of beings comes ever anew to be; at fall of night it dissolves away all helpless; at dawn of day it rises up again.

The Unmanifest beyond the Unmanifest

(20) But beyond that there is [yet] another mode of being—beyond the Unmanifest [another] Unmanifest (*masc.*), primeval: this is he who does not fall to ruin when all contingent beings are destroyed. (21) Unmanifest [is he], surnamed 'Imperishable': this, men say, is the highest way and, this once won, there is no more returning: this is my highest home. (22) But that highest *Person* is to be won by love-and-worship directed to none other. In Him do all beings subsist; by Him this universe is spun.

The Fate of the Soul at Death

(23) Some to return, some never to return, athletes of the spirit set forth when they pass on; the times [and seasons] of them all I shall [now] declare. (24) Fire, light, day, [the moon's] light [fortnight], the six months of the [sun's] northern course,—dying in these to Brahman do they go, the men who Brahman know. (25) Smoke, night, [the moon's] dark [fortnight], the six months of the [sun's] southern course,—[dying] in these an athlete of the spirit wins the light of the moon, and back he comes again. (26) For these two courses—light and dark—are deemed to be primeval [laws] on earth. One leads to [the place of] no return, by the other one returns again. (27) Knowing these two courses no athlete of the spirit whatever is perplexed; so, Arjuna, be integrated by spiritual exercise (*yoga-yukta*) at all times. (28) For knowledge of the Veda, for sacrifice, for grim austerities, for gifts of alms a meed of merit is laid down: all this the athlete of the spirit leaves behind who knows this [secret teaching; and knowing it] he draws right nigh to the exalted primal state.

CHAPTER IX

God and His Creation

The Blessed Lord said:

(1) But most secret-and-mysterious is this wisdom I will [now] reveal,—[a wisdom] based on holy writ and consonant with experience: to you [will I proclaim it,] for in you there is no envy; and knowing it you shall be freed from ill. (2) Science of kings, mystery of kings is this, distilling the purest essence, to the understanding evident, with righteousness enhanced—how easy to carry out! [Yet] it abides forever. (3) Men who put no faith in this law of righteousness fail to reach Me and must return to the road of recurring death.

(4) By Me, Unmanifest in form, all this universe was spun: in Me subsist all beings, I do not subsist in them. (5) And [yet] contingent beings do not subsist in Me,—behold my sovereign skill-in-works (*yoga*): my Self sustains [all] beings, It does not subsist in them; It causes them to be-and-grow. (6) As in [wide] space subsists the mighty wind blowing [at will] ever and everywhere, so do all contingent beings subsist in Me: so must you understand it. (7) All contingent beings pour into material Nature which is mine when a world-aeon comes to an end; and then again when [another] aeon starts, I emanate them forth. (8) Subduing my own material Nature ever again I emanate this whole host of beings—powerless [themselves], from Nature comes the power.

(9) These works [of mine] neither bind-nor-limit Me: as one indifferent I sit among these works, detached. (10) [A world of] moving and unmoving things material Nature brings to birth while I look-on-and-supervise: this is the cause [and this the means] by which the world revolves.

God's Incarnation as Krishna

(11) For that a human form I have assumed fools scorn Me, knowing nothing of my higher state,—great Lord of contingent beings. (12) Vain their hopes and vain their deeds, vain their 'gnosis', vain their wit; a monstrous devilish nature they embrace

which leads [them far] astray. (13) But great-souled men take up their stand in a nature that is divine; and so with minds intent on naught but [Me], they love-and-worship Me, knowing [Me to be] the beginning of [all] contingent beings, as Him who passes not away. (14) Me do they ever glorify, [for Me] they strive, full firm their vows; to Me do they bow down, devoted-in-their-love, and integrated ever [in themselves] they pay Me worship. (15) Others again with wisdom's sacrifice make sacrifice to Me and worship Me as One and yet as Manifold, in many a guise with face turned every way.

Some Essential Attributes of God

(16) I am the rite, the sacrifice, the offering for the dead, the healing herb; I am the sacred formula, the sacred butter am I: I am the fire and I the oblation offered [in the fire]. (17) I am the father of this world, mother, ordainer, grandsire, [all] that need be known; vessel of purity [am I, the sacred syllable] Oṁ, and the Rig-, Sāma-, and Yajur-Vedas too. (18) [I am] the Way, sustainer, Lord, and witness, [true] home and refuge, friend,—origin and dissolution and the stable state [between],—a treasure-house, the seed that passes not away. (19) It is I who pour out heat, hold back the rain and send it forth: deathlessness am I and death, what IS and what is not.

Different Cults

(20) Trusting in the three Vedas the Soma-drinkers, purged of [ritual] fault, worship Me with sacrifice, seeking to go to paradise: these win through to the pure world of the lord of the gods and taste in heaven the gods' celestial joys. (21) [But] once they have [to the full] enjoyed the broad expanse of paradise, their merit exhausted, they come [back] to the world of men. And so it is that those who stick fast to the three Vedas receive [a reward] that comes and goes; for it is desire that they desire.

(22) For those men who meditate on Me, no other [thought in mind], who do Me honour, ever persevere, I bring attainment and possession of what has been attained. (23) [Yet] even those who lovingly devote themselves to other gods and sacrifice to them, full filled with faith, do really worship Me though the rite may differ from the norm. (24) For it is I who of all sacrifices am recipient and Lord, but they do not know Me as I really am, and so they fall

[back into the world of men]. (25) To the gods go the gods' devotees, to the ancestors their votaries, to disembodied spirits go the worshippers of these, but those who worship Me shall come to Me.

The Rewards of Loving Devotion

(26) Be it a leaf or flower or fruit or water that a zealous soul may offer Me with love's devotion, that do I [willingly] accept, for it was love that made the offering. (27) Whatever you do, whatever you eat, whatever you offer in sacrifice or give away in alms, whatever penance you may perform, offer it up to Me. (28) So from [those] bonds which works [of their very nature forge], whose fruits are fair and foul, you will be freed: [your]self [now] integrated by renunciation and spiritual exercise, set free (*vimukta*), you will draw nigh to Me. (29) In all contingent beings the same am I; none do I hate and none do I fondly love; but those who commune with Me in love's devotion (*bhajanti bhaktyā*) [abide] in Me, and I in them.

(30) However evil a man's livelihood may be, let him but worship Me with love and serve no other, then shall he be reckoned among the good indeed, for his resolve is right. (31) Right soon will his self be justified and win eternal rest. Arjuna, be sure of this: none who worships Me with loyalty-and-love is lost to Me. (32) For whosoever makes Me his haven, base-born though he may be, yes, women too and artisans, even serfs, theirs it is to tread the highest way. (33) How much more, then, Brāhmans pure-and-good, and royal seers who know devoted love. Since your lot has fallen in this world, impermanent and joyless, commune with Me in love. (34) On Me your mind, on Me your loving-service, for Me your sacrifice, to Me be your prostrations: now that you have thus integrated self, your striving bent on Me, to Me you will [surely] come.

CHAPTER X

Krishna, the Origin of All

The Blessed Lord said:

(1) Now once again, [my] strong-armed [friend], give ear to my all-highest word which I shall speak to you [alone], for therein is your delight and your welfare is my wish.

(2) None knows from whence I came—not the gods' celestial host nor yet the mighty seers: for I am the beginning of the gods [themselves] as of the mighty seers and all in every way. (3) Whoso shall know Me as unborn, beginningless, great Lord of [all] the worlds, shall never know delusion among men, from every evil freed.

(4) Intellect (*buddhi*), wisdom, freedom from delusion, long-suffering, truth, restraint, tranquillity, pleasure and pain, coming to be and passing away, fear and fearlessness as well, (5) refusal to do harm, equanimity, content, austerity, open-handedness, fame and infamy—[such are] the dispositions of contingent beings, and from Me in all their diversity they arise.

(6) The seven mighty seers of old, likewise the Manus four, sharing in my mode of being, were born [the children] of [my] mind; from them [arose] these creatures in the world.

(7) Whoso should know this my far-flung power and how I use it (*yoga*), [whoso should know these] as they really are, is [truly] integrated; and this his integration (*yoga*) can never be undone. Herein there is no doubt.

(8) The source of all am I; from Me all things proceed: this knowing, wise men commune with Me in love (*bhaj-*), full filled with warm affection. (9) On Me their thoughts, their life they would sacrifice for Me; [and so] enlightening one another and telling my story constantly they take their pleasure and delight. (10) To these men who are ever integrated and commune with Me in love I give that integration of the soul by which they may draw nigh to Me. (11) Out of compassion for those same men [all] darkness born of ignorance I dispel with wisdom's shining lamp, abiding [ever] in my own [true] nature.

Arjuna confesses Krishna as the All-Highest

Arjuna said:

(12–13) [All-]Highest Brahman, highest home, [all-]highest vessel of purity are You. All seers agree that You are the Person eternal and divine, primeval God, unborn and all-pervading Lord. So too Nārada, the godly seer, Asita, Devala, and Vyāsa [have declared]; and You Yourself do tell me so. (14) All this You tell me is true; so, Krishna, I believe, for, Blessed Lord, neither gods nor demons acknowledge [this] manifest [world] as yours. (15) By [your] Self You yourself do know [your] Self, O You all-highest Person, You who bestow being on contingent beings, Lord of [all] beings, God of gods, and Lord of [all] the world.

(16) Tell me, I beg You, leaving nothing unsaid—for divine are the far-flung powers [that centre] on [your] Self by which You pervade these worlds, standing [unchanged the while]. (17) How am I to know You, [great] athlete of the spirit, though I think about You always? And in what several modes of being should I think about You, Blessed Lord. (18) Tell me again in detail full of your far-flung power [that centres] on [your] Self and how You use it (*yoga*); for as I listen to your undying [words] I cannot have enough.

God, the Quintessence of all Essences

The Blessed Lord said:

(19) Lo, I will tell you—for divine are my far-flung powers [that centre] on [my] Self,—[I will tell you] what is most fundamental, for of the details there is no end.

(20) I am the Self established in the heart of all contingent beings: I am the beginning, the middle, and the end of all contingent beings too.

(21) Among the Ādityas I am Vishnu, among lights the radiant sun, among the Maruts I am Marīci, among stars I am the moon. (22) Of the Vedas I am the Sāma-Veda, I am Indra among the gods; among the senses I am the mind, amongst contingent beings thought. (23) Among the Rudras Śiva am I, among sprites and monsters the Lord of Wealth; among the Vasus I am fire, among mountains I am Meru. (24) And of household priests know that I am the chief, Brihaspati; among war-lords I am Skanda, among lakes I am the Ocean. (25) Among the great seers I am Bhrigu, among utterances the single syllable [Oṁ]; among sacrifices I am

the sacrifice of muttered prayer, among things immovable the Himalayas; (26) among all trees the holy fig-tree, Nārada among the celestial seers, among the heavenly minstrels Citraratha, among perfected beings Kapila, the silent sage. (27) Among horses know that I am Uccaihśravas, [Indra's steed,] from nectar born, among princely elephants [Indra's, called] Airāvata, among men the king. (28) Among weapons I am the thunderbolt, of cows the milch-cow of desires; and I am Kandarpa, [god of love,] generating [seed], among serpents I am Vāsuki, [the serpent king]. (29) Of Nāga-serpents I am [their chief,] Ananta, of water-dwellers Varuna, [their lord,] am I; of the ancestors I am Aryaman, among those who subdue I am Yama, [god of death]. (30) Among demons I am Prahlāda, among those who reckon I am Time; among beasts I am [the lion,] the king of beasts, and among birds Garuda, [Vishnu's bird]. (31) Among those who purify I am the wind, Rāma I am among men at arms; among water-monsters I am the crocodile, among rivers I am the Ganges. (32) Among emanations the beginning and the end and the middle too am I; among sciences I am the science concerned with Self, among those who speak [their very] speech am I. (33) Among the letters of the alphabet I am 'A', among grammatical compounds the *dvandva.* Truly I am imperishable Time, I, the Ordainer, with face turned every way.

(34) And I am Death that snatches all away, and the origin of creatures yet to be. And among feminine nouns [I am] fame, fortune, speech, memory, intelligence, steadfastness, long-suffering. (35) Again among chants I am the Great Chant, among metres the Gāyatrī, among months I am [the first,] Mārgaśīrsha, among seasons flower-bearing [spring].

(36) I am the dicing of tricksters, glory of the glorious am I; I am victory and I am firm resolve, and the courage of the brave am I. (37) Among the Vrishni clansmen I am [Krishna,] Vasudeva's son, among Pāndu's sons [I am] Arjuna; among silent sages I am Vyāsa, among psalmists I am the psalmist Uśanas. (38) Of those who subdue the rod-of-chastisement am I, I am the statecraft of those who seek the upper hand; the very silence of hidden, secret things am I, and I am the wisdom of the wise.

(39) And what is the seed of all contingent beings, that too am I. No being is there, whether moving or unmoving, that exists or could exist apart from Me. (40) Of [these] my far-flung powers divine there is no end; as much as I have said concerning them must

serve as an example. (41) Whatever being shows wide power, prosperity, or strength, be sure that this derives from [but] a fragment of my glory.

(42) But where's the use for you to know so much, Arjuna? This whole universe I hold apart [supporting it] with [but] one fragment of [Myself], yet I abide [unchanging].

CHAPTER XI

Arjuna asks to see Krishna's Universal Form

Arjuna said:

(1) Out of your gracious favour for me You have uttered the highest mystery called 'what appertains to Self', and by that word of yours this my perplexity has gone. (2) For I have heard of the coming to be and passing away of contingent beings: [this] You have told me in detail full, as well as the majesty of [your own] Self which does not pass away. (3) Even as You have described [your] Self to be, so must it be, O Lord Most High; [but] fain would I *see* the form of You as *Lord*, O [All-]Highest Person. (4) If, Lord, You think that I can see You thus, then show me, Lord of creative power (*yoga*), [this] Self [of yours] which does not pass away.

Krishna gives Arjuna a Celestial Eye

The Blessed Lord said:

(5) Son of Prithā, behold my forms in their hundreds and their thousands; how various they are, how divine, how many-hued and multiform! (6) Ādityas, Vasus, Rudras, the Aśvins twain, and the Maruts too, behold them! Marvels never seen before—how many!—Arjuna, behold them! (7) Do you today the whole universe behold centred here in One, with all that it contains of moving and unmoving things; [behold it] in my body, and whatever else you fain would see.

(8) But never will you be able to see Me with this your [natural] eye. A celestial eye I'll give you, behold my power (*yoga*) as Lord!

Krishna's Transfiguration

Sanjaya said:

(9) So saying Hari, the great Lord of power-and-the-skilful-use-of-it (*yoga*), revealed to the son of Prithā his highest sovereign form—(10) [a form] with many a mouth and eye and countless marvellous aspects; many [indeed] were its divine adornments, many the celestial weapons raised on high. (11) Garlands and robes

celestial He wore, fragrance divine was his anointing. [Behold this] God whose every [mark] spells wonder, the Infinite, facing every way!

(12) If in [bright] heaven together should arise the shining brilliance of a thousand suns, then would that perhaps resemble the brilliance of that [God] so great of Self.

(13) Then did the son of Pāndu see the whole [wide] universe in One converged, there in the body of the God of gods, yet divided out in multiplicity. (14) Then filled with amazement Arjuna, his hair on end, hands joined in reverent greeting, bowing his head before the God, [these words] spake out.

Arjuna said:

(15) O God, the gods in your body I behold and all the hosts of every kind of being; Brahmā, the lord, [I see] throned on the lotus-seat, celestial serpents and all the [ancient] seers. (16) Arms, bellies, mouths and eyes all manifold—so do I see You wherever I may look—infinite your form! End, middle, or again beginning I cannot see in You, O Monarch Universal, [manifest] in every form! (17) Yours the crown, the mace, the discus—a mass of glory shining on all sides—so do I see You—yet how hard are You to see,—for on every side there is brilliant light of fire and sun. Oh, who should comprehend it? (18) You are the Imperishable, [You] wisdom's highest goal; You, of this universe the last prop-and-resting-place, You the changeless, [You] the guardian of eternal law, You the primeval Person; [at last] I understand. (19) Beginning, middle, or end You do not know,—how infinite your strength! How numberless your arms,—your eyes the sun and moon! So do I see You,—your mouth a flaming fire, burning up this whole universe with your blazing glory. (20) By You alone is this space between heaven and earth pervaded,—all points of the compass too; gazing on this, your marvellous, frightening form, the three worlds shudder, [All-]Highest Self!

(21) Lo! these hosts of gods are entering into You: some, terror-struck, extol You, hands together pressed; great seers and men perfected in serried ranks cry out, 'All hail,' and praise You with copious hymns of praise. (22) Rudras, Ādityas, Vasus, Sādhyas, All-gods, Aśvins, Maruts, and [the ancestors] who quaff the steam, minstrels divine, sprites, demons, and the hosts of perfected saints gaze upon You, all utterly amazed.

(23) Gazing upon your mighty form with its myriad mouths, eyes, arms, thighs, feet, bellies, and sharp, gruesome tusks, the worlds [all] shudder [in affright],—how much more I! (24) Ablaze with many-coloured [flames] You touch the sky, your mouths wide open, [gaping,] your eyes distended, blazing: so do I see You and my inmost self is shaken: I cannot bear it, I find no peace, O Vishnu!

(25) I see your mouths with jagged, ghastly tusks reminding [me] of Time's [devouring] fire: I cannot find my bearings, I cannot find a refuge; have mercy, God of gods, home of the universe!

(26) Lo, all these sons of Dhritarāshtra accompanied by hosts of kings,—Bhīshma, Drona, and [Karna,] son of the charioteer, and those foremost in battle of our party too, (27) rush [blindly] into your [gaping] mouths that with their horrid tusks strike [them] with terror. Some stick in the gaps between your teeth,—see them!—their heads to powder ground!

(28) As many swelling, seething streams rush headlong into the [one] great sea, so do these heroes of the world of men enter into your blazing mouths. (29) As moths in bursting, hurtling haste rush into a lighted blaze to [their own] destruction, so do the worlds, well-trained in hasty violence, pour into your mouths to [their own] undoing!

(30) On every side You lick, lick up,—devouring,—worlds, universes, everything,—with burning mouths. Vishnu! your dreadful rays of light fill the whole universe with flames-of-glory, scorching [everywhere]. (31) Tell me, who are You, your form so cruel? Homage to You, You best of gods, have mercy! Fain would I know You as You are in the beginning, for what You are set on doing I do not understand.

Krishna reveals Himself as Time

The Blessed Lord said:

(32) Time am I, wreaker of the world's destruction, matured,—[grimly] resolved here to swallow up the worlds. Do what you will, all these warriors shall cease to be, drawn up [there] in their opposing ranks. (33) And so stand up, win glory, conquer your enemies and win a prosperous kingdom! Long since have these men in truth been slain by Me: yours it is to be the mere occasion.

(34) Drona, Bhīshma, Jayadratha, Karna, and all the other men of war are [as good as] slain by Me. Slay them then,—why falter? Fight! [for] you will conquer your rivals in the battle.

Sanjaya said:

(35) Hearing these words of Krishna, [Arjuna,] wearer of the crown, hands joined in veneration, trembling, bowed down to Krishna and spake again with stammering voice, as terrified he did obeisance.

Arjuna's Hymn of Praise

Arjuna said:

(36) Full just is it that in praise of You the world should find its pleasure and its joy, that monsters struck with terror should scatter in all directions, and that all the hosts of men perfected should do You homage. (37) And why should they not revere You, great [as is your] Self, more to be prized even than Brahman, first Creator, Infinite, Lord of the gods, home of the universe? You are the Imperishable, what IS and what is not and what surpasses both. (38) You are the Primal God, Primeval Person, You of this universe the last prop-and-resting-place, You the knower and what is to be known, [You our] highest home, O You whose forms are infinite, by You the whole universe was spun.

(39) [You are the wind-god,] Vāyu, Yama, [the god of death,] Agni, [the god of fire,] Varuna, [the god of water,] and the moon: Prajāpati are You and the primordial ancestor: all hail, all hail to You, [all hail] a thousandfold, and yet again, all hail, all hail to You! (40) All hail [to You] when I stand before You, [all hail] when I stand behind You, all hail to You wherever I may be, [all hail to You,] the All! How infinite your strength, how limitless your prowess! All things You bring to their consummation: hence You are All.

(41) How rashly have I called You comrade, for so I thought of You, [how rashly said,] 'Hey Krishna, hey Yādava, hey comrade!' Little did I know of this your majesty; distraught was I . . . or was it that I loved You? (42) Sometimes in jest I showed You disrespect as we played or rested or sat or ate at table, sometimes together, sometimes in sight of others: I crave your pardon, O [Lord,] unfathomable, unfallen!

(43) You are the father of the world of moving and unmoving

things, You their venerable teacher, most highly prized; none is there like You,—how could there be another greater?—in the three worlds. Oh, matchless is your power. (44) And so I bow to You, prostrate my body, crave grace of You, [my] Lord adorable: bear with me, I beg You, as father [bears] with son, or friend with friend, or lover with the one he loves, O God!

(45) Things never seen before I have seen, and ecstatic is my joy; yet fear-and-trembling perturb my mind. Show me, then, God, that [same human] form [I knew]; have mercy, Lord of gods, home of the universe! (46) Fain would I see You with [your familiar] crown and mace, discus in hand, just as You used to be; take up again your four-armed form, O thousand-armed, to whom every form belongs.

The Blessed Lord said:

(47) Because I desired to show you favour, Arjuna, by my Self's own power (*yoga*) I have shown you my highest form,—glorious, all-embracing, infinite, primeval, which none but you has ever seen before. (48) Not by the Vedas, not by sacrifice, not by [much] study or the giving of alms, not by rituals or grim ascetic practice can I be seen in such a form in the world of men: to you alone [have I revealed it,] champion of the Kurus. (49) You need not tremble nor need your spirit be perplexed though you have seen this form of mine, so awful, grim. Banish all fear, be glad at heart: behold again that [same familiar] form [you knew].

Krishna assumes His Human Form again

Sanjaya said:

(50) Thus speaking did the son of Vasudeva show his [human] form to Arjuna again, comforting him in his fear. For once again the great-souled [Krishna] assumed the body of a friend.

Arjuna said:

(51) Now that I see [again] this your human form, friendly-and-kind, I have returned to my senses and regained my normal state.

The Blessed Lord said:

(52) Right hard to see is this my form which you have seen: this is the form the gods themselves forever crave to see. (53) Not by

the Vedas or grim-ascetic-practice, not by the giving of alms or sacrifice can I be seen in such a form as you did see Me; (54) but by worship-of-love addressed to [Me,] none other, Arjuna, can I be known and seen in such a form and as I really am: [so can my lovers] enter into Me.

(55) Do works for Me, make Me your highest goal, be loyal-in-love to Me, cut off all [other] attachments, have no hatred for any being at all: for all who do thus shall come to Me.

CHAPTER XII

Personal God and Impersonal Absolute

Arjuna said:

(1) Of those who are thus ever integrated and serve You with loyal devotion, and those who [revere] the Imperishable Unmanifest, which are the most experienced in spiritual exercise?

The Blessed Lord said:

(2) Those I deem to be most integrated who fix their thoughts on Me and serve Me, ever integrated [in themselves], filled with the highest faith. (3) But those who revere the indeterminate Imperishable Unmanifest, unthinkable though coursing everywhere, sublime, aloof (*kūṭastha*), unmoving, firm, (4) who hold in check the complex of the senses, in all things equal-minded, taking pleasure in the weal of all contingent beings, these too attain to Me. (5) [But] greater is the toil of those whose thinking clings to the Unmanifest; for difficult [indeed] it is for embodied men to reach-and-tread the unmanifested way.

Exclusive Devotion to the Personal God

(6) But those who cast off all their works on Me, solely intent on Me, and meditate on Me in spiritual exercise, leaving no room for others, [and so really] do Me honour, (7) these will I lift up on high out of the ocean of recurring death, and that right soon, for their thoughts are fixed on Me.

(8) On Me alone let your mind dwell, stir up your soul to enter Me; thenceforth in very truth in Me you will find your home. (9) But if you are unable in all steadfastness to concentrate your thoughts on Me, then seek to win Me by effort unremitting. (10) And if for such effort you lack the strength, then work-and-act for Me, make this your goal; for even if you work only for my sake, you will receive the prize. (11) And then again if even this exceeds your powers, gird up your loins, renounce the fruit of all your works with self restrained. (12) For better is wisdom than [mere] effort, better than wisdom meditation; and [better] than

meditation to renounce the fruits of works: renunciation leads straightway to peace.

Whom God Loves

(13) Let a man feel hatred for no contingent being, let him be friendly, compassionate; let him be done with thoughts of 'I' and 'mine', the same in pleasure as in pain, long-suffering, (14) content and ever integrated, his self restrained, his purpose firm, let his mind and soul be steeped in Me, let him worship Me with love: then will I love him [in return].

(15) That man I love from whom the people do not shrink and who does not shrink from them, who is free from exaltation, fear, impatience, and excitement. (16) I love the man who has no expectation, is pure and skilled, indifferent, who has no worries and gives up all [selfish] enterprise, loyal-and-devoted to Me. (17) I love the man who hates not nor exults, who mourns not nor desires, who puts away both pleasant and unpleasant things, who is loyal-devoted-and-devout. (18–19) I love the man who is the same to friend and foe, [the same] whether he be respected or despised, the same in heat and cold, in pleasure as in pain, who has put away attachment and remains unmoved by praise or blame, who is taciturn, contented with whatever comes his way, having no home, of steady mind, [but] loyal-devoted-and-devout. (20) But as for those who reverence these deathless [words] of righteousness which I have just now spoken, putting their faith [in them], making Me their goal, my loving-devotees,—these do I love exceedingly.

CHAPTER XIII

The Field and the Knower of the Field

Arjuna said:

(0) [What is] Nature? [What the] 'person'? [What] the 'field' and [what] the 'knower of the field'? This, Krishna, would I know. [What too is] knowledge? [What] that which should be known?

The Blessed Lord said:

(1) The body is called the 'field' and he who knows it is the 'knower of the field', or so it has been said by those who know it. (2) And know that I am the 'knower of the field' in every field; knowledge of [this] field and [this] knower of the field I deem to be [true] knowledge. (3) What that field is and what it is like, what are its changes and which derives from which, and who He is, [the knower of the field,] and what his powers, hear [now] from Me in brief. (4) In many ways has it been sung by seers, in varied hymns each in its separate way, in aphoristic verses concerning Brahman, well reasoned and conclusive.

(5) Gross elements, the ego, intellect (*buddhi*), the Unmanifest, the eleven senses, and the five [sense-objects] on which the senses thrive, (6) desire, hate, pleasure, pain, *sensus communis*, thought and constancy,—these, in briefest span, are called the field together with their changes.

Knowledge

(7) To shun conceit and tricky ways, to wish none harm, to be long-suffering and upright, to reverence one's teacher, purity, steadfastness, self-restraint, (8) detachment from the senses' objects and no sense of 'I' most certainly, insight into birth, death, old age, disease, and pain, and what constitutes their worthlessness, (9) to be detached and not to cling to sons, wives, houses, and the like, a constant equal-mindedness whatever happens, pleasing or unpleasing, (10) unswerving loyalty-and-love for Me with spiritual exercise on no other bent, to dwell apart in desert places, to take no pleasure in the company of men, (11) constant attention to the wisdom that appertains to self, to see where knowledge of

reality must lead, [all] this is 'knowledge',—or so it has been said. Ignorance is what is otherwise than this.

The Real Object of Knowledge

(12) [And now] I will tell you that which should be known: once a man knows it, he attains to immortality. The highest Brahman it is called,—beginningless,—It is not Being nor is It Not-Being. (13) Hands and feet It has on every side, on every side eyes, heads, mouths, and ears; in the world all things encompassing [changeless] It abides. (14) Devoid of all the senses, It yet sheds light on all their qualities, [from all] detached, and yet supporting all; free from Nature's constituents, It yet experiences them. (15) Within all beings, yet without them; unmoved, It yet moves indeed; so subtle is It you cannot comprehend It; far off It stands, and yet how near It is! (16) Undivided in beings It abides, seeming divided: this is That which should be known,—[the one] who sustains, devours, and generates [all] beings. (17) Light of lights, 'Beyond the Darkness' It is called: [true] knowledge, what should be known, accessible to knowledge, established in the heart of all.

(18) And so in brief I have explained the 'field' and 'knowledge' and 'that which should be known'; the man who loves-and-worships Me, on knowing this, becomes fit to [share in] my own mode of being.

Matter and Spirit (Prakṛti *and* Puruṣa)

(19) 'Nature' and 'Person': know that these two are both beginningless: and know that change and quality arise from Nature. (20) Material Nature, they say, is [itself] the cause of cause, effect, and agency, while 'person' is said to be the cause in the experience of pleasure and of pain. (21) For 'person' is lodged in material Nature, experiencing the 'constituents' that arise from it; because he attaches himself to these he comes to birth in good and evil wombs.

(22) [And yet another One there is who,] surveying and approving, supports and [Himself] experiences [the constituents of Nature], the Mighty Lord: 'Highest Self' some call Him, the 'Highest Person' in this body. (23) Whoever knows 'person', material Nature, and its constituents to be such, in whatever state he be, he is not born again.

(24) By meditation some themselves see self in self, others by putting sound reason into practice, yet others by the exercise (*yoga*) of works. (25) But some, not knowing thus, hear it from others and revere it; and even these, taking their stand on what they hear, overcome death indeed.

(26) Whatever being comes to be, be it motionless or moving, [derives its being] from the union of 'field' and 'knower of the field': this know.

God Immanent in His Creatures

(27) The same in all contingent beings, abiding [without change], the Highest Lord, when all things fall to ruin, [Himself] is not destroyed: who sees Him sees [indeed]. (28) For seeing Him, the same, the Lord, established everywhere, he cannot of himself to [him]self do hurt, hence he treads the highest way.

(29) Nature it is which in every way does-work-and-acts; no agent is the self: who sees it thus he sees [indeed]. (30) When once a man can see [all] the diversity of contingent beings as abiding in One [alone] and their radiation out of It, then to Brahman he attains. (31) Because this Highest Self knows no beginning, no constituents, it does not pass away: though abiding in [many] a body, it does not act nor is it defiled. (32) Just as the ether, roving everywhere, knows no defilement, so subtle [is its essence], so does [this] Self, though everywhere abiding embodied, know no defilement. (33) As the one sun lights up this whole universe, so does the 'owner of the field' illumine the whole 'field'.

(34) Whoso with wisdom's eye discerns the difference between 'field' and 'knower of the field', and knows deliverance from material Nature to which [all] contingent beings are subject, goes to the further [shore].

CHAPTER XIV

The Blessed Lord said:

(1) [And now] again I shall proclaim the highest wisdom, best of doctrines; on knowing this all sages, when they passed on hence, attained the highest prize. (2) With this wisdom as their bulwark they reached a rank [in the order of existence] equivalent to my own, and even when [the universe is once again] engendered, they are not born [again], and when [again] it is dissolved, they know no trepidation.

'Great Brahman is My Womb'

(3) Great Brahman is to Me a womb, in it I plant the seed: from this derives the origin of all contingent beings. (4) In whatever womb whatever form arises-and-grows-together, of [all] those [forms] Great Brahman is the womb, I the father, giver of the seed.

The Three Constituents of Nature

(5) Goodness—Passion—Darkness: these are the [three] constituents from Nature sprung that bind the embodied [self] in the body though [the self itself] is changeless. (6) Among these Goodness, being immaculate, knowing no sickness, dispenses light, [and yet] it binds by [causing the self] to cling to wisdom and to joy. (7) Passion is instinct with desire, [this] know. From craving and attachment it wells up. It binds the embodied [self] by [causing it] to cling to works. (8) But from ignorance is Darkness born: mark [this] well. All embodied [selves] it leads astray. With fecklessness and sloth and sleepiness it binds. (9) Goodness causes [a man] to cling to joy, Passion to works; but Darkness, stifling wisdom, attaches to fecklessness. (10) Once it dominates Passion and Darkness, Goodness waxes strong; so Passion and Darkness when they dominate the other two.

(11) When at all the body's gates wisdom's light arises, then must you know that Goodness has increased. (12) When Passion is waxing strong, these [states] arise: greed, [purposeful] activity, committing oneself to works, disquiet, and ambition. (13) When

Darkness is surging up, these [states] arise: unlighted [darkness], unwillingness to act, fecklessness, delusion.

(14) But when an embodied [self] comes face to face with [the body's] dissolution and Goodness prevails, then will he reach the spotless worlds of those who know the highest. (15) [Another] goes to his demise when Passion [predominates]; he will be born among such men as cling to works: and as to him who dies when Darkness [has the upper hand], he will be born in the wombs of deluded fools.

(16) Of works well done, they say, the fruits belong to Goodness, being without spot: but pain is the fruit of Passion, ignorance the fruit of Darkness. (17) From Goodness wisdom springs, from Passion greed, from Darkness fecklessness, delusion, and ignorance—how not? (18) Upward is the path of those who abide in Goodness, in the middle stand the men of Passion. Stuck in the modes of the vilest constituent the men of Darkness go below.

(19) When the watching [self] sees there is no agent other than [these] constituents and knows what is beyond them, then will he come to [share in] that mode of being which is mine. (20) Transcending these three constituents which give the body its existence, from the sufferings of birth, death, and old age delivered, the embodied [self] wins immortality.

Arjuna said:

(21) What signs, Lord, mark him out,—[this man] who has transcended these three constituents? How does he behave? And how does he step out beyond these three constituents?

The Man who has transcended the Constituents

The Blessed Lord said:

(22) Radiance—activity—yes, delusion too,—when these arise he hates them not; and when [in turn] they cease he pines not after them. (23) As one indifferent he sits, by the constituents unruffled: 'So the constituents are busy': thus he thinks. Firm-based is he, unquavering. (24) The same in pleasure as in pain and self-assured, the same when faced with clods of earth or stones or gold; for him, wise man, are friend and foe of equal weight, equal the praise or blame [with which men cover him]. (25) Equal [his mind] in honour and disgrace, equal to ally and to enemy, he

renounces every [busy] enterprise: 'He has transcended the constituents': so must men say.

(26) And as to those who do Me honour with spiritual exercise, in loyalty-and-love undeviating, passed [clean] beyond these constituents, to becoming Brahman they are conformed. (27) For I am the base supporting Brahman,—immortal [Brahman] which knows no change,—[supporting] too the eternal law of righteousness and absolute beatitude.

CHAPTER XV

The Eternal Fig-tree

The Blessed Lord said:

(1) With roots above and boughs beneath, they say, the undying fig-tree [stands]: its leaves are the Vedic hymns: who knows it knows the Veda. (2) Below, above, its branches straggle out, well nourished by the constituents; sense-objects are the twigs. Below its roots proliferate inseparably linked with works in the world of men. (3) No form of it can here be comprehended, no end and no beginning, no sure abiding-place: this fig-tree with its roots so fatly nourished—[take] the stout axe of detachment and cut it down!

(4) And then search out that [high] estate to which, when once men go, they come not back again. 'I fly for succour to that primeval Person from whom flowed forth primordial creativity.' (5) Not proud, not fooled, [all] taint of attachment crushed, ever abiding in what appertains to self, desire suppressed, released from [all] dualities made known in pleasure as in pain, the undeluded march ahead to that state which knows no change. (6) That [state] is not illumined by sun or moon or fire: once men go thither, they come not back again, for that is my highest home.

The Transmigrating Self

(7) In the world of living things a minute part of Me, eternal [still], becomes a living [self], drawing to itself the five senses and the mind which have their roots in Nature. (8) When [this] sovereign [self] takes on a body and when he rises up therefrom, he takes them [with him] and moves on as the wind [wafts] scents away from their proper home. (9) Ear, eye, touch, taste, and smell he turns to due account,—so too the mind; [with these] he moves along the objects of sense. (10) Whether he rise up [from the body] or remain [therein], or whether, through contact with the constituents, he tastes experience, fools do not perceive him, but whoso possesses wisdom's eye sees him [indeed]. (11) And athletes of the spirit, fighting the good fight, see him established in [them]selves;

not so the men whose self is unperfected, however much they strive, witless, they see him not.

The Immanent God

(12) The splendour centred in the sun which bathes the whole world in light, [the splendour] in the moon and fire,—know that it [all] is mine. (13) [Thus] too I penetrate the earth and so sustain [all] beings with my strength; becoming [the moon-plant] Soma, I, the very sap [of life], cause all healing herbs to grow. (14) Becoming the [digestive] fire in [the bodies of] all men I dwell in the body of all that breathes; conjoined with the inward and outward breaths I digest the fourfold food. (15) I make my dwelling in the hearts of all: from Me stem memory, wisdom, the dispelling [of doubt]. Through all the Vedas it is I who should be known, for the maker of the Vedas' end am I, and I the Vedas know.

The Two Persons and the Transcendent God

(16) In the world there are these two persons,—perishable the one, Imperishable the other: the 'perishable' is all contingent beings, the 'Imperishable' they call the 'sublime, aloof (*kūṭastha*)'. (17) But there is [yet] another Person, the [All-]Sublime, surnamed 'All-Highest Self': the three worlds He enters-and-pervades, sustaining them,—the Lord who passes not away. (18) Since I transcend the perishable and am more exalted than the Imperishable itself, so am I extolled in Vedic as in common speech as the 'Person [All-]Sublime'. (19) Whoever thus knows Me, unconfused, as the Person [All-]Sublime, knows all and [knowing all] communes with Me with all his being, all his love. (20) And so have I [at last] revealed this most mysterious doctrine: let a man but understand it, for then he will be a man who [truly] understands, his [life's] work done.

CHAPTER XVI

The Cardinal Virtues and the Deadly Sins

The Blessed Lord said:

(1) Fearless and pure in heart, steadfast in the exercise of wisdom, open-handed and restrained, performing sacrifice, intent on studying Holy Writ, ascetic and upright, (2) none hurting, truthful, from anger free, renouncing [all], at peace, averse to calumny, compassionate to [all] beings, free from nagging greed, gentle, modest, never fickle, (3) ardent, patient, enduring, pure, not treacherous nor arrogant,—such is the man who is born to [inherit] a godly destiny.

(4) A hypocrite, proud of himself and arrogant, angry, harsh and ignorant is the man who is born to [inherit] a devilish destiny.

(5) A godly destiny means deliverance, a devilish one enslavement; this is the usual view. [But] do not worry, Arjuna, [for] you are born to a godly destiny. (6) There are two orders of beings in this world,—the godly and the devilish. Of the godly I have discoursed at length; now listen to [my words about] the devilish.

Of Human Devils

(7) Of creative action and its return to rest the devilish folk know nothing; in them there is no purity, no morality, no truth. (8) 'The world is devoid of truth,' they say, 'it has no ground, no ruling Lord; it has not come to be by mutual causal law; desire alone has caused it, nothing else.' (9) Holding fast to these views, lost souls with feeble minds, they embark on cruel-and-violent deeds, malignant [in their lust] for the destruction of the world. (10) Insatiate desire is their starting-point,—maddened are they by hypocrisy and pride, clutching at false conceptions, deluded as they are: impure are their resolves. (11) Unmeasured care is theirs right up to the time of death, [for] they have no other aim than to satisfy their lusts, convinced that this is all. (12) Bound by hundreds of fetters forged by hope, obsessed by anger and desire, they seek to build up wealth unjustly to satisfy their lusts.

(13) 'This have I gained today, this whim I'll satisfy; this

wealth is mine and much more too will be mine as time goes on. (14) He was an enemy of mine, I've killed him, and many another too I'll kill. I'm master [here]. I take my pleasure [as I will]; I'm strong and happy and successful. (15) I'm rich and of good family. Who else can match himself with me? I'll sacrifice and I'll give alms: [why not?] I'll have a marvellous time!' So speak [fools] deluded in their ignorance.

(16) [Their minds] unhinged by many a [foolish] fancy, caught up in delusion's net, obsessed by the satisfaction of their lusts, into foul hell they fall. (17) Puffed up with self-conceit, unbending, maddened by their pride in wealth, they offer sacrifices that are but sacrifice in name and not in the way prescribed,—the hypocrites! (18) Selfishness, force and pride, desire and anger, [these do] they rely on, envying and hating Me who dwell in their bodies as I dwell in all.

(19) Birth after birth in this revolving round, these vilest among men, strangers to [all] good, obsessed with hate and cruel, I ever hurl into devilish wombs. (20) Caught up in devilish wombs, birth after birth deluded, they never attain to Me: and so they tread the lowest way.

The Triple Gate of Hell

(21) Desire—Anger—Greed: this is the triple gate of hell, destruction of the self: therefore avoid these three. (22) When once a man is freed from these three gates of darkness, then can he work for [his] self's salvation, thence tread the highest way. (23) Whoso forsakes the ordinance of Scripture and lives at the whim of his own desires, wins not perfection, [finds] no comfort, [treads] not the highest way. (24) Therefore let Scripture be your norm, determining what is right and wrong. Once you know what the ordinance of Scripture bids you do, you should perform down here the works [therein prescribed].

CHAPTER XVII

The Unorthodox

Arjuna said:

(1) [And yet there are some] who forsake the ordinance of Scripture and offer sacrifice full filled with faith, where do they stand? On Goodness, Passion, or Darkness?

The Blessed Lord said:

(2) Threefold is the faith of embodied [selves]; each [of the three] springs from [a man's] own nature. [The first is] of Goodness, [the second] of Passion, of Darkness [is the third]. Listen to this.

(3) Faith is connatural to the soul of every man: man is instinct with faith: as is his faith, so too must he be. (4) To the gods do men of Goodness offer sacrifice, to sprites and monsters men of Passion, to disembodied spirits and the assembled spirits of the dead the others,—men of Darkness,—offer sacrifice.

Exaggerated Asceticism

(5–6) And this know too. Some men there are who, without regard to Scripture's ordinance, savagely mortify [their flesh], buoyed up by hypocrisy and self-regard, yielding to the violence of passion and desire, and so torment the mass of [living] beings whose home their body is, the witless fools,—and [with them] Me Myself within [that same] body abiding: how devilish their intentions!

The Three Constituents of Nature

(*a*) *In Food*

(7) Threefold again is food,—[food] that agrees with each [different type of] man: [so too] sacrifice, ascetic practice, and the gift of alms. Listen to the difference between them.

(8) Foods that promote a fuller life, vitality, strength, health, pleasure, and good-feeling, [foods that are] savoury, rich in oil and firm, heart-gladdening,—[these] are agreeable to the man of

Goodness. (9) Foods that are pungent, sour, salty, stinging hot, sharp, rough, and burning,—[these] are what the man of Passion loves. They bring pain, misery, and sickness. (10) What is stale and tasteless, rotten and decayed,—leavings, what is unfit for sacrifice, is food agreeable to the man of Darkness.

(*b*) *In Sacrifice*

(11) The sacrifice approved by [sacred] ordinance and offered up by men who would not taste its fruits, who concentrate their minds on this [alone]: 'In sacrifice lies duty': [such sacrifice] belongs to Goodness. (12) But the sacrifice that is offered up by men who bear its fruits in mind or simply for vain display,—know that [such sacrifice] belongs to Passion. (13) The sacrifice in which no proper rite is followed, no food distributed, no sacred words recited, no Brāhmans' fees paid up, no faith enshrined,—[such sacrifice] men say belongs to Darkness.

(*c*) *In Ascetic Practice*

(14) [Due] reverence of gods and Brāhmans, teachers and wise men, purity, uprightness, chastity, refusal to do harm,—[this] is [true] penance of the body. (15) Words that do not cause disquiet, [words] truthful, kind, and pleasing, the constant practice too of sacred recitation,—[this] is the penance of the tongue. (16) Serenity of mind and friendliness, silence and self-restraint, and the cleansing of one's affections,—this is called the penance of the mind.

(17) When men possessed of highest faith, integrated and indifferent to the fruits [of what they do], do penance in this threefold wise, men speak of [penance] in Goodness' way. (18) Some mortify themselves to win respect, honour, and reverence, or from sheer hypocrisy: here [on earth] this must be called [penance] in Passion's way,—fickle and unsure. (19) Some mortify themselves following perverted theories, torturing themselves, or to destroy another: this is called [penance] in Darkness' way.

(*d*) *In Alms-giving*

(20) Alms given because to give alms is a [sacred] duty to one from whom no favour is expected in return at the [right] place and time and to a [fit] recipient,—this is called alms [given] in Goodness' way. (21) But [alms] given in expectation of favours in

return, or for the sake of fruits [to be reaped] hereafter, [alms given] too against the grain,—this is called alms [given] in Passion's way. (22) Alms given at the wrong place and time to an unworthy recipient without respect, contemptuously,—this is called [alms given] in Darkness' way.

OṀ – THAT – IT IS

(23) OṀ — THAT — IT IS: This has been handed down, a three-fold pointer to Brahman: by this were allotted their proper place of old Brāhmans, Veda, and sacrifice. (24) And so [all] acts of sacrifice, the giving of alms, and penance enjoined by [sacred] ordinances and ever again [enacted] by Brahman's devotees begin with the utterance of [the one word] Oṁ.

(25) THAT: [so saying] do men who hanker for deliverance perform the various acts of sacrifice, penance, and the gift of alms, having no thought for the fruits [they bring].

(26) IT IS: in this the meanings are conjoined of 'Being' and of 'Good'; so too the [same] word *sat* is appropriately used for works that call forth praise. (27) In sacrifice, in penance, in the gift of alms [the same word] *sat* is used, meaning 'steadfastness': and works performed with these purposes [in mind], [these] too are surnamed *sat*. (28) Whatever offering is made in unbelief, whatever given, whatever act of penance undertaken, whatever done,—of that is said *asat*, 'It is not:' for naught it is in this world or the next.

CHAPTER XVIII

Renunciation and Self-Surrender

Arjuna said:

(1) Krishna, fain would I know the truth concerning renunciation and apart from this [the truth] of self-surrender.

The Blessed Lord said:

(2) To give up works dictated by desire, wise men allow [this] to be renunciation; surrender of all the fruits that [accrue] to works discerning men call self-surrender.

(3) '[All] works must be surrendered, for [works themselves] are tainted with defect:' so say some of the wise; but others say that [works of] sacrifice, the gift of alms, and works of penance are not to be surrendered.

(4) Hear [then] my own decision in this matter of surrender: for threefold is self-surrender; so has it been declared. (5) [Works of] sacrifice, the gift of alms, and works of penance are not to be surrendered; these must most certainly be done: it is sacrifice, alms-giving, and ascetic practice that purify the wise. (6) But even these works should be done [in a spirit of self-surrender], for [all] attachment [to what you do] and [all] the fruits [of what you do] must be surrendered. This is my last decisive word.

(7) For to renounce a work enjoined [by Scripture] is inappropriate; deludedly to give this up is [the way] of Darkness. This [too] has been declared. (8) The man who gives up a deed simply because it causes pain or because he shrinks from bodily distress, commits an act of self-surrender that accords with Passion['s way]: assuredly he will not reap the fruit of self-surrender. (9) But if a work is done simply because it should be done and is enjoined [by Scripture], and if [all] attachment, [all thought of] fruit is given up, then that is surrender in Goodness[' way], I deem.

(10) The self-surrendered man, suffused with Goodness, wise, whose [every] doubt is cut away, hates not his uncongenial work nor cleaves to the congenial. (11) For one still in the body it is not possible to surrender up all works without exception; rather it is

he who surrenders up the *fruit* of works who deserves the name, 'A self-surrendered man.'

(12) Unwanted—wanted—mixed: threefold is the fruit of work, —[this they experience] at death who have not surrendered [self], but not at all such men as have renounced.

The Five Causes

(13) In the system of the Sāṁkhyas these five causes are laid down; by these all works attain fruition. Learn them from Me.

(14) Material basis, agent, material causes of various kinds, the vast variety of motions, and fate, the fifth and last. (15) These are the five causes of whatever work a man may undertake,—of body, speech, or mind,—no matter whether right or wrong. (16) This being so, the man who sees self isolated [in itself] as the agent, does not see [at all]. Untrained is his intelligence (*buddhi*) and evil are his thoughts. (17) A man who has reached a state where there is no sense of 'I', whose soul (*buddhi*) is undefiled,—were he to slaughter [all] these worlds,—slays nothing. He is not bound.

The Three Constituents again

(*a*) *In Metaphysical Doctrine*

(18) Knowledge—its object—knower: [these form] the threefold instrumental cause of action. Instrument—action—agent: [such is] action's threefold nexus.

(19) Knowledge—action—agent: [these too are] three in kind, distinguished by 'constituent'. The theory of constituents contains it [all]: listen to the manner of these [three].

(20) That [kind of] knowledge by which one sees one mode of being, changeless, undivided in all contingent beings, divided [as they are], is Goodness' [knowledge]. Be sure of this. (21) But that [kind of] knowledge which in all contingent beings discerns in separation all manner of modes of being, different and distinct,—this, you must know, is knowledge born of Passion. (22) But that [kind of knowledge] which sticks to one effect as if it were all,—irrational, not bothering about the Real as the [true] object [of all knowledge, thinking of it as] finite,—this [knowledge] belongs to Darkness. So is it laid down.

(*b*) *In Works*

(23) The work prescribed [by Scripture] from [all] attachment free, performed without passion, without hate, by one who hankers

not for fruits, is called [the work] of Goodness. (24) But the work in which much effort is expended by one who seeks his own pleasure-and-desire or again thinks, 'It is I who do it,' such [work] is assigned to Passion. (25) The work embarked on by a man deluded who has no thought of consequence, nor [care at all] for the loss and hurt [he causes others] or for the human part [he plays himself], is called [a work] of Darkness.

(*c*) *In the Agent*

(26) The agent who, from attachment freed, steadfast and resolute, remains unchanged in failure and success and never speaks of 'I', is called [an agent] in Goodness' way. (27) The agent who pursues the fruit of works, passionate, greedy, intent on doing harm, impure, a prey to exaltation as to grief, is widely known [to act] in Passion's way. (28) The agent, inept and vulgar, stiff-and-proud, a cheat, low-spoken, slothful, who is subject to depression, who procrastinates, is called [an agent] in Darkness' way.

(*d*) *In the Intellect*

(29) Divided threefold too are intellect and constancy according to the constituents. Listen [to Me, for I shall] tell it forth in all its many forms, omitting nothing.

(30) The intellect that distinguishes between activity and its cessation, between what should be done and what should not, between danger and security, bondage and release, is [an intellect] in Goodness' way. (31) The intellect by which lawful-right and lawless-wrong, what should be done and what should not, are untruly understood, is [an intellect] in Passion's way. (32) The intellect which, by Darkness overcast, thinks right is wrong, law lawlessness, all things their opposite, is [an intellect] in Darkness' way.

(*e*) *In Constancy*

(33) The constancy by which a man holds fast in check the works of mind and breath and sense, unswerving in spiritual exercise, is constancy in Goodness' way. (34) But the constancy by which a man holds fast [in balance] pleasure, self-interest, and righteousness, yet clings to them, desirous of their fruits, is constancy in Passion's way. (35) [The constancy] by which a fool will not let go sleep, fear, or grief, depression or exaltation, is constancy in Darkness' way.

(*f*) *In Pleasure*

(36) Threefold too is pleasure: Arjuna, hear this now from Me. [That pleasure] which a man enjoys after much effort [spent], making an end thereby of suffering, (37) which at first seems like poison but in time transmutes itself into what seems to be ambrosia, is called pleasure in Goodness' way, for it springs from that serenity which comes from apperception of the self. (38) [That pleasure] which at first seems like ambrosia, arising when the senses meet the objects of sense, but in time transmutes itself into what seems to be poison,—that pleasure, so it is said, is in Passion's way. (39) That pleasure which at first and in the sequel leads the self astray, which derives from sleep and sloth and fecklessness, has been declared as [pleasure] in Darkness' way.

(40) There is no existent thing in heaven or earth or yet among the gods which is or ever could be free from these three constituents from Nature sprung.

The Four Great Classes of Society

(41) To Brāhmans, princes, peasants-and-artisans, and serfs works have been variously assigned by [these] constituents, and they arise from the nature of things as they are.

(42) Calm, self-restraint, ascetic practice, purity, long-suffering and uprightness, wisdom in theory as in practice, religious faith,—[these] are the works of Brāhmans, inhering in their nature. (43) High courage, ardour, endurance, skill, in battle unwillingness to flee, an open hand, a lordly mien,—[these] are the works of princes, inhering in their nature [too]. (44) To till the fields, protect the kine, and engage in trade, [these] are the works of peasants-and-artisans, inhering in their nature; but works whose very soul is service inhere in the very nature of the serf.

(45) By [doing] the work that is proper to him [and] rejoicing [in the doing], a man succeeds, perfects himself. [Now] hear just how a man perfects himself by [doing and] rejoicing in his proper work. (46) By dedicating the work that is proper [to his caste] to Him who is the source of the activity of all beings, by whom this whole universe was spun, a man attains perfection-and-success. (47) Better [to do] one's own [caste-] duty, though devoid of merit, than [to do] another's, however well performed. By doing the work prescribed by his own nature a man meets with no

defilement. (48) Never should a man give up the work to which he is born, defective though it be: for every enterprise is choked by defects, as fire by smoke.

'Becoming Brahman'

(49) With soul detached from everything, with self subdued, [all] longing gone, renounce: and so you will find complete success, perfection, works transcended. (50) Perfection found, now learn from Me how you may reach Brahman too: [this I will tell you] briefly; it is wisdom's highest bourne.

(51) Let a man be integrated by his soul [now] cleansed, let him restrain [him]self with constancy, abandon objects of sense,—sound and all the rest,—passion and hate let him cast out; (52) let him live apart, eat lightly, restrain speech, body, and mind; let him practise meditation constantly, let him cultivate dispassion; (53) let him give up all thought of 'I', force, pride, desire and anger and possessiveness, let him not think of anything as 'mine', at peace;—[if he does this,] to becoming Brahman is he conformed.

From Brahman to God

(54) Brahman become, with self serene, he grieves not nor desires; the same to all contingent beings he gains the highest love-and-loyalty to Me. (55) By love-and-loyalty he comes to know Me as I really am, how great I am and who; and once he knows Me as I am, he enters [Me] forthwith. (56) Let him then do all manner of works continually, putting his trust in Me; for by my grace he will attain to an eternal, changeless state.

Arjuna's Personal Case

(57) Give up in thought to Me all that you do, make Me your goal: relying on the integration of the soul, think on Me constantly. (58) Thinking on Me you will surmount all dangers by my grace; but if through selfishness you will not listen, then will you [surely] perish. (59) [But if,] relying on your ego, you should think, 'I will not fight', vain is your resolve, [for] Nature will constrain you. (60) You are bound by your own works which spring from your own nature; [for] what, deluded, you would not do, you will do perforce. (61) In the region of the heart of all contingent beings dwells

the Lord, twirling them hither and thither by his uncanny power (*māyā*) [like puppets] mounted on a machine.

(62) In Him alone seek refuge with all your being, all your love; and by his grace you will attain an eternal state, the highest peace. (63) Of all the mysteries the most mysterious, this wisdom have I told you; ponder it in all its amplitude, then do whatever you will.

'I love you Well'

(64) And now again give ear to this my highest Word, of all the most mysterious: 'I love you well.' Therefore will I tell you your salvation.

(65) Bear Me in mind, love Me and worship Me, sacrifice, prostrate yourself to Me: so will you come to Me, I promise you truly, for you are dear to Me. (66) Give up all things of law, turn to Me, your only refuge, [for] I will deliver you from all evils; have no care.

The Supreme Value of the Teaching of the Gītā

(67) Never must you tell this word to one whose life is not austere, to one devoid of love-and-loyalty, to one who refuses to obey, or to one who envies Me. (68) [But] whoever shall proclaim this highest mystery to my loving devotees, showing the while the highest love-and-loyalty to Me, shall, nothing doubting, come to Me indeed. (69) No one among men can render Me more pleasing service than a man like this; nor shall any other man on earth be more beloved by Me than he. (70) And whoso shall read this dialogue which you and I have held concerning what is right, it will be as if he had offered Me a sacrifice of wisdom: so do I believe. (71) And the man of faith, not cavilling, who listens [to this my Word], he too shall win deliverance, and attain to the goodly worlds of those whose works are pure.

(72) Have you listened, Arjuna, [to these my words] with a mind intent on them alone? And has the confusion [of your mind] that stemmed from ignorance been dispelled?

Arjuna said:

(73) Destroyed is the confusion; and through your grace I have regained a proper way of thinking: with doubts dispelled I stand ready to do your bidding.

Epilogue

Sanjaya said:

(74) So did I hear this wondrous dialogue of [Krishna,] Vasudeva's son, and the high-souled Arjuna, [and as I listened] I shuddered with delight. (75) By Vyāsa's favour have I heard this highest mystery, this spiritual exercise from Krishna, the Lord of spiritual exercise (*yoga*) himself as He in person told it. (76) O King, as often as I recall this marvellous, holy dialogue of Arjuna and Krishna, I thrill with joy, and thrill with joy again. (77) And as often as I recall that form of Vishnu,—so utterly marvellous,—how great is my amazement! I thrill with joy, and thrill with joy again. (78) Wherever Krishna is, the Lord of spiritual exercise, wherever Arjuna, holder of the bow, there is good fortune, victory, success, sound policy assured. This do I believe.

TRANSLITERATION
TRANSLATION
AND
COMMENTARY

CHAPTER I

The Setting

Dhṛtarāṣṭra uvāca:

1. *dharma-kṣetre kuru-kṣetre samavetā yuyutsavaḥ*
māmakāḥ Pāṇḍavāś c'aiva: kim akurvata, Saṁjaya?

Dhritarāshtra said:

On the field of justice, the Kuru-field, my men and the sons of Pāndu too [stand] massed together ready for the fight. What, Sanjaya, did they do?

Saṁjaya uvāca:

2. *dṛṣṭvā tu Pāṇḍav'ānīkaṁ vyūḍhaṁ Duryodhanas tadā*
ācāryam upasaṁgamya rājā vacanam abravīt.

Sanjaya said:

Then did Duryodhana, the king, seeing the ranks of Pāndu's sons drawn up [for battle], approach the teacher, [Drona,] with these words:

3. *paśy'aitāṁ Pāṇḍu-putrāṇām, ācārya, mahatīṁ camūm*
vyūḍhāṁ Drupada-putreṇa tava śiṣyeṇa dhīmatā.

'Teacher, behold this mighty host of Pāndu's sons drawn up [in ranks] by the son of Drupada, your own wise pupil.'

4. *atra śūrā maheṣvāsā Bhīm'ārjuna-samā yudhi*
Yuyudhāno Virāṭaś-ca Drupadaś ca mahā-rathaḥ,

Here are brave men, great archers, the equal of Bhīma and Arjuna in battle,—Yuyudhāna, Virāta, and Drupada, the mighty charioteer,

5. *Dhṛṣṭaketuś Cekitānaḥ Kāśī-rājaś ca vīryavān,*
Purujit Kuntibhojaś ca Śaibyaś ca nara-puṁgavaḥ,

Dhristiketu, Cekitāna, the Kāśīs' valiant king, Purijit, Kuntibhoja, and the king of the Śibis, foremost of fighting men,

6. *Yudhāmanyuś ca vikrānta Uttamaujāś ca vīryavān,*
Saubhadro Draupadeyāś ca, sarva eva mahā-rathāḥ.

Brave Yudhāmanyu and valiant Uttamaujas, Subhadrā's son, and the sons of Draupadī, all of them mighty charioteers.

7. *asmākaṁ tu viśiṣṭā ye, tān nibodha, dvij'ottama,*
nāyakā mama sainyasya; saṁjñ' ārthaṁ tān bravīmi te.

Listen too, great Brāhman, to [the list of] those outstanding on our side, the captains of my army; I will enumerate them so that you may be kept informed.

8. *bhavān Bhīṣmaś ca Karṇaś ca Kṛpaś ca samitiṁ-jayaḥ,*
Aśvatthāmā Vikarṇaś ca Saumadattis tath' aiva ca;

Yourself, Bhīshma, Karna, and Kripa, victorious in battle, Aśvatthāman, Vikarna, and Somadatta's son as well,

9. *anye ca bahavaḥ śūrā mad-arthe tyakta-jīvitāḥ*
nānā-śastra-praharaṇāḥ sarve yuddha-viśāradāḥ.

And many another fighting man will lay down his life for me. Various are their arms and weapons, and all are skilled in war.

10. *aparyāptaṁ tad asmākaṁ balaṁ Bhīṣm' ābhirakṣitam,*
paryāptaṁ tv idam eteṣāṁ balaṁ Bhīm' ābhirakṣitam.

Imperfect are those our forces, though Bhīshma [himself] protects them, but perfect are these their forces which Bhīma guards.

This appears to be what the text means. The words are spoken by Duryodhana who is much given to boasting and come somewhat unnaturally from his lips. Hence, Rk., following some ancient and modern commentators, translates *aparyāptam* as 'unlimited' and *paryāptam* as 'limited'. He does not, however, quote any parallel for such a use of the word. Some MSS. reverse the order of *Bhīṣma-* and *Bhīma*, thus giving the required sense.

11. *ayaneṣu ca sarveṣu yathā-bhāgam avasthitāḥ*
Bhīṣmam ev' ābhirakṣantu bhavantaḥ sarva eva hi.

So stand firm in all your goings, each in his appointed place. Guard Bhīshma above all others, every one of you.

12. *tasya saṁjanayan harṣaṁ Kuru-vṛddhaḥ pitāmahaḥ*
siṁha-nādaṁ vinady' occhaiḥ śaṅkhaṁ dadhmau pratāpavān.

To give him cheer, [Bhīshma,] the aged grandsire of the Kuru clan, roared like a lion, loud [and strong], and undaunted blew his conch.

13. *tataḥ śaṅkhāś ca bheryaś ca paṇav'ānaka-gomukhāḥ*
sahas'aiv'ābhyahanyanta: sa śabdas tumulo 'bhavat.

Then conchs, drums, cymbals, trumpets, and kettledrums burst into sudden sound: tumultuous was the din.

14. *tataḥ śvetair hayair yukte mahati syandane sthitau*
Mādhavaḥ Pāṇḍavaś c'aiva divyau śaṅkhau pradadhmatuḥ.

Then too did [Krishna,] Madhu's scion and [Arjuna,] son of Pāndu, standing [erect] on their great chariot yoked to white steeds, their godly conchs blow.

15. *Pāñcajanyaṁ hṛṣīkeśo, Devadattaṁ dhanaṁjayaḥ*
Pauṇḍraṁ dadhmau mahā-śaṅkhaṁ bhīma-karmā vṛk'odaraḥ.

[The conch called] Pāncajanya did Krishna blow, [that called] Devadatta Arjuna; the mighty conch [called] Paundra blew wolf-bellied [Bhīma,] doer of dreadful deeds.

16. *Anantavijayaṁ rājā Kuntī-putro Yudhiṣṭhiraḥ,*
Nakulaḥ Sahadevaś ca Sughoṣa-Maṇipuṣpakau:

[The conch called] Anantavijaya blew Kuntī's son, Yudhishthira, the king: Sughosha and Manipushpaka [blew] Nakula and Sahadeva:

17. *Kāśyaś ca param'eṣvāsaḥ Śikhaṇḍī ca mahā-rathaḥ*
Dhṛṣṭadyumno Virāṭaś ca Sātyakiś c'āparājitaḥ,

And the Kāśis' king, archer supreme, and Śikhandin, the great charioteer, and Dhrishtadyumna, Virāta, and unconquered Sātyaki,

18. *Drupado Draupadeyāś ca sarvaśaḥ, pṛthivī-pate,*
Saubhadraś ca mahā-bāhuḥ śaṅkhān dadhmuḥ pṛthak-pṛthak.

Drupada and the sons of Draupadī and Subhadrā's strong-armed son, each blew his conch [resounding] from every side.

19. *sa ghoṣo Dhārtarāṣṭrāṇāṁ hṛdayāni vyadārayat*
nabhaś ca pṛthivīṁ c'aiva tumulo vyanunādayan.

The tumultuous din [they made] rent the hearts of Dhritarāshtra's sons, making heaven and earth resound.

20. *atha vyavasthitān dṛṣṭvā Dhārtarāṣṭrān kapi-dhvajaḥ*
pravṛtte śastra-saṁpāte dhanur udyamya Pāṇḍavaḥ,

Then Pāndu's son, whose banner is an ape, scanning [the ranks of] Dhritarāshtra's men drawn up, took up his bow: the clash of arms was on.

21. *hṛṣīkeśaṁ tadā vākyam idam āha, mahī-pate,*
senayor ubhayor madhye: rathaṁ sthāpaya me, 'cyuta,

Then between the two armies, Sire, he addressed Krishna in these words: 'Halt the chariot, unfallen [Lord],

22. *yāvad etān nirīkṣe 'haṁ yoddhu-kāmān avasthitān,*
kair mayā saha yoddhavyam asmin raṇa-samudyame.

That I may scan these men drawn up, spoiling for the fight, [that I may see] with whom I must do battle in this enterprise of war.

23. *yotsyamānān avekṣe 'haṁ ya ete 'tra samāgatāḥ*
Dhārtarāṣṭrasya durbuddher yuddhe priya-cikīrṣavaḥ.

I see them here assembled, ready to fight, seeking to please Dhritarāshtra's baleful son, by waging war.

24. *evam ukto hṛṣīkeśo guḍākeśena, Bhārata,*
senayor ubhayor madhye sthāpayitvā rath'ottamam,

Thus addressed by Arjuna, Krishna brought that splendid chariot to a halt between the two armies

25. *Bhīṣma-Droṇa-pramukhataḥ sarveṣāṁ ca mahī-kṣitām*
uvāca: Pārtha, paśy' aitān samavetān Kurūn iti.

In front of Bhīshma and Drona and all the rulers of the earth, Said he: 'Son of Prithā, behold these Kurus assembled [here].

26. *tatr' āpaśyat sthitān Pārthaḥ pitṝn atha pitāmahān*
ācāryān mātulān bhrātṝn putrān pautrān sakhīṁs tathā,

There as they stood the son of Prithā saw fathers, grandsires, teachers, uncles, brothers, sons, grandsons, and comrades,

27. *śvaśurān suhṛdaś c' aiva senayor ubhayor api;*
tān samīkṣya sa Kaunteyaḥ sarvān bandhūn avasthitān,

Fathers-in-law and friends in both armies; and seeing them, all his kinsmen, [thus] arrayed, the son of Kuntī

28. *kṛpayā parayā'viṣṭo viṣīdann idam abravīt:*
dṛṣṭv'emān svajanān, Kṛṣṇa, yuyutsūn samavasthitān

Was filled with deep compassion and, desponding, spoke these [words]: 'Krishna, when I see these mine own folk standing [before me], spoiling for the fight,

29. *sīdanti mama gātrāṇi mukhaṁ ca pariśuṣyati*
vepathuś ca śarīre me roma-harṣaś ca jāyate.

My limbs give way, my mouth dries up, trembling seizes upon my body, and my [body's] hairs stand up in dread.

30. *Gāṇḍīvaṁ sraṁsate hastāt tvak c'aiva paridahyate,*
na ca śaknomy avasthātuṁ bhramatī'va ca me manaḥ.

[My bow,] Gāndīva, slips from my hand, my very skin is all ablaze; I cannot stand and my mind seems to wander.

31. *nimittāni ca paśyāmi viparītāni, Keśava,*
na ca śreyo 'nupaśyāmi hatvā svajanam āhave.

Krishna, adverse omens too I see, nor can I discern aught good in striking down in battle mine own folk.

32. *na kāṅkṣe vijayaṁ, Kṛṣṇa, na ca rājyaṁ sukhāni ca:*
kiṁ no rājyena, Govinda, kiṁ bhogair jīvitena vā ?

Krishna, I do not long for victory nor for the kingdom nor yet for things of pleasure. What should I do with a kingdom? What with enjoyments or [even] with life?

33. *yeṣām arthe kāṅkṣitaṁ no rājyaṁ bhogāḥ sukhāni ca,*
ta ime 'vasthitā yuddhe prāṇāṁs tyaktvā dhanāni ca,—

Those for whose sake we covet kingdom, enjoyments, things of pleasure, stand [here arrayed] for battle, surrendering life and wealth,—

kāṅkṣitaṁ no: var. *jīvitaṁ me.*

dhanāni ca, 'and wealth': var. *sudustyajān*, 'difficult to give up' (agreeing with 'life').

34. *ācāryāḥ pitaraḥ putrās tath'aiva ca pitāmahāḥ,*
mātulāḥ śvaśurāḥ pautrāḥ śyālāḥ saṁbandhinas tathā.

Teachers, fathers, sons, and grandsires too; uncles, fathers-in-law, grandsons, brothers-in-law,—kinsmen all.

35. *etān na hantum icchāmi ghnato 'pi, Madhusūdana,*
api trailokya-rājyasya hetoḥ, kiṁ nu mahī-kṛte ?

Krishna, though they should slay [me], yet would I not slay them, not for the dominion over the three worlds, how much less for the earth [alone]!

36. *nihatya Dhārtarāṣṭrān naḥ kā prītiḥ syāj, Janārdana ?*
pāpam ev'āśrayed asmān hatv'aitān ātatāyinaḥ.

Should we slaughter Dhritarāshtra's sons, Krishna, what sweetness then is ours? Evil, and only evil, would come to dwell with us, should we slay them, hate us as they may.

37. *tasmān n'ārhā vayaṁ hantuṁ Dhārtarāṣṭrān sabāndhavān;*
svajanaṁ hi kathaṁ hatvā sukhinaḥ syāma, Mādhava ?

Therefore we have no right to kill the sons of Dhritarāshtra and their kin. For, Krishna, were we to lay low our own folk, how could we be happy?

sabāndhavān, 'and their kin': var. *svabāndhavān*, 'our own kin'.

38. *yady apy ete na paśyanti lobh'opahata-cetasaḥ*
kula-kṣaya-kṛtaṁ doṣaṁ mitra-drohe ca pātakam,

And even if, bereft of sense by greed, they cannot see that to ruin a family is wickedness and to break one's word a crime,

39. *kathaṁ na jñeyam asmābhiḥ pāpād asmān nivartitum*
kula-kṣaya-kṛtaṁ doṣaṁ prapaśyadbhir, Janārdana ?

How should we not be wise enough to shun this evil thing, for we clearly see that to ruin a family is wickedness?

40. *kula-kṣaye praṇaśyanti kula-dharmāḥ sanātanāḥ:*
dharme naṣṭe kulaṁ kṛtsnam adharmo 'bhibhavaty uta.

Once the family is ruined, the primeval family laws collapse. Once law is destroyed, then lawlessness overwhelms all [that is known as] family.

41. *adharm'ābhibhavāt, Kṛṣṇa, praduṣyanti kula-striyaḥ;*
strīṣu duṣṭāsu, Vārṣṇeya, jāyate varṇa-saṁkaraḥ.

With lawlessness triumphant, Krishna, the family's women are debauched; once the women are debauched, there will be a mixing of caste.

42. *saṁkaro narakāy' aiva kula-ghnānāṁ kulasya ca;*
patanti pitaro hy eṣāṁ lupta-piṇḍ'odaka-kriyāḥ.

The mixing of caste leads to hell,—[the hell prepared] for those who wreck the family and for the family [so wrecked]. So too their ancestors fall down [to hell], cheated of their offerings of food and drink.

43. *doṣair etaiḥ kula-ghnānāṁ varṇa-saṁkara-kārakaiḥ*
utsādyante jāti-dharmāḥ kula-dharmāś ca śāśvatāḥ.

These evil ways of men who wreck the family, [these evil ways] that cause the mixing of caste, [these evil ways] bring caste-law to naught and the eternal family laws.

44. *utsanna-kula-dharmāṇāṁ manuṣyāṇāṁ, Janārdana,*
narake niyataṁ vāso bhavatī'ty anuśuśruma.

A sure abode in hell there is for men who bring to naught the family laws: so, Krishna, have we heard.

45. *aho bata mahat pāpaṁ kartuṁ vyavasitā vayam*
yad rājya-sukha-lobhena hantuṁ svajanam udyatāḥ.

Ah! Ah! so are we [really] bent on committing a monstrous evil deed? intent as we are on slaughtering our own folk because we lust for the sweets of sovereignty.

'Sweets of sovereignty': or, 'sovereignty and joy'.

46. *yadi mām apratīkāram aśastraṁ śastra-pāṇayaḥ*
Dhārtarāṣṭrā raṇe hanyus, tan me kṣemataraṁ bhavet.

O let the sons of Dhritarāshtra, arms in hand, slay me in battle though I, unarmed myself, will offer no defence; therein were greater happiness for me.'

47. *evam uktvā 'rjunaḥ saṁkhye ratho'pastha upāviśat*
visṛjya saśaraṁ cāpaṁ śoka-saṁvigna-mānasaḥ.

So saying Arjuna sat down upon the chariot-seat [though] battle [had begun], let slip his bow and arrows, his mind distraught with grief.

CHAPTER II

THE first chapter provides the setting of the Bhagavad-Gītā. Krishna, the incarnate God, after having exhausted all his powers of mediation, is now determined that the Kauravas must be destroyed, and it is Arjuna, his bosom-friend, who is to be the principal agent of their destruction. This is the divine plan and it is ruthlessly brought home later in the dialogue:

> And so stand up, [Krishna will say] win glory, conquer your enemies and win a prosperous kingdom! Long since have these men in truth been slain by Me; yours it is to be the mere occasion. (11.33)

Arjuna, however, had shrunk from the mass slaughter of his kinsmen of which he was to be the 'occasion':

> Should we slaughter Dhritarāshtra's sons, [he had said,] what sweetness then is ours? Evil, and only evil, would come to dwell with us, should we slay them, hate us as they may. . . . And even if, bereft of sense by greed, they cannot see that to ruin a family is wickedness and to break one's word a crime, how should we not be wise enough to shun this evil thing, for we clearly see that to ruin a family is wickedness? (1.36–9)

In support of this very natural reluctance to take the life of his kinsmen, he appeals to the *dharma*, the religious law current in his time: family strife leads to the ruin of the family itself and of the laws that keep the social structure of which the family is the basis together. The inevitable result of this must be that there will be a mixing of caste, and there can be no worse evil than this:

> These evil ways of men who wreck the family, [these evil ways] that cause the mixing of caste, [these evil ways] bring caste-law to naught and the eternal family laws. A sure abode in hell there is for men who bring to naught the family laws; so, Krishna, have we heard. (1.43–4)

Accordingly Arjuna lets his bow and arrows slip and dejectedly sits down on his chariot-seat. It is now up to Krishna to explain why this fratricidal war must go on, and in Chapter II the dialogue begins.

Verses 1–10 are the natural sequence of Chapter I. Arjuna, after appealing to Krishna to instruct him, suddenly makes up his mind: 'I will not fight'. (2. 9)

In verses 11–37 Krishna advances four reasons why Arjuna should fight. (*a*) The 'embodied self' is immortal and is not destroyed when the body is destroyed (12–25), (*b*) what is born must die and what dies must be born again (26–9), (*c*) it is the duty of the princely (*kṣatriya*) class to fight in a just war (31–3), and (*d*) Arjuna would lose face in backing out of the battle at the last moment and would be accused of cowardice (34–7).

Of these four reasons (*a*) and (*b*) hang together as do (*c*) and (*d*). The first two are concerned with the nature of the human 'self', the second two with the specific duties and characteristics of a member of the princely class. The first two are concerned with the human condition as it is understood by the Hindus and looks forward to Krishna's teaching concerning human bondage and release: the second two adumbrate the principles which should guide a man (in this case a warrior of the princely class) in his journey from the bondage of this mundane world of action (*karma*) to his final release, liberation (*mukti*, *mokṣa*) and eternal rest (*śānti*). Throughout the dialogue the two themes will alternate and combine, but there can be no question, as we shall see later, of action being commended for its own sake: man must never be *committed* to any action, however apparently worthwhile—he may only use 'works' (*karma*) as a means to transcending works themselves: for 'works' of their very nature 'bind' (3. 9, 31: 4. 14: 9. 28: 18. 60).

Up to this point we are still firmly in the context of the Epic. Krishna is persuading Arjuna to fight and the reasons he advances are directed towards this very practical goal. In 39–72, however, we are taken out of the immediate practical context and enter into a more speculative sphere.

Verses 39–53 are concerned with what is called *buddhi-yoga*—the 'Yoga' of the contemplative intellect or what we in the West would call the soul (below, p. 143), while verses 54–72 describe the 'man of steady wisdom'.

As scholars have not been slow to point out, the transition from a purely practical argumentation aimed at persuading Arjuna to go to war to a consideration of the contemplative life by which Arjuna will 'put away the bondage that is inherent in [all] works' (2. 39), seems harsh, but it is not really so as we shall see in the sequel. Though there is no 'salvation' in 'works', they must nevertheless be performed because the 'world', though it falls far short of absolute value, is yet maintained in existence by God and it is not his will that it should cease to be. As Krishna himself will say:

If I were not tirelessly to busy Myself with works, then would men everywhere follow in my footsteps. If I were not to do my work, these worlds would fall to ruin, and I should be a worker of confusion, destroying these [my] creatures. (3.23–4)

What Krishna demands is that a man should give up all *attachment* to works and their 'fruits'. This precept he repeats again and again, and if there is one virtue that stands out above all others in the Gītā it is detachment and renunciation: and this is a Buddhist virtue.

Krishna Protests

Saṁjaya uvāca:

1. *taṁ tathā kṛpayā'viṣṭam aśru-pūrṇ'ākul'ekṣaṇam*
viṣīdantam idaṁ vākyam uvāca Madhusūdanaḥ:

Sanjaya said:

To him thus in compassion plunged, his eyes distraught and filled with tears, [to him] desponding Krishna spoke these words:

Śrībhagavān uvāca:

2. *kutas tvā kaśmalam idaṁ viṣame samupasthitam*
anārya-juṣṭam asvargyam akīrtikaram, Arjuna ?

The Blessed Lord said:

Whence comes this faintness on you [now] at this crisis-hour? This ill beseems a noble, wins none a heavenly state, [but] brings dishonour, Arjuna.

3. *klaibyaṁ mā sma gamaḥ, Pārtha, n'aitat tvayy upapadyate:*
kṣudraṁ hṛdaya-daurbalyaṁ tyaktv'ottiṣṭha, paraṁtapa.

Play not the eunuch, son of Prithā, for this ill beseems you: give up this vile faint-heartedness. Stand up, chastiser of your foes!

'I will not Fight'

Arjuna uvāca:

4. *kathaṁ Bhīṣmam ahaṁ saṁkhye Droṇaṁ ca, Madhusūdana,*
iṣubhiḥ pratiyotsyāmi pūj'ārhāv, arisūdana ?

Arjuna said:

Krishna, how can I fight Bhīshma and Drona in battle, [how assail them] with [my] arrows? for they are worthy of respect.

5. *gurūn ahatvā hi mahā'nubhāvān*
śreyo bhoktuṁ bhaikṣyam apī'ha loke:
hatvā'rtha-kāmāṁs tu gurūn ih'aiva
bhuñjīya bhogān rudhira-pradigdhān.

For better were it here on earth to eat a beggar's food than to slay [our] teachers of great dignity. Were I to slay [my] teachers, ambitious though they be, then should I be eating blood-sullied food.

[*a*]*rtha-kāmāṁs*, 'ambitious though they be': is most naturally taken with *gurūn* (so Ś., R.). Some (e.g. Barnett) take it with *bhogān*. The meaning would then be: 'Were I to slay my teachers, then should I be enjoying the delights of wealth and pleasure though sullied with their blood.' *Artha* and *kāma*, the pursuit of wealth and pleasure, are, along with *dharma*, 'duty', the three legitimate goals of life prescribed in the law-books and Epics. All three are superseded by and subsumed in *mokṣa*, 'liberation' or 'spiritual freedom'.

Var. *na tv artha-kāmas tu gurūn nihatya*, 'Were I, ambitious, to slay my teachers . . .' .

6. *na c'aitad vidmaḥ kataran no garīyo*
yad vā jayema yadi vā no jayeyuḥ:
yān eva hatvā na jijīviṣāmas,
te 'vasthitāḥ pramukhe Dhārtarāṣṭrāḥ.

Besides we do not know which is for us the better part, whether that we should win the victory or that they should conquer us. There facing us stand Dhritarāshtra's sons. Should we kill them, we should hardly wish to live.

pramukhe Dhārtarāṣṭrāḥ: var. *pratyanīkeṣu yodhāḥ.*

7. *kārpaṇya-doṣ'opahata-svabhāvaḥ*
pṛcchāmi tvā dharma-saṁmūḍha-cetāḥ:
yac chreyaḥ syān, niścitaṁ brūhi tan me,
śiṣyas te 'haṁ, śādhi māṁ tvāṁ prapannam.

My very being is oppressed with compassion's harmful taint. With mind perplexed concerning right [and wrong] I ask you which is the better course? Tell me [and let your words be] definite [and clear]. I am your pupil and put all my trust in you. So teach me.

'Put all my trust in you': or simply, 'who have come to you'.

8. *na hi prapaśyāmi mam' āpanudyād*
yac chokam ucchoṣaṇam indriyāṇām
avāpya bhūmāv asapatnam ṛddhaṁ
rājyaṁ surāṇām api c' ādhipatyam.

For I cannot see what could dispel my grief, [this] parching of the senses, not though on earth I were to win a prosperous, unrivalled empire or sovereignty over the gods themselves.

Saṁjaya uvāca:

9. *evam uktvā hṛṣīkeśaṁ guḍākeśaḥ, paraṁtapa,*
na yotsya iti Govindam uktvā tuṣṇīṁ babhūva ha.

Sanjaya said:

These [were the words that] Arjuna addressed to Krishna, and then he said to him: 'I will not fight!' And having spoken held his peace.

paraṁtapa (voc.) ['O scorcher of the foe']: var. *paraṁtapaḥ* (nom.).

10. *tam uvāca hṛṣīkeśaḥ prahasann iva, Bhārata,*
senayor ubhayor madhye viṣīdantam idaṁ vacaḥ.

[Standing] between the two armies, Krishna, faintly smiling, spoke these words to Arjuna in his [deep] despondency.

Śrī-bhagavān uvāca:

11. *aśocyān anvaśocas tvaṁ prajñā-vādāṁś ca bhāṣase:*
gat' āsūn agat' āsūṁś ca n' ānuśocanti paṇḍitāḥ.

The Blessed Lord said:

You sorrow for men who do not need your sorrow and [yet] speak words that [in part] are wise. Wise men do not sorrow for the living or the dead.

prajñā-vādāṁś, 'words that [in part] are wise': as in 1. 41 ff. on the mixing of caste (so R.). E. quotes MBh. 2. 61. 38 where *prajñā-vādika* means 'pretending or claiming to be wise' (so S.). D. 'wenn auch deine Reden verständig sein mögen'. Var. *prajñāvan n' ābhibhāṣase*, 'you do not talk like a wise man'.

Some MSS. add here:

tvaṁ mānuṣyeṇ' opahat' āntarātmā
viṣāda-moh' ābhibhavād visaṁjñaḥ
kṛpā-gṛhītaḥ samavekṣya bandhūn
abhiprapannān mukham antakasya.

Vanquished by dejection and delusion, devoid of wit, your inmost self has been upset by what is [all too] human; pity has seized upon you because you see your kinsmen enter into the jaws of death.

The Undying Self

12. *na tv ev'āhaṁ jātu n'āsaṁ, na tvaṁ, n'eme jan'ādhipāḥ;*
na c'aiva na bhaviṣyāmaḥ sarve vayam ataḥ param.

Never was there a time when I was not, nor you, nor yet these princes, nor will there be a time when we shall cease to be,— all of us hereafter.

R. argues that the clear distinction made between 'I', 'you', and 'these princes' proves that the Bhagavad-Gītā assumes a plurality of 'selves' (*ātman*) which are subject to transmigration from time without beginning to time without end unless and until 'liberation' is achieved. Ś., however, glosses: 'All of us in time past, present, and future are eternal (*nitya*) after the body is destroyed because the self is what it is (i.e. eternal by definition). The plural form refers to distinction (*bheda*) of bodies and does not mean that there is a distinction between one self [and another].' The obvious sense of the verse would seem to support R.

Krishna is here speaking of the transmigration of individual selves (including himself as *incarnate* God)—a process that has no beginning and, unless final 'liberation' supervenes, no end. He is not yet speaking of the 'Self' or 'selves' as eternal beings outside time—a subject which he broaches in verse 16.

13. *dehino 'smin yathā dehe kaumāraṁ yauvanaṁ jarā*
tathā deh'āntara-prāptir: dhīras tatra na muhyati.

Just as in this body the embodied [self] must pass through childhood, youth, and old age, so too [at death] will it assume another body: in this a thoughtful man is not perplexed.

14. *mātrā-sparśās tu, Kaunteya, śīt'oṣṇa-sukha-duḥkha-dāḥ*
āgam'āpāyino 'nityās, tāṁs titikṣasva, Bhārata.

But contacts with the objects of sense give rise to heat and cold, pleasure and pain: they come and go, impermanent. Put up with them [then], Arjuna.

mātrā-, 'objects of sense': so, following Ś., i.e. the *tanmātras* of the Sāṁkhya system. E. prefers 'matter': D. 'mit dem Stofflichen'.

[*a*]*nityās*, 'impermanent': a typical Buddhist term. The senses, the objects of sense, and the link between the two are all *anicca* (Pāli for *anitya*), 'impermanent', *dukkha*, 'painful', and *anattā*, 'void of self'. This is a recurring theme in the Pāli Canon and becomes almost obsessional in *Saṁyutta* iv. 1–204. It is through the senses that Māra, the Buddhist Devil, operates (S. iv. 178). The impermanence of the world,

however, is rarely emphasized in the Upanishads because the world, for them, participates in the supreme principle, Brahman, or is derived from It, or indeed *is* It—the All and the One frequently being synonymous. The total separation of the 'permanent' (*nibbāna, nirvāṇa*) from the 'impermanent' (*saṁsāra, anicca*) which is typical of the Sāṁkhya system too, seems to originate with the Buddha. The term *anitya* itself does not appear in the Upanishads until the *Kaṭha* on which the Gītā is to some extent dependent. There too, as in this and the following two stanzas, a contrast is made between the impermanent and the permanent, what becomes and what *is*. For the Buddhists there was a gulf fixed between the two, and the *Kaṭha* (2. 10) provisionally accepts this:

> I know that what's called treasure is impermanent,
> For by things unstable the Stable cannot be obtained.
> Have I, then, builded up the Nāciketa fire,—
> By things impermanent have I the Permanent attained?

So too the Gītā (2. 16) will draw a firm distinction between what becomes and what *is* only to reconcile them later in God, for as Krishna later says (14. 27):

> I am the base supporting Brahman,—immortal [Brahman] which knows no change,—[supporting] too the eternal law of righteousness and absolute beatitude.

15. *yaṁ hi na vyathayanty ete puruṣaṁ, puruṣ'arṣabha,*
sama-duḥkha-sukhaṁ dhīraṁ, so 'mṛtatvāya kalpate.

For wise men there are, the same in pleasure as in pain, whom these [contacts] leave undaunted: such are conformed to immortality.

'The same in pleasure as in pain': the root meaning of *sama* is 'the same'. As such it is a proper epithet of Brahman *quâ* absolute Being which remains ever the same when all else changes. In man this abiding essence is the *ātman* or 'self'—the same in every contingent being. But so long as this self is imprisoned in a body and all that properly belongs to a body including mind and what we call 'soul' (see 2. 41), its 'sameness' manifests itself as 'sameness' towards pleasure and pain and all the other pairs of opposites. This idea is fully developed in 5. 18–21:

> [These] wise ones see the selfsame thing in a Brāhman wise and courteous as in a cow or in an elephant, nay, as in a dog or outcaste. While yet in this world they have overcome [the process of] emanation [and decay], for their minds are stilled in that-which-is-ever-the-same: for devoid of imperfection and ever-the-same is Brahman: therefore in Brahman [stilled] they stand.
>
> Winning some pleasant thing [the sage] will not rejoice, nor shrink disquietened when the unpleasant comes his way: steadfast-and-still his soul, [all] unconfused, he will know Brahman, in Brahman [stilled] he'll stand. [His] self detached from contacts with the outside world, in [him]self he finds his joy, [his] self in Brahman integrated by spiritual exercise (*yoga*), he finds unfailing joy.

The 'sameness' that is Brahman is reflected in the 'sameness' or 'equanimity' of the enlightened sage: he is 'the same in pleasure as in pain' (2. 15, 38: 6. 7: 12. 13, 18: 14. 24), in heat and cold (2. 14: 6. 7: 12. 18), in success and failure (2. 48: 4. 22: 6. 7), the same to friend and foe (6. 9: 12. 18: 14. 24–25). This 'sameness' is the same unchanging principle within himself which he sees in the outside world (5. 18–19): 'the same in everything he sees' (6. 29). This principle is Brahman, that changeless Being which is common to God and man. 'Who knows himself, knows his Lord', a Muslim tradition has it, and so Krishna too declares:

Who sees Me everywhere, who sees the All in Me, for him I am not lost, nor is he lost to Me. Who standing firm on unity communes-in-love with Me as abiding in all beings, in whatever state he be, that athlete of the spirit abides in Me. By analogy with self who sees the same [Brahman] everywhere, be it as pleasure or as pain, he is the highest athlete of the spirit, or so men think (6. 30–2).

But this is to anticipate. Suffice to say now that God, in so far as He is Brahman, that is, changeless immanent Being, is 'the same' root and ground that inheres and indwells every single contingent being in this 'impermanent' phenomenal world. As such He, like the perfected sage, is impassible:

In all contingent beings the same am I; none do I hate and none do I fondly love (9. 29). . . . The same in all contingent beings, abiding [without change], the Highest Lord, when all things fall to ruin, [Himself] is not destroyed: who sees Him sees [indeed] (13. 27).

Those who are 'the same in pleasure as in pain' are 'conformed to immortality'. The word *kalpate* is frequently used with the dative case in the sense of 'being conformed to' (the root meaning of the word is to 'form'). So in KaU. 3. 17 and ŚU. 5. 9 the 'wise man' on the one hand and the 'living self' on the other, though themselves a point without magnitude, are both 'conformed to infinity'. Similarly in the Gītā (14. 26) Krishna's devotees are 'conformed to becoming Brahman'—Brahman thus being equated with 'immortality' and 'infinity'.

16. *n'āsato vidyate bhāvo, n'ābhāvo vidyate sataḥ:*
ubhayor api dṛṣṭo 'ntas tv anayos tattva-darśibhiḥ.

Of what is not there is no becoming; of what is there is no ceasing to be: for the boundary-line between these two is seen by men who see things as they really are.

The translation is not absolutely certain here. The word *bhāva* normally means 'nature, mode of existence, state of being' or simply 'creature' (cf. *sva-bhāva*); for 'becoming' one would rather expect *bhava, bhavana,* or indeed *saṁsāra*. The sentence might then mean: 'What does not exist can have no essence, nor can what exists lack an essence.'

In the Gītā itself *bhāva* is always used in the sense of 'nature': 7. 12 *sāttvikā bhāvā*: 7. 13 *guṇamayair bhāvair*: 8. 4 *kṣaro bhāvaḥ*: 8. 6 *yaṁ yaṁ . . . smaran bhāvaṁ* ('whatever state of being a man may bear in mind'): 8. 20 *paras tasmāt tu bhāvo 'nyo,* 'but beyond that there is another mode of being'. In 10. 5 the *bhāvas* of contingent beings are enumerated: these consist of *buddhi,* various virtues, and some vices including, strangely enough, *bhava* and *abhāva* ('becoming' and 'the lack of *bhāva*'!) Here the word is probably best translated as 'characteristic'. In 10. 17 again Arjuna asks Krishna in what *bhāvas* ('aspects') He is to be meditated on. In 18. 17 we have *yasya n'āhaṁkṛto bhāvo,* 'whose nature is not egoized', and in 18. 20 *ekaṁ bhāvam avyayam,* 'the one mode of existence which is not transient'. Upanishadic usage is similar and in MuU. 2. 1. 1 and ŚU. 6. 4 the word means 'mode of being' or simply 'creature'.

In the Gītā *mad-bhāva* ('my mode of being') is (when Krishna is speaking) also used to mean God's mode of being, i.e. his divinity. This will be discussed at 4. 10 where it occurs for the first time.

Against all this we have *abhāva* used as the opposite of *bhava,* 'becoming' in 10. 4. Here *abhāva* must mean 'un-becoming', that is, 'ceasing to be as a phenomenal or contingent being'. Normally, it should be noted, it means simply 'absence'.

Ś. takes *bhāva* to mean 'existence' (*bhavana, astitā*) and says that there is no existence of the 'unreal' (*asat*) by which he understands the body and the pairs of opposites: only Ātman-Brahman really exists (*sat*) and this can never cease to exist. This seems tautologous. On balance I prefer to stick to the translation adopted in the text.

Moreover, the following verses seem to give some clue to what this verse really means. 'What is' is clearly the indestructible 'That' of the next line. This is confirmed by the formula *Oṁ tat sat* which appears in 17. 23 and which is said to describe Brahman and recalls the *etad vai tat,* 'This in truth is That', which is the refrain of KaU. 4 and 5, and the *tat tvam asi,* 'That you are', of ChU. 6. 8. 7 ff. In both these cases as elsewhere *tat,* 'that', expresses the supreme Brahman.

It is not so easy to see what is meant by *asat* in this passage. Both Ś. and R. take it to mean the body, that is, by extension the whole of material Nature elsewhere called *prakṛti* in accordance with Sāṁkhya usage. This they presumably infer from verse 18: 'Finite, they say, are these [our] bodies [indwelt] by an eternal embodied [self]'. But it is the very nature of bodies as of all the phenomenal world to 'become' or 'develop' or 'have an essence', which, however we translate *bhāva* here, is denied to *asat.*

In the two or three passages in the Gītā where the words *sat* and *asat* are contrasted *sat* would appear to refer to eternal Being beyond space and time, that is, Ātman-Brahman, *asat* to Nature or the phenomenal world. Thus in 9. 19 Krishna says: 'Deathlessness am I and death, what IS and what is not (*sad-asat*)' implying that 'what is not' is equivalent to death and 'what IS' to deathlessness or immortality as in BU. 1. 3. 28 ('by *asat* [he means] death, by *sat* immortality'). So too in the Gītā 'death' is equivalent to the ever-dying world of material Nature and 'immortality' to the changeless category of Ātman-Brahman. In 11. 37 Arjuna goes beyond this and confesses to Krishna: 'You are the Imperishable, what IS and what is not and what surpasses both'. In other words He is both the phenomenal and the eternal and at the same time transcends both.

On the contrary in 13. 12 Brahman is described as being neither *sat* nor *asat*. This probably means, as in 'negative' theology in all religions, that the Absolute cannot be defined in any way without thereby being made finite. This will be more fully discussed ad loc.

In our present passage, however, it seems that the use of the word *asat* cannot be explained by parallel passages in the Gītā itself because it is expressly stated that *asat* has no *bhāva*: it does not become or develop nor has it any 'nature' of its own. We must, then, look outside the Gītā to the Upanishads and beyond.

The concept of *sad-asat*, 'Being and Not-Being', is already present in RV. 10. 129. 1: 'Then neither Being nor Not-Being was. . . .' This is one of the most beautiful, most deeply impressive, most profound, and most profoundly obscure of the Rig-Vedic hymns, and it would be futile to seek to impose upon it one or other exclusive interpretation. In Upanishadic speculation, however, distinct views on the nature of Not-Being (*asat*) developed.

For TU. 2. 7 Not-Being is the ultimate principle from which Being is born. The meaning seems to be that the original principle is primal matter which, as with most Greek philosophers, can scarcely be said to exist at all: from this primal matter Being, that is pure spirit (Ātman-Brahman), arises.

This position is specifically attacked in ChU. 6. 2. 1–2 where the possibility of anything being born from Not-Being is roundly denied: ontological primacy can only belong to Being, and so the Upanishad says:

> In the beginning, my dear, this [universe] was Being only,—one only,—without a second. True, some say that in the beginning this [universe] was Not-Being only,—one only,—without a second, and that from that Not-Being Being was born.
>
> But, my dear, whence could this be? . . . How could Being be born from Not-Being? No, it was Being alone that was this [universe] in the beginning,—one only, without a second.

Asat here is plainly not primal matter but what does not exist absolutely—nothing, and this must surely be the idea that the Gītā is taking up here. From 'nothing' there can be no becoming or development: what does not exist cannot have an essence since existence necessarily precedes essence as in Aristotle. This accords fully with 17. 23–27, in which *tat sat*, 'That which IS', is synonymous with Brahman, and with KaU. 6. 12–13 in which the supreme Self (already personal in this Upanishad since He 'elects' those whom He is pleased to set free) cannot 'be understood unless we say—HE IS'. This is the position that the Gītā seems to be taking up here.

17. *avināśi tu tad viddhi yena sarvam idaṁ tatam:*
vināśam avyayasy'āsya na kaścit kartum arhati.

Yes, indestructible [alone] is That,—know this,—by which this whole universe was spun: no one can bring destruction on That which does not pass away.

tad, 'That': this refers to Brahman (so Ś. and see previous note). R. interprets it as *ātma-tattva*, the 'essence or category of [individual] selves' and (like Ś. and almost all modern translators) takes *tatam* ('spun') to mean 'pervaded' (*vyāptam*).

yena sarvam idaṁ tatam, 'by which this whole universe was spun'. A favourite refrain in the Gītā. *Tatam* literally means 'spun' or 'spread out' (so D.: cf. *tantu*, 'thread'). The idea is that the universe emerges from the First Principle as a spider's web emerges from a spider. We find this idea twice in the classical Upanishads:

> As a spider emerges [from itself] by [spinning] threads [out of its own body], as small sparks rise up from a fire, so too from this Self do all the life-breaths, all the worlds, all the gods, and all contingent beings rise up in all directions (BU. 2. 1. 20).

> As a spider emits and re-absorbs [its threads],
> As plants grow up upon the earth,
> As hair [grows] on the body and head of a living man,
> So does everything on earth arise from [this] Imperishable.
> (MuU. 1. 1. 7.)

As always in traditional Hinduism creation is not *ex nihilo*. Brahman is the material as well as the efficient cause of the world. It is both the weaver as here and the warp and woof across which all phenomenal existence is woven (BU. 3. 6).

Here the 'weaver' is 'That', the neuter Brahman, 'by which this whole universe was spun'. In 8. 22 it is the highest 'Person' not yet unequivocally identified with Krishna. In 9. 4 it is Krishna Himself who thereby identifies Himself with the highest 'Person' of 8. 22 who is also the 'Unmanifest beyond the Unmanifest' (8. 20), the 'Imperishable', and the 'highest way' (8. 21); and in 11. 38 Arjuna hails Him as (among other things) 'You whose forms are infinite, by [whom] the whole universe was spun'. The phrase is used for the last time in 18. 46 where again it seems to refer to Krishna.

As will become apparent in the sequel Krishna absorbs and transcends all that had previously been ascribed to Brahman and to Purusha, the [highest] 'Person'.

na kaścit, 'no one': var. *na kiṁcit*, 'nothing'.

18. *antavanta ime dehā nityasy'oktāḥ śarīriṇaḥ*
anāśino 'prameyasya: tasmād yudhyasva, Bhārata.

Finite, they say, are these [our] bodies [indwelt] by an eternal embodied [self],—[for this self is] indestructible, incommensurable. Fight then, scion of Bharata.

śarīriṇaḥ, '*an* embodied [self]': or '*the* embodied [self'], since there is no article in Sanskrit. The first would seem to be preferable in this context at least, since verse 12 presupposes a plurality of embodied selves ('Never was there a time when I was not, nor you, nor yet these princes'). It might, however, be argued that it is more easily referred to the *tad*,

'That', of the previous line (so D.) and this would mean that there is, in fact, no plurality of selves. This, however, is quite contrary to the main trend of the Gītā's thought, and both in the *Kaṭha* and *Śvetāśvatara* Upanishads the word *dehin* (the more usual word for 'embodied' [self] (as against *śarīrin* here, both *deha* and *śarīra* meaning 'body')) is used in the sense of the individual not the universal self (KaU. 5. 4, 7: ŚU. 2. 14: 5. 11–12).

We meet with the 'embodied self' again in 3. 40 where it is 'fooled' or 'led astray' by desire. The idea is further developed in 14. 5 where it is 'bound' in the body by the three constituents of Nature though in its essence it is changeless. The *dehin* or *śarīrin*, then, is the 'empirical or individual self': it is subject to bondage in this world but wins immortality when it succeeds in transcending it: 'Transcending these three constituents which give the body its existence, from the sufferings of birth, death, and old age delivered, the embodied [self] wins immortality' (14. 20.)

The distinction between God or the supreme Ātman-Brahman, who is unaffected by the world, the transmigratory process or action (*karma*), and the empirical self, which *is* affected by all these, is by no means always made clear. In 15. 7, however, the distinction is made quite plain:

> In the world of living things a minute part of Me, eternal [still], becomes a living [self], drawing to itself the five senses and the mind which have their roots in Nature.

This 'living [self]' (*jīva*) is, of course, identical with the *dehin* or 'embodied [self]'. The 'self', seen as distinct from the body it assumes, being a 'minute part' of God, is eternal and in its inmost essence remains unaffected by the world process and *karma* (cf. 3. 17–18: 5. 14, etc.).

The distinction between the self as it is in its essence and as it 'becomes' when it is connected with a body and the world is most clearly made in MaiU. 2. 7: 3. 2.

> This self . . . wanders around on earth in body after body, apparently unaffected by the fruits of [his] works, be they white or black. Because he is unmanifest, subtile, invisible, impalpable, and possesses nothing, he must surely be impermanent and a worker in what is not Being (*asat*, i.e. the phenomenal world); and yet he is in no sense a worker [nor does he do anything] (*akartṛ*): he is permanent [and abiding]. He is indeed the pure, the stable, the unmoved, the unaffected, unflurried, free from desire, standing still like a spectator, self-subsistent. . . .
>
> [But] there is indeed another, different [self]: he is known as the 'elemental' [or individual] self (*bhūt'ātman*) which [really] is affected by the fruits of [his own] works, be they white or black, and who must [ever again] enter into the wombs of good or evil [women], thus ascending or descending [in the order of existence], wandering around at the mercy of [all manner of] dualities.

This distinction between the 'self-in-itself' and the self as it is individuated in a human being must be borne in mind throughout the Gītā.

[*a*]*prameyasya*, 'incommensurable': or 'unfathomable, incomprehensible' by the ordinary means of knowledge (Ś., R.).

tasmād yudhyasva, 'fight then' or 'therefore'. The causal connexion is not clear. The fact that no self-in-itself can be destroyed because it is eternal and timeless can scarcely be accounted a sufficient reason for going to war since it cannot ultimately matter whether one kills another's body or not. The only valid reason Krishna produces in this chapter is in verse 31 where he appeals to Arjuna's caste-duty.

19. *ya enaṁ vetti hantāraṁ yaś c'ainaṁ manyate hatam,*
ubhau tau ne vijānīto: n'āyaṁ hanti na hanyate.

Who thinks this [self] can be a slayer, who thinks that it can be slain, both these have no [right] knowledge: it does not slay nor is it slain.

This stanza is based on KaU. 2. 19, the second line being identical. For the first line KaU. has: 'Should the killer think, "I kill", or the killed, "I have been killed". . . .' The Gītā gives the more satisfactory sense since *enaṁ*, 'he', must refer to the embodied self already mentioned.

20. *na jāyate mriyate vā kadācin*
n'āyaṁ bhūtvā bhavitā vā na bhūyaḥ:
ajo nityaḥ śāśvato 'yaṁ purāṇo,
na hanyate hanyamāne śarīre.

Never is it born nor dies; never did it come to be nor will it ever come to be again: unborn, eternal, everlasting is this [self],—primeval. It is not slain when the body is slain.

This again is taken from the *Kaṭha* Upanishad (2. 18), the second line again being identical. For the first line KaU. has: 'This wise one is not born nor dies; from nowhere has He [sprung] nor has He anyone become.' The difference is that the *Kaṭha* is speaking of the supreme Self whereas the Gītā is speaking of the individual self.

This stanza would seem to contradict verse 13 in which Krishna says that the embodied self takes on a new body at death, that is, it *is* reborn and *does* die. In fact there is no contradiction. Rather, two different ideas succeed each other rather confusedly.

(i) The self-in-itself, since its being is eternal and beyond space and time, thereby participating in or being identical with the timeless Brahman, cannot be born or die, nor can it be said to have come to be in the past or that it will come to be in the future. As it is in itself it is never involved in the process of transmigration or in action (*karma*) of any kind: 'he is not stained by evil as a lotus-petal [is not stained] by water' (5. 10). Being beyond time it is wholly static.

(ii) In so far as the self-in-itself is, as a matter of empirical fact, constantly involved in the world process (*saṁsāra*) and is associated with an individual psycho-somatic mechanism—in so far, that is, as it is a *dehin*, it is always being born and dying again until it is ultimately released. This is the theme of verses 12–13. 14–15 indicate how the link between the self-in-itself and the outside world can be severed, while 16–18 assert the absolute independence of what *is* from what becomes though the former is, even so, the source of the latter.

21. *ved'āvināśinaṁ nityaṁ ya enam ajam avyayam*
kathaṁ sa puruṣaḥ, Pārtha, kaṁ ghātayati hanti kam ?

If a man knows it as indestructible, eternal, unborn, never to pass away, how and whom can he cause to be slain or slay?

22. *vāsāṁsi jīrṇāni yathā vihāya*
navāni gṛhṇāti naro 'parāṇi
tathā śarīrāṇi vihāya jīrṇāny
anyāni saṁyāti navāni dehī.

As a man casts off his worn-out clothes and takes on other new ones, so does the embodied [self] cast off its worn-out bodies and enters other new ones.

We now return to the self as it is in the transmigrating process. Rebirth is, perhaps a little illogically, regarded as a progress from a less developed state to a more developed one: 'just as in this body the embodied [self] must pass through childhood, youth, and old age, so too [at death] will it assume another body' (2. 13). The embodied self takes with it all the 'fruits' of the actions it has performed in this and previous lives and with it go its psychic and intellectual faculties. It is only the old body that is left behind: all the rest—intellect, will, and mind—accompany the embodied self in its endless journey through time. In its new birth 'it is united with the intellect-and-will (*buddhi*) as it had matured in its former body' (6. 43).

The clearest account of *what* transmigrates (apart from the fruits of one's actions of which we shall be hearing very much more later) is found in BU. 4. 4. 1–6:

(1) When this self grows weak and seems all confused, then do the bodily faculties gather round him. He collects around him those elements of light and descends right down into the heart. When the 'person' present in the eye turns away, back [towards the sun], he no longer recognizes forms.

(2) 'He is becoming one, he does not see', they say. 'He is becoming one, he does not smell', they say. 'He is becoming one, he does not taste', they say. 'He is becoming one, he does not speak', they say. 'He is becoming one, he does not hear', they say. 'He is becoming one, he does not think', they say. 'He is becoming one, he does not feel', they say. 'He is becoming one, he does not understand', they say.

The apex of the heart lights up, and [lighted] by this light the self departs through the eye or the head or some other part of the body. As he departs, the breath of life follows after him; and as the breath of life departs, all the bodily faculties follow after it. He is then [re-]united with the understanding (*vijñāna*, ability to recognize things), and follows after the understanding. His wisdom and his works and his knowledge of the past lay hold of him.

(3) As a caterpillar, drawing near to the tip of a blade of grass, prepares its next step and draws itself up towards it, so does this self, striking the body aside and dispelling ignorance, prepare its next step and draw itself up [in readiness to be born again].

(4) As a goldsmith, making use of the material of a [golden] object, forges another new and more beautiful form, so does this self, striking the body aside and dispelling ignorance, devise another new and more beautiful form,—be it [the form] of one of the ancestors or of a Gandharva or of a god or of one in the Prajāpati[-world] or of one in the Brahman[-world] or of any other being.

(5) This self is Brahman indeed (Brahman as the All, rather than the One, the Absolute): it consists of understanding, mind, breath, sight, and hearing; of earth, water, wind and space, light and darkness, desire and desirelessness, anger and the lack of it, right and wrong: it consists of all things. . . .

As a man acts, as he behaves, so does he become. Whoso does good, becomes good: whoso does evil, becomes evil. By good works a man becomes holy, by evil [works] he becomes evil.

But some have said: 'This "person" consists of desire alone. As is his desire, so will his will be; as is his will, so will he act; as he acts, so will he attain.

(6) On this there is this verse:

To what his mind [and] character are attached,
To that attached a man goes with his works:
Whatever deeds he does on earth,
Their rewards he reaps.
From the other world he comes back here,—
To the world of deed-and-work.

The self, then, on leaving one body for another, takes with it the mental and psychic equipment it had developed in its last existence, and this in turn is conditioned by the nature of its previous works. A similar though less satisfactory account of what the self takes with it on its onward course will be found in ŚU. 5. 7–12.

23. *n'ainaṁ chindanti śastrāṇi, n'ainaṁ dahati pāvakaḥ,*
na c'ainaṁ kledayanty āpo, na śoṣayati mārutaḥ.

Weapons do not cut it nor does fire burn it, the waters do not wet it nor does the wind dry it.

24. *acchedyo 'yam adāhyo 'yam akledyo 'śoṣya eva ca,*
nityaḥ sarvagataḥ sthāṇur acalo 'yaṁ sanātanaḥ.

Uncuttable, unburnable, unwettable, undryable it is,—eternal, roving everywhere, firm-set, unmoved, primeval.

sarvagataḥ, 'roving everywhere, omnipresent'. Though the *dehin* is by etymology and definition associated with the body, it is not confined to it. In itself it is beyond space and time and can thus be said to rove everywhere just as the wind roves through space though it 'abides' (*sthita*), that is, remains as it were static within it (9. 6): in the same way all contingent beings abide in God (ibid.).

The closest parallel, however, is 12. 3 which has these epithets in common with this and the following verse—*sarvagata* (*sarvatraga*), 'roving everywhere', *acintya*, 'unthinkable', *acala*, 'unmoving', *avyakta*, 'unmanifest'. Moreover, the *dhruva* of 12. 3 is identical in meaning with *sthāṇu* here ('firm-set'). Suffice it to say at this stage that the entity referred to in 12. 3 is Brahman conceived of as the Absolute, the still, static, stable, absolutely motionless and changeless ground of the universe. In so far as the self-in-itself shares these characteristics and is divorced from all that moves or acts in any way, it *is* Brahman in this sense. In so far as it is contingent, of course, it is not. But of this later.

25. *avyakto 'yam acintyo 'yam avikāryo 'yam ucyate,*
tasmād evaṁ viditv' ainaṁ n' ānuśocitum arhasi.

Unmanifest, unthinkable, immutable is it called: then realize it thus and do not grieve [about it].

avyakto, 'unmanifest': this is usually the term used to denote primal matter in its totally undeveloped state (8. 18: 13. 5, etc.). In the Gītā the term is used in a variety of ways and we shall deal with them as they come up. Here, however, we are still dealing with the embodied self which in its essence is unaffected by matter in any form. Hence, Ś. rightly glosses: 'because it is inaccessible to the senses, it cannot be expressed'. R.: 'it cannot be expressed in terms applicable to objects that can be cut, etc.'.

26. *atha c' ainaṁ nitya-jātaṁ nityaṁ vā manyase mṛtam*
tathā 'pi tvaṁ, mahā-bāho, n' ainaṁ śocitum arhasi.

And even if you think that it is constantly [re-]born and constantly [re-]dies, even so you grieve for it in vain.

Here we are firmly back in concept (ii) of our note on 2. 20. The self is here regarded as eternal in time, without beginning and without end. It is not the 'firm-set, unmoving, unthinkable, and immutable' essence that Krishna has been speaking of in the last two verses.

27. *jātasya hi dhruvo mṛtyur, dhruvaṁ janma mṛtasya ca:*
tasmād aparihārye 'rthe na tvaṁ śocitum arhasi.

For sure is the death of all that is born, sure is the birth of all that dies: so in a matter that no one can prevent you have no cause to grieve.

For the great majority of Hindus transmigration appears as a self-evident fact, not just as a theory.

28. *avyakt' ādīni bhūtāni vyakta-madhyāni, Bhārata,*
avyakta-nidhanāny eva: tatra kā paridevanā ?

Unmanifest are the beginnings of contingent beings, manifest their middle course, unmanifest again their ends: what cause for mourning here?

29. *āścaryavat paśyati kaścid enam,*
āścaryavad vadati tath' aiva c' ānyaḥ:
āścaryavac c' ainam anyaḥ śṛṇoti,
śrutvā 'py enaṁ veda na c' aiva kaścit.

By a rare privilege may someone behold it, and by a rare privilege indeed may another tell of it, and by a rare privilege may such another hear it, yet even having heard there is none that knows it.

āścaryavat, 'by a rare privilege': or, 'as a wonder'. Cf. KaU. 2. 7:

> Many there are who never come to hear of Him,
> Many, though hearing of Him, know Him not:
> Blessed (*āścarya*) the man who, skilled therein, proclaims Him, grasps Him;
> Blessed the man who learns from one so skilled and knows Him!

Ś. and R. take the word to mean 'very rarely': Ś., 'one in thousands'. R. refers the stanza to God rather than the individual self; yet oddly enough in the Gītā it is not so much God who is unknowable as the self. Thus the possibility of knowing God is mentioned in 7. 3 and 7. 30, but it is a remote one. In 9. 13 it is *bhakti*, love and devotion, that enables man to know God as the eternal source of all things, and in 15. 19 it is by love that a man comes to know God as the 'Person [All-]Sublime' who is 'more exalted than the Imperishable [Brahman] itself'. Similarly in his final message in 18. 55 Krishna says: 'By love-and-loyalty [a man] comes to know Me as I really am, how great I am and who; and once he knows Me as I am, he enters [Me] forthwith.' Knowledge of God, then, would appear to be dependent on love and not vice versa. The self, on the other hand, whether you think of it as your own eternal, timeless essence or as the eternal substrate of all things, cannot be loved because it is 'indeterminate', 'for difficult [indeed] is it for embodied men to reach-and-tread the unmanifested way' (12. 5).

30. *dehī nityam avadhyo 'yaṁ dehe sarvasya, Bhārata,*
tasmāt sarvāṇi bhūtāni na tvaṁ śocitum arhasi.

Never can this embodied [self] be slain in the body of anyone [at all]: and so you have no need to grieve for any contingent being.

sarvasya, 'anyone [at all]': more literally 'in the body of all'. For Ś. there is only one Self, the Absolute, and it cannot be slain in any individual person because it is omnipresent and without parts.

Caste Duty and Honour

31. *svadharmam api c'āvekṣya na vikampitum arhasi,*
dharmyād dhi yuddhāc chreyo 'nyat kṣatriyasya na vidyate.

Likewise consider your own [caste-]duty, then too you have no cause to quail; for better than a fight prescribed by law is nothing for a man of the princely class.

dharmyād, 'prescribed by law': the word might equally be translated as 'just' or 'righteous'. Hindu society was originally divided into four 'classes' (*varṇa*, 'colour'): (i) the Brāhmans or sacerdotal class; (ii) the *Kshatriyas*, the royal, princely, and warrior class; (iii) the *Vaiśyas*, agriculturalists, merchants, and artisans; and (iv) the *Śūdras*, serfs. Their respective duties are succinctly enumerated in 18. 41–44. Krishna claims to have introduced the system Himself (4. 13).

32. *yadṛcchayā c'opapannaṁ svarga-dvāram apāvṛtam*
sukhinaḥ kṣatriyāḥ, Pārtha, labhante yuddham īdṛśam.

Happy the warriors indeed who become involved in such a war as this, presented by pure chance and opening the doors of paradise.

For a *Kshatriya* to be killed in battle facing the enemy is a sure way to gain paradise. *Pace* Radhakrishnan it seems to make not the slightest difference whether one is fighting in a just or an unjust cause. It is generally agreed that Duryodhana's cause was not just, yet because he died in battle facing the enemy, he straightway entered paradise. His opponent, Yudhishthira, Arjuna's brother and leader of the Pāndavas, himself the incarnation of Righteousness (*dharma*), found him there seated in the lap of luxury, 'shining like the sun, encompassed by the rich glory of the brave, and accompanied by resplendent gods and saints whose deeds were pure' (MBh. 18. 1. 4–5). Yudhishthira, who represents a more just and compassionate moral code, was filled with righteous indignation.

33. *atha cet tvam imaṁ dharmyaṁ saṁgrāmaṁ na kariṣyasi*
tataḥ svadharmaṁ kīrtiṁ ca hitvā pāpam avāpsyasi.

But if you will not wage this war prescribed by [your caste-] duty, then, by casting off both duty and honour, you will bring evil on yourself.

pāpam avāpsyasi, 'you will bring evil on yourself': or, 'incur guilt'. *pāpa* means 'evil' not 'sin' as Rk. and others translate it.

34. *akīrtiṁ c'āpi bhūtāni kathayiṣyanti te 'vyayām,*
saṁbhāvitasya c'ākīrtir maraṇād atiricyate.

And [all] creatures will recount your dishonour which will never pass away; and dishonour in a man well trained [to honour is an evil] surpassing death.

35. *bhayād raṇād uparataṁ maṁsyante tvāṁ mahā-rathāḥ,*
yeṣāṁ ca tvaṁ bahu-mato bhūtvā yāsyasi lāghavam.

'From fear he fled the battlefield'—so will they think of you, the mighty charioteers. Greatly esteemed by them before, you will bring contempt upon yourself.

36. *avācya-vādāṁś ca bahūn vadiṣyanti tav'āhitāḥ*
nindantas tava sāmarthyaṁ: tato duḥkhataraṁ nu kim ?

And many a word that is better left unsaid will such men say as wish you ill, disputing your capacity. What could cause [you] greater pain than this?

This appeal to *amour propre* seems rather out of joint with the main teaching of the Gītā. Even at this stage Arjuna has been told that he should be 'the same in pleasure as in pain' (2. 15). He will later learn that he must be equally indifferent to praise and blame, honour and disgrace (6. 7: 12. 18–19: 14. 24–25). It seems strange that Krishna should have left this most 'worldly' argument to the end.

37. *hato vā prāpsyasi svargaṁ jitvā vā bhokṣyase mahīm:*
tasmād uttiṣṭha, Kaunteya, yuddhāya kṛta-niścayaḥ.

If you are slain, paradise is yours, and if you gain the victory, yours is the earth to enjoy. Stand up, then, son of Kuntī, resolute for the fight.

Be the Same in All Things

38. *sukha-duḥkhe same kṛtvā lābh'ālābhau jay'ājayau,*
tato yuddhāya yujyasva: n'aivaṁ pāpam avāpsyasi.

Hold pleasure and pain, profit and loss, victory and defeat to be the same: then brace yourself for the fight. So will you bring no evil on yourself.

same kṛtvā, 'hold . . . to be the same': that is, make no difference between them, since from the absolute point of view they *are* the same, for Brahman Itself is 'the same' (5. 19), the common ground of all contingent beings. See also note on 2. 15.

yuddhāya yujyasva, 'brace yourself for the fight'. The root *yuj-*, from which *yoga* is derived, is perhaps the keyword of the Gītā. Here it is used as it is in the non-religious parts of the Epic in a purely secular sense, 'get ready for battle'. The basic meaning of the word is 'unite' (cf. Latin *jungere*, 'join', *jugum*, 'yoke'; Greek ζεύγνυμι, ζύγον; English 'yoke', etc.). Here the form is imperative middle, 'yoke yourself for', i.e. 'get ready for'. The noun *yoga*, then, means first 'yoking', then 'preparation'. These are, however, only the primary meanings: there are many, many others. The Gītā plays on all of these with extraordinary skill and this makes it almost impossible to convey the various nuances in translation. In the commentary, however, I will do my best to relate and co-ordinate the different meanings and uses of the root and its derivatives with what seems to me to be the basic doctrine of the Gītā.

The Soul's Practice of Contemplation

39. *eṣā te 'bhihitā sāṁkhye buddhir; yoge tv imāṁ śṛṇu*
buddhyā yukto yayā, Pārtha, karma-bandhaṁ prahāsyasi.

This wisdom has [now] been revealed to you in theory; listen now to how it should be practised. If you are controlled by the soul, you will put away the bondage that is inherent in [all] works.

eṣā . . . buddhir, 'this wisdom': *buddhi* normally means 'intellect' or, in the Gītā, what we normally understand by 'soul' (see 2. 41). Here, however, it must mean 'wisdom' as Ś. rightly interprets it (*jñānam*). In the very next hemistich, however, (*buddhyā yukto*, see below) there is a shift in the meaning which looks forward to the definition of the word in 2. 41. The 'wisdom' referred to is presumably Krishna's teaching concerning the dual immortality of the self.

sāṁkhye, 'theory': the word literally means 'enumeration'. *Sāṁkhya*, however, is also the name of one of the six schools of Indian philosophy, as is *Yoga*. This leads to considerable confusion since neither the 'Sāṁkhya' nor the 'Yoga' of the Gītā corresponds exactly to the 'classical' texts of Sāṁkhya and Yoga respectively—the *Sāṁkhya-kārikā* of Iśvarakrishna on the one hand and the *Yoga-sūtras* of Patañjali on the other. These two 'schools' of philosophy are closely allied, Sāṁkhya providing the theoretical basis for 'Yoga' which is the practical method devised for the achievement of 'liberation'. Hence the two terms are legitimately translated as 'theory' and 'practice' respectively. Sāṁkhya is concerned with the true nature of reality and Yoga is the means of realizing it, as Ś. rightly points out. The two hang inseparably together (5. 4), so much so indeed that they are often jointly referred to as *Sāṁkhya-Yoga*—a combination which first appears in ŚU. 6. 13. *Sāṁkhya-Yoga*, however, as understood in the *Śvetāśvatara* Upanishad and the Gītā, both of which are strongly theistic, differs quite considerably from the basic texts of both Sāṁkhya and Yoga, for the Sāṁkhya admits of no supreme Being at all whereas Yoga, while admitting its existence, denies its relevance in the supreme experience of liberation.

Since the Gītā is permeated through and through with Sāṁkhya terminology, let us now summarize the essential tenets of that system.

Unlike the Upanishads where a clear distinction is rarely drawn between spirit and matter, Sāṁkhya draws the clearest possible distinction. There are two orders of reality, spirit on the one hand which is immutable, unchanging, beyond time, space, and causation, and material Nature on the other which is in a perpetual state of flux, without beginning and without end.

Spirit is not one, and it is therefore in no way comparable to the Brahman of the Upanishads. It is multiple: there are innumerable spiritual monads called *puruṣa*s or 'male persons' in the *Sāṁkhya-kārikā* and it is their unexplained misfortune to become entangled in the material world. This is not natural to them, and their 'salvation' consists in returning to that state which is really theirs—one of complete isolation both from material Nature and from one another. This state of liberation is called *kaivalyam*, 'isolation'.

Material Nature (*prakṛti*) on the other hand is complex—compounded of different elements. From a primal state of rest called the 'Unmanifest' it evolves in the following way. The first evolute is *buddhi*, 'intellect' or 'consciousness', also called the 'great' (*mahat*). From this arises *ahaṁkāra*, the ego, the apparent centre of personality; and from the ego derive the mind (*manas*) which roughly corresponds to the *sensus communis* of the schoolmen, the five senses, the five 'motor' organs (speech, handling, walking, evacuation, and reproduction), the five 'subtle' elements, that is, the objects of the five senses, and the five 'gross' elements—space or ether, air, fire, water, and earth. In all, then, there are twenty-five categories including spirit or *puruṣa*; and the whole scheme can best be illustrated by a diagram, thus:

1. *Puruṣa* (Spirit, the spiritual monads) 2. Material Nature (the 'Unmanifest')

3. *Buddhi-Mahat* (consciousness, intellect)

4. Ego

5. Mind 6–10. The senses 11–15. The motor organs

16–20. The subtle elements

21–25. The gross elements

More fundamental to the structure of material Nature, however, are the three 'constituents', the so-called *guṇa*s or 'strands'. These constituents are called *sattva*, *rajas*, and *tamas* which play an enormous part in the Gītā. I have translated them as Goodness, Passion, and Darkness which, in non-technical contexts, is what they usually mean. Since the later chapters of the Gītā deal with these 'constituents' exhaustively, there is little we need say here except that (in the Gītā at least) all of them 'bind' the embodied self—the *dehin* which in the Gītā corresponds to the *puruṣa* of the Sāṁkhya. Even 'Goodness' does this. To anticipate what the Gītā will say let us introduce these three constituents of Nature now since they will be continually recurring:

Goodness—Passion—Darkness: these are the [three] constituents from Nature sprung that bind the embodied [self] in the body though [the self itself] is changeless.

Among these Goodness, being immaculate, knowing no sickness, dispenses light, [and yet] it binds by [causing the self] to cling to wisdom and to joy. Passion is instinct with desire, [this] know. From craving and attachment it wells up. It binds the embodied [self] by [causing it] to cling to works. But from ignorance is Darkness born: mark [this] well. All embodied [selves] it leads astray. With fecklessness and sloth and sleepiness it binds (14. 5–8).

All this is accepted by the 'Yoga' school. The only difference in the theory is that in addition to the twenty-five categories of the Sāṁkhya it admits a twenty-sixth—God, the 'Lord'. This Lord, the *Yoga-sūtras* say (1. 24–26), 'is a special type of spiritual monad which is untouched by care, works (*karma*), the ripening of works, or hope. In him the seed of omniscience is perfect. He is the *guru* even of the ancients since he is not limited by time.'

Yoga, however, as everyone knows, is not only the name of one of the six 'schools' of philosophy but also a technique for achieving spiritual 'liberation': it uses matter, that is, the body, to enable the spiritual monad to divest itself of matter once and for all. Liberation, however, does not mean union with God as Christians might expect. True, contemplation of God as the Yogin's ideal in that he is 'untouched by care, works, the ripening of works, or hope', is recommended as a means towards achieving liberation or isolation, but once this goal of 'isolation' has been reached, God, having served his purpose, disappears from the Yogin's ken, for he is now himself absolute and alone (*kevala*). So much for the 'classical' Sāṁkhya and Yoga.

By *Sāṁkhya* the Gītā understands 'classical' Sāṁkhya, but with one very considerable difference,—over and above both material Nature and the spiritual monads (usually called 'embodied [selves]' or simply 'selves' (*ātman*) in the Gītā) stands the one God, Krishna. Moreover, the spiritual monads or selves are not independent entities as they are in the classical Sāṁkhya and Yoga but 'minute parts' of God (15. 7) and his 'seed' (14. 3). Moreover, salvation or liberation does not consist in the total isolation of each self from all others, from Nature, and from God, as in the Yoga system, but in 'becoming Brahman' (an originally Buddhist expression which we shall explain later (5. 24 n.)) and in realizing the unity of all things in oneself and then in God (4. 35: 6. 29–30).

The word *yoga* in the Gītā is used in a vast number of senses which we shall be considering later. When opposed to the term *sāṁkhya*, however, it means putting into practice the theory of Sāṁkhya as that word is understood in the Gītā, and that is what it means in this verse.

buddhyā yukto yayā, 'if you are controlled by the soul': *yukto* is the past participle passive of the root *yuj-* (p. 138) from which *yoga* is derived. Thus, following on what had been said in the previous hemistich, it should mean 'practised, exercised, influenced, or controlled by this wisdom (*buddhi*)'. The phrase, however, looks not only back but forwards—to 2. 41 where *buddhi*, 'intellect', is said to have the nature of will, and to 2. 48–51 where the *yoga* of *buddhi* and the *buddhi-yukta* are discussed. So the phrase here, in addition to meaning 'influenced etc. by this wisdom' also means 'controlled or integrated by the intellect-and-will'. Thus controlled or integrated Arjuna 'will put away the bondage that is inherent in [all] works'.

40. *n'eh'ābhikrama-nāśo 'sti, pratyavāyo na vidyate:*
svalpam apy asya dharmasya trāyate mahato bhayāt.

Herein no effort goes to seed nor is there any slipping back: even a very little of this discipline will protect [you] from great peril.

mahato bhayāt, 'great peril': Ś. and R. gloss this as *saṁsāra*, 'phenomenal existence, the round of birth and death'. This passage, as well as 15. 1–3, derives from KaU. 6. 1–3:

(1) With roots above and boughs beneath
This immortal fig-tree [stands];
That is the Pure, that Brahman,
That the Immortal, so men say:
In it all the worlds are stablished;
Beyond it none can pass.

(2) This whole moving world, whatever is,
Stirs in the breath of life, deriving from it:
The great fear (*mahad bhayaṁ*) [this], the upraised thunderbolt;
Whoso shall know it [thus], becomes immortal.

(3) For fear of it the fire burns bright,
For fear [of it] the sun gives forth its heat,
For fear [of it] the gods of storm and wind,
And Death, the fifth, [hither and thither] fly.

In the Gītā the emphasis has changed no doubt under Sāṁkhya influence. Both the immortal fig-tree which reappears in 15. 1–3 and the 'great fear' or 'peril' here are *saṁsāra*, transient existence, seen not so much as rooted in the Absolute Brahman but as separate or at least to be separated from It. Elsewhere in the Gītā, as we shall see, the two are reconciled in God.

41. *vyavasāy'ātmikā buddhir ek'aiva, Kuru-nandana,*
bahu-śākhā hy anantāś-ca buddhayo 'vyavasāyinām.

The essence of the soul is will, and it is really single, but many-branched and infinite are the souls of men devoid of will.

ek'aiva, 'it is really single': so following a variant. The *textus receptus* has *ek'eha*, 'single here [on earth]', but the sense surely is that *buddhi* as the highest evolute of Nature and therefore the nearest to the immortal 'self' is single, simple, one, because its true function is contemplation of the eternal. Hence, Krishna gives *buddhi-yoga* to those who 'commune with

Him in love' (10. 10), and it is through *buddhi-yoga* that Krishna's devotees meditate on Him.

'The essence of the soul is will': on the strength of this passage I have taken the liberty of translating *buddhi* as 'soul', for in the Christian tradition it is the soul that is the responsible element in man; it is the soul that is saved or damned, for in it are both intellect and will. This seems to me to be exactly what the Gītā understands by *buddhi*. Apart from the *ātman* or 'self' it is man's highest faculty and is or should be directed towards God. Once in the MBh. (12. 240. 3) it is said to be identical with the self (*buddhir ātmā manuṣyasya*).

In the *Sāṁkhya-kārikā* (23) *buddhi* is defined as *adhyavasāya*, 'determination' or 'cognition'.

Vedic Religion

42–4. *yām imāṁ puṣpitāṁ vācaṁ pravadanty avipaścitaḥ*
vedavāda-ratāḥ, Partha, n'ānyad astī'ti vādinaḥ
kām'ātmānaḥ svarga-parā janma-karma-phala-pradām
kriyā-viśeṣa-bahulāṁ bhog'aiśvarya-gatiṁ prati
bhog'aiśvarya-prasaktānāṁ tayā 'pahṛta-cetasām
vyavasāy'ātmikā buddhiḥ samādhau na vidhīyate.

The essence of the soul is will,—[but the souls] of men who cling to pleasure and to power, their minds seduced by flowery words, are not attuned to enstasy. Such men give vent to flowery words, lacking discernment, delighting in the Veda's lore, saying there is naught else. Desire is their essence, paradise their goal,—their words preach [re-]birth as the fruit of works and expatiate about the niceties of ritual by which pleasure and power can be achieved.

samādhau, 'enstasy': by 'enstasy' I understand that type of 'introverted' mystical experience in which there is experience of nothing except an unchanging, purely static oneness. It is the exact reverse of ecstasy which means to get outside oneself and which is often characterized by a breaking down of the barriers between the individual subject and the universe around him.

'Paradise their goal': paradise or heaven (*svarga*) is not the mystic's goal. It is at best a *pis aller* since it too belongs to the phenomenal world which must be transcended.

45. *traiguṇya-viṣayā vedā: nistraiguṇyo bhav'ārjuna,*
nirdvandvo nitya-sattva-stho niryogakṣema ātmavān.

[All Nature is made up of] the three 'constituents': these are the Veda's goal. Have done with them, Arjuna: have done with

[all] dualities, stand ever firm on Goodness. Think not of gain or keeping the thing gained, but be yourself!

-sattva-, 'Goodness'; the constituent of that name. So Ś. and R. Some modern commentators translate 'reality', 'truth', 'purity', or 'courage' on the grounds that Krishna would scarcely ask Arjuna to take his stand on 'Goodness' since he had already been told to have done with all three constituents. No doubt this slight inconsistency also occurred to Ś. and R., but it plainly did not seem unnatural to them since 'Goodness', though one of the constituents, is none the less attached to the self (MBh. 12. 290. 22) and the self lives in the *ambiance* of Goodness just as a fish lives in water, a gnat in a fig, or pith in grass (ibid. 12. 240. 20–22).

ātmavān, 'be yourself': Ś. glosses *apramatta*, 'recollected'. E., 'self-possessed': H., 'master of thy soul': S., 'maître de toi'.

46. *yāvān artha udapāne sarvataḥ saṁplut'odake*
tāvān sarveṣu vedeṣu brāhmaṇasya vijānataḥ.

As much use as there is in a water-tank flooded with water on every side, so much is there in all the Vedas for the Brāhman who discerns.

There has been much discussion on this verse because it seems to reject the Vedas *in toto*. The difficulty disappears, however, once one realizes that Krishna is here speaking of a 'Brāhman who discerns'. Arjuna is not a Brāhman but a *Kshatriya*, a warrior, and it is not for him in this life at least to seek to emulate the perfected Brāhman who is already *buddhi-yukta*, 'controlled or integrated by the soul'. For in the very next stanza Arjuna is told that work alone is his proper business; and works are the proper sphere of the Vedas since they are inseparable from the three constituents of Nature which alone really act (3. 28: 14. 19, 23).

There is indeed nothing particularly surprising in Krishna's depreciation of the Vedas as distinct from the Upanishads of which he claims to be the author (15. 15). The Vedas have their uses in the phenomenal world, but they do not lead to liberation: only the 'Veda's end', the Upanishads, do that. This theme had already been clearly enunciated in MuU. 1. 2. 1–12:

(1) The [ritual] acts that the seers beheld in the sacred formulas
Were spread abroad on the threefold [fire]:
O ye who long for truth, perform them constantly,
This is for you the path of [work] well done on earth.

But this is not enough, for:

(7) Unstable are these barks, the eighteenfold,
In the form of sacrifice
In which an inferior [ritual] act is uttered:
Deluded men who hail it as the best
Return again to old age and death.

(8) Self-wise, puffed up with learning,
Passing their days in the midst of ignorance,
They wander round, the fools, doing themselves much hurt,
Like blind men guided by the blind.

(9) Passing their days in ignorance in many and diverse ways,
'Our goal is won,' say they, childish in their conceit.
By that which in their passion they do not recognize as truth,
Though busy all the while, they are oppressed
And, losing the worlds [for which they long],
They come hurtling down [again].

(10) Thinking that sacrifice and merit are the highest good,
Deluded men, they nothing better know:
On heaven's vault they'll first enjoy their works well done
But then come back to this world,—or to another—worse.

(11) But those who in penance and in faith dwell in the forest,
Tranquil and wise, living a beggar's life,
Pass on, immaculate, through the doorway of the sun
To where that deathless Person dwells, of changeless Self.

(12) When he surveys the worlds built up by ritual works,
A Brāhman must despair.
Between what 's made and what 's unmade there's no connexion.

Works, then, in the form of sacrifice (see 3. 10–16: 4. 23 ff., 'he works for sacrifice [alone]') have their place in Krishna's scheme of things, but *of themselves* they cannot bring about release (*mokṣa*).

On the difficulties that commentators have found in this stanza see Hill ad loc.

Action is Arjuna's Duty

47. *karmaṇy ev'ādhikāras te mā phaleṣu kadācana:*
mā karma-phala-hetur bhūr, mā te saṅgo 'stv akarmaṇi.

[But] work alone is *your* proper business, never the fruits [it may produce]: let not your motive be the fruit of works nor your attachment to [mere] worklessness.

All work is or should be a sacrifice (3. 10–16) and Arjuna's business is war, and war is the sacrificial fire of which the warriors are the priests (MBh. 5. 139. 29 ff. etc.): but whatever he does he must do it in a spirit of detachment. This is drummed in again and again throughout the Gītā.

48. *yoga-sthaḥ kuru karmāṇi saṅgaṁ tyaktvā, dhanaṁjaya,*
siddhy-asiddhyoḥ samo bhūtvā. samatvaṁ yoga ucyate.

Stand fast in
{Yoga
the control the soul (*buddhi*) exercises over you
the integration of self
sameness-and-indifference},

surrendering attachment; in success and failure be the same and then get busy with your works. Yoga means 'sameness-and-indifference'.

yoga: here again the meaning of the word is imperceptibly shifting. The last time the word was used (2. 39) it meant 'practice' as opposed to theory (*sāṁkhya*), yet immediately afterwards the past participle passive of the same root had come to mean 'controlled' or 'integrated'. Here the word *yoga* looks both back to the idea of the *buddhyā yukta*, the man who is 'controlled' or 'integrated by the soul', and forward to the new definition in the second hemistich where *yoga* is defined as 'sameness-and-indifference'. This sameness-and-indifference is the hallmark of the Absolute, Brahman (5. 18–21, see note on 2. 15); and *yoga* is the 'practice' of this same holy indifference in the phenomenal world, the preparation for the ultimate 'sameness' which is Brahman, and the 'yoking' or integration of the whole man by the *buddhi* or soul.

Some MSS. add the following stanza here:

yasya sarve samārambhā nirāśīr, bandhanās tv iha,
tyāge yasya hutaṁ sarvaṁ, sa tyāgī sa ca buddhimān.

He who undertakes all enterprises without hope,—for therein are fetters,—who sacrifices all to self-surrender, he is [truly] self-surrendered and [truly] wise.

The Soul's Practice of Contemplation again

49. *dūreṇa hy avaraṁ karma buddhi-yogād, dhanaṁjaya,*
buddhau śaraṇam anviccha: kṛpaṇāḥ phala-hetavaḥ.

For lower far is [the path of] active work [for its own sake]

than { integration through the soul / the spiritual exercise of the soul / the indifference of the soul [to all dualities] }. Seek

refuge in the soul! How pitiful are they whose motive is the fruit [of works]!

yoga again: here E. and Rk. translate 'discipline', H. has 'method'. Both are right in this and many other contexts. Thus the three 'Yogas' generally attributed to the Gītā, *jñāna-yoga*, *karma-yoga*, and *bhakti-yoga* can well be translated as the 'discipline' of wisdom (or knowledge), of works, and of love and devotion. 'Method' will do equally well. I would, however, prefer to translate it as 'spiritual exercise' first because 'exercise' preserves the sense of activity which is always present in the word *yoga* when it is opposed to *sāṁkhya*, and secondly because 'spiritual exercise' recalls the *Spiritual Exercises* of Ignatius Loyola—the *yoga* of the Jesuits. All the other translations I have suggested, however, are inherent in this protean word.

The superiority of *buddhi-yoga* over *karma*, 'action', seems to be contradicted in 3. 8 where work (*karma*) is said to be better than doing no work at all (*akarman*) which is another word for *saṁnyāsa* ('renunciation'). Krishna, however, is now speaking of works *tout court*: He has not yet fully expounded his doctrine of performing actions without regard to their fruits or results. This, because of the total detachment it entails, is equivalent to doing nothing at all. All this will become clearer in the sequel.

50. *buddhi-yukto jahātī'ha ubhe sukṛta-duṣkṛte:*
tasmād yogāya yujyasva; yogaḥ karmasu kauśalam.

Whoso { is integrated by the soul / performs spiritual exercise with the soul / is united with the soul (?) } discards here [and now] both good and evil works: brace yourself then for { Yoga / spiritual exercise }; for Yoga is [also] skill in [performing] works.

buddhi-yukto, 'united with the soul (?)'. A possible translation, but scarcely fits into the general context. The author is probably still thinking back to the *buddhyā yukto* of 2. 39 where the man who is 'controlled or integrated by the soul puts away the bondage that is inherent in [all] works'. In this passage he does just the same. Similarly, in the résumé of the whole of the doctrine of the Gītā in 18. 51 the 'man who is integrated by his soul (*buddhyā*) [now] cleansed' casts off passion and hate just as here he casts off 'both good and evil works'. The idea remains the same, and it is simply to disregard the context and the whole use of the words *yukta* and *yoga* in the Gītā to translate *buddhi-yukta* as 'one who has yoked his intelligence (with the Divine)' as Rk. does. Deussen is equally at sea when he translates *yoga* throughout this passage as 'Hingebung'.

'Discards both good and evil works': once liberation is won and the spirit is free, morality ceases to have any meaning. This to us rather disconcerting idea was already well established in the Upanishads. In TU. 2. 9 it is said of the man who knows Brahman:

> That from which [all] words recoil together with the mind,
> Unable to attain it,—
> That is the bliss of Brahman; knowing it,
> A man has naught to fear from anywhere.

Such a man is not worried [by the thought]: 'Why did I not do good? Why did I do evil?' Knowing [good and evil] in this way he saves [him]self.

Cf. BU. 4. 3. 23: 5. 14. 8.

Similarly in MuU. 3. 1. 3 (cf. MaiU. 6. 18):

When a seer beholds the Maker, Lord,
The Person golden-hued, whose womb is Brahman,
Then does he understand: immaculate
He shakes off good and evil, reaches the highest,
The same manner of being [as is His].

It might be supposed that once one has reached the 'state of Brahman' (2. 72), which is a state of absolute static Being beyond becoming and therefore beyond all action, what actions one still performs while yet in the body must *eo ipso* be absolutely good, for, as with St. Thomas Aquinas, 'Being' and 'good' are interchangeable terms (17. 26). On balance, however, this is not the view of the Upanishads or the later texts of classical Hinduism. This is brutally brought home by the god Indra's proud boast in KauU. 3. 1:

Indra did not swerve from the truth, for Indra *is* truth. So he said: 'Know me, then, as I am. This indeed is what I consider most beneficial for mankind—that they should know me. I killed the three-headed son of Tvashtri, I threw the Arunmukha ascetics to the hyenas. Transgressing many a compact, I impaled the people of Prahlāda to the sky, the Paulomas to the atmosphere, and the Kālakānjas to the earth, and I did not lose a single hair in the process.'

The man who knows me as I am loses nothing that is his, whatever he does, even though he should slay his mother or his father, even though he steal or procure an abortion. Whatever evil he does, he does not blanch.

yogāya yujyasva, 'brace yourself for spiritual exercise': once again a play on the different meanings of the root *yuj-*. In 2. 38 we had the phrase *yuddhāya yujyasva*, 'brace yourself for the fight'. This coincidence can scarcely be fortuitous: fighting, that is war, is the *yoga* or 'spiritual exercise' most suitable to a member of the warrior class. Ideally, however, as Krishna points out, it should be performed with 'sameness-and-indifference' (*yoga*) and with 'skill' as he now defines *yoga*. For:

'Yoga is [also] skill in [performing] works.' Thus for *yoga* we now have the following meanings:

(i) practice as opposed to theory (2. 39);
(ii) spiritual exercise (2. 39);
(iii) control and/or integration (2. 39, 48–50);
(iv) sameness-and-indifference (2. 48—defined);
(v) skill in performing works (2. 50—defined).

These five meanings derive either from the root meaning of (*a*) 'yoking' or from the derived meaning (*b*) 'preparation, activity'. (*a*) accounts for (iii) and derives from the idea of a yoke controlling oxen, while (ii) and (iv) are further clarification of what is meant by 'control'. (i) and (v) derive from (*b*), whereas both (*a*) and (*b*) are implicit in (ii) 'spiritual exercise', perhaps the basic meaning of *yoga* in the Gītā.

51. ***karma-jaṁ buddhi-yuktā hi phalaṁ tyaktvā manīṣiṇaḥ***
janma-bandha-vinirmuktāḥ padaṁ gacchanty anāmayam.

For those wise men who are controlled-and-integrated by the soul, who have renounced the fruit that is born of works, these will be freed from the bondage of [re-]birth and fare to that region that knows no ill.

buddhi-yuktā hi: one MS. has *buddhi-yukt'ātmā*, 'whose self is controlled or integrated by the soul' (*buddhi*). This must be wrong since a plural form is required.

janma-, 'birth': var. *karma-*, 'works, action'. Birth of course, like works or action of any kind, constitutes a bond: it ties you to the material world of Nature and deflects you from your eternal destiny which is a total freedom of the spirit beyond space and time and action.

padaṁ . . . anāmayam, 'the region that knows no ill'. This is the region of liberation (so Ś. rightly).

52. *yadā te moha-kalilaṁ buddhir vyatitariṣyati*
tadā gantā 'si nirvedaṁ śrotavyasya śrutasya ca.

When your soul passes beyond delusion's turbid quicksands, then will you learn disgust for what has been heard [ere now] and for what may yet be heard.

śrutasya, 'what has been heard': *śruti* (which appears in the next line and which is the verbal noun of *śruta* of which *śrutasya* is gen. sing.) is one of the ordinary words for the Veda—excluding apparently in this case the Upanishads. Krishna's teaching supersedes the purely verbal instruction of the Vedas (cf. 6. 44). What is meant by *śrotavyasya*, 'what may yet be heard', is not so clear.

53. *śruti-vipratipannā te yadā sthāsyati niścalā*
samādhāv acalā buddhis, tadā yogam avāpsyasi.

When your soul, by scripture once bewildered, stands motionless and still, immovable in enstasy, then will you attain to { integration [under the direction of the soul] / Yoga, sameness-and-indifference }.

śruti-vipratipannā, 'by scripture once bewildered'. E. 'averse to traditional lore ("heard" in the Veda)'. The Veda once again is considered worthless for the attainment of *samādhi*, 'enstasy' which, as this passage shows along with many others to come, is a state of absolute quiescence—motionless and static. To emphasize this the Gītā here uses two synonyms for 'motionless'—*niścalā* and *acalā*. *Buddhi*, the soul, is by nature single, simple, one (2. 41), and by realizing itself as such it can become immersed in enstasy—static and still like the 'self-in-itself' with which it now seems to have reached identity. *Samādhi* or 'enstasy' cannot be obtained by those who delight in the Vedas (2. 42–44).

The Man of Steady Wisdom

Arjuna uvāca:

54. *sthita-prajñasya kā bhāṣā samādhi-sthasya, Keśava ?*
sthita-dhīḥ kiṁ prabhāṣeta, kim āsīta, vrajeta kim ?

Arjuna said:

What is the mark of the man of steady wisdom immersed in enstasy? How does he speak, this man of steadied thought? How sit? How walk?

Śrī-bhagavān uvāca:

55. *prajahāti yadā kāmān sarvān, Pārtha, mano-gatān,*
ātmany ev'ātmanā tuṣṭaḥ sthita-prajñas tad'ocyate.

The Blessed Lord said:

When a man puts from him all desires that prey upon the mind, himself contented in self alone, then is he called a man of steady wisdom.

'When a man puts from him all desires': desire for the Gītā as for the Buddhists is the active manifestation of evil: it forces you to do evil against your will (3. 37) and, when thwarted, gives rise to anger, which in turn sets off a disastrous chain reaction (2. 62–63). Krishna does not preach an easy way any more than did the Buddha. 'Give up' is the practical purport, the *Yoga*, which corresponds to the theory, the *Sāṁkhya*, that the natural habitat of the self is timeless eternity, not the world of time and of action which is conditioned by time, for the self is 'firm-set, unmoved, primeval, . . . immutable' (2. 24–25). To realize it as such a man must 'give up, deny himself': he must give up the 'bondage that is inherent in [all] works' (2. 39); 'the same in success and failure' (2. 48) he must give up attachment; he must give up *all* works, both good and evil, and, of course, 'the fruit that is born of works' (2. 51). Now he is asked to give up 'desire' though this is inseparable from the human condition itself (2. 62: cf. 2. 60 n.).

ātmany ev'ātmanā tuṣṭaḥ, 'himself contented in self alone': this is the first time that the self has appeared under its own name (*ātman*). *Ātman* in classical Sanskrit is a reflexive pronoun and when used in the instrumental case (*ātmanā*) it means simply 'oneself, yourself', etc., in such phrases as 'Do it yourself' (*ātmanā kuru*) or 'What do you yourself think?' (*ātmanā kiṁ manyase?*). One might then think that *ātmany* (loc.) . . . *tuṣṭaḥ* meant simply 'pleased with oneself'. This is not so, for *ātman* also means what I have called 'self-in-itself', the timeless being that inhabits every body, the *dehin* or 'embodied [self]' with which we are now familiar (2. 13–30). Being beyond space and time and action which is conditioned by both, it is not a responsible entity: and so 'let a man take pleasure in self alone, in self his satisfaction find, in self alone content: [for then] there is naught he needs to *do*' (3. 17).

56. *duḥkheṣv anudvigna-manāḥ, sukheṣu vigata-spṛhaḥ,*
vīta-rāga-bhaya-krodhaḥ sthita-dhīr munir ucyate.

Whose mind is undismayed [though beset] by many a sorrow, who for pleasures has no further longing, from whom all passion, fear, and wrath have fled, such a man is called a man of steadied thought, a silent sage.

57. *yaḥ sarvatr'ānabhisnehas tat-tat prāpya śubh'āśubham*
n'ābhinandati na dveṣṭi, tasya prajñā pratiṣṭhitā.

Who has no love for any thing, who rejoices not at whatever good befalls him nor hates the bad that comes his way,—firm-stablished is the wisdom of such a man.

'Who has no love for any thing': 'such as body and life' (Ś.). Love (*sneha*) is as much to be rejected as hate: cf. MBh. 12. 185. 3: 277. 7; 287. 33: 308. 52: 316. 31: 317. 5: 290. 62 ('the mud of love'). Love, like *karma* itself, is a 'snare' (*pāśa*).

58. *yadā saṁharate c'āyaṁ kūrmo 'ṅgānī'va sarvaśaḥ*
indriyāṇī'ndriy'ārthebhyas, tasya prajñā pratiṣṭhitā.

And when he draws in on every side his senses from their proper objects as a tortoise [might draw in] its limbs,—firm-stablished is the wisdom of such a man.

This simile is frequently repeated in the didactic portions of the MBh. (references will be found in the critical edition) and also occurs in the Buddhist canon (S. i. 7). Here the Gītā parts company with the classical Sāṁkhya. 'Liberation', or in this case 'salvation' in the sense of 'making whole', is attained not by the separation of the self from the Sāṁkhya categories deriving from material Nature—ego, mind, senses, and the rest, but by their absorption and concentration (*samādhi*) into the self. The human personality becomes one as it does at death (BU. 4. 4. 2, 'He is becoming one, he does not see' etc., see 2. 22 n.).

59. *viṣayā vinivartante nirāhārasya dehinaḥ*
rasa-varjaṁ: raso 'py asya paraṁ dṛṣṭvā nivartate.

For the embodied [self] who eats no more objects of sense must disappear,—save only the [recollected] flavour,—and that too must vanish at the vision of the highest.

nirāhārasya, 'who eats no more': in Sanskrit the word *āhāra* normally means 'food', and E. takes it so literally: the man who fasts even so retains the 'flavour' of food, but 'when he sees the highest' he ceases even to feel hungry. Both Ś. and R., however, take *āhāra* to mean the 'objects of the senses' and they are almost certainly right, for in the first six chapters of the Gītā we are continually coming across Buddhist ideas and Buddhist terms which do not naturally fit into the Gītā's Upanishadic background. *Āhāra* is one of these. It does not occur in the classical Upanishads, but is a stock idea in the Buddhist Pāli canon. There it means not only bodily food, but also the food of the senses by contact (*phassāhāro*), of the mind-and-will, and of consciousness (*viññāna*) (see the Pali Text Society's *Pali–English Dictionary*, p. 117: S. v. 102 ff.). This is clearly what it means here.

paraṁ, 'the highest': the root meaning appears to be 'other', hence 'beyond'. R. takes it to mean simply 'beyond the objects of sense'. For Ś. it is 'the transcendent reality (*paramārtha-tattvam*), Brahman'.

In the Upanishads, if neuter, it means Brahman or (what is synonymous with it) the 'Imperishable'. In TU. 2. 1 'Whoso knows Brahman, wins the *param*', while in KaU. 3. 2 'what is *param*' is equated with the 'Imperishable Brahman'. So too in the same Upanishad 2. 16 it is the Imperishable, and it is by the 'higher' (*para*) science only that the Imperishable can be understood (MuU 1. 1. 5). Cf. PU. 1. 1: 6. 7 (*paraṁ Brahma*): 4. 10 (*param akṣaram*, 'highest Imperishable'): 4. 7 (*para ātmani*): 4. 9 (*pare 'kṣare ātmani*).

By the time of the Gītā, then, *param* had come to mean the 'Imperishable', Brahman, and Ātman, that is, Being beyond space and time whether this is associated with God or man or the universe.

60. *yatato hy api, Kaunteya, puruṣasya vipaścitaḥ*
indriyāṇi pramāthīni haranti prasabhaṁ manaḥ.

And yet however much a wise man strive, the senses' tearing violence may seduce his mind by force.

vipaścitaḥ, 'wise': var. *avipaścitaḥ*, 'unwise, one who does not discern'.

According to the Buddhist Pāli canon the attainment of Nirvāna, that is, the total release from the human condition as we know it—in other words, life—cannot be achieved until all contact between the senses and their objects has been severed (see esp. S. iv. 1–210). It is this contact which gives rise to attachment, not the senses or the objects of sense alone. For example, if a black ox were yoked or tied to a white one, no one could say that either was the connecting-link between the two; rather the link is the yoke or cord which unites them. So too it is the mutual attraction (*chandarāga*) between the two which causes this disastrous connexion (S. iv. 282–3). The Gītā takes on this idea from Buddhism: it is not in the least typical of the Upanishads and makes its first appearance in the relatively late *Kaṭha* Upanishad to which the Gītā is closely related.

61. *tāni sarvāṇi saṁyamya yukta āsīta mat-paraḥ:*
vaśe hi yasy'endriyāṇi tasya prajñā pratiṣṭhitā.

Let him sit, curbing them all, integrated, intent on Me: for firmly established is that man's wisdom whose senses are subdued.

yukta, 'integrated': this meaning of *yukta*, *yoga*, is now becoming preponderant. *Buddhi*, the soul, is the agent of integration and *yoga* or integration is itself the goal (2. 50, 53). In this and similar passages Ś. glosses *samāhita* ('concentrated [in *samādhi*]'). 'Integrated', then, seems to be the best translation, for the process is likened to the drawing in of the limbs of a tortoise into itself. This is precisely what *buddhi* does: it draws the senses, mind, and ego into itself in order to concentrate them in a unified whole upon the eternal centre of the human personality—the self.

mat-paraḥ, 'intent on Me': var. *tat-paraḥ*, 'intent on That', meaning presumably Brahman: *mat-paraḥ*, however, is the better attested reading.

This is the first time that Krishna has mentioned Himself as in any way connected with these essentially Buddhistic and Sāṁkhya-Yoga exercises in detachment. In this first instance He is not at all offering Himself as an object of loving devotion and veneration, but merely as a definite object on which to direct what is elsewhere called 'one-pointed' (*ekāgra*, cf. *Yoga-sūtras* 3. 11, 12) concentration. This is all part and parcel of the technique of the classical [Sāṁkhya-]Yoga. There the technique of concentration is in three stages. First, the body must be brought under control; then follows the repetition of the sacred formula through which the deity invoked in the formula becomes present to the mind; and thirdly, by concentration on God as the one spiritual monad who is permanently unaffected by what goes on in the phenomenal world, one becomes like him, that is, 'free' (*mukta*, liberated) and 'isolated' (*kevala*) in one's own absolute essence. There is no suggestion that there is any form of communion with God any more than there is in Buddhism—a system in which there is no God at all, whether personal or impersonal. Here Krishna makes no claims to devotion, nor does He yet present Himself as the Absolute as Person: He presents Himself simply as the 'Lord' as He is understood in the *Yoga-sūtras*, 'a special type of spiritual monad which is untouched by care, works, the fruits of works, or hope, in whom the seed of omniscience is perfect, and who is the *guru* even of the ancients because he is unlimited in time' (*Yoga-sūtras* 1. 24–26). Indeed, when it comes to the *practice* of contemplation, it matters little whether the Yogin concentrates on the God described in the passage just quoted, or whether he selects whatever god he prefers as the object on which to direct his one-pointed concentration (ibid. 2. 44–45): for the final aim of the Yogin of the *Yoga-sūtras* must be detachment not only from all that springs from material Nature but also from other spiritual monads and therefore from God himself. Hence, at the end of this chapter which from now on describes the ascent of the self to full liberation, there is no further mention of Krishna as God: the goal is not God, but Nirvāna, the Buddha's goal.

62. *dhyāyato viṣayān puṁsaḥ saṅgas teṣū'pajāyate,*
saṅgāt saṁjāyate kāmaḥ, kāmāt krodho 'bhijāyate.

Let a man [but] think of the objects of sense,—attachment to them is born: from attachment springs desire, from desire is anger born.

'From desire is anger born': when desire is thwarted a man gets angry with his neighbour (Ś., R.).

63. *krodhād bhavati saṁmohaḥ, saṁmohāt smṛti-vibhramaḥ,*
smṛti-bhraṁśād buddhi-nāśo, buddhi-nāśāt praṇaśyati.

From anger comes bewilderment, from bewilderment wandering of the mind, from wandering of the mind destruction of the soul: once the soul is destroyed the man is lost.

saṁmohaḥ, 'bewilderment': Ś., R., 'inability to distinguish right from wrong'.

'Destruction of the soul': that is, the destruction of both the intellect and will and their dissipation (2. 41). This is presumably what we would now call a nervous breakdown.

praṇaśyati, 'the man is lost': *naś-* means both 'to be destroyed' and 'to be lost', both 'damnation' and 'perdition'.

64. *rāga-dveṣa-viyuktais tu viṣayān indriyaiś caran*
ātma-vaśyair vidhey'ātmā prasādam adhigacchati.

But he who roves among the objects of sense, his senses subdued to self and disjoined from passion and hate, and who is self-possessed [himself], draws nigh to calm serenity.

rāga-dveṣa-, 'passion and hate': together with *moha*, 'delusion' or 'bewilderment' (cf. *saṁ-moha* of the previous stanza) these are the three cravings (*taṇhā*) denounced by the Buddhists. The total uprooting of the three is, among other things, Nirvāna (S. iv. 251, 297, etc.). This seems to be Buddhist influence once again.

ātma-vaśyair, 'subdued to self': the native commentators draw a sharp distinction between the 'self' as it truly is, that is, like the Sāṁkhya *puruṣa*, beyond space and time, and the 'lower' self—what in the Christian West we would call the 'carnal self' which is continually at war with the higher self. The Gītā is aware of this distinction and it is forcefully expressed in 6. 5–6 where the enmity between the two is graphically described, but on the whole the higher 'self' is not sharply distinguished from the psychosomatic organism to which it is temporarily attached; on the contrary even when 'purified' it is 'integrated' (*yukta*, 5. 7–8), not dissociated from *buddhi*, *manas*—soul, mind—and the rest. Rather it absorbs them into itself just as God absorbs the universe into Himself at the end of a world-cycle.

65. *prasāde sarva-duḥkhānāṁ hānir asy'opajāyate:*
prasanna-cetaso hy āśu buddhiḥ paryavatiṣṭhate.

And from him thus becalmed all sorrows flee away: for once his thoughts are calmed, his soul stands firmly [in its ground].

'His soul stands firmly [in its ground]': Ś., 'stands motionless, conformed (*rūpeṇa*) to the self'.

66. *n'āsti buddhir ayuktasya na c'āyuktasya bhāvanā,*
na c'ābhāvayataḥ śāntir: aśāntasya kutaḥ sukham ?

The man who is not integrated has no soul, in him there is no development: for the man who does not develop there is no peace. Whence should there be joy to a peaceless man?

Since it is *buddhi*, the soul, which controls and integrates a man (2. 39), the man who is not integrated can be said to have no soul in that it goes to pieces and sprawls all over the place like the branches of a tree (2. 41). Since he is dissipated in this way he cannot 'develop' towards final integration and spiritual freedom (*mokṣa*), and if he cannot develop, he cannot attain to peace which is the very essence of the 'state of Brahman' (2. 71–2).

bhāvanā, 'development': modern commentators seem to have gone badly astray in interpreting this word. Translations have varied between 'perseverance in the pursuit of knowledge' (Telang translating Ś.), 'Verinnerlichung' (D.), 'inspiration' (Barnett), 'conceptual ideation' (Rangacarya), 'méditation' (S.), 'reflection' (Hill), 'power of concentration' (Rk.), and 'efficient-force' (E.). These meanings are also assigned by the respective translators to the *abhāvayataḥ* of the following hemistich. Both in Sanskrit and Pāli the normal meaning of *bhāvaya-* is 'nourish' or 'develop'. In the Gītā itself (3. 11) the word is used of the sacrifice to the gods. By sacrifice man *nourishes* the gods and the gods in turn nourish man. The word is common in the MBh. in the sense of 'nourish' and 'develop'. This too is its normal meaning in Pāli.

67. *indriyāṇāṁ hi caratāṁ yan mano 'nuvidhīyate,*
tad asya harati prajñāṁ vāyur nāvam iv'āmbhasi.

Hither and thither the senses rove, and when the mind is attuned to them, it sweeps away [whatever of] wisdom a man may possess, as the wind [sweeps away] a ship on the water, *mano*, 'mind': according to the *Sāṁkhya-kārikā* (27) *manas*, 'mind', is *saṁkalpakam*, a difficult word to translate. It means both 'imagination', 'conception', and 'determination'. The last seems to be what is meant in the *Kārikā* since, theoretically at least, it determines how the senses should act. It is also regarded as being the sixth of the senses (as it is in Buddhism) corresponding more or less to what the Schoolmen called *sensus communis*. In the Gītā its principal job seems to be to control the senses (3. 7: 6. 24), but unless it is firmly controlled itself, the senses will master it (2. 60, 67). It is the seat of memory (3. 6) but extremely fickle (6. 26, 34, 35) and itself needs to be controlled (6. 14). In the parable of the chariot in the *Kaṭha* Upanishad (3. 3–4) *buddhi*, the soul, is the charioteer, *manas* the reins, and the senses the horses. Being classed with the senses *manas* naturally looks in their direction, whereas *buddhi* naturally looks towards the self. Hence, if it is to fulfil its proper function of restraining the senses, it must itself be held in check (6. 14) so that it too may finally come to rest in the self (6. 25) and so be dedicated to God (12. 2, 8).

68. *tasmād yasya, mahā-bāho, nigṛhītāni sarvaśaḥ*
indriyāṇī'ndriy'ārthebhyas, tasya prajñā pratiṣṭhitā.

And so whose senses are withheld from the objects proper to them, wherever he may be, firm-stablished is the wisdom of such a man.

On withholding the senses from the objects proper to them see 2. 58 and 2. 60 n.

69. *yā niśā sarva-bhūtānāṁ tasyāṁ jāgarti saṁyamī:*
yasyāṁ jāgrati bhūtāni sā niśā paśyato muneḥ.

In what for all [other] folk is night, therein is the man of self-restraint [wide-]awake. When all [other] folk are awake, that is night for the sage who sees.

paśyato, 'who sees [in truth]': 'seeing' is elsewhere elaborated as:

(i) seeing the self (2. 29);
(ii) seeing the highest (2. 59 and n.);
(iii) seeing inactivity in action (i.e. the eternal in the temporal) (4. 18);
(iv) seeing all beings in the self (4. 35: 6. 29);
(v) seeing all beings in God (4. 35: 6. 30);
(vi) seeing that Sāṁkhya and Yoga (theory and practice) are one (5. 5);
(vii) seeing self in self (6. 20: 13. 24);
(viii) seeing self in all beings (6. 29);
(ix) seeing God everywhere (6. 30: 13. 27);
(x) seeing 'the same' everywhere (6. 32: 13. 27–28);
(xi) seeing self as not being an agent (13. 29: 18. 16);

(xii) seeing self in transmigration (15. 10) and as established in the [empirical] self (15. 11).

How this twelvefold vision is finally co-ordinated we shall see in the sequel.

70. *āpūryamāṇam acala-pratiṣṭhaṁ*
samudram āpaḥ praviśanti yadvat,
tadvat kāmā yaṁ praviśanti sarve
sa śāntim āpnoti na kāma-kāmī.

As the waters flow into the sea, full filled, whose ground remains unmoved, so too do all desires flow into [the heart of] man: and such a man wins peace,—not the desirer of desires.

In ChU. 6. 10. 1, MuU. 3. 2. 8, and PU. 6. 5 we also find the almost universal mystical symbol of the rivers and the sea, signifying the loss of man's individuality in the infinity of the Absolute. This passage, however, is talking about something different: it is desires that are absorbed into the total personality. They are not destroyed but sublimated into tranquillity. The idea appears to be based on two passages from the *Bṛhadāraṇyaka* Upanishad. The first (4. 3. 32) compares the seer to an ocean in which he finds his highest bliss:

An ocean, One, the seer becomes, without duality: this, sire, is the Brahman-world. . . . This is his highest path, this his highest prize, this his highest world, this his highest bliss. This is that bliss of his on but a fraction of which other beings live.

So too the enlightened Buddha is compared to an ocean (S. iv. 376–7):

Freed from form, sense-perception, feeling, habitual tendencies, and consciousness he is deep, incommensurable, unfathomable like the great ocean.

The second passage is BU. 4. 3. 21 in which it is shown how all desires can be reduced to the desire for the Self which is the consummation of all desires:

This is that form of his which is beyond desire, free from evil, free from fear. Just as a man, closely embraced by his loving wife, knows nothing without, nothing within, so does this 'person', closely embraced by the Self that consists of wisdom, know nothing without, nothing within. That is his [true] form in which [all] his desires are fulfilled, in which Self [alone] is his desire, in which he has no desire, no sorrow.

This, as the Gītā says, constitutes peace.

71. *vihāya kāmān yaḥ sarvān pumāṁś carati niḥspṛhaḥ*
nirmamo nirahaṁkāraḥ sa śāntim adhigacchati.

The man who puts away all desires and roams around from longing freed, who does not think, 'This I am', or 'This is mine', draws near to peace.

The philosophical transition in this stanza and the next is abrupt. In the last stanza the attainment of 'peace' was seen as a true integration of the personality in which all desires were transmuted into that tranquillity which is characteristic of the 'self-in-itself'. Here we not only return to the Buddhistic ideal of the total severance of the temporal (*saṁsāra*) from the eternal (*nirvāṇa*), which in practice means the total *suppression* of desire, but we also come up against terminology that is unmistakably Buddhist.

nirmamo nirahaṁkāraḥ, 'who does not think, "This I am", or "This is mine" ': this is the *ahaṁkāra-mamaṁkāra* of the Pāli canon (e.g. M. iii. 19, 32: S. ii. 252, 275; iii. 80, 236). The concepts of 'I' and 'mine' are illusory: neither the body nor the mind nor the senses nor feeling nor perception nor consciousness nor anything associated with life in this world can be described as 'I' or 'mine'. *n'etaṁ mama n'eso 'ham asmi na m'eso attā*: 'This is not mine, this is not I, this is not my self' (M. i. 185: S. iv. 1 ff. and more or less *passim*). Examples could be endlessly multiplied, for it is cardinal doctrine of Theravāda Buddhism that nothing transient can be called 'I', 'mine', or 'self'. The three terms *anicca, dukkha, anattā*, 'impermanent', 'sorrow', and 'void of self' are interchangeable. Nothing that you can think of as 'I', 'mine', or 'myself' is really 'you', 'yours', or 'yourself'. Whether or not early Buddhism believed in a 'self-in-itself', the corner-stone of Hindu ontology, is still a matter of dispute. What is important, however, is that the Buddhist refusal to countenance the idea that anything in time and space can be called 'I', 'mine', or 'self' made its way into Hinduism for the first time in the Bhagavad-Gītā. In the rest of the MBh. and not only in the didactic portions (which are almost certainly late) the idea has already become part and parcel of Hinduism. In fact no less a person than Yudhishthira, the 'king of righteousness' and Arjuna's elder brother, makes this doctrine his own (MBh. 12. 9. 14: 12. 17. 12, etc.) and for that he is accused of being an 'atheist' (*nāstika*), a term used also of the Buddhists (ibid. 12. 14. 33).

In Chapters II, V, and VI of the Gītā the Buddhist ideal of total detachment and selflessness, as well as Nirvāna which is the goal to which they lead, is wholly accepted. It is Krishna's task to fit it into a scheme of things which also makes room for a personal God.

72. *eṣā brāhmī sthitiḥ, Pārtha, n'aināṁ prāpya vimuhyati:*
sthitvā 'syām antakāle 'pi brahma-nirvāṇam ṛcchati.

This is the fixed, still state of Brahman; he who wins through to this is nevermore perplexed. Standing therein at the time of death, to Nirvāna that is Brahman too he goes.

brāhmī sthitiḥ, 'the fixed, still state of Brahman': as in 2. 53 where the perfected soul (*buddhi*) 'stands motionless and still, immovable in enstasy', here too this immobility (*sthitiḥ, sthitvā*, 'standing still') is emphasized. E. catches the same idea by translating 'fixation' (so too D. 'Feststehen') and suggests an alternative translation, 'resulting in the attainment of Brahman', which however represents the original less faithfully.

Nirvāṇa is a Buddhist, not a Hindu term and only becomes acclimatized in Hinduism after its adoption in the Gītā: it does not occur in the classical Upanishads. *Brahma-* used in compounds is also a Buddhist term and is therefore likely to be used in the sense that the Buddhists use it both because it is directly attached to the word *nirvāṇa* and because much of the terminology and ideology of this section is in any case Buddhist.

What the Buddhists understand by Nirvāna is simply the cessation of phenomenal existence. The word literally means 'blowing out' and Nirvāna is thus the 'blowing out' of the lamp or fire of existence (Sn. 235: D. ii. 266: M. i. 487; iii. 245: S. ii. 85; iv. 213, etc.). This means the cessation of sensation of any kind; sensation will have 'grown cold' (S. iv. 213. Cf. M. i. 341; ii. 159; iii. 245: S. i. 141, 212, etc.). It is the extinction of becoming, craving, and pain (*Udāna* 33: Sn. 1109: Iti. 44: M. i. 294: S. iii. 179, 190, 193, etc.). It is the peace (Sn. 933) of eternity which can only be won by detachment from (*virāga*), disgust at (*nibbidā*), and the bringing to an end of (*nirodha*) phenomenal existence, by the tranquillizing (*upasamā*) of the senses, wisdom (*abhiññā*), and enlightenment (*saṁbodhi*) (D. i. 189: M. i. 485: the formula is common throughout the Pāli canon). It is the end of anything we can conceive of as personality, so much so that the commonest phrase used to express the state of a man who has attained Nirvāna, of the man who is *nibbuta*, 'brought to a standstill' or 'extinguished' in a purely phenomenal sense, is *vimuttasmiṁ vimuttaṁ*, 'what is liberated in liberation', 'what is set free in freedom' (S. iv. 3 and *passim* in S. iv; common elsewhere).

The term *brahma-nirvāṇa* does not occur in the Pāli canon and seems to have been coined by the author of the Gītā from the two Buddhist terms *brahma-bhūta* 'become Brahman' (see 5. 24 n.) and *nirvāṇa*.

So ends the introductory chapter of the Gītā. The gist of Krishna's teaching is that Arjuna must not shirk the coming war because, though he may think he will be killing his kinsmen, he will in fact be doing no such thing because every man's soul is immortal in eternity as well as in time. He should fight because it is his caste-duty to do so (there will be much more about this later), but he must learn to fight as he must learn to engage in any action whatsoever without regard to result: he must learn Yoga which is both 'skill in works' and 'sameness-and-indifference' to the outcome of what he does. By cultivating the 'Yoga' of 'sameness' he will come to realize the eternal 'sameness', that is, the unvarying presence of timeless Being in and behind all that comes to be and passes away. This is what the Buddhists understand by *brahma-* and *nirvāṇa*; it is the Yoga of 'sameness' that can only be reached by the Yoga of 'skill in works' which means the total detachment of the senses from their objects or their absorption by the mind into the soul and by the soul into the timeless self that is the core of every man's being. This introductory chapter is, then, concerned with the nature of man. The *ambiance* is Buddhistic and Sāṁkhya-Yogin (with the exceptions we have already pointed out). Krishna is in no hurry to reveal his true nature as 'God of gods' (11. 13).

CHAPTER III

KRISHNA's eulogy of the 'spiritual exercise directed by the soul' (*buddhi-yoga*) and his apparent disparagement of action very naturally lead Arjuna to ask Him why He urges him to commit a violent deed (1–2). Krishna explains that it is in fact quite impossible to live at all without acting and that all action should be regarded as a sacrifice (3–9). Then comes a digression on the institution and utility of sacrifice and the origin of the whole world-process (10–16).

Here, surprisingly enough in the context, follow two verses in praise of the man who, since he finds pleasure in the immortal self alone, has no need to perform any action at all (17–18). Returning to his main theme, Krishna again bids Arjuna to act but without attachment just as He Himself as God Almighty does. In this he should set an example to others just as He Himself does (19–26).

Moreover, man does not really act himself, it is the constituents of Nature that act through him; hence he should resign all his actions to God (to whom they really belong) and so he will be released from action itself and all its effects. Everyone acts in accordance with his own nature, and since one's nature corresponds to the caste into which one is born, one should rigorously perform the duties appropriate to one's own caste (27–35).

Why, then, Arjuna asks, do men do evil against their will? This, Krishna replies, is due to desire and anger, 'brigands on the road'. The chapter ends with an exhortation to know the self which is yet higher than the soul. Only so can he conquer his arch-enemy, desire (36–43).

This chapter is traditionally called *karma-yoga*, the 'Yoga of action or works'.

Why?

Arjuna uvāca:

1. *jyāyasī cet karmaṇas te matā buddhir, Janārdana,*
tat kiṁ karmaṇi ghore māṁ niyojayasi, Keśava?

Arjuna said:

If you think that [the contemplative life of] the soul is a loftier [course] than [the mere performance of] acts, then why do you command me to do a cruel deed?

buddhir: Ś. glosses *jñānam*, '[transcendent] wisdom', as he does on 2. 39. The two are in fact closely associated and there is really no difference between the *buddhi-yoga* of the last chapter and the *jñāna-yoga* of the following one.

2. *vyāmiśreṇ'aiva vākyena buddhiṁ mohayasī'va me:*
tad ekaṁ vada niścitya yena śreyo 'ham āpnuyām.

You confuse my soul [and intellect], or so it seems, with distinctly muddled words: so tell me with authority the one [simple way] whereby I can attain the better part.

vyāmiśreṇ'aiva vākyena, 'with distinctly muddled words': this is the reading of the critical edition of the MBh. Most MSS. have *vyāmiśreṇ'eva* (-*a iva*), 'with seemingly muddled words'.

buddhiṁ, '[you confuse my] soul [and intellect]': this is a grave charge and the word is surely not selected at random. Arjuna remembers that Krishna had said of *buddhi* in 2. 41: 'The essence of the soul is will and it is really single, but many-branched and infinite are the souls of men devoid of will.' Krishna's apparently equivocal words, then, seem to Arjuna designed to confuse the singleness and simplicity of his soul and thereby to lead it to its destruction and ultimate perdition (2. 63).

śreyo, 'the better part': this would seem to mean little more than 'to do the right thing'. E. has 'welfare', D. 'Heil', while Rk.'s 'highest good' would seem to be flying rather too high for this stage of the dialogue.

Work and Bodily Life are Inseparable

Śrī-bhagavān uvāca:

3. *loke 'smin dvividhā niṣṭhā purā proktā mayā, 'nagha,*
jñāna-yogena sāṁkhyānāṁ, karma-yogena yoginām.

The Blessed Lord said:

Of old did I proclaim the twofold law [that holds sway] in this world,—for men of theory the spiritual exercise of wisdom, for men of action the spiritual exercise through works.

jñāna-yogena, 'spiritual exercise of wisdom' [for the men of theory, —*sāṁkhyas*]. This takes us back to 2. 39 where it is *buddhi*, the 'soul' or 'contemplative intellect', rather than wisdom (*jñāna*) that is the privilege of the 'man of theory'. The transition is natural enough, for wisdom is inherent in *buddhi* and according to the *Sāṁkhya-kārikā* (23) is identical with it.

Throughout the Gītā *jñāna*, 'wisdom', is contrasted with *karma*, 'action'. It means the apperception of transcendent reality as distinct from the phenomenal world (so Ś.): this is the function of *buddhi*, the 'soul'. It is from the same root as the Greek *gnōsis*, and just as the gnoses of the various Gnostic sects are as various as the sects themselves, so are the *jñāna*s of the Indian 'schools' of philosophy. It might, then, be as well to consider at this point what the Gītā itself understands by this word. This is stated at some length in 13. 7–11:

> To shun conceit and tricky ways, to wish none harm, to be long-suffering and upright, to reverence one's teacher, purity, steadfastness, self-restraint, detachment from the senses' objects and no sense of 'I' most certainly, insight into birth, death, old age, disease, and pain, and what constitutes their worthlessness, to be detached and not to cling to sons, wives, houses, and the like, a constant equal-mindedness whatever happens, pleasing or unpleasing, unswerving loyalty-and-love for Me with spiritual exercise on no other bent, to dwell in desert places, to take no pleasure in the company of men, constant attention to the wisdom that appertains to self, to see where knowledge of reality must lead, [all] this is 'wisdom'.

Wisdom, then, amounts to *de*tachment from all that is transient and a loving *at*tachment of the immortal self to God, for in that both self and God are eternal they coincide in that both are ultimately not bound by space, time, action, and causation. Hence the man whose 'works [are] burnt up in wisdom's fire' (4. 19) 'beholds [all] beings in [him]self—every one of them—and then in' God (4. 35). By true wisdom 'one sees one mode of being, changeless, undivided in all contingent beings, divided [as they are]' (18. 20). This wisdom or knowledge is in a sense identical with the one supreme object of knowledge—the 'highest Brahman', that is, God (13. 12). This is:

> Within all beings, yet without them; unmoved, It yet moves indeed; so subtle is It you cannot comprehend It; far off It stands, and yet how near It is! Undivided in beings It abides, seeming divided: this is That which should be known—[the one] who sustains, devours, and generates [all] beings. Light of lights, 'Beyond the Darkness' It is called: [true] knowledge (wisdom), what should be known, accessible to knowledge, established in the heart of all (13. 15–17).

yoginām: var. *karmiṇām*, 'men of action'. This is also Ś.'s gloss on the term and Rk. rightly translates it so.

4. *na karmaṇām anārambhān naiṣkarmyaṁ puruṣo 'śnute,*
na ca saṁnyasanād eva siddhiṁ samadhigacchati.

Not by leaving works undone does a man win freedom from [the bond of] works, nor by renunciation alone can he win perfection's prize.

karmaṇām, 'works': Ś. interprets this as meaning ritual actions like sacrifice which are designed to cause wisdom to arise and to eliminate the effects of evil deeds committed in the past. R. too restricts these 'works' to works prescribed by scripture. There seems to be no reason so to restrict the meaning of the word.

naiṣkarmyaṁ, 'freedom from [the bond of] works': lit. 'actionlessness' (E.), 'worklessness' (H.). It is, however, distinct from *akarman* (3. 8: 'inaction' (Rk., E.)) which means to do nothing at all. Ś. glosses 'absence (*śūnyatā*) of activity, the essential state of the self which does not act'. This again is a Buddhist technical term (Pāli *nekkhamma*) meaning 'self-abnegation, detachment, passionlessness, freedom from desire' (so defined in *Dīgha*, iii. 275). This is clearly what the word means here, not just 'actionlessness'. The use of the word in this sense shows once again how deeply the first chapters of the Gītā are influenced by Buddhism.

siddhiṁ, 'perfection's prize', or simply 'success'. According to Ś. this means *naiṣkarmya* as interpreted by himself. This is almost certainly right, for 18. 49 speaks of the man who 'all longing gone finds the highest *naiṣkarmya-siddhi*' by means of renunciation (*saṁnyāsa*) after having fulfilled his caste duties. This does not contradict our present passage where renunciation *alone* is condemned. The use of the terms 'all longing gone' and 'renunciation' confirm that the word *naiṣkarmya* is used in its Buddhist, not in its etymological sense.

5. *na hi kaścit kṣaṇam api jātu tiṣṭhaty akarma-kṛt,*
kāryate hy avaśaḥ karma sarvaḥ prakṛti-jair guṇaiḥ.

For not for a moment can a man stand still and do no work, for every man is powerless and made to work by the constituents born of Nature.

guṇaiḥ, 'constituents of Nature': see above, pp. 140–1. Action is the province of material Nature and its constituents. Cf. 3. 28 'constituents on constituents act': 14. 19, 'there is no agent other than the constituents'. Men only think they act because their ego which regards itself as being the agent *par excellence* fools them into this absurd belief (3. 27), for 'what, deluded, you would not do you will do perforce' (18. 60).

6. *karm'endriyāṇi saṁyamya ya āste manasā smaran*
indriy'ārthān vimūḍh'ātmā mithy'ācāraḥ sa ucyate.

Whoso controls his limbs through which he acts but sits remembering in his mind sense-objects, deludes [him]self: he is called a hypocrite.

karm'endriyāṇi, 'limbs through which he acts': these are the so-called organs of action or motor organs, that is, voice, hands, feet, anus, and private parts (*Sāṁkhya-kārikā*, 26).

vimūḍh'ātmā, 'deludes [him]self', or 'whose self is deluded'. Theoretically the self, at least as it is *per se*, cannot be deluded, and the commentators, in contexts like this, usually gloss *ātman* as *manas*, 'mind' (cf. 2. 67 n.).

It is doubtful, however, whether the author of the Gītā thought in such watertight compartments about the nature of human personality.

7. *yas tv indriyāṇi manasā niyamy' ārabhate, 'rjuna,*
karm' endriyaiḥ karma-yogam asaktaḥ, sa viśiṣyate.

But more excellent is he who with the mind controls those limbs (or senses) and through these limbs [themselves] by which he acts embarks on the spiritual exercise of works, remaining detached the while.

The whole theory of Yoga in all its manifestations is to *use* the body and its faculties to free the spirit for ever from its material envelope, and this can only be done by detaching oneself *from* the body by means of the mind now 'bent on contemplation of the self' (R.).

8. *niyataṁ kuru karma tvaṁ, karma jyāyo hy akarmaṇaḥ;*
śarīra-yātrā 'pi ca te na prasidhyed akarmaṇaḥ.

Do the work that is prescribed [for you], for to work is better than to do no work at all; for without working you will not succeed even in keeping your body in good repair.

niyataṁ, 'prescribed': Ś., 'work for which one is fitted (*adhikṛta*) but which is not designed to produce results (fruit)'. Arjuna's 'proper business (*adhikāra*)' is 'work alone, never the fruits [it may produce]' (2. 47).

karma jyāyo hy akarmaṇaḥ, 'work is better than not to work at all', 'action is loftier than inaction'. This seems to contradict 2. 49 (cf. 3. 1) where action is said to be greatly inferior to *buddhi-yoga* (*buddhi*, 'soul', being correctly glossed by Ś. as *jñāna*, 'wisdom,' in 3. 1), and according to Ś. (*passim*) *jñāna* in the sense of intuitive apprehension of the Absolute completely transcends all works. Hence he takes *akarman*, 'worklessness', to mean just doing nothing at all, and from the mundane point of view this is greatly inferior to performing works while remaining detached. This point has already been made in 3. 4 where *naiṣkarmya* in the Buddhist sense of 'passionlessness' is clearly distinguished from doing nothing.

Karma, 'work, action', is a deep mystery to the Hindus, and 'action' and 'inaction' are a pair of opposites which, like all pairs of opposites, must be both transcended and fused: 'the man who sees worklessness in work [itself], and work in worklessness, is wise among his fellows, integrated, performing every work' (4. 18). There, however, *akarman* is used to mean 'worklessness' in the sense of transcending works as distinct from *vikarman*, 'work ill done'.

9. *yajñ' ārthāt karmaṇo 'nyatra loko 'yaṁ karma-bandhanaḥ;*
tad-arthaṁ karma, Kaunteya, mukta-saṅgaḥ samācara.

This world is bound by bonds of work save where that work is done for sacrifice. Work to this end, then, Arjuna, from [all] attachment freed.

Karma(n) means literally 'work', but in the Veda and Upanishads it is frequently specialized in the sense of 'ritual act, sacrifice'. The transition from the idea of 'work' or 'action' to that of 'sacrifice' is, then, given the Vedic background, in no way forced. Arjuna's present work in hand is to go to war, and war itself is a sacrifice (see 2. 47 n.).

Sacrifice

10. *saha-yajñāḥ prajāḥ sṛṣṭvā pur'ovāca Prajāpatiḥ:*
anena prasaviṣyadhvam; eṣa vo 'stv iṣṭa-kāmadhuk.

Of old the Lord of Creatures said, emitting creatures and with them sacrifice: 'By this shall ye prolong your lineage, let this be to you the cow that yields the milk of all that ye desire.

Prajāpatiḥ, 'the Lord of Creatures': Prajāpati is the 'creator' god *par excellence*. Cf. *Śatapatha Brāhmaṇa* 11. 1. 8. 2–3: 'Prajāpati gave himself up to [the gods] and the sacrifice [thereby] became theirs; for the sacrifice is the food of the gods. After giving himself up to the gods, he emitted his own counterpart, the sacrifice. Hence people say: "The sacrifice is Prajāpati".'

kāmadhuk, 'the cow that yields the milk of all that ye desire': a cow specially connected with the god Indra (ibid. 4. 2. 3. 6).

11. *devān bhāvayat'ānena; te devā bhāvayantu vaḥ:*
parasparaṁ bhāvayantaḥ śreyaḥ param avāpsyatha.

With this shall ye sustain the gods so that the gods may sustain you [in return]. Sustaining one another [thus] ye shall achieve the highest good.

śreyaḥ param, 'the highest good'; one would expect this to mean 'liberation', and R. duly glosses it thus. Ś. is reluctant to admit this and glosses, 'by attaining to transcendent wisdom (*jñāna*) gradually' and suggests *svarga*, 'heaven', as an alternative. This is more in line with the thinking of the Gītā elsewhere. Worship of the gods does not lead to final liberation, the gods can merely satisfy man's worldly desires (7. 20–22), and even sacrifice to Krishna himself will take one no further than Indra's heaven if that is the sacrificer's intention (9. 20).

12. *iṣṭān bhogān hi vo devā dāsyante yajña-bhāvitāḥ:*
tair dattān apradāy'aibhyo yo bhuṅkte, stena eva saḥ.

For, [so] sustained by sacrifice the gods will give you the food of your desire. Whoso enjoys their gift yet gives nothing [in return] is a thief, no more nor less.'

13. *yajña-śiṣṭ'āśinaḥ santo mucyante sarva-kilbiṣaiḥ;*
bhuñjate te tv aghaṁ pāpā ye pacanty ātma-kāraṇāt.

Good men who eat the leavings of the sacrifice are freed from every taint, but evil are they and evil do they eat who cook [only] for their own sakes.

14. *annād bhavanti bhūtāni, parjanyād anna-saṁbhavaḥ,*
yajñād bhavati parjanyo, yajñaḥ karma-samudbhavaḥ.

From food do [all] contingent beings derive and food derives from rain; rain derives from sacrifice and sacrifice from works.

annād, 'from food': Ś. glosses, 'from food when eaten and converted into blood and semen'. The idea of food as primal matter goes back to the *Taittirīya* Upanishad 2 and 3. There (2. 2) we read:

From food indeed do creatures come to birth,
Whatever [creatures] dwell on earth.
Then again by food they live,
And again pass into it in the end.
For food is the chief of beings,
Hence is it called the elixir of all.
All food most certainly do they attain
Who reverence Brahman as food.
For food is the chief of beings,
Hence is it called the elixir of all.
From food do beings come to birth,
When born, by food they grow.
Eaten, it eats [all] beings;
Hence is it known as food (*an-na*, 'eatable').

And again ibid. 3. 7: 'Food should not be despised. That is the sacred rule.'

yajñād, '[rain derives] from sacrifice': presumably in answer to the sacrificer's prayer. Both Ś. and R. quote *Manu* 3. 76: 'The oblation duly thrown into the fire reaches the sun. From the sun rain is born, from rain food, from [food living] creatures.'

karma-, '[sacrifice from] works': Ś., 'from the activity of the two sacrificial priests', which makes good sense. R., 'from human activity like making money', which, since the priest's fees had to be paid up (cf. 17. 13), seems equally logical. *Karma* here almost certainly has its specialized meaning of 'sacrificial action'.

15. *karma brahm'odbhavaṁ viddhi, brahm'ākṣara-samudbhavam:*
tasmāt sarvagataṁ brahma nityaṁ yajñe pratiṣṭhitam.

From Brahman work arises, know this, and Brahman is born from the Imperishable; therefore is Brahman, penetrating everywhere, forever based on sacrifice.

'Brahman . . . the Imperishable': the word *Brahman*, besides meaning the Absolute, can also mean the Veda or (more rarely, cf. 14. 3) material Nature. If it means the Veda, then it would be natural to take *akṣara* ('the Imperishable') to mean the syllable Oṁ of which it is a synonym (cf. 8. 13: ChU. 1. 1. 1, etc.). If, however, *Brahman* means 'material Nature' as it certainly does in 14. 3, then the 'Imperishable' must be the imperishable source of all things which we encounter for the first time in BU. 3. 8. 8 and which we will encounter often again in the Gītā starting at 8. 3 where it is roundly identified with Brahman.

Ś. takes *brahman* to mean the Veda and *akṣara* 'Brahman, the supreme Self from which the Veda arises like breath from a man'. R., quoting 14. 3, takes it to mean material Nature or the body and *akṣara* to mean the individual self (*jīvātman*).

'Therefore is Brahman . . .': depending on which way one takes the previous line, this means either that the Veda depends on the sacrifice, presumably because if sacrifice were to cease it would no longer be recited, or that material Nature depends for its continued existence on the sacrifice, since sacrifice and the world process are one and the same thing. This to us rather strange idea originates in RV. 10. 90 where Primal Man, *Puruṣa*, the macrocosm, is immolated and from his dismembered body the whole cosmos in its wide variety comes to be.

It is of course possible to understand *brahman* as meaning *both* the Veda *and* material Nature, and *akṣara* as meaning *both* the syllable Oṁ *and* imperishable being.

16. *evaṁ pravartitaṁ cakraṁ: n'ānuvartayatī'ha yaḥ*
aghāyur indriy'ārāmo moghaṁ, Pārtha, sa jīvati.

So was the wheel in motion set: and whoso here fails to match his turning [with the turning of the wheel], living an evil life, the senses his pleasure-ground, lives out his life in vain.

cakraṁ, 'the wheel': the wheel of Brahman described in ŚU. 1. 4–6:

> [We understand] him [as a wheel]
> With one felly, with a triple tyre, . . .
>
> This is the great wheel of Brahman
> Giving life and livelihood to all,
> Subsists in all:
> In it the swan [of the soul] is hither and thither tossed.

Satisfaction in Self alone

17. *yas tv ātma-ratir eva syād ātma-tṛptaś ca mānavaḥ*
ātmany eva ca saṁtuṣṭas, tasya kāryaṁ na vidyate.

Nay, let a man take pleasure in self alone, in self his satisfaction find, in self alone content: [for then] there is naught he needs to do.

This stanza does not seem to follow very naturally on the previous one. Arjuna is urged to 'match his turning [with the turning of the wheel]', that is to say, to engage in action consonant with his caste-duty and the world process in general. The connecting link seems to be the idea of what one takes one's pleasure in. The sensual man makes 'the senses his pleasure-ground' whereas the man who has achieved liberation takes pleasure in self alone—he takes pleasure in what is by definition eternal, timeless, beyond cause and effect and all activity, and there is therefore nothing he *need* do just as there is nothing God need do (3. 22). Even so, God acts just the same, and so, Krishna will say, man must emulate Him in this too (3. 25). Once works have ceased to 'bind' him, his very works will also be effortless and free—he 'will have freedom of movement in every state of being' (ChU. 8. 1. 6).

The 'pleasure' (*rati*) the liberated man takes in the self is vividly described in ChU. 7. 25. 2:

> The man who sees and thinks and understands in this way (i.e. realizes that his inmost self has an eternal and infinite dimension) has pleasure in the self, plays with the self, copulates with the self, and has his joy with the self.

This joy in one's own eternal being, though it makes one aware that there is absolutely nothing one *need* do, does not for that reason absolve one from action, for the man 'whose sport is self, whose joy is self, *a man of works*, of all who Brahman know is the most highly to be prized' (MuU. 3. 1. 4).

18. *n'aiva tasya kṛten'ārtho n'ākṛten'eha kaścana,*
na c'āsya sarva-bhūteṣu kaścid artha-vyapāśrayaḥ.

In works done and works undone on earth he has no interest,—no [interest] in all contingent beings: on such interest he does not depend.

In other words he passes beyond good and evil in so far as these must be manifested in works: he 'is not worried [by the thought]: "Why did I not do good? Why did I do evil?" Knowing [good and evil] in this way he saves [him]self' (TU. 2. 9: see also 2. 50 n.).

Act without Attachment as God does

19. *tasmād asaktaḥ satataṁ kāryaṁ karma samācara;*
asakto hy ācaran karma param āpnoti pūruṣaḥ.

Therefore detached, perform unceasingly the works that must be done, for the man detached who labours on to the highest must win through.

tasmād, 'therefore': the gist of the present stanza scarcely seems to follow on from what has been said in the last two stanzas. It would, however, follow quite naturally on stanza 16 and it is therefore tempting to regard stanzas 17–18 as being a later interpolation. The argument, however, seems to be this:

'Conform your works to the world process of which you are part, but do not take pleasure in worldly things. Take pleasure in the immortal self alone which will make you independent of the works you have to do. Therefore detach yourself from any interest that binds you to what you do and do it because (as I, Krishna, am about to tell you) that is precisely what I who am God do.'

param, 'the highest': that is, the Imperishable Brahman or Self. Ś. glosses 'liberation' (see 2. 59 n.). As Ś. points out, Arjuna has to *work* out his salvation because he is not yet 'liberated'.

20. *karmaṇ' aiva hi saṁsiddhim āsthitā Janakādayaḥ:*
loka-saṁgraham evā'pi saṁpaśyan kartum arhasi.

For only by working on did Janaka and his like attain perfection's prize. Or if again you consider the welfare [and coherence] of the world, then you should work [and act].

'Janaka': king of Videha, a philosopher king prominent in BU. 4. 1–4 and renowned for his generosity (ibid. 2. 1. 1: KauU. 4. 1).

saṁsiddhim, 'perfection's prize', or 'success': Ś. glosses *mokṣa*.

saṁgraham, 'welfare': Ś. glosses *prayojana*, 'profit'. Modern translators differ. E. has 'control', Rk. 'maintenance', H. 'guidance'; but 'welfare' (S., 'le bien du monde') seems to be the obvious meaning at least in MBh. 12. 251. 25 where *dharma* is instituted by God, the Ordainer, as 'associated with the *saṁgraha* of the world'. Perhaps 'coherence' might be a better translation more consonant with the etymology of the word.

21. *yad-yad ācarati śreṣṭhas, tad-tad ev' etaro janaḥ:*
sa yat pramāṇaṁ kurute, lokas tad anuvartate.

Whatever the noblest does, that too will others do: the standard that he sets all the world will follow.

22. *na me, Pārth', āsti kartavyaṁ triṣu lokeṣu kiṁcana,*
n' ānavāptam avāptavyaṁ, varta eva ca karmaṇi.

In the three worlds there is nothing that I need do, nor anything unattained that I need to gain, yet work [is the element] in which I move.

23. *yadi hy ahaṁ na varteyaṁ jātu karmaṇy atandritaḥ,*
mama vartm' ānuvartante manuṣyāḥ, Pārtha, sarvaśaḥ.

For if I were not tirelessly to busy Myself with works, then would men everywhere follow in my footsteps.

R. takes this to refer to Krishna's works in his incarnation, particularly his conformity to caste-law. This seems a rather narrow interpretation of the passage, the gist of which is to persuade Arjuna that he must conform to God not only in his timeless essence but also in his incessant activity within the 'created' order.

24. *utsīdeyur ime lokā na kuryāṁ karma ced aham,*
saṁkarasya ca kartā syām, upahanyām imāḥ prajāḥ.

If I were not to do my work, these worlds would fall to ruin, and I should be a worker of confusion, destroying these [my] creatures.

saṁkarasya, 'confusion': this probably refers to the *varṇa-saṁkara*, 'mixture of castes', mentioned in 1. 41–43, which, according to Arjuna, leads straight to hell. So R., here as elsewhere, emphasizes the necessity to adhere to the caste-law laid down in the law-books and to family tradition. According to Ś. it is the duty even of the liberated man who knows full well that there is nothing that he *need* do, to engage in action for the sake of others.

25. *saktāḥ karmaṇy avidvāṁso yathā kurvanti, Bhārata,*
kuryād vidvāṁs tathā 'saktaś cikīrṣur loka-saṁgraham.

As witless [fools] perform their works attached to the work [they do], so, unattached, should the wise man do, longing to bring about the welfare [and coherence] of the world.

saṁgraham, 'welfare, coherence': see 3. 20 n.

26. *na buddhi-bhedaṁ janayed ajñānāṁ karma-saṅginām,*
joṣayet sarva-karmāṇi vidvān yuktaḥ samācaran.

Let not a wise man split the soul of witless men attached to work: let him encourage all [manner of] works, himself though busy, acting as an integrated man.

buddhi-bhedaṁ, 'split the soul': *buddhi*, the soul, is naturally simple, single, one (2. 41), and to split it is to dissipate it (ibid.) and ultimately to destroy it (2. 63). Literally this word might well be translated 'schizophrenia'; and this is indeed what it means. It is the condition of the man described in KaU. 4. 14:

> As rain that falls in craggy places
> Loses itself, dispersed throughout the mountains,
> So does the man who sees things as diverse,
> [Himself] become dispersed in their pursuit.

joṣayet, 'encourage' (so S.): Ś., 'cause to be performed': R., 'generate love for': E. 'let them enjoy': Rk. (following Ś.), 'set others to act': H., 'approve': D. 'veranlassen . . . mit Freudigkeit zu tun'.

yuktaḥ, 'integrated': one MS. has *muktaḥ*, 'liberated'. *Yukta* presumably means what it meant in 2. 61 where it takes up the *buddhi-yukta* of 2. 51, 'the man integrated by the soul or contemplative intellect'. This is how R. glosses it. In 2. 50 Arjuna was told to engage in action (*yoga*), that is, the spiritual exercise appropriate to a warrior, while keeping in mind the *buddhi-yukta* who discards both good and evil works. The two forms of 'spiritual exercise', the life of pure contemplation and the life of action controlled and integrated by the contemplative intellect, are not mutually exclusive. Hence whether you are sitting still (2. 61) in contemplation or whether you are as here busy and active and encouraging others to act even for unworthy motives, that is, in the hope of enjoying the fruits of their actions (so Ś.), the common denominator remains: you must be *yukta*, 'controlled and integrated'.

Material Nature is the sole Real Agent

27. *prakṛteḥ kriyamāṇāni guṇaiḥ karmāṇi sarvaśaḥ;*
ahaṁkāra-vimūḍh'ātmā kartā 'ham iti manyate.

It is material Nature's [three] constituents that do all works wherever [works are done]; [but] he whose self is by the ego fooled thinks, 'It is I who do'.

prakṛteḥ, 'material Nature' and its constituents: see 2. 39 n. According to 2. 45 the bulk of the Veda (apart from the Upanishads) is concerned with the three constituents of Nature, only the Upanishads are concerned with pure spirit (*puruṣa*). In this passage the underlying theory is almost pure *Sāṁkhya*—an almost complete dualism of spirit and matter. Material Nature alone acts through its three constituents: spirit (*puruṣa* or *ātman*), when united with Nature, experiences but does not act (13. 20), *but* although by itself it is incapable of action, through its union with material Nature it *seems* to act (*Sāṁkhya-kārikā*, 20); and, as here, it is the ego that deceives and deludes it. It is the ego which, according to Ś. on the present passage, identifies the psychosomatic organism (*kārya-karaṇa-saṁghāta*) of which it considers itself to be the centre, with the self. The self is thereby deluded. Ś. unnecessarily glosses *-ātmā* as *antaḥ-karaṇa*, 'the internal sense', that is, the mind. In the Sāṁkhya system and in the Gītā the [individual] self or 'person' may and does experience anything and everything so long as it is in contact with material Nature (13. 20). Self and psychosomatic organism are according to the *Sāṁkhya-kārikā* (21) like a lame man mounted on the shoulders of a blind man—the one sees and the other acts: spirit sees and experiences, but it is the psychosomatic organism which is a microcosm of material Nature that alone acts. The subject will be taken up again in Chapters VII, IX, XIII, and XIV.

28. *tattva-vit tu, mahā-bāho, guṇa-karma-vibhāgayoḥ,*
guṇā guṇeṣu vartanta iti matvā na sajjate.

But he who knows how constituents and works are parcelled out in categories, seeing things as they are, thinks thus: 'Constituents on constituents act', [and thus thinking] remains unattached.

'Constituents on constituents act': similarly in 14. 23 where the 'self' or spirit is described as 'indifferent' (*udāsīna*), the very word Gaudapāda uses of him in his commentary on *Sāṁkhya-kārikā* 20.

29. *prakṛter guṇa-saṁmūḍhāḥ sajjante guṇa-karmasu:*
tān akṛtsna-vido mandān kṛtsna-vin na vicālayet.

By the constituents of Nature fooled are men attached to the constituents' works. Such men, dull-witted, only know in part. Let not the knower of the whole upset [the knower of the part].

The 'knower of the whole' and the 'knower in part': these are described in 18. 20–21:

> That [kind of] knowledge by which one sees one mode of being, changeless, undivided in all contingent beings, divided [as they are], is Goodness['knowledge]. Be sure of this. But that [kind of] knowledge which in all contingent beings discerns in separation all manner of modes of being, different and distinct—this, you must know, is knowledge born of Passion.

'Goodness' and 'Passion' are, of course, the highest and the midmost of the three constituents of Nature (see 2. 39 n.).

30. *mayi sarvāṇi karmāṇi saṁnyasy'ādhyātma-cetasā*
nirāśīr nirmamo bhūtvā yudhyasva vigata-jvaraḥ.

Cast all your works on Me, your thoughts [withdrawn] in what appertains to self; have neither hope nor thought that 'This is mine': cast off this fever! Fight!

'Cast all your works on Me': we have already had the word *saṁ-ny-as-*, 'cast off, give up, renounce', in 3. 4. One cannot attain to true dispassion simply by 'giving up' or 'renouncing' works. A more fruitful way of 'giving them up' is here suggested: give them up by casting them on to the Lord (the same word *saṁ-ny-as-* is used). Give them up to Him or rather give them back to Him since it is really He who is the agent working through material Nature and its constituents; through them He acts though works do not affect or bind Him (4. 6, 14: 9. 8, 9). Or else, as Ś. suggests, the words may mean that you should offer up whatever you do to God as a servant offers up his service to his master. This is what is meant when action (*karma*) is identified with sacrifice (3. 9): you offer back to God the actions which seem to be your own but which are really initiated by God 'consorting with material Nature which is his' (4. 6).

adhyātma-cetasā, 'your thoughts [withdrawn] in what appertains to self': so R. Ś. paraphrases in the sense of the last paragraph. In 8. 3, however, *adhyātmam* is defined as *svabhāva* ('own being' or 'inherent nature') and it is this that initiates action in 5. 14. So Ś. on 8. 3 takes *adhyātmam* to mean the 'Self in its relationship to the body, active as the individual self'. R. simply glosses as 'material Nature'. This verse (8. 3) is one of the most obscure in the Gītā and we shall have to defer a full discussion of the term *adhyātmam* until we come to it.

Leaving this controversial passage aside for the moment let us consider the use of cognate terms in the Gītā itself. In 10. 32 Krishna says that among 'sciences' (*vidyā*) He is the 'science concerned with self' (*adhyātma-vidyā*). In 13. 11 *jñāna* is defined as 'constant attention to the wisdom that appertains to self (*adhyātma-jñāna*)' and 'to see where knowledge of reality must lead'. Similarly in 15. 5 we read:

Not proud, not fooled, [all] taint of attachment crushed, *ever abiding in what appertains to self* (*adhyātma-nitya*), desire suppressed, released from [all] dualities made known in pleasure as in pain, the undeluded march ahead to that state which knows no change.

It seems then plain that *adhyātma*, 'what appertains to self', is in fact that form of existence in which the self-in-itself has its being, namely, in a timeless eternity otherwise known as the Imperishable Brahman (cf. 8. 3 again!). E.'s 'over-soul' (which he had presumably borrowed from Emerson) introduces a wholly new concept and is quite unjustified. Moreover, the idea is already adumbrated in KaU. 2. 12:

Let a wise man think upon that God (i.e. the Self),
Let him engage in spiritual exercise related to the self (*adhyātma-yoga*). . . .

Here *adhyātma* simply means the *ambiance* of both the microcosmic and macrocosmic self, and that is what it means in our present passage, anticipating 6. 18, 20, 25 which describe the progressive stages on the way to liberation. Let us see what those stanzas say:

6. 18: When thought, held well in check, is stilled in self alone, then is a man from longing freed though all desires assail him.

6. 20–21: When thought by spiritual exercise is checked and comes to rest, and when of [one]self one sees the self in self and finds content therein (cf. 3. 17), that is the utmost joy which transcends [all things of] sense and which soul [alone] can grasp.

6. 25: By soul held fast in steadfastness he must make the mind [too] subsist in the self; then little by little will he come to rest; he must think of nothing at all.

Here you have the full teaching on the stages a man must go through on his journey to full liberation which is complete tranquillity and stillness, the 'bringing to a standstill of discursive thought', as *Yoga-sūtras* 1. 1 puts it. Our present stanza points forward to this.

Arjuna is told to do two things in this passage: (i) he must cast all his works on Krishna, and (ii) he must withdraw his thoughts into the [individual] self. Self, then, the eternal being immanent within him, is the immediate goal of his contemplation, whereas the personal God is acknowledged only as the initiator of all action in the phenomenal world and therefore really responsible for the fighting that Arjuna must, willy-nilly, engage in: God acts (4. 13), Arjuna is 'the mere occasion' (11. 33). Certainly, in 2. 61 Krishna speaks of the contemplative as being 'intent on' Him, but this is merely a passing phase prescribed in the *Yoga-sūtras* with a view to concentrating the mind on one point. This is transcended in 6. 25 where the adept is told that 'he must think of nothing at all'. At this stage of the argument, then, God is regarded as being all-powerful in the phenomenal world, but almost irrelevant in that other world which is beyond time. There it is the 'self' that must be sought out, not yet God.

nirmamo, 'have no thought that "This is mine"': the Buddhist term again: see 2. 71 n.

31. *ye me matam idaṁ nityam anutiṣṭhanti mānavāḥ*
śraddhāvanto 'nasūyanto mucyante te 'pi karmabhiḥ.

Whatever men shall practise constantly this my doctrine, firm in faith, not envying, [not cavilling,] they too will find release from works.

karmabhiḥ, 'from works': the case is instrumental, and so Deussen and others translated '*through* works', but this is quite out of tune with the whole doctrine of the Gītā. Moreover, the use of the instrumental for the ablative is quite normal: cf. 3. 13: 12. 15: ŚU. 2. 15: 4. 16: 5. 13: 6. 13, etc.

32. *ye tv etad abhyasūyanto n'ānutiṣṭhanti me matam,*
sarva-jñāna-vimūḍhāṁs tān viddhi naṣṭān acetasaḥ.

But whoso refuses to perform this my doctrine, envious [yet and cavilling], of every [form of] wisdom fooled, is lost, the witless [dunce]! Be sure of that.

33. *sadṛśaṁ ceṣṭate svasyāḥ prakṛter jñānavān api:*
prakṛtiṁ yānti bhūtāni; nigrahaḥ kiṁ kariṣyati?

As is a man's own nature, so must he act, however wise he be. [All] creatures follow Nature: what will repression do?

svasyāḥ prakṛter, 'a man's own nature'. A man's 'own nature' is that parcel of the whole material cosmos which has attached itself to his individual self, 'the aggregate of righteous and unrighteous action performed in past lives and manifested right from one's present birth', as Śankara puts it.

'All creatures follow Nature': so H. following R. E., Rk., 'follow (their own) nature'. The first version seems preferable since in 3. 27–29 all action of any kind has been attributed to the constituents of Nature. This point is again made very clearly indeed in 18. 59:

[But if,] relying on your ego, you should think, 'I will not fight', vain is your resolve, [for] Nature will constrain you.

34. *indriyasy' endriyasy' ārthe rāga-dveṣau vyavasthitau:*
tayor na vaśam āgacchet, tau hy asya paripanthinau.

In [all] the senses passion and hate are seated, [turned] to their proper objects: let none fall victim to their power, for these are brigands on the road.

rāga-dveṣau, 'passion and hate': together with *moha*, 'delusion', these form the three root sins of Buddhism. Their destruction is Nirvāna (S. iv. 359, 362, etc.). The usual Hindu equivalents are *kāmakrodha*, 'desire and anger', as in 3. 37.

This stanza seems to contradict the last in that it allows a certain amount of free will to man, and Ś. seems conscious of this. Passion and hate (attraction and repulsion) are natural in man, he says, but they must be used to restrain each other, and this can only be done within the frame of one's own caste and the laws that govern it.

35. *śreyān svadharmo viguṇaḥ para-dharmāt svanuṣṭhitāt:*
svadharme nidhanaṁ śreyaḥ; para-dharmo bhay' āvahaḥ.

Better one's own duty [to perform], though void of merit, than to do another's well: better to die within [the sphere of] one's own duty: perilous is the duty of other men.

This maxim is again rubbed in at the end of the discourse (18. 47). In ethical matters Krishna is not an innovator; in each incarnation He merely re-establishes the old *dharma* when it is in decline (4. 7–8).

Our Enemy Desire

Arjuna uvāca:

36. *atha kena prayukto 'yaṁ pāpaṁ carati pūruṣaḥ,*
anicchann api, Vārṣṇeya, balād iva niyojitaḥ?

Arjuna said:

Then by what impelled does [mortal] man do evil unwilling though he be? He is driven to it by force, or so it seems to me.

Śrī-bhagavān uvāca:

37. *kāma eṣa, krodha eṣa, rajo-guṇa-samudbhavaḥ,*
mah' āśano mahā-pāpmā: viddhy enam iha vairiṇam.

The Blessed Lord said:

Desire it is: Anger it is,—arising from the constituent of Passion,—all devouring, mightily wicked, know that this is [your] enemy on earth.

kāma, 'desire': Ś., 'the enemy of all the world'. This total condemnation of desire is untypical of the earlier literature: this again reflects Buddhist influence.

Some MSS. add the following couplets here:

Arjuna uvāca:
bhavaty eṣa kathaṁ, Kṛṣṇa, kathaṁ c'aiva vivardhate?
kim-ātmakaḥ, kim-ācāras? tan mam'ācakṣva pṛcchataḥ.

Śrī-bhagavān uvāca:
eṣa sūkṣmaḥ paraḥ śatrur dehinām indriyaiḥ saha,
sukha-tantra iv'āsīno mohayan, Pārtha, tiṣṭhati;
kāma-krodhamayo ghoraḥ stambha-harṣa-samudbhavaḥ
ahaṁkāro 'bhimān'ātmā dustaraḥ pāpa-karmabhiḥ.
harṣam asya nivarty'aiṣa śokam asya dadāti ca,
bhayaṁ c'āsya karoty eṣa mohayaṁs tu muhur-muhuḥ.
sa eṣa kaluṣaḥ kṣudraś chidra-prekṣī, dhanaṁjaya,
rajaḥ-pravṛtto moh'ātmā manuṣyāṇām upadravaḥ.

Arjuna said:

How does it arise, Krishna, and how increase? What is its essence, and how does it behave? As I ask you, tell me.

The Blessed Lord said:

Subtle is he, the deadliest foe of embodied [selves] together with the senses. There he is, son of Prithā, seated, it seems, in a web of pleasure, deluding [men]. Cruel he is, compounded of desire and anger, author of doltish joy—the ego, masquerading as the self. Evil-doers have difficulty in passing him by. [Soon] does he deprive [a man] of joy and give him grief [instead]: and ever again perplexing him he brings him fear. Turbid is he and vile, a peeper into keyholes, from Passion sprung, his essence delusion, he is the plague of men.

38. *dhūmen'āvriyate vahnir yathā'darśo malena ca,*
yath'olben'āvṛto garbhas, tathā ten'edam āvṛtam.

As fire is swathed in smoke, as a mirror is [fouled] by grime, as an embryo is all covered up by the membrane envelope, so is this [world] obscured by that.

idam, 'this [world]': *idam* standing alone frequently means 'this world': so R., *jantu-jātam*, 'living creatures'. Ś. supplies *jñānam*, 'wisdom', from the following line: cf. 3. 42–43 where the pronoun *saḥ* seems to anticipate *ātmānam* in the following stanza.

39. *āvṛtaṁ jñānam etena jñānino nitya-vairiṇā*
kāma-rūpeṇa, Kaunteya, duṣpūreṇ'ānalena ca.

This is the wise man's eternal foe; by this is wisdom overcast, whatever form it takes, a fire insatiable.

kāma-rūpeṇa, 'whatever form it takes': the phrase could also mean 'in the form of desire', but this is tautologous.

40. *indriyāṇi mano buddhir asy' ādhiṣṭhānam ucyate;*
etair vimohayaty eṣa, jñānam āvṛtya, dehinam.

Sense, mind, and soul, they say, are the places where it lurks; through these it smothers wisdom, fooling the embodied [self].

The soul (*buddhi*), though the highest faculty of all the evolutes of Nature, is even so not immune to the attacks of desire, nor, for that matter, is the individual self so long as it is associated with Nature. It is fooled by desire just as it is fooled by the ego (3. 27), and all but the totally detached can be described as *kām' ātmā*, 'desire their very self' (2. 43).

41. *tasmāt tvam indriyāṇy ādau niyamya, Bharat' arṣabha,*
pāpmānaṁ prajahi hy enaṁ jñāna-vijñāna-nāśanam.

Therefore restrain the senses first: strike down this evil thing! destroyer alike of what we learn from holy books and what we learn from life.

jñāna-vijñāna: my translation follows Ś.'s interpretation.

42. *indriyāṇi parāṇy āhur, indriyebhyaḥ paraṁ manaḥ,*
manasas tu parā buddhir, yo buddheḥ paratas tu saḥ.

Exalted are the senses, or so they say; higher than the senses is the mind; yet higher than the mind the soul: what is beyond the soul is he.

saḥ, 'he': Ś. and practically all other commentators both ancient and modern take this to mean the *ātman* which occurs in the following stanza (cf. *dehinam*, 'embodied [self]', in verse 40). R. takes it as referring to desire in strict accord with the grammatical context. This seems most unlikely since the whole passage is based on KaU. 6. 7–8, where we read:

> Higher than the senses is the mind,
> Higher than the mind the soul (*sattva*),
> Higher than the soul the self, the great,
> Higher than [this] 'great' the Unmanifest.
>
> Higher than [this] Unmanifest the 'Person' (*puruṣa*),
> Pervading all, untraceable.

Almost identical with this is ibid. 3. 10–11 except that the word for 'soul' there is *buddhi* (as in the Gītā), not *sattva*, 'Goodness', the highest of the constituents of which *buddhi*, the soul, is ideally composed.

The schema both in the Gītā and in the *Kaṭha* Upanishad differs from the Sāṁkhya schema as tabulated on p. 140 above. In the *Kaṭha*, *Puruṣa*, the 'Person', is pure spirit—God: He emits the 'Unmanifest'—material

Nature as it is before there is any differentiation—primal matter. Then appears the 'great' self, that is, the individual self from which proceed soul, mind, and the senses. The Gītā stops here—its 'self' presumably being identical with the 'great self' of the *Kaṭha*, that is, the individual self.

What the *Kaṭha* has done is to subordinate the Sāṁkhya category of *puruṣa*, the multiplicity of individual spirits which it calls 'great selves', to both Unmanifest Nature and transcendent Spirit (*Puruṣa* used in a quite different sense from the Sāṁkhya *puruṣa* which is equivalent to the 'great self' of the *Kaṭha* and the 'self' of this passage in the Gītā), and to split the Sāṁkhya category of *buddhi* (also called *mahat*, the 'great') into two—(i) the 'great self' which may mean either the individual self or an eternal and timeless essence which permeates and pervades all that derives from Unmanifest Nature, the mysterious '[Nature] developed into life' we will meet in 7. 5; and (ii) *buddhi*, the contemplative intellect or soul alternatively called *sattva*, that 'Goodness' whose nature is to illumine and to 'bind' to wisdom and to joy (14. 6).

Thus we have the following hierarchy of being:

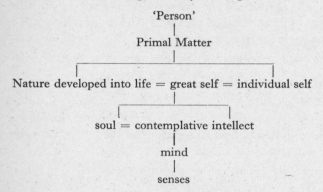

'Person'
|
Primal Matter
|
Nature developed into life = great self = individual self
|
soul = contemplative intellect
|
mind
|
senses

Ś. here enumerates the functions of 'mind' and 'soul', and since these are in substantial agreement both with what the Gītā says and with what the other didactic sections of the MBh. say, it would not be out of place to quote them. 'Mind' is responsible for concepts (*saṁkalpa*) and doubt (*vikalpa*), while 'soul' is characterized by *niścaya*, 'determination', both in the sense of defining objects as they really are and in determining a course of action.

43. *evaṁ buddheḥ paraṁ buddhvā saṁstabhy' ātmānam ātmanā*
jahi śatruṁ, mahā-bāho, kāma-rūpaṁ durāsadam.

So know him who is yet higher than the soul, and make firm [this] self yourself. Vanquish the enemy, Arjuna! [Swift is he] to change his form, and hard is he to conquer.

ātmanā, 'yourself': see 2. 55 n.

ātmānam, '[this] self': R. glosses *manas*, 'mind'. Theoretically the 'self' is always stable, static, and still, experiencing sensations as a spectator (*sākṣin*, *Sāṁkhya-kārikā*, 19), as a spectator at the ballet 'experiences' the ballet (ibid. 59). This, however, does not appear to prevent it from being deluded into thinking that it actually participates (3. 27): hence the need to make it firm and stabilize it.

kāma-rūpaṁ: see 3. 39 n.

CHAPTER IV

KRISHNA opens this chapter by saying that the doctrine He had expounded in the last chapter had already been revealed by Him to Vivasvat, the primal ancestor of the human race. He then explains that because the doctrines proclaimed of old grow stale with time He must become incarnate from time to time (1–8).

There here follows an apparent digression in which Krishna explains how a true understanding of his works can cause a man to draw near to Him and to share in his own mode of being (9–11). At this point Krishna again takes up the theme of 3. 27–35 (already adumbrated in 2. 47–48) on the necessity of performing works in a spirit of total detachment just as He himself does (12–23).

As in Chapter III works are again identified with sacrifice and there follows another digression on the various types of sacrifice (24–32).

The chapter finishes up with a eulogy of wisdom which 'reduces all works to ashes'. What precisely is understood by 'wisdom' is left unsaid, and the chapter is therefore not very appropriately named *jñāna-yoga*, the 'Yoga of Wisdom'.

The Divine Incarnations

Śrī-bhagavān uvāca:

1. *imaṁ Vivasvate yogaṁ proktavān aham avyayam,*
Vivasvān Manave prāha, Manur Ikṣvākave 'bravīt.

The Blessed Lord said:

This changeless mode of life I to Vivasvat [once] proclaimed;
to Manu Vivasvat told it, and Manu to Ikshvāku told it [again].

yogaṁ: again a slight shift of meaning. 'Mode of life' is probably the best translation here.

Vivasvat: a sun-god, father of Manu who is himself the origin of the human race.

2. *evaṁ paraṁpar' āprāptam imaṁ rāja' rṣayo viduḥ;*
sa kālen' eha mahatā yogo naṣṭaḥ, paraṁtapa.

Thus was the tradition from one to another handed on, the royal seers came to know it; [but] in the long course of time this mode of life here was lost.

3. *sa ev'āyaṁ mayā te 'dya yogaḥ proktaḥ purātanaḥ;*
bhakto 'si me sakhā c'eti, rahasyaṁ hy etad uttamam.

This is the same primeval mode of life that I preach to you today; for you are loyal, devoted, and my comrade, and this is the highest mystery.

bhakto, 'loyal, devoted': this is the first time that the root *bhaj-*, from which *bhakti*, usually translated as 'loving devotion', derives, occurs. *Bhakta* is a past participle and here means 'loyal and devoted'. The root meaning of *bhaj-* is 'to share in, participate in'. This root idea is never quite lost, but in classical Sanskrit it comes to mean increasingly 'to participate in something or someone through affection'. In the Epics the following meanings are attested:

(i) 'inhere in, attend on': MBh. 1. 6676 (vulgate), *kṣamā māṁ bhajate*, 'patience inheres in me'. Ibid. 12. 326. 21 (critical edition), *na guṇās taṁ bhajanti vai*, 'the constituents do not inhere in him'. Ibid. 3. 239. 4, *na bhajanti nṛpaṁ śriyaḥ*, 'prosperity does attend on the king'.

(ii) 'belong to': Rām. 7. 61. 14, *bhavataḥ putram ekaṁ tu śūlam etad bhajiṣyate*, 'this stake shall belong to your son alone'.

(iii) 'cultivate, enjoy': Rām. 6. 9. 22, *bhajasva dharmam*, 'cultivate justice': ibid. 2. 11. 28, *Bharato bhajatām adya yauvarājyam akaṇṭakam*, 'let Bharata today enjoy the office of heir apparent without let or hindrance'.

(iv) 'to be loyal, devoted': MBh. 17. 3. 7, *ayaṁ śvā . . . bhakto māṁ nityam eva*, 'this dog is ever loyal and devoted to me'. This usually refers to the loyalty of an inferior to a superior, but the opposite relationship is sometimes also indicated. Cf. Rām. 2. 45. 29:

bhaktimanti hi bhūtāni jaṅgam'ājaṅgamāni ca:
yācamāneṣu teṣu tvaṁ bhaktiṁ bhakteṣu darśaya.

Both moving and unmoving creatures are devoted and loyal to you: show an [answering] loyalty to these loyal men who supplicate you.

Very frequently it is used as here in a religious sense. MBh. 3. 286. 1, *bhagavantam ahaṁ bhakto*, 'I am loyally devoted to you' (Karna to his divine father, the Sun).

(v) 'sexual love': e.g. the very frequently occurring *bhaja māṁ bhajamānāṁ*, 'make love to me who love you', a direct invitation to sexual intercourse (MBh. 1. 92. 7 and often).

The last sense is never present in the Gītā, but it becomes prominent in the later Krishna cult. In the Gītā *bhakta* almost invariably means 'loyal, devoted, and devout'.

I am indebted to Fr. M. Dhavamony, S.J., for the above analysis of the semantics of *bhaj-* and *bhakti*.

Arjuna uvāca:

4. *aparaṁ bhavato janma, paraṁ janma Vivasvataḥ:*
katham etad vijānīyāṁ, tvam ādau proktavān iti?

Arjuna said:

Later is your birth, earlier Vivasvat's: how should I understand your words that in the beginning You did proclaim it?

Krishna had already told Arjuna that reincarnation stretches back endlessly in time for everyone (2. 12 ff.). Moreover, if the Gītā is taken in its over-all context within the Epic, Arjuna and everyone else already know that Krishna is the great God Vishnu incarnate. According to R., Arjuna wishes to know whether Krishna's incarnations are real or merely Docetic—*indrajālavat*, 'like a conjuring trick'. 'If real, what is the manner of his birth, what is the nature of his body, what is the reason for his birth, where and why was He born?' For R., Vishnu's incarnations are real, there is nothing docetic about them at all.

Śrī-bhagavān uvāca:

5. *bahūni me vyatītāni janmāni tava c'ārjuna:*
tāny ahaṁ veda sarvāṇi, na tvaṁ vettha, paraṁtapa.

The Blessed Lord said:

Many a birth have I passed through, and [many a birth] have you: I know them all but you do not.

6. *ajo 'pi sann avyay'ātmā, bhūtānām īśvaro 'pi san,*
prakṛtiṁ svām adhiṣṭhāya saṁbhavāmy ātma-māyayā.

Unborn am I, changeless is my Self, of [all] contingent beings I am the Lord! Yet by my creative energy I consort with Nature—which is mine—and come to be [in time].

prakṛtiṁ svām adhiṣṭhāya, 'I consort with Nature—which is mine'. Here for the first time Krishna begins to assert Himself as Supreme Being. Hitherto we seem to have been moving in a dualist Sāṁkhya world in which spirit and matter, the embodied self and the body it is forced to inhabit (2. 13–25), *buddhi* and *karma* (soul and the realm of action—2. 49–72), wisdom and action (3. 3–8), the autarchic self (3. 17–18) and the activity of material Nature (3. 27–29, 33), are or appear to be incompatible. They are in their own way equally real: the one is eternity outside time and infinity beyond space, the other is never-ending time and never-ending space, both without beginning and both going on for ever. God himself is introduced only as an object of contemplation (2. 61) and as someone to whom human beings can safely leave the responsibility for their actions (3. 30). It is not yet clear whether that is because He is really their author or whether He is merely a convenient depositary for actions and their 'fruits' from which human beings desire to free themselves.

In 3. 27–28 we were told that material Nature, acting through the three constituents, was alone responsible for all activity in the phenomenal world, whether cosmic or individual. We now learn, however, that Nature does not do this of itself but under the impulse of Krishna, the Lord.

adhiṣṭhāya, 'I consort with . . .': Ś. glosses *vaśī-kṛtya*, 'brings under his power', and this would appear to be about right. E., 'resorting to': Rk., 'establishing Myself in': H., 'governing': D., 'indem ich eingehe'. In ChU. 5. 19. 2 to 5. 23. 2 the word seems to mean 'rule over' while in PU. 3. 4 it certainly means to 'govern' a group of villages.

In ŚU., as we might expect, the word is used in more 'theological' passages. Here again 'govern', 'preside over', or 'direct' seems to fit. In ŚU. 1. 3 God 'governs' all causes, and in 5. 5 He 'governs' the whole universe. So too in 5. 4 we should probably translate: 'He governs (holds sway over) whatever creature issues from the womb' (*yoni-svabhāva*, which could, however, mean no more than 'causes and essences'). Slightly less obvious is ŚU. 4. 11 where we read: *yoniṁ yonim adhitiṣṭhaty eko*, which may either mean, 'He alone governs every cause', or 'He alone approaches every womb'. This second translation seems the more likely since the same idea is expressed in the Gītā 14. 3 where Krishna says: 'Great Brahman (meaning here "material Nature") is to Me a womb, in it I plant the seed.' As usual in such cases I prefer to think that the author of the Gītā had both senses in mind.

ātma-māyayā, 'by my creative energy': the word *māyā* has practically entered the English language in the sense of 'world illusion'. This is unfortunate, for even for Śankara, the first and greatest of the Indian monists, *māyā* only means illusion from the point of view of Absolute Reality which is One without a second. Empirically it is real. Thus, for him, Brahman as Absolute Reality is the *one* thing-in-itself, all else is appearance; and sense-perception and what we deduce from it can therefore only have access to appearance ('manifestation'), they cannot penetrate through to the One, Absolute Reality, Thing-in-itself. It is true that the term *māyā* is used as early as the Rig-Veda to mean 'uncanny power', thence 'magic' and 'deceit', but the word is only once used in the Upanishads in a cosmological sense: this is in ŚU. 4. 10 where we read:

> *Māyā* is material Nature (*prakṛti*), this must be known,
> And He who possesses it is the Mighty Lord.

This is what the word means: it *is* material Nature, and one's translation of the word will depend on what view one takes of material Nature. Even Śankara is not so extreme in this respect as he is sometimes made out to be. For instance, commenting on the word *prakṛti* in this passage he says: '[this means the God] Vishnu's *māyā*, which is essentially the three constituents of Nature through whose compulsion the world goes round. Deluded by it [the world] does not recognize Krishna as its own

[real] Self.' For Rāmānuja *māyā* is the divine wisdom (*jñāna*) and will (*saṁkalpa*): this is surely a very long way from 'illusion'. He goes on to say that by becoming incarnate in a real man, Krishna, God (Vishnu) does not thereby give up his divine attributes which are wholly devoid of evil and subsume all that is good.

7. *yadā yadā hi dharmasya glānir bhavati, Bhārata,*
abhyutthānam adharmasya tadā'tmānaṁ sṛjāmy aham.

For whenever the law of righteousness withers away and lawlessness arises, then do I generate Myself [on earth].

dharmasya, 'the law of righteousness': both Ś. and R. take this to mean the ancient Hindu system of the four classes and the four stages of life that the three superior classes were supposed to observe. In this they are almost certainly right since in 4. 13 Krishna claims to have founded the system himself.

sṛjāmy, 'I generate' or 'emit': this seems to be more accurate than 'send forth' (E., Rk.) or 'create' (H.).

8. *paritrāṇāya sādhūnāṁ vināśāya ca duṣkṛtām*
dharma-saṁsthāpan'ārthāya saṁbhavāmi yuge yuge.

For the protection of the good, for the destruction of evildoers, for the setting up of the law of righteousness I come into being age after age.

To know God is to share in His Mode of Being

9. *janma karma ca me divyam evaṁ yo vetti tattvataḥ*
tyaktvā dehaṁ punar-janma n'aiti, mām eti so, 'rjuna.

Who knows my godly birth and mode of operation thus as they really are, he, his body left behind, is never born again: he comes to Me.

mām eti, 'he comes to Me': whatever a man worships, to that he will go. 'To the gods go the gods' devotees, to the ancestors their votaries, to disembodied spirits go the worshippers of these, but those who worship Me shall come to Me' (9. 25). Again man is conformed to what he believes in: 'man is instinct with faith: as is his faith, so too must he be' (17. 3).

Ś. glosses 'he comes to Me' as *mucyate*, 'he is liberated'. R., on the other hand, interprets it as: 'taking refuge in Me, loving Me alone, thinking of Me alone, he possesses (*prāpnoti*) Me indeed'. Both interpret the passage (as indeed they do almost all others) in accordance with their own philosophy. As interpretations of what the Gītā actually means, they are of minimal value.

Just as in the last chapter (3. 17–18) the ascetic ideal of the man 'in self alone content' suddenly obtrudes itself into Krishna's discourse on the desirability of leading an active life, presumably to serve as a reminder that action must always be balanced by contemplation, so too here, *pace* Śankara, a new idea (or rather two) is introduced. By meditating on Krishna's incarnation and his deeds both as God and as man, one comes to know Him as the God who acts, the Lord of history as Protestant theologians would put it. Secondly in 4. 10, as if to restore the balance, the ascetic ideal of detachment and contemplative wisdom is once again proclaimed: as in 2. 55–72 and 3. 37–43 desire and anger, passion and hatred must be put aside. The result, however, is not the Buddhist Nirvāna 'which is Brahman too' of 2. 72 but access to Krishna's 'mode of being' as yet undefined. Finally, in 4. 11 the idea of *bhakti* is introduced for the first time (for in 4. 3 the word *bhakta* means little more than a loyal friend) meaning here the love which God returns to his devotees. Thus by contemplating God's activity one knows God as agent, by assimilating oneself to Him one participates in his mode of being which, though at present undefined, must surely mean his timeless Being which is in fact Nirvāna, and by humbly approaching Him, one wins his love. This, in three stanzas, may be said to sum up the whole teaching of the Gītā.

10. *vīta-rāga-bhaya-krodhā manmayā mām upāśritāḥ*
bahavo jñāna-tapasā pūtā mad-bhāvam āgatāḥ.

Many are they who, passion, fear, and anger spent, inhere in Me, making Me their sanctuary; made pure by wisdom and hard penances, they come to [share in] my own mode of being.

See previous note.

vīta- . . . -krodhā, 'passion, fear, and anger spent': these are the qualities of the 'man of steadied thought' (2. 56 ff.), who, though 'intent on God' (2. 61), reaches not God himself but the 'Nirvāna which is Brahman too' (2. 72).

jñāna-tapasā, 'by wisdom and hard penances', or, 'by the hard penance that consists in wisdom'.

mad-bhāvam, 'my own mode of being': that is, God's 'higher state' which is 'changeless, all-highest' (7. 24), 'one mode of being, changeless, undivided in all contingent beings, divided [as they are]' (18. 20). This is only accessible to those who love God devotedly (13. 18).

11. *ye yathā māṁ prapadyante, tāṁs tath'aiva bhajāmy aham:*
mama vartm'ānuvartante manuṣyāḥ, Pārtha, sarvaśaḥ.

In whatsoever way [devoted] men approach Me, in that same way do I return their love. [Whatever their occupation and] wherever they may be, men follow in my footsteps.

prapadyante, '[devoted] men approach Me': the insertion of '[devoted]' is justified, for *prapad-* means not only to approach but also to be utterly devoted to somebody. Unlike *bhakti* it is an emotional attitude that is only possible from an inferior to a superior: this humble devotion is rewarded by God's returning the love that is shown Him (see 4. 3 n.).

bhajāmy, 'I return their love': Ś., *anugṛhṇāmi*, 'I show favour to them', so E., H.: R., 'I reveal Myself [to them]': Rk., 'I accept them': S., 'à chacun je fais ma part': D. (whom I follow), 'in demselben Masse liebe ich sie wieder'. Only the last translation corresponds to the Epic usage of the root *bhaj-* (see 4. 3 n.).

According to Ś. God rewards different people in different ways: He grants the desires ('fruits', *phala*) of the self-interested, gives wisdom (right knowledge, *jñāna*) to those who aspire after liberation, and liberation itself to wise men who utterly renounce all works and their fruits (*saṁnyāsins*). In other words He grants to each what he wants, not necessarily what is good for him. What is good for him is, of course, liberation, but most men are interested in success (the 'fruit' of their works), and this is strictly incompatible with a genuine desire for liberation.

The second hemistich is identical with the second hemistich of 3. 23 where it fits a great deal better. The sense here seems to be that although all men must follow in God's footsteps because they are forced to act in accordance with the laws of Nature and its constituents (3. 33), it is only those who realize that Nature itself is subject to God (4. 6) and that God himself becomes incarnate in a material body 'for the protection of the good, for the destruction of evil-doers' (4. 8)—it is only these who willingly conform their lives to God's will. Consideration of the divine incarnation, purification from the passions, inherence in God's eternal and timeless being, and finally submission to God's holy will enable a man to *be* with God in eternity and to *work* and walk in his footsteps in time.

Action and Inaction—Human and Divine

12. *kāṅkṣantaḥ karmaṇāṁ siddhiṁ yajanta iha devatāḥ,*
kṣipraṁ hi mānuṣe loke siddhir bhavati karma-jā.

Desiring success in their (ritual) acts men worship here the gods; for swiftly in the world of men comes success engendered by the act [itself].

13. *cāturvarṇyaṁ mayā sṛṣṭaṁ guṇa-karma-vibhāgaśaḥ;*
tasya kartāram api māṁ viddhy akartāram avyayam.

The four-caste system did I generate with categories of 'constituents' and works; of this I am the doer, [the agent,]—this know,—[and yet I am] the Changeless One who does not do [or act].

According to Ś. the four 'classes' correspond to the three constituents of Nature. The 'stuff' (*pradhāna*) of the Brāhmans is Goodness and it is displayed in the virtues of quietness, self-control, and asceticism. The warrior or princely class is compounded of Passion with an admixture of Goodness; the resultant virtues are valour and 'guts' (*tejas*). The 'commons' (*vaiśya*) are compounded of Passion again but with an admixture of Darkness; the result is agriculture and similar occupations. Serfs, on the other hand, are compounded of Darkness with an admixture of Passion; hence service is all that can be expected of them.

From the empirical point of view—the point of view of *māyā*—God is the only true agent and therefore, in accordance with the law of *karma* which 'binds' the agent to and by what He does, He must himself be 'bound', that is, limited (since to define is to make finite); He must be associated with the result of what He does. All this is true enough (I am paraphrasing Śankara), but from the absolute point of view God, being by definition changeless, cannot be regarded as an agent: He does not act because in eternity there is no such thing as action. This is how Śankara interprets the passage. It is an over-simplification as any purely logical and philosophical explanation of religious truth is bound to be; for religion is of its very nature paradoxical and cannot be expressed in any logical formula. Hinduism in particular resists any 'either/or' approach, it is essentially a religion of 'both/and'. The Sāṁkhya system sought neatly to divide time from eternity, the phenomenal from the Absolute: what the Gītā sets out to do is to bring the two together again in a more or less coherent whole—to bring religion back to the spirit of the Upanishads for which the supreme Principle is not a static monad but a dynamic reality which is at the same time eternally at rest:

> Unmoving—One—swifter than thought—
> The gods could not seize hold of It as It sped before [them];
> Standing, It overtakes [all] others as they run;
> In It the wind incites activity.
>
> It moves. It moves not.
> It is far, yet It is near:
> It is within this whole universe,
> And yet It is without it. (*Iśā* Upanishad, 4–5.)

14. *na māṁ karmāṇi limpanti, na me karma-phale spṛhā,*
iti māṁ yo 'bhijānāti karmabhir na sa badhyate.

Works can never affect Me. I have no yearning for their fruits. Whoso should know that this is how I am will never be bound by works.

To 'know' God as He really is, that is as both changeless and perpetually active yet not bound by and therefore not committed to what He does, is to identify oneself with Him, and thereby to accede to his 'mode of being' (4. 10).

15. *evaṁ jñātvā kṛtaṁ karma pūrvair api mumukṣubhiḥ:*
kuru karm'aiva tasmāt tvaṁ pūrvaiḥ pūrvataraṁ kṛtam.

Knowing this the ancients too did work though seeking [all the while] release [from temporal life]: so do you work [and act] as the ancients did in days of old.

Those who have not yet realized the eternal self within them, should act in accordance with their caste duty in order to purify themselves, while those who have reached knowledge of the truth should work for the welfare of the world (Ś., cf. 3. 20). The appeal to tradition is typical of Krishna's essential conservatism (cf. 3. 20: 4. 1–3).

16. *kiṁ karma, kim akarm'eti, kavayo 'py atra mohitāḥ.*
tat te karma pravakṣyāmi yaj jñātvā mokṣyase 'śubhāt.

What is work? What worklessness? Herein even sages are perplexed. So shall I preach to you concerning work; and once you have understood my words, you will find release from ill.

[*a*]*śubhāt*, 'from ill': Ś., R., 'phenomenal existence (*saṁsāra*)'.

17. *karmaṇo hy api boddhavyaṁ, boddhavyaṁ ca vikarmaṇaḥ,*
akarmaṇaś ca boddhavyaṁ, gahanā karmaṇo gatiḥ.

For a man must understand [the nature] of work, of work ill done, and worklessness [all three]: profound [indeed] are the ways of work.

karmaṇo, 'work': Ś., 'prescribed by scripture': R., 'with a view to liberation'.

vikarmaṇaḥ, 'works ill done': R., 'like making money'. In MBh. 3. 198. 25 ff. it means doing what is not one's caste duty.

akarmaṇaś, 'worklessness': Ś., 'silence': R., 'wisdom'.

18. *karmaṇy akarma yaḥ paśyed akarmaṇi ca karma yaḥ,*
sa buddhimān manuṣyeṣu, sa yuktaḥ kṛtsna-karma-kṛt.

The man who sees worklessness in work [itself], and work in worklessness, is wise among his fellows, integrated, performing every work.

akarmaṇi, 'worklessness': R., 'wisdom, knowledge of the self'. He further explains: 'he who sees actions in their performance as being conformed (*-ākāra*) to wisdom because they inhere in the very essence of the self and who sees wisdom as being conformed to action because it indwells it (*antargata*). . . '. This seems to me to render admirably the meaning of the verse.

buddhimān . . . yuktaḥ, 'wise . . . integrated': this is plainly a throw-back to the *buddhyā yukto* of 2. 39, 50, the 'man integrated by and through the soul or contemplative intellect' who performs actions while at the same time renouncing them. The present stanza is an advance on this in that it sees action and rest, time and eternity, and, in Arjuna's case, war and peace, as being inseparably connected. This is the *naiṣkarmya*, 'passionlessness', of 3. 4.

19. *yasya sarve samārambhāḥ kāma-saṁkalpa-varjitāḥ,*
jñān'āgni-daghda-karmāṇaṁ tam āhuḥ paṇḍitaṁ budhāḥ.

When all a man's emprises are free from desire [for fruit] and motive, his works burnt up in wisdom's fire, then wise men call him learned.

-saṁkalpa-varjitāḥ, 'have . . . nor motive': var. *-krodha-vivarjitāḥ*, 'have . . . nor anger'.

'His works burnt up in wisdom's fire': R., 'the fire of wisdom which means that the very essence of the self indwells action'. In 'wisdom' which, in the technical sense in which the Gītā uses the word, means timeless Being, 'all works find their consummation' (4. 33). This would seem to contradict both our present passage and 4. 37 where 'the fire of wisdom reduces all works to ashes' and 4. 23 where all works are said 'entirely to melt away'. This is, however, the eternal paradox of all 'positive' mysticism. By denying yourself you fulfil yourself, and equally by fulfilling yourself you deny yourself.

The equation of 'wisdom' or 'knowledge' with eternal Being and that of 'ignorance' with phenomenal existence seem odd to us. It seems to derive from two parallel stanzas in the *Īśā* Upanishad (9, 12):

Blind darkness enter they
Who revere the uncompounded:
Into a darkness blinder yet
[Go they] who delight in the compounded.

Blind darkness enter they
Who reverence unwisdom:
Into a darkness blinder yet
[Go they] who delight in wisdom.

20. *tyaktvā karma-phal'āsaṅgaṁ nitya-tṛpto nirāśrayaḥ*
karmaṇy abhipravṛtto'pi n'aiva kiṁcit karoti saḥ.

When he has cast off [all] attachment to the fruits of works, ever content, on none dependent, though he embarks on work [himself], in fact he does no work at all.

nitya-tṛpto, 'ever content': R., 'content in his own eternal self'. Cf. 3. 17, 'in self alone content'.

nirāśrayaḥ, 'on none dependent': this scarcely accords with 4. 10 where men 'made pure by wisdom and hard penances' are encouraged to take refuge in Krishna. Hence, Ś. says that it means not to rely on anything visible or invisible for the gaining of worldly ends. R., 'having no sense of dependence on unstable Nature'.

21. *nirāśīr yata-citt'ātmā tyakta-sarva-parigrahaḥ*
śārīraṁ kevalaṁ karma kurvan n'āpnoti kilbiṣam.

Nothing hoping, his thought and self controlled, giving up all possessions, he only does such work as is needed for his body's maintenance, and so he avoids defilement.

-citt'ātmā, 'thought and self': Ś. takes *citta* to mean the mind and *ātmā* (incredibly) to mean the 'external aggregate of effects and organs' which apparently means the body. R. glosses *ātmā* as mind, his usual practice when it does not mean the self-in-itself. The phrase, however, is reminiscent of 3. 30: 'Cast all your works on Me, your thoughts [withdrawn] in what appertains to self (*adhyātma-cetasā*); have neither hope nor thought that "This is mine".'

'He only does such work as is needed for his body's maintenance': because 'without working you will not succeed even in keeping your body in good repair' (3. 8).

22. *yadṛcchā'lābha-saṁtuṣṭo dvandv'ātīto vimatsaraḥ*
samaḥ siddhāv asiddhau ca kṛtvā 'pi na nibadhyate.

Content to take whatever chance may bring his way, surmounting [all] dualities, knowing no envy, the same in success and failure, though working [still] he is not bound.

'Surmounting [all] dualities (or pairs of opposites)': a constant theme throughout the Gītā. Cf. 2. 45: 5. 3: 7. 27–28: 15. 5.

'The same in success and failure': Arjuna has already been told to be the same in success and failure for 'Yoga means sameness-and-indifference' (2. 48), the very quality that can be affirmed of the Absolute (5. 19). To be equal-minded, the 'same' to all, is to reflect the unchanging and unchangeable essence of Brahman which is at the heart of all contingent beings (13. 17). See 2. 15 n.

23. *gata-saṅgasya muktasya jñān'āvasthita-cetasaḥ*
yajñāy'ācarataḥ karma samagraṁ pravilīyate.

Attachment gone, deliverance won, his thoughts are fixed on wisdom: he works for sacrifice [alone], and all the work [he ever did] entirely melts away.

muktasya, 'deliverance won (liberated)': one MS. reads *yuktasya*, 'integrated'. Deliverance, liberation, release (*mukti, mokṣa*), S. here says means the disappearance of all bonds or ties (*bandha*). These bonds include righteousness, morality, duty, religion, and religious law (*dharma*) quite as much as the reverse. He is very insistent on this point.

'His thoughts are fixed on wisdom': cf. 3. 30, 'your thoughts [withdrawn] in what appertains to self', that is, eternal being, the Imperishable Brahman. *Jñāna* throughout this chapter (and indeed generally) means intuitive knowledge of eternal, timeless Being, as the comparison of these two passages shows.

'He works for sacrifice [alone]': cf. 3. 9 ff., 'This world is bound by bonds of work save where that work is done for sacrifice'.

'All the work [he ever did] entirely melts away': this is scarcely the same as 'is destroyed' (Ś.) or 'annihilated without remainder' (R.). Though your works may be burnt up (4. 19) or reduced to ashes (4. 37) by 'wisdom', they also melt into it as here or are consummated in it (4. 33). This surely is the whole point of the equation of works with sacrifice. Whether the sacrifice takes the form of gift (3. 11–12) or whether it means the immolation of a living thing to a higher power, the expectation is that what is lost will be restored in another and higher form. Our 'works' are offered up to God (3. 30) and burnt up in his 'wisdom' like a burnt-offering; they are dissolved in Him and thereby find their consummation in Him. By offering up our works we gain 'wisdom'—intuitive knowledge of the Eternal—and what in our works is valueless is reduced to ashes.

Works as Sacrifice

24. *brahm' ārpaṇaṁ, brahma havir brahm' āgnau brahmaṇā hutam;*
brahm' aiva tena gantavyaṁ brahma-karma-samādhinā.

The offering is Brahman, Brahman the [sacrificial] ghee offered by Brahman in Brahman's fire: who sinks himself in this [sacrificial] act which is Brahman, to Brahman must he thereby go.

What is meant by Brahman in this context? Oddly enough we have heard very little about Brahman so far. We were told about the 'still, fixed state of Brahman' (*brāhmī sthitiḥ*) and of the 'Brahman that is Nirvāna too' in 2. 72. This 'state' and this 'Nirvāna' are clearly the 'peace' mentioned in 2. 70–71. On the other hand, we meet with a very different conception of Brahman in 3. 15. There the sacrifice is said to arise from works, works from Brahman, and Brahman from the Imperishable which there seems to be the highest principle. 'Therefore', it is said, 'is Brahman, penetrating everywhere, forever based on sacrifice.' Clearly, then, it would seem, it is with this sacrificial Brahman that we are here concerned; but here there is a difference. Brahman is not only *based* on the sacrifice but *is* the sacrifice and everything to do with it, just as Primal Man (*Puruṣa*) is in RV. 10. 90 and Prajāpati or Vishnu in the Brāhmaṇas. Brahman, however, is the link between (sacrificial) action (*karma*) on the one hand and the

Imperishable on the other (3. 15), the link between the eternal and the temporal, hence its presence 'penetrating everywhere' (*sarvagata*) links the world of action (whether sacrificial or otherwise) with the imperishable sphere of 'wisdom'. And so the man who 'sinks himself in this [sacrificial] act which is Brahman' must thereby *go* to Brahman, just as in 2. 70–72 the 'man of steady wisdom' *goes* to the 'Nirvāna that is Brahman too', that is, 'draws near' to peace and wins peace.

Nirvāna, as everyone knows, is a Buddhist term: it is the negation of action, sensation, even of consciousness as normally understood: it is the negation of the human condition as we know it. Brahman *is* Nirvāna, but it is also sacrificial action; and it is therefore just as possible to achieve 'enstasy' (*samādhi*) in Brahman seen as (sacrificial) act as it is for the soul or contemplative intellect to 'stand motionless and still, immovable in enstasy' whereby it reaches that *Yoga* (2. 53) which, defined as 'sameness-and-indifference' (2. 48), is nothing less than Brahman (5. 19). Through the contemplation of Brahman as sacrifice one reaches the Brahman which is the Imperishable (8. 3).

Ś. is unusually obscure on this passage. What he seems to be saying is that everything *is* Brahman in so far as it *is*, but in so far as anything shows diversity of any sort it is as non-existent as the silver for which a man may mistake mother-of-pearl. On his realizing the mistake the 'silver' is simply annihilated. So with the phenomenal world, once one has realized Brahman, the One, it is seen to be simply nothing. All this is very far from the thought of the Gītā.

R. is more interesting. 'The man who sinks himself in the idea that all action is instinct with Brahman (*brahmamaya*)', he says, 'because its very essence is Brahman, is the *brahma-karma-samādhi* (mentioned in the text). And because its very essence is Brahman he must go to it because it has become Brahman [for him] and has the essential nature (*svarūpa*) of the self.'

25. *daivam ev'āpare yajñaṁ yoginaḥ paryupāsate,*
brahm'āgnāv apare yajñaṁ yajñen'aiv'opajuhvati.

Some adepts offer sacrifice to the gods as their sole object; in the fire of Brahman others offer sacrifice as sacrifice [which has merit in itself].

yoginaḥ, 'adepts': more accurately 'performers of *karma-yoga* (spiritual exercise through works)'. So R.

'Sacrifice to the gods': this can satisfy man's worldly desires (7. 20–22).

'In the fire of Brahman': what precisely this means is much disputed. It would, however, seem reasonable to suppose that the 'fire' of Brahman in this passage is the same as the 'fire' of transcendent wisdom mentioned in verses 19 and 37. This should be obvious if one is prepared to take the Gītā as an organic whole and not as a collection of bits and pieces put together anyhow. H. lists an abundance of opinions on this passage to which those interested may turn.

26. *śrotrādīnī'ndriyāṇy anye saṁyam'āgniṣu juhvati,*
śabdādīn viṣayān anya indriy'āgniṣu juhvati.

Yet others offer the senses,—hearing and the rest,—in the fires of self-restraint; others the senses' proper objects,—sounds and the like,—in the fires of the senses.

What exactly the second class of adept is supposed to be doing is not clear. The words seem to mean that this class of adept pampers the senses. Neither Ś. nor R., however, like this, Ś. saying that it means to take cognizance of unforbidden (*aviruddha*) objects, and R. saying that this class of adepts 'strives to check the proneness of the senses to objects of sense'.

27. *sarvāṇī'ndriya-karmāṇi prāṇa-karmāṇi c'āpare*
ātma-saṁyama-yog'āgnau juhvati jñāna-dīpite.

Others offer up all works of sense and works of vital breath in the fire of the spiritual exercise of self-control kindled by wisdom.

-indriya-karmāṇi, 'all works of sense': this applies as much to the 'organs of action' (3. 6, 7 and n.) as to the senses proper.

prāṇa-karmāṇi, 'works of vital breath': the offering of the five 'vital breaths' to the self. This is an allegorical interpretation of the *Agnihotra* or fire-sacrifice described in ChU. 5. 19–24. The five 'vital breaths' which occur repeatedly throughout the Upanishads are *prāṇa*, 'in-breath'; *apāna*, 'out-breath'; *vyāna*, 'diffused breath'; *udāna*, 'upper breath'; and *samāna*, 'concentrated breath'. According to Ś. commenting on BU. 1. 5. 3 the 'in-breath' is a function (*vṛtti*) of the heart converging on the mouth and nose; the 'out-breath' is a function of the lower part of the body located in the navel which assists excretion; the 'diffused breath' correlates the 'in-breath' and the 'out-breath' and brings about actions that require strength; the 'upper breath' is a function located throughout the body from the soles of the feet up to the skull and has an upward tendency; the 'concentrated breath', located in the belly, digests food and drink.

'The fire of the spiritual exercise of self-control': this is clearly a reference to 3. 7: 'More excellent is he who with the mind controls those limbs (or senses) and through these limbs [themselves] by which he acts embarks on the spiritual exercise of works, remaining detached the while.'

'Kindled by wisdom': cf. 4. 19, 'his works burnt up in wisdom's fire', and 4. 37, 'so does the fire of wisdom reduce all works to ashes'. Cf. also 4. 23: 'Attachment gone, deliverance won, his thoughts are fixed on wisdom: he works for sacrifice [alone], and all the work [he ever did] entirely melts away.' So in this passage Ś. glosses, 'they cause [all works . . .] to melt away (*pravilāpayanti*)'. See notes on 4. 19, 23, and 37.

28. *dravya-yajñās tapo-yajñā yoga-yajñās tathā'pare*
svādhyāya-jñāna-yajñāś ca yatayaḥ saṁśita-vratāḥ.

Some offer up their wealth, some their hard penances, some spiritual exercise, and some again make study and knowledge [of scripture] their sacrifice,—religious men whose vows are strict.

yoga-, 'spiritual exercise': it is not clear in what exact sense the word is used here. Ś., 'breath-control, etc.': R., 'pilgrimages'.

29. *apāne juhvati prāṇaṁ, prāṇe'pānaṁ tathā'pare,*
prāṇ'āpāna-gatī ruddhvā prāṇāyāma-parāyaṇāḥ.

Some offer the in-breath in the out-breath, likewise the out-breath in the in-breath, checking the flow of both, on breath-control intent.

'Breath-control': one of the eight 'limbs' of the classical Yoga described in *Yoga-sūtras* 2. 49–52.

30. *apare niyat'āhārāḥ prāṇān prāṇeṣu juhvati.*
sarve 'py ete yajña-vido yajña-kṣapita-kalmaṣāḥ.

Others restrict their food and offer up breaths in breaths. All these know the [meaning of] sacrifice, and by sacrifice [all] their defilements are made away.

31. *yajña-śiṣṭ'āmṛta-bhujo yānti brahma sanātanam.*
n'āyaṁ loko 'sty ayajñasya, kuto 'nyaḥ, Kuru-sattama ?

Eating of the leavings of the sacrifice, the food of immortality, they come to primeval Brahman. This world is not for him who performs no sacrifice,—much less the other [world].

We have already heard that 'good men who eat the leavings of the sacrifice are freed from every taint' (3. 13). Here every form of sacrifice is equated with the official cult. These different forms of sacrifice not only free from taint or defilement but also bring one to the primeval Brahman, the immortal nexus between the static Imperishable and the phenomenal world of action (4. 24 n.). It is perhaps worth noting that the word *sanātana*, 'primeval' or 'eternal', does contain the idea of time rather than of a static eternity, for it derives from *sana* = Lat. *senex*, 'old'. Hence the Gītā speaks of the *sanātana* 'family laws' (1. 40) which clearly can operate only in time.

'This world . . . the other [world]': R. glosses, 'the world of material Nature connected with [the three legitimate human activities according to the Hindu law-books,] the pursuit of righteousness (*dharma*), worldly success (*artha*), and pleasure (*kāma*)': the other world is that of 'liberation' (*mokṣa*).

32. *evaṁ bahuvidhā yajñā vitatā brahmaṇo mukhe.*
karma-jān viddhi tān sarvān, evaṁ jñātvā vimokṣyase.

So, many and various are the sacrifices spread out athwart the mouth of Brahman. They spring from work, all of them: be sure of this; for once you know this, you will win release.

'Spread out athwart the mouth (or face) of Brahman)': Ś. takes 'Brahman' to mean the Veda. R. allegorizes: 'are established as a means for getting possession of the very essence of the self'. The phrase could equally mean 'offered in the presence of Brahman'. For further views see H.'s note. E. suggests, 'are performed before Brahman'. All these interpretations are plausible enough except, perhaps, Śankara's. The Gītā, however, is merely making the point it made in 3. 14–15. There is an upward progression from sacrifice as here elaborated through *karma* ('sacrificial action' and more generally 'action, works') to Brahman which is the 'mouth' or door to the Imperishable, later defined indeed as the 'Imperishable Brahman' (8. 3).

'Once you know this, you will win release': Ś. takes this to mean that once you realize that sacrifice, works, and everything to do with them are wholly foreign to the Self, you will win release from the bondage of phenomenal existence (*saṁsāra*). This is very far indeed from what the Gītā says. Rather, Brahman which both is the source of the sacrifice and *is* the sacrifice acts as a link between 'this world' of time and 'the other' world of timelessness.

33. *śreyān dravyamayād yajñāj jñāna-yajñaḥ, paraṁtapa,*
sarvaṁ karm' ākhilaṁ, Pārtha, jñāne parisamāpyate.

Better than the sacrifice of wealth is the sacrifice of wisdom. All works without exception in wisdom find their consummation.

'The sacrifice of wisdom (knowledge)': this could and probably does refer to the 'sacrifice of study and knowledge [of scripture]' mentioned in 4. 28, although Ś. there takes *svādhyāya* to refer to the Vedas and *jñāna* to refer to the *śāstras*, religious treatises not in the Vedic canon. It may also mean the 'sacrifice that consists in wisdom', in which case it would mean that type of sacrifice which has no earthly goal as its object, thus anticipating the following stanzas.

'All works without exception in wisdom find their consummation': Ś., 'are contained in'. In 'wisdom' or intuitive insight into Reality all works are both obliterated (4. 19, 23 and nn.) and sublimated.

Transcendent Wisdom

34. *tad viddhi praṇipātena paripraśnena sevayā;*
upadekṣyanti te jñānaṁ jñāninas tattva-darśinaḥ.

Learn to know this by humble reverence [of the wise], by questioning, by service, [for] the wise who see things as they really are will teach you wisdom.

The next stanza tells us what is meant by 'seeing things as they really are'.

35. *yaj jñātvā na punar moham evaṁ yāsyasi, Pāṇḍava,*
yena bhūtāny aśeṣeṇa drakṣyasy ātmany atho mayi.

Once you have known this you will never again be perplexed as you are now: by [knowing] this you will behold [all] beings in [your]self—everyone of them—and then in Me.

This is a crucial verse in the development of the Gītā's theology, since for the first time it brings God and the self-in-itself into juxtaposition: moreover, it is an anticipation of the rather clearer formulation of the same doctrine in 6. 29–32. Both Ś. and R. are worth quoting here as their respective comments lucidly illustrate the fundamental difference that separates them on the question of the nature of mystical experience and the reality that that experience is supposed to represent.

Ś.: 'By this wisdom you will see in an act of immediate awareness (*sākṣāt*) all contingent beings without exception from [the god] Brahmā to a clump of grass, that is, these contingent beings which subsist in Me (Krishna), in [your]self, that is the "individual" Self (*pratyag-ātmani*); and then you will see them in Me, Krishna, the supreme Lord, since the oneness of Self (*kṣetra-jña*, "knower of the field", see 13. 2 n.) and the supreme Lord is attested in all the Upanishads.'

R.: 'By this [wisdom] you will really see all contingent beings in your own self, not [indeed] schematized in [separate] forms as gods, men, and other categories of being, [but rather you will see] the sameness or identity (*sāmyam*) between you and other contingent beings which are separated by material Nature in that you all share the one "form" of wisdom (intuitive insight).'

We now have liberation conceived of in four different ways:

(i) In 2. 70–72 the goal is peace (cf. 4. 39), the 'fixed, still state of Brahman' and the 'Nirvāna that is Brahman too'. God is only a convenient object on which to fix one's contemplative intellect.

(ii) In 3. 17 it is implied that the self-in-itself is autarchic, for in it are pleasure, satisfaction, and contentment, and hence 'there is naught it needs to do'.

(iii) In 4. 9–11 knowledge of the divine incarnations, reliance on God, and inhering in Him cause a man to share in his mode of being.

(iv) In this passage by *jñāna*, 'transcendent wisdom', by 'seeing things as they really are', one sees all beings in the self-in-itself, and then in God.

This mere catalogue must suffice for the moment, as the whole concept of liberation will be occupying us during the next two chapters.

36. *api ced asi pāpebhyaḥ sarvebhyaḥ pāpa-kṛttamaḥ*
sarvaṁ jñāna-plaven'aiva vṛjinaṁ saṁtariṣyasi.

Even though you were the very worst among all evil-doers, [yet once you have boarded] wisdom's bark, you will surmount all [this] tortuous [stream of life].

37. *yath' aidhāṁsi samiddho 'gnir bhasmasāt kurute, 'rjuna,*
jñān' āgniḥ sarva-karmāṇi bhasmasāt kurute tathā.

As a kindled fire reduces its fuel to ashes, so does the fire of wisdom reduce all works to ashes.

Cf. 4. 19, 23, 33, and nn. All works are both destroyed and find their consummation in wisdom because both works and sacrifice derive from Brahman, and Brahman derives from the Imperishable (3. 14–15). Sacrifice 'spread out athwart the mouth of Brahman' (4. 32) transmutes the sacrificial offering of work into the very substance of eternal wisdom just as a man by eating transforms food into the living substance of his own body. This transformation of one substance into another—of food into the eater—had a strange fascination for the authors of the Upanishads. According to MaiU. 6. 10: 'He who is the mouth of the Unmanifest is Agni (the sacrificial fire)', and we remember that it is 'athwart the mouth of Brahman' that the sacrifice is spread (4. 32). By becoming (sacrificial) food one's essence is transmuted into that of the eater, in this case Brahman: sacrifice is swallowed up in action, action in Brahman, and Brahman in Imperishable Wisdom. The destruction of life is no real destruction but a transformation. Works 'entirely melt away' (4. 23) in a greater reality, as food 'melts away' into the eater—Brahman. 'This indeed is the great, unborn Self, eater of food, giver of good things. . . . This indeed, the great, unborn Self, that knows neither age nor death nor fear, is Brahman—yes, Brahman, free from fear!' (BU. 4. 4. 24–25). To put it briefly, the destruction of the ego leads to the manifestation of the timeless self.

38. *na hi jñānena sadṛśaṁ pavitram iha vidyate;*
tat svayaṁ yoga-saṁsiddhaḥ kālen' ātmani vindati.

For nothing on earth resembles wisdom in its power to purify; and this in time a man himself may find within [him]self—a man perfected in spiritual exercise.

Wisdom is the 'form' of the self-in-itself according to R.

39. *śraddhāvāṁl labhate jñānaṁ tat-paraḥ saṁyat' endriyaḥ;*
jñānaṁ labdhvā parāṁ śāntim acireṇ' ādhigacchati.

A man of faith, intent on wisdom, his senses [all] restrained, wins wisdom; and, wisdom won, he will come right soon to perfect peace.

tat-paraḥ, 'intent on [wisdom]': one MS. has *mat-paraḥ*, 'intent on Me'.

śraddhāvāṁl, 'a man of faith': faith in what? This adjective is elsewhere applied to faith in Krishna (3. 31: 6. 47: 18. 71). The noun *śraddhā*, 'faith', is frequently used of faith in one or other of the gods (7. 21–22: 9. 23: 17. 1) or in Krishna (12. 2). In 17. 2 and 17. 17 there is nothing to indicate what the object of faith is, while in 6. 37 faith seems to mean faith in the possibility of ultimate liberation. Similarly here it would seem to mean faith in the possibility of possessing wisdom.

40. *ajñaś c'āśraddadhānaś ca saṁśay'ātmā vinaśyati:*
n'āyaṁ loko 'sti na paro na sukhaṁ saṁśay'ātmanaḥ.

The man, unwise, devoid of faith, of doubting self, must perish: this world is not for the man of doubting self, nor the next [world] nor yet happiness.

'Of doubting self': both Ś. and R. gloss 'self' as 'mind'. Sacrifice, faith, and a desire for wisdom are thus necessary if perdition is to be avoided.

41. *yoga-saṁnyasta-karmāṇaṁ jñāna-saṁchinna-saṁśayam*
ātmavantaṁ na karmāṇi nibadhnanti, dhanaṁjaya.

Let a man in spiritual exercise [all] works renounce, let him by wisdom [all] doubts dispel, let him be himself, and then [whatever] his works [may be, they] will never bind him [more].

yoga-saṁnyasta-karmāṇaṁ, 'renouncing [all] works in *yoga*': the phrase is rather strange. In 3. 30 and 12. 6 works are cast (*saṁ-ny-as-*) on God, and in 5. 10 they are 'placed on' Brahman. Here again, I venture to think, the author is deliberately playing on the different meanings of *yoga*. In 5. 1 *yoga* is directly contrasted with *saṁnyāsa*—doing with renouncing—and in the very next stanza here (4. 42) *yoga* certainly means 'action'. How, then, can one cast off one's actions on action? The clue seems to be in the use of *yukta* in 4. 18 and in its frequent use in the next two chapters. Certainly in 4. 42 *yoga* means 'action' and nothing else, but the *yogin* is necessarily (if for no other than etymological reasons) a *yukta*, a 'disciplined' and 'integrated' man, and *yoga* is not only 'action' but disciplined and integrated action. And so it is natural for Arjuna to address Krishna Himself as 'Yogin' (10. 17) and as 'Lord of Yoga' (11. 4), and at the very end of the book this is how Sanjaya speaks of him too (18. 75, 78). Hence *yoga* here would appear to mean God's never-ceasing and integrated activity. This prepares us for the wholly 'secular' use of the word in the next stanza.

42. *tasmād ajñāna-saṁbhūtaṁ hṛt-sthaṁ jñān'āsinā'tmanaḥ*
chittv'ainaṁ saṁśayaṁ yogam ātiṣṭh'ottiṣṭha, Bhārata.

And so [take up] the sword of wisdom and with it cut this doubt of yours, unwisdom's child, still lurking in your heart: prepare for action now, stand up!

ātmanaḥ: Ś. 'doubt concerning your own self'. H. (taking it with *jñān'āsinā*), 'thy Self's sword of knowledge'. I prefer to take it as a simple reflexive which seems more in accordance with the peremptory command that is to come.

yogam ātiṣṭha: this is the ordinary epic term for to 'get going', and this is certainly what it means here. Naturally the other senses of *yoga* listed in 2. 51 n. are also at the back of the author's mind.

CHAPTER V

IN 3. 2 Arjuna had accused Krishna of 'confusing his soul . . . with distinctly muddled words', and had asked him for an authoritative decision as to whether he should engage in action, that is, go to war, or pursue the way of contemplation—'spiritual exercise controlled by the soul'. Arjuna, like most Europeans, thinks in 'either/or' categories: he has not yet realized that Krishna's categories and those of the religion he inherits and further develops are not 'either/or' but 'both/and'. Opposites do not exclude each other but complement each other. So this chapter opens with Arjuna asking once again for clear guidance.

Krishna replies that both renunciation and action (as understood and qualified by Himself) lead to the highest good. You cannot, however, really separate them since *saṁnyāsa*, 'renunciation', is a state of mind in which the man of action (*yoga*, verse 5) too must share. Such a man he calls *yoga-yukta*, 'a man integrated by spiritual exercise'. This is Krishna's ideal, and both this chapter and the next are devoted to him. Whatever he may do, he reminds himself that he is not really the agent: he attributes all his actions to God (Brahman, verse 10 and n. ad loc.), renouncing all attachment. Solely intent on transcendent wisdom he attains the 'highest'. His soul steadfast and stilled he will abide in Brahman—the word *Brahman* being used in the sense of the 'fixed, still state of Brahman' of 2. 72—and he will find joy only in the self-in-itself within him. And so he 'becomes Brahman and attains to the 'Brahman that is Nirvāna too'. The whole chapter is thus an elaboration of 2. 54–72 which presents the 'man of steady wisdom' as the ideal human being and 'Nirvāna which is Brahman too' as the one all-satisfying goal. This is the Buddhist ideal, and Krishna absorbs it, but in the very last line He again obtrudes Himself into this atmosphere of perfect, static peace; and claims that it is rather by knowing Him as 'great Lord of all the worlds' that one attains to peace.

This is, perhaps, the most homogeneous of all the chapters of the Gītā. Traditionally it is called 'The Yoga of action and renunciation': it would be better described as the chapter of 'the man integrated into Brahman'.

The Unity of Theory and Practice—Renunciation and Action

Arjuna uvāca:

1. *saṁnyāsaṁ karmaṇāṁ, Kṛṣṇa, punar yogaṁ ca śaṁsasi*
yac chreya etayor ekaṁ tan me brūhi suniścitam.

Arjuna said:

'Renounce [all] works': [such is the course] You recommend: and then again [You say]: 'Perform them'. Which *one* is the better of the two? Tell me this [in clear,] decisive [words].

yogaṁ, 'perform them': *yoga* is obviously used in the sense of *yogam ātiṣṭha*, 'prepare for action' in the last stanza of the last chapter. Arjuna emphatically demands a clear-cut answer. Which *one* of the two alternatives is he to follow: is he to become a professional *saṁnyāsin*, an ascetic who has wholly put the world behind him, or is he to 'get going' and lead his elder brother Yudhishthira's armies into war? Krishna's discourses in Chapters III and IV have, as far as he is concerned, confused the issue even further. Certainly Krishna has told him quite clearly that he must act and how he must act. He must act without any attachment to what he is doing or to what is likely to be the result of his action (3. 7, 19: 4. 14–15), for by so doing what he does—his works—will no longer bind him (4. 14–15, 20–23, 41). This is what the ancients did (3. 20: 4. 15), and this is the example that Krishna himself sets (3. 22–24: 4. 14). Moreover, mere renunciation does not bring about success (3. 4) and inaction is never better than action (3. 8). On the other hand, Arjuna is told to fight and cast his actions on Krishna (3. 30) apparently in order to evade responsibility. In any case, he is told, wisdom utterly destroys mere deeds (4. 19), reducing them to ashes (4. 37), and that for the perfected sage 'in self alone content' (3. 17) there is absolutely nothing that he need do. The only reason he has been told to fight is that his elders and betters (the 'ancients' and the Man-God) did and do so: he has been given no *moral* justification for doing so except that it is his caste duty (2. 31–33). As far as he can see (and just now he has something of the moral fibre of his elder brother, Yudhishthira) he is merely being asked to initiate mass slaughter and to shirk the moral consequences with an unruffled conscience. His doubt persists, nor will it dissolve until Krishna shows him the awful majesty of God whose ways it is futile to question, just as Yahweh did to Job in the Old Testament.

Śrī-bhagavān uvāca:

2. *saṁnyāsaḥ karma-yogaś ca niḥśreyasa-karāv ubhau;*
tayos tu karma-saṁnyāsāt karma-yogo viśiṣyate.

The Blessed Lord said:

Renouncing works,—performing them [as spiritual exercise],—

both lead to the highest goal; but of the two to engage in works is more excellent than to renounce them.

saṁnyāsaḥ karma-yogaś ca, 'renouncing works—performing them': renunciation in itself does not lead to that 'passionlessness' which is the *sine qua non* of the man who is set on liberation (3. 4); and although works in themselves are greatly inferior to the 'spiritual exercise controlled by the soul' (2. 49), the content of which is wisdom (*prajñā*, 2. 54 ff.: *jñāna*, 4. 33–42), and although 'nothing on earth resembles wisdom in its power to purify' (4. 38), it is still better to 'perform works' because 'performance' is *yoga*, and *yoga* has been defined both as 'sameness-and-indifference' (2. 48)—which, since this is equally an epithet of the Imperishable Brahman (5. 19), must be an absolute value—and as 'skill in [performing] works' (2. 50). Hence the {performance of / skill in performing / spiritual exercise consisting in sameness-and-indifference brought to the performance of} works must be superior to the mere renouncing of them. *Yoga* is indeed a wonderful word!

3. *jñeyaḥ sa nitya-saṁnyāsī yo na dveṣṭi na kāṅkṣati:*
nirdvandvo hi, mahā-bāho, sukhaṁ bandhāt pramucyate.

This is the mark of the man whose renunciation is abiding: he hates not nor desires, for, devoid of all dualities, how easily is he released from bondage.

'He hates not nor desires': like God who neither hates nor loves anyone (9. 29, but see n. ad loc.).

'Bondage': i.e. the bondage of works on which Krishna has insisted so much during the last chapter.

4. *sāṁkhya-yogau pṛthag bālāḥ pravadanti na paṇḍitāḥ.*
ekam apy āsthitaḥ samyag ubhayor vindate phalam.

'There must be a difference between theory and practice', so say the simple-minded, not the wise. Apply yourself to only one whole-heartedly and win the fruit of both.

sāṁkhya-yogau, 'theory and practice': in 2. 39 these two terms meant simply 'theory' and 'practice'. 3. 3 is more explicit: 'wisdom' is the province of *sāṁkhya* ('theory', now merging into 'contemplation'), action that of *yoga* (the meaning there remains 'practice'). Here, however, while *yoga* is still connected with action, *sāṁkhya* appears to be identified with renunciation. As Ś. rightly says, the Lord has merely changed his terminology—a practice all too common in the Hindu sacred books and the Gītā in particular. Very roughly we can say:

Sāṁkhya in the Gītā = wisdom = *buddhi* in Chapter II = renunciation of action in so far as it binds.

Yoga (as the opposite of *Sāṁkhya*) = the performance of action qualified by a total dissociation from its fruits.

Sāṁkhya, then, = pure contemplation leading to intuitive apprehension of reality: *Yoga* = leading an active life without a trace of ambition, in preparation for pure contemplation which will come later. This, at least, is how Ś. interprets it, and in the main he would seem to be right.

5. *yat sāṁkhyaiḥ prāpyate sthānaṁ tad yogair api gamyate;*
ekaṁ sāṁkhyaṁ ca yogaṁ ca: yaḥ paśyati sa paśyati.

[True,] the men of [contemplative] theory attain a [high] estate, but that [same estate] achieve the men of practice too; for theory and practice are all one: who sees [that this is true], he sees [indeed].

sthānaṁ, '[high] estate': one MS. has *jñānaṁ*, 'wisdom'.

'Who sees [that this is true], he sees [indeed]': the phrase occurs again in 13. 27 and there we are told what the seer sees: 'The same in all contingent beings, abiding [without change], the Highest Lord, when all things fall to ruin, [Himself] is not destroyed: who sees Him sees [indeed].'

The repetition of the words *yaḥ paśyati sa paśyati* in the later passage does not seem to me to be fortuitous, for the author of the Gītā is here describing that highest 'estate' to which *Sāṁkhya* ('contemplation') and *Yoga* ('disinterested action') both lead;—they must do so for they cannot legitimately be separated (5. 4). In *Sāṁkhya* terms this is the Imperishable Brahman, 'the same in all contingent beings' (cf. 5. 19, 'ever-the-same is Brahman'), 'abiding' (*tiṣṭhantam*, lit. 'standing': cf. 2. 72, *brāhmī sthitiḥ*, 'the fixed, still state of Brahman'), which, 'when all things fall to ruin, [itself] is not destroyed' (cf. 8. 20 where almost identical words are used of the 'Unmanifest beyond the Unmanifest'). In *Yoga* terms the 'same' 'estate' is the Highest Lord, that is, Krishna, the 'Lord of Yoga' (11. 4: 18. 75, 78).

Transcending Works by purifying the Self

6. *saṁnyāsas tu, mahā-bāho, duḥkham āptum ayogataḥ:*
yoga-yukto munir brahma nacireṇ'ādhigacchati.

But hard to attain is [true] renunciation without [the practice of some] spiritual exercise: the sage { well versed in spiritual exercise / integrated by spiritual exercise / by integration integrated } right soon to Brahman comes.

yoga-yukto: none of the modern translations are adequate. E., 'disciplined in discipline': Rk., 'earnest in yoga': H., 'whose way is practice': D., 'der dem Yoga sich hingebende'. Only E. gives *yukto* its proper force as a past participle passive—a sense it clearly retains as the phrase *buddhyā yukto*, 'integrated by the soul', in 2. 39 shows. Ś. glosses: 'endowed (*yukta*) with Vedic *karma-yoga* dedicated to the Lord and without regard for the fruits [of his works]'.

'To Brahman comes': R., 'obtains the self': Ś. (oddly), 'Brahman means renunciation because it is characterized by the attainment of intuitive apprehension (*jñāna*) of the highest Self'. The phrase, however, can scarcely be separated from the *brahma . . . gantavyam*, 'to Brahman must he go', of 4. 24 where, as we have seen, Brahman is the eternal seen as present in the sacrifice. Sacrifice is based on works (*karma*, 3. 15) and hence it is only natural that the *yoga-yukta*, the 'man integrated, etc. by the Yoga *of works*' should go to the Brahman which is the link between works and 'imperishable wisdom', before he finally expires in the 'Nirvāna which is Brahman too' (5. 24–26 where this concept which we had already encountered in 2. 72 is more fully elaborated). That 'Brahman' does not here mean the 'highest Self' of Ś. or even the 'self' of R. seems clear not only from 4. 24 (the last time the word was used) but also from 5. 10 (q.v.) where it clearly means the divine *in operation*, not the 'fixed, still state of Brahman' of 2. 72. This will only be reached later.

7. *yoga-yukto viśuddh'ātmā vijit'ātmā jit'endriyaḥ*
sarva-bhūt'ātma-bhūt'ātmā kurvann api na lipyate.

Well-versed in spiritual exercise, his self made pure, his self and senses quelled, his self become the [very] self of every contingent being, though working still, he is not defiled.

viśuddh'ātmā, 'his self made pure': Ś. glosses *ātmā* as *sattva*, 'Goodness', the highest constituent of Nature. This seems rather imperceptive since 'Goodness' of its very nature is 'immaculate' (14. 6). R., as usual in contexts where the self is referred to as being subject to action of any kind, glosses 'mind'. This seems to be drawing too fine a distinction. The self is like a mirror, and just as dirt accumulates on a mirror without the mirror thereby being identified with the dirt, so does the self need cleaning from the 'defilement' it suffers from contact with the senses and the organs of action (5. 10–11). This is clearly and beautifully expressed in ŚU. 2. 14:

> Even as a mirror with dirt begrimed
> Shines brightly once it is well cleaned,
> So too the embodied [self], once it has seen
> Self as it really is,
> Becomes one, its goal achieved, from sorrow free.

vijit'ātmā, 'his self . . . quelled': var. *saṁyat'ātmā*, 'with self restrained'. Ś. takes 'self' to mean 'body', and this seems fair enough, though the use of the word in such different senses in one hemistich is a little disconcerting. The idea of a 'higher' and a 'lower' self is, however, not foreign to the Gītā. It is clearly formulated in 6. 5–6:

> Raise self by self, let not the self droop down; for self's friend is self indeed, so too is self self's enemy. Self is the friend to the self of him whose self is by the self subdued; but for the man bereft of self self will act as an enemy indeed.

The self which is quelled or subdued is clearly the whole psychosomatic complex in which the 'higher self' (6. 7) inheres. So too in the Buddhist texts 'self' must be conquered (Dhp. 103, 104), tamed (ibid. 80, 159, 160: M. ii. 105) and purged (Dhp. 88, 165).

'His self become the [very] self of every contingent being': Ś. seems to find this to us rather surprising statement self-evident as he offers no commentary. R., for whom this appears altogether too pantheistic, says that this realization of the true essence of the self means no more than that all selves have one 'form' (*ākāra*)—that of 'wisdom', by which he means eternal being beyond space, time, and action. Diversity is due to material Nature. For him the self is the *puruṣa* of the Sāṁkhya system (p. 140) except that its being is grounded in God. Together with material Nature selves form the 'body' of God, God himself being the 'soul' of the universe and as such different in kind from both selves and Nature.

Be this as it may, what the Gītā is describing is in fact the common experience of 'nature mystics': 'without and within glide into each other', as Karl Joel succinctly put it (R. C. Zaehner, *Mysticism Sacred and Profane*, p. 38), or as Forrest Reid puts it better than anyone else who has come to my attention (ibid., p. 41):

> It was as if everything that had seemed to be external and around me were suddenly within me. The whole world seemed to be within me. It was within me that the trees waved their green branches, and it was within me that the skylark was singing, it was within me that the hot sun shone, and that the shade was cool.

This is what the *Chāndogya* Upanishad (7. 1–14) calls 'freedom of movement', or in the words of the same Upanishad (8. 1. 3–5):

> (3) As wide as this space [around us], so wide is the space within the heart. In it both sky and earth are concentrated, both fire and wind, both sun and moon, lightning and stars, what a man possesses on earth and what he does not possess: everything is concentrated in this [tiny space within the heart].
>
> (4) If they should say to him: 'If all this is concentrated within this city of Brahman—all beings and all desires—what is left of it all when old age overtakes it and it falls apart?'
>
> (5) Then should he say: 'It does not grow old with [the body's] ageing nor is it slain when [the body] is slain. This is the true city of Brahman; in it are concentrated [all] desires. This is the Self, exempt from evil, untouched by age or death or sorrow, untouched by hunger or thirst: [this is the Self] whose desire is the real, whose idea is the real.'

8. *n'aiva kiṁcit karomī'ti yukto manyeta tattva-vit*
paśyañ śṛṇvan spṛśañ jighrann aśnan gacchan svapañ śvasan,

'Lo, nothing do I do': so thinks the integrated man who knows things as they really are, seeing the while and hearing, touching, smelling, eating, walking, sleeping, breathing,

'Lo, nothing do I do': cf. 4. 18–20 (seeing 'action in inaction and inaction in action'). The same paradox is expressed in BU. 4. 3. 23 ff.:

Though he does not see, yet it is by seeing that he does not see; for there is no disjunction between seer and sight since [both] are indestructible. But there is no second thing other than himself and separate that he might see it. (And so on for the other senses.)

yukto, 'integrated': Ś. glosses here and in similar contexts *samāhita*, 'concentrated' or even 'integrated' (from the same root as *samādhi*). Such a man, he adds, sees the insubstantiality (*abhāva*) of action just as he would recognize a mirage for what it is. Rk's 'united with the Divine' is wrong as all the parallel passages in this and the following chapter plainly show.

svapañ śvasan, 'sleeping, breathing'; var. *śvasañ japan*, 'breathing, talking'. For the last four participles one MS. has, 'eating, walking, breathing, smiling'.

9. *pralapan visṛjan gṛhṇann unmiṣan nimiṣann api*
indriyāṇī'ndriy'ārtheṣu vartanta iti dhārayan.

Talking, evacuating, grasping, opening and shutting the eyes. 'The senses are busied with their proper objects: [what has that to do with me?' This is the way] he thinks.

'The senses are busied with their proper objects': cf. 3. 28: 'Constituents on constituents act.' The 'constituents' of course operate through the senses and the mind.

10. *brahmaṇy ādhāya karmāṇi saṅgaṁ tyaktvā karoti yaḥ,*
lipyate na sa pāpena padma-pattram iv'āmbhasā.

And on he works though he has [long] renounced attachment, ascribing his works to Brahman; [yet] is he not stained by evil as a lotus-petal [is not stained] by water.

'Ascribing his works to Brahman': the obvious parallel is 3. 30, cf. 12. 6, where Arjuna is urged to resign or give up all his works to Krishna. So Ś. glosses *brahmaṇy* as *īśvare*, 'on the Lord', adding 'like a servant: he renounces all works and attachment to the fruits [of his action], *even liberation*, for the sake of his master'. R. referring to 14. 3 where the word *brahman* obviously means 'material Nature', glosses it as such. All this seems to miss the point. Brahman, as we have seen, is in Chapters III–V of the Gītā the bridge between this world and the next, between the world of action and the still, tranquil world of Nirvāna. Hence it is natural to attribute one's actions to Brahman which both operates in Nature and has its true being in eternity. The relationship between Brahman and God is not yet clear: this will emerge with greater clarity as we read on.

'[Yet] is he not stained by evil as a lotus-petal [is not stained] by water': this metaphor was in all probability originally Buddhist. Cf. S. iii. 140: 'Just as a lotus born of the water, grown up in water, passing up above the water, is not stained by the water, so is the Tathāgata (Buddha), though he has grown up in the world and conquered it, not stained by the world.' The same phrase also occurs in ChU. 4. 14. 3: 'As water does not stick to a lotus-petal, so do evil deeds not stick to the man who knows this.'

11. *kāyena manasā buddhyā kevalair indriyair api*
yoginaḥ karma kurvanti saṅgaṁ tyaktvā'tma-śuddhaye.

With body, mind, soul, and senses alone-and-isolated [from the self] do men engaged in spiritual exercise engage in action renouncing attachment for the cleansing of the self.

-ātma-śuddhaye, 'for the cleansing of the self': var. *ātma-siddhaye*, 'for the perfection of the self', but cf. 5. 7 and n. This passage seems to be based on KaU. 6. 10–11, perhaps the earliest reference to Yoga as a technique:

> When the five senses stand, [their action stilled,]
> Likewise the mind; and when the soul (*buddhi*)
> No longer moves or acts—
> Such, have men said, is the all-highest way.
>
> 'Yoga', this is how they think of it—
> [It means] to check the senses firmly, still them:
> Then is a man freed from heedlessness,
> For Yoga is origin and end.

12. *yuktaḥ karma-phalaṁ tyaktvā śāntim āpnoti naiṣṭhikīm.*
ayuktaḥ kāma-kāreṇa phale sakto nibadhyate.

The integrated man, renouncing the fruit of works, gains an abiding peace: the man not integrated, whose works are prompted by desire, being attached to fruits, is bound.

yuktaḥ, 'the integrated man': Rk., 'earnest (or devoted)' although he had translated the same word as 'united with the Divine' in verse 8. For *ayuktaḥ* in this stanza he again has 'he whose soul is not in union with the Divine'. 'With the Divine' is, of course, in either case his own addition for which there is no justification.

'Abiding peace': Ś., 'this means liberation'. R., 'gains that still, static (*sthira*) state of pure inactivity (*nirvṛtti*) in which one experiences the self'. This perfect peace which is enjoyed in Nirvāna we have already encountered in 2. 70–72 and 4. 39 where it is the fruit of wisdom.

No Agent is the Self

13. *sarva-karmāṇi manasā saṁnyasy'āste sukhaṁ vaśī*
nava-dvāre pure dehī n'aiva kurvan na kārayan.

[And so,] all works renouncing with the mind, quietly he sits in full control,—the embodied [self] within the city with nine gates: he neither works nor makes another work.

dehī, 'the embodied [self]': var. *dehe*, 'in the body': *gehe*, 'in the house'. The term 'embodied [self]' takes us right back to the beginning (2. 13 ff.) where Krishna first discourses on the immortality of the soul.

'The city of nine gates': i.e. the body. Cf. ŚU. 3. 18:

> In the city of nine gates the embodied [self]
> [Like] a great bird flutters outward,
> Though the whole world 's in its power,
> What moves and what stands still.

Cf. also ChU. 8. 1. 3–5 quoted above p. 205.

14. *na kartṛtvaṁ na karmāṇi lokasya sṛjati prabhuḥ*
na karma-phala-saṁyogaṁ, svabhāvas tu pravartate.

Neither agency nor worldly works does [the body's] lord engender, nor yet the bond that works to fruit conjoins: it is inherent Nature that initiates the action.

na karmāṇi lokasya sṛjati prabhuḥ, 'nor worldly works does [the body's] lord engender': or, 'nor works does the lord of the world engender'. Ś. takes *lokasya* with *karmāṇi* and glosses: 'The self does not originate those works which are most coveted by the world such as chariots, vessels, palaces, etc.' He then identifies the self with the 'embodied [self]' by which he presumably means the empirical self viewed from the empirical point of view. This fits in with his commentary on the previous line where he compares the self to a monarch and the bodily faculties to his subjects. R. also interprets *prabhuḥ* as meaning the individual self. *Pace* Senart and Rk. who translate 'le Seigneur du monde' and 'the Sovereign Self' respectively, this must be right, for the whole argument in Chapters III and IV has been that it is not the individual self that acts but the constituents of Nature that act through it (3. 5, 27–28: cf. 5. 9). Ultimately it is God who 'engenders' works (7. 4–6: 9. 8–9) just as He engenders Himself out of material Nature (4. 6–7). Certainly the use of the word *prabhu* for the individual self is unusual but far less shocking than *īśvara* used in the same sense in 15. 8 where that word is used quite specifically of the individual transmigrating self which is described as a 'part' of God.

One MS. has *n'ākartṛtvaṁ* for *na kartṛtvaṁ*, and *na kartṛtvaṁ* for *na karmāṇi*.

15. *n'ādatte kasyacit pāpaṁ na c'aiva sukṛtaṁ vibhuḥ.*
ajñānen' āvṛtaṁ jñānaṁ; tena muhyanti jantavaḥ.

He takes not on the good and evil works of anyone at all,—[that] all-pervading lord. By ignorance is wisdom overspread; thereby are creatures fooled.

vibhuḥ, '[that] all-pervading lord': here Ś. switches from the empirical to the absolute (*paramārthika*) standpoint and attacks devotional religion as being ultimately pointless: 'he does not receive the good or evil deeds performed by anyone devoted to him (*bhakta*)'. R. rightly takes *vibhuḥ* to refer to the individual self and comments: 'he does not receive or reject the good or evil deeds performed by people he respects such as his son simply because they are related to him'. *Vibhu*, meaning 'all-pervading', is indeed quite suitably used of the individual self since that self has 'become the [very] self of every contingent being' (5. 7).

ādatte, 'takes on', is the same word as that used for 'ascribing' works to Brahman in 5. 10. The individual self in other words neither initiates works nor accepts their consequences: all this must be ascribed to Brahman seen as the nodal point and 'womb' from which the multiplicity of Nature arises (14. 3).

The Light of Wisdom

16. *jñānena tu tad ajñānaṁ yeṣāṁ nāśitam ātmanaḥ,*
teṣām ādityavaj jñānaṁ prakāśayati tat param.

But some there are whose ignorance of self by wisdom is destroyed. Their wisdom, like the sun, illumines that [all-] highest.

'Illumines that [all-]highest': R. takes *tat param* with *jñānaṁ* and paraphrases: 'That supreme wisdom which inheres within them (*svābhāvika*) and which is infinite and unconfined, illumines everything as it really is (*yathā'vasthita*)'. He further defines ignorance as 'the accretion of endless works performed from time without beginning'.

'That [all-]highest': i.e. the 'Imperishable Brahman' (see 2. 59 n.).

17. *tad-buddhayas tad-ātmānas tan-niṣṭhās tat-parāyaṇāḥ*
gacchanty apunar-āvṛttiṁ jñāna-nirdhūta-kalmaṣāḥ.

Souls [bent on] that, selves [bent on] that, with that their aim and that their aspiration, they stride [along the path] from which there is no return, [all] taints by wisdom washed away.

'Souls [bent on] that': Ś., 'their soul (intellect) enters into that [wisdom] . . . and for them the Self is the highest Brahman'. R., 'their wills (cf. 2. 41) intent on seeing the self as that . . . and making that the object of their minds'.

Three MSS. insert the following stanza:

smaranto 'pi muhus tv etat spṛśanto 'pi sva-karmaṇi,
saktā api na sajjanti paṅke ravi-karā iva.

Though reflecting on this repeatedly and touching it even while they act, though they are [still] attached, they are not [really] attached any more than the sun's rays [are attached] to the puddle [in which they are reflected].

Brahman and Nirvāna

18. *vidyā-vinaya-saṁpanne brāhmaṇe, gavi, hastini,*
śuni c'aiva śvapāke ca paṇḍitāḥ sama-darśinaḥ.

[These] wise ones see the selfsame thing in a Brāhman wise and courteous as in a cow or an elephant, nay, as in a dog or outcaste.

'See the self-same thing': Rk. prefers 'see with an equal eye'. The 'self-same thing', however, is defined in the next stanza as Brahman, and that is how Ś. and R. interpret it. R. glosses: 'because wisdom has one and the same form everywhere'.

19. *ih'aiva tair jitaḥ sargo yeṣāṁ sāmye sthitaṁ manaḥ:*
nirdoṣaṁ hi samaṁ brahma; tasmād brahmaṇi te sthitāḥ.

While yet in this world they have overcome [the process of] emanation [and decay], for their minds are stilled in that-which-is-ever-the-same: for devoid of imperfection and ever-the-same is Brahman: therefore in Brahman [stilled] they stand.

sargo, '[the process of] emanation [and decay]': var. *svargo*, 'heaven'. This is clearly wrong for heaven is the reward not of the man who has abandoned all worldly desires, but of the man 'whose essence is desire' (2. 43). Ś. reads *sargo* and glosses simply 'birth'.

'In Brahman [stilled] they stand': R., 'for Brahman is the stuff (*vastu*) of self: . . . standing still in Brahman means the conquest of temporal existence (*saṁsāra*)'. This is, of course, the *brāhmī sthitiḥ*, 'the fixed, still state of Brahman' of 2. 72. Rk. translates *brahman* as 'God', which is a fallacious over-simplification.

20. *na prahṛṣyet priyaṁ prāpya, n'odvijet prāpya c'āpriyam;*
sthira-buddhir asaṁmūḍho brahma-vid brahmaṇi sthitaḥ.

Winning some pleasant thing [the sage] will not rejoice, nor shrink disquietened when the unpleasant comes his way: steadfast-and-still his soul, [all] unconfused, he will know Brahman, in Brahman [stilled] he'll stand.

'Winning some pleasant thing . . .': the whole of this passage is a further elaboration of the concept of the 'man of steady wisdom' of 2. 55–72. Cf. 2. 56: 'Whose mind is undismayed [though beset] by many a sorrow, who for pleasures has no further longing, from whom all passion, fear, and wrath have fled, such a man is called a man of steadied thought, a silent sage.'

sthira-buddhir, 'steadfast-and-still his soul': cf. 2. 65: *buddhiḥ parya-vatiṣṭhate*, 'his soul stands firmly [in its ground]'. Ś. rather unnecessarily glosses *sthira-* as 'free from doubt': R., 'whose soul is in the steadfast-and-still self'. H.'s 'steadfast in judgement', and Rk.'s 'firm of under-standing' are misleading. Better S., 'l'âme toujours égale'.

sthitaḥ, '[stilled] he'll stand': Brahman *qua* the Imperishable, being a *state* of being beyond space and time is essentially static: hence the repeated use of derivatives of the root *sthā-* (Latin *stare*, English 'stand' etc.): *sthitaṁ manaḥ*, 'the mind stilled'; *brahmaṇi sthitāḥ*, 'in Brahman stilled they stand'; *sthira-buddhir*, 'steadfast-and-still his soul'. Rk.'s 'established in God' for *brahmaṇi sthitāḥ* is rather a paraphrase than a translation and quite fails to convey the wholly static quality of the timeless aspect of Brahman which Krishna is emphasizing here. Ś. is less naïve: '*sthitaḥ*', he says, means 'not doing anything, renouncing all actions'. R. too comments, 'constant (*vyava-sthita*) in the static (*sthira*) experience of his loving contemplation of the self'.

21. *bāhya-sparśeṣv asakt'ātmā vindaty ātmani yat sukham,*
sa brahma-yoga-yukt'ātmā sukham akṣayam aśnute.

[His] self detached from contacts with the outside world, in [him]self he finds his joy, [his] self in Brahman integrated by spiritual exercise he finds unfailing joy.

brahma-yoga-yukt'ātmā, '[his] self in Brahman integrated by spiritual exercise': in splitting the compound into its grammatical components I follow Ś. As usual in this chapter Ś. glosses *yoga* and *yukta* as *samādhi* and *samāhita* respectively: this almost exactly corresponds to the English 'integrated'. E. prefers, 'his self disciplined in Brahman-discipline': H., 'his self controlled by contemplating Brahman' (there is nothing about contemplation in the Sanskrit): Rk., 'self-controlled in Yoga on God': D., 'der Hingebung an Brahman mit ganzer Seele ergeben' (again more a paraphrase than a translation): S., 'intimement uni à Brahman', but in this chapter and the next *yukta-* never means 'united'.

In 5. 7 the so-called extraverted form of mystical experience was described—the mystic's self becomes 'the [very] self of every contingent being'. From here on the 'introverted' experience will be described, the discovery of 'the kingdom of God within you'. The discovery of this immortal element within the human personality is beautifully described in KaU. 4. 1:

The self-existent [Lord] bored holes facing the outside world;
Therefore a man looks outward, not into [him]self.
A certain sage, in search of immortality,
Turned his eyes inward and saw the self within.

22. *ye hi saṁsparśa-jā bhogā duḥkha-yonaya eva te*
ādy-antavantaḥ, Kaunteya, na teṣu ramate budhaḥ.

For the pleasures men derive from contacts assuredly give rise to pain, having a beginning and an end. In these a wise man takes no delight.

As with so much in this chapter the idea that pleasure is only pain in disguise is pure Buddhism: 'pleasant sensations should be seen as pain' (S. iv. 207) because all pleasures are transient and what is transient is painful because it has no core to it—it 'has no self' (*anattā*, S. iii. 28 ff. and *passim*). The 'beginning', according to Ś., is the contact established by one of the senses with its proper object, the 'end' is their disjunction: this again is originally a Buddhist idea (S. iv. 31, etc.), and the Gītā will make it its own in 6. 23 where *yoga* (originally 'joining') is defined as the '*disjunction* of the joining with pain'!

23. *śaknotī'h'aiva yaḥ soḍhuṁ prāk śarīra-vimokṣaṇāt*
kāma-krodh'odbhavaṁ vegaṁ, sa yuktaḥ, sa sukhī naraḥ.

Only the man who [remains] in this world and, before he is released from the body, can stand fast against the onset of desire and anger, is [truly] integrated, [truly] happy.

'Desire and anger': man's deadliest enemies on earth. The reader will remember Krishna's fierce attack on these in 3. 37–41.

yuktaḥ, 'integrated': var. *yogī*.

24. *yo 'ntaḥ-sukho 'ntar-ārāmas tathā 'ntar-jyotir eva yaḥ,*
sa yogī brahma-nirvāṇaṁ brahma-bhūto 'dhigacchati.

His joy within, his bliss within, his light within, the man who-is-integrated-in-spiritual-exercise becomes Brahman and draws nigh to Nirvāna that is Brahman too.

sa yogī brahma-nirvāṇaṁ: var. *sa, Pārtha, paramaṁ yogaṁ*, substituting 'the highest Yoga' for 'Nirvāna that is Brahman too'.

brahma-nirvāṇaṁ, 'Nirvāna that is Brahman too'; Rk.'s 'the beatitude of God' is thoroughly misleading. The term *nirvāṇa* is, of course, essentially Buddhist and does not appear in the classical Upanishads. Even in the fifty-four Upanishads from which G. A. Jacob compiled his concordance it only occurs three times, and the Upanishads from which the quotations are taken are almost certainly very late. Ś. is well aware that this is a Buddhist term, for he glosses it as *brahmaṇi nirvṛti*, 'cessation of activity in Brahman'. This is interesting, as *nirvṛti* (as opposed to the usual Sanskrit word for 'cessation of activity, *nivṛtti*) is a Sanskritization of the Pāli *nibbuti*, a very common synonym for *nibbāna* (the Pāli form of *nirvāṇa*). The compound *brahma-nirvāṇa*, however, seems to originate with the Gītā and is rarely found except in the other didactic treatises in the MBh. which are largely dependent on the Gītā. We have, of course, already met the term in 2. 72 and the remainder of this chapter is largely an amplification of what we read there.

The Gītā starts by taking Buddhism and the Buddhist conception of liberation fully into account: it adopts much of its terminology and accepts its conclusions and ultimate goal (Nirvāna), but it goes further than this in that it seeks to adopt the Buddhist ideal into its own essentially theistic framework.

It is frequently said that the Buddhist Nirvāna is an essentially negative concept. This, however, is very much less true of the earlier texts (e.g. *Suttanipāta*, *Udāna*, and *Itivuttaka*) than it is of the later ones (especially the rather artificial constructions of the *Saṁyutta* and *Anguttara Nikāyas*). Etymologically the word means 'blowing out'—specifically the blowing out of the fire [of craving, *taṇhā*] (D. ii. 157, 266: M. i. 188, 487; iii. 245: S. i. 159; ii. 85; iii. 126, etc.); it means 'peace' (Sn. 933) and the 'cooling off' [of all desire] (D. ii. 266: M. i. 171, 341; ii. 159; iii. 245: S. i. 141; iii. 126; iv. 213, etc.). It is the unborn (Ud. 81: Iti. 37: M. i. 163), the deathless (Sn. 204, 228: Iti. 46, 62: M. i. 227 and *passim*): it is health, the Buddha being the surgeon who makes health possible (M. ii. 260). It is an individual experience (S. iv. 23: D. i. 36; iii. 28: M. i. 251–2, etc.), but so emphatic are the Pāli texts in not identifying anything that can be called the 'self' with anything at all that is transient that one of the formulas they prefer to use to describe the state of Nirvāna is *vimuttaṁ vimuttasmiṁ*, 'something that is liberated in what is liberated [or free]' (M. iii. 280, 287: S. ii. 245; iii. 50, 83 and countless other times). What in fact is liberated is *citta* or *paññā*, 'transcendent reason' or 'wisdom' (D. i. 156, 167, 251: S. ii. 214, 239; iv. 120, etc., etc.). Nirvāna means the bringing to end of phenomenal existence, 'disgust, detachment, cessation, tranquillization, wisdom, and enlightenment' (M. i. 166, 485; iii. 114 and *passim*); in particular it is the destruction of the three root evils—passion, hatred, and delusion (S. iv. 160, 297, 359, etc.), of craving (Ud. 33: Sn. 1109: Iti. 44: M. i. 294: S. iii. 190, etc.), of becoming (Iti. 39, 44: S. i. 2; ii. 117). This means nothing less than the destruction of life, of the human condition as we know it. Indeed the man who has brought all activity to a standstill differs from a dead man only in so far as he retains physical life, heat, and senses: his only characteristics are indifference (*samatha*) and insight (S. iv. 294–5). Nirvāna, then, is certainly extinction of life as we know it, but it is also a state of liberation, of spiritual freedom uninhibited by space, time, or causation. It is like a level (*sama* again) and charming countryside (S. iii. 109) or the scent of a flower (S. iii. 130), and this freeing of transcendent reason and wisdom from the bondage of the *āsavas* of passion, hatred, and delusion is compared to a man detachedly observing oysters, shells, and fish in limpid water (M. ii. 22). It is seeing things as they really are *sub specie aeternitatis*:

Who sees contingent being as it really is
And [then] transcends it,
He is set free in existence as it really is
By the destruction of the craving to become.
If a mendicant has gained insight
Into contingent being,
All craving gone for what becomes and what un-becomes,
By making contingent being cease to become,
He will never be born again. (Iti. 44.)

The destruction of becoming, however, does not mean extinction, but the setting free of 'transcendent reason' in an atmosphere where there is complete freedom of movement as the *Chāndogya* Upanishad (p. 205) puts it. It is the abandonment of individuality in a great peace that is boundless as the ocean:

Just as—whatever streams flow into the mighty ocean and whatsoever floods fall from the sky, there is no shrinkage or overflow seen thereby in the mighty ocean, even so . . . though many mendicants pass finally away into that condition of Nirvāna which has no remainder, yet there is no shrinkage nor overflow in that condition of Nirvāna seen thereby. (Ud. 55.)

brahma-bhūto, 'become Brahman': what is meant by 'becoming Brahman? In the present context we would be justified in looking to the Buddhist texts for an explanation, for this chapter is clearly influenced by Buddhist ideas and Buddhist terminology: and in fact the word *brahma-bhūta* in these texts is one of the stock epithets of the man who has achieved liberation and therefore entered Nirvāna. The word as such does not occur in the classical Upanishads. We do, however, twice meet the phrase *brahma bhavati*, 'becomes Brahman', once in BU. 4. 4. 25 and once in MuU. 3. 2. 9, which, however, seems to be a later addition because it is in prose and does not easily fit in with the rest of this section which is entirely in verse. *Brahma-bhūta*, however, is a stock phrase in the Pāli canon and appears most frequently in the phrase *brahma-bhūtena attanā* (= Skt. *ātmanā*). The commonest phrase in which it occurs is: *nicchāto nibbuto sīti-bhūto sukha-paṭisaṁvedī brahma-bhūtena attanā*, 'without craving, appeased, cooled, experiencing joy, with his self become Brahman' (D. iii. 233: M. i. 341, 412, 413; ii. 159, etc.). It is used of the Buddha (Sn. 561: D. iii. 84: M. i. 111; iii. 195: S. iv. 94: A. v. 226, etc.) and of *arahats* who have attained enlightenment (A. ii. 206; S. iii. 83, etc.). In S. iv. 94–95 the Buddha is described as 'having become [all] eye, [all] wisdom, having become the Buddhist "Norm" (*dhamma*) itself, and having become Brahman'. As such he is the 'giver of immortality'. The Pāli *brahma-* in compounds also means merely 'excellent'.

The phrase *brahma-bhūta* seems to have been taken on in the Gītā in its Buddhist sense of entering a form of existence which is unconditioned by space, time, and causation, the very 'flavour' of Nirvāna. The phrase too is common in the MBh. in general and is equivalent to 'becoming immortal' (e.g. 5. 42. 5: 12. 231. 18). Whereas most men become *brahma-bhūta* (this being a synonym of liberation), Krishna is always *brahma-bhūta*

(13. 6817, 6875 (vulgate)) and was so born in his present incarnation (13. 6838 (vulgate)). Similarly at the beginning of each world-cycle all men are *brahma-bhūta* (3. 181. 12).

The Buddhist idea of the man who is *brahma-bhūta*, whose natural habitat is in the Buddhist Nirvāna, does not however fit in with what we have come to learn about Brahman in the Gītā itself. In 3. 15 it sprang from the Imperishable and itself originated action and sacrifice; and in 4. 24 it was identified with the latter two. 'Who sinks himself in this [sacrificial] act which is Brahman, to Brahman must he thereby go.' This is the primeval Brahman to which the eaters of the remains of the sacrifice also go (4. 31): it is the Brahman of action rather than the Brahman of eternal peace, though it is also the 'mouth' (4. 32) which joins the two; and even in 5. 6 and 5. 10 the sage well versed in spiritual *exercise*, who ascribes all action to Brahman, goes to Brahman. It is only in 5. 19 that we meet with a Brahman which is beyond the 'Brahman of sacrificial action', that Brahman which is 'ever the same', in which the liberated man stands stilled. This is no longer the Brahman of action but the 'Brahman which is Nirvāna too'—the groundless peace of eternity. This ambivalent nature of Brahman is not new in the Gītā. We already have it in *Iśā* Up. 9, 12 (p. 189) and more explicitly in ŚU. 5. 1:

> In the imperishable, infinite city (reading *pure*) of Brahman
> Two things there are—
> Wisdom and unwisdom, hidden, established there:
> Perishable is unwisdom, but wisdom is immortal:
> Who over wisdom and unwisdom rules, He is Another.

In Chapter V of the Gītā we are taken from the purely pantheistic view of Brahman as the very principle of the cosmic flux to the Buddhistic idea of a state that is utterly beyond flux.

25. *labhante brahma-nirvāṇam ṛṣayaḥ kṣīṇa-kalmaṣāḥ*
chinna-dvaidhā yat'ātmānaḥ sarva-bhūta-hite ratāḥ.

Nirvāna that is Brahman too win seers in whom [all] taint-of-imperfection is destroyed; their doubts dispelled, with self controlled, they take their pleasure in the weal of all contingent beings.

yat'ātmānaḥ, 'with self controlled': var. *jit'ātmānaḥ*, 'with self subdued'. This variant is fairly frequent.

'They take their pleasure in the weal . . .': repeated in 12. 4. Total detachment from the world is not incompatible with a general benevolence. This particular phrase probably originated in the Gītā. It gained immense popularity and is endlessly repeated in the didactic portions of the MBh. (for references see MBh., critical edition, ad loc.).

The emphasis on compassion and benevolence is new, since in the Upanishads we hear rather more about transcending good and evil (see 2. 50 n.), and this may be due to Buddhist influence with its emphasis on 'passionless compassion' (*mettā-(karuṇā-)ceto-vimutti*, D. 1. 251, etc.). Yet even in 3. 20 Arjuna has clearly been told to work for the welfare of the world.

26. *kāma-krodha-viyuktānāṁ yatīnāṁ yata-cetasām*
abhito brahma-nirvāṇaṁ vartate vidit'ātmanām.

Around these holy men whose thoughts are [fast] controlled, estranged from anger and desire, knowing [at last] the self, fares Nirvāna that is Brahman too.

-viyuktānāṁ, 'estranged': var. *vimuktānāṁ*, 'released'.

vidit'ātmanām, 'knowing the self': var. *vijit'ātmanām*, 'who have conquered self'.

abhito, 'around': Ś., 'on both sides, both when living and when dead'.

vartate, 'fares': R., 'lies in their hands (*hasta-sthaṁ*)'.

27. *sparśān kṛtvā bahir bāhyāṁś cakṣuś c'aiv'āntare bhruvoḥ,*
prāṇ'āpānau samau kṛtvā nās'ābhyantara-cāriṇau.

[All] contact with things outside he puts away, fixing his gaze between the eyebrows; inward and outward breaths he makes the same as they pass up and down the nostrils.

'Fixing his gaze between the eyebrows': according to MBh. 3. 178. 22 this is where the self is located.

28. *yat'endriya-mano-buddhir munir mokṣa-parāyaṇaḥ*
vigat'ecchā-bhaya-krodho yaḥ sadā, mukta eva saḥ.

With senses, mind, and soul restrained, the silent sage, on deliverance intent, who has forever banished fear, anger, and desire, is truly liberated.

yat'endriya-, 'with senses . . . restrained': var. *jit'endriya-*, 'who has conquered the senses'.

-krodho, 'anger': var. *-dveṣo*, 'hatred'.

The sense of this line seems to be that the sage 'intent on deliverance or liberation' is in fact already liberated once he has conquered the passions.

29. *bhoktāraṁ yajña-tapasāṁ sarva-loka-maheśvaram*
suhṛdaṁ sarva-bhūtānāṁ jñātvā māṁ, śāntim ṛcchati.

Knowing Me to be the proper object of sacrifice and mortification, great Lord of all the worlds, friend of all contingent beings, he reaches peace.

bhoktāraṁ, 'proper object [of sacrifice]': lit., 'he who enjoys or experiences'. This very abrupt introduction of the personal God as the only true recipient and experiencer of the sacrifice and religious practices in general is surprising, as it does not seem to fit in with the rest of the chapter which is otherwise quite coherent. Perhaps we should interpret the verse in connexion with 4. 24 where Brahman is described as the offering, the sacrificial ghee offered by Brahman in Brahman's fire. Brahman in fact is everything connected with the sacrifice *except* its recipient, and in this Krishna excels it, for, as He says in 9. 24: 'It is I who of all sacrifices am recipient and Lord.' Thus, after developing the idea of the twofold Brahman which is both operative and still, both temporal and eternal, He proposes Himself as being in this respect different from and superior to it—He is the proper object of all sacrifice, which must, of course, include self-sacrifice. To know Him as such brings the same peace as the realization of the 'Nirvāna that is Brahman too'.

'Friend of all contingent beings': this is also to anticipate, though God's love for man had already been hinted at in 4. 11: 'In whatsoever way [devoted] men approach Me, in that same way do I return their love.' Thus, it would seem, Krishna already claims to be everything that the impersonal Brahman is, but in addition He is the sole true object of sacrifice and the 'friend' of all contingent beings. For the first time He proposes Himself to our attention as something other than both the Brahman of action and the Brahman that is Nirvāna.

CHAPTER VI

This chapter is a further elaboration of the previous one. Theory and practice, renunciation and the active life are not mutually exclusive, they complement each other, and the first is the culmination of the second (1–4).

There are two selves in man. The higher one must be uplifted, the lower one suppressed: only so can true equanimity be achieved (5–9). With the goal thus briefly etched the practical means of attaining it are now outlined, both the physical and the psychic. Anticipating a little, Krishna now produces a new definition of the liberated state: this is 'that peace which has Nirvāna as its end and which subsists in Me' (15). Krishna, having thus for the first time asserted his total paramountcy, goes on to describe the various ways in which liberation may be experienced (20–32):

(i) it is to see the self in self, and this seems to be a 'prize beyond all others';
(ii) it is the 'unlinking of the link with suffering and pain';
(iii) it is the descent of the highest joy on to the man who has stilled his passions and become Brahman—the 'Nirvāna that is Brahman too' described in the last chapter, unbounded joy, and 'Brahman's [saving] touch';
(iv) by means of it a man 'sees the self in all beings abiding, all beings in the self'; and
(v) by analogy with himself he sees 'the same [Brahman] everywhere', 'sees [God] everywhere and sees the All in [God]'; but despite the apparent identity of self and God, God is not lost to the self, nor is the self lost to God.

Two immensely important points emerge from this: first the Buddhist 'Nirvāna which is [the Hindu] Brahman too' subsists in God, and secondly even the liberated self which, by transcending space, 'sees all beings in the self' is not thereby lost to or destroyed in God, nor is God lost to or obliterated in the self:

> Who standing firm on unity communes-in-love with Me as abiding in all beings, in whatever state he be, that athlete of the spirit abides in Me (31).

This is the climax of the chapter, and Arjuna is overawed both by the magnitude of the goal and the arduousness of the path that leads to it. He pleads the fickleness of his mind and thereby sees little hope for himself (33–34). Krishna replies that it is all a matter of self-control and passionlessness. Arjuna, however, is still not happy and asks what happens to the man who, despite his faith, has failed in the spiritual exercise called Yoga. Krishna comforts him with the promise of a happy life in heaven and rebirth in a spiritually advanced family. Then, as the fruits of his past actions wear away, he will ultimately 'tread the highest path'.

To rub in the new teaching outlined in this chapter—the teaching, that is, that both the Buddhist Nirvāna and the Brahman of the Upanishads, the two 'absolutes' of Indian religion, 'subsist in' Krishna, the personal and incarnate God, and are therefore ontologically dependent on Him—and to point the corollary of this teaching, namely, that even the man who has 'become Brahman' and who has experienced 'all beings in [him]self' and '[him]self in all beings' is not thereby lost to, that is, merged into or swallowed up in the Infinite even if the Infinite is objectified as a personal God, He ends up by exalting the Yogin described in this chapter above all others—the man of spiritual exercise, the real athlete of the spirit, over against the mere ascetic, the 'gnostic' 'man of wisdom', and the mere man of action, however detached he may be. Finally, he states categorically that 'of all [such] athletes of the spirit the man of faith who loves-and-honours Me, *his inmost self absorbed in Me*, is the most fully integrated' of them all.

The chapter is traditionally called the 'Yoga of Meditation'. It might more fittingly be called the 'Chapter of Brahman and Him who is beyond'.

The Unity of Renunciation and Spiritual Exercise

Śrī-bhagavān uvāca:

1. *anāśritaḥ karma-phalaṁ kāryaṁ karma karoti yaḥ,*
sa saṁnyāsī ca yogī ca, na niragnir na c'ākriyaḥ.

The Blessed Lord said:

The man who does the work that is his to do, yet covets not its fruits, he it is who at once renounces and yet works on, not the man who builds no sacrificial fire and does not work.

2. *yaṁ saṁnyāsam iti prāhur yogaṁ taṁ viddhi, Pāṇḍava;*
na hy asaṁnyasta-saṁkalpo yogī bhavati kaścana.

What men call renunciation is also {spiritual exercise / practice}: you must know this. For without renouncing [all set] purpose no one can {engage in spiritual exercise / act [in the manner explained in the preceding chapter]}.

-saṁkalpo, 'purpose'. So E., Rk., H.: D., 'Wünschen': S., 'désir'. Ś. glosses 'attachment to the fruits [of action]'. The word *saṁkalpa* oscillates in meaning between 'imagination', 'idea', purpose', and 'will'. Hence R. paraphrases, 'conceiving of self as being in material Nature which is other than self'. The Gītā knows nothing of 'commitment, involvement, tension, unconditional concern' or any of the other shibboleths of contemporary existentialism and neo-orthodox Protestantism. Even when it comes to speak of the love of God it is a love in which tension is utterly resolved.

3. *ārurukṣor muner yogaṁ karma kāraṇam ucyate;*
yog'ārūḍhasya tasy'aiva śamaḥ kāraṇam ucyate.

For the silent sage who would climb [the ladder of] spiritual exercise works are said to be the means; but for that same [sage] who has reached {the state of integration / [the goal of] spiritual exercise} they say quiescence is the means.

śamaḥ, 'quiescence': Ś., R., 'ceasing to act'.

4. *yadā hi n'endriy'ārtheṣu na karmasv anuṣajjate*
sarva-saṁkalpa-saṁnyāsī yog'ārūḍhas tad'ocyate.

For when a man knows no attachment to objects of sense or to the deeds [he does], when he has renounced all purpose, then has he reached {the state of integration / [the goal of] spiritual exercise}, or so they say.

The Two Selves in Man

5. *uddhared ātmanā'tmānaṁ, n'ātmānam avasādayet;*
ātm'aiva hy ātmano bandhur, ātm'aiva ripur ātmanaḥ.

Raise self by self, let not the self droop down; for self's friend is self indeed, so too is self self's enemy.

More precisely: 'Let a man by his { [spiritual] self [conjoined with soul (*buddhi*)] / own efforts } raise up his [carnal] self. Let him not allow the [carnal] self to sink down; for the [carnal] self is the friend of the [spiritual] self[-in-itself], so too is the [carnal] self the enemy of the [spiritual] self[-in-itself].' The 'carnal self' is the combination of soul (*buddhi*), mind, ego, and the senses, and the two selves correspond more or less exactly to what St. Paul calls 'spirit' and 'flesh'. The next stanza makes the author's meaning abundantly clear.

6. *bandhur ātmā'tmanas tasya yen'ātm'aiv'ātmanā jitaḥ;*
anātmanas tu śatrutve vartet'ātm'aiva śatruvat.

> Self is the friend to the self of him whose self is by the self subdued; but for the man bereft of self self will act as an enemy indeed.

Again more precisely: 'The [carnal] self is the friend of the [spiritual] self[-in-itself] of him whose [carnal] self is subdued by { the [spiritual] self [conjoined with the soul] / his own efforts }, but for the man bereft of [spiritual] self[-in-itself] the [carnal] self will act as an enemy indeed.' The 'friend' and the 'enemy' must be the carnal self since the true spiritual self does not itself act at all; this is the sphere of the constituents of Nature (3. 28) and of the senses (5. 8–9) or of the whole physico-psychic complex of body, mind, soul, and sense. So Ś., 'the complex of body (*kārya*) and senses'.

anātmanas, 'bereft of self': Ś., 'those who have not subdued themselves'. There seems no reason why this should not be taken literally. The 'carnal' self which includes what we would call 'soul', which is conditioned by its works in this and previous lives, and which transmigrates, can be 'lost' or 'destroyed' (2. 63) by the combined assaults of desire, anger, and greed (16. 21)—an eternal alienation from the centre of its being and therefore from God (16. 20). Such a person is literally *anātman*, 'bereft of self'. In Christian terms he is damned. 'Hell', as the modern American Trappist monk, Thomas Merton, puts it in what must be one of the most pregnant footnotes of all time—' "Hell" can be described as a perpetual alienation from our true being, our true self, which is in God' (*New Seeds of Contemplation*, London, Burns and Oates, 1962, p. 6).

The Spiritual Self

7. *jit'ātmanaḥ praśāntasya param'ātmā samāhitaḥ*
śīt'oṣṇa-sukha-duḥkheṣu tathā mān'āpamānayoḥ.

The higher self of the self-subdued, quietened, is rapt in enstasy,—in cold as in heat, in pleasure as in pain, likewise in honour and disgrace.

param'ātmā samāhitaḥ, 'the highest self . . . rapt in enstasy' or, more conventionally, 'concentrated'. Ś., 'the supreme Self is present without any mediation (*sākṣāt*) as self'. This is, however, no more than a paraphrase. R., 'here *param'ātmā* means the individual self . . . : or the sentence could be read as *ātmā paraṁ samāhitaḥ*, "the self is supremely concentrated"'. H. (who also separates *param* from *ātmā*) translates 'remains absorbed in contemplation of the Highest': S., 'parfaitement recueilli'. Rk. (who here takes up an extreme monist position) translates, 'his Supreme Self abides ever concentrate'. E. does much the same while avoiding capital letters. D. (improbably), 'in dem hat das höchste Selbst Wohnung genommen'.

It is true that *param'ātmā* would normally mean the 'highest Self', that is God *qua* timeless, eternal Brahman, as it certainly does in 13. 22 where it is equated with the 'highest Lord', and in 15. 17 where it is equated with the 'highest Person or Spirit'. The only other place it occurs in the Gītā is 13. 31 where it might mean either self-in-itself or God-in Himself, assuming that this distinction is valid throughout the Gītā and not only in the greater part of it in which it is too obvious to be swept under the carpet. Moreover, we have seen that both *prabhu* and *vibhu*, words normally applied to God, are in all probability used of the individual self in 5. 14–15 and that the word *īśvara*, 'Lord'—God's title *par excellence*—is certainly used of the individual self in 15. 8. Moreover, in this passage at least, following immediately upon one of those rare passages in Hindu scripture where two selves are clearly distinguished, it seems both legitimate and natural to take *param'ātmā* to mean the individual self-in-itself.

8. *jñāna-vijñāna-tṛpt'ātmā kūṭa-stho vijit'endriyaḥ*
yukta ity ucyate yogī sama-loṣṭ'āśma-kāñcanaḥ.

With self content in wisdom learnt from holy books and wisdom learnt from life, with sense subdued, sublime, aloof, [this] {man of integration / man of spiritual exercise / athlete of the spirit} [stands]: 'Integrated', so is he called; the same to him are clods of earth, stones, gold.

jñana-vijñāna-, 'wisdom learnt from holy books and wisdom learnt from life': so Ś. whom I follow here. R. interprets *jñāna* as meaning immediate knowledge of self and *vijñāna* as meaning knowledge of the self as being different in kind from material Nature.

kūṭa-stho, 'sublime, aloof': the word means literally 'standing on a peak'. Ś. glosses 'unshakeable': R. merely paraphrases. In 12. 3 and 15. 16 it is used of the Imperishable Brahman *qua* static, immovable, and therefore timeless principle. Here, however, it refers to the total detachment of the self from what is other than self. The simile is used in MBh. 12. 242. 16–18 where the self's crossing of the fearful river of *saṁsāra*, the world of time, is described:

> Once you have crossed this, you will be freed (liberated) from every side, clean, knowing [your] self as pure; firmly relying on the highest part of your soul (*uttamā buddhi*) you will become Brahman, for you will have transcended all defilements, your self serene, immaculate. As one standing on a mountain (*parvata-stha*) survey those beings still living in the plains (*bhūmi*).

Similarly ibid. 12. 17. 19: 'As a man standing on a rock (*adri*) might look on men living in the plains (*jagatī*), so does he who has scaled the battlements of wisdom [look down] on folk of little wit who mourn for men who do not need their mourning.' Cf. ibid. 12. 172. 6: 'Among men preoccupied with their affairs involving duty, pleasure, and profit who are [all the time] being carried off by the flood [of time], you will stand out as one standing on a peak (*kūṭa-stha*).'

yukta . . . yogī: *yukta* has now firmly settled down in the meaning 'integrated' (*samāhita* according to Ś.), and *yoga* is both the 'spiritual exercise' by which this state is attained and the state of 'integration' to which that spiritual exercise leads. Hence, since a *yogin* is one possessed of *yoga* in every sense of that protean word, I have now translated him as 'athlete of the spirit'.

sama-, 'the same to him are . . .': because they are all Brahman which is by definition 'the same' (5. 19) and Yoga itself is *samatva*, 'sameness-and-indifference'. Cf. 5. 18: '[These] wise ones see the selfsame thing in a Brāhman wise and courteous as in a cow or an elephant, nay, as in a dog or outcaste.'

9. *suhṛn-mitr'āry-udāsīna-madhyastha-dveṣya-bandhuṣu*
sādhuṣv api ca pāpeṣu sama-buddhir viśiṣyate.

Outstanding is he whose soul views in the selfsame way friends, comrades, enemies, those indifferent, neutrals, men who are hateful and those who are his kin,—the good and the evil too.

sama-buddhir: var. *sama-dṛṣṭir*, 'seeing as the same'.

viśiṣyate, 'outstanding is': var. *vimucyate*, 'liberated is'.

Some MSS. (most appropriately) repeat 5. 19 here:

> While yet in this world they have overcome [the process of] emanation [and decay], for their minds are stilled in that-which-is-ever-the-same: for devoid of imperfection and ever-the-same is Brahman: therefore in Brahman [stilled] they stand.

Spiritual Exercise and its Physical Conditions

10. *yogī yuñjīta satatam ātmānaṁ rahasi sthitaḥ*
ekākī yata-citt'ātmā nirāśīr aparigrahaḥ.

Let the athlete of the spirit ever integrate [him]self standing in a place apart, alone, his thoughts and self restrained, devoid of [earthly] hope, possessing nothing.

ātmānaṁ, '[him]self': Ś., as is usual in such contexts, 'mind'.

yata-citt'ātmā, 'his thoughts and self restrained': var. *jita-citt'ātmā*, 'his thoughts and self subdued'. With unusual perversity Ś. here glosses *ātman* as 'body' and *citta* as 'mind'.

11. *śucau deśe pratiṣṭhāpya sthiram āsanam ātmanaḥ*
n'ātyucchritaṁ n'ātinīcaṁ cail'ājina-kuś'ottaram.

Let him set up for [him]self a steady seat in a clean place, neither too high nor yet too low, bestrewn with cloth or hide or grass.

This and the following stanzas are closely parallel to ŚU. 2. 8–10.

12. *tatr'aikāgraṁ manaḥ kṛtvā yata-citt'endriya-kriyaḥ*
upaviśy'āsane yuñjyād yogam ātma-viśuddhaye.

There let him sit and make his mind a single point, let him restrain the operations of his thought and senses and {practise integration / concentrate on spiritual exercise} to purify the self.

ekāgraṁ manaḥ kṛtvā, 'make his mind a single point': 'single-pointedness' of mind is mentioned in *Yoga-sūtras* 2. 41 as being one of the fruits of 'possessing nothing' (cf. verse 10 here), along with 'purity of soul (*sattva*)', joyousness, conquest of sense, and a capacity to 'see' the self. Here (6. 14) it is Krishna who is the object of this one-pointed concentration. This stanza is closely parallel to 5. 11.

yata-: var. *jita-*.

yuñjyād yogam, 'practise integration', etc.: R., 'practise contemplation of the self'. For him the essence of the Yogic experience is the 'vision' of the self.

13. *samaṁ kāya-śiro-grīvaṁ dhārayann acalaṁ sthiraḥ*
saṁprekṣya nāsik'āgraṁ svaṁ diśaś c'ānavalokayan.

[Remaining] still, let him keep body, head, and neck in a straight line, unmoving; let him fix his eye on the tip of his nose, not looking round about him.

By holding himself perfectly still he imitates the total stillness of Brahman: for 'devoid of imperfection and ever-the-same is Brahman: therefore in Brahman [stilled] they stand. . . . Steadfast-and-still his soul, [all] unconfused, he will know Brahman, in Brahman [stilled] he'll stand' (5. 19–20).

By fixing his gaze on the tip of his nose or between the eyebrows (5. 27) the Yogin matches one-pointedness of mind with one-pointedness of vision. In the next stanza we are told that Krishna is the single object of his meditation (cf. 2. 61: 4. 10). This is the great difference between Chapters V and VI. In V there is no reference to the personal God until the very last stanza: in VI, on the other hand, this God obtrudes Himself ever more insistently until Nirvāna itself is shown to have value only in so far as it subsists in Him (6. 15).

14. *praśānt'ātmā vigata-bhīr brahmacāri-vrate sthitaḥ,*
manaḥ saṁyamya mac-citto yukta āsīta mat-paraḥ.

[There] let him sit, [his] self all stilled, his fear all gone, firm in his vow of chastity, his mind controlled, his thoughts on Me, integrated, [yet] intent on Me.

15. *yuñjann evaṁ sadā'tmānaṁ yogī niyata-mānasaḥ*
śāntiṁ nirvāṇa-paramāṁ mat-saṁsthām adhigacchati.

Thus let the athlete of the spirit be constant in integrating [him]self, his mind restrained; then will he approach that peace which has Nirvāna as its end and which subsists in Me.

'His mind restrained': the mind (*manas*) is naturally orientated towards the senses which are liable to sweep it away (2. 60, 67), while the soul (*buddhi*) is by nature stable (being the locus of the constituent of Nature called 'Goodness', cf. 2. 41, 45) and as such can alone among the faculties comprehend and 'see' the self (6. 20–21).

'Peace which has Nirvāna as its end': peace is the reward of the true Buddhist who has passed beyond all thought of 'I' and 'mine' (2. 71); it is the reward of that 'wisdom' which apprehends timeless Reality (4. 39), finally, it is the reward of the 'integrated' man who has renounced all purposive action (5. 12). It is not the final goal but only a stage on the way 'which has Nirvāna as its end'; and Nirvāna (that is Brahman too), we are now told, itself subsists in the personal God.

16. *n'ātyaśnatas tu yogo 'sti na c'aikāntam anaśnataḥ*
na c'āti-svapna-śīlasya jāgrato n'aiva c'ārjuna.

But [this] {way of integration / spiritual exercise} is not for him who eats too much, nor yet for him who does not eat at all, nor for him who is all too prone to sleep, nor yet for him who [always] stays awake.

17. *yukt'āhāra-vihārasya yukta-ceṣṭasya karmasu*
yukta-svapn'āvabodhasya yogo bhavati duḥkha-hā.

[Rather] is [this] {way of integration / spiritual exercise} for him who knows-the-mean in food and recreation, who knows-the-mean in his deeds and gestures, who knows-the-mean in sleeping as in waking; [this] {practice-of-the-mean / spiritual exercise} [it is] that slaughters pain.

yukta-, 'who-knows-the-mean': another shift of emphasis in this amazing word. The 'integrated' man is also the man who knows the mean between extremes because he is *sama-*, remains 'the same-and-indifferent' between the various pairs of opposites—pleasure and pain, honour and disgrace, and the rest. Ś. glosses 'moderate', R., 'measured'.

18. *yadā viniyataṁ cittam ātmany ev'āvatiṣṭhate*
niḥspṛhaḥ sarva-kāmebhyo, yukta ity ucyate tadā.

When thought, held well in check, is stilled in self alone, then is a man from longing freed though all desires assail him: then do men call him 'integrated'.

ātmany: Ś., 'in his own self'.

avatiṣṭhate, 'is stilled': so Ś., 'he gains stillness or stability (*sthiti*)': R. 'remains motionless'.

19. *yathā dīpo nivāta-stho n'eṅgate, s'opamā smṛtā*
yogino yata-cittasya yuñjato yogam ātmanaḥ.

As a lamp might stand in a windless place, unflickering,—this likeness has been heard of such {men of integration / athletes of the spirit} who control their thought and practise integration of the self.

The simile of the lamp reappears in MBh. 12. 46. 6; 240. 15; 304. 19.

yata-, 'control': var. *jita-*, 'subdue'.

yuñjato yogam ātmanaḥ, 'practise integration of the self': we have had the same idea in 6. 10, 12, and 15. One both practises integration and is integrated by that very practice (5. 6–7): both result in the purification of the self (5. 7: 6. 12) and lead to Nirvāna (6. 15) or to Brahman (5. 6) which is the same thing. Integration and purification of the self are really the same thing: integration means the assimilation of the whole physico-psychic complex to the changeless peace, the sameness-and-indifference, of the self, while purification means the removal from the self of all the tendencies naturally inherent in the faculties—desire and anger, love and hate, and all the other pairs of opposites.

The Goal of Spiritual Exercise

20. *yatr'oparamate cittaṁ niruddhaṁ yoga-sevayā,*
yatra c'aiv'ātmanā'tmānaṁ paśyann ātmani tuṣyati,

When thought by {the practice of integration / spiritual exercise} is checked and comes to rest, and when of [one]self one sees the self in self and finds content therein,

'When of [one]self one sees the self in self and finds content therein': this may either mean seeing the individual self-in-itself in the now integrated human personality, or seeing the supreme Self (God *qua* timeless Brahman) in the individual self. The former seems preferable because the second phrase, 'finds content therein', obviously refers back to 3. 17: 'Nay, let a man take pleasure in self alone, in self his satisfaction find, in self alone content: [for then] there is naught he needs to do.'

This accords with 15. 7–11 where it is said that 'a minute part of [God], eternal [still], becomes a living [self]', and then proceeds to transmigrate. 'Fools do not perceive him, but whoso possesses wisdom's eye sees him [indeed]' (15. 10). On the other hand, our passage must be based on BU. 4. 4. 23, where we read:

> 'Hence the man who thus knows will be at peace, tamed, quietly contented, long-suffering, recollected, for he will see the Self in [him]self: he will see all things as the Self.'

So too in *Iśā* 6 we have:

> Those who see all beings in the Self,
> And the Self in all beings
> Will never shrink from It.

Here the 'Self' is the 'great unborn Self' who 'lies in the space within the heart, the Ruler of all, the Lord of all, the King of all' (BU. 4. 4. 22), in other words, God. The Gītā, however, though here it no doubt bases itself on this passage, elsewhere distinguishes clearly between the individual self and God. This comes out clearly in 6. 29–30 where it is said that the liberated self seen in all things is not lost to God who is in all things too.

Further, the whole passage from here to verse 30 recalls ŚU. 2. 14–15 which distinguishes three phases in the process of liberation—(i) seeing self as it really is and thereby becoming one, (ii) seeing Brahman as it really is, and, finally, (iii) knowing God who is 'beyond all essences as they really are'. We shall discuss this more fully at 6. 30.

tuṣyati, 'finds content': var. *tiṣṭhati*, 'stands'.

21\. *sukham ātyantikaṁ yat tad buddhi-grāhyam atīndriyam*
vetti yatra, na c'aiv'āyaṁ sthitaś calati tattvataḥ,

That is the utmost joy which transcends [all things of] sense and which soul [alone] can grasp. When he knows this and [knowing it] stands still, moving not an inch from the reality [he sees],

buddhi-grāhyam, 'which soul alone can grasp': Ś. glosses, 'in so far as it disregards the senses'. R., '*buddhi* (consciousness) of self.'

atīndriyam, 'which transcends [all things of] sense': Ś., 'since it is not produced by objects of sense'. *Buddhi*, the 'soul', alone whose nature is both pure intellect and unitary will (2. 41) can *see* the self. This idea seems to derive from KaU. 3. 12:

> This is the self, deep-hidden in all beings,
> [The self that] shines not forth—
> Yet it *can* be seen by men who see things subtle,
> By the subtle soul (*buddhi*), [man's] noblest [part].

calati, 'moving': var. *cyavati*, 'falling'.

22\. *yaṁ labdhvā c'āparaṁ lābhaṁ manyate n'ādhikaṁ tataḥ*
yasmin sthito na duḥkhena guruṇā 'pi vicālyate.

He wins a prize beyond all others,—or so he thinks. Therein he [firmly] stands, unmoved by any suffering, however grievous it may be.

labdhvā, 'wins': var. *dṛṣṭvā*, 'sees'.

'Or so he thinks': surely this is significant. For the monist who identifies the human self completely with the ground of the universe because (in his opinion) the One alone IS and all diversity is imaginary—for such a monist the experience of unfractionable oneness can only mean to experience the One which alone IS. Obviously if this is so, one will have reached ultimate reality, and it would be quite impossible to pass beyond the absolutely Absolute. This, however, is not the view of the Gītā. Unity of Being in the Gītā as in the majority of the Upanishads is a unity in diversity, not an absolute One that absolutely excludes all diversity and multiplicity. In the theophany of Chapter XI (verse 13) Arjuna *sees* this with the divine eye Krishna has bestowed on him:

> Then did the son of Pāndu see the whole [wide] universe in One converged, there in the body of the God of gods, yet divided out in multiplicity.

Similarly in 13. 30 after the vision may have somewhat faded in his memory, Krishna reminds him once again that reality is one (the 'same') manifesting itself in a multitude of forms: 'When once a man can see [all] the diversity of contingent beings as abiding in One [alone] and their radiation out of It, then to Brahman he attains.' What is meant by Brahman in this passage we shall return to in our note *ad loc.*

23. *taṁ vidyād duḥkha-saṁyoga-viyogaṁ yoga-saṁjñitam;*
sa niścayena yoktavyo yogo 'nirviṇṇa-cetasā.

This he should know is what is meant by 'spiritual exercise',—the unlinking of the link with suffering-and-pain. This is the {act-of-integration / spiritual exercise} that must be brought about with [firm] resolve and mind all undismayed.

'The unlinking of the link with suffering-and-pain': this new definition of *yoga* is purely Buddhistic. From the standpoint of the timeless and deathless, that is, Nirvāna, all phenomenal existence has the three marks of transience, suffering, and insubstantiality (i.e. it has no 'self'). The realm of becoming is the realm of Māra (the Devil who is at the same time Death) (S. iv. 128) and the senses themselves *are* Māra (ibid. 39, 92) but it is the contact, the linking of sense to object of sense that is really the cause of bondage (ibid. 162–3). Once the senses are withdrawn from their objects and the contemplative intellect is set free (*ceto-vimutti*), that is Nirvāna (S. ii. 172; iii. 45; iv. 9, etc.). In our present passage *duḥkha* is surely used in the technical Buddhist sense: it is a synonym for 'transient' (*anicca*). This vision of the self, equated with Nirvāna is, the Gītā implies, the highest joy that a Buddhist can imagine; for the Buddhists themselves, though it is still maintained by many that they acknowledged nothing equivalent to the Hindu 'self', continually speak of 'self' as an 'island' or 'refuge', and so on (Sn. 514: D. ii. 100; iii. 58, etc.) just as they speak of the Buddhist *dhamma* in the same terms (ibid.). The Gītā, however, goes on to describe stages in liberated existence beyond this.

[*a*]*nirvinna-cetasā*, 'with mind all undismayed': var. *nirviṇṇa-cetasā*, 'with mind dismayed', i.e. at all that is transient. In a Buddhist context this makes excellent sense, 'dismay' or 'disgust' at the phenomenal world being a corollary of Nirvāna.

24. *saṁkalpa-prabhavān kāmāṁs tyaktvā sarvān aśeṣataḥ,*
manas' aiv' endriya-grāmaṁ viniyamya samantataḥ,

Let him renounce all desires whose origin lies in the will,—all of them without remainder; let him restrain in every way by mind alone the senses' busy throng.

saṁkalpa-, 'will': for the different meanings of *saṁkalpa* see 6. 2 n.

25. *śanaiḥ śanair uparamed, buddhyā dhṛti-gṛhītayā,*
ātma-saṁsthaṁ manaḥ kṛtvā, na kiṁcid api cintayet.

By soul held fast in steadfastness he must make the mind [too] subsist in the self; then little by little will he come to rest; he must think of nothing at all.

buddhyā dhṛti-gṛhītayā, 'by soul held fast in steadfastness': I prefer to take this with the following *ātma-saṁsthaṁ manaḥ kṛtvā*, 'making the mind subsist in self' thereby giving the full instrumental sense to *buddhyā*. E. takes it to mean 'little by little let him come to rest thru the consciousness, held with firmness; keeping the thought-organ fixed in the self, he should think of nothing at all'. If, however, we take *buddhyā* etc. with what follows we get a much more satisfactory sense, for these two stanzas will now describe the exact process of integration. Mind must control sense, and the soul must in its turn absorb mind—and the senses with it—into the self. This is precisely what the simile of the tortoise illustrated in 2. 58: the faculties of sense and the mind are all withdrawn into the self by the '*yoga* of *buddhi*', the process of integration of the whole personality which the soul initiates and controls. This in no way conflicts with the new definition of *yoga* as 'the unlinking of the link with suffering-and-pain', for what is happening is the absorption of the total personality into its immortal and timeless centre—the self. It is, if you like, the 'sacrifice' of the human personality as it exists and had developed in time to the individual self which, in the case of the individual, is the 'mouth of Brahman' alluded to in 4. 32.

26. *yato yato niścarati manaś cañcalam asthiram,*
tatas tato niyamy'aitad ātmany eva vaśaṁ nayet.

Wherever the fickle mind unsteady roves around, from thence [the soul] will bring it back and subject it to the self.

vaśaṁ, 'subjection': var. *śamaṁ*, 'peace'.

27. *praśānta-manasaṁ hy enaṁ yoginaṁ sukham uttamam*
upaiti śānta-rajasaṁ brahma-bhūtam akalmaṣam.

For upon this athlete of the spirit whose mind is stilled the highest joy descends: [all] passion laid to rest, free from [all] stain, Brahman he becomes.

'Highest joy': cf. 5. 21, 'in [him]self he finds his joy, [his] self in Brahman integrated by spiritual exercise, he finds unfailing joy'. Cf. also 6. 21 and the following stanza.

upaiti, 'descends': lit. 'approaches'. Var. *abhyeti*: cf. 5. 26 *abhito . . . vartate*, 'fares around'.

brahma-bhūtam, 'Brahman he becomes': cf. 5. 24 n. where we pointed out that the term *brahma-bhūta* is in all probability of Buddhist origin: it means the final transcendence of phenomenal existence, the cutting off of all contacts with the phenomenal world. Here everything is the 'same' and there seems no possibility of differentiation, for differentiation comes from material Nature, not from spirit.

28. *yuñjann evaṁ sadā'tmānaṁ yogī vigata-kalmaṣaḥ*
sukhena brahma-saṁsparśam atyantaṁ sukham aśnute.

[And] thus [all] flaws transcending, the athlete of the spirit, constant in integrating [him]self, with ease attains unbounded joy, Brahman's [saving] touch.

'Constant in integrating self': the leitmotiv of this whole chapter (cf. 6. 10, 12, 15, 19).

yogī vigata-kalmaṣaḥ, 'the Yogin, [all] flaws transcending': var. *yogī niyata-mānasaḥ*, 'the Yogin with mind controlled': *mad-bhaktau n'ānya-mānasaḥ*, '[a man] with mind [devoted] to nothing except love-and-devotion to Me'.

-saṁsparśam, 'touch, contact': var. *-saṁyogam*, 'union'.

sukham aśnute, 'attains joy': var. *adhigacchati*: 'draws near to'.

How is it, one may ask, that the fully integrated self which has already 'become Brahman' can also attain to 'Brahman's [saving] touch', or, according to the variant, to 'union with Brahman'? The answer would seem to be that this process of integration which presses and concentrates all that can be 'saved' in the human personality into its timeless centre, the self, described in the Upanishads as 'more minute than the minute' (KaU. 2. 20: ŚU. 3. 20: MaiU. 6. 20: MuU. 2. 2. 2: cf. below 8. 9), causes this same personality, now liberated and free from all the bonds of earthly life, to take part in, to make 'contact' with everything else that shares this quite different mode of being: this is 'Brahman's [saving] touch' which brings unbounded, infinite joy. It is a 'touch' of which the Buddhists know nothing, yet the most real of all the 'unions of opposites' —that of the point without magnitude which is the human self and of the utterly unmeasured and unmeasurable, the inconceivably great—the two immensities of which Pascal spoke and over against which finite man seemed to make no sense. By the maximum concentration of all that is within us into the infinitely small—the timeless self which is 'but a part of a hundredth part of the tip of a hair divided a hundred times' one finds that this 'nothing' is nevertheless 'conformed to infinity' (ŚU. 5. 9). It might almost be said that when this grinding process of integration, this total introversion, reaches its goal, there is an explosion and the self bursts asunder and finds itself utterly free through Brahman's saving touch. The interconnexion and interpenetration of all things that is now revealed was not at all what the classical Sāṁkhya had conceived of: it had, however, been beautifully adumbrated in the passage of the *Chāndogya* Upanishad we quoted at 5. 7 and in the even better-known passage from the same Upanishad, 3. 14:

This whole universe is Brahman. . . . He who consists of mind, whose body is the breath of life, whose form is light, whose idea is the real, whose self is space, through whom are all works, all desires, all scents, all tastes, who encompasses all this universe, who does not speak and has no care—he is my Self within the heart, smaller than a grain of rice or a barley-corn, or a mustard-seed, or a grain of millet, or the kernel of a grain of millet; this is my Self within my heart, greater than the earth, greater than the atmosphere, greater than the sky, greater than all these worlds.

All works, all desires, all scents, all tastes belong to it: it encompasses all this universe, does not speak and has no care. This my Self within the heart is that Brahman. When I depart from hence I shall merge into it. He who believes this will never doubt.

In the following verse the Gītā describes how its 'athlete of the spirit' *sees* and knows that this is so.

29. *sarva-bhūta-stham ātmānaṁ sarva-bhūtāni c'ātmani*
īkṣate yoga-yukt'ātmā sarvàtra sama-darśanaḥ.

With self integrated by { spiritual exercise / the unlinking of the link with the transient }
[now] he sees the self in all beings standing, all beings in the self: the same in everything he sees.

'He sees the self in all beings standing, all beings in the self': Are we still talking of the individual self-in-itself or of the supreme Self who is God, the 'highest Person in this body' of whom the Gītā is later to speak? (13. 22). Or is no difference now made between the two? If we are to grant even a minimum of consistency to the Gītā, it would seem that we cannot separate the 'self' which has been integrated with so much self-sacrifice from the omnipresent self mentioned in this passage. How, then, are we to interpret it? The stages enumerated in this chapter have been as follows:

(i) 'When thought by spiritual exercise is checked and comes to rest, and when of [one]self one sees the self in self and finds content therein, that is the utmost joy which transcends [all things of] sense and which soul [alone] can grasp. When he knows this and [knowing it] stands still, moving not an inch from the reality [he sees], he wins a prize beyond all others—or so he thinks. Therein he [firmly] stands' (6. 20–22). This is the 'fixed, still state of Brahman', the 'Nirvāna that is Brahman too' (2. 72)—a state of complete interiority and introversion, in which 'his joy [is] within, his bliss within, his light within' (5. 24) and in which he 'becomes Brahman'. This is the Buddhist Nirvāna, and the 'highest Brahman' of the Upanishads is identified with it. It is the *ambiance*, the proper atmosphere, in which liberated beings naturally dwell. In itself it is static and still because it is eternal and beyond time, and since this is so it necessarily means the 'unlinking of the link with suffering-and-pain', because 'suffering and pain', according to the Buddhists, is identified with the stuff of the phenomenal world which, being transient and void of substance, is therefore painful.

(ii) Secondly, the athlete of the spirit 'constant in integrating [him]self, with ease attains unbounded joy, Brahman's [saving] touch' (6. 28); or again the very same person, 'constant in integrating [him]self (the very same words are used) . . . will approach that peace which has Nirvāna as its end and which subsists in Me' (6. 15). In both these passages there is a new element: the man who is fully integrated and made one becomes aware of something that is other than himself—in the one case the 'touch' or 'contact' with Brahman, in the other a Person who stands behind and supports the timeless peace of Nirvāna.

(iii) This 'touch' dissolves the total personality now 'oned' in the 'more minute than the minute' and liberates it in the 'greater than the great'. This approach to Brahman (5. 6) as an external reality which is at the same time an entry into contact with it, is 'easy' so long as one is already integrated (5. 6 : 6. 28), and the result is that one 'sees' [one]self, because Brahman is essentially the 'same' eternal Being manifest in all things (5. 19), as having 'become the [very] self of every being' (5. 7). To make contact with Brahman means to resume contact with everything: detachment from outside contacts (*sparśa*) (5. 21) has been replaced by contact (*saṁsparśa*) with the omnipresent Brahman and through Brahman with all things—but in a new dimension and a new light. Hence the athlete of the spirit 'sees the self in all beings standing, all beings in the self: the same [Brahman] in everything he sees'. By detaching himself from all things he becomes Brahman, he sees 'self in self', he sees himself solely and simply as immortal, eternal, static, beyond time, One: but 'contact' with Brahman as other than himself transforms the vision from one of completely static en-stasy into one of all-comprehending ec-stasy: the cosmos flows into him, and he flows into the cosmos: the unity remains, but there is boundless diversity too.

This passage seems to be based on *Īśā* Up. 6–7 which we shall have to refer to again in our note on 6. 31. This is what it says:

> Those who see all beings in the self,
> And the self in all beings
> Will never shrink from it.
>
> When once one understands that in oneself
> The self's become all beings,
> When once one's seen the unity,
> What room is there for sorrow? What room for perplexity?

Of interest in this context is MBh. 3. 202. 13–14:

> Whoso possesses both the higher and the lower knowledge sees self as extended throughout the world and the world [as abiding] in the self: if attached, he sees all contingent beings [as objects]; but the man who has become Brahman, though he never stops seeing all contingent beings in all their [manifold] conditions, suffers nothing untoward through this contact [with them].

In other words the man who has this 'pan-en-henic' vision of all things in One and One in all, can nevertheless lead a perfectly normal life, untroubled and free.

sama-darśanaḥ, 'the same . . . he sees': that is, Brahman (5. 19). R., 'he sees the same in selves everywhere which, separated though they be thanks to material Nature, nevertheless have only one form—the form of wisdom'. Ś. prefers not to comment.

30. *yo māṁ paśyati sarvatra sarvaṁ ca mayi paśyati,*
tasy' āhaṁ na praṇaśyāmi, sa ca me na praṇaśyati

Who sees Me everywhere, who sees the All in Me, for him I am not lost, nor is he lost to Me.

The first hemistich would seem to mean that Krishna and the integrated self who has 'become Brahman' are identical, but this is flatly contradicted by the second line, for if they *were* identical, then how could Krishna go on to say, 'For him I am not lost, nor is he lost to Me'? Clearly, in this passage at least, 'to become the [very] self of every being' (5. 7) does not mean the loss of a personal relationship with God, and therefore probably with other liberated beings as well. This is in line with at least one type of Upanishadic thought typified in the dialogue between Indra and Prajāpati in ChU. 8. The relevant passage is 8. 12. 1–3:

Bountiful One! For sure this body is mortal, held in the grip of death. Yet it is the dwelling-place of the immortal, incorporeal self. [And this self,] while still in the body, is held in the grip of pleasure and pain; and so long as it remains in the body there is no means of ridding it of pleasure and pain. But once it is freed from the body, pleasure and pain cannot [so much as] touch it.

The wind has no body. Clouds, thunder, and lightning—these too have no body. So, just as these arise from [the broad expanse of] space up there and plunge into the highest light, revealing themselves each in its own form, so too does this deep serenity arise out of this body and plunge into the highest light, revealing itself in its own form. Such a one is a superman (*uttara puruṣa*); and there he roves around, laughing, playing, taking his pleasure with women, chariots, or friends and remembering no more that excrescence [which was] his body.

So too in the Gītā even in the state of liberation which transcends matter and all that depends on it, persons continue to exist and the relationship between them is not lost. The importance of this stanza can scarcely be exaggerated. But here again this is no clear-cut case of *either* absorption into the Absolute and a consequent identification of the individual self with the cosmic Self *or* a continuing relationship even in the state of liberation of the self and the Person who has already declared Himself to be the ground in which Nirvāna itself subsists (6. 15). Both are in a sense true, but at this stage it is the self's existence as Brahman and its consciousness of having 'become the [very] self of every contingent being' through Brahman, that is felt to be the overriding reality. That this should be true of Krishna too not only as God but also as a 'self' is, then, not at all difficult to understand. What, however, given these premisses, *is* difficult to understand is that in this mode of existence in which all personal distinctions seem to melt away and in which therefore there can be no relationship of one person to another, God yet remains distinct. Hence Krishna's categorical assurance: 'For him I am not lost, nor is he lost to Me.'

This, as Ś. himself points out, means that neither God 'disappears' from the sight of the integrated self nor does the integrated self disappear from the sight of God 'because He and I are one Self and one's self is always dear to [one]self'. But if that is so, how can one speak of 'vision' which implies duality? R. comments: 'He sees that all self-stuff as it is in itself (*svarūpeṇa*) and after it has shaken off good and evil, is the same in Me', that is, 'untrammelled wisdom' (on 6. 31). This seems to me to miss the point: 'all beings' are not obliterated in God, nor is God obliterated in 'the All', hence neither is 'lost' or 'destroyed'. This is what the Gītā says, and it is the great divide between the 'pantheistic' and 'theistic' portions of the poem.

Liberation is no longer the 'isolation' of the classical Sāṁkhya-Yoga: rather it is the end of what Christian mystics call the *via purgativa*, the way of the *viśuddh'ātmā*, the 'purified self' (5. 7: cf. 5. 11: 6. 12). It is the beginning of the personal encounter of the integrated and liberated self with God.

31. *sarva-bhūta-sthitaṁ yo māṁ bhajaty ekatvam āsthitaḥ*
sarvathā vartamāno 'pi sa yogī mayi vartate.

Who standing firm on unity {participates in / communes-in-love with / belongs to} Me as abiding in all beings, in whatever state he be, that {integrated man / athlete of the spirit} abides in Me.

'Standing firm on unity': the 'unity' or 'oneness' Krishna is referring to must surely be both the oneness of all beings in the self and of all beings in Himself, that is, in God. Because the point of reference of *any* experience must be oneself, this integral vision of reality must first be seen with reference to oneself, only in the second place with reference to God (cf. 4. 35). Knowledge of the true self-in-itself precedes knowledge of God: as the Muslim tradition puts it: 'Who knows himself, knows his Lord.' This self, however, is now seen not merely as the 'fixed, still state of Brahman' (2. 72) which precludes all relationship and all interpenetration, but as inextricably mingled with all things. Brahman—what Rāmānuja calls 'self-stuff'—is not only at rest but also perpetually in movement, not only static but also dynamic. As the *Iśā* Upanishad (4, 5) puts it:

Unmoving—One—swifter than thought—
The gods could not seize hold of it as it sped before [them]:
Standing, it overtakes [all] others as they run;
In it the wind incites activity.

It moves. It moves not.
It is far, yet it is near:
It is within this whole universe,
And yet it is without it.

And then switching from the unnamed neuter to the masculine (universal) Self which is here conterminous with it, the Upanishad goes on to say:

Those who see all beings in the Self,
And the Self in all beings
Will never shrink from It.

When once one understands that in oneself
The Self's become all beings,
Whcn oncc onc's seen the unity,
What room is there for sorrow? What room for perplexity?

The first of these two stanzas is quite clearly responsible for BhG. 6. 29; equally the second is responsible for 5. 7c ('his self become the [very] self of every contingent being') and for the 'standing firm on unity' of the present passage. Is there anything in the *Iśā* corresponding to the switch from self to God that we have here in the Gītā?

The *Iśā* opens with the words: 'This whole universe must be pervaded by a Lord.' This is the first and last time that this Lord is actually named. But immediately after the description of the omnipresent self, we come upon the following words (§ 8):

He, the wise Sage, all-conquering, self-existent,
Encompassed that which is resplendent,
    Incorporeal, invulnerable,
Devoid of sinews, pure, unpierced by evil:
[All] things He ordered each according to its nature
    For years unending.

This is quite clearly what the text must mean grammatically though Hume, Rk., and even Deussen quite arbitrarily confuse masculine forms with neuters, nominatives with accusatives. Grammatically, however, the text says that the 'wise Sage'—clearly the 'Lord' of the opening stanza—'encompassed that which is resplendent, incorporeal, invulnerable', etc.; and in addition He 'ordered all things each according to its nature'. This can only mean that the Lord transcends both what moves and what does not move—that is, Brahman-Self in both its eternal and its temporal aspects—and that He puts all things in order and sustains them. This is exactly what the Gītā will tell us later; and it is surely with this verse of the *Iśā* in mind that the Gītā now says:

Who standing firm on unity {participates in / communes-in-love with / belongs to} Me as abiding in all beings, in whatever state he be, that {integrated man / athlete of the spirit} abides in Me.

'In whatever state he be': the same words occur in 13. 23. They probably do not mean 'whatever his station in life', but rather whether he has realized himself as pure spirit, as a self-in-itself, or whether he is still immersed in material Nature. This seems more natural in the context. Moreover, this seems to accord with verses 9 and 10 of the *Iśā* on which the Gītā here seems to depend:

Blind darkness enter they
Who revere the uncompounded:
Into darkness blinder yet
[Go they] who delight in the compounded.

Other, they say, than what becomes,
Other, they say, than what does not become:
So from wise men have we heard
Who instructed us therein.

The import of this seems to be that while it would be obviously wrong to revere the unitary principle of the universe (Brahman-Self) as the 'compounded', that is, as what the Sāṁkhya-Yoga was later to call 'material Nature', it would be only slightly less erroneous to revere it as the 'uncompounded'—as the Buddhist Nirvāna, the Sāṁkhya *puruṣa* or 'spirit', or what Rāmānuja would call 'self-stuff'; for not only is Brahman one, uniting within itself what moves with what does not move, but there is also a higher principle different from Brahman in both its aspects which 'encompasses' them and 'orders all things each according to its nature'. Hence Krishna says in our present passage that the athlete of the spirit who has had the integral vision of reality must first 'stand firm on the unity' of his own integrated self now seen as diffused throughout the universe, and then he should approach the 'Other'—Himself—in fellowship, communion, and love. What the exact nuance of the word *bhaj-* is here it is too early to say (see above 4. 3 n.).

mayi vartate, 'abides in Me': one MS. has *na nivartate*, 'does not return [to earth]', presumably by analogy with 13. 23 *na sa bhūyo 'bhijāyate*, 'he is not born again'.

32. *ātm'aupamyena sarvatra samaṁ paśyati yo 'rjuna*
sukhaṁ vā yadi vā duḥkhaṁ sa yogī paramo mataḥ.

By analogy with self who sees the same [Brahman] everywhere, be it as pleasure or as pain, he is the highest athlete of the spirit, or so men think.

'Be it as pleasure or as pain': the integrated man is 'rapt in enstasy—in cold as in heat, in pleasure as in pain' (6. 7). He is unaffected by them because they are epiphenomena on the same one eternal 'self-stuff', Brahman. This was the very first lesson Krishna taught Arjuna, the wisdom He called *buddhi*—the wisdom that is native to a rightly orientated soul, the one virtue that truly reflects Brahman: 'Hold pleasure and pain, profit and loss, victory and defeat to be the same: then brace yourself for the fight. So will you bring no evil on yourself' (2. 38). This 'sameness' the integrated man no longer receives on trust from authority, but sees to be true with his own spiritual eyes. Both Ś. and R. give this a humanitarian twist (oddly perhaps in the case of Ś. who never tires of telling us that both good and evil actions, both righteousness and unrighteousness, bind), and say that by analogy with oneself one sees that what is pleasant or painful to oneself must also be pleasant or painful to others, and that one should therefore refrain from harming them. This scarcely seems to fit in with the doctrine that Krishna had preached from the very beginning, namely, that it is impossible to hurt the embodied self since it is of its very nature inviolate (2. 12–30).

Arjuna's Inadequacy

Arjuna uvāca:

33. *yo 'yaṁ yogas tvayā proktaḥ sāmyena, Madhusūdana,*
etasy'āhaṁ na paśyāmi cañcalatvāt sthitiṁ sthirām.

Arjuna said:

So fickle [is my mind] that I cannot descry this still, firm-stablished state of this spiritual exercise which You have preached as 'being the same [in everything]'.

sthirām, 'firm-stablished': var. *parām*, 'highest'. 'Sameness' and the 'still, firm-stablished state' are one and the same thing, the 'fixed, still state of Brahman' of 2. 72 and the 'Brahman that is Nirvāna too' (ibid. 5. 24, 25, 26: cf. 6. 15). 'Sameness', it will be remembered, was also a definition of Yoga (2. 48).

34. *cañcalaṁ hi manaḥ, Kṛṣṇa, pramāthi, balavad dṛḍham:*
tasy'āhaṁ nigrahaṁ manye vāyor iva suduṣkaram.

For fickle is the mind, impetuous, exceeding strong: how difficult to curb it! As difficult as to curb the wind, I would say.

pramāthi, 'impetuous': in 2. 60 it is the senses that are *pramāthin*, 'impetuous', but the mind of itself will follow the senses unless it is itself controlled by *buddhi*, the 'soul'. The relationship between all these is beautifully illustrated in the well-known simile of the chariot in KaU. 3. 3-4:

> The self is the owner of the chariot,
> The chariot is the body,
> Soul is the [body's] charioteer,
> Mind the reins [that curb it].
>
> Senses, they say, are the [chariot's] steeds,
> Their objects the tract before them.

Mind, then, will be swayed by whichever is stronger—the charioteer or the horses, the soul or the senses. Unless it is itself controlled it is helpless.

Śrī-bhagavān uvāca:

35. *asaṁśayaṁ, mahā-bāho, mano durnigrahaṁ calam;*
abhyāsena tu, Kaunteya, vairāgyeṇa ca gṛhyate.

The Blessed Lord said:

Herein there is no doubt, hard is the mind to curb and fickle, but by untiring effort and by transcending passion it can be held in check.

abhyāsena, 'untiring effort': defined in *Yoga-sūtras* 1. 13 as 'effort towards stillness (*sthiti*)'.

36. *asaṁyat'ātmanā yogo duṣprāpa iti me matiḥ,*
vaśy'ātmanā tu yatatā śakyo 'vāptum upāyataḥ.

Hard to come by is this {spiritual exercise / integrated state / sameness-and-indifference} by one whose self is not restrained; this [too] I think; but a man who strives, his self controlled, can win it if he but use [the appropriate] means.

Justification by Faith

Arjuna uvāca:

37. *ayatiḥ śraddhay'opeto yogāc calita-mānasaḥ*
aprāpya yoga-saṁsiddhiṁ kāṁ gatiṁ, Kṛṣṇa, gacchati?

Arjuna said:

[Suppose] a man of faith should strive in vain, his restless mind shying away from {integration / spiritual exercise / sameness-and-indifference}: he fails to win the perfect prize of {integration / spiritual exercise / sameness-and-indifference}

—what path does he tread [then]?

gatiṁ, 'path': lit. 'going'. The word also means 'goal' or 'refuge'.

Some MSS. add:

lipsamānaḥ satāṁ mārgaṁ pramūḍho brahmaṇaḥ pathi
aneka-citto vibhrānto mohasy'aiva vaśaṁ gataḥ.

[What] of the man who tries to find the way [that] good men [tread], but is confused on Brahman's path, his thoughts not unified, distracted, a prey to error?

Brahman here as in the following line means *saṁsāra*, the path of phenomenal existence: cf. the 'wheel of Brahman' (ŚU. 1. 6: 6. 1).

38. *kaccin n'obhaya-vibhraṣṭaś chinn'ābhram iva naśyati*
apratiṣṭho, mahā-bāho, vimūḍho brahmaṇaḥ pathi?

Does he, both objects unachieved, come crashing down and perish like a riven cloud, his [firm] foundation gone, bemused on Brahman's path?

'Both objects': Ś., 'the way of action and the way of *yoga*'. It must, however, surely refer to the renunciation and *yoga* ('practice') of the opening verses.

vimūḍho brahmaṇaḥ pathi, 'bemused on Brahman's path': var. *vināśaṁ vā'dhigacchati*, 'or meet with destruction'.

'Brahman's path': Ś., 'the path leading to the possession of Brahman'. But see the previous note.

39. *etan me saṁśayaṁ, Kṛṣṇa, chettum arhasy aśeṣataḥ;*
tvad-anyaḥ saṁśayasy' āsya chettā na hy upapadyate.

Krishna, this doubt You can dispel for me so that none of it remains, for there seems to be no other who can dispel this doubt [of mine].

Śrī-bhagavān uvāca:

40. *Pārtha, n'aiv'eha n'āmutra vināśas tasya vidyate:*
na hi kalyāṇa-kṛt kaścid durgatiṁ, tāta, gacchati.

The Blessed Lord said:

Not in this world nor in the next is such a man destroyed-or-lost: for no doer of fair works will tread an evil path, my friend, no, none whatever.

41. *prāpya puṇya-kṛtāṁl lokān uṣitvā śāśvatīḥ samāḥ*
śucīnāṁ śrīmatāṁ gehe yoga-bhraṣṭo 'bhijāyate.

The worlds of doers of good works he'll win and dwell there countless years: and then will he be born again, this man who failed in spiritual exercise, in the house of holy men by fortune blest.

42. *athavā yoginām eva kule bhavati dhīmatām;*
etad dhi durlabhataraṁ loke janma yad īdṛśam.

Or else he will be born in a family of men well-advanced-in-spiritual-exercise, possessed of insight; but such a birth as this on earth is yet harder to obtain.

dhīmatām, 'possessed of insight': var. *nirmale*, 'immaculate' (loc. agreeing with *kule*, 'family').

43. *tatra taṁ buddhi-saṁyogaṁ labhate paurvadehikam,*
yatate ca tato bhūyaḥ saṁsiddhau, Kuru-nandana.

There is he united with the soul as it had matured in his former body; and once again he strives to win perfection's prize.

buddhi-saṁyogaṁ, 'union with the soul': probably nothing to do with the *buddhi-yoga*, 'integration of the soul', of 2. 39 ff. Rather it means the reassumption by the transmigrating self of the psychosomatic faculties it had acquired in its former body. Cf. BU. 4. 4. 2: 'As [the self] departs, the breath of life follows after him; and as the breath of life departs, all the bodily faculties follow after it. He is then [re-]united with the understanding and follows after the understanding. His wisdom and his works and his knowledge of the past lay hold on him.'

44. *pūrv'ābhyāsena ten'aiva hriyate hy avaśo 'pi saḥ;*
jijñāsur api yogasya śabda-brahm'ātivartate.

By [the force of] that same struggle he had waged in former times he is carried away though helpless [of himself]; for even he who only wants to know what {integration / spiritual exercise} is, transcends that 'Brahman' which is [no more than] wordy rites.

'That "Brahman" which is [no more than] wordy rites': Ś., 'the Veda which is concerned with the performance of actions and their fruits'. Krishna has already castigated the Veda in 2. 42–46, 52–53.

45. *prayatnād yatamānas tu yogī saṁśuddha-kilbiṣaḥ*
aneka-janma-saṁsiddhas tato yāti parāṁ gatim.

But cleansed of taint [that] athlete of the spirit strives on with utmost zeal, through many, many births [at last] perfected; and then the highest path he treads.

'The highest path he treads'; see 6. 37 n. This phrase is constantly occurring, and alternative translations will no longer be noted. *Gati*, 'going, way, goal, refuge' is exactly parallel to the 'Way' of John xiv. 6, 'I am the way and the truth and the life'.

46. *tapasvibhyo 'dhiko yogī jñānibhyo 'pi mato 'dhikaḥ*
karmibhyaś c'ādhiko yogī: tasmād yogī bhav'ārjuna.

Higher than the [mere] ascetic is the athlete of the spirit held to be, yes, higher than the man of wisdom, higher than the man of works: be, then, a spiritual athlete, Arjuna!

'Man of wisdom': described in 4. 34–39.

'Man of works': described in 3 *passim*. Both Ś. and R. unnecessarily confine 'works' to sacrificial works.

47. *yoginām api sarveṣāṁ mad-gaten'āntarātmanā*
śraddhāvān bhajate yo māṁ, sa me yuktatamo mataḥ.

But of all athletes of the spirit the man of faith who loves-and-honours Me, his inmost self absorbed in Me,—he is the most fully integrated: this do I believe.

bhajate, 'loves-and-honours': var. *labhate*, 'obtains'.

'Athletes of the spirit': that is, *yogins*. Throughout this chapter *yogin* has meant specifically the 'integrated man' who finishes up by obtaining an 'integral' vision of the universe and of himself. By *yoga* we have been taught to understand (i) 'sameness-and-indifference', or 'equanimity' (2. 48), (ii) 'skill in [performing] works' (2. 50), and (iii) the 'unlinking of the link with suffering-and-pain' (6. 23). This corresponds almost exactly with the Stoic ideal in Europe; but one thing, Krishna says, is lacking, and that is commitment to a God who, wholly immanent though He is, is yet other than yourself. This was already announced in 6. 31, but in the context it seemed almost an afterthought. Here we are told with the utmost clarity that no integration of the personality around its admittedly eternal and divine centre can be complete until it is combined with the adoration of God transcendent. In Christian terminology, we whose bodies are the temples of the Holy Spirit are not thereby exempted from adoration of the Father.

'His inmost self absorbed in Me': the word *ātman*, 'self', as we know, is often loosely used and, in contexts where it appears to be an agent, both Ś. and R. usually gloss it as 'mind'. In this passage this is clearly not legitimate since Krishna goes out of his way to say '*inmost* self', and this can only mean the individual 'timeless' self which is at the same time Brahman. Communion with God in love (*bhakti*), then, is only fully possible to the self who is already 'integrated', 'liberated', and 'purified'—already in Nirvāna. From this point on we leave the Buddhist ideal behind, or rather, having absorbed it, we are invited to go yet further: we are asked not only to accept the infinite in silence but also, so far as it is possible even for a God when He speaks to finite minds, to chart it.

CHAPTER VII

According to Rāmānuja the first six chapters of the Gītā are devoted to the acquisition of true knowledge of the individual self as being immortal and of the 'stuff' of Brahman, while the next six are devoted to the knowledge of God. In modern terms, then, the subject-matter of the first six chapters would be psychology, that of the second six theology. This is only very roughly true as the attentive reader will have noticed, the first half of Chapter IV, for instance, being devoted almost entirely to Krishna both as incarnate God and as the universal agent. Nevertheless from the present chapter until the tremendous theophany in Chapter XI we shall be increasingly concerned with Krishna as God, less with the self's realization of itself as having its real existence outside space and time.

Krishna announces in the opening stanza that He will teach Arjuna everything about Himself, though He immediately warns him that practically no one comes to know Him as He really is (1–3). He then goes on to speak of his two material Natures (4–7) (hitherto we had only heard about one (4. 6: cf. 3. 27, 29, 33)) and of what He considers to be most essential and typical among his attributes (8–11). He is the source of the constituents of Nature and therefore of good and evil (12–15).

He then discusses the different types of men who offer Him loving devotion and also the worshippers of other gods (16–23); and in the final section He speaks of his own incarnation and his ability and willingness to lead men out of this world of time into the freedom of 'liberation'. This chapter is commonly called the '*Yoga* of Wisdom and Experience'.

The Two Natures of God

Śrī-bhagavān uvāca:

1. *mayy āsakta-manāḥ, Pārtha, yogaṁ yuñjan mad-āśrayaḥ*
asaṁśayaṁ samagraṁ māṁ yathā jñāsyasi tac chṛṇu.

The Blessed Lord said:

Attach your mind to Me: engaging [still] in spiritual exercise put your trust in Me: [this doing] listen how you may come to know Me in my entirety, all doubt dispelled.

'Attach your mind to Me': this is utterly new and apparently at variance with the whole content of the last two chapters. There we had been told almost *ad nauseam* that we had to *de*tach ourselves from everything: only by total detachment could liberation be won. Meditate on God certainly as a means of concentrating your mind, as the *Yoga-sūtras* recommend, but do not *attach* yourself to Him or anything else because 'liberation' is clearly incompatible with attachment of any kind. Here, however, Arjuna is told most bluntly that this is not so: the true athlete of the spirit who has succeeded in integrating his personality and in becoming Brahman must now not only continue his spiritual exercise unremittingly, he must also attach his whole personality in all its new-found fullness and freedom to Krishna who is God and, being God, transcends the immortal Brahman as much as He transcends the phenomenal world. Continued spiritual exercise preserving the integrated personality intact, attachment to God, and total trust in Him are what Krishna demands in this stanza.

2. *jñānaṁ te 'haṁ savijñānam idaṁ vakṣyāmy aśeṣataḥ*
yaj jñātvā n'eha bhūyo 'nyaj jñātavyam avaśiṣyate.

This wisdom [derived from sacred writ] and the wisdom [of experience] I shall proclaim to you, leaving nothing unsaid. This known, never again will any other thing that needs to be known here remain.

'This wisdom' etc.: my interpretation follows Ś. and R.

3. *manuṣyāṇāṁ sahasreṣu kaścid yatati siddhaye;*
yatatām api siddhānāṁ kaścin māṁ vetti tattvataḥ.

Among thousands of men but one, maybe, will strive for [self-]perfection, and even among [these] athletes who have won perfection['s crown] but one, maybe, will come to know Me as I really am.

siddhaye, '[self-]perfection'. Ś. rightly glosses, 'liberation'. This rams in the point of 6. 47, namely, that 'liberation' does not necessarily mean to know the personal God in his entirety (7. 1): this is reserved to only the rarest saints.

4. *bhūmir āpo 'nalo vāyuḥ khaṁ mano buddhir eva ca*
ahaṁkāra itī'yaṁ me bhinnā prakṛtir aṣṭadhā.

Eightfold divided is my Nature,—thus: earth, water, fire and air, space, mind, and also soul,—and the ego.

'Earth, water', etc.: the so-called gross elements. In man, the microcosm, they correspond to the five senses—earth to smell, water to taste, fire to sight, air to touch, space (or ether) to sound. This is the normal Sāṁkhya classification.

5. *apar'eyam, itas tv anyāṁ prakṛtiṁ viddhi me parām*
jīva-bhūtāṁ, mahā-bāho, yay'edaṁ dhāryate jagat.

This is the lower: but other than this I have a higher Nature; this too must you know. [And this is Nature] developed into life by which this world is kept in being.

jīva-bhūtāṁ, '[Nature] developed into life': one MS. has *bīja-bhūtāṁ*, 'become or in the form of seed' (cf. 7. 10). Ś. interprets the word as meaning *kṣetra-jña*, 'the knower of the field' of Chapter XIII, which is a synonym for *ātman*, 'self', and which for him means the one absolute reality. The lower nature he interprets as *māyā-śakti*, 'the power of *māyā*' which for him means the 'power of illusion' (cf. p. 183 n.). R. takes the lower to mean unconscious matter, the higher, 'living' nature to mean conscious matter the nature of which is to experience unconscious matter. H. takes it to mean 'a single principle of life, inclusive of or identical with each separate *puruṣa* or *ātman*'. Rk. translates 'soul' and glosses 'the totality of the conscious', following R. in this. D., 'eine lebendige Seele'.

The stanza, however, must be read in connexion with 3. 42 where we read: 'Exalted are the senses, or so they say; higher than the senses is the mind; yet higher than the mind the soul: what is beyond the soul is he.' 'He', as we saw when we were discussing that passage, must be the [individual] self. This seemed to emerge quite clearly from KaU. 6. 7–8 where an entity call the 'great self' appears as higher than the soul, and higher than this again is the 'Unmanifest'. It would, then, seem that this Nature 'developed into life' must correspond to the 'self' of 3. 43. The difference is no more than what one would expect, for in this passage Krishna is speaking in terms of the universe, the macrocosm, while in 3. 42 He was speaking of man, the microcosm. Hence, as R. rightly saw, 'Nature developed into life' must mean the totality of conscious matter as opposed to the 'self' of 3. 43 which is the individual, conscious self. This totality of conscious matter keeps the world in being because each individual, conscious self is a 'part' of God (15. 7), and to sustain the world is, of course, one of God's prime functions (9. 5 etc.).

In 15. 7 ff. the word *jīva-bhūta* is used of the 'parts' of Krishna which are the eternal, conscious selves of every human being and which are linked with a whole psychosomatic complex in the course of transmigration. They are selves-in-themselves, but they are not God in his fullness. They are the objects that are 'seen' when a man achieves liberation

(15. 11: cf. 6. 20, 29), they are the 'great self' or selves of the *Kaṭha* Upanishad 6. 7–8 which are separated from the highest 'Person' or 'Spirit' by the 'Unmanifest'. This is the position taken up in MBh. 12. 238 which is closely dependent on the Gītā (as its use of the simile of the lamp in a windless place (MBh. 12. 238. 11 = BhG. 6. 19) clearly shows). Almost the same hierarchy of being appears: lowest are the senses, then come the objects of sense, the mind, the soul (*buddhi*), and finally the 'great self'. Beyond the 'great self' again is the 'Unmanifest', and beyond that the 'Deathless' (*amṛtam*, neut.): 'beyond the Deathless there is nothing else at all: that is the goal (*kāṣṭhā*), that is the highest Way. And so the self is hidden in all beings and does not shine forth, but it is seen by means of the subtle apex of the soul (*agryayā buddhyā*) by people who see things as they really are. Withdrawing the five senses and their objects together with the mind by means of the soul (*medhayā*) into the inmost self and not thinking much about anything that can be thought, the man whose self is stilled (*praśānta*) will bring his meditation to a halt, infuse the mind with wisdom (*vidyā*), acknowledging none as his master (*anīśvara*, if the reading is right). Then he will go on to that state which is the Deathless' (MBh. 12. 238. 4–7).

If our interpretation of the 'higher Nature' of Krishna is right, liberation as described in Chapters V and VI will mean no more than the realization by each individual self of its own eternal essence as a 'part' of God, as what the *Kaṭha* Upanishad calls the 'great self', not as the supreme 'Person' or 'Spirit' of the same Upanishad which is elsewhere said to be 'beyond the beyond' (MuU. 3. 2. 8).

6. *etad-yonīni bhūtāni sarvāṇī'ty upadhāraya,*
ahaṁ kṛtsnasya jagataḥ prabhavaḥ pralayas tathā.

To all beings these [two Natures] are [as] a womb; be very sure of this. Of this whole universe the origin and the dissolution too am I.

etad-yonīni, etc., 'to all beings these [two Natures] are [as] a womb': *etad-* in compounds can be taken as either singular or plural. Ś. and R. take it to refer to both Natures of God. In this they are followed by most modern translators. E. prefers to refer it to the higher Nature only, and translates, 'beings spring from it, all of them'. Yet it would surely be more natural to take *etad-* to refer to Nature in general, both the higher and the lower.

Yoni, of course, originally means 'womb', then by extension 'origin'. It seems to me more natural to take the word in its literal sense since Krishna refers to Himself as 'the primeval seed of all contingent beings' in 7. 10 and more explicitly He says in 14. 3, 'Great Brahman is to Me a womb, in it I plant the seed'—'great Brahman' there corresponding to the two 'Natures' in this passage and, it would seem, to the 'great self' of KaU. 6. 7 and MBh. 12. 238 quoted in the note to the last stanza.

7. *mattaḥ parataraṁ n'ānyat kiṁcid asti, dhanaṁjaya;*
mayi sarvam idaṁ protaṁ sūtre maṇi-gaṇā iva.

Higher than I there is nothing whatsoever: on Me this universe is strung like clustered pearls upon a thread.

'Clustered pearls upon a thread': the same simile is used in Mbh. 12. 199. 1 of Brahman. The idea probably goes back to BU. 3. 8. 6–8 (cf. 3. 6):

She said: 'Yājñavalkya, that which is above the sky, which is below the earth, which is between sky and earth—that which men speak of as past, present, and future: on what is *that* woven, warp and woof?'

He said: 'Gārgī, that which is above the sky, which is below the earth, which is between sky and earth—that which men speak of as past, present, and future: that is woven on space, warp and woof.'

'On what, then, is space woven, warp and woof?' said she.

He said: 'Gārgī, that is what Brāhmans call the "Imperishable".'

This 'Imperishable', identified by the Gītā (8. 3) with the 'highest Brahman', is there described both negatively and positively (see 8. 3 n.).

The idea of the 'thread' on which all things are strung together again occurs in BU. 3. 7. 2 where it is identified with the wind: 'By this thread, which is the wind, this world and the next world and all beings are strung together.'

Some Essential Attributes of God

8. *raso 'ham apsu, Kaunteya, prabhā 'smi śaśi-sūryayoḥ,*
praṇavaḥ sarva-vedeṣu, śabdaḥ khe, pauruṣaṁ nṛṣu.

In water I am the flavour, in sun and moon the light, in all the Vedas [the sacred syllable] Oṁ, in space [I am] sound, in men [their] manliness am I.

'In water I am the flavour' etc.: cf. 7. 4 n.

9. *puṇyo gandhaḥ pṛthivyāṁ ca, tejaś c'āsmi vibhāvasau,*
jīvanaṁ sarva-bhūteṣu, tapaś c'āsmi tapasviṣu.

Pure fragrance in the earth am I, flame's onset in the fire: [and] life am I in all contingent beings, in ascetics [their] fierce austerity.

10. *bījaṁ māṁ sarva-bhūtānāṁ viddhi, Pārtha, sanātanam:*
buddhir buddhimatām asmi, tejas tejasvinām aham.

Know that I am the primeval seed of all contingent beings: insight in men of insight, glory in the glorious am I.

bījaṁ . . . sanātanam, 'primeval seed': for *sanātana*, 'primeval' rather than 'eternal' see 4. 31 n. As 'seed' Krishna is the eternal origin of the whole world process: cf. 9. 18: '[I am] . . . the seed that passes not away.'

buddhir, 'insight': better than 'reason' as I translated in the Everyman's Library *Hindu Scriptures*. In this I followed Ś. who glosses, 'the power of discrimination in the mind (*antaḥkaraṇa*)'.

11. *balaṁ balavatāṁ c'āhaṁ kāma-rāga-vivarjitam:*
dharm'āviruddho bhūteṣu kāmo 'smi, Bharata'rṣabha.

Power in the powerful am I,—[such power] as knows neither desire nor passion: desire am I in contingent beings, [but such desire as] does not conflict with righteousness.

'Power'; Ś. glosses, 'only such power as is needed to sustain the body etc.': similarly he confines desire to the craving for what one does not possess. This is plainly to whittle away Krishna's words. The whole of Chapter XI is a magnificent revelation of Krishna as absolute power, whereas in MBh. 14. 13. 9–17 Krishna explains to Yudhishthira, a natural *sannyāsin* if ever there was one, just how He is desire:

In [this] world men do not commend a man whose very self is desire, and [yet] there can be no progress (*pravṛtti*) without desire; for the gift of alms, study of the Veda, ascetic practices, and the Vedic sacrificial acts [are all motivated] by desire. Whoever knowingly undertakes a religious vow, performs sacrifice or any other religious duty, or engages in the spiritual exercise of meditation without desire, [does all this in vain(?)]. Whatever a man desires, that is [to him his] duty (*dharma*): it cannot be sound to curb one's duty.

This is the song which knowers of ancient lore celebrate as having been sung by Desire. Listen [to me], Yudhishthira; [I] will recite it to you in full:

'I cannot be slain by any being whatever since he is wholly without the means. If a man should seek to slay me, putting his trust in the strength of a weapon, then do I appear again in the very weapon he uses. If a man should seek to slay me by offering sacrifices and paying all manner of fees, then do I appear again as the "self that dwells in all action" in moving things. If a man should seek to slay me by means of the Vedas and the ways of perfection [prescribed] in the Vedas' end, then do I appear as the "stilled, quiet self (*śānt'ātman*)" in unmoving things. If a man should seek to slay me by steadfastness, a very paladin of truth, then do I become his very nature, unaware of me though he is. If a man should seek to slay me by ascetic practice, strict in his vows, then do I appear again in his very ascetic practice. If a man should seek to slay me, wise and bent on liberation, then do I dance and laugh before him as he abides in the bliss (*rati*) of liberation. Of all beings I alone cannot be slain, eternal [as I am].'

This may not be immediately recognizable as the Krishna of the Gītā, but it is all of one piece with Krishna as he is depicted in the bulk of the Epic.

God and the Constituents of Nature

12. *ye c'aiva sāttvikā bhāvā rājasās tāmasāś ca ye,*
matta ev'eti tān viddhi; na tv ahaṁ teṣu, te mayi.

Know too that [all] states of being whether they be of [Nature's constituent] Goodness, Passion, or Darkness proceed from Me; but I am not in them, they are in Me.

'[Nature's constituent(s)]': the three 'constituents' of Nature which according to 3. 5 and 3. 27 were alone responsible for action, are here named for the first time. The nature of these three constituents is described in great detail in 14. 5–19: 17. 2–22: 18. 7–9 and 18–40. Although the constituents are described as the sole agent in 3. 27 and will be so described again in 14. 19, they in fact proceed from God.

'I am not in them, they are in Me': Ś., 'I am not dependent on them or in their power: as belonging to the world of flux (*saṁsāra*) they are "in Me"—in my power and dependent on Me.' R., '"in Me", as being my body'. Whereas, he goes on to say, bodies belong to the self and the self makes use of bodies, God depends on nothing and the only use He has for contingent existence is as a sport (*līlā*).

13. *tribhir guṇamayair bhāvair ebhiḥ sarvam idaṁ jagat*
mohitaṁ, n'ābhijānāti mām ebhyaḥ param avyayam.

By these three states of being inhering in the constituents this whole universe is led astray and does not understand that I am far beyond them and that I neither-change-nor-pass-away.

According to R. God is present in all effects, causes, and bodies, but He is higher than they because He is the [first] cause, author of differentiation (*śeṣin*), and possessed of every conceivable perfection in which no creature shares.

14. *daivī hy eṣā guṇamayī mama māyā duratyayā.*
mām eva ye prapadyante māyām etāṁ taranti te.

For [all] this is my creative power, composed of the constituents, divine, hard to transcend. Whoso shall put his trust in Me alone, shall pass beyond this [my] uncanny power.

daivī . . . māyā, 'divine . . . creative power', 'uncanny power': being 'composed of the constituents' *māyā* is still a synonym for *prakṛti*, 'material Nature' as in ŚU. 4. 10 and BhG. 4. 6 (see note ad loc.). '*Māyā*', says R., 'is formed by God as He begins to sport': it does not mean 'false'.

15. *na māṁ duṣkṛtino mūḍhāḥ prapadyante nar'ādhamāḥ*
māyayā 'pahṛta-jñānā āsuraṁ bhāvam āśritāḥ.

Doers of evil, deluded, base, put not their trust in Me; their wisdom swept away by [this] uncanny power, they cleave to a devilish mode of existence.

māyayā, 'by [this] uncanny power': there is only a very slight shift of meaning here, for the constituents of Nature blind man to the true nature of reality. R. who at 4. 6 had equated *māyā* with *jñāna*, 'wisdom', now glosses it as 'tricky arguments'! This is quite unnecessary since in the Gītā *māyā* is real: it depends on God and is therefore called 'divine' but at the same time distracts man's attention from Him.

āsuraṁ bhāvam, 'devilish mode of existence': this is fully described in 16. 6-20. There contingent beings are divided into sheep and goats, the 'divine' and the 'devilish'. Similarly it might be said that Nature or *māyā* may be seen as either 'divine' or 'devilish': seen as dependent on God and not as an independent principle (as in the Sāṁkhya system) it is divine, but in so far as it stands between the individual self and God and distracts it from Him, it is 'devilish'. In itself, as in the Sāṁkhya, it is morally neutral and only assumes a moral and/or immoral character once the constituents are differentiated.

One MS. inserts 16. 20 here: 'Caught up in devilish wombs, birth after birth deluded, they never attain to Me: and so they tread the lowest way.'

Different Types of Devotee

16. *catur-vidhā bhajante māṁ janāḥ sukṛtino, 'rjuna,*
ārto, jijñāsur, arth'ārthī jñānī ca, Bharata'rṣabha.

Fourfold are the doers of good who love-and-worship Me,—the afflicted, the man who seeks wisdom, the man who strives for gain, and the man who wisdom knows.

jñānī, 'the man who wisdom knows': R., 'the man who knows that the eternal self is totally different from material Nature, who desires the Lord and considers Him to be the final goal'.

17. *teṣāṁ jñānī nitya-yukta eka-bhaktir viśiṣyate,*
priyo hi jñānino 'tyartham ahaṁ, sa ca mama priyaḥ.

Of these the man of wisdom, ever integrated, who loves-and-worships One alone excels: for to the man of wisdom I am exceeding dear and he is dear to Me.

nitya-yukta, 'ever integrated': this is of course the *yoga-yukto*, 'the man integrated in spiritual exercise' who was celebrated throughout Chapters V (6, 7, 12, 21, 23) and VI (8, 10, 12, 14, 15, 18, 19, 28), the man 'who ever integrates the self' (6. 10, 15, 28). In translating 'in constant union with the Divine' Rk. is merely reading his own ideas into the text: the Gītā is not here speaking of 'union with the Divine' but of integration of the personality—the truly massive theme of Chapters V and VI. This verse in fact links up with 6. 46-47 where the *yogin*, the 'athlete of the spirit', is exalted above all other types:

> Higher than the [mere] ascetic is the athlete of the spirit held to be, yes, higher than the man of wisdom, higher than the man of works. . . . But of all athletes of the spirit the man of faith who loves-and-honours Me, his inmost self absorbed in Me—he is the most fully integrated: this do I believe.

Here too Krishna insists, as He had done in 7. 1-3, that the integrated man who, even after liberation, does not cease to practise spiritual exercise, must also be possessed of correct knowledge concerning the timeless nature of the self; and in addition he must love and worship Him alone. The integrated man is, as we saw in the last chapter, also 'liberated, Brahman-become' (6. 27–28), and as such 'there is nothing he needs to do' (3. 17), yet all this is not enough without a loving devotion to God. *Mokṣa* means 'liberation' from the bonds of time and action: the 'liberated' man is thereby free, and what Krishna demands is therefore the love of a free and disinterested self. The 'afflicted', the 'man who seeks wisdom', and the 'man who strives for gain' each in their different way want something out of God—relief, true wisdom, or simply wealth and power; but the 'man who wisdom knows' and who 'is ever integrated' needs nothing. His love and devotion are, then, an act of pure, disinterested self-giving, and this love-in-communion, Krishna has already said, He will return in full (4. 11).

18. *udārāḥ sarva ev'aite, jñānī tv ātm'aiva me matam;*
āsthitaḥ sa hi yukt'ātmā mām ev'ānuttamāṁ gatim.

All these are noble-and-exalted, but the man of wisdom is [my] very self, so do I hold, for with self [already] integrated he puts his trust in Me, the one all-highest Way.

ātm'aiva, '[my] very self': Ś., of course, takes this literally: 'the man whose self is integrated, i.e. whose thoughts are concentrated, is convinced that he is the Blessed Lord, son of Vasudeva, and no other'. To emphasize the identity of Krishna and the 'highest Brahman' he glosses *mām*, 'Me', in the next line as 'the highest Brahman'. R. goes to the other extreme—'the maintenance of my (God's) very self is dependent on him'. God, moreover, according to R. *is* as dependent on the individual self as the latter is on Him. This seems to be totally at variance with the whole tone of the Gītā, for the man who has realized his own self in the 'Nirvāna that is Brahman too' is thereby free and dependent on nothing just as God is (3. 22), and the love between man and God which Krishna is now beginning to reveal must be a free love—freely given and freely accepted. The phrase 'is my very self' probably means no more than 'he is the apple of my eye'.

mām, 'Me': var. *mama*, 'my [all-highest Way]'.

19. *bahūnāṁ janmanām ante jñānavān māṁ prapadyate,*
Vāsudevaḥ sarvam iti, sa mah'ātmā sudurlabhaḥ.

At the end of many a birth the man of wisdom gives himself up to Me, [knowing that Krishna,] Vasudeva's son, is All: so great a self is exceeding hard to find.

The 'man of wisdom' is essentially the man who burns out all works and their fruits in the 'fire' of wisdom (4. 19, 37: cf. 4. 23, 33 where works are either melted into wisdom or find their consummation in it). Krishna, however, is the God of action (3. 23–24: 4. 13–14) as well as the principle of eternal repose; and hence it takes the 'man of wisdom' 'many births' to realize not only that his own Nirvāna subsists in Krishna (6. 15) but that the whole phenomenal world which has its *raison d'être* in works is also God seen under another aspect: He is both time (11. 32) and eternity (7. 24: 11. 37, etc.). The man of wisdom has trained himself to live only in eternity.

Worship of Other Gods

20. *kāmais tais tair hṛta-jñānāḥ prapadyante 'nya-devatāḥ*
taṁ taṁ niyamam āsthāya prakṛtyā niyatāḥ svayā.

[All] wisdom swept away by manifold desires, men put their trust in other gods, relying on diverse rules-and-precepts: for their own nature forces them thereto.

svayā, 'their own [nature]': var. *tvayā*, 'by you'. Cf. 5. 14: 'Neither agency nor worldly works does [the body's] lord engender, nor yet the bond that work to fruit conjoins: it is inherent Nature that initiates the action.'

More immediately the phrase recalls 7. 15 where men's 'wisdom' is 'swept away' by God's *māyā*. *Māyā* and *prakṛti*, 'creative power' and 'material Nature' are, as we know, synonymous; and just as they operate on the cosmic scale, so do they operate on the individual level. Each man has a nature of his own which is the result of the deeds he has done in past lives: he is conditioned by these and they may force him to do things he does not want to do. So, in the great theophany of Chapter XI, Krishna tells Arjuna: 'Yours it is to be the mere occasion' (11. 33); and again in 18. 59 He tells him that even if he makes up his mind not to fight, 'Nature will constrain you'.

21. *yo yo yāṁ yāṁ tanuṁ bhaktaḥ śraddhayā 'rcitum icchati*
tasya tasy'ācalāṁ śraddhāṁ tām eva vidadhāmy aham.

Whatever form, [whatever god,] a devotee with faith desires to honour, that very faith do I confirm in him [making it] unswerving-and-secure.

On the worshippers of other gods cf. 9. 23–25: 17. 3–4 ('Man is instinct with faith: as is his faith, so too must he be').

22. *sa tayā śraddhayā yuktas tasy'ārādhanam īhate,*
labhate ca tataḥ kāmān may'aiva vihitān hi tān.

Firm-stablished in that faith he seeks to reverence that [god] and thence he gains his desires, though it is I who am the true dispenser.

23. *antavat tu phalaṁ teṣāṁ tad bhavaty alpa-medhasām:*
devān deva-yajo yānti, mad-bhaktā yānti mām api.

But finite is the reward of such men of little wit: whoso worships the gods, to the gods will [surely] go, but whoso loves-and-worships Me, to Me will come indeed.

'To the gods will [surely] go': some MSS. add here: 'Those devoted to perfected saints (or the ancestors) will go to them, worshippers of ghosts will go to the ghosts.' This addition is based on 9. 25.

According to R. the worshipper achieves union (*sāyujya*) with what he worships, and since the pleasures of the gods are limited in time, the worshipper must be reincarnated along with them when their store of merit is exhausted.

The Unknown God

24. *avyaktaṁ vyaktim āpannaṁ manyante mām abuddhayaḥ,*
paraṁ bhāvam ajānanto mam'āvyayam anuttamam.

Fools think of Me as one unmanifest [before] who has reached [the stage of] manifestation: they know nothing of my higher state, the Changeless, All-Highest.

The first sentence seems to mean that Krishna, like any other mortal, 'appears' at birth and 'disappears' at death. This very simple idea He had already exposed in 2. 28 (and Ś. interprets accordingly): 'Unmanifest are the beginnings of contingent beings, manifest their middle course, unmanifest again their ends.'

'Unmanifest', however, is also the term used for 'primal, undifferentiated matter' in the Sāṁkhya system (*Kārikā*, 10 ff.) from which intellect (*buddhi*), mind, ego, the senses, etc., proceed (p. 140). This has been briefly mentioned in 2. 25 and will be causing us some trouble in 8. 18–21. Here, however, Krishna surely means that fools think He is a human being like everyone else, here today and gone tomorrow.

paraṁ bhāvam, 'higher state or mode of being': the state already mentioned in 4. 10 which is reached by Krishna's devotees. This is never defined, but presumably means God's eternal Being, the source of Nirvāna itself (6. 15), the 'one mode of being, changeless, undivided in all contingent beings, divided [as they are]' (18. 20).

25. *n'āhaṁ prakāśaḥ sarvasya yoga-māyā-samāvṛtaḥ:*
mūḍho 'yaṁ n'ābhijānāti loko mām ajam avyayam.

Since [my] creative power and the way I use it conceal Me, I am not revealed to all; this world, deluded, knows Me not,—[Me,] the Unborn and Changeless.

yoga-māyā-: a number of interpretations are possible. I have translated 'creative power and the way I use it' because that corresponds to the way the two words have been used in the Gītā hitherto. Ś. glosses, 'the *māyā* (sc. delusion) which consists in association with the constituents'; R. 'the *māyā* (sc. power) which consists in the union of the complex which makes up [the body of a] man and the self which [essentially] has nothing in common with it'. The trouble is that *yoga*, though its root meaning is 'joining' ('union, association') is scarcely ever used in this sense in the Gītā which in this sense prefers *saṁyoga* (cf. 6. 23: 13. 26: 18. 38). Nor is *yoga* used in the Gītā to denote the supernatural power attributed to the advanced Yogin in the *Yoga-sūtras*. E.'s 'magic trick-of-illusion' avoids the issue.

Even so, it should be emphasized that although *māyā* has so far been synonymous with *prakṛti*, 'material Nature' as in ŚU. 4. 9–10, it does also mean 'deceit' in the later Vedic literature: cf. PU. 1. 16, *na yeṣu jihmam anṛtaṁ na māyā ca*, 'in whom there is neither crookedness, nor falsehood, nor deceit'. In the RV. it usually means 'magic power'.

26. *ved'āhaṁ samatītāni vartamānāni c'ārjuna,*
bhaviṣyāṇi ca bhūtāni: māṁ tu veda na kaścana.

[All] beings past and present and yet to come I know: but there is no one at all that knows Me.

Krishna had already claimed to know all his and Arjuna's previous incarnations in 4. 5: here He lays claim to complete omniscience.

'There is no one at all who knows Me': this would seem to be at variance with 7. 1 where Arjuna is told to 'listen how you may come to know Me in my entirety'. Moreover, Krishna had said in 7. 3 that perhaps one in a million comes to know Him 'as He really is'. Hence both Ś. and R. make exceptions to this unqualified statement. Ś. (surprisingly) excepts Krishna's devotees while R. merely says that the man who really knows Krishna is rare indeed. The meaning, however, surely is that however much you may be taught *about* God (and Arjuna will be taught a great deal), you can never come to know Him because He is, according to ŚU. 2. 15, 'beyond all essences as they really are (*atattva*)'; and what has no essence cannot be defined.

27. *icchā-dveṣa-samutthena dvandva-mohena, Bhārata,*
sarva-bhūtāni saṁmohaṁ sarge yānti, paraṁtapa.

By dualities are men confused, and these arise from desire and hate; thereby are all contingent beings bewildered the moment they are born.

28. *yeṣāṁ tv anta-gataṁ pāpaṁ janānāṁ puṇya-karmaṇām,*
te dvandva-moha-nirmuktā bhajante māṁ dṛḍha-vratāḥ.

But some there are for whom [all] ill is ended, doers of what is good-and-pure: released [at last] from the confusion of duality, steady in their vows, they love-and-worship Me.

'Released [at last] from the confusion of duality': we already know that the man who has surmounted duality, that is, all the pairs of opposites, is no longer bound (4. 22): 'how easily is he released from bondage' (5. 3). To transcend the pairs of opposites means the total integration of the personality, its unification around and in the immortal, timeless self; and this is the essential prelude to achieving a true love and devotion to God.

Who standing firm on unity communes-in-love with Me as abiding in all beings, in whatever state he be, that athlete of the spirit abides in Me (6. 31: cf. 7. 17).

It is also implied in this passage, in contradistinction to all that has gone before, that 'good works' can save though, even so, one must assume that they are performed in a spirit of total detachment and disinterestedness. The 'man of wisdom', we may remember, has no such worries:

Even though you were the very worst among all evil-doers, [yet once you have boarded] wisdom's bark, you will surmount all [this] tortuous [stream of life] (4. 36).

29. *jarā-maraṇa-mokṣāya mām āśritya yatanti ye,*
te brahma tad viduḥ kṛtsnam adhyātmaṁ karma c'ākhilam,

Whoso shall strive to win release from old age and death, putting his trust in Me, will come to know that Brahman in its wholeness,—as it appertains to self, the whole [mystery] of works,

The point of this passage seems to be that while the service and love offered by the man who is already integrated and free from earthly bonds is alone perfect, Krishna can and will aid all who are still seeking liberation. Since they are striving primarily for liberation pure and simple which is described as the 'fixed, still state of Brahman' (2. 72) or the 'Nirvāna that is Brahman too' (ibid.: 5. 24–26), Krishna promises to reveal to them 'Brahman in its wholeness', part of which, as we shall see, is very much involved with the phenomenal world.

yatanti, 'strive': var. *yajanti*, 'worship'; *bhajanti*, 'love-and-worship'.

adhyātmaṁ, 'what appertains to self'. E.'s 'over-soul' and H.'s 'Essential Self' are surely wrong since they ignore the voluminous Upanishadic usage of this word and of *adhibhūtam* and *adhidaivam* in the following stanza. Only Senart's translation is reasonably accurate here. See 8. 3, 4, nn.

30. *sādhibhūt'ādhidaivaṁ māṁ sādhiyajñaṁ ca: ye viduḥ*
prayāṇa-kāle 'pi ca māṁ, te vidur yukta-cetasaḥ.

As it appertains to contingent beings, and to the divine,—and Me [too] as I appertain to sacrifice. And whoso shall know

Me [thus] even at the time of passing on, will know [Me] with an integrated mind.

At this stage we can but note the discrepancies in this chapter on whether or not it is possible to know God. The opening and closing verses of the chapter are optimistic, but verse 3 says that perhaps one in a million can know God as He really is, while verse 26 says flatly that no one can know Him at all. Perhaps the meaning is that God can be known as eternal Being because every liberated self participates in this, but He cannot be known as He operates through *māyā* because it is the very function of *māyā*, of matter, to bewilder and confuse (7. 14–15, 25). As Śankara would say, *māyā* is something you cannot pin down or adequately describe (*anirvacanīya*); it neither is nor is not; yet in the Gītā it is inextricably intertwined with the being of God.

'Brahman in its wholeness', as we shall see in the next chapter, comprises (i) the 'Imperishable' (see 8. 3 n.), (ii) the law of *karma* which gives rise to individuality, (iii) material Nature, and (iv) eternal individual selves. In addition there is God who is especially connected with the sacrifice (see 8. 4 n.). Each of these categories can be learnt *in theory* by those who 'strive to win release from old age and death'. The totality of them all in God can only be 'known' once a man's mind and thoughts are fully integrated. This, however, is not to know in the ordinary sense of the word, but an intuitive apprehension beyond all discursive thought. The *Kena* Upanishad 2. 2–3 has the last word to say on this 'knowledge' or 'wisdom':

I do not think, 'I know It well',
I do not know, 'I do not know';
He of us who knows It, knows It,
He does not know, 'I know It not'.

Who thinks not on It, by him It's thought:
Who thinks upon It, does not know—
Ununderstood by those who understand,
By those who understand not understood.

For the punctuation of this passage see 8. 3–4 nn. *Adhyātmaṁ* and *sādhibhūt'ādhidaivaṁ* must surely be taken together in accordance with Upanishadic practice. From the purely grammatical point of view too *māṁ sādhiyajñaṁ ca* is best taken with what precedes to avoid the tautologous repetition of *māṁ* in the following line.

CHAPTER VIII

THIS chapter opens with Arjuna asking Krishna to define some unusual words he had used at the end of the last. Krishna does so though, from our point of view, rather inadequately. He then goes on to impress on Arjuna the supreme importance of one's last thoughts at death as they will determine our future existence (1–7). Hence he must fix his thoughts on God, the 'highest Person' (8–10) or on the 'Imperishable' (11–13): this will guarantee him against rebirth (14–16).

Krishna then speaks of the 'day and night' of Brahman, the world cycles which repeatedly emerge from the 'Unmanifest' and are repeatedly reabsorbed into it. Beyond this Unmanifest, however, there is another which is identical both with the 'higher' or 'exalted Person' and the 'Imperishable' (17–22).

In the final section (23–8) Krishna speaks of the two paths that are open to the soul at death. This chapter is traditionally but inappropriately called the 'Yoga of the imperishable Brahman'. It might more appropriately be called the 'Chapter of the different aspects of the Lord'.

Some Definitions

Arjuna uvāca:

1. *kiṁ tad brahma, kim adhyātmaṁ, kiṁ karma, puruṣ'ottoma,*
adhibhūtaṁ ca kiṁ proktam, adhidaivaṁ kim ucyate ?

Arjuna said:

What is That Brahman? What that which appertains to self? [And] what, O best of men, are works? What is that called which appertains to contingent beings? What that which appertains to the divine?

2. *adhiyajñaḥ kathaṁ ko 'tra dehe 'smin, Madhusūdana ?*
prayāṇa-kāle ca kathaṁ jñeyo 'si niyat'ātmabhiḥ ?

Who and in what manner is He who appertains to the sacrifice here in this body? And how, at the time of passing on, can You be known by men of self-restraint?

Śrī-bhagavān uvāca:

3. *akṣaraṁ brahma paramaṁ, svabhāvo 'dhyātmam ucyate*
bhūta-bhāv'odbhava-karo visargaḥ karma-saṁjñitaḥ.

The Blessed Lord said:

The Imperishable is the highest Brahman; it is called 'inherent nature' in so far as it appertains to [an individual] self,—as the creative force known as 'works' which gives rise to the [separate] natures of contingent beings.

akṣaraṁ, 'the Imperishable': this can either refer to the supreme principle Brahman, either as connected with or as distinct from the 'perishable' (8. 4: cf. 15. 16), or to the sacred syllable Oṁ (8. 13). In fact it almost certainly refers to both since Oṁ *is* Brahman (TU. 1. 8: MāU. 1–2). Ś. prefers to take it in the former sense only in order to distinguish it from 'Oṁ' in verse 13. R. interprets it as the 'Knower of the field' (i.e. the self, see 13. 3 ff.) in its universal form.

We have already met the 'Imperishable' in the Gītā at 3. 15 where Brahman is said to arise out of it (if indeed the passage is not referring to the syllable Oṁ and the Veda as arising from it). Here, however, Brahman is roundly identified with the Imperishable, and the Imperishable also seems to be identified with the 'higher' or 'exalted' Person (8. 21–2); moreover, Krishna implies though He does not clearly state that He is identical with both. In any case Arjuna so understands Him as both during the great theophany (11. 37–8), only to learn later that He transcends both the perishable and the Imperishable (15. 17).

In BU. 3. 8. 8–9 the 'Imperishable' is quite clearly the supreme Being—both the indescribable Eternal and the source of all phenomenal existence:

[The Imperishable] is not coarse nor fine; not short nor long; not red (like fire) nor adhesive (like water). It casts no shadow, is not darkness. It is not wind nor is it space. It is not attached to anything. It is not taste or smell; it is not eye or ear; it is not voice or mind; it is not light or life; it has no face or measure; it has no 'within', no 'without'. Nothing does it consume nor is it consumed by anyone at all.

At the behest of this Imperishable . . . sun and moon are held apart and so abide. At the behest of this Imperishable . . . sky and earth are held apart and so abide. At the behest of this Imperishable . . . seconds and minutes, days and nights, fortnights and months, seasons and years are held apart and so abide. At the behest of this Imperishable . . . some rivers flow from the white mountains to the east, others to the west, each pursuing its [appointed] course. At the behest of this Imperishable . . . men praise the open-handed, gods depend upon the sacrificer and the ancestors on the rites offered for the dead.

Here the 'Imperishable' is clearly God in every sense of the word, the God of St. Anselm 'than whom nothing higher can be thought'. With the advance of theism in the later Upanishadic period, however, the personal God, the 'Person' (*puruṣa*) of the *Muṇḍaka* and the Rudra-Śiva of the *Śvetāśvatara*, tends to be elevated above the Imperishable which is now contrasted with, and therefore limited by, the 'perishable':

What is here conjoined together—
Perishable and imperishable,
Manifest and unmanifest—
All this doth the Lord sustain. (ŚU. 1. 8.)

Perishable is Nature,
Immortal and imperishable [the self]:
Both the perishable and the self
Doth the One God Hara rule. (ibid. 1. 10.)

In the imperishable, infinite city (reading *pure*) of Brahman
Two things there are—
Wisdom and unwisdom, hidden, established there:
Perishable is unwisdom, but wisdom is immortal:
Who over wisdom and unwisdom rules, He is Another. (ibid. 5. 1.)

In MuU, 2. 1. 1–2, however, the Imperishable is not eternal Being as in ŚU., but the source of all that is perishable:

As a thousand sparks from a blazing fire
Leap forth each like the other,
So, friend, from the Imperishable, modes of being
Variously spring forth and return again thereto.

For divine and formless is the Person:
What is without and what within are his:
Unborn [is He]—pure, brilliant.
He is not breath nor mind,
He, the All-highest, beyond the Imperishable [itself].

Similarly in the Gītā Krishna, the personal God, will be extolled as 'more exalted than the Imperishable itself' (15. 18) which, as *kūṭa-stha*, 'subline, aloof' (cf. 12. 3) must be the 'highest Brahman' of this passage.

svabhāvo, 'inherent nature': *sva-bhāva* means 'own-being'. H.'s translation, 'Its Being', owing to the capital letters, is misleading.

[*a*]*dhyātmam*, 'in so far as it appertains to [an individual] self': modern translators have gone strangely wrong here. E.'s 'over-soul' which he would distinguish from the supreme Self and matter, H.'s 'Essential Self', Rk.'s 'Self', and Barnett's 'One over Self' all ignore not only Ś. but the combined witness of Upanishadic usage. Ś. correctly translates, 'with reference to self, i.e. the body'. D. and S. alone with their 'unter dem eigenen Selbste' and 'ce Brahman universel et individu' are not wide of the mark.

adhyātmam, *adhibhūtam*, and *adhidaivatam* are all common Upanishadic adverbs meaning 'with reference to the individual' (= exactly Pāli *ajjhattaṁ*), 'with reference to creatures or contingent beings in general', and 'with reference to the gods or external phenomena': see G. A. Jacob's *Concordance* ad loc. Here they may be treated as adverbs or as adjectives agreeing with *brahman*. To translate them as if they were independent substantives is quite contrary to Upanishadic usage and therefore inadmissible. *Adhyātmam* is in fact used in the sense indicated thirty-seven times in the classical Upanishads, *adhibhūtam* four times, and *adhidaivatam* fourteen times. *Adhyātmam* and *adhidaivatam* are regularly contrasted (twelve times) while the three terms appear together in BU. 3. 7. 14–15, *adhidaivatam* referring (as always) to what is outside man (earth, water, sky, sun, etc.), *adhyātmam* to what is inside man, while *adhibhūtam* refers to contingent beings in general.

It is true that in 11. 1 Arjuna thanks Krishna for having revealed to him the 'highest *adhyātma* mystery', but this is obviously not referring to this passage (in which he learns very little indeed) but to all that he has been taught about Krishna's own 'highest' Self. Similarly in the MBh. 12. 239. 1 and elsewhere an *adhyātma* doctrine is spoken of, and it turns out to be almost identical in content with the doctrine of the first six chapters of the Gītā—the same Sāṁkhya physiology and psychology and much the same account of liberation.

visargaḥ, 'creative force': so approximately E., H., Rk., Barnett, Otto, etc. D. (very oddly) 'fliessendes Sein'. Ś. takes the word to mean offerings to the gods which, according to 3. 14, produce rain which in turn produces food. As such it can be regarded as the 'seed' of all beings. R. takes it to mean sexual intercourse, and he is probably right since the ordinary meaning of *visarga* is 'excretion'. If this is so, the 'Imperishable Brahman' must be thought of not as the 'sublime, aloof, unmoving, firm' of 12. 3, but as the source of all contingent beings as in MuU. 2. 1. 1 quoted above and in the Gītā itself (3. 15). *Visarga* will then mean the emission by Krishna of his seed into 'Great Brahman' which is his 'womb' (14. 3).

Visargaḥ is best taken as being in apposition to *svabhāvo*. As far as the individual is concerned (*adhyātmam*) Brahman is its own 'inherent nature' which is itself a creative impulse which gives rise to individuation and which is itself the manifestation of *karma*. *Svabhāva*, *visarga*, and *karma* are then the manifestations in the individual (*adhyātmam*) of *kṣaro bhāvaḥ*, 'perishable nature', which is Brahman as generally manifested in the phenomenal world (*adhibhūtam*, see next stanza).

bhūta-bhāva-: not 'beings' (H., Rk.), but '[separate] natures of contingent beings' or 'states of beings' (E.).

4. *adhibhūtaṁ kṣaro bhāvaḥ, puruṣaś c'ādhidaivatam,*
adhiyajño 'ham ev'ātra dehe, deha-bhṛtāṁ vara.

In so far as it appertains to [all] contingent beings, it is [their] perishable nature, and in so far as it appertains to the gods, [it is] 'person (spirit)'. In so far as it appertains to sacrifice [it is] I here in this body, O best of men who bodies bear.

kṣaro bhāvaḥ, 'perishable nature': all contingent beings come to be and pass away, but this does not effect the sum of material beings which remains 'imperishable'. The 'Imperishable', it seems, is here the 'Imperishable' of the *Muṇḍaka* Upanishad, the source of all contingent being, rather than that of the *Śvetāśvatara* Upanishad which contrasts it starkly with the 'perishable' as the Sāṁkhya system does.

puruṣaś, 'person': this is the 'Person' of the Upanishads which derives from the *Puruṣa-sūkta* (RV. 10. 90), the supreme cosmic 'Male Person' whose dismemberment in sacrifice is the origin of the universe. In this passage this cosmic Person can be regarded as the sum-total of all individual selves (the *puruṣa*s of the Sāṁkhya), the sum-total of what R. calls the 'stuff of selves'.

adhiyajño, 'in so far as it appertains to sacrifice': it is not at all clear why Krishna here chooses to identify Himself with the sacrifice. In 4. 24 it was Brahman that was identified with the sacrifice in all its aspects: the only thing that is not claimed for it is that it is the *recipient* of the sacrifice. Krishna, in fact, by claiming to be Brahman 'in so far as it appertains to the sacrifice', means that to whatever god sacrifice may be offered, He alone is its proper recipient and object. This comes out clearly in Chapter IX where Krishna claims not only to be the sacrifice in all its aspects (9. 16), but also to be the one true recipient of every sacrifice (9. 23–4), thereby exalting Himself above Brahman—*adhiyajño*—'as far as sacrifice is concerned'. This is how R. too understands the passage. Ś. merely refers to *Taittirīya Saṁhitā* (1. 7. 4) which equates Vishnu with sacrifice; cf. MaiU. 6. 16:

> Offerer, recipient, oblation, sacred formula,
> Sacrifice, Vishnu, Prajāpati,
> The Lord is everyone who exists, the Witness
> Who shines in the circle [of the sun] up there.

ev'ātra dehe, 'here in the body': Ś., 'because sacrifice has to be performed by the body, it is inherent in the body'. R., 'because I am really present in Indra and the other gods who form my body and because sacrifice is [really] dedicated to Me'. This is probably what the Gītā means. Sacrifice is always offered up to some personal entity—even the Christian sacrifice is offered up to the 'Father', a 'Person' if ever there was one. Moreover, Krishna is personally present in the body of every living thing—man, ghost, or god—and it is there that He is either loved or hated (cf. 16. 18: 'envying and hating Me who dwell in their bodies as I dwell in all').

Where to direct your Thoughts at Death

5. *anta-kāle ca mām eva smaran muktvā kalevaram*
yaḥ prayāti, sa mad-bhāvaṁ yāti: n'āsty atra saṁśayaḥ.

Whoso at the hour of death, abandoning his mortal frame, bears Me in mind and passes on, accedes to my own mode of being: there is no doubt of this.

'My own mode of being': presumably God's 'higher' mode of being, the 'Unchangeable, All-Highest'. See 7. 24 n.

6. *yaṁ yaṁ v'āpi smaran bhāvaṁ tyajaty ante kalevaram*
taṁ tam ev'aiti, Kaunteya, sadā tad-bhāva-bhāvitaḥ.

Whatever state a man may bear in mind when in the end he casts his mortal frame aside, even to that state does he accede, for ever does that state make him grow into itself.

tad-bhāva-, 'that state': var. *mad-bhāva-*, 'my state'; *sad-bhāva-*, 'state of reality'.

-bhāvitaḥ: past part. pass. caus. of *bhū-*, 'to become': this word (in the causative) frequently means 'train'. Ś. glosses, 'projecting himself (or rather, "being projected") by bearing it in mind into that state'. This is not quite right, as it is the state or mode of being (*bhāva*) that does the projecting. The word-play on *bhāva* and *bhāvita* is difficult to render into English, but the sense of 'growing into' another form of being is clearly there. What you worship and what you believe in exercise a powerful fascination over you and make you grow into them. The same idea is expressed in 7. 23 where the worshippers of the gods are said to go to the gods and the worshippers of Krishna to go to Krishna, and again in 9. 25. Even more striking is the assertion in 17. 3: 'Man is instinct with faith: as is his faith, so too must he be.'

7. *tasmāt sarveṣu kāleṣu mām anusmara yudhya ca:*
mayy arpita-mano-buddhir, mām ev'aiṣyasy asaṁśayaḥ.

Then muse upon Me always and fight; for if you fix your mind and soul on Me, you will, nothing doubting, come to Me.

'You will . . . come to Me': R., 'you will reach Me in the form you covet'.

asaṁśayaḥ, 'nothing doubting': var. *asaṁśayam*, 'no doubt'. The first seems preferable since it is Arjuna's doubt about the ethics of fighting at all that is the occasion for the Gītā itself. By fixing his mind on Krishna even his mind, the very source of doubt (MBh. 12. 239. 15), is set at rest.

8. *abhyāsa-yoga-yuktena cetasā n'ānya-gāminā*
paramaṁ puruṣaṁ divyaṁ yāti, Pārth'ānucintayan.

Let a man's thoughts be integrated by spiritual exercise and constant striving: let them not stray to anything else at all; so by meditating on the divine exalted Person, [that man to that Person] goes.

abhyāsa-yoga-, 'spiritual exercise and constant striving' (so R.): or, 'the spiritual exercise of constant striving' (so Ś.).

'The divine exalted Person': see 8. 3 n. Krishna implies that He *is* the 'divine exalted Person' though He does not actually say so. Ś. takes 'divine' to mean the god 'in the circle of the sun', not, it would seem, the supreme Brahman. R. simply identifies him with Krishna. But see below

15. 16–17 where the 'imperishable Person' is subordinated to 'another Person, the [All-]Sublime, surnamed "All-highest Self"'.

9. *kaviṁ purāṇam anuśāsitāram*
aṇor aṇīyāṁsam anusmared yaḥ
sarvasya dhātāram acintya-rūpam
āditya-varṇaṁ tamasaḥ parastāt,

The Ancient Seer, Governor [of all things, yet] smaller than the small, Ordainer of all, in form unthinkable, sun-coloured beyond the darkness,—let a man meditate on Him [as such].

This stanza is based on different texts from the Upanishads: 'The Ancient Seer, Governor (of all things], . . . Ordainer of all', derives from *Īśā* Up. 8:

> He, the wise Sage, all-conquering, self-existent,
> Encompassed that which is resplendent,
> Incorporeal, invulnerable,
> Devoid of sinews, pure, unpierced by evil:
> [All] things He ordered each according to its nature
> For years unending.

'Smaller than the small': this is derived from KaU. 2. 20 = ŚU. 3. 20:

> Smaller than the small, greater than the great,
> The Self is hidden in the heart of creatures [here].

acintya-rūpam, 'in form unthinkable' (var. *acintya-śaktim*, 'of unthinkable power'): cf. MuU. 3. 1. 7:

> Vast, heavenly, unthinkable its form,
> Smaller than the small, forth it shines.

āditya-varṇaṁ, 'sun-coloured' (var. *āditya-rūpaṁ*, 'of the form of the sun'), 'beyond the darkness': cf. 13. 17 where 'beyond the darkness' is used of Brahman, and ŚU. 3. 8:

> I know that mighty Person,
> Sun-coloured beyond the darkness.

dhātāram, 'Ordainer': H., D., 'Creator': Rk., 'supporter': E., 'establisher': S., 'auteur'. Ś. glosses, 'who allots actions and their fruits in all their variety to living creatures and after allotting them gives [them to them]'. R., 'emanator of all'.

10. *prayāṇa-kāle manasā 'calena*
bhaktyā yukto yoga-balena c'aiva
bhruvor madhye prāṇam āveśya samyak,
so taṁ paraṁ puruṣam upaiti divyam.

With mind unmoving at the time of passing on, by love-and-devotion integrated and by the power of spiritual exercise too, forcing the breath between the eyebrows duly, so will that man draw nigh to that divine exalted Person.

yoga-balena, 'by the power of spiritual exercise': Ś. glosses, 'steadiness of thought brought about by the accumulation of the elements of concentration'. Yoga, 'spiritual exercise', is not enough, it must be accompanied by love and devotion which is itself an integrating force.

'Forcing the breath between the eyebrows duly': cf. 5. 27: 'fixing his gaze between the eyebrows, inward and outward breaths he makes the same as they pass up and down the nostrils'.

11. *yad akṣaraṁ veda-vido vadanti,*
viśanti yad yatayo vīta-rāgāḥ,
yad icchanto brahmacaryaṁ caranti,
tat te padaṁ saṁgraheṇa pravakṣye.

The imperishable state of which the Vedic scholars speak, which sages enter, their passion spent, desiring which men lead a life of chastity, that state will I proclaim to you in brief.

padaṁ, 'state': or, 'word', since the 'imperishable' here is both the 'state' of the liberated self and the syllable Oṁ (8. 13). The verse is taken from KaU. 2. 15 (with a slight change in the first line and a different second line). One MS. adds the *Kaṭha* text after this stanza:

> The single word announced by all the Vedas,
> Proclaimed by all ascetic practices . . . .

Ś. compares meditation on the syllable Oṁ to the statue of a god; it is only of assistance to the immature.

12. *sarva-dvārāṇi saṁyamya mano hṛdi nirudhya ca*
mūrdhny ādhāy' ātmanaḥ prāṇam āsthito yoga-dhāraṇām,

Let a man close up all [the body's] gates, stem his mind within the heart, fix his breath within the head, engrossed in Yogic concentration.

hṛdi, 'within the heart': in the Upanishads as in all mystical traditions the heart not the mind or the head is the seat of contemplation. R. comments, 'in Me, the Imperishable, who dwell in the lotus of the heart'. Krishna dwells in the bodies of all (16. 18): 'In the region of the heart of all contingent beings dwells the Lord' (18. 61).

'Fix his breath within the head': cf. 5. 27: 8. 10 q.v.

-dhāraṇām: '[Yogic] concentration': I have kept the word 'Yogic' as *dhāraṇā* is a technical term in the Yoga system and means 'concentration of thought on one particular field' (*Yoga-sūtras*, 3. 1). R., 'he reaches a motionless state in Me'.

13. *om ity ek'ākṣaraṁ brahma vyāharan mām anusmaran*
yaḥ prayāti tyajan dehaṁ, sa yāti paramāṁ gatim.

Let him utter [the word] Oṁ, Brahman {the One Imperishable / in one syllable}, keeping Me in mind; then, when he departs, leaving aside the body, he will tread the highest way.

As we have seen, verse 10 is taken from KaU. 2. 15. That Upanishad then goes on to identify the 'Imperishable' (see 8. 3 n.) with the syllable Oṁ (N.B. the word for 'imperishable' and 'syllable' is the same in Sanskrit):

Oṁ—this is it.

The Imperishable Brahman this,
This the Imperishable Beyond:
Whoso this Imperishable comes to know—
What he desires is his.

tyajan dehaṁ, 'leaving aside the body': one MS. has *sa mad-bhāvaṁ*, 'towards my mode of being', and instead of *paramāṁ gatim*, 'the highest way', has *n'āsty atra saṁśayaḥ*, 'there is no doubt about it'.

sa yāti paramāṁ gatim, 'he will tread the highest way': R., 'he will attain to the self in dissociation from material Nature, which means not being born again and sharing in the same form [of being] as Myself'.

14. *ananya-cetāḥ satataṁ yo māṁ smarati nityaśaḥ,*
tasy'āhaṁ sulabhaḥ, Pārtha, nitya-yuktasya yoginaḥ.

How easily am I won by him who bears Me in mind unceasingly, thinking of nothing else at all,—an athlete of the spirit ever integrated [in himself].

yoginaḥ, 'athlete of the spirit': var. *dehinaḥ*, 'embodied [self]'.

'How easily am I won . . .': the 'athlete of the spirit ever integrated [in himself]' has now reached 'that peace which has Nirvāna as its end and which subsists in Me' (6. 15); but as this stanza, like 6. 47 and 7. 28, points out, the achievement of 'integration' and 'liberation' does not yet mean full participation in the life of God. R. is continually stressing this, and he is right to do so since there really can be no doubt that this is perhaps the most crucial of all the teachings of the Gītā. What R. perhaps does not make equally clear is that though there may be other ways of reaching God, the way preferred by Krishna is that of 'spiritual exercise' (*yoga*) which, based on right knowledge (*jñāna*), must lead to integration and the vision of one's own immortal and changeless self: this is, so to speak, the base from which the direct spiritual apprehension of God as Person can most fruitfully be made. R., with his wonted enthusiasm, goes much further than the Gītā itself and puts these words into Krishna's mouth: 'Unable to bear separation from [this athlete of the spirit] I choose him and grant him the fruition of that worship (*upāsana*) which had predisposed him towards winning through to Me—[a fruition] which thrusts away all that is antagonistic to it, and which, among other things, includes a boundless love of Me.'

15. *mām upetya punar-janma duḥkh'ālayam aśāśvatam*
n'āpnuvanti mah'ātmānaḥ saṁsiddhiṁ paramāṁ gatāḥ.

Coming right nigh to Me these great of self are never born again, [for rebirth is] the abode of suffering, knows nothing that abides: [free from it now] they attain the highest prize.

'The highest prize': Ś., 'liberation': R. again lets himself go: 'Their wisdom conformed to Me as I really am, out of the excess of the love they bear Me, they are unable to sustain the existence of their very selves without Me; their minds attached to Me, putting their trust in Me and worshipping Me, they win through to Me who am their highest prize.'

16. *ā brahma-bhuvanāl lokāḥ punar-āvartino, 'rjuna,*
mām upetya tu, Kaunteya, punar-janma na vidyate.

The worlds right up to Brahmā's realm [dissolve and] evolve again; but he who comes right nigh to Me shall never be born again.

The Day and Night of Brahmā

17. *sahasra-yuga-paryantam ahar yad brahmaṇo viduḥ,*
rātriṁ yuga-sahasr'āntāṁ te 'ho-rātra-vido janāḥ.

For a thousand ages lasts [one] day of Brahmā, and for a thousand ages [one such] night: this knowing, men will know [what is meant by] day and night.

yuga-, 'ages': a 'great *yuga*' lasts 4,320,000 earthly years.

18. *avyaktād vyaktayaḥ sarvāḥ prabhavanty ahar-āgame;*
rātry-āgame pralīyante tatr'aiv'āvyakta-saṁjñake.

At the day's dawning all things manifest spring forth from the Unmanifest; and then at nightfall they dissolve [again] in that same thing called 'Unmanifest'.

The 'Unmanifest' is the *pradhāna*, 'primal matter' or 'undifferentiated primal Nature' of the Sāṁkhya system (*Sāṁkhya-kārikā*, 10–11). Unlike all that evolves from it it is uncaused, eternal, all-pervasive, inactive, one, relying on itself alone, without characteristics, without parts, and independent. All these qualities, or rather the lack of them, it has in common with the *puruṣas*, the 'persons', 'spirits', or 'selves' of that system, but unlike them it is productive and dynamic: its eternity is an eternity of endless duration, not of timeless Being. It is constant under all the 'manifestations' that proceed from it in that quantitatively it remains ever the same. In the myth of the day and night of Brahmā it corresponds to the night when the whole universe is reabsorbed into a total unconsciousness. In the Upanishads, as we have seen (3. 42 n.), it is subordinated to a cosmic *Puruṣa* who is God.

19. *bhūta-grāmaḥ sa ev'āyaṁ bhūtvā bhūtvā pralīyate*
rātry-āgame 'vaśaḥ, Pārtha, prabhavaty ahar-āgame.

Yes, this whole host of beings comes ever anew to be; at fall of night it dissolves away all helpless; at dawn of day it rises up again.

'All helpless': R., 'because of *karma*': those selves which have 'drawn nigh' to God are, however, excepted from this universal process.

The Unmanifest beyond the Unmanifest

20. *paras tasmāt tu bhāvo 'nyo 'vyakto 'vyaktāt sanātanaḥ*
yaḥ, sa sarveṣu bhūteṣu naśyatsu na vinaśyati.

But beyond that there is [yet] another mode of being,—beyond the Unmanifest [another] Unmanifest (*masc.*), primeval: this is he who does not fall to ruin when all contingent beings are destroyed.

'vyakto 'vyaktāt, 'beyond the Unmanifest [another] Unmanifest': var. *'vyakt'āvyaktaḥ*, 'unmanifest to the unmanifest(?)'; *puruṣ'ākhyaḥ*, 'called Person'; *vyakt'āvyaktaḥ*, 'unmanifest to the manifest'.

This second 'Unmanifest' is possibly the 'exalted Person' of 8. 22. This passage seems to derive from KaU. 6. 7–8 (cf. ibid. 3. 10–11. BhG. 3. 42 n.):

Higher than the senses is the mind,
Higher than mind the soul (*sattva*),
Higher than soul, the self, the 'great',
Higher than [this] 'great', the Unmanifest.

Higher than [this] Unmanifest the 'Person',
Pervading all, untraceable (or, not possessing a subtle body).

In the Gītā the word *avyakta*, 'unmanifest', has already been used of the individual self-in-itself (2. 25): 'Unmanifest, unthinkable, immutable is it called: realize it thus and do not grieve [about it].' This individual self (*masc.*) forms part of or is identical with what R. would call 'self-stuff' (*neut.*) which is 'indestructible' and 'does not pass away' (2. 17), in other words, 'primeval Brahman' (4. 31: cf. 8. 3).

21. *avyakto 'kṣara ity uktas; tam āhuḥ paramāṁ gatim,*
yaṁ prāpya na nivartante: tad dhāma paramaṁ mama.

Unmanifest [is he], surnamed 'Imperishable': this, men say, is the highest way and, this once won, there is no more returning: this is my highest home.

The 'Unmanifest beyond the Unmanifest' is, then, identical with the 'Imperishable' Brahman of 8. 3 of which it is the personalized form. This 'Imperishable' is presumably that of BU. 3. 8. 8–9, the supreme Being in every sense, rather than the attenuated form of it we find in ŚU. 1. 10 and 5. 1 or of MuU. 2. 1. 1–2 (see 8. 3 n.), for in KaU. 3. 11 on which this passage is based we read:

> Than 'Person' there is nothing higher;
> He is the goal, He *the highest way* (as here).

Further he is Krishna's 'highest home', by which is presumably meant his 'higher state, the Changeless, All-Highest' (7. 24). *Dhāma* is a word only rarely used in the Upanishads though common in the Rig-Veda where it usually means 'home' or 'law'. In KauU. 3. 1 it is used of 'Indra's well-loved abode'. Krishna's *dhāma* would, then, seem to be the *ambiance* in which He has his being, that is, timeless bliss; and so Arjuna considers it appropriate to call Krishna himself 'highest Brahman, highest home' (10. 12: cf. 11. 38). According to R. God has three *dhāmas*, 'abodes' or 'states'. The first is Krishna's lower Nature (7. 4) which is unconscious, the second is his 'living' Nature (7. 5) which is the state of selves which are still involved in this lower Nature, and lastly the state of released selves which is a state of pure spirit undefiled by matter. It is this state that Krishna is speaking of here, and this state, like the other two is subject to his control. Alternatively, he says, *dhāma* can mean 'light'.

R.'s analysis of the three 'abodes' or 'states' of the supreme Being of the Gītā is ingenious and interesting, but it does raise difficulties. *Unless* we are prepared to separate the 'Person' of the next stanza from the 'Unmanifest (*masc.*) beyond the unmanifest (*neut.*)' of this and the preceding stanzas, this second Unmanifest can only be God. The two 'unmanifests' mentioned here are not the two 'Natures' of Krishna mentioned in 7. 4–5 as R. rightly saw. The first 'Unmanifest' is the material Nature of the Sāṁkhya system from which everything that is conditioned by time including what we call soul (*buddhi*), mind, and individuality proceed and into which they all dissolve. This applies equally to 'living Nature' which, as R. rightly says, is composed of human selves still enmeshed in matter; *but* this 'living Nature', as we saw at 7. 5, must also include individual selves as they are in themselves and as they are seen by *buddhi*, what the *Kaṭha* Upanishad misleadingly calls the 'great self'. These, by the mere fact that they are 'seen' by *buddhi*, still retain a link with that element. As MBh. 12. 240. 20–2 puts it:

The one (*sattva* = *buddhi*) emits qualities, the other does not. Though in the natural state of affairs the two are [theoretically] separate, they are always linked together. Just as a fish is other than water, even so are these two linked together; or again as a gnat is [indissolubly] linked with the fig [in which it lives], or again as the pith is both separate from and united with the grass [of which it is the pith], so are these two united and established in each other.

This, then, would appear to be the position of the 'great self' of the *Kaṭha* Upanishad which is the same as the 'living Nature' of BhG. 7. 5. Along with everything else it must lose its identity in 'unmanifest Nature' at the end of a world era. The Gītā, however, is now speaking in cosmic terms, not in terms of the individual: it is affirming the existence of one single 'Person' beyond the Unmanifest, of one single Spirit beyond primal matter from which both mind and individuality and what we call soul originate. It is not speaking of individual selves as the next stanza shows, but of one spiritual principle beyond 'unmanifest' material Nature. This is the Person 'beyond the darkness' of 8. 9, since 'darkness' is not only the name of the lowest of the constituents of Nature, but also a synonym for the Sāṁkhya 'Unmanifest' (cf. MBh. 12. 335. 14).

22. *puruṣaḥ sa paraḥ, Pārtha, bhaktyā labhyas tv ananyayā*
yasy'āntaḥsthāni bhūtāni, yena sarvam idaṁ tatam.

But that highest *Person* is to be won by love-and-worship directed to none other. In Him do all beings subsist; by Him this universe is spun.

Some MSS. add: *yaṁ prāpya na punar-janma labhante yogino, 'rjuna* 'once athletes of the spirit have achieved Him, Arjuna, they are not born again'.

ananyayā, 'directed to none other': or, 'in no other way'. The first is preferable since wisdom and spiritual integration are required in addition to love and devotion.

'In Him all beings subsist': the same phrase is used of Krishna in 9. 4.

'By Him this universe is spun': cf. 2. 17 where the phrase is used of the 'indestructible [Brahman]'. Ś. there as here glosses *tatam*, 'spun' as *vyāptam*, 'pervaded'. The phrase is later applied to Krishna Himself (9. 4: 11. 38: 18. 46).

Let us now resume the claims the Gītā makes on behalf of the 'exalted Person' in these three stanzas. This 'Person' is the supreme 'Person' of the Upanishads with whom Krishna clearly identifies Himself in the following chapter.

He is—

(i) the 'Unmanifest beyond the Unmanifest', that is to say, the 'Person' of the *Kaṭha* Upanishad 'than whom there is nothing higher';

(ii) the 'Indestructible' principle of Gītā 2. 17 which 'does not pass away', that is, the highest Brahman;
(iii) the 'Imperishable' of BU. 3. 8. 8–9 of which nothing positive can be predicated, but at whose 'behest sun and moon are held apart and so abide';
(iv) the 'highest way', identified in KaU. 3. 11 with the 'Person';
(v) Krishna's 'highest home', that is, his highest mode of being;
(vi) finally, the highest or exalted 'Person' to whom alone love and devotion are due, who indwells all beings and by whom 'this universe is spun'.

All these epithets except the last might apply to the liberated selves or to the aggregate of them, particularly if we remember that the 'Imperishable' had suffered a diminution in the *Muṇḍaka* and *Śvetāśvatara* Upanishads which are far more closely related to the Gītā than is the *Bṛhadāraṇyaka*, that the 'highest way' is generally no more than a synonym for 'liberation', and that on the face of it Krishna's 'highest home' can scarcely be fully identical with Krishna Himself. R., whose commentary is really obscure here, nevertheless distinguishes between two 'ways' which have one thing in common, namely, that they both put a stop to rebirth. One is the way of the man who gets to know the self-in-itself as it really is, the other is the way that leads to the supreme Lord as its final goal. It seems to me, however, that there is a deliberate ambiguity here, and the Gītā is content to keep the reader guessing as to whether this 'Person beyond the darkness' is the liberated self or rather the aggregate of liberated selves, or whether it is Krishna, supreme God and Supreme Lord, to whom alone love and devotion are due. This ambiguity ceases in verse 22 since the 'Person' here is defined as He who 'is won by love-and-worship directed to none other'.

There would therefore be no difficulty in referring the whole passage to the personal God, did we not find in 15. 16–17 that this 'imperishable Person' is again referred to, and there this 'imperishable Person' is sharply contrasted with the 'perishable' as also happens in the *Śvetāśvatara* Upanishad. Since there is there an 'ultimate' (*uttama*) Person as well—Krishna, who transcends both the 'Imperishable' and the 'perishable'—the 'Imperishable' must refer to liberated individual selves or to the aggregate of them which together form one spiritual block—the 'fixed, still state of Brahman' of 2. 72. This is there also called *kūṭa-stha*, 'sublime, aloof'—a term that is applied to the integrated man in 6. 8 (q.v.) and to the 'Imperishable Unmanifest' in 12. 3 which is plainly another way of speaking of the 'fixed, still state of Brahman' or the 'Nirvāna that is Brahman too' of 2. 72 and 5. 24–6.

Hence it would seem that verse 22 should be separated from the two preceding stanzas, and this does not seem unnatural in view of the use of the particle *tu*, 'but'. This at least obviates the difficulty of identifying Krishna with his *dhāma*, his 'home' or 'highest state' which can scarcely be an object of loving devotion any more than Nirvāna can be, or indeed the 'Imperishable Unmanifest' as understood in 12. 3.

The Fate of the Soul at Death

23. *yatra kāle tv anāvṛttim āvṛttiṁ c'aiva yoginaḥ*
prayātā yānti, taṁ kālaṁ vakṣyāmi, Bharata'rṣabha.

Some to return, some never to return, athletes of the spirit set forth when they pass on; the times [and seasons] of them all I shall [now] declare.

24. *agnir jyotir ahaḥ śuklaḥ ṣaṇmāsā uttar'āyaṇam,—*
tatra prayātā gacchanti brahma brahma-vido janāḥ.

Fire, light, day, [the moon's] light [fortnight], the six months of the [sun's] northern course,—dying in these to Brahman do they go, the men who Brahman know.

This is based on ChU. 5. 10. 1–2 = BU. 6. 2. 14:

Those who know thus as well as those who worship in the forest knowing that self-mortification is the same as faith, merge into the flame [of the funeral pyre]; from the flame [they pass on] into the day, from the day into the half-month of the full moon, from the half-month of the full moon into the six months during which the sun moves northwards, from [those] months into the year, from the year into the sun, from the sun into the moon, from the moon into the lightning. There, there is a Person who is other than human. He leads them on to Brahman. This path is the 'way of the gods'.

25. *dhūmo rātris tathā kṛṣṇaḥ ṣaṇmāsā dakṣiṇ'āyanam,—*
tatra cāndramasaṁ jyotir yogī prāpya nivartate.

Smoke, night, [the moon's] dark [fortnight], the six months of the [sun's] southern course,—[dying] in these an athlete of the spirit wins the light of the moon, and back he comes again.

ChU. 5. 10. 3–6 = BU. 6. 2–15:

But those who in their villages lay great store by sacrifice, good works, and the giving of alms, merge into smoke, from smoke [they pass on] into the night, from the night into the latter half of the month, from the latter half of the month into the six months in which the sun moves southwards. These do not reach the year. From [those] months they [merge] into the world of the ancestors, from the world of the ancestors into space, from space into the moon which is King Soma, the food of the gods. This the gods eat up.

There they remain until the residue [of their good works] is exhausted, and then they once again return on the same path. [They merge] into space, and from space into the wind. After becoming wind, they become smoke; after becoming smoke, they become mist; after becoming mist, they become cloud; after becoming cloud, they pour forth as rain. [Then] they are born here as rice or barley, herbs or trees, sesame or beans. To emerge from these is very difficult. For only if someone or other eats [him as] food and pours [him out as] semen, can he be born again.

26. *śukla-kṛṣṇe gatī hy ete jagataḥ śāśvate mate;*
ekayā yāty anāvṛttim, anyayā 'vartate punaḥ.

For these two courses—light and dark—are deemed to be primeval [laws] on earth. One leads to [the place of] no return, by the other one returns again.

mate, 'are deemed to be': var. *same*, 'are the same'.

27. *n'aite sṛtī, Pārtha, jānan yogī muhyati kaścana;*
tasmāt sarveṣu kāleṣu yoga-yukto bhav'ārjuna.

Knowing these two courses no athlete of the spirit whatever is perplexed; so, Arjuna, be integrated by spiritual exercise at all times.

28. *vedeṣu yajñeṣu tapaḥsu c'aiva*
dāneṣu yat puṇya-phalaṁ pradiṣṭam
atyeti tat sarvam, idaṁ viditvā
yogī paraṁ sthānam upaiti c'ādyam.

For knowledge of the Veda, for sacrifice, for grim austerities, for gifts of alms a meed of merit is laid down: all this the athlete of the spirit leaves behind who knows this [secret teaching; and knowing it] he draws right nigh to the exalted primal state.

ādyam, 'primal': Ś. refers this to Brahman as cause.

CHAPTER IX

In this Chapter Krishna develops more fully what He had adumbrated in 7. 4–7, 12–14, 24–6, namely, that He is God in every sense of the word: He is the highest Brahman and the highest Person of the Upanishads and of the earlier chapters of the Gītā itself, the ground and support of the universe (4–6). He creates the world out of matter which is his own (lower) Nature (7–8) though He remains forever unaffected by his creative activity.

He then goes on to speak of his incarnation and how this deceives many. Those sincerely devoted to Him on the other hand find in it an additional reason for glorifying Him, and men of wisdom see in Him the One who manifests Himself in the many (11–15).

As in 7. 8–11 there is an interlude here in which Krishna lists some of his essential characteristics (16–19): both interludes will be developed at length in the next chapter where Krishna identifies Himself with whatever is most excellent in any form of cosmic or human existence.

In 20–5 Krishna develops again what had already been stated in 7. 20–3; but whereas there He had said of the worshippers of other gods that He actually strengthened their faith in them though their goals remained finite, He here goes a step further and says that all worship is really directed towards Himself, though the worshipper may not realize it.

Even the humblest act of worship receives its reward, and if men make of all their doing and all their living an offering to Himself, they will thereby be released from the 'bonds of works' and draw nigh to Him (26–9). Loving devotion wipes out all sin and, unlike the religion of the Vedas, is accessible even to serfs and women (30–2). He finally urges Arjuna to love and adore Him and with integrated self to make Him alone his goal. The chapter is traditionally known as the 'Yoga of Royal Knowledge and the Royal Mystery'; it is in fact a chapter of love and devotion.

God and His Creation

Śrī-bhagavān uvāca:

1. *idaṁ tu te guhyatamaṁ pravakṣyāmy anasūyave*
jñānaṁ vijñana-sahitaṁ yaj jñātvā mokṣyase 'śubhāt.

The Blessed Lord said:

But most secret-and-mysterious is this wisdom I will [now] reveal,—[a wisdom] based on holy writ and consonant with experience: to you [will I proclaim it,] for in you there is no envy; and knowing it you shall be freed from ill.

jñānaṁ . . ., 'a wisdom based on holy writ . . .': following Ś. and R. on 7. 2. Here too Ś. interprets *vijñāna* as 'experience', but interprets *jñāna*, 'wisdom', in accordance with his own philosophical predilections: 'Krishna is All; the Self is this All'. R. does the same: for him *jñāna* means *bhakti*, 'love-and-devotion' and *vijñāna* 'worship'!

[*a*]*śubhāt*, 'from ill': Ś., 'the bondage of phenomenal existence (*saṁsāra*)'.

2. *rāja-vidyā rāja-guhyaṁ pavitram idam uttamam*
pratyakṣ'āvagamaṁ dharmyaṁ susukhaṁ kartum avyayam.

Science of kings, mystery of kings is this, distilling the purest essence, to the understanding evident, with righteousness enhanced,—how easy to carry out! [Yet] it abides forever.

uttamam, 'highest': var. *adbhutam*, 'marvellous'.

3. *aśraddadhānāḥ puruṣā dharmasy'āsya, paraṁtapa,*
aprāpya māṁ nivartante mṛtyu-saṁsāra-vartmani.

Men who put no faith in this law of righteousness fail to reach Me and must return to the road of recurring death.

dharmasy[*a*], 'law of righteousness': var. *jñānasy*[*a*], 'wisdom'. The difference is minimal since both words in the context mean 'teaching'.

4. *mayā tatam idaṁ sarvaṁ jagad avyakta-mūrtinā:*
mat-sthāni sarva-bhūtāni, na c'āhaṁ teṣv avasthitaḥ.

By Me, Unmanifest in form, all this universe was spun: in Me subsist all beings, I do not subsist in them.

'Unmanifest in form': or, 'in the form of the Unmanifest'. It is not clear whether Krishna is referring to what is normally called the 'Unmanifest', that is, the 'primal matter' of the Sāṁkhya system or to the 'Unmanifest beyond the Unmanifest' of 8. 20. Ś. seems to think it is the latter. He is probably right since 'this universe was spun' by the 'Indestructible [Brahman]' in 2. 17 and by the 'highest Person' who is almost certainly to be identified with Krishna in 8. 22. Against this Krishna is certainly speaking of the lower 'Unmanifest' in verses 6–8.

'In Me subsist all beings': Ś., 'they subsist in Me as essential Self [themselves]'. R., 'they exist in Me as their Inner Controller' (BU 3. 7. 3 ff.). Krishna here identifies Himself with the 'highest Person' of 8. 22, 'in Him do all beings subsist'.

'I do not subsist in them': Ś., 'because I have no contact with them as corporeal things do'. R., 'my continued existence does not depend on them, and because their continued existence depends on Me, I do not need them in any way'.

5. *na ca mat-sthāni bhūtāni, paśya me yogam aiśvaram:*
bhūta-bhṛn, na ca bhūta-stho mam'ātmā bhūta-bhāvanaḥ.

And [yet] contingent beings do not subsist in Me,—behold my sovereign $\left\{\begin{array}{l}\text{skill-in-works}\\ \text{activity}\end{array}\right\}$: my Self sustains [all] beings, It does not subsist in them; It causes them to be-and-grow.

'Contingent beings do not subsist in Me': Ś., 'He is speaking of Self in its essence'. R., 'not because He contains them like water in a pot, but [because He maintains them in existence] by his will (*saṁkalpa*)'.

yogam, $\left\{\begin{array}{l}\text{`skill-in-works'}\\ \text{`activity'}\end{array}\right\}$: *yoga* was defined as 'skill in [performing] works' at 2. 50, and this is probably what it means here, perhaps with overtones of uncanny power. The point surely is that contingent beings do not 'subsist' or 'abide' in God because they are of themselves transient: they can only be said to subsist in Him in the sense that the wind, the most fickle and unstable of all elements, subsists in space (see the next stanza).

'My Self sustains [all] beings, It does not subsist in them': Ś., 'He sustains them though He is unattached to them'. When Krishna speaks of his 'Self' as being active as he does here, Ś. says, He is using popular terminology. R., for whom there is no real inconsistency between God as pure Being and God as providence and will, glosses: 'my very Self, my will which is akin to mind, brings contingent beings into existence, keeps them in existence and controls them'. So too for Ś. *-bhāvanaḥ* means 'to bring into existence and to cause to grow'. This whole passage should be compared to 13. 14–16 where very much the same is said of Brahman.

According to Ś. and R. Krishna 'does not subsist in beings' because, as they have both pointed out, He does not depend on them nor has He any need of them. As in the *Iśā* Upanishad it is impossible to confine God either to the world of eternity—the *ambiance* of liberated selves—or to the world of time—the universe as we know it. God's 'Self' both operates in time because it *is* Time (11. 32) and *is* the changeless Absolute, the 'same' Lord dwelling everywhere in the body (13. 28, 32).

mam'ātmā, 'my Self': var. *bhūt'ātmā*, 'the Self in contingent beings': *dharm'ātmā*, 'having the essence of righteousness'.

One MS. adds here:

sarva-gaḥ sarvavac c'ādyaḥ sarva-kṛt sarva-darśanaḥ
sarva-jñaḥ sarva-darśī ca sarv'ātmā sarvato-mukhaḥ.

'Penetrating everywhere, made up of all, primeval, doer of all, all-seeing, all-knowing, all-descrying, Self of all, facing in all directions.'

6. *yath'ākāśa-sthito nityaṁ vāyuḥ sarvatra-go mahān,*
tathā sarvāṇi bhūtāni mat-sthānī'ty upadhāraya.

As in [wide] space subsists the mighty wind blowing [at will] ever and everywhere, so do all contingent beings subsist in Me: so must you understand it.

See previous note. Several MSS. add here:

evaṁ hi sarva-bhūteṣu carāmy anabhilakṣitaḥ
bhūta-prakṛtim āsthāya sah'aiva ca vin'aiva ca.

'For thus I rove in all contingent beings unobserved: consorting with the material nature of each of them, I am truly both with them and without them.'

7. *sarva-bhūtāni, Kaunteya, prakṛtiṁ yānti māmikām*
kalpa-kṣaye, punas tāni kalp'ādau visṛjāmy aham.

All contingent beings pour into material Nature which is mine when a world-aeon comes to an end; and then again when [another] aeon starts, I emanate them forth.

The day and night of Brahmā described in 8. 17–18. Cf. also the two 'Natures' of Krishna described in 7. 4–6 where the material Nature of the Sāṁkhya system is only Krishna's 'lower' Nature. The 'higher' Nature is in fact that aspect of God which keeps the world in being—his higher Nature 'developed into life by which this world is kept in being' (7. 5). This 'higher Nature', then, is what Krishna understands by his 'Self' in 9. 5. It is akin to the 'seed', the male principle, He mentions in 7. 10 and which in 14. 3 He will speak of as being emitted into 'great Brahman' as into a womb. 'Living Nature' is, then, the result of the fusion of God's seed, the spiritual principle with his lower Nature—matter.

8. *prakṛtiṁ svām avaṣṭabhya visṛjāmi punaḥ punaḥ*
bhūta-grāmam imaṁ kṛtsnam avaśaṁ prakṛter vaśāt.

Subduing my own material Nature ever again I emanate this whole host of beings,—powerless [themselves], from Nature comes the power.

avaṣṭabhya, 'subduing': I follow Ś. who glosses *vaśīkṛtya*, 'subduing'. One MS. reads *adhiṣṭhāya* as in 4. 6, 'consort with'. The idea is certainly the same. In 4. 6 Krishna consorts with 'his own' Nature in order to be born as the incarnate God; here He 'subdues', 'relies on', or 'consorts with' her in order to produce the entire phenomenal world. The phrase in both passages has a sexual connotation which becomes explicit in 14. 3: 'Great Brahman is to Me a womb, in it I plant the seed: from this derives the origin of all contingent beings.' The phenomenal world, then, is the result of the sexual union of God the Father and God the Mother (cf. 9. 17, 'I am the father of this world, [its] mother'), that is, of spirit and matter.

9. *na ca māṁ tāni karmāṇi nibadhnanti, dhanaṁjaya,*
udāsīnavad āsīnam asaktaṁ teṣu karmasu.

These works [of mine] neither bind-nor-limit Me: as one indifferent I sit among these works, detached.

'Works neither bind-nor-limit Me': a now familiar theme. There is nothing Krishna need do nor is there anything to be attained that He does not already possess (3. 22); hence works can never affect Him nor does He yearn for their fruits (4. 14). Like the *puruṣa*, 'person' or 'spirit' of the Sāṁkhya He is 'as one indifferent' (*Saṁkhya-kārikā*, 20). There is, however, a slight difference: the Sāṁkhya *puruṣa is* indifferent while the God of the Gītā is *udāsīna-vat*, '*as* one indifferent'. Hence, though He may neither love nor hate any contingent being (9. 29), this does not prevent Him 'loving' the man of wisdom who is devoted to Him (7. 17) and indeed all who have transcended passion and hate and who reach precisely that 'indifference' He claims as his own. The divine indifference does not preclude a love based on approval, for the God of the Gītā, as must already be apparent, is as firmly established in this world of change and action as He is in the 'fixed, still state of Brahman'.

10. *mayā 'dhyakṣeṇa prakṛtiḥ sūyate sacar'ācaram;*
hetunā 'nena, Kaunteya, jagad viparivartate.

[A world of] moving and unmoving things material Nature brings to birth while I look-on-and-supervise: this is the cause [and this the means] by which the world revolves.

God is not quite so indifferent as the last stanza would have us believe: He supervises and controls the world, and this, according to R., He does in accordance with the past actions of each individual. Thus God is never responsible for evil; evil is the result of bad actions performed in former lives. The idea of God controlling the world goes back to BU. 3. 7. 3 ff.:

> He who, abiding in the earth, is other than the earth, whom the earth does not know, whose body is the earth, who controls the earth from within—He is the Self within you, the Inner Controller, the Immortal.

God's Incarnation as Krishna

11. *avajānanti māṁ mūḍhā mānuṣīṁ tanum āśritam*
paraṁ bhāvam ajānanto mama bhūta-mah'eśvaram.

For that a human form I have assumed fools scorn Me, knowing nothing of my higher state,—great Lord of contingent beings.

mūḍhā, 'fools': lit. 'deluded'. R., 'by their evil deeds', but we have already been told that it is the constituents of Nature or Nature itself, also called the divine *māyā*, which 'deludes' man and conceals his own self and God, the supreme Self, from him (7. 13–15). God's incarnation is a snare that conceals his 'higher state', the 'Changeless, All-Highest' (7. 24).

mama bhūta-mah'eśvaram, 'my . . .—great Lord of contingent beings': var. *mam'āvyayam anuttamam*, 'my [highest state], the Changeless, All-Highest' (as in 7. 24): *sarva-bhūta-mah'eśvaram*, 'great Lord of all contingent beings'.

God's 'higher state' which in 7. 24 was 'the Changeless, All-Highest' has now become that of the 'great Lord of contingent beings'. He is not only that which never changes when all else changes but also the Lord and master of all that changes too, the Lord of human 'selves' as much as He is the Lord of the changing universe. As in BU. 2. 5. 15 He is at once the centre and the circumference of the wheel of existence and thereby the Lord of all:

This Self is indeed the Lord of all contingent beings, king of all beings. Just as the spokes of a wheel are together fixed on to the hub and felloe, so are all contingent beings, all gods, all worlds, all vital breaths and all these selves together fixed in this Self.

12. *mogh'āśā mogha-karmāṇo mogha-jñānā vicetasaḥ*
rākṣasīm āsurīṁ c'aiva prakṛtiṁ mohinīṁ śritāḥ.

Vain their hopes and vain their deeds, vain their 'gnosis', vain their wit; a monstrous devilish nature they embrace which leads [them far] astray.

'A monstrous devilish nature': 'Nature' is still *prakṛti* and therefore still derives from Krishna as God. Both the 'eightfold' material Nature of the Sāṁkhya system and the 'living Nature' which is that same Nature ensouled by individual selves (7. 4–5) belong to Krishna; both are pervaded by the three constituents of Nature which is synonymous with *māyā*. It is of the essence of material Nature or *māyā* to lead astray through the constituents (7. 13) even when it is considered as beneficent or 'divine' (7. 14), for, when all is said and done, Krishna, like the man 'integrated by soul' (2. 50), is beyond good and evil.

Whether material Nature is called 'divine' or 'devilish', it remains Krishna's own Nature: it becomes 'devilish' to those whose deeds in past lives had lowered them in the cosmic scale of value, 'divine' to those who had risen high. One's disposition and destiny depend on past *karma* which determines one's present character: 'a godly destiny means deliverance, a devilish one enslavement (bondage)' (16. 5). R. is very insistent that evil does not exist in God and that it is entirely the fruit of evil deeds performed in past lives and maturing in this one.

13. *mah'ātmānas tu māṁ, Pārtha, daivīṁ prakṛtim āśritāḥ*
bhajanty ananya-manaso jñātvā bhūt'ādim avyayam.

But great-souled men take up their stand in a nature that is divine; and so with minds intent on naught but [Me], they love-and-worship Me, knowing [Me to be] the beginning of [all] contingent beings, as Him who passes not away.

'Knowing Me . . .': see 7. 30 n. No one can know God as He really is (7. 26), but it is possible to know Him in part as the beginning of all things for instance. 'Although the true nature of my name and activity (*karma*) are inaccessible to voice or mind, they love-and-worship Me in my incarnation in human form which takes place because of my tender compassion and for the protection of the good' (R.). The signs of the man who 'takes his stand in a nature that is divine' are 'tranquillity, self-control, compassion, and faith' (Ś.).

14. *satataṁ kīrtayanto māṁ yatantaś ca dṛḍha-vratāḥ*
namasyantaś ca māṁ bhaktyā nitya-yuktā upāsate.

Me do they ever glorify, [for Me] they strive, full firm their vows; to Me do they bow down, devoted-in-their-love, and integrated ever [in themselves] they pay Me worship.

This stanza rubs in the lesson of 8. 14: 'How easily am I won by him who bears Me in mind unceasingly, thinking of nothing else at all—an athlete of the spirit ever integrated [in himself].' And this again takes up 7. 28 and 6. 31: 'Some there are for whom [all] ill is ended, doers of what is good-and-pure: released [at last] from the confusion of duality, steady in their vows, they love-and-worship Me.' 'Who standing firm on unity communes-in-love with Me as abiding in all beings, in whatever state he be, that athlete of the spirit abides in Me.'

The essential point, however, was most clearly stated in 6. 47: 'But of all athletes of the spirit the man of faith who loves-and-honours Me, his *inmost self* absorbed in Me—he is the most fully integrated: this do I believe.'

This is the highest form of loving devotion, the *parā bhakti* which in 18. 54 God bestows on the man who has already become Brahman. It should, then, be absolutely clear that for the Gītā integration of the personality which unveils the marvels of the naked human self as it is *in* God is only a stage on its journey *to* God.

The lower stages of loving devotion are outlined later in this chapter (verses 26–32).

15. *jñāna-yajñena c'āpy anye yajanto mām upāsate*
ekatvena pṛthaktvena bahudhā viśvato-mukham.

Others again with wisdom's sacrifice make sacrifice to Me and worship Me as One and yet as Manifold, in many a guise with face turned every way.

'As One and yet as Manifold': unity *in* multiplicity is the consistent doctrine of the Gītā. First, the unity of the self-in-itself must be recognized, realized, experienced (6. 31), then comes participation and communion (*bhakti*) with the whole and through the whole with God (ibid.). God is One, yet really present everywhere (11. 13: 13. 16: 18. 20) and eminently present in the human heart (18. 61: cf. 13. 17) even though the owner of that heart may hate Him (16. 18). For R. the universe of unconscious matter, conscious beings still dependent on matter, and selves as they are eternally in themselves together form the one infinitely varied body of God who is Himself the One Great Self of the whole universe.

Some Essential Attributes of God

16. *ahaṁ kratur, ahaṁ yajñaḥ, svadhā 'ham, aham auṣadham,*
mantro 'ham, aham ev'ājyam, aham agnir, ahaṁ hutam.

I am the rite, the sacrifice, the offering for the dead, the healing herb; I am the sacred formula, the sacred butter am I: I am the fire and I the oblation offered [in the fire].

Krishna, it will be remembered, specifically identifies Himself with the sacrifice (8. 4) and hence with Brahman, the sacrificial link between this world and eternity (4. 24 n.). This identification will be extended in later chapters and particularly in 13. 12–17.

17. *pitā 'ham asya jagato, mātā dhātā pitāmahaḥ*
vedyaṁ pavitram oṁ-kāra ṛk sāma yajur eva ca.

I am the father of this world, mother, ordainer, grandsire, [all] that need be known; vessel of purity [am I, the sacred syllable] Oṁ, and the Rig-, Sāma-, and Yajur-Vedas too.

dhātā, 'ordainer': or, 'creator, supporter'. Ś., 'He who allots the fruits of their works to living creatures'. R. thinks it refers principally to the conscious principle which, apart from the role of father and mother, causes the coming-to-be of conscious beings.

'Rig-, Sāma-, and Yajur-Vedas': one MS. manages to fit in the Atharva-Veda too.

18. *gatir bhartā prabhuḥ sākṣī nivāsaḥ śaraṇaṁ suhṛt*
prabhavaḥ pralayaḥ sthānaṁ nidhānaṁ bījam avyayam.

[I am] the Way, sustainer, Lord, and witness, [true] home and refuge, friend,—origin and dissolution and the stable state [between],—a treasure-house, the seed that passes not away.

gatir, 'the Way': or 'goal, refuge'.

bhartā, 'sustainer': or, 'husband'.

bījam, 'seed': cf. 7. 10: 'Know that I am the primeval seed of all contingent beings.' So too 10. 39.

19. *tapāmy aham, ahaṁ varṣaṁ nigṛhṇāmy utsṛjāmi ca:*
amṛtaṁ c'aiva mṛtyuś ca, sad asac c'āham, Arjuna.

It is I who pour out heat, hold back the rain and send it forth: deathlessness am I and death, what IS and what is not.

sad asac ca, 'what IS and what is not': in this passage *sat*, 'what is', and *asat*, 'what is not' almost certainly mean immortality and death. This seems to be directly borrowed from BU. 1. 3. 28:

> From what is not lead me to what IS!
> From darkness lead me to the light!
> From death lead me to deathlessness!

Here the Upanishad glosses: 'By "what is not" [he means] death, by "what IS" deathlessness.' In other Upanishadic passages *sat* and *asat* seem to mean very nearly spirit and matter. See 2. 16 n.

In 11. 37 Arjuna confesses that Krishna is 'what IS and what is not and what surpasses both', while in 13. 12 both Being and Not-Being are denied to the omnipresent Brahman—an anomaly we shall be discussing ad loc.

Different Cults

20. *traividyā māṁ soma-pāḥ pūta-pāpā*
yajñair iṣṭva svar-gatiṁ prārthayante,
te puṇyam āsādya sur'endra-lokam
aśnanti divyān divi deva-bhogān.

Trusting in the three Vedas the Soma-drinkers, purged of [ritual] fault, worship Me with sacrifice, seeking to go to paradise: these win through to the pure world of the lord of the gods and taste in heaven the gods' celestial joys.

21. *te taṁ bhuktvā svarga-lokaṁ viśālaṁ*
kṣīṇe puṇye martya-lokaṁ viśanti;
evaṁ trayī-dharmam anuprapannā
gat'āgataṁ kāma-kāmā labhante.

[But] once they have [to the full] enjoyed the broad expanse of paradise, their merit exhausted, they come [back] to the world of men. And so it is that those who stick fast to the three Vedas receive [a reward] that comes and goes; for it is desire that they desire.

The Vedas help only in the phenomenal world which is governed by the three constituents of Nature (2. 45) and the gods can only grant finite joys (3. 12: 4. 12: 7. 22–3). Even they must return to earth as do their devotees (see 7. 23 n.).

22. *ananyāś cintayanto māṁ ye janāḥ paryupāsate,*
teṣāṁ nity'ābhiyuktānāṁ yoga-kṣemaṁ vahāmy aham.

For those men who meditate on Me, no other [thought in mind], who do Me honour, ever persevere, I bring attainment and possession of what has been attained.

23. *ye 'py anya-devatā-bhaktā yajante śraddhayā 'nvitāḥ,*
te 'pi mām eva, Kaunteya, yajanty avidhi-pūrvakam.

[Yet] even those who lovingly devote themselves to other gods and sacrifice to them, full filled with faith, do really worship Me though the rite may differ from the norm.

Cf. 7. 20–3 where Krishna says that He strengthens the faith of people who worship other gods. The reason is, as He here reveals, that they are really worshipping Him.

24. *ahaṁ hi sarva-yajñānāṁ bhoktā ca prabhur eva ca;*
na tu mām abhijānanti tattven'ātaś cyavanti te.

For it is I who of all sacrifices am recipient and Lord, but they do not know Me as I really am, so they fall [back into the world of men].

Krishna as *adhiyajña*, 'appertaining to the sacrifice' (8. 4), is also the recipient and proper object of all sacrifice and mortification because He is the 'great Lord of all the worlds' (5. 29).

25. *yānti deva-vratā devān, pitṝn yānti pitṛ-vratāḥ,*
bhūtāni yānti bhūt'ejyā, yānti mad-yājino 'pi mām.

To the gods go the gods' devotees, to the ancestors their votaries, to disembodied spirits go the worshippers of these, but those who worship Me shall come to Me.

Cf. 7. 23: 'Whoso worships the gods, to the gods will [surely] go, but whoso loves-and-worships Me, to Me will come indeed.'

The manner of men's worship will depend on which of the three constituents of Nature predominates in his character. So we read in 17. 4:

> To the gods do men of Goodness offer sacrifice, to sprites and monsters men of Passion, to disembodied spirits and the assembled spirits of the dead the others—men of Darkness—offer sacrifice.

The Rewards of Loving Devotion

26. *pattraṁ puṣpaṁ phalaṁ toyaṁ yo me bhaktyā prayacchati,*
tad ahaṁ bhakty-upahṛtam aśnāmi prayat'ātmanaḥ.

Be it a leaf or flower or fruit or water that a zealous soul may offer Me with love's devotion, that do I [willingly] accept, for it was love that made the offering.

27. *yat karoṣi, yad aśnāsi, yaj juhoṣi, dadāsi yat,*
yat tapasyasi, Kaunteya, tat kuruṣva mad-arpaṇam.

Whatever you do, whatever you eat, whatever you offer in sacrifice or give away in alms, whatever penance you may perform, offer it up to Me.

yat karoṣi, 'whatever you do': 'whatever *karma* you perform'. In the earlier literature *karma* and kindred words (*kriyā* etc.) were primarily used in the sense of 'sacred' action: 'action' was regarded as being predominantly sacrificial action, and even in the Gītā sacrifice depends on action (3. 14: 4. 32) and both proceed from Brahman (3. 15) over whose mouth, the sacrificial fire, all sacrifices are extended. The very existence of the world depends on sacrifice (3. 10) because in primitive thought sacrifice must automatically bear its appropriate fruit. You sacrifice to the gods because you expect the gods to give you something in return (3. 11–12) whether it be long life, abundance of sons, prosperity, or victory over your enemies. This theory was then extended to works in general: 'as a man acts, as he behaves, so does he become. Whoso does good, becomes good: whoso does evil, becomes evil. By good works a man becomes holy, by evil [works] he becomes evil' (BU. 4. 4. 5).

In the Gītā this idea is superseded, and throughout the first four chapters it is drummed in that all actions must be done in a totally disinterested spirit because action, even good action, 'binds'. Hence action must once again be assimilated to sacrifice—but not sacrifice as formerly understood but *self*-sacrifice, the giving of something without expecting anything in return: 'the sacrifice approved by [sacred] ordinance and offered up by men who would not taste its fruits, who concentrate their minds on this [alone]: "In sacrifice lies duty": [such sacrifice] belongs to Goodness' (17. 11). This must apply to every action, for unless action is offered as a sacrifice, it merely sucks you deeper into the quagmire of temporal existence, for 'this world is bound by bonds of work save where that work is done for sacrifice' (3. 9). Hence all work must be done as an offering to God either as an offering of the free will or because it is God who in the last analysis is the only real agent, operating as He does through the constituents of Nature, his 'creative power' or *māyā* (3. 28: 7. 13–14). It is, then, both realistic and praiseworthy to offer all one does and is to God (3. 30) or to ascribe it to Brahman (5. 10) which, in the context, means much the same thing.

tat kuruṣva mad-arpaṇam, 'offer it up to Me': you offer it up because the act of offering is itself Brahman (4. 24), the gateway between time and eternity, and the whole ritual *is* Brahman and through Brahman God (4. 24: 9. 16). Brahman, however, is the pantheistic 'All': seen either as the 'One' or the 'All', it cannot be a proper *object* of sacrifice. This can only be a personal god: hence men offer their sacrifices to a variety of gods inherited from their forbears. There is, however, only one eternal, self-subsistent, omnipotent, and omniscient Lord who is at the same time not only Brahman but also the 'ground' of Brahman (14. 27), and that is Krishna, the incarnation of the supreme God, Vishnu. Hence He is *adhiyajña* (8. 4), 'He who assists at the sacrifice' and the only true Recipient and Enjoyer of sacrifice and of gifts given as *self*-sacrifice (5. 29: 9. 24). Thus all disinterested giving even of a leaf or flower is a true sacrifice to the one true God through Brahman, the means and intermediary of the sacrificial ritual itself.

28. *śubh'āśubha-phalair evaṁ mokṣyase karma-bandhanaiḥ;*
saṁnyāsa-yoga-yukt'ātmā vimukto mām upaiṣyasi.

So from [those] bonds which works [of their very nature forge], whose fruits are fair and foul, you will be freed: [your]self [now] integrated by renunciation and spiritual exercise, set free, you will draw nigh to Me.

Works, as we know, are really the product of the three constituents of Nature, and since these are the very stuff of the phenomenal world, they 'bind'. This is even true of the highest of them—Goodness, for it binds 'to wisdom and to joy' (14. 6), the very condition of a liberated man (4. 39 and Chapters V and VI *passim*). Hence one must already be liberated, free from all attachment to mortal life, in order to approach God. See 9. 14 n.

saṁnyāsa-yoga-, 'renunciation and spiritual exercise': or, 'the spiritual exercise consisting in renunciation'; or, 'in renunciation by spiritual exercise'. R. takes *saṁnyāsa* as meaning casting off one's actions on God. It does not seem to matter very much which way you take the compound since, as Krishna has said, only the simple-minded try to draw any hard and fast distinction (5. 4: cf. 6. 2). The whole phrase recalls 5. 21 *brahma-yoga-yukt'ātmā*, '[his] self in Brahman integrated by spiritual exercise'. *Saṁnyāsa* (which in Chapter V is equated with 'wisdom' and 'theory' (*sāṁkhya*)) may very well be the equivalent of Brahman here and of the 'fixed, still state of Brahman' of 2. 72.

29. *samo 'haṁ sarva-bhūteṣu, na me dveṣyo 'sti na priyaḥ;*
ye bhajanti tu māṁ bhaktyā, mayi te, teṣu c'āpy aham.

In all contingent beings the same am I; none do I hate and none do I fondly love; but those who commune with Me in love's devotion [abide] in Me, and I in them.

samo, 'the same': here again Krishna identifies Himself with Brahman which is 'devoid of imperfection and ever-the-same' (5. 19). 'The same', however, also means that He shows no partiality, He is no 'respecter of persons': He is as 'indifferent' as He expects the perfected athlete of the spirit whom He describes in 12. 13–19 to be: and yet He goes on to say that 'those who commune with Me in love's devotion [abide] in Me, and I in them'. So too in 12. 15 He says: 'That man I *love* from whom the people do not shrink and who does not shrink from them, who is free from exaltation, fear, impatience, and excitement', and He goes on to list a great many other equal-minded men whom He loves. This may be a paradox, but it is a paradox we meet with in all religions; it is the *sainte indifférence* of St. François de Sales which, though it excludes partial and, of course, passionate love, does not at all exclude disinterested love which Christians call *agape*. In the Gītā *bhakti*, loving devotion and communion with the divine, transcends the 'fixed, still state of Brahman'. The philosophical puzzle of whether it is proper to say that contingent beings subsist in God or do not subsist in Him, is here transcended because *bhakti* introduces a new dimension. Love means giving, sharing, participation, total self-giving, and total interpenetration, and so God abides in his lovers and they in Him. There can no longer be any question of the 'isolation' of the eternal element in man as in the Sāṁkhya system nor even of the 'fixed, still state of Brahman'. In *bhakti* there is a complete and personal indwelling of God and this can be experienced only by the man who has already achieved liberation.

Ś. remarks here, very appropriately, that God remains the same always. Like a fire He warms those who draw near to Him, but those far away must remain in the cold. *Bhakti* is the natural culmination of any mystical theory which makes room for the many as well as the One; for what could hold together the many in the One if it is not love, the universal mutual attraction of all things to their centre, the One, and through the One to each other? It should not be forgotten, moreover, that Krishna has already said of Himself: '*Desire* am I in contingent beings, [but such desire as] does not conflict with righteousness' (7. 11).

30. *api cet sudurācāro bhajate mām ananya-bhāk,*
sādhur eva sa mantavyaḥ, samyag vyavasito hi saḥ.

However evil a man's livelihood may be, let him but worship Me with love and serve no other, then shall he be reckoned among the good indeed, for his resolve is right.

This stanza is, of course, to be read in conjunction with the next. The evil-doer is changed by his love of God just as Mary Magdalene and most of the more attractive Christian saints were.

31. *kṣipraṁ bhavati dharm'ātmā, śaśvac-chāntiṁ nigacchati:*
Kaunteya, pratijānīhi, na me bhaktaḥ praṇaśyati.

Right soon will his self be justified and win eternal rest. Arjuna, be sure of this: none who worships Me with loyalty-and-love is lost to Me.

me bhaktaḥ, 'who worships Me with loyalty-and-love . . . to Me': var. *mad-bhaktaḥ*. The reading of the text is preferable since *me* can be taken with both *bhaktaḥ* and *praṇaśyati*, '*my* devotee is not lost to *Me*', which nicely recalls 6. 30: 'Who sees Me everywhere, who sees the All in Me, for him I am not lost, nor is he lost to Me.'

32. *māṁ hi, Pārtha, vyapāśritya ye 'pi syuḥ pāpa-yonayaḥ,*
striyo vaiśyās tathā śūdrās, te 'pi yānti parāṁ gatim.

For whosoever makes Me his haven, base-born though he may be, yes, women too and artisans, even serfs, theirs it is to tread the highest way.

The Vedic religion was not open to the lower classes or to women. The religion of *bhakti*, like Buddhism, is open to all.

33. *kiṁ punar brāhmaṇāḥ puṇyā bhaktā rāja-rṣayas tathā:*
anityam asukhaṁ lokam imaṁ prāpya bhajasva mām.

How much more, then, Brāhmans pure-and-good, and royal seers who know devoted love. Since your lot has fallen in this world, impermanent and joyless, commune with Me in love.

'Impermanent and joyless': two typically Buddhist terms. Krishna now proposes an alternative to the Buddhist 'Nirvāna that is Brahman too'· 'Commune with Me in love.'

34. *man-manā bhava mad-bhakto mad-yājī, māṁ namas-kuru:*
mām ev' aiṣyasi yuktv' aivam ātmānaṁ mat-parāyaṇaḥ.

On Me your mind, on Me your loving-service, for Me your sacrifice, to Me be your prostrations: now that you have thus integrated self, your striving bent on Me, to Me you will [surely] come.

yuktv' aivam, 'now that you have thus integrated self': once again 'integration' is seen as an indispensable condition for the pursuit of what Krishna will call the 'highest *bhakti*' (18. 54). So little is this to Śankara's taste that his interpretation violates the perfectly straightforward grammar of the last sentence.

yuktvā which obviously governs *ātmānaṁ*, 'having integrated self', he takes to mean *samādhāya cittam*, 'having integrated [your] thought', *evam*, 'so', *eṣyasi*, 'you will come', *ātmānaṁ*, 'to the Self, (for I am the Self of all beings, the highest Way, the highest path, that is,) to Me as Self'.

This would, perhaps, be a good point at which to analyse the relationship between 'liberation' and 'loving devotion' in what we have read so far.

Even in the earlier passages Krishna recommends that the aspirant should fix his thoughts on Him as an object of contemplation. This follows the classical Yoga tradition which recommends 'meditation on the Lord' as being one of the means of achieving the true Yogic 'isolation' or, in the Gītā, the Buddhist Nirvāna. So in 2. 61 where we have the first account of liberation we read:

(i) 'Let a man sit curbing all [his senses], integrated, intent on Me.'

The final liberation is described in 2. 71–2:

'The man who puts away all desires and roams around from longing freed, who does not think, "This I am", or "This is mine", draws near to peace. This is the *fixed, still state of Brahman*; he who wins through to this is nevermore perplexed. Standing therein at the time of death, *to Nirvāna that is Brahman too he goes.*'

There is here no question of drawing nigh to God; it is rather an introversion of the whole personality into the still centre which is the 'fixed, still state of Brahman'.

In 4. 9–11 we have the opposite side of the picture though somewhat feebly etched:

(ii) 'Who knows my godly birth and mode of operation thus as they really are, he, his body left behind, is never born again: *he comes to Me*. Many are they who, passion, fear, and anger spent, *inhere in Me*, making Me their sanctuary; *made pure by wisdom* and hard penances, *they come to [share in] my own mode of being*. In whatsoever way [devoted] men approach Me, *in that same way do I return their love.*'

Here meditation on the birth and incarnate life of God (rather like the Jesuit *Spiritual Exercises*) and a real concentration on the being of God is combined with the stilling of the passions and with 'wisdom'—an intuitive apprehension of the Eternal. The result is, then, not the 'Nirvāna that is Brahman too', but the drawing near to God and to his eternal mode of being. This is an approach of person to Person with no mention this time of *yoga*, 'integration'.

The third example is purely negative: it describes the discovery of 'wisdom' in the self, which means the total destruction of 'works', that is to say, the elimination of all that takes place in space and time from the consciousness. It occurs in 4. 37–9:

(iii) 'As a kindled fire reduces its fuel to ashes, so does the fire of wisdom reduce all works to ashes. For nothing on earth resembles wisdom in its power to purify; and this in time a man may find within [him]self—a man perfected in spiritual exercise. A man of faith, intent on wisdom, his senses [all] restrained, wins wisdom; and, wisdom won, he will come right soon to perfect peace.'

Here again it is 'peace, stillness, rest' that is emphasized, the 'fixed, still state of Brahman' of (i), and there is no mention at all of the Lord.

The fourth major example comprises the bulk of Chapter V. It is an elaboration of (i) and the liberation it describes is the 'Nirvāna that is

Brahman too'. It consists of 5. 12, 16–17, 19–21, 24–6, and 28–9. To this long passage 4. 21–3 acts, so to speak, as a curtain-raiser.

(iv) 4. 21–3: 'Nothing hoping, his thought and self controlled, giving up all possessions, he only does such work as is needed for his body's maintenance, and so he avoids defilement. Content to take whatever chance may bring his way, surmounting [all] dualities, knowing no envy, the same in success and failure, though working [still] he is not bound. Attachment gone, deliverance won, his thoughts are fixed on wisdom: he works for sacrifice [alone], and all the work [he ever did] entirely melts away.'

5. 12 etc.: 'The integrated man, renouncing the fruit of works, gains an abiding peace. . . . But some there are whose ignorance of self by wisdom is destroyed. Their wisdom, like the sun, illumines that [all-]highest. Souls [bent on] that, selves [bent on] that, with that their aim and that their aspiration, they stride [along the path] from which there is no return, [all] taints by wisdom washed away. . . . While yet in this world they have overcome [the process of] emanation [and decay], for *their minds are stilled in that-which-is-ever-the-same: for devoid of imperfection and ever-the-same is Brahman: therefore in Brahman [stilled] they stand.* Winning some pleasant thing [the sage] will not rejoice, nor shrink disquietened when the unpleasant comes his way: *steadfast-and-still* his soul, [all] unconfused, he will know Brahman, *in Brahman [stilled] he'll stand.* [His] self detached from contacts with the outside world, in [him]self he finds his joy, [*his*] *self in Brahman integrated* by spiritual exercise, he finds unfailing joy. . . . His joy *within*, his bliss *within*, his light *within*, the man who-is-integrated-in-spiritual-exercise *becomes Brahman and draws nigh to Nirvāna that is Brahman too.* Nirvāna that is Brahman too win seers in whom [all] taint-of-imperfection is destroyed; their doubts dispelled, with self controlled, they take their pleasure in the weal of all contingent beings. Around these holy men whose thoughts are [fast] controlled, estranged from anger and desire, *knowing [at last] the self, fares Nirvāna that is Brahman too.* . . . With senses, mind, and soul restrained, the silent sage, on deliverance intent, who has forever banished fear, anger, and desire, is *truly liberated. Knowing Me to be the proper object of sacrifice and mortification*, great Lord of all the worlds, friend of all contingent beings, *he reaches peace.*'

The brusque introduction of the Lord into the last stanza comes as a shock because, after what has gone before, He seems quite irrelevant. Unlike (ii) where knowledge of God as active in the world quite naturally brought the adept near to God, there seems no reason why 'knowing God as the proper object of sacrifice' should bring the peace of Nirvāna except as a surety that sacrifice and therefore works and therefore the whole phenomenal world have nothing whatever to do with the man who has won release in the Nirvāna that is Brahman too. All this can be left to God and indeed must be left to God (3. 30). Even here God is recognized for what (among other things) He is, omnipotent and beneficent Lord, but omnipotence implies ability to *do* (that is, *karma*), but in Nirvāna 'the fire of wisdom reduces all works (*karma*) to ashes' (4. 37).

The fullest description of spiritual liberation and the first one to point out its connexion with the love of God is 6. 8, 10, 14–15, 18–23, 27–32, and 46–7:

(v) 'With self content in wisdom learnt from holy books and wisdom learnt from life, with sense subdued, *sublime, aloof*, [this] athlete of the spirit [stands]:

"*Integrated*", so is he called; the same to him are clods of earth, stones, gold. . . . Let the athlete of the spirit ever *integrate* [*him*]*self* standing in a place apart, alone, his thoughts and self restrained, devoid of [earthly] hope, possessing nothing. . . . [There] let him sit, [his] self all stilled, his fear all gone, firm in his vow of chastity, . . . *integrated*, [*yet*] *intent on Me*. Thus let the athlete of the spirit be *constant in integrating* [*him*]*self*, his mind restrained; *then will he approach that peace which has Nirvāna as its end and which subsists in Me*. . . .

'When thought, held well in check, *is stilled in self alone*, then is a man from longing freed though all desires assail him: *then do men call him "integrated"*. As a lamp might stand in a windless place, unflickering—this likeness has been heard of such athletes of the spirit who control their thought and practise integration of the self.

'When *thought* by spiritual exercise is checked and *comes to rest*, and when of [one]self *one sees the self in self* and finds content therein, that is *the utmost joy which transcends* [*all things of*] *sense* and which soul [alone] can grasp. When he knows this and [knowing it] *stands still*, moving not an inch from the reality [he sees], *he wins a prize beyond all others—or so he thinks*. Therein he [firmly] stands, unmoved by any suffering, however grievous it may be. This he should know is what is meant by "spiritual exercise"—*the unlinking of the link with suffering-and-pain*. This is the act-of-integration that must be brought about with [firm] resolve and mind all undismayed. . . . For upon this athlete of the spirit whose mind is stilled the highest joy descends: [all] passion laid to rest, free from [all] stain, *Brahman he becomes*. [And] thus [all] flaws transcending, the athlete of the spirit, *constant in integrating* [*him*]*self*, with ease attains unbounded joy, *Brahman's* [*saving*] *touch*. With self integrated by spiritual exercise [now] *he sees the self in all beings standing, all beings in the self: the same in everything he sees*.

'*Who sees Me everywhere, who sees the All in Me, for him I am not lost, nor is he lost to Me. Who standing firm on unity communes-in-love with Me as abiding in all beings*, in whatever state he be, *that athlete of the spirit abides in Me*. By analogy with self who sees the same [Brahman] everywhere, . . . he is the highest athlete of the spirit, *or so men think*. . . . [For] higher than the [mere] ascetic is the athlete of the spirit held to be, yes, *higher than the man of wisdom*, higher than the man of works: be, then, a spiritual athlete, Arjuna! But of all athletes of the spirit *the man of faith who loves-and-honours Me, his inmost self absorbed in Me—he is the most fully integrated*: this do I believe.'

The mere juxtaposition of these five passages, and the order in which they occur, surely amounts to proof that in the eyes of the author of the Gītā the old largely Buddhistic idea of liberation—the transcending of the phenomenal—is not the goal of the mystical life, but only the end of what is called in the West the *via purgativa*. Once won, however, the experience of the 'transcendental' self must never be abandoned. This is emphasized throughout the Gītā and is recapitulated with splendid clarity at the end of the last chapter.

For the convenience of the reader let us list here the remaining relevant passages which occur after Chapter VI.

(vi) 7. 17: 'Of these the man of wisdom, ever integrated, *who loves-and-worships One alone excels*: for to the man of wisdom I am exceeding dear and he is dear to Me.'

(vii) 7. 28: 'But some there are for whom [all] ill is ended, doers of what is good-and-pure: *released* [at last] *from the confusion of duality*, steady in their vows, *they love-and-worship Me*.'

(viii) 8. 14: 'How easily am I won by him who bears Me in mind unceasingly, thinking of nothing else at all—an athlete of the spirit *ever integrated* [in himself].'

(ix) 9. 14: 'Me do they ever glorify, [for Me] they strive, full firm their vows; to Me do they bow down, devoted-in-their-love, and *integrated ever* [*in themselves*] *they pay Me worship*.'

(x) 9. 28: 'So from [those] bonds which works [of their very nature forge], whose fruits are fair and foul, *you will be freed:* [*your*]*self* [*now*] *integrated by renunciation and spiritual exercise, set free, you will draw nigh to Me*.'

(xi) 9. 34 (our present passage): 'On Me your mind, on Me your loving service, for Me your sacrifice, to Me be your prostrations: *now that you have thus integrated self*, your striving bent on Me, *to Me you will* [*surely*] *come*.'

(xii) 10. 10–11: 'To these men *who are ever integrated and commune with Me in love I give that integration of the soul by which they may draw nigh to Me*. Out of compassion for those same men [all] darkness born of ignorance I dispel with wisdom's shining lamp, abiding [ever] in my own [true] nature.'

(xiii) 11. 54–5: 'But by worship-of-love addressed to [Me,] none other, Arjuna, *can I be known and seen* in such a form and as I really am: [*so can my lovers*] *enter into Me*. Do works for Me, make Me your highest goal, be loyal-in-love to Me, cut off all [other] attachments, have no hatred for any being at all: *for all who do thus shall come to Me*.'

(xiv) 14. 26–7: 'And as to those who do Me honour with spiritual exercise, in *loyalty-and-love* undeviating, passed [clean] beyond these constituents, *to becoming Brahman they are conformed. For I am the base supporting Brahman*—immortal [Brahman] which knows no change—[supporting] too the eternal law of righteousness and absolute beatitude.'

(xv) 15. 19: 'Whoever thus knows Me, unconfused, as the Person [All-] Sublime, knows all and [knowing all] *communes with Me with all his being, all his love*.'

Finally, and most clearly of all:

(xvi) 18. 51–5: 'Let a man be *integrated by his soul* [*now*] *cleansed*, let him restrain [him]self with constancy, abandon objects of sense—sound and all the rest—passion and hate let him cast out; let him live apart, eat lightly, restrain speech, body, and mind; let him practise meditation constantly, let him cultivate dispassion; let him give up all thought of "I", force, pride, desire and anger and possessiveness, let him not think of anything as "mine", *at peace*;—[if he does this,] *to becoming Brahman is he conformed*.

'*Brahman become*, with self serene, he grieves not nor desires; the same to all contingent beings he *gains the highest love-and-loyalty to Me. By love-and-loyalty he comes to know Me as I really am*, how great I am and who; and once he knows Me as I am, *he enters* [*Me*] *forthwith*.'

CHAPTER X

THIS chapter opens with a clear declaration by Krishna that He is the supreme Being, 'Great Lord of [all] the worlds' (1–3). He is the source of all virtue, all created dispositions, and of the ancient sages (4–7); and He should be lovingly revered by wise men as the origin of all (8). These loving devotees of his He will reward with *buddhi-yoga*, 'integration by means of the soul', and the darkness of their ignorance He will dispel with the lamp of wisdom (9–11).

Overwhelmed by such unequivocal claims to supreme divinity Arjuna acknowledges Him as 'Highest Brahman', the 'Person eternal and divine' and as every other traditional concept applicable to supreme Divinity. In his enthusiasm he asks Krishna to enumerate his manifold powers so that he may the better meditate on Him (12–18). In the rest of the chapter Krishna, elaborating on what He had already said in 7. 8–11 and 9. 16–19, speaks of Himself as the foremost representative of various classes of being and as the specific virtues of virtuous men. He ends up by claiming that he holds apart and sustains the whole universe with but a fraction of Himself. The scene is now set for the great theophany of Chapter XI. This chapter is traditionally and appropriately called the 'Yoga of Far-flung Power'.

Krishna, the Origin of All

Śrī-bhagavān uvāca:

1. *bhūya eva, mahā-bāho, śṛṇu me paramaṁ vacaḥ*
yat te 'haṁ prīyamāṇāya vakṣyāmi hita-kāmyayā.

The Blessed Lord said:

Now once again, [my] strong-armed [friend], give ear to my all-highest word which I shall speak to you [alone], for therein is your delight and your welfare is my wish.

'Therein is your delight': or, 'you are beloved [to Me]'.

2. *na me viduḥ sura-gaṇāḥ prabhavaṁ, na maha'rṣayaḥ:*
aham ādir hi devānāṁ maha'rṣīṇāṁ ca sarvaśaḥ.

None knows from whence I came,—not the gods' celestial host nor yet the mighty seers: for I am the beginning of the gods [themselves] as of the mighty seers and all in every way.

prabhavaṁ, 'origin': var. *prabhāvaṁ*, 'lordly power'. *Prabhava* can also mean 'lordly power' as Ś. and R. point out. In the context 'origin' fits very much better and is always used in this sense elsewhere in the Gītā.

3. *yo mām ajam anādiṁ ca vetti loka-mah'eśvaram,*
asaṁmūḍhaḥ sa martyeṣu sarva-pāpaiḥ pramucyate.

Whoso shall know Me as unborn, beginningless, great Lord of [all] the worlds, shall never know delusion among men, from every evil freed.

anādiṁ, 'beginningless': according to R. this epithet distinguishes God from liberated selves which are also 'unborn'. What he seems to mean by this is that they are 'unborn' in the sense that from time without beginning they have existed in association with matter (*heya*, 'evil'), but they are not 'beginningless' in that they are originated by God since they depend on Him. The distinction will scarcely stand since both the Sāṁkhya *puruṣas* (i.e. 'selves') and material Nature are said to be 'beginningless' in 13. 19.

'From every evil freed': 'freed' (*pramuc-*) is of course one of the usual terms for 'liberation' in the technical sense. Here, however, the 'evils' from which Krishna promises to free those who acknowledge Him as God, are probably the purely mundane evils that beset mortal life. Although they follow Ś. in this H. and Rk. are probably wrong in translating the word *pāpa* as 'sin' since that word means exactly what the English word 'evil' means: it is both the evil we do and the evil we suffer. If this 'liberation from evil' does indeed refer to 'liberation' as understood in the cases we discussed at the end of the last chapter, however, the way in which that liberation will be achieved through divine grace will be explained in verses 8–11.

R., quite arbitrarily, takes *-pāpaiḥ* to mean monistic conceptions which identify God with anything and everything.

4. *buddhir jñānam asaṁmohaḥ kṣamā satyaṁ damaḥ śamaḥ*
sukhaṁ duḥkhaṁ bhavo 'bhāvo bhayaṁ c'ābhayam eva ca,

Intellect, wisdom, freedom from delusion, long-suffering, truth, restraint, tranquillity, pleasure and pain, coming to be and passing away, fear and fearlessness as well,

bhavo 'bhāvo, 'coming to be and passing away': Ś., as in my translation: R., 'exaltation and depression'. Ś. is almost certainly right.

5. *ahiṁsā samatā tuṣṭis tapo dānaṁ yaśo 'yaśaḥ*
bhavanti bhāvā bhūtānāṁ matta eva pṛthag-vidhāḥ.

Refusal to do harm, equanimity, content, austerity, open-handedness, fame and infamy,—[such are] the dispositions of contingent beings, and from Me in all their diversity they arise.

6. *maha'rṣayaḥ sapta pūrve catvāro manavas tathā*
mad-bhāvā mānasā jātā yeṣāṁ loka imāḥ prajāḥ.

The seven mighty seers of old, likewise the Manus four, sharing in my mode of being, were born [the children] of [my] mind; from them [arose] these creatures in the world.

'The Manus four': Manu is the founder of the human race. There are four corresponding to the four world ages (*yuga*) which make up a world-cycle (*kalpa*).

'Sharing in my mode of being': as elsewhere in the Gītā. Some translate 'originate from Me'.

7. *etāṁ vibhūtiṁ yogaṁ ca mama yo vetti tattvataḥ,*
so 'vikampena yogena yujyate, n'ātra saṁśayaḥ.

Whoso should know this my far-flung power and how I use it, [whoso should know these] as they really are, is [truly] integrated; and this his integration can never be undone. Herein there is no doubt.

Here once again the Gītā is playing on the various meanings of the word *yoga* and its verbal root *yuj-*: if a man knows God's far-flung power and his *yoga*—his mode of operation, his way of putting it into practice—if his knowledge is not merely theoretical but a practical participation in it (cf. 2. 39 n.: 2. 50 n.: 5. 4 n.), then he himself will be 'exercised by an unshakable spiritual exercise (an integration that can never be undone)', that is, firmly integrated within himself. In other words God's *yoga* in the universe is like the *yoga* conducted by the *buddhi*, the 'soul', in man: it is the orderly integration of all things about their immortal centre. To take the analogy a stage further, it might be said that God's 'far-flung power' corresponds to the senses in man: He controls and integrates it into an orderly and unitary whole just as the soul co-ordinates and integrates the senses into and around the immortal self. This play on the word *yoga* is not only exceedingly subtle, but also throws a flood of light onto the central philosophy of the Gītā—the ultimate inseparability of eternal being from existence in time, and the interdependence of man's integration of himself and the cosmic integration around him and in God.

Just how the mere acceptance of the supremacy and total independence of God from all that is other than Himself produces personal integration is explained in verses 8–11.

8. *ahaṁ sarvasya prabhavo, mattaḥ sarvaṁ pravartate:*
iti matvā bhajante māṁ budhā bhāva-samanvitāḥ.

The source of all am I; from Me all things proceed: this knowing, wise men commune with Me in love, full filled with warm affection.

bhāva-, 'warm affection': *bhāva*, when it does not mean simply 'mode of being', usually means 'affection'. So R., 'eager desire'. Ś. equates it with *bhāvanā* which he interprets as 'perseverance (*abhiniveśa*) in seeking the supreme reality'. E.'s (proper) state (of mind)' seems to get us nowhere, while S. and Rk.'s 'conviction' is scarcely a translation of *bhāva*. D. and H. have simply 'love' which is perhaps a little too strong.

9. *mac-cittā mad-gata-prāṇā bodhayantaḥ parasparam*
kathayantaś ca māṁ nityaṁ tuṣyanti ca ramanti ca.

On Me their thoughts, their life they would sacrifice for Me; [and so] enlightening one another and telling my story constantly they take their pleasure and delight.

10. *teṣāṁ satata-yuktānāṁ bhajatāṃ prīti-pūrvakam*
dadāmi buddhi-yogaṁ taṁ yena mām upayānti te.

To these men who are ever integrated and commune with Me in love I give that integration of the soul by which they may draw nigh to Me.

On the combination of integration and love (*bhakti*) see 9. 34 n.

'That integration of the soul': presumably that described in 2. 39–41, 49–72, but with a difference, for whereas the integration of the soul described there results in the 'fixed, still state of Brahman', here the love of God must be integrated into the self too, for the goal is now God Himself: hence our athlete of the spirit must once again move outward—must 'draw nigh' to God. The same idea occurs in the same sequence in 18. 51–54.

11. *teṣām ev'ānukamp'ārtham aham ajñāna-jaṁ tamaḥ*
nāśayāmy ātma-bhāva-stho jñāna-dīpena bhāsvatā.

Out of compassion for those same men [all] darkness born of ignorance I dispel with wisdom's shining lamp, abiding
{ [ever] in my own [true] nature
{ in the state of being peculiar to the self }.

Translators opt for one or other version in the bracketed passage. H. has 'abiding in *their* souls' ignoring *bhāva*: Rk., E., following S., 'remaining in *my own* true state': D., 'gehe ich in ihr Wesen ein', which is scarcely a translation. As usual both meanings are probably intended. God always 'dwells in the region of the heart of all contingent beings' (18. 61) in his 'self-nature', that is, in that aspect of Himself which he shares with selves-in-themselves, eternal Being, his 'higher state' (7. 24) of which they are ignorant even after release. As R. rightly says *jñāna* here means knowledge of God. The lamp with which he enlightens the total personality is itself the self: 'As a lamp might stand in a windless place, unflickering—this likeness has been heard of such athletes of the spirit who control their thought and practise integration of the self' (6.19). This revelation of God in the self might be called the 'highest wisdom' corresponding to the 'highest love-and-loyalty' to God mentioned in 18. 54.

Arjuna confesses Krishna as the All-Highest

Arjuna uvāca:

12. ***paraṁ brahma, paraṁ dhāma, pavitraṁ paramaṁ bhavān.***
puruṣaṁ śāśvataṁ divyam ādi-devam ajaṁ vibhum

13. *āhus tvām ṛṣayaḥ sarve deva'rṣir Nāradas tathā*
Asito Devalo Vyāsaḥ, svayaṁ c'aiva bravīṣi me.

Arjuna said:

[All-]Highest Brahman, highest home, [all-]highest vessel of purity are You. All seers agree that You are the Person eternal and divine, primeval God, unborn and all-pervading Lord. So too Nārada, the godly seer, Asita, Devala, and Vyāsa [have declared]; and Your Yourself do tell me so.

'[All-]Highest Brahman': identified with the 'Imperishable' in 8. 3.

'Highest home': identified with the 'Unmanifest beyond the Unmanifest', the 'Imperishable', and the 'highest Way' in 8. 21. In that passage Krishna does not identify Himself with it but claims it as his own. Ś. and R. again gloss, 'light'.

'[All-]highest vessel of purity': the word *pavitra* is used of wisdom in 4. 38. Arjuna is simply repeating without fully understanding what Krishna has already taught.

'The Person eternal and divine': the 'highest Person' of 8. 22 identified with the 'Unmanifest beyond the Unmanifest' and the 'Imperishable'.

ādi-devam: 'primeval God', used here for the first time.

'Vyāsa': the mythical author of the *Mahābhārata*.

14. *sarvam etad ṛtaṁ manye yan māṁ vadasi, Keśava,*
na hi te, bhagavan, vyaktiṁ vidur devā na dānavāḥ.

All this You tell me is true; so, Krishna, I believe, for, Blessed Lord, neither gods nor demons acknowledge [this] manifest [world] as yours.

na dānavāḥ, 'nor demons': var. *maha'rṣayaḥ*, 'great sages'.

vyaktiṁ, '[this] manifest [world]': this is how Ś. seems to take it: he glosses, *prabhava*, 'origin', by which he seems to mean that neither gods nor demons know Krishna as the origin of the phenomenal world. The word 'manifestation' might perhaps more naturally refer to Krishna's incarnation (cf. 7. 24). Var. *vyaktaṁ*, 'the manifest'; *bhaktiṁ*, 'devotion'.

15. *svayam ev'ātman'ātmānaṁ vettha tvaṁ, puruṣ'ottama,*
bhūta-bhāvana bhūt'eśa deva-deva jagat-pate.

By [your] Self You yourself do know [your] Self, O You all-highest Person, You who bestow being on contingent beings, Lord of [all] beings, God of gods, and Lord of [all] the world.

16. *vaktum arhasy aśeṣeṇa, divyā hy ātma-vibhūtayaḥ*
yābhir vibhūtibhir lokān imāṁs tvaṁ vyāpya tiṣṭhasi.

Tell me, I beg You, leaving nothing unsaid,—for divine are the far-flung powers [that centre] on [your] Self by which You pervade these worlds, standing [unchanged the while].

divyā hy ātma-vibhūtayaḥ: var. *vibhūtīr ātmanaḥ śubhāḥ* (acc.) without the particle *hi*, 'for'. This gives an easier construction.

17. *kathaṁ vidyām ahaṁ, yogiṁs, tvāṁ sadā paricintayan,*
keṣu keṣu ca bhāveṣu cintyo 'si, bhagavan, mayā?

How am I to know You, You {athlete of the spirit / who make good use [of your far-flung powers]}, though I think about You always? And in what several modes of being should I think about You, Blessed Lord.

yogiṁs (voc.): Krishna is both the perfect 'athlete of the spirit' and the controller of the universe. Both senses of the word *yoga* are implied, both 'sameness-and-indifference' (2. 48) and 'skill in [performing] works' (2. 50). Var. *yogī* (nom.) which R. accepts and glosses, 'intent on the *yoga* of loving devotion', as one might expect.

18. *vistareṇ'ātmano yogaṁ vibhūtiṁ ca, janārdana,*
bhūyaḥ kathaya, tṛptir hi śṛṇvato n'āsti me 'mṛtam.

Tell me again in detail full of your far-flung power [that centres] on [your] Self and how You use it; for as I listen to your undying [words] I cannot have enough.

yogaṁ, 'how You use it': see 10. 7 n.

[*a*]*mṛtam*, 'undying [words]': or, 'nectar'.

God, the Quintessence of all Essences

Śrī-bhagavān uvāca:

19. *hanta te kathayiṣyāmi,—divyā hy ātma-vibhūtayaḥ,—*
prādhānyataḥ, Kuru-śreṣṭha, n'āsty anto vistarasya me.

The Blessed Lord said:

Lo, I will tell you,—for divine are my far-flung powers [that centre] on [my] Self,—[I will tell you] what is most fundamental, for of the details there is no end.

divyā hy ātma-vibhūtayaḥ: see 10. 16 n.

20. *aham ātmā, Guḍākeśa, sarva-bhūt'āśaya-sthitaḥ,*
aham ādiś ca madhyaṁ ca bhūtānām anta eva ca.

I am the Self established in the heart of all contingent beings: I am the beginning, the middle, and the end of all contingent beings too.

āśaya-, 'heart': lit. 'place where one lies down'. For God within the heart cf. 15. 15: 18. 61.

21. *Ādityānām ahaṁ Viṣṇur, jyotiṣāṁ ravir aṁśumān,*
Marīcir Marutām asmi, nakṣatrāṇām ahaṁ śaśī.

Among the Ādityas I am Vishnu, among lights the radiant sun, among the Maruts I am Marīci, among stars I am the moon.

'Ādityas': a group of celestial deities.

'Vishnu': the supreme God of the Gītā of whom Krishna is the incarnation.

'Maruts': a group of storm-gods closely associated with the lightning and with Indra, the 'king of the gods'.

22. *vedānāṁ sāma-vedo 'smi, devānām asmi Vāsavaḥ,*
indriyāṇāṁ manaś c'āsmi, bhūtānām asmi cetanā.

Of the Vedas I am the Sāma-Veda, I am Indra among the gods; among the senses I am the mind, amongst contingent beings thought.

'Indra': see 10. 21 n.

'The mind': in the Sāṁkhya system the mind (*manas*) is reckoned as the sixth sense.

23. *Rudrāṇāṁ Śaṁkaraś c'āsmi, vitt'eśo yakṣa-rakṣasām,*
Vasūnāṁ pāvakaś c'āsmi, Meruḥ śikhariṇām aham.

Among the Rudras Śiva am I, among sprites and monsters the Lord of Wealth; among the Vasus I am fire, among mountains I am Meru.

'Rudras': another name of the Maruts (10. 21).

'Śiva': the later name of the Vedic Rudra whose relationship with the 'Rudras' or Maruts is tenuous. For his worshippers Śiva was the supreme God. Hence Krishna who is the incarnation of Vishnu who also claims to be the supreme God, identifies Himself with him. The philosophical identification of the two supreme Gods is frequent in the MBh., but their rivalry in the field of mythology is very real.

'The Lord of Wealth': Kuvera, the king of the underworld who very closely resembles the Greek Pluto.

'Vasus': a group of deities originally associated with Indra. In BU. 3. 9. 3 they are fire, earth, wind, atmosphere, sun, sky, moon, and stars. Fire is their mouth (ChU. 3. 6. 1).

'Meru': a mythical mountain, enormously high, which stands in the middle of the world.

24. *purodhasāṁ ca mukhyaṁ māṁ viddhi, Pārtha, Bṛhaspatim;*
senānīnām ahaṁ Skandaḥ, sarasām asmi sāgaraḥ.

And of household priests know that I am the chief, Brihaspati; among war-lords I am Skanda, among lakes I am the Ocean.

'Brihaspati': the chief priest of the gods.

'Skanda': son of Śiva and god of war.

25. *maha'rṣīṇāṁ Bhṛgur ahaṁ, girām asmy ekam akṣaram,*
yajñānāṁ japa-yajño 'smi, sthāvarāṇāṁ Himālayaḥ,

Among the great seers I am Bhrigu, among utterances the single syllable [Oṁ]; among sacrifices I am the sacrifice of muttered prayer, among things immovable the Himalayas;

[Oṁ]: cf. 8. 13, 'Oṁ, Brahman in one syllable'.

26. *aśvatthaḥ sarva-vṛkṣāṇāṁ, deva'rṣīṇāṁ ca Nāradaḥ,*
gandharvāṇāṁ Citrarathaḥ, siddhānāṁ Kapilo muniḥ.

Among all trees the holy fig-tree, Nārada among the celestial seers, among the heavenly minstrels Citraratha, among perfected beings Kapila, the silent sage.

'Kapila': the reputed founder of the Sāṁkhya system.

27. *Uccaiḥśravasam aśvānāṁ viddhi mām amṛt'odbhavam,*
Airāvataṁ gaj'endrāṇāṁ, narāṇāṁ ca nar'ādhipam.

Among horses know that I am Uccaihśravas, [Indra's steed,] from nectar born, among princely elephants [Indra's, called] Airāvata, among men the king.

28. *āyudhānā, ahaṁ vajraṁ, dhenūnām asmi kāma-dhuk,*
prajanaś c'āsmi Kandarpaḥ, sarpāṇām asmi Vāsukiḥ.

Among weapons I am the thunderbolt, of cows the milch-cow of desires; and I am Kandarpa, [god of love,] generating [seed], among serpents I am Vāsuki, [the serpent king].

prajanaś, 'generating [seed]': Ś. 'generator': R. 'cause of generation'. Krishna is the seed (7. 10: 9. 18: 10. 39) and the giver of the seed (14. 4), father and grandsire (9. 17) of all things. As such He is the God of love and desire itself (7. 11).

29. *Anantaś c'āsmi nāgānāṁ, Varuṇo yādasām aham,*
pitṝṇām Aryamā c'āsmi, Yamaḥ saṁyamatām aham.

Of Nāga-serpents I am [their chief,] Ananta, of water-dwellers Varuna, [their lord,] am I; of the ancestors I am Aryaman, among those who subdue I am Yama, [god of death].

'Ananta': the cosmic serpent on which Vishnu falls asleep at the end of a cosmic aeon.

30. *Prahlādaś c'āsmi daityānāṁ, kālaḥ kalayatām aham,*
mṛgāṇāṁ ca mṛg'endro 'haṁ, Vainateyaś ca pakṣiṇām.

Among demons I am Prahlāda, among those who reckon I am Time; among beasts I am [the lion,] the king of beasts, and among birds Garuda, [Vishnu's bird].

'Prahlāda': he was saved by becoming a votary of Vishnu.

'Time': it is as Time that Vishnu-Krishna reveals Himself in the next chapter (11. 32).

31. *pavanaḥ pavatām asmi, Rāmaḥ śastra-bhṛtām aham,*
jhaṣāṇāṁ makaraś c'āsmi, srotasām asmi Jāhnavī.

Among those who purify I am the wind, Rāma I am among men at arms; among water-monsters I am the crocodile, among rivers I am the Ganges.

'Rāma': either Rāma, the hero of the shorter of the two Hindu epics, the *Rāmāyaṇa*, who is Vishnu's seventh incarnation, or Paraśu-Rāma, 'Rāma with the axe', his sixth incarnation. The purpose of Vishnu's incarnation as Paraśu-Rāma was to extirpate the princely or warrior class. Since this is largely the purpose of his incarnation as Krishna too, it is quite likely that it is this Rāma who is referred to here.

'Crocodile': or perhaps 'shark' or 'dolphin'.

32. *sargāṇām ādir antaś ca madhyaṁ c'aiv'āham, Arjuna,*
adhyātma-vidyā vidyānāṁ, vādaḥ pravadatām aham.

Among emanations the beginning and the end and the middle too am I; among sciences I am the science concerned with Self, among those who speak [their very] speech am I.

'Speech': this seems to be the obvious translation of *vādaḥ*. So E.; Rk., following Ś., 'dialectic': S. and H. (unaccountably), 'la vérité', 'the True': D. 'die These der Disputierenden'.

33. *akṣarāṇām akāro 'smi, dvandvaḥ sāmāsikasya ca,*
aham ev'ākṣayaḥ kālo, dhātā 'haṁ viśvato-mukhaḥ.

Among the letters of the alphabet I am 'A', among grammatical compounds the *dvandva*. Truly I am imperishable Time, I, the Ordainer, with face turned every way.

'A': the first letter of the alphabet in Sanskrit as in Latin and Greek.

dvandva: two substantives run together, e.g. 'Peter-Paul' for 'Peter and Paul'.

'Ordainer': or 'creator' or 'sustainer'.

34. *mṛtyuḥ sarva-haraś c'āham udbhavaś ca bhaviṣyatām,*
kīrtiḥ śrīr vāk ca nārīṇāṁ, smṛtir medhā dhṛtiḥ kṣamā.

And I am Death that snatches all away, and the origin of creatures yet to be. And among feminine nouns [I am] fame, fortune, speech, memory, intelligence, steadfastness, long-suffering.

'Feminine nouns': lit. 'women': all these nouns are feminine in Sanskrit.

35. *bṛhat-sāma tathā sāmnāṁ, gāyatrī chandasām aham,*
māsānāṁ mārgaśīrṣo 'ham, ṛtūnāṁ kusum'ākaraḥ.

Again among chants I am the Great Chant, among metres the Gāyatrī, among months I am [the first,] Mārgaśīrsha, among seasons flower-bearing [spring].

Some MSS. add either here or after 10. 38 the following lines:

auṣadhīnāṁ yavaś c'āsmi, dhātūnām asmi kāñcanam,
saurabheyo gavām asmi, snehānāṁ sarpir apy aham,
sarvāsāṁ tṛṇa-jātīnāṁ darbho 'ham, Pāṇḍu-nandana.

Among plants I am barley, among metals I am gold, among cows I am the bull, among fats I am butter, among all species of grass I am the *darbha* grass, son of Pāndu.

36. *dyūtaṁ chalayatām asmi, tejas tejasvinām aham,*
jayo 'smi, vyavasāyo 'smi, sattvaṁ sattvavatām aham.

I am the dicing of tricksters, glory of the glorious am I; I am victory and I am firm resolve, and the courage of the brave am I.

'The dicing of tricksters': this must be a reference to the fatal game of dice which lost Yudhishthira, Arjuna's elder brother, his kingdom. According to the MBh. (2. 51. 16, 22; 52. 14; 60. 13; 67. 3; 72. 11 and *passim*) Yudhishthira was impelled to this by Fate, Time, or the 'Ordainer'; and Krishna is all of these. Had Yudhishthira not lost his kingdom, there would have been no war and Krishna's purpose would have remained unfulfilled.

sattva, 'courage': the word can also mean the constituent of Nature, 'Goodness', so Ś.: also 'magnanimity' (so R.) or simply 'life'.

37. *Vṛṣṇīnāṁ Vāsudevo 'smi, Pāṇḍavānāṁ dhanaṁjayaḥ,*
munīnām apy ahaṁ Vyāsaḥ, kavīnām Uśanā kaviḥ.

Among the Vrishni clansmen I am [Krishna,] Vasudeva's son, among Pāndu's sons [I am] Arjuna; among silent sages I am Vyāsa, among psalmists I am the psalmist Uśanas.

'Vrishni': the name of Krishna's clan.

'Arjuna': in the main body of the Epic Krishna and Arjuna are such intimate friends that they are frequently called *kṛṣṇau*, 'the two Krishnas'.

38. *daṇḍo damayatām asmi, nītir asmi jigīṣatām,*
maunaṁ c'aiv'āsmi guhyānāṁ, jñānaṁ jñānavatām aham.

Of those who subdue the rod-of-chastisement am I, I am the statecraft of those who seek the upper hand; the very silence of hidden, secret things am I, and I am the wisdom of the wise.

39. *yac c'āpi sarva-bhūtānāṁ bījaṁ tad aham, Arjuna,*
na tad asti vinā yat syān mayā bhūtaṁ car'ācaram.

And what is the seed of all contingent beings, that too am I. No being is there, whether moving or unmoving, that exists or could exist apart from Me.

Ś. comments: 'If anything were withdrawn from Me or abandoned by Me, it would be without self and void: . . . everything has Me as its self.' R.: 'All things in whatever state they be, are united with Me as self.'

40. *n'ānto 'sti mama divyānāṁ vibhūtīnāṁ, paraṁtapa,*
eṣa tū'ddeśataḥ prokto vibhūter vistaro mayā.

Of [these] my far-flung powers divine there is no end; as much as I have said concerning them must serve as an example.

mama, 'my': var. *śubha-*, 'fair'.

41. *yad yad vibhūtimat sattvaṁ śrīmad ūrjitam eva vā,*
tat tad evā'vagaccha tvaṁ mama tejo'ṁśa-saṁbhavam.

Whatever being shows wide power, prosperity, or strength, be sure that this derives from [but] a fragment of my glory.

42. *athavā bahun'aitena kiṁ jñātena tavā'rjuna ?*
viṣṭabhy'āham idaṁ kṛtsnam ek'āṁśena sthito jagat.

But where's the use for you to know so much, Arjuna? This whole universe I hold apart [supporting it] with [but] one fragment [of Myself], yet I abide [unchanging].

CHAPTER XI

THIS chapter is the climax of the Gītā. In it Krishna reveals Himself in all his terrifying majesty.

Arjuna, not content with the account of Krishna's 'far-flung powers' of which he had heard in the last chapter, asks to *see* his 'Self which does not pass away' (1–4).

Krishna grants his request and gives him a 'celestial eye' with which he may behold his transfiguration (5–8). The rest of the chapter is an account of the tremendous vision in which the universe in all its variety is seen as Krishna's body—all its multiplicity converging onto One (9–13). Arjuna then describes what he sees: the entire world is rushing headlong into Krishna's mouths (15–31).

Krishna then explains that He is all-consuming Time and that as such He has already killed the Kaurava hosts: Arjuna is to be but the occasion (32–4). Arjuna, in terrified ecstasy, now confesses Him as God (35–46). The vision over, Krishna resumes his human form, and ends up by telling Arjuna once again to worship Him with love that he may enter into Him (47–55).

Arjuna asks to see Krishna's Universal Form

Arjuna uvāca:

1. *mad-anugrahāya paramaṁ guhyam adhyātma-saṁjñitam*
yat tvay'oktaṁ vacas, tena moho 'yaṁ vigato mama.

Arjuna said:

Out of your gracious favour for me You have uttered the highest mystery called 'what appertains to Self', and by that word of yours this my perplexity has gone.

adhyātma-, 'what appertains to Self': see 8. 3 n. (p. 259).

2. *bhav'āpyayau hi bhūtānāṁ śrutau vistaraśo mayā*
tvattaḥ, kamala-pattr'ākṣa, māhātmyam api c'āvyayam.

For I have heard of the coming to be and passing away of contingent beings: [this] You have told me in detail full, as well as the majesty of [your own] Self which does not pass away.

3. *evam etad yath'āttha tvam ātmānaṁ, param'eśvara,*
draṣṭum icchāmi te rūpam aiśvaraṁ, puruṣ'ottama.

Even as You have described [your] Self to be, so must it be, O Lord Most High; [but] fain would I *see* the form of You as *Lord*, O [All-]Highest Person.

4. *manyase yadi tac chakyaṁ mayā draṣṭum iti, prabho,*
yog'eśvara, tato me tvaṁ darśay'ātmānam avyayam.

If, Lord, You think that I can see You thus, then show me, Lord of creative power, [this] Self [of yours] which does not pass away.

yog'eśvara, 'Lord of creative power': 'creative power' seems to be the meaning of *yoga* here. It is the *yoga* of 10. 7, 18 the 'practical use' that God makes of his 'far-flung powers'.

Krishna gives Arjuna a Celestial Eye

Śrī-bhagavān uvāca:

5. *paśya me, Pārtha, rūpāṇi śataśo 'tha sahasraśaḥ*
nānā-vidhāni divyāni nānā-varṇ'ākṛtīni ca.

The Blessed Lord said:

Son of Prithā, behold my forms in their hundreds and their thousands; how various they are, how divine, how many-hued and multiform.

6. *paśy'ādityān, Vasūn, Rudrān, Aśvinau, Marutas tathā,*
bahūny adṛṣṭa-pūrvāṇi paśy'āścaryāṇi, Bhārata.

Ādityas, Vasus, Rudras, the Aśvins twain, and the Maruts too, behold them! Marvels never seen before,—how many!—Arjuna, behold them.

'Ādityas' etc.: see 10. 21, 23 nn.

'Aśvins': twin gods not unlike Castor and Pollux. Among other things they are heavenly physicians.

7. *ih'aika-sthaṁ jagat kṛtsnaṁ paśy'ādya sacar'ācaram*
mama dehe, Guḍākeśa, yac c'ānyad draṣṭum icchasi.

Do you today the whole universe behold centred here in One, with all that it contains of moving and unmoving things; [behold it] in my body, and whatever else you fain would see.

8. *na tu māṁ śakṣyase draṣṭum anen' aiva sva-cakṣuṣā*
divyaṁ dadāmi te cakṣuḥ, paśya me yogam aiśvaram.

But never will you be able to see Me with this your [natural] eye. A celestial eye I'll give you, behold my power as Lord!

cakṣuh, 'eye': see 11. 4 n. Var. *rūpaṁ*, 'form'.

Krishna's Transfiguration

Saṁjaya uvāca:

9. *evam uktvā tato, rājan, mahā-yog' eśvaro hariḥ*
darśayām āsa Pārthāya paramaṁ rūpam aiśvaram,

Sanjaya said:

So saying Hari, the great Lord of power-and-the-skilful-use-of-it, revealed to the son of Prithā his highest sovereign form,—

'Hari': a name of Vishnu.

yoga-, 'power-and-the-skilful-use-of-it': bearing 10. 7, 18 in mind and the definition of 2. 50: 'Yoga is "skill in [performing] works".'

10. *aneka-vaktra-nayanam anek' ādbhuta-darśanam*
aneka-divy' ābharaṇaṁ divy' ānek' odyat' āyudham,

[A form] with many a mouth and eye and countless marvellous aspects; many [indeed] were its divine adornments, many the celestial weapons raised on high.

11. *divya-māly' āmbara-dharaṁ divya-gandh' ānulepanam*
sarv' āścaryamayaṁ devam anantaṁ viśvato-mukham.

Garlands and robes celestial He wore, fragrance divine was his anointing. [Behold this] God whose every [mark] spells wonder, the Infinite, facing every way!

12. *divi sūrya-sahasrasya bhaved yugapad utthitā*
yadi bhāḥ, sadṛśī sā syād bhāsas tasya mah' ātmanaḥ.

If in [bright] heaven together should arise the shining brilliance of a thousand suns, then would that perhaps resemble the brilliance of that [God] so great of Self.

13. *tatr' aika-sthaṁ jagat kṛtsnaṁ pravibhaktam anekadhā*
apaśyad deva-devasya śarīre Pāṇḍavas tadā.

Then did the son of Pāndu see the whole [wide] universe in One converged, there in the body of the God of gods, yet divided out in multiplicity.

14. *tataḥ sa vismay'āviṣṭo hṛṣṭa-romā dhanaṁjayaḥ*
praṇamya śirasā devaṁ kṛt'āñjalir abhāṣata.

Then filled with amazement Arjuna, his hair on end, hands joined in reverent greeting, bowing his head before the God, [these words] spake out.

Arjuna uvāca:

15. *paśyāmi devāṁs tava, deva, dehe*
sarvāṁs tathā bhūta-viśeṣa-saṁghān,
Brahmāṇam īśaṁ kamal'āsana-stham
ṛṣīṁś ca sarvān uragāṁś ca divyān.

Arjuna said:

O God, the gods in your body I behold and all the hosts of every kind of being; Brahmā, the lord, [I see] throned on the lotus-seat, celestial serpents and all the [ancient] seers.

'Brahmā': the creator-god *par excellence*. At the beginning of each world-aeon a lotus emerges from the navel of the recumbent Vishnu and Brahmā is seated on it. He then proceeds to create the universe anew. He must not be confused with the neuter 'Brahman' with which we have become acquainted in the Gītā. It is, however, only in the nominative and accusative cases that the two can be grammatically distinguished.

16. *aneka-bāhū'dara-vaktra-netraṁ*
paśyāmi tvāṁ sarvato 'nanta-rūpam:
n'āntaṁ na madhyaṁ na punas tav'ādiṁ
paśyāmi, viśv'eśvara, viśva-rūpa.

Arms, bellies, mouths, and eyes all manifold,—so do I see You wherever I may look,—infinite your form! End, middle, or again beginning I cannot see in You, O Monarch Universal, [manifest] in every form!

17. *kirīṭinaṁ gadinaṁ cakriṇaṁ ca*
tejo-rāśiṁ sarvato dīptimantam
paśyāmi tvāṁ durnirīkṣyaṁ samantād
dīpt'ānal'ārka-dyutim aprameyam.

Yours the crown, the mace, the discus,—a mass of glory shining on all sides,—so do I see You,—yet how hard are You to see,—for on every side there is brilliant light of fire and sun. Oh, who should comprehend it?

18. *tvam akṣaraṁ paramaṁ veditavyaṁ,*
tvam asya viśvasya paraṁ nidhānam,
tvam avyayaḥ śāśvata-dharma-goptā,
sanātanas tvaṁ puruṣo mato me.

You are the Imperishable, [You] wisdom's highest goal; You, of this universe the last prop-and-resting-place, You the changeless, [You] the guardian of eternal law, You the primeval Person; [at last] I understand.

'The Imperishable' (*neut.*): that is, the 'highest Brahman' (8. 3), identical with the 'Unmanifest beyond the Unmanifest' (8. 20). The adjective *paramaṁ* qualifies both *akṣaraṁ*, 'Imperishable', and *veditavyaṁ*, 'wisdom's goal'.

nidhānam, 'prop-and-resting-place': or 'treasure-house' (9. 18). Ś., 'vessel (into which something is put)': R., 'support'.

'Primeval Person': the 'highest Person' of 8. 8, 10, 22: the 'Person eternal and divine' whom Arjuna had already confessed in 10. 12.

'Guardian of eternal law (*dharma*)': the protection of the existing *dharma* is indeed the purpose of Vishnu's incarnations: 'for whenever the law of righteousness withers away and lawlessness arises, then do I generate myself [on earth]' (4. 7).

19. *anādi-madhy'āntam ananta-vīryam*
ananta-bāhuṁ śaśi-sūrya-netram
paśyāmi tvāṁ dīpta-hutāśa-vaktraṁ
sva-tejasā viśvam idaṁ tapantam.

Beginning, middle, or end You do not know,—how infinite your strength! How numberless your arms,—your eyes the sun and moon! So do I see You,—your mouth a flaming fire, burning up this whole universe with your blazing glory.

'Sun and moon': for R. the moon represents God's grace, the sun his wrath: the fire is the fire of Time which consumes the world at the end of each world-aeon.

20. *dyāvā-pṛthivyor idam antaraṁ hi*
vyāptaṁ tvay'aikena diśaś ca sarvāḥ:
dṛṣṭvā 'dbhutaṁ rūpam ugraṁ tav'edaṁ
loka-trayaṁ pravyathitaṁ, mah'ātman.

By You alone is this space between heaven and earth pervaded, —all points of the compass too; gazing on this, your marvellous, frightening form, the three worlds shudder, [All-] Highest Self!

21. *amī hi tvāṁ sura-saṁghā viśanti;*
kecid bhītāḥ prāñjalayo gṛṇanti;
svastī'ty uktvā maha'rṣi-siddha-saṁghāḥ
stuvanti tvāṁ stutibhiḥ puṣkalābhiḥ.

Lo! these hosts of gods are entering into You: some, terror-struck, extol You, hands together pressed; great seers and men perfected in serried ranks cry out, 'All hail', and praise You with copious hymns of praise.

22. *Rudr'ādityā, Vasavo, ye ca Sādhyā,*
Viśve, 'śvinau, Marutaś c'oṣma-pāś ca,
Gandharva-Yakṣ'āsura-siddha-saṁghā
vīkṣante tvāṁ vismitāś c'aiva sarve.

Rudras, Ādityas, Vasus, Sādhyas, All-gods, Aśvins, Maruts, and [the ancestors] who quaff the steam, minstrels divine, sprites, demons, and the hosts of perfected saints gaze upon You, all utterly amazed.

'Rudras' etc.: see 10. 21, 23 nn.

'Sādhyas': an inferior class of deity who dwell between heaven and earth.

'Aśvins': see 11. 6 n.

23. *rūpaṁ mahat te bahu-vaktra-netraṁ,*
mahā-bāho, bahu-bāh'ūru-pādam
bah'ūdaraṁ bahu-daṁṣṭrā-karālaṁ
dṛṣṭvā lokāḥ pravyathitās, tathā 'ham.

Gazing upon your mighty form with its myriad mouths, eyes, arms, thighs, feet, bellies, and sharp, gruesome tusks, the worlds [all] shudder [in affright],—how much more I!

24. *nabhaḥ-spṛśaṁ dīptam aneka-varṇaṁ*
vyātt'ānanaṁ dīpta-viśāla-netram,
dṛṣṭvā hi tvāṁ pravyathit'āntarātmā
dhṛtiṁ na vindāmi śamaṁ ca, Viṣṇo.

Ablaze with many-coloured [flames] You touch the sky, your mouths wide open, [gaping,] your eyes distended, blazing: so do I see You and my inmost self is shaken: I cannot bear it, I find no peace, O Vishnu!

'My inmost self is shaken': both Ś. and R. gloss 'inmost self' as 'mind'. This would be justifiable in the case of *ātman*, but scarcely in the case of *antar-ātman*, the '*inmost* self' which can only be the individual 'self-in-itself', that 'inmost' self that is at the same time Brahman. This self—the true self of the liberated man—is nevertheless capable either of being absorbed in God (6. 47) or of being terrified by his awful power.

25. *daṁṣṭrā-karālāni ca te mukhāni*
dṛṣṭv' aiva kāl' ānala-saṁnibhāni,
diśo na jāne na labhe ca śarma:
prasīda, dev' eśa, jagan-nivāsa.

I see your mouths with jagged, ghastly tusks reminding [me] of Time's [devouring] fire: I cannot find my bearings, I cannot find a refuge; have mercy, God of gods, home of the universe!

'Time's [devouring] fire': the fire that burns the world up at the end of a world-aeon.

śarma, 'refuge': this is what it normally means, yet both Ś. and R. gloss *sukham*, 'anything pleasant'. H. and Rk., following them, translate 'happiness' and 'peace' respectively.

26. *amī ca tvāṁ Dhṛtarāṣṭrasya putrāḥ*
sarve sah' aiv' āvani-pāla-saṁghaiḥ,
Bhīṣmo, Droṇaḥ, sūta-putras tathā 'sau
sahā' smadīyair api yodha-mukhyaiḥ,

Lo, all these sons of Dhritarāshtra accompanied by hosts of kings,—Bhīshma, Drona, and [Karna,] son of the charioteer, and those foremost in battle of our party too,

27. *vaktrāṇi te tvaramāṇā viśanti*
daṁṣṭrā-karālāni bhay' ānakāni.
kecid vilagnā daśan' āntareṣu
saṁdṛśyante cūrṇitair uttam' āṅgaiḥ.

Rush [blindly] into your [gaping] mouths that with their horrid tusks strike [them] with terror. Some stick in the gaps between your teeth,—see them!—their heads to powder ground!

After the first half-stanza some MSS. add:
sahasra-sūryāta [sic]*-saṁnibhāni*
tathā jagad-grāsa-kṛta-kṣaṇāni.

'Like unto a thousand suns biding their time to devour the world.'

After the whole stanza some MSS. add:

nānā-rūpaiḥ puruṣair vadhyamānā
viśanti te vaktram acintya-rūpam
Yaudhiṣṭhirā Dhārtarāṣṭrāś ca yodhāḥ
śastraiḥ kṛttā vividhaiḥ sarva eva
tvat-tejasā nihatā nūnam ete:
tathā hī'me tvac-charīraṁ praviṣṭāḥ.

Slain by divers other men they enter into your mouth of form unthinkable—all Yudhishthira's and Dhritarāshtra's fighting men slashed by every kind of weapon, and at the same time killed by your blazing glory. So do these men enter into your body.

28. *yathā nadīnāṁ bahavo 'mbu-vegāḥ*
samudram ev'ābhimukhā dravanti,
tathā tav'āmī nara-loka-vīrā
viśanti vaktrāṇy abhijvalanti.

As many swelling, seething streams rush headlong into the [one] great sea, so do these heroes of the world of men enter into your blazing mouths.

29. *yathā pradīptaṁ jvalanaṁ pataṅgā*
viśanti nāśāya samṛddha-vegāḥ,
tath'aiva nāśāya viśanti lokās
tav'āpi vaktrāṇi samṛddha-vegāḥ.

As moths in bursting, hurtling haste rush into a lighted blaze to [their own] destruction, so do the worlds, well-trained in hasty violence, pour into your mouths to [their own] undoing!

30. *lelihyase grasamānaḥ samantāl*
lokān samagrān vadanair jvaladbhiḥ:
tejobhir āpūrya jagat samagraṁ
bhāsas tav'ogrāḥ pratapanti, Viṣṇo.

On every side You lick, lick up,—devouring,—worlds, universes, everything,—with burning mouths. Vishnu! your dreadful rays of light fill the whole universe with flames-of-glory, scorching [everywhere].

31. *ākhyāhi me ko bhavān ugra-rūpo:*
namo 'stu te, deva-vara, prasīda.
vijñātum icchāmi bhavantam ādyaṁ,
na hi prajānāmi tava pravṛttim.

Tell me, who are You, your form so cruel? Homage to You, You best of gods, have mercy! Fain would I know You as You are in the beginning, for what You are set on doing I do not understand.

'What You are set on doing': so R., *kiṁ kartuṁ pravṛttaḥ*. Arjuna does not yet understand the terrible side to his nature displayed by Krishna which is capable even of upsetting the still self that has won liberation (11. 24 n.). Nothing in Krishna's teaching had prepared him for this. He would sooner know Him 'as He is in the beginning', in his eternal rest, rather than his incomprehensible and seemingly savage activity. Krishna now tells him that the reality is quite as fearful as it seems.

Krishna reveals Himself as Time

Śrī-bhagavān uvāca:

32. *kālo 'smi loka-kṣaya-kṛt pravṛddho,*
lokān samāhartum iha pravṛttaḥ:
ṛte 'pi tvāṁ na bhaviṣyanti sarve
ye 'vasthitāḥ pratyanīkeṣu yodhāḥ.

The Blessed Lord said:

Time am I, wreaker of the world's destruction, matured,— [grimly] resolved here to swallow up the worlds. Do what you will, all these warriors shall cease to be, drawn up [there] in their opposing ranks.

ṛte tvāṁ, 'do what you will': this could mean, 'except you', as some translators have taken it. However, at the end of the Epic it is only Yudhishthira who, because of his blameless life, ascends to heaven without having suffered bodily death. Arjuna, like his three other brothers, falls by the way. The meaning is surely that Krishna has every intention of destroying the whole warrior class without Arjuna's assistance if necessary.

33. *tasmāt tvam uttiṣṭha, yaśo labhasva,*
jitvā śatrūn bhuṅkṣva rājyaṁ samṛddham:
may' aiv' aite nihatāḥ pūrvam eva:
nimitta-mātraṁ bhava, savya-sācin.

And so stand up, win glory, conquer your enemies and win a prosperous kingdom! Long since have these men in truth been slain by Me: yours it is to be the mere occasion.

God is the sole agent as He makes brutally clear again at the end of the poem: 'If, relying on your ego, you should think, "I will not fight", vain is your resolve, [for] Nature will constrain you. . . . In the region of the heart of all contingent beings dwells the Lord, twirling them hither and thither by his uncanny power [like puppets] mounted on a machine (18. 59, 61).

34. *Droṇaṁ ca Bhīṣmaṁ ca Jayadrathaṁ ca*
Karṇaṁ tathā 'nyān api yodha-vīrān
mayā hatāṁs tvaṁ jahi, mā vyathiṣṭhā:
yudhyasva, jetā'si raṇe sapatnān.

Drona, Bhīshma, Jayadratha, Karna, and all the other men of war are [as good as] slain by Me. Slay them then,—why falter? Fight! [for] you will conquer your rivals in the battle.

Saṁjaya uvāca:

35. *etac chrutvā vacanaṁ Keśavasya*
kṛt'āñjalir vepamānaḥ kirīṭī
namas-kṛtvā bhūya ev'āha Kṛṣṇaṁ
sagadgadaṁ bhīta-bhītaḥ praṇamya.

Sanjaya said:

Hearing these words of Krishna, [Arjuna,] wearer of the crown, hands joined in veneration, trembling, bowed down to Krishna and spake again with stammering voice, as terrified he did obeisance.

Arjuna's Hymn of Praise

Arjuna uvāca:

36. *sthāne, Hṛṣīkeśa, tava prakīrtyā*
jagat prahṛṣyaty anurajyate ca:
rakṣāṁsi bhītāni diśo dravanti,
sarve namasyanti ca siddha-saṁghāḥ.

Arjuna said:

Full just is it that in praise of You the world should find its pleasure and its joy, that monsters struck with terror should scatter in all directions, and that all the hosts of men perfected should do You homage.

37. *kasmāc ca te na nameran, mah'ātman,*
garīyase brahmaṇo 'py ādi-kartre:
ananta, dev'eśa, jagan-nivāsa,
tvam akṣaraṁ sad asat tat-paraṁ yat.

And why should they not revere You, great [as is your] Self, more to be prized even than Brahman, first Creator, Infinite, Lord of the gods, home of the universe? You are the Imperishable, what IS and what is not and what surpasses both.

Brahmaṇo, 'than Brahman': practically all the commentators, both ancient and modern, take *brahmaṇo* as the genitive of *Brahmā*, the creator-god of 11. 15. This seems to me unlikely since Brahmā has only been mentioned once, whereas Brahman is a concept that has been gaining increasing importance throughout the previous chapters. As against this it may be argued that the 'Imperishable' with which Arjuna identifies Krishna here is identified with the 'highest Brahman' in 8. 3 and that he identifies Krishna Himself with the latter in 10. 12. To this we may reply that in 3. 15 Brahman is itself subordinated to the 'Imperishable', that Arjuna can scarcely be regarded as an exact theologian, and finally—a really strong argument—that Krishna has already said that Nirvāna (which is Brahman too) 'subsists in' Him (6. 15), that in this very passage Krishna not only is the Imperishable, but surpasses it, and that He is to say in 14. 27 that He is 'the base supporting Brahman', just as He supports *dharma*, 'the eternal law of righteousness' and 'absolute beatitude'. Moreover, there is nothing new in this. The same idea had already appeared in ŚU. 5. 1:

> In the imperishable, infinite city of Brahman
> Two things there are—
> Wisdom and unwisdom, hidden, established there:
> Perishable is unwisdom, but wisdom is immortal:
> Who over wisdom and unwisdom rules, He is Another.

This would seem to be an elaboration of the deeply cryptic stanza 13 of *Iśā* Up.:

> Other, they say, than wisdom,
> Other than unwisdom [too], they say:
> So from the wise have we heard
> Who instructed us therein.

Again in ŚU. 3. 7 we read *tataḥ paraṁ brahma-paraṁ bṛhantaṁ . . . īśam*, where translators, blindly following Śankara and Deussen, have read *brahma*(-)*paraṁ* as two words, thereby obtaining the sense, 'higher than that is the highest Brahman'. It seems far more natural (as well, apparently, as being in accordance with the majority of the MSS.) to read *brahma-paraṁ* as one word and to take *paraṁ* in the same sense in the two phrases, 'beyond this, beyond Brahman'. The whole stanza should therefore be translated thus:

> Higher than this, than Brahman higher, the mighty [God],
> Hidden in all beings, in each according to his kind,
> The One, all things encompassing, the Lord—
> By knowing Him a man becomes immortal.

Similarly in ŚU. 2. 15 the usual translation (e.g. Hume) makes nonsense of the passage in that it fails to see that God and Brahman are here distinct. So we are asked to believe that 'a practiser of Yoga beholds the nature (*tattva*) of Brahman . . . from every nature free'! If, however, one reads the stanza in a way that is natural to the grammar, the logical absurdity of a Brahman which both has a *tattva* and is *a-tattva*, free from any *tattva*, will be avoided. In its place we find a clear graduation of being rising from 'self' through Brahman to God. Thus—

> When by means of self as it really is as with a lamp
> An integrated man sees Brahman as it really is,
> [Then will he know] the unborn, undying God, the Pure,
> Beyond all essences as they really are,
> [And] knowing Him, from all fetters he'll be freed.

This is the straight reading of the text as, I think, anyone who is more interested in grammar and syntax than in his own theological bias would agree. The straightforward translation, as we have seen, avoids the absurdity of attributing an essence to Brahman in one breath and depriving it of it in the next.

Only in 13. 12–17 does the 'highest Brahman' seem to be wholly equated with the supreme God. True, it is not hailed, as Krishna here is, as 'what IS and what is not *and what surpasses both*', but as neither 'what IS (Being)' nor as 'what is not (Not-Being)'. It would be disingenuous to argue that this double negation in fact reduces Brahman to what Śankara calls *māyā*—that which neither *is* nor is not absolutely—in other words the phenomenal world, since the rest of the passage rules this out. In the Gītā, alas, the word *brahman* is used to mean both the 'Imperishable', material Nature, the sacrifice, and in 13. 12–17 the Imperishable seen as indwelling the perishable. Whether this is identical with the God revealed in the rest of the Gītā will be discussed there.

Finally, it should be noted that the phrase *garīyase brahmaṇo 'py ādi-kartre* can also be taken to mean 'most highly to be prized first Creator even of Brahmā (or Brahman)'. So Ś. and R. (referring to Brahmā, of course, not Brahman).

'Home of the universe': cf. 11. 25 and 9. 18 'home (*nivāsa* as here) and refuge'.

akṣaraṁ, 'Imperishable': see 11. 18 n.

sad asat, 'what IS and what is not': 'Being and Not-Being'. As we have seen (2. 16 n.) *sat* seems usually to mean 'eternal being', *asat* 'conditioned or contingent being'. This is in accordance with Upanishadic usage and is almost certainly what Krishna means when in 9. 19 (q.v.) He says that He is 'deathlessness and death, what IS and what is not', death being the hallmark of the contingent and deathlessness of the absolute and eternal.

tat-paraṁ yat, 'what surpasses both': so Rk., E., following Ś. and R. H., following D., divides *tat paraṁ yat* and translates 'That Supreme'. In this case either *tat* or *yat* is otiose. Moreover, the variants *sad-asattaḥ paraṁ* and *sad-asatoḥ paraṁ* show that the copyists too understood the phrase to mean 'what is beyond both'. Ś. takes the whole in apposition to *akṣaraṁ*, 'the Imperishable which is beyond that, viz., what IS and what is not', while R. comments, 'what is beyond and other than material Nature and individual selves still bound up in it, that is, the category of liberated selves'. It seems, however, perfectly clear that Arjuna is hailing Krishna as being beyond both contingent and 'imperishable' being (cf. ŚU. 5. 1).

38. *tvam ādi-devaḥ, puruṣaḥ purānas,*
tvam asya viśvasya paraṁ nidhānam;
vettā 'si vedyaṁ ca paraṁ ca dhāma:
tvayā tataṁ viśvam, ananta-rūpa.

You are the Primal God, Primeval Person, You of this universe the last prop-and-resting-place, You the knower and what is to be known, [You our] highest home, O You whose forms are infinite, by You the whole universe was spun.

'Primeval Person': see 11. 18 and n.

'Last prop-and-resting-place': the phrase is repeated from 11. 18.

'[Our] highest home': so 10. 12 where Arjuna hails Krishna as 'highest Brahman, highest home', although Krishna had previously said (8. 21) that the Imperishable [Brahman] was *his* 'highest home' (*dhāma* in all cases) and therefore not identical with Him.

'By You the whole universe was spun (or pervaded)': the phrase first appears in 2. 17 where it is used of the 'Indestructible' (sc. Brahman). In 8. 22 it is the 'highest Person' who 'spins' out the universe, while in 9. 4 and here it is Krishna Himself as it would appear to be in 18. 46.

39. *Vāyur, Yamo, 'gnir, Varuṇaḥ, śaśāṅkaḥ,*
Prajāpatis tvaṁ prapitāmahaś ca:
namo namas te 'stu sahasra-kṛtvaḥ
punaś ca bhūyo 'pi namo namas te.

[You are the wind-god,] Vāyu, Yama, [the god of death,] Agni, [the god of fire,] Varuna, [the god of water,] and the moon: Prajāpati are You and the primordial ancestor: all hail, all hail to You, [all hail] a thousandfold, and yet again, all hail, all hail to You!

'Prajāpati': the 'lord of creatures', a creator god interchangeable with Brahmā (11. 15).

Some MSS. insert the following couplet here:

anādimān apratima-prabhāvaḥ
sarv'eśvaraḥ sarva-mahā-vibhūte.

Beginningless, matchless in glory, Lord of all, O You whose great and far-flung powers [encompass] all.

40. *namaḥ purastād atha pṛṣṭhatas te,*
namo 'stu te sarvata eva, sarva:
ananta-vīry' āmita-vikramas tvaṁ;
sarvaṁ samāpnoṣi: tato 'si sarvaḥ.

All hail [to You] when I stand before You, [all hail] when I stand behind You, all hail to You wherever I may be, [all hail to You,] the All! How infinite your strength, how limitless your prowess! All things You bring to their consummation: hence You are All.

After *sarva* some MSS. add the following couplet:

na hi tvad-anyaḥ kaścid apī'ha, deva,
loka-traye dṛśyate 'cintya-karmā.

O God whose works cannot be conceived of, no other but You can be seen here in the three worlds.

samāpnoṣi, 'bring to their consummation': the word means 'to complete'. H.'s 'fill' is therefore adequate. Neither S., Rk. 'penetrate' nor E. 'attain' nor D. 'durchdringst' will do. We have already had the idea expressed in 4. 33: 'All works without exception in wisdom find their consummation (*parisamāpyate*).' Everything finite finds its end and justification in the Infinite.

41. *sakh' eti matvā prasabhaṁ yad uktaṁ,*
he Kṛṣṇa, he Yādava, he sakh' eti,
ajānatā mahimānaṁ tav' edaṁ
mayā pramādāt praṇayena vā 'pi,

How rashly have I called You comrade, for so I thought of You, [how rashly said,] 'Hey Krishna, hey Yādava, hey comrade!' Little did I know of this your majesty; distraught was I . . . or was it that I loved You?

42. *yac c' āvahās' ārtham asatkṛto 'si*
vihāra-śayy' āsana-bhojaneṣu
eko 'thavā 'py, acyuta, tat-samakṣaṁ
tat kṣāmaye tvām aham aprameyam.

Sometimes in jest I showed You disrespect as we played or rested or sat or ate at table, sometimes together, sometimes in sight of others: I crave your pardon, O [Lord,] unfathomable, unfallen!

aprameyam, 'unfathomable': or, 'boundless'. Var. *īśam īḍyam*, 'adorable Lord'.

43. *pitā 'si lokasya car'ācarasya,*
tvam asya pūjyaś ca gurur garīyān;
na tvat-samo 'sty abhyadhikaḥ kuto 'nyo
loka-traye 'py apratima-prabhāva.

You are the father of the world of moving and unmoving things, You their venerable teacher, most highly prized; none is there like You,—how could there be another greater?—in the three worlds, Oh, matchless is your power.

44. *tasmāt praṇamya, praṇidhāya kāyaṁ,*
prasādaye tvām aham īśam īḍyam:
pit' eva putrasya, sakh' eva sakhyuḥ,
priyaḥ priyāy' ārhasi, deva, soḍhum.

And so I bow to You, prostrate my body, crave grace of You, [my] Lord adorable: bear with me, I beg You, as father [bears] with son, or friend with friend, or lover with the one he loves, O God!

īśam īḍyam, 'Lord adorable': var. *aprameyam*, 'unfathomable'.

Some MSS. add here:

divyāni karmāṇi tav'ādbhutāni
pūrvāṇi pūrve 'py ṛṣayaḥ smaranti:
n'ānyo 'sti kartā jagatas, tvam eko
dhātā vidhātā ca vibhur bhavaś ca.
tav'ādbhutaṁ kiṁ nu bhaved asahyaṁ,
kiṁ vā' śakyaṁ? paruluḥ kīrtayiṣye?
kartā 'si sarvasya: yataḥ svayaṁ vai,
vibho, tataḥ sarvam idaṁ tvam eva.
atyadbhutaṁ karma na duṣkaraṁ te,
karm'opamānaṁ na hi vidyate te.
na te guṇānāṁ parimāṇam asti,
na tejaso, n'āpi balasya na'rddheḥ.

The ancient seers recount the deeds You did of old, marvellous and divine. No other maker of the world is there; You alone are Ordainer, Dispenser, Lord, and Origin. What marvel could there be beyond your endurance or beyond your power? Should I [then] ascribe it to another? Maker of all are You: in that You most surely [exist] yourself, O all-pervading Lord, so are You surely this whole universe. No deed, however marvellous, is difficult for You, for with You there is no standard of comparison in what You do. No limit is there to your attributes, to your glory, power, and riches.

One MS. has one stanza only based on the above.

45. *adṛṣṭa-pūrvaṁ hṛṣito 'smi dṛṣṭvā*
bhayena ca pravyathitaṁ mano me.
tad eva me darśaya, deva, rūpaṁ;
prasīda, dev' eśa, jagan-nivāsa.

Things never seen before I have seen, and ecstatic is my joy; yet fear-and-trembling perturb my mind. Show me, then, God, that [same human] form [I knew]; have mercy, Lord of gods, home of the universe!

46. *kirīṭinaṁ gadinaṁ cakra-hastam*
icchāmi tvāṁ draṣṭum ahaṁ tath' aiva;
ten' aiva rūpeṇa catur-bhujena,
sahasra-bāho, bhava, viśva-mūrte.

Fain would I see You with [your familiar] crown and mace, discus in hand, just as You used to be; take up again your four-armed form, O thousand-armed, to whom every form belongs.

catur-bhujena, 'four-armed': var. *bhuja-dvayena*, 'two-armed'.

Śri-bhagavān uvāca:

47. *mayā prasannena tav' ārjun' edaṁ*
rūpaṁ paraṁ darśitam ātma-yogāt
tejomayaṁ viśvam anantam ādyaṁ
yan me tvad-anyena na dṛṣṭa-pūrvam.

The Blessed Lord said:

Because I desired to show you favour, Arjuna, by my Self's own power I have shown you my highest form,—glorious, ell-embracing, infinite, primeval, which none but you has ever seen before.

ātma-yogāt, 'by my Self's own power' (and how I use it): cf. 10. 7 n.

48. *na veda-yajñ' ādhyayanair na dānair*
na ca kriyābhir na tapobhir ugraiḥ
evaṁ-rūpaḥ śakya ahaṁ nṛ-loke
draṣṭuṁ tvad-anyena, Kuru-pravīra.

Not by the Vedas, not by sacrifice, not by [much] study or the giving of alms, not by rituals or grim ascetic practice can I be seen in such a form in the world of men: to you alone [have I revealed it,] champion of the Kurus.

nṛ-loke, 'world of men': var. *tri-loke*, 'the three worlds'.

49. *mā te vyathā mā ca vimūḍha-bhāvo*
dṛṣṭvā rūpaṁ ghoram īdṛṅ mam' edam:
vyapeta-bhīḥ prīta-manāḥ punas tvaṁ
tad eva me rūpam idaṁ prapaśya.

You need not tremble nor need your spirit be perplexed though you have seen this form of mine, so awful, grim. Banish all fear, be glad at heart: behold again that [same familiar] form [you knew].

Krishna assumes His Human Form again

Saṁjaya uvāca:

50. *ity Arjunaṁ Vāsudevas tath'oktvā*
svakaṁ rūpaṁ darśayām āsa bhūyaḥ,
āśvāsayām āsa ca bhītam enaṁ
bhūtvā punaḥ saumya-vapur mah'ātmā.

Sanjaya said:

Thus speaking did the son of Vasudeva show his [human] form to Arjuna again, comforting him in his fear. For once again the great-souled [Krishna] assumed the body of a friend.

Arjuna uvāca:

51. *dṛṣṭv'edaṁ mānuṣaṁ rūpaṁ tava saumyaṁ, janārdana,*
idānīm asmi saṁvṛttaḥ sacetāḥ prakṛtiṁ gataḥ.

Arjuna said:

Now that I see [again] this your human form, friendly-and-kind, I have returned to my senses and regained my normal state.

Śrī-bhagavān uvāca:

52. *sudurdarśam idaṁ rūpaṁ dṛṣṭavān asi yan mama:*
devā apy asya rūpasya nityaṁ darśana-kāṅkṣiṇaḥ.

The Blessed Lord said:

Right hard to see is this my form which you have seen: this is the form the gods themselves forever crave to see.

53. *n'āhaṁ vedair na tapasā na dānena na c'ejyayā*
śakya evaṁ-vidho draṣṭuṁ dṛṣṭavān asi māṁ yathā.

Not by the Vedas or grim-ascetic-practice, not by the giving of alms or sacrifice can I be seen in such a form as you did see Me;

54. *bhaktyā tv ananyayā śakya aham evaṁ-vidho, 'rjuna,*
jñātuṁ draṣṭuṁ ca tattvena praveṣṭuṁ ca, paraṁtapa.

But by worship-of-love addressed to [Me,] none other, Arjuna, can I be known and seen in such a form and as I really am: [so can my lovers] enter into Me.

'Addressed to [Me], none other': the love of God excludes all other love: cf. 8. 14: 9. 13, 22, 30: 12. 6: 13. 10.

'Enter into Me': this is the privilege of the *bhākta*, the lover of God. It is never used of the 'man of wisdom' except in 12. 4 where the devotees of the Unmanifest are said to 'reach' God. To 'enter into' God, however, implies an even more intimate relationship.

55. *mat-karma-kṛn mat-paramo mad-bhaktaḥ saṅga-varjitaḥ*
nirvairaḥ sarva-bhūteṣu yaḥ, sa mām eti, Pāṇḍava.

Do works for Me, make Me your highest goal, be loyal-in-love to Me, cut off all [other] attachments, have no hatred for any being at all: for all who do thus shall come to Me.

'Do works for Me': cf. 9. 27: 'Whatever you do, whatever you eat, whatever you offer in sacrifice or give away in alms, whatever penance you may perform, offer it up to Me.'

'Make Me your highest goal': cf. 10. 9, 'On Me their thoughts, their life they would sacrifice for Me.' The lesson of total and exclusive love of God is repeated as God's 'highest' and 'most mysterious' doctrine at the very end of the Gītā (18. 64–5): 'Bear Me in mind, love Me and worship Me, sacrifice, prostrate yourself to Me: so will you come to Me, I promise you truly, for you are dear to Me.'

'[other]': the addition is obviously necessary since the total detachment of the first six chapters has been replaced and 'filled' by a total attachment to God. The change comes abruptly and with telling force in 7. 1: 'Attach your mind to Me. . . '.

CHAPTER XII

THE opening of this chapter must be one of the biggest anti-climaxes in literature. After what has gone before Arjuna asks in the most detached tones whether those who revere the personal god, Krishna, whose terrifying reality he has just witnessed, or those who revere the 'imperishable Unmanifest' are in fact the 'most experienced in spiritual exercise'.

Krishna, not surprisingly, replies that his own devotees are to be preferred, but grants that those who revere the 'Unmanifest' also reach Him. This is, however, the harder way (1–5). He recommends Arjuna to consign all his works to Himself, to meditate on Him to the exclusion of all others, then he will come to dwell in Him (6–8). Should he be unable to do this, then he should resort to other methods (9–12).

The rest of the chapter is devoted to an enumeration of the classes of people who are particularly dear to Krishna. All of them are characterized by the virtues of self-control, dispassion, indifference, and loving devotion to God. The chapter is traditionally and appropriately called the 'Yoga of Loving Devotion'.

Personal God and Impersonal Absolute

Arjuna uvāca:

1. *evaṁ satata-yuktā ye bhaktās tvāṁ paryupāsate*
ye c'āpy akṣaram avyaktaṁ, teṣāṁ ke yoga-vittamāḥ ?

Arjuna said:

Of those who are thus ever integrated and serve You with loyal devotion, and those who [revere] the Imperishable Unmanifest, which are the most experienced in spiritual exercise?

In the first half of this stanza Arjuna takes up Krishna's thought in 10. 10, while in the second half he returns to 8. 20–1—just as if the theophany had never taken place at all! So closely does the first half of this stanza fit in with 10. 10 and so little has it to do with the theophany of Chapter XI which immediately precedes it, that one is tempted to rearrange the text in what seems a more rational manner. In 10. 10 Krishna had said: 'To these men who are ever integrated (*satata-yukta*) and commune with

Me in love I give that integration of the soul (*buddhi-yoga*) by which they may draw nigh to Me.'

In our note on 10. 10 we suggested that whereas the 'integration of the soul' of 2. 39–41 etc., leads only to the 'fixed, still state of Brahman', there Krishna grants a higher or at least a different type of 'integration of the soul' which makes room for the love of God and which draws it out of its timeless immobility into an affective relation with God seen as transcendent and 'other'. This (assuming that my interpretation is correct) Arjuna had not understood, and so he now contrasts integration and loving devotion on the one hand with reverence for the Imperishable Unmanifest on the other. The question, however, was worth asking since Krishna's reply supplements what He had already said in 10. 10 and 8. 20–2.

paryupāsate, 'revere': Ś., meditate on'.

akṣaram, 'Imperishable': Ś., 'Brahman . . . seen as devoid of all illusory adjuncts (*upādhi*)': R., 'in the form of the individual self'. See 12. 3 n.

avyaktaṁ: Ś., R., 'not accessible to the senses'.

Śrī-bhagavān uvāca:

2. *mayy āveśya mano ye māṁ nitya-yuktā upāsate*
śraddhayā paray'opetās te me yuktatamā matāḥ.

The Blessed Lord said:

Those I deem to be most integrated who fix their thoughts on Me and serve Me, ever integrated [in themselves], filled with the highest faith.

Krishna here repeats in slightly different words what He had emphatically stated in 6. 47: 'Of all athletes of the spirit the man of faith who loves-and-honours Me, *his inmost self absorbed in Me*—he is the most fully integrated: this do I believe.' This man, it will be remembered, had already 'become Brahman' (6. 27) and 'seen the self in all beings standing, all beings in the self': he had seen 'the same in everything'. Despite all this (or perhaps because of it) Krishna does not say at that stage that he had thereby reached God Himself in his transcendence.

3. *ye tv akṣaram anirdeśyam avyaktaṁ paryupāsate*
sarvatra-gam acintyaṁ ca kūṭa-stham acalaṁ dhruvam,

But those who revere the indeterminate Imperishable Unmanifest, unthinkable though coursing everywhere, sublime, aloof, unmoving, firm,

paryupāsate, 'revere' or 'serve': var. *māṁ upāsate*, 'revere Me as'. The variant is significant in that it completely identifies Krishna with the 'Imperishable Unmanifest'. Ś. interprets *paryupāsate* thus: 'by focussing one's attention on an object recommended by Scripture and drawing near to it, one remains in its presence for a long time [sustained] by the current of constant intention as by a stream of oil'.

anirdeśyam, 'indeterminate': R., 'it cannot be defined as "god" or anything else because it is different from a material body'.

akṣaram, 'Imperishable': R., 'the "form" (*svarūpa*) of the individual self'. The 'Imperishable', as we know, was identified with the 'highest Brahman' in 8. 3 and the method of reaching it is discussed in 8. 11–13 (see 12. 4 n.). In 8. 21 it is identified with the 'Unmanifest beyond the Unmanifest' and that again with the 'highest' or 'exalted Person'. In 11. 18 and 37 Arjuna hailed Krishna Himself as the 'Imperishable'.

So too in BU. 3. 8. 8–9 the 'Imperishable' is quite clearly the supreme Being—'indeterminate' and 'unthinkable' in that it can only be described in negative terms, 'not coarse, not fine, not short, not long; . . . it has no "within", no "without"', etc.; but at the same time it is God in act: 'At the behest of the Imperishable . . . sun and moon stand apart and so abide' etc.: see further 8. 3 n. On the other hand, both in ŚU. and MuU. the Imperishable is no longer the supreme Being in that it is either contrasted with its opposite, the 'perishable' (ŚU. 1. 8: 5. 1) and, having thus become no more than one pole of a pair of opposites, it is subjected to the Lord, the one God Hara (1. 10) who is 'Another' (5. 1), or it is equated with what the Sāṁkhya system calls the 'Unmanifest', the hidden source from which the visible universe proceeds (MuU. 2. 1. 1), and as such it is again subjected to the 'highest Person . . . beyond the Imperishable [itself]' (ibid. 2. 1. 2).

Later in the Gītā (15. 16) an 'imperishable' and a 'perishable' 'person' are contrasted and once again subjected to a 'supreme Person' who is, of course, Vishnu-Krishna. This is fully in line with the thought of the *Śvetāśvatara* Upanishad. The 'Imperishable' in our present passage must, I think, be that of the *Śvetāśvatara* rather than that of the *Bṛhadāraṇyaka* Upanishad: it is static, eternal, timeless Being, divorced from all contact with or taint of the finite. This seems to be proved by the other epithets applied to it here. It is our old friend, the 'fixed, still state of Brahman' of 2. 72 and the 'Nirvāna that is Brahman too' of 5. 24–6.

avyaktaṁ, 'unmanifest': the term is first used of the individual self in 2. 25 where it is also called 'unthinkable' as here. In KaU. 6. 7 it is equated with the 'Unmanifest' of the Sāṁkhya system (see 3. 42 n.), that is, primal matter, but in 8. 20 we meet with the 'Unmanifest (*masc.*) beyond the Unmanifest' which we discussed ad loc. This corresponds to the 'Person' of KaU. 6. 8 and the 'self' of BhG. 3. 43, that is, the individual self or the eternal Brahman at least as it is on the scale of the microcosm.

sarvatra-gam, 'coursing everywhere, omnipresent': this is the very condition of the liberated self (2. 24) as it is of Brahman in so far as it is connected with the sacrifice (3. 15).

acintyaṁ, 'unthinkable': again used of the self-in-itself in 2. 25.

kūṭa-stham, 'sublime, aloof': we have already met with this word in 6. 8 where it is applied to the 'athlete of the spirit' who has conquered his senses and reached a state of holy indifference characteristic of the spiritually free—the liberated man. Later in 15. 16 the same word is equated with the 'imperishable' as opposed to the 'perishable' 'person' who, as we have seen, is here subject to the 'Person [All-]Sublime', Vishnu-Krishna.

There is no doubt at all about the meaning of this word as the parallels from the MBh., a few of which were cited in our note on 6. 8, show. Many more could be cited both from the MBh. and from the Pāli canon where the Pāli form *kūṭa-ttha* is used in the same sense. It is, then, all the more surprising that Ś., usually so careful in matters of philology and semantics, should interpret the word in the following way: 'standing in *kūṭa* (the crooked), that is, something that has the quality of being visible and has an internal defect, that is to say, the seed of repeated reincarnation originating in [cosmic] ignorance . . . also known as *māyā*: . . . [the Self] abides in this as an onlooker (*adhyakṣa*)'. Alternatively he suggests 'standing like a heap'. These extraordinary interpretations he repeats at 15. 16, though at 6. 8 he rightly glosses 'unshakable'.

R. takes *acintyaṁ* and *kūṭa-stham* to mean that selves cannot be thought of in separate 'forms' because they are different in kind from whatever has form or shape. They are all alike in that they are not subject to change.

acalaṁ, 'unmoving': this again occurs in 2. 24 on which this whole stanza seems to be based. There Krishna is talking about the immortality of the individual self, more particularly and quite concretely of Arjuna's and of those of his opponents whom he is about to slay. The following words are common to the two passages: *avyakta*, 'unmanifest'; *sarvatra-ga* (*sarva-gata*), 'omnipresent'; *acintya*, 'unthinkable'; and *acala*, 'unmoving'. *Akṣara*, 'imperishable', *kūṭa-stha*, 'sublime, aloof', and *dhruva*, 'firm' do not occur in the parallel passage, but in their place we have *avikārya*, 'not susceptible to modification', *sthāṇu*, 'firm as a pillar', and *nitya*, 'eternal, abiding'.

All that this amounts to is that Krishna here is speaking of the individual self in its timeless being which Arjuna rightly sees as something different from the God who has revealed Himself as all-destroying Time. At the same time although the Gītā makes a progressive distinction between Brahman as the timeless 'stuff' in which individual selves participate and as the material source of the universe on the one hand and Krishna as the wholly transcendent and immanent God on the other, it is made increasingly clear that by 'becoming Brahman', that is, by entering into the transcendent world beyond space and time, one must *ipso facto* draw nearer to the transcendent God. Herein lies the sharp difference between the 'Yoga' of the Gītā and that of the *Yoga-sūtras* where 'isolation' not 'communion' is the goal.

4. *saṁniyamy' endriya-grāmaṁ sarvatra sama-buddhayaḥ,*
te prāpnuvanti mām eva sarva-bhūta-hite ratāḥ.

Who hold in check the complex of the senses, in all things equal-minded, taking pleasure in the weal of all contingent beings, these too attain to Me.

saṁniyamy'endriya-grāmaṁ, 'who hold in check the complex of the senses': practically the same phrase is used in 6. 24: 'let him restrain by mind alone the complex of the senses'. This is the exercise that leads directly to 'becoming Brahman'.

sama-buddhayaḥ, 'equal-minded' (lit. 'same-souled'): the word occurs along with *kūṭa-stha*, 'sublime, aloof' in 6. 8–9. 'With self content in wisdom learnt from holy books and wisdom learnt from life, with sense subdued, *sublime, aloof*, [this] athlete of the spirit [stands]: "Integrated", so is he called; *the same* to him are clods of earth, stones, gold. Outstanding is *he whose soul views in the selfsame way* (*sama-buddhi*) friends, comrades, enemies, those indifferent, neutrals, men who are hateful and those who are his kin—the good and the evil too.'

sarva-bhūta-hite ratāḥ, 'taking pleasure in the weal of all contingent beings': this is the positive side to *sama-buddhi*, viewing all things equally, sublime indifference, and it is the result of attaining to the state of Nirvāna (5. 25): 'Nirvāna that is Brahman too win seers in whom [all] taint-of-imperfection is destroyed; their doubts dispelled, with self controlled, *they take their pleasure in the weal of all contingent beings*.'

Comparing the passage we have just quoted with our present stanza we cannot help being struck by the very close resemblance between the two. The only real difference seems to be that in the one case the goal achieved is 'Nirvāna that is Brahman too' while in the other it is Krishna, the personal God. The inference, then, would seem to be that there is no real distinction between the two; and this impression is strengthened if we compare the two passages with 8. 11–13 where Krishna is speaking precisely about the Imperishable and how to attain it:

The imperishable state of which the Vedic scholars speak, which sages enter, their passion spent, desiring which men lead a life of chastity, that state will I proclaim to you in brief. . . . Let [a man] utter [the word] Oṁ, Brahman {the One Imperishable / in one syllable}, keeping Me in mind; then, when he departs, leaving aside the body, he will tread the highest way.

Here again we cannot help feeling that there is no real distinction between the One Imperishable syllable Oṁ (Brahman) which the dying man utters and the God whom he bears in mind as he utters it. Moreover, the 'Imperishable' is itself the 'highest way' as we learn from 8. 21, but here there is a distinct shift of emphasis:

Unmanifest [is he], surnamed 'Imperishable': this, men say, is the highest way and, this once won, there is no more returning: this is my highest home. *But* that *highest Person* is to be won by love-and-worship directed to none other. In Him do all beings subsist; by Him this universe is spun.

This passage (if my interpretation of it is right, see note ad loc.) seems to throw light on the meaning of our present passage. The 'highest

Person', the personal God, the 'Person [All-]Sublime' of 15. 17 cannot himself be won except by love and devotion 'directed to none other': none of the techniques devised for 'becoming Brahman' are in themselves enough. However 'integrated' and spiritually free, however 'liberated' one may be, God must still dispel what darkness remains, and so 'to these men who are ever integrated and commune with Me in love I give that integration of the soul by which they may draw nigh to Me. Out of compassion for those same men [all] darkness born of ignorance I dispel with wisdom's shining lamp' (10. 10–11).

Thus, the realization of the identity in eternity of the self-in-itself with the Imperishable Brahman as a mere preliminary to the self's subsequent encounter with the personal God can be deduced from the comparison of the relevant texts themselves *in the order in which they occur*. Yet, admittedly, an element of doubt remains. This, however, is finally dispelled when we turn to the last chapter where all the apparent ambiguities of the earlier chapters are cleared up. There what we have been arguing all along is clearly stated, namely, that the 'highest' love of God and the highest devotion to Him are the *last* fruits of liberation which prepare the liberated self to 'enter into' God, not merely into Brahman, God's 'highest home':

> Let a man be *integrated by his soul now cleansed*, . . . let him give up all thought of 'I', force, pride, desire and anger and possessiveness, let him think of nothing as 'mine', *at peace*;—[if he does this,] *to becoming Brahman is he conformed. Brahman become*, with self serene, he grieves not nor desires; *the same* to all contingent beings *he gains the highest love-and-loyalty to Me* (18. 51–4).

This explains how in our present passage the man who reveres the 'Imperishable Unmanifest' also reaches God who transcends both the Imperishable and the perishable. He does so by receiving the highest *bhakti*, the 'lamp of wisdom' which dispels all remaining darkness. This final grace he obtains because, as the second half of this chapter will tell us, God himself loves the 'athlete of the spirit' who has steeled himself in the hard school of 'integration' and has thereby won release from all earthly bonds.

māṁ prāpnuvanti, 'attain to Me': R., presumably wishing to emphasize the distinction between God and the self-in-itself to the last, glosses: 'they attain to the self as it is when no longer in the wheel of birth and death (*asaṁsārin*) which has the same form as I do'. This distorts the 'middle way' of the Gītā in a dualist direction just as Ś. distorts it in attempting to make it conform to his own extreme type of monism.

5. *kleśo 'dhikataras teṣām avyakt'āsakta-cetasām,*
avyaktā hi gatir duḥkhaṁ dehavadbhir avāpyate.

[But] greater is the toil of those whose thinking clings to the Unmanifest; for difficult [indeed] it is for embodied men to reach-and-tread the unmanifested way.

'Greater is the toil of those whose thinking clings to the Unmanifest': obviously, for how can you think of the 'unthinkable' and 'indeterminate'?

Exclusive Devotion to the Personal God

6. *ye tu sarvāṇi karmāṇi mayi saṁnyasya mat-parāḥ*
ananyen' aiva yogena māṁ dhyāyanta upāsate,

But those who cast off all their works on Me, solely intent on Me, and meditate on Me in spiritual exercise, leaving no room for others, [and so really] do Me honour,

'Cast off their works on Me': so already 3. 30.

'Leaving no room for others': despite Krishna's positive encouragement of the worship of other gods (7. 21: cf. 9. 23) He becomes increasingly insistent in the latter half of the Gītā that worship, meditation, and love should be directed to Him alone:

8. 14: 'How easily am I won by him who bears Me in mind unceasingly, thinking of nothing else at all.'

8. 22: 'But that highest Person is to be won by love-and-worship directed to none other.'

9. 13: 'With minds intent on nought but [Me], they love-and-worship Me.'

9. 22: 'For those men who meditate on Me, no other [thought in mind], who do me honour, ever persevere, I bring attainment and possession of what has been attained.'

9. 30: 'However evil a man's livelihood may be, let him but worship Me with love and serve no other. . . .'

11. 54: 'By worship-of-love addressed to [Me,] none other, can I be known and seen. . . .'

13. 10–11: 'Unswerving loyalty-and-love for Me with spiritual exercise on no other bent, . . . this is "knowledge".'

7. *teṣām ahaṁ samuddhartā mṛtyu-saṁsāra-sāgarāt*
bhavāmi nacirāt, Pārtha, mayy āveśita-cetasām.

These will I lift up on high out of the ocean of recurring death, and that right soon, for their thoughts are fixed on Me.

Both in Buddhism and the classical Yoga man must reach his goal, whether it be Nirvāna or 'isolation' by his own efforts, and in the earlier part of the Gītā this is equally true, for the word *ātmanā*—the instrumental case of *ātman*—used in so many passages dealing with liberation, means 'by your own efforts'—'yourself' in the sense that we might say, 'Do it *yourself*'. This is what it means in 2. 55: 3. 43: 6. 20: 13. 24. So too we are told in 6. 5 that a man should 'raise self by self, let not the self droop down; for self's friend is self indeed, so too is self self's enemy'. Krishna, however, is not only the 'Imperishable' and even 'what is beyond it' but also a God of grace who assists the self of man in every stage of his development. This is something quite new in Hinduism.

8. *mayy eva mana ādhatsva, mayi buddhiṁ niveśaya,*
nivasiṣyasi mayy eva ata ūrdhvaṁ, na saṁśayaḥ.

On Me alone let your mind dwell, stir up your soul to enter Me; thenceforth in very truth in Me you will find your home.

ata ūrdhvaṁ, na saṁśayaḥ, 'thenceforth in very truth': var. *yogam uttamam āsthitaḥ,* 'engaging in the highest spiritual exercise'.

9. *atha cittaṁ samādhātuṁ na śaknoṣi mayi sthiram*
abhyāsa-yogena tato mām icch'āptuṁ, dhanaṁjaya.

But if you are unable in all steadfastness to concentrate your thoughts on Me, then seek to win Me by effort unremitting.

abhyāsa-yogena, 'by effort unremitting': lit. 'by practice of application': recommended in 6. 35 as a method of controlling the mind. Ś., 'concentrating thought on one object, withdrawing it from all [else] and repeatedly checking it'.

10. *abhyāse 'py asamartho 'si mat-karma-paramo bhava,*
mad-artham api karmāṇi kurvan siddhim avāpsyasi.

And if for such effort you lack the strength, then work-and-act for Me, make this your goal; for even if you work only for my sake, you will receive the prize.

'work-and-act for Me': cf. 3. 30: 12. 6. R., 'acts of devotion like building temples, parks, etc.'.

siddhim, 'the prize': var. *muktim,* 'liberation'.

'The prize': R., 'obtaining Me'.

11. *ath'aitad apy aśakto 'si kartum udyogam āśritaḥ,*
sarva-karma-phala-tyāgaṁ tataḥ kuru yat'ātmavān.

And then again if even this exceeds your powers, gird up your loins, renounce the fruit of all your works with self restrained.

udyogam āśritaḥ, 'gird up your loins': lit. 'taking refuge in effort'. The better attested reading, however, is *mad-yogam,* 'my spiritual exercise', the meaning of which is not clear to me. Ś. takes it to mean the performance of actions and casting them off on to God. R., for no apparent reason, takes it to mean that one should concentrate on the 'imperishable' nature of the individual self which automatically gives rise to the highest loving devotion.

12. *śreyo hi jñānam abhyāsāj, jñānād dhyānaṁ viśiṣyate,*
dhyānāt karma-phala-tyāgas, tyāgāc chāntir anantaram.

For better is wisdom than [mere] effort, better than wisdom meditation; and [better] than meditation to renounce the fruits of works: renunciation leads straightway to peace.

This stanza does not seem to fit in naturally with what has gone before, and it worried Hill greatly. Assuming it does fit in, however, then we must take 'wisdom' to mean 'concentrating one's thoughts on God'; 'meditation' to mean 'meditation on God in spiritual exercise' (so verse 6); and 'the abandonment of the fruit of works' to mean not what has been mentioned in the last stanza but the 'casting off of all works on God' again referred to in verse 6. Then the 'renouncing of the fruit of all your works' of verse 11 would mean the renouncing of them without reference to God. This would seem to make sense since, as this chapter tirelessly points out, the classic virtues of detachment and indifference are only perfected if they are complemented by the love of God.

Whom God Loves

13. *adveṣṭā sarva-bhūtānāṁ maitraḥ karuṇa eva ca*
nirmamo nirahaṁkāraḥ sama-duḥkha-sukhaḥ kṣamī,

Let a man feel hatred for no contingent being, let him be friendly, compassionate; let him be done with thoughts of 'I' and 'mine', the same in pleasure as in pain, long-suffering,

The virtues listed here are the typical *Buddhist* virtues. *Maitra* and *karuṇa* are the Buddhist *mettā* and *karuṇā*, the virtues with which the Buddhist monk suffuses the whole universe in the first and second of the four Buddhist *brahma-vihāras*, 'sublime states' (D. ii. 186 etc.), while the abandonment of all thought of 'I' and 'mine' (because for the Buddhists no such entities really exist) is basic to all Buddhism (see 2. 71 n.). Krishna here adopts and accepts the typically Buddhist virtues of self-denial and gives them their due place in his own theistic system: for Him the Buddhist is not and cannot be perfected unless and until he both accepts the existence of God and learns to love Him.

adveṣṭā, 'feel no hatred': var. *aceṣṭā*, 'doing nothing'. Ś., a man feels no hatred for others 'because he sees them as [him]self'. R., on the other hand, explains it as meaning that in whatever way others offend you, you should accept the offence as being ultimately caused by the Lord.

14. *saṁtuṣṭaḥ satataṁ yogī yat'ātmā dṛḍha-niścayaḥ*
mayy arpita-mano-buddhir yo mad-bhaktaḥ, sa me priyaḥ.

Content and ever integrated, his self restrained, his purpose firm, let his mind and soul be steeped in Me, let him worship Me with love: then will I love him [in return].

15. *yasmān n'odvijate loko, lokān n'odvijate ca yaḥ,*
harṣ'āmarṣa-bhay'odvegair mukto yaḥ, sa ca me priyaḥ.

That man I love from whom the people do not shrink and who does not shrink from them, who is free from exaltation, fear, impatience, and excitement.

-udvegair, 'excitement': var. *-krodhair*, 'anger'.

16. *anapekṣaḥ śucir dakṣa udāsīno gata-vyathaḥ*
sarv'ārambha-parityāgī yo mad-bhaktaḥ, sa me priyaḥ.

I love the man who has no expectation, is pure and skilled, indifferent, who has no worries and gives up all [selfish] enterprise, loyal-and-devoted to Me.

-parityāgī, 'who . . . gives up': var. *-phala-tyāgī*, 'who gives up the fruit of . . .'.

17. *yo na hṛṣyati na dveṣṭi na śocati na kāṅkṣati*
śubh'āśubha-parityāgī bhaktimān yaḥ, sa me priyaḥ.

I love the man who hates not nor exults, who mourns not nor desires, who puts away both pleasant and unpleasant things, who is loyal-devoted-and-devout.

na śocati, 'does not mourn': R., 'e.g. at the loss of wife, child, or fortune'. Cf. 2. 11 ff.: 'You sorrow for men who do not need your sorrow. . . .' As with the Buddhists mourning for the dead is not only useless but stupid.

parityāgī: see 12. 16 n.

18–19. *samaḥ śatrau ca mitre ca tathā mān'āvamānayoḥ*
śīt'oṣṇa-sukha-duḥkheṣu samaḥ saṅga-vivarjitaḥ
tulya-nindā-stutir maunī saṁtuṣṭo yena kenacit
aniketaḥ sthira-matir bhaktimān me priyo naraḥ.

I love the man who is the same to friend and foe, [the same] whether he be respected or despised, the same in heat and cold, in pleasure as in pain, who has put away attachment and remains unmoved by praise or blame, who is taciturn, contented with whatever comes his way, having no home, of steady mind, [but] loyal-devoted-and-devout.

samaḥ, 'the same, indifferent': just as Brahman is always 'the same' (5. 19) and *yoga* is 'sameness' (2. 48 and n.). This passage (16–19) has much in common with 2. 56–7, 6. 7–9, and even more with 14. 23–6.

aniketaḥ, 'having no home': i.e. a wandering Sannyāsin.

20. *ye tu dharmy'āmṛtam idaṁ yath'oktaṁ paryupāsate*
śraddadhānā mat-paramā bhaktās, te 'tīva me priyāḥ.

But as for those who reverence these deathless [words] of righteousness which I have just now spoken, putting their faith [in them], making Me their goal, my loving-devotees,—these do I love exceedingly.

CHAPTER XIII

THIS chapter is certainly the most confused in the whole of the Gītā, but at least it falls neatly into sections each of which deals with an aspect of reality which, however, sometimes seems to be at variance with different aspects of reality promulgated in other sections. The chapter can be divided into four sections:

(i) The first subject discussed is the 'field' and the 'knower of the field'. The field is the body and everything that derives from material Nature: the 'knower of the field' is God (1–6).

(ii) What is knowledge and what is the real object of knowledge? Knowledge is, surprisingly, at first identified with a series of (Buddhistic) virtues—honesty, 'non-violence', self-restraint, detachment, etc. To these *bhakti*, loving devotion to God, is now added.

It seems, then, rather strange that the true object of knowledge is now defined not in terms of the personal God but of the more abstract 'highest Brahman', seen both as the 'One' and as the source of the 'many'. Knowledge of Brahman, however, must be supplemented by love and devotion to God (7–18).

(iii) A Sāṁkhya episode: what are 'person' and 'material Nature', *puruṣa* and *prakṛti*? Nature causes, 'person' experiences. God, the 'highest Self' and 'highest Person' surveys, approves, and supports both individual 'persons' or selves, and Nature (19–25).

(iv) In 26 there is abrupt return to the 'field' and the 'knower of the field' which are now fairly clearly identified with 'Person' and material Nature. God, the 'highest Lord' must be seen as the one 'Indestructible' among the 'many' who perish. It is Nature that acts, and not the [individual] self. All multiplicity has its source in the One which is God, whether you wish to think of Him as 'highest Person', 'highest Self', or 'highest Brahman'; and God indwells all bodies. As 'Knower of the field' and 'highest Person' He does not act. Salvation, we are finally told, consists in being able to distinguish between the 'field' and the 'knower of the field' (26–34).

The Field and the Knower of the Field

Arjuna uvāca:

0. *prakṛtiṁ puruṣaṁ c'aiva kṣetraṁ kṣetra-jñam eva ca,*
etad veditum icchāmi, jñānaṁ jñeyaṁ ca, Keśava.

Arjuna said:

[What is] Nature? [What the] 'person'? [What] the 'field' and [what] the 'knower of the field'? This, Krishna, would I know. [What too is] knowledge? [What] that which should be known?

This stanza is omitted in many MSS. One adds another stanza in which Krishna says he will answer the question exactly as Arjuna has asked it.

Śrī-bhagavān uvāca:

1. *idaṁ śarīraṁ, Kaunteya, kṣetram ity abhidhīyate:*
etad yo vetti, taṁ prāhuḥ kṣetra-jña iti tad-vidaḥ.

The Blessed Lord said:

The body is called the 'field' and he who knows it is the 'knower of the field', or so it has been said by those who know it.

kṣetra-jña, 'knower of the field': the term is already used in the Upanishads (ŚU. 6. 16: MaiU. 2. 5). In both these passages the 'knower of the field' is not God but the individual self. In ŚU. 6. 16 the word is used as if it were generally understood to be an alternative word for the *puruṣa* of the Sāṁkhya system, the spiritual monad that indwells every human being. The purpose of that passage is to exalt God (Rudra-Śiva) over both material Nature and the *puruṣa*s or spiritual monads of the Sāṁkhya:

> Maker of all is He, all-knowing, source of selves,
> He knows, He the architect of Time,
> Possessed of [all] attributes, omniscient:
> Lord of primeval Nature, [Lord of all] knowers of the field,
> Lord of the constituents of Nature,
> Cause of the round of birth and death,
> [Cause of] deliverance,
> [Cause of our] sojourn here and of [our] imprisonment.

It is true that this passage is the earliest source in which the term 'knower of the field' occurs, but *a-kṣetra-jña*, 'one who does *not* know the field' occurs in ChU. 8. 3. 1, and from this passage it is possible to see how the term came to acquire the technical sense of 'individual self' or 'spiritual monad'. The *Chāndogya* Upanishad, as is its way, is very down to earth. This is what it says:

Just as [a group of people] who do not know the country (*a-kṣetra-jña*) might wander about and pass over a hidden hoard of gold time and again without finding it, so too do all these creatures go on day after day without finding the Brahman-world within them, for they are led astray by unreality (*anṛta*).

The *kṣetra-jña*, then, is the 'man who knows the local country', the 'man who knows his own field' as we would say in English meaning the 'man who knows his own subject'. And it is interesting to note that in secular language this is precisely what *kṣetra-jña* means (e.g. MBh. 1. 84. 12: 1. 85. 13: 1. 87. 8 *kṣetra-jñaṁ tasya dharmasya*, 'an expert in this matter': cf. ibid. 1. 87. 13: 1. 88. 1, etc.). One's 'field', then, one's 'subject' is oneself as a psychosomatic complex, but under the field there is a 'hidden hoard of gold', the Brahman-world, which lies latent in the heart of all of us, and so one can only be said to be a true 'knower of the field' if one has discovered this treasure. The treasure is, of course, the self; for as the Upanishad goes on to say:

> Truly, this self is in the heart. . . . Then this deep serenity which, rising up from the body, attains the highest light, reveals itself in its own [true] form: this is the self. . . . This is the immortal, [this] freedom from fear: this is Brahman. And the name of Brahman is this—what-is-real-and-what-is-true.

This self is not the universal Self of God, but the individual self-in-itself as it is when freed from all contact with matter. This is as certain as anything can be since the same passage is repeated and amplified in ChU. 8. 12. 3: 'So too does this deep serenity, rising up from the body, attain the highest light, revealing itself in its own [true] form. Such a one is a superman (*uttara puruṣa*); and there he roves around, laughing, playing, taking his pleasure with women, chariots, or friends and remembering no more that excrescence [which was] his body.'

Here the 'knower of the field' is, as it was to be later in the *Śvetāśvatara* Upanishad, the individual self, not the universal Spirit or God.

In the *Maitrī* Upanishad 2. 5 this is made very explicit indeed:

> Here [in the body] this subtle, impalpable, invisible one known as 'Person' begins to move, or rather a fraction of himself does so, though there was no awareness [of him] beforehand, just as when a sleeper awakes there is no awareness of the awakening beforehand.
>
> Assuredly, this part of him is pure consciousness, reflecting the Person himself; [it is] the 'knower of the field' whose subtle body is made up of conception, will, and self-consciousness, Prajāpati under the name of 'common to all men'. By consciousness is this body set up so that it really appears to be conscious [itself]: he it is who impels it [into action].

This, then, is the background against which the author of the Gītā was writing.

2. *kṣetra-jñaṁ c'āpi māṁ viddhi sarva-kṣetreṣu, Bhārata,*
kṣetra-kṣetrajñayor jñānaṁ yat, taj jñānaṁ mataṁ mama.

And know that I am the 'knower of the field' in every field; knowledge of [this] field and [this] knower of the field I deem to be [true] knowledge.

'I am the knower of the field': this is new. God is the 'knower of the field' in every field. According to R. this means that God knows all 'fields' and 'knowers of the field', all bodies and individual selves which together constitute his favourite concept of the 'body of the Lord'. In this I think he is right not because he interprets the passage in accordance with his own philosophy, but because we must assume that the author of the Gītā was familiar with the passage from the *Chāndogya* Upanishad which we have just quoted: the 'field' includes the 'hidden hoard of gold' just as the body includes the 'self within the heart'. Thus the Gītā does not contradict the Upanishads but merely asserts again that there is One who, as the *Śvetāśvatara* puts it, is 'Lord of primeval Nature, [Lord of all] knowers of the field'. 'Knowledge' or 'wisdom' means to be able to distinguish God as 'knower of every field' from both individual selves and from material Nature.

3. *tat kṣetraṁ yac ca yādṛk ca yad-vikāri yataś ca yat,*
sa ca yo yat-prabhāvaś ca, tat samāsena me śṛṇu.

What that field is and what it is like, what are its changes and which derives from which, and who He is, [the knower of the field,] and what his powers, hear [now] from Me in brief.

-prabhāvaś, 'powers': var. *-svabhāvaś*, 'nature'.

4. *ṛṣibhir bahudhā gītaṁ chandobhir vividhaiḥ pṛthak*
brahma-sūtra-padaiś c'aiva hetumadbhir viniścitaiḥ.

In many ways has it been sung by seers, in varied hymns each in its separate way, in aphoristic verses concerning Brahman, well reasoned and conclusive.

brahma-sūtra-padaiś, 'aphoristic verses concerning Brahman': some commentators take this to refer to the *Brahma-sūtras* of Bādarāyana, the basic classic of the Vedānta philosophy on which all the great ancient commentators have written commentaries. E. doubts whether they existed at the time of the Gītā. That, however, is anyone's guess. It is, for instance, generally thought that the *Sāṁkhya-kārikā* and the *Yoga-sūtras* did not exist in their present form at the time that the Gītā was first composed, but Sāṁkhya and Yoga ideas were certainly in the air as the Gītā itself proves. The same is probably true of the *Brahma-sūtras*: they may not have existed in their present form, but it seems more than likely that collections of aphorisms concerning the nature of Brahman, that is, the nature of the Absolute, were already in circulation.

5. *mahā-bhūtāny ahaṁkāro buddhir avyaktam eva ca*
indriyāṇi daś'aikaṁ ca pañca c'endriya-gocarāḥ,

Gross elements, the ego, intellect (*buddhi*), the Unmanifest, the eleven senses, and the five [sense-objects] on which the senses thrive,

'Gross elements': these are earth, water, fire, air, and space (ether): cf. 7. 4 where they are enumerated.

'The Unmanifest': that is, primal matter in the Sāṁkhya system. Cf. 8. 18 n.

'The eleven senses': the five senses as normally understood, the mind, and the five 'organs of action'—hands, feet, voice, anus, and genitals.

6. *icchā dveṣaḥ sukhaṁ duḥkhaṁ saṁghātaś cetanā dhṛtiḥ,*
etat kṣetraṁ samāsena savikāram udāhṛtam.

Desire, hate, pleasure, pain, *sensus communis*, thought and constancy,—these, in briefest span, are called the field together with their changes.

saṁghātaś, '*sensus communis*': the word normally means 'aggregate'. Ś. glosses, 'the bringing together of the bodily senses', that is, the *sensus communis* of the Schoolmen, and I follow him in this. Most modern commentators understand the word to mean the 'body' or some equivalent term. R. reads with some MSS. *saṁghātaś cetan'ādhṛtiḥ* which he takes to mean 'the aggregate of elements necessary to support consciousness'. H., E., 'association'.

dhṛtiḥ, 'constancy' or 'consistence'. The word usually means 'steadfastness'.

It is strange that after promising to give a brief account of the 'field' and the 'knower of the field' the author of the Gītā stops short after he has described the 'field'. He adds nothing to what he has said about the 'knower of the field' in verse 2, and the word does not appear again until verse 26. It is, then, quite possible that verses 7–25 are an interpolation introduced perhaps at the time when verse 0 which is missing in many MSS. first became current. This seems all the more probable in that the definition of 'knowledge' in 7–11 is totally different from that in verses 2 and 34. There it is to know the 'field' and the 'knower of the field', that is to say, to know how to distinguish between them, whereas the 'knowledge' or 'wisdom' of 7–11 is simply a list of virtues and clearly is not at all what is meant by 'wisdom' in the rest of the Gītā, that is, a direct intuition of eternal Being.

Knowledge

7. *amānitvam adambhitvam ahiṁsā kṣāntir ārjavam*
ācāry'opāsanaṁ śaucaṁ sthairyam ātma-vinigrahaḥ,

To shun conceit and tricky ways, to wish none harm, to be long-suffering and upright, to reverence one's teacher, purity, steadfastness, self-restraint,

-dambhitvam, 'tricky ways': or, 'ostentation' (Ś., R.).

sthairyam, 'steadfastness': var. *maunam*, 'silence'.

8. *indriy'ārtheṣu vairāgyam anahaṁkāra eva ca*
janma-mṛtyu-jarā-vyādhi-duḥkha-doṣ'ānudarśanam,

Detachment from the senses' objects and no sense of 'I' most certainly, insight into birth, death, old age, disease, and pain, and what constitutes their worthlessness,

9. *asaktir anabhiṣvaṅgaḥ putra-dāra-gṛhādiṣu*
nityaṁ ca sama-cittatvam iṣṭ'āniṣṭ'opapattiṣu,

To be detached and not to cling to sons, wives, houses, and the like, a constant equal-mindedness whatever happens, pleasing or unpleasing,

10. *mayi c'ānanya-yogena bhaktir avyabhicāriṇī,*
vivikta-deśa-sevitvam, aratir jana-saṁsadi,

Unswerving loyalty-and-love for Me with spiritual exercise on no other bent, to dwell apart in desert places, to take no pleasure in the company of men,

'With spiritual exercise on no other bent': see 12. 6 n.

11. *adhyātma-jñāna-nityatvaṁ, tattva-jñān'ārtha-darśanam,*
etaj jñānam iti proktam, ajñānaṁ yad ato 'nyathā.

Constant attention to the wisdom that appertains to self, to see where knowledge of reality must lead, [all] this is 'knowledge',—or so it has been said. Ignorance is what is otherwise than this.

adhyātma-jñāna-, 'the wisdom that appertains to self': see 8. 3 n. For *-jñāna-* there is a variant, *-dhyāna-*, 'meditation'.

-darśanam, 'to see': var. *cintanam*, 'to think'.

The Real Object of Knowledge

12. *jñeyaṁ yat tat pravakṣyāmi yaj jñātvā 'mṛtam aśnute:*
anādimat paraṁ brahma, na sat tan n'āsad ucyate.

[And now] I will tell you that which should be known: once a man knows it, he attains to immortality. The highest Brahman It is called,—beginningless,—It is not Being nor is It Not-Being.

jñeyaṁ, 'that which should be known': in 11. 38 this (*vedyaṁ*) is Krishna, the personal God.

[*a*]*mṛtam*, 'immortality', or 'the immortal': R. takes this to refer to the individual self. In the Gītā the phrase *amṛtatvāya kalpate* (2. 15), 'is conformed to immortality', is a synonym for *brahma-bhūyāya kalpate* (14. 26: 18. 53), 'is conformed to becoming Brahman'.

anādimat paraṁ, 'highest [Brahman] . . . beginningless': var. *anādi mat-paraṁ*, '[Brahman,] dependent on Me, beginningless'. In Śankara's time both readings were extant. The first reading presents no difficulty. If, however, you read the second, he says, it must mean, 'Brahman is beginningless, and I, Krishna, am its highest power (*śakti*)'—a very forced interpretation of the text. R. reads *anādi mat-paraṁ* as we might expect, but glosses *ahaṁ paro yasya*, 'beyond whom I am', which is grammatically quite as forced as Ś. *Mat-para*, however, would more naturally mean 'dependent on Me', 'intent on Me', or quite as plausibly 'beyond Me'!

It is not easy to say which reading should be followed, but, as so often in the Gītā, it seems to me that the ambiguity may well have been intentional. Brahman, as here described, is both the material cause of the universe and the eternal spirit immanent in the universe, rather than the 'fixed, still state of Brahman' of 2. 72. It is Krishna's material Nature (14. 3) which He, as male, 'subdues' or 'consorts with' (9. 8: 4. 6), remaining unattached the while. As 'highest Brahman' it is the 'Imperishable' (8. 3) and therefore the 'Unmanifest beyond the Unmanifest' (8. 20–1), the 'living Nature' of Krishna (7. 5) which Ś. himself identifies with the 'knower of the field' and Krishna's 'pure Nature . . . which exists in order to sustain living creatures'. It is the pantheistic world-soul indwelling all that derives from matter and Nature, it is then both spirit and matter. As the following chapter says, it is a 'womb' to Krishna in which He plants the seed (14. 3). So long as the universe exists, then, it is 'unmanifest' matter fertilized by spirit, but it is also the fixed, still state of Brahman—an idea that seems to come to the Gītā from Buddhism (see 2. 71, 72 nn.), and it is what man 'becomes' once he is freed from matter (5. 24: 6. 27: 14. 26: 18. 53–4). Thus the Upanishadic idea of Brahman as the 'All' has been confused with the Buddhistic concept of the *brahma-bhūta* man, which in Buddhism means a man who has achieved a 'sublime' form of existence.

The problem of the Gītā was how to fit these two contrasting aspects of Brahman into a single whole. On the one side we have the Upanishadic tradition which sees in Brahman the material cause of the universe, its 'Inner Controller' which is yet 'other' than mind-bearing matter both in the macrocosm and in the microcosm (BU. 3. 7. 3–23), while on the other we have the Buddhistic idea of the *brahma-bhūta*, the liberated man who has 'become Brahman'; and the two seem incompatible since the Buddhists use the word *brahma-* in a quite different sense.

Now in the Upanishads there are three common ways of expressing the Supreme Being—*brahman*, *ātman*, and *puruṣa*—Brahman, Self, and Person, and it is quite obviously the intention of the Gītā to show that Vishnu's incarnation, Krishna, not only *is* all three but is also *beyond* all three. Just as He is the 'Person' beyond the 'Unmanifest beyond the Unmanifest' (8. 22, if my interpretation is correct), so is He beyond the *puruṣa*, the aggregate of the spiritual monads of the Sāṁkhya system (13. 22), beyond the 'Imperishable Person' (15. 17): He is the 'Highest Self' (13. 22) as well as the 'Highest Lord' (13. 27). Similarly the Buddhist conception of Nirvāna which enters into Hinduism for the first time in the Gītā must in its turn be subjected to the new God in whom it is made to 'subsist' (6. 15).

Brahman, however, was a more difficult problem since the word had come to mean the Absolute, the unconditioned and wholly divine. But even Brahman had to be subordinated to this highly personal God who had come with a totally new message of devotion and love; and so we read in 14. 27 that Krishna is 'the base supporting Brahman—immortal [Brahman] which knows no change—[supporting] too the eternal law of righteousness and absolute beatitude'. And the Brahman referred to is both that Brahman which plays the female to Krishna's male (14. 3) and the state of absolute beatitude which the Buddhists called *brahma-* in the expression *brahma-bhūta*, 'Brahman-become' (14. 26).

All these considerations, however, do not convince me that Rāmānuja is right in reading *anādi mat-paraṁ brahma*, 'Brahman is the beginningless, dependent on Me', rather than *anādimat paraṁ brahma*, 'the supreme Brahman is beginningless'. I prefer to think that the author of the Gītā who is a master of subtle gradation leaves the division of the words entirely open to the theological bias of the reader, only to make his own position unequivocally clear at the end of the following chapter. Commentators have not been slow to fall into this well-laid trap.

'It is not Being nor is It Not-Being': unlike Krishna who is both and what is beyond them (11. 37). By 'Being' and 'Not-Being' we should presumably understand unconditioned, eternal Being on the one hand and being in time, that is becoming, on the other. In 9. 19 Krishna is 'deathlessness and death, what IS and what is not (Being and Not-Being)', the two pairs being regarded as identical (see note ad loc.), whereas in 11. 37 He is Being and Not-Being and what is beyond both, just as He is beyond the Imperishable and the perishable in 15. 16–17.

What, however, is meant by Brahman being neither Being nor Not-Being? According to Ś. you cannot define Brahmaṅ as either Being or Not-Being because it necessarily eludes all definitions. As BU. 3. 9. 26 etc., says you can only say 'No' to any definition:

> This Self—[what can one say of it but] 'No, no!' It is impalpable, for it cannot be grasped; indestructible, for it cannot be destroyed; free from attachment, for it is not attached [to anything], not bound. It does not quaver nor can it be hurt.

He further quotes *Kena* Up. 1. 3 ('Other it is, for sure, than what is known, beyond [the scope of] the unknown too') and ŚU. 6. 19 ('No parts has He, no part in action, tranquil, unblemished and unflecked'), but this in fact refers to the personal God, Rudra-Śiva, not to the impersonal Brahman; and neither of the quotations is strictly parallel. Much more to the point is ŚU. 4. 18 where the personal God, Rudra-Śiva, is exalted above both Being and Not-Being:

> When there is no darkness, no day nor night,
> No Being, no Not-Being—Śiva alone [is this].

Yet even this is not an exact parallel for quite clearly Brahman, as described in our present passage, is simply the cosmos seen as the aggregate of mind-bearing matter ensouled by eternal spirit. It does not transcend either matter or spirit as Śiva does in the *Śvetāśvatara* Upanishad and as Krishna does in the Gītā. It simply *is* both. Why then, one might justifiably ask, does the Gītā say here that it is neither? We might be tempted to answer that the two terms 'Being' and 'Not-Being' mean what they mean in 2. 16 where we read: 'Of what is not (Not-Being) there is no becoming; of what is (Being) there is no ceasing to be.' Here, as we pointed out ad loc., 'Being' must mean absolute Being, Not-Being absolute non-existence, a total impossibility or contradiction in terms like a child of a barren woman, to use a favourite Hindu example. This idea goes back to ChU. 6. 2. 2: 'How could Being be born from Not-Being? No, it was Being alone that was this [universe] in the beginning—one only, without a second.'

Now, Brahman in this passage is certainly not the 'One without a second': rather it corresponds to the 'body' of the supreme God, Vishnu, which Arjuna had been privileged to see (11. 9 ff.), the 'unmanifest form' of the same God (9. 4), his twin Nature (7. 4–6), and his 'womb'. It is the One as manifested in the many (13. 16) as is Krishna's transfigured body in 11. 13, 'what should be known' and thus identical with Krishna as the one true object of knowledge (11. 38), the proper subject-matter of all theology (*Brahma-sūtras* 1. 1. 1).

13. *sarvataḥ-pāṇi-pādaṁ tat, sarvato'kṣi-śiro-mukham*
sarvataḥ-śrutimal loke sarvam āvṛtya tiṣṭhati.

Hands and feet It has on every side, on every side eyes, heads, mouths, and ears; in the world all things encompassing [changeless] It abides.

This verse is lifted straight out of ŚU. 3. 16 which itself is a modification of RV. 10. 81. 3. Throughout this passage the Gītā draws heavily on the Upanishads and particularly the *Śvetāśvatara*.

'It abides': because as 'living Nature' it supports the whole world (7. 5). Both Ś. and R. develop their pet theories here at great length.

14. *sarv'endriya-guṇ'ābhāsaṁ sarv'endriya-vivarjitam*
asaktaṁ sarva-bhṛc c'aiva nirguṇaṁ guṇa-bhoktṛ ca.

Devoid of all the senses, It yet sheds light on all their qualities, [from all] detached, and yet supporting all; free from Nature's constituents, It yet experiences them.

The first line again is borrowed from ŚU. 3. 17.

'It yet sheds light on all their qualities': or, 'has the semblance of their qualities'. *Guṇa* probably means simply 'quality' here, not the three constituents of Nature.

asaktaṁ, 'detached': just as Krishna himself is detached (9. 8–9): 'Subduing my own material Nature ever again I emanate this whole host of beings—powerless [themselves], from Nature comes the power. These works [of mine] neither bind-nor-limit Me: as one indifferent I sit among these works, detached'.

By 'subduing his material Nature', that is, by casting his seed into the 'Great Brahman' (14. 3) Krishna emanates the phenomenal world which is his 'living Nature' (7. 5) in which spirit and matter are inextricably mixed up. However, just as Krishna, as highest 'Person', as highest 'Male', is in his essence detached, so is Brahman in so far as It is impregnated with Krishna's seed which is spirit.

'Supporting all': see 13. 16 n.

'Free from Nature's constituents': the terminology now becomes Sāṁkhya. Just as the *puruṣas*, the spiritual monads, of the Sāṁkhya system are 'free from the constituents' (Gaudapāda on *Sāṁkhya-kārikā*, 11), so is Brahman in so far as It is the depository of Krishna's seed. Similarly It 'experiences' the constituents just as the Sāṁkhya monads do: 'It is conscious of pleasure, pain, and delusion and knows them' (ibid.). Brahman is, in fact, the combination of the Sāṁkhya *puruṣa* and *prakṛti* which appear in the following section (19–25), the twofold Brahman of ŚU. 5. 1, which perhaps we may be forgiven for quoting again:

In the imperishable, infinite city of Brahman
    Two things there are—
Wisdom and unwisdom, hidden, established there:
Perishable is unwisdom, but wisdom is immortal:
Who over wisdom and unwisdom rules, He is Another.

15. *bahir antaś ca bhūtānām acaraṁ caram eva ca:*
sūkṣmatvāt tad avijñeyaṁ; dūrasthaṁ c'āntike ca tat.

Within all beings, yet without them; unmoved, It yet moves indeed; so subtle is It you cannot comprehend It; far off It stands, and yet how near It is!

This is based on *Īśā* Up. 5:

It moves, It moves not.
It is far, yet It is near.

Moving and unmoving, far and near, it is both the 'imperishable' and the 'perishable'. But just as the 'imperishable' and the 'perishable' are subject to 'Another' in the *Śvetāśvatara*, so are the 'unmoved' and the 'moving' dependent on Krishna's seed (10. 39): 'What is the seed of all contingent beings, that too am I. No being is there, *whether moving or unmoving*, that exists or could exist apart from Me.' Similarly in 11. 43 Arjuna salutes Krishna as the 'father of the world of moving and unmoving things': 'You are the father of the world of moving and unmoving things, You their venerable teacher, most highly prized; none is there like You—how could there be another greater?—in the three worlds. Oh, matchless is your power.'

Certainly in the later literature the compound word *car'ācaram* came to mean little more than moving and unmoving things, organic and inorganic matter if you like, but it seems likely that for the author of the Gītā the two components 'moving' and 'unmoving' meant what they meant in the Upanishads, the 'perishable' and the 'imperishable'.

16. *avibhaktaṁ ca bhūteṣu vibhaktam iva ca sthitam,*
bhūta-bhartṛ ca taj jñeyaṁ, grasiṣṇu prabhaviṣṇu ca.

Undivided in beings It abides, seeming divided: this is That which should be known,—[the one] who sustains, devours, and generates [all] beings.

'Undivided in beings' etc.: cf. 11. 13: 'Then did the son of Pāndu see the whole [wide] universe in One converged, there in the body of the God of gods, yet divided out in multiplicity.' Brahman, then, as Rāmānuja is never tired of pointing out, *is* the 'body of the Lord'. It is the whole universe, spiritual and material, static and dynamic, in space and beyond space, in time and out of time, *puruṣa* and *prakṛti*, but still it is not God, for God is the 'Mighty Lord' who 'surveys It and approves' (13. 22).

'[The one] who sustains': so too Krishna, 'Unmanifest in form', 'sustains [all] beings' (9. 4–5), both in his lower Nature and in his 'living Nature' (7. 4–5) which, like Brahman, are his womb (7. 6).

grasiṣṇu, 'devours': cf. 11. 30: 'On every side You lick, lick up—devouring—worlds, universes, everything—with burning mouths. Vishnu! your dreadful rays of light fill the whole universe with flames-of-glory, scorching [everywhere].' Again it is Krishna's transfigured *body* of which Arjuna is speaking.

prabhaviṣṇu, 'generates': Krishna is the origin of the universe through his two Natures (7. 6: cf. 9. 8: 10. 8).

17. *jyotiṣām api taj jyotis, tamasaḥ param ucyate,*
jñānaṁ jñeyaṁ jñāna-gamyaṁ hṛdi sarvasya dhiṣṭhitam.

Light of lights, 'Beyond the Darkness' It is called: [true] knowledge, what should be known, accessible to knowledge, established in the heart of all.

In this stanza no clear distinction is made between Brahman and the Lord; or rather perhaps one should say that Brahman here is no longer the 'body of the Lord' so much as the 'fixed, still state of Brahman' that manifests itself at the moment of liberation and which is the 'highest mode of being' of the Lord Himself (7. 24).

'Light of lights': this is borrowed from BU. 4. 4. [15–]16:

Should a man descry Him suddenly,
This Self, this God,
Lord of what was and what is yet to be,
How should he shrink from Him?

Before whose face the year
Revolves with [all] its days—
To Him the gods pay homage—
Life, *light of lights*, and immortality.

'Beyond the darkness': borrowed from MuU. 2. 2. 6:

In this [Self all] nerves are [harmoniously] compacted
As spokes in the hub of a chariot-wheel:
He [it is who] operates within,
Coming to birth in many a form and place.
So must you ponder on the Self, [uttering it] as Oṁ:
Good luck to you! May you pass *beyond the darkness*.

Cf. BhG. 8. 9 where the 'divine exalted Person' is described as 'sun-coloured beyond the darkness'. So too ŚU. 3. 8:

I know that mighty Person,
Sun-coloured *beyond the darkness*:
By knowing Him indeed a man surpasses death;
No other path is there on which to go.

And in more graphic detail MaiU. 6. 24:

The body is a bow, Oṁ the arrow, the mind its tip, *darkness the target*. Pierce the darkness, and you will come to that which is not shrouded in darkness. Pierce that [again], and you will see as it were a wheel of sparks, throbbing, of the colour of the sun, mighty in power and vigour—*Brahman beyond the darkness*, shining in the sun up there, [shining] in the moon and lightning. And seeing Him, you will draw nigh to immortality.

'Established in the heart': this again seems to be based on ŚU. 3. 13: 4. 20:

The Person of the measure of a thumb, the Inmost Self,
Forever dwells within the hearts of men,
By heart and thought and mind to be conceived of:
Whoso knows this becomes immortal.

His form cannot be glimpsed,
None can see Him with the eye:
Whoso should know Him with heart and mind
As dwelling in the heart, becomes immortal!

From these parallel passages it is clear that Brahman *here* is identical in all respects with Krishna, the personal God: this is the Brahman of the *Brahma-sūtras*, the recognized God of theology, the Brahman of 17. 23–8, pure Being. Krishna is, then, the 'Highest Brahman' (cf. 10. 12) just as He is the 'Highest Person' and 'Highest Self' (13. 22); but just as He is distinct from all other 'persons' and all other 'selves' so is He superior to all other Brahmans, the Brahman manifested in the phenomenal world (14. 3), the Brahman of sacrifice, and the eternal Brahman which the liberated man becomes (14. 26–7).

18. *iti kṣetraṁ tathā jñānaṁ jñeyaṁ c'oktaṁ samāsataḥ;*
mad-bhakta etad vijñāya mad-bhāvāy'opapadyate.

And so in brief I have explained the 'field' and 'knowledge' and 'that which should be known'; the man who loves-and-worships Me, on knowing this, becomes fit to [share in] my own mode of being.

The 'field', 'knowledge', and 'that which should be known' have all been explained, but there is still no mention of the 'knower of the field', further details about whom were promised in 13. 3. We can only assume that since the 'field' corresponds exactly to the Sāṁkhya *prakṛti* (material Nature) which will be discussed in the next section, the 'knower of the field' must correspond to the Sāṁkhya *puruṣa* or spiritual monad which is discussed along with it.

'My mode of being': this phrase has already occurred in 4. 10 and 8. 5 and will occur again in 14. 19. Both Ś. and R. take it to mean liberation, that is, changeless immortality (7. 24: 18. 20). It is, however, an immortality that includes love as the word *mad-bhakta* shows. This is what distinguishes Krishna's 'mode of being' from the 'fixed, still state of Brahman'. Cf. 4. 10–11:

Many are they who, passion, fear, and anger spent, inhere in Me, making Me their sanctuary; made pure by wisdom and hard penances, they come to [share in] my own mode of being. In whatsoever way [devoted] men approach Me, in that same way do I return their love.

So too in 12. 14–20 Krishna emphasizes his love for the self-controlled, and right at the end of the book (18. 64) He confesses to Arjuna that He 'loves him well' or, more literally, 'desires' him.

Matter and Spirit

19. *prakṛtiṁ puruṣaṁ c'aiva viddhy anādī ubhāv api:*
vikārāṁś ca guṇāṁś c'aiva viddhi prakṛti-saṁbhavān.

'Nature' and 'Person': know that these two are both beginningless: and know that change and quality arise from Nature.

'"Nature" and "Person"': according to Ś. these are the same as the two 'Natures' of Krishna described in 7. 4–5: they are also the same as the 'field' and the 'knower of the field'. His second statement is true, his first probably not.

'Quality': Ś., R., the qualities listed in 13. 6 ff. Since this whole section is purely Sāṁkhya, the word is more likely to mean the three constituents of Nature.

20. *kārya-kāraṇa-kartṛtve hetuḥ prakṛtir ucyate,*
puruṣaḥ sukha-duḥkhānāṁ bhoktṛtve hetur ucyate.

Material Nature, they say, is [itself] the cause of cause, effect, and agency, while 'person' is said to be the cause in the experience of pleasure and of pain.

-kāraṇa-, 'cause': var. *-karaṇa-*, 'instrument'. Ś. and R. take *kārya* to mean the body, *kāraṇa* or *karaṇa* to mean the senses, mind, etc. This is quite unnecessary. All the text says is that material Nature is the seat of causality whereas the spiritual monad alone experiences. This is orthodox Sāṁkhya teaching.

21. *puruṣaḥ prakṛti-stho hi bhuṅkte prakṛti-jān guṇān;*
kāraṇaṁ guṇa-saṅgo 'sya sad-asad-yoni-janmasu.

For 'person' is lodged in material Nature, experiencing the 'constituents' that arise from it; because he attaches himself to these he comes to birth in good and evil wombs.

prakṛti-stho: var. *sukha-duḥkho* '[experiencing] pleasure and pain'. In the Sāṁkhya system the *puruṣa*s or spiritual monads are infinite in number. This seems to be the view of the Gītā too, though the whole category of spirit (what R. calls 'self-stuff') is sometimes referred to as one (cf. 2. 17 where a neuter 'indestructible' turns up alongside a plurality of 'embodied [selves]').

22. *upadraṣṭā 'numantā ca bhartā bhoktā mah'eśvaraḥ*
param'ātm'eti c'āpy ukto dehe 'smin puruṣaḥ paraḥ.

[And yet another One there is who,] surveying and approving, supports and [Himself] experiences [the constituents of Nature], the Mighty Lord: 'Highest Self' some call Him, the 'Highest Person' in this body.

'Surveying and approving': we have had the same idea in 9. 10: '[A world of] moving and unmoving things material Nature brings to birth while I look-on-and-supervise (*adhyakṣeṇa*).' This is what distinguishes the personal God from the impersonal Brahman of 13. 12–17. Brahman comprises both the *puruṣa* and *prakṛti* of the Sāṁkhya system but does not appear to affect them. The personal God 'surveys and approves' the world-process for which, through his own Nature, He is directly responsible but from which He remains permanently detached since 'works do not bind Him' (9. 9 etc.).

bhartā, 'supports': var. *kartā*, 'maker'. As Nature he 'supports', as 'Person' he experiences, as does Brahman (13. 14). Only as the One who 'surveys and approves' is He to be distinguished from Brahman.

23. *ya evaṁ vetti puruṣaṁ prakṛtiṁ ca guṇaiḥ saha*
sarvathā vartamāno 'pi na sa bhūyo 'bhijāyate.

Whoever knows 'person', material Nature, and its constituents to be such, in whatever state he be, he is not born again.

24. *dhyānen' ātmani paśyanti kecid ātmānam ātmanā,*
anye sāṁkhyena yogena, karma-yogena c' āpare.

By meditation some themselves see self in self, others by putting sound reason into practice, yet others by the exercise of works.

dhyānen[*a*], 'by meditation': var. *jñānen*[*a*], 'by wisdom'.

'Some themselves see self in self': so 6. 20 where the vision of the self is said to constitute 'the utmost joy which transcends [all things of] sense and which soul [alone] can grasp'. The 'self' seen in the 'self' is probably not the 'Highest Self' of 13. 22 but the individual self which is only a 'minute part' of God (15. 7) and which Yogins '*see* established in [them]selves' (15. 11).

ātmani, 'in self': Ś., 'in the soul (*buddhi*)': R., 'in the body'.

'Exercise of works': without attachment to their fruits as taught throughout Chapters II–IV.

This and the following stanza appear to bear no relation whatever either to what precedes or to what follows.

25. *anye tv evam ajānantaḥ śrutvā 'nyebhya upāsate,*
te 'pi c' ātitaranty eva mṛtyuṁ śruti-parāyaṇāḥ.

But some, not knowing thus, hear it from others and revere it; and even these, taking their stand on what they hear, overcome death indeed.

śruti-, 'what they hear': the word is also commonly used to mean the Vedas, but, following so closely on *śrutvā*, it would seem unlikely that it is used in this sense here. In any case Krishna goes out of his way to disparage the Vedas (2. 42–4, 52–3) because, being concerned with Nature and its constituents (2. 45), they cannot help anyone to overcome death.

26. *yāvat saṁjāyate kiṁcit sattvaṁ sthāvara-jaṅgamam*
kṣetra-kṣetrajña-saṁyogāt tad viddhi, Bharata'rṣabha.

Whatever being comes to be, be it motionless or moving, [derives its being] from the union of 'field' and 'knower of the field': this know.

Here at last we return to the 'knower of the field': but here it appears to be identical with the 'spiritual monad' of the Sāṁkhya system, and not with God as it is in verse 2.

saṁyogāt, 'union': in ŚU. this is practically a technical term meaning the 'union' ('conjoining') of spirit and matter. So ŚU. 1. 8:

What is here conjoined together—
Perishable and imperishable,
Manifest and unmanifest—
All this doth the Lord sustain.

So too ŚU. 6. 5: 'He is the Beginning, the efficient cause of the conjoining.'

God Immanent in His Creatures

27. *samaṁ sarveṣu bhūteṣu tiṣṭhantaṁ param'eśvaram*
vinaśyatsv avinaśyantaṁ yaḥ paśyati, sa paśyati.

The same in all contingent beings, abiding [without change], the Highest Lord, when all things fall to ruin, [Himself] is not destroyed: who sees Him sees [indeed].

'The same': that is, Brahman as the 'Imperishable' (8. 3) 'Unmanifest' (8. 21). Cf. 5. 19: 'While yet in this world they have overcome [the process of] emanation [and decay], for their minds are stilled in that-which-is-ever-the-same: for devoid of imperfection and ever-the-same is Brahman: therefore in Brahman [stilled] they stand.'

'[Himself] is not destroyed': like the 'Imperishable Unmanifest beyond the Unmanifest' in 8. 20: cf. 2. 17.

'Who sees Him sees [indeed]': see 5. 5 n. where it is suggested that the *Sāṁkhya*, the pure contemplative, sees only the same eternal substratum underlying all beings, while the *Yogin*, the more active 'athlete of the spirit' sees God as a Person, identical with Brahman yet transcending It.

28. *samaṁ paśyan hi sarvatra samavasthitam īśvaram*
na hinasty ātmanā'tmānaṁ, tato yāti parāṁ gatim.

For seeing Him, the same, the Lord, established everywhere, he cannot of himself to [him]self do hurt, hence he treads the highest way.

'[Him]self': the Highest Self in which all selves participate is timeless and cannot be destroyed, therefore this must apply to all selves. Hence once you realize this you yourself become invulnerable. E., in one of his rare comments, says: 'Since the same Lord (= soul, cf. v. 15) is in all beings, the self of others is one's own self, and if he injures others, he injures himself. That this is the meaning seems obvious to me; but for some reason, it has escaped all commentators and modern interpreters examined by me except Deussen.' I fail to understand the logic of this. What E. presumably means is that since he can *not* injure others, he can *not* injure himself. According to Ś. the mere performance of action whether good or bad (*dharma* or *adharma*) causes the destruction of one psychosomatic complex after another. The real 'self' is also 'killed' in the sense that it has no existence for the man who remains in ignorance of it.

29. *prakṛty'aiva ca karmāṇi kriyamāṇāni sarvaśaḥ;*
yaḥ paśyati tathā'tmānam akartāraṁ, sa paśyati.

Nature it is which in every way does-work-and-acts; no agent is the self: who sees it thus he sees [indeed].

Nature acts through the three constituents. Cf. 3. 5: 'Every man is powerless and made to work by the constituents born of Nature.' Cf. 3. 27–8. So 14. 19: 'There is no agent other than [these] constituents.'

ātmānam akartāraṁ, 'no agent is the self': here presumably the individual self is meant which is usually deluded enough to *think* it acts when it is really the constituents of Nature acting and reacting on each other (3. 27–8).

30. *yadā bhūta-pṛthag-bhāvam eka-stham anupaśyati,*
tata eva ca vistāraṁ, brahma saṁpadyate tadā.

When once a man can see [all] the diversity of contingent beings as abiding in One [alone] and their radiation out of It, then to Brahman he attains.

Cf. 11. 13: 'Then did the son of Pāndu see the whole [wide] universe in One converged, there in the body of the God of gods, yet divided out in multiplicity.' The same is said of Brahman in 13. 16. Also 6. 29–30: 'With self integrated by spiritual exercise [now] he sees the self in all beings standing, all beings in the self: the same in everything he sees. Who sees Me everywhere, who sees the All in Me, for him I am not lost, nor is he lost to Me.' God indwells the self as the eternal 'fixed, still state of Brahman' just as He 'ensouls' the universal Brahman which comprises both material Nature and the countless individual spiritual monads or selves and which is God's body. See 13. 12 n.

'To Brahman he attains': Ś., 'becomes Brahman indeed', presumably in the Buddhistic sense of this word.

31. *anāditvān nirguṇatvāt param'ātmā 'yam avyayaḥ*
śarīra-stho 'pi, Kaunteya, na karoti, na lipyate.

Because this Highest Self knows no beginning, no constituents, it does not pass away: though abiding in [many] a body, it does not act nor is it defiled.

anāditvān, 'knows no beginning': var. *anantatvān*, 'knows no end'.

nirguṇatvāt, 'knows . . . no constituents (or qualities)': var. *nirmalatvāt*, 'immaculate'. The copyist presumably had 14. 6 in mind where this word occurs in the same grammatical form.

At first sight the statement that the Highest Self, which here must surely mean God, does not act seems surprising since in 3. 22 Krishna said that that work or action was the very element in which He moves and that if He were to cease to act the whole universe would collapse. Things, however, are not as simple as this since all opposites must meet and dissolve into each other. So Krishna tells us (4. 13–14) that although He generated the four-class system with categories of 'constituents' and works and is thereby the agent *par excellence*, He is at the same time no-agent, for no action can affect or defile Him since He is totally disinterested in whatever He does; hence He is never bound. 'Profound [indeed] are the ways of work!' (4. 17.)

The individual self, as we know, does not act except in so far as it is associated with the constituents of Nature. Similarly God as 'knower of the field' in all fields, as Absolute Being, does not act; but in conjunction with material Nature He does. As 'Lord' He consorts with Nature (4. 6) and by 'subduing' her emanates the whole universe (9. 8). He is the eternal Male (*Puruṣa*, for that is the literal meaning of the word), Nature the female (14. 3). So in MBh. 12. 293. 12 we are told that the 'Imperishable' and the 'perishable' are linked together like man and woman.

'Though abiding in [many] a body': Krishna, like Brahman (13. 17), abides in the heart of all creatures (15. 15: 18. 61). Alternatively it may simply mean that He abides in his own body which is the total universe of spirit and matter (11. 13).

32. *yathā sarva-gataṁ saukṣmyād ākāśaṁ n'opalipyate,*
sarvatr'āvasthito dehe tathā'tmā n'opalipyate.

Just as the ether, roving everywhere, knows no defilement, so subtle [is its essence], so does [this] Self, though everywhere abiding embodied, know no defilement.

dehe, 'embodied': lit. 'in a body': var. *dehī*, 'embodied', a standard synonym for the individual self (2. 13 ff.). Here presumably the Gītā is still speaking of the Highest Self.

33. *yathā prakāśayaty ekaḥ kṛtsnaṁ lokam imaṁ raviḥ,*
kṣetraṁ kṣetrī tathā kṛtsnaṁ prakāśayati, Bhārata.

As the one sun lights up this whole universe, so does the 'owner of the field' illumine the whole 'field'.

kṣetrī, 'owner of the field': God not only *knows* the whole universe composed of his two Natures, they are also his very own (4. 6: 7. 5–6). R. quite unnecessarily refers this to the individual self.

34. *kṣetra-kṣetrajñayor evam antaraṁ jñāna-cakṣuṣā*
bhūta-prakṛti-mokṣaṁ ca ye vidur, yānti te param.

Whoso with wisdom's eye discerns the difference between 'field' and 'knower of the field', and knows deliverance from material Nature to which [all] contingent beings are subject, goes to the further [shore].

CHAPTER XIV

THIS chapter has little connexion with the last. It starts off with an account of creation in purely sexual terms. Krishna, the eternal Male (*Puruṣa*), casts his seed into 'Great Brahman' which here means material Nature. From this primal sexual act the whole universe comes into being (1–4).

Without any link or connexion we now pass on to a detailed study of the three constituents of Nature—Goodness, Passion, and Darkness—which from now until the final summing up at the end of Chapter XVIII largely dominate the scene. Liberation, which is immortality, means final release from the three constituents. Krishna then describes the characteristics of the man who is so released (22–6), and these are very similar to those of the 'man He loves' described in 12. 13–20 and the 'man of steady wisdom' of 2. 54–72, except that the latter, who represents the Buddhist ideal, knows nothing of *bhakti*, the love of God. Finally, Krishna makes his absolute and unqualified claim to be the base supporting Brahman as well as the eternal law of righteousness (*dharma*) and absolute beatitude. The chapter is aptly called the 'Yoga of the Distinction of the Three Constituents'.

Śrī-bhagavān uvāca:

1. *paraṁ bhūyaḥ pravakṣyāmi jñānānāṁ jñānam uttamam*
yaj jñātvā munayaḥ sarve parāṁ siddhim ito gatāḥ.

The Blessed Lord said:

[And now] again I shall proclaim the highest wisdom, best of doctrines; on knowing this all sages, when they passed on hence, attained the highest prize.

2. *idaṁ jñānam upāśritya mama sādharmyam āgatāḥ*
sarge 'pi n'opajāyante pralaye na vyathanti ca.

With this wisdom as their bulwark they reached a rank [in the order of existence] equivalent to my own, and even when [the universe is once again] engendered, they are not born [again], and when [again] it is dissolved, they know no trepidation.

'Great Brahman is My Womb'

3. *mama yonir mahad brahma, tasmin garbhaṁ dadhāmy aham:*
saṁbhavaḥ sarva-bhūtānāṁ tato bhavati, Bhārata.

Great Brahman is to Me a womb, in it I plant the seed: from this derives the origin of all contingent beings.

This stanza amplifies what had already been said in 4. 6 and 9. 8, namely, that Krishna, by consorting with or subduing his own material Nature, produces all contingent beings. In Vishnu–Krishna, then, the male and female principles, spirit and matter, the *puruṣa* and *prakṛti* of the Sāṁkhya system are unified as they are in Vishnu's rival, Śiva. The apparent dualism of much of the last chapter is thereby put into its proper perspective. Krishna is both He who plants the seed and the seed itself (7. 10: 9. 18: 10. 39). Even in the Upanishads Brahman appears as the universal womb (MuU. 3. 1. 3):

> When a seer beholds the Maker, Lord,
> The Person golden-hued, whose womb is Brahman,
> Then does he understand.

The compound *brahma-yoni* could also mean 'source of Brahman (or Brahmā)' and this is how most modern translators have taken it, but our present passage makes this interpretation most unlikely.

dadhāmy, 'I plant' (lit. 'place'): var. *dadāmy*, 'I give'.

4. *sarva-yoniṣu, Kaunteya, mūrtayaḥ saṁbhavanti yāḥ,*
tāsāṁ brahma mahad yonir, ahaṁ bīja-pradaḥ pitā.

In whatever womb whatever form arises-and-grows-together, of [all] those [forms] Great Brahman is the womb, I the father, giver of the seed.

The Three Constituents of Nature

5. *sattvaṁ, rajas, tama iti guṇāḥ prakṛti-saṁbhavāḥ*
nibadhnanti, mahā-bāho, dehe dehinam avyayam.

Goodness—Passion—Darkness: these are the [three] constituents from Nature sprung that bind the embodied [self] in the body though [the self itself] is changeless.

There is no exact translation for *sattva, rajas,* and *tamas* in English. Perhaps Hill's 'purity' is better than 'Goodness' since it is this constituent that helps the embodied self to final release from matter itself, and this means the severing of all worldly ties. *Rajas* is the active principle which promotes action (*karma*) and which is characterized by purpose. *Tamas,* which literally means 'darkness', is almost identical with what we would call 'sloth'. Since the Gītā devotes most of this chapter and of Chapters XVII and XVIII to an analysis of the three constituents, there seems little point in anticipating what it has to say.

6. *tatra sattvaṁ nirmalatvāt prakāśakam anāmayam*
sukha-saṅgena badhnāti jñāna-saṅgena c'ānagha.

Among these Goodness, being immaculate, knowing no sickness, dispenses light, [and yet] it binds by [causing the self] to cling to wisdom and to joy.

nirmalatvāt, 'being immaculate': var. *nirmamatvāt,* 'being devoid of a sense of "mine"'.

jñāna-, 'wisdom': according to Ś. the wisdom referred to is the pursuit of happiness, not the intuitive wisdom of the self. H. and Rk. follow him in this, but it is doubtful whether the author of the Gītā made any such distinction, for it is legitimate to attach oneself to God (7. 1) or to the Unmanifest Brahman (12. 5) which is synonymous with the 'highest wisdom'. In MBh. 12. 240. 19–22 'Goodness' and the 'knower of the field' can only be distinguished in thought: in practice they are always interfused (see pp. 268–9). Attachment to wisdom and joy, however, is wrong if, once having experienced their 'radiance', one sorrows when the ecstatic state passes (14. 22).

7. *rajo rāg'ātmakaṁ viddhi tṛṣṇa-saṅga-samudbhavam;*
tan nibadhnāti, Kaunteya, karma-saṅgena dehinam.

Passion is instinct with desire, [this] know. From craving and attachment it wells up. It binds the embodied [self] by [causing it] to cling to works.

rāg[*a*], 'desire': for R. this means 'sexual desire'.

tṛṣṇā-, 'craving' (lit. 'thirst'): according to Buddhism the root sin of mankind. For Ś. it means craving for what you have not got while 'attachment' means hanging on to what you already have.

8. *tamas tv ajñāna-jaṁ viddhi mohanaṁ sarva-dehinām,*
prmād'ālasya-nidrābhis tan nibadhnāti, Bhārata.

But from ignorance is Darkness born: mark [this] well. All embodied [selves] it leads astray. With fecklessness and sloth and sleepiness it binds.

pramād[*a*]-, 'fecklessness': R., 'avoiding one's duty'.

9. *sattvaṁ sukhe sañjayati, rajaḥ karmaṇi, Bhārata,*
jñānam āvṛtya tu tamaḥ pramāde sañjayaty uta.

Goodness causes [a man] to cling to joy, Passion to works; but Darkness, stifling wisdom, attaches to fecklessness.

10. *rajas tamaś c'ābhibhūya sattvaṁ, Bhārata, vardhate;*
rajaḥ sattvaṁ tamaś c'aiva, tamaḥ sattvaṁ rajas tathā.

Once it dominates Passion and Darkness, Goodness waxes strong; so Passion and Darkness when they dominate the other two.

Bhārata, vardhate, '(O Bhārata,) waxes strong': var. *bhavati, Bhārata* (the better attested reading), 'comes to be, (O Bhārata)'. Both Ś. and R. read the latter and gloss as if it were the former.

11. *sarva-dvāreṣu dehe 'smin prakāśa upajāyate*
jñānaṁ yadā, tadā vidyād vivṛddhaṁ sattvam ity uta.

When at all the body's gates wisdom's light arises, then must you know that Goodness has increased.

'The body's gates': 'the senses' (Ś., R.).

12. *lobhaḥ pravṛttir ārambhaḥ karmaṇām aśamaḥ spṛhā,*
rajasy etāni jāyante vivṛddhe, Bharata'rṣabha.

When Passion is waxing strong, these [states] arise: greed, [purposeful] activity, committing oneself to works, disquiet, and ambition.

aśamaḥ spṛhā, 'disquiet and ambition': var. *manasaḥ spṛhā,* 'ambition of the mind'; *aśamaś ca tṛṭ,* 'disquiet and craving'.

13. *aprakāśo 'pravṛttiś ca pramādo moha eva ca,*
tamasy etāni jāyante vivṛddhe, Kuru-nandana.

When Darkness is surging up, these [states] arise: unlighted [darkness], unwillingness to act, fecklessness, delusion.

14. *yadā sattve pravṛddhe tu pralayaṁ yāti deha-bhṛt,*
tad'ottama-vidāṁ lokān amalān pratipadyate.

But when an embodied [self] comes face to face with [the body's] dissolution and Goodness prevails, then will he reach the spotless worlds of those who know the highest.

amalān, 'spotless': one MS. has *acalān,* 'unmoving'.

15. *rajasi pralayaṁ gatvā karma-saṅgiṣu jāyate,*
tathā pralīnas tamasi mūḍha-yoniṣu jāyate.

[Another] goes to his demise when Passion [predominates]; he will be born among such men as cling to works: and as to him who dies when Darkness [has the upper hand], he will be born in the wombs of deluded fools.

mūḍha-, 'deluded fools': Ś., 'such as domestic animals': R., 'such as dogs and pigs'.

16. *karmaṇaḥ sukṛtasy'āhuḥ sāttvikaṁ nirmalaṁ phalam;*
rajasas tu phalaṁ duḥkham, ajñānaṁ tamasaḥ phalam.

Of works well done, they say, the fruits belong to Goodness, being without spot: but pain is the fruit of Passion, ignorance the fruit of Darkness.

duḥkham, 'pain, suffering': the fruit of Passion appears pleasurable enough at first; it is only later that its true nature shows itself. So 18. 38: '[That pleasure] which at first seems like ambrosia, arising when the senses meet the objects of sense, but in time transmutes itself into what seems to be poison—that pleasure, so it is said, is in Passion's way.'

17. *sattvāt saṁjāyate jñānaṁ, rajaso lobha eva ca,*
pramāda-mohau tamaso bhavato 'jñānam eva ca.

From Goodness wisdom springs, from Passion greed, from Darkness fecklessness, delusion, and ignorance—how not?

lobha, 'greed': R. refers this particularly to a hankering for heaven.

18. *ūrdhvaṁ gacchanti sattva-sthā, madhye tiṣṭhanti rājasāḥ,*
jaghanya-guṇa-vṛtti-sthā adho gacchanti tāmasāḥ.

Upward is the path of those who abide in Goodness, in the middle stand the men of Passion. Stuck in the modes of the vilest constituent the men of Darkness go below.

'Upward . . . in the middle . . . below': for Ś. 'upward' means rebirth as a god, 'in the middle' as a human, and 'below' rebirth as an animal. For R. 'upward' means gradual release from the world of *saṁsāra*, while 'below' means rebirth as a worm or an insect or even as a tree, bush, stone, or grass.

19. *n'ānyaṁ guṇebhyaḥ kartāraṁ yadā draṣṭā 'nupaśyati*
guṇebhyaś ca paraṁ vetti, mad-bhāvaṁ so 'dhigacchati.

When the watching [self] sees there is no agent other than [these] constituents and knows what is beyond them, then will he come to [share in] that mode of being which is mine.

The constituents of Nature as sole agent: cf. 3. 27–8: 14. 23.

mad-bhāvaṁ, 'that mode of being which is mine': God's 'higher' state or mode of being (7. 24: 9. 11) which is 'changeless' (7. 24), 'one mode of being, changeless, undivided in all contingent beings, divided [as they are]' (18. 20). See 13. 18 n.

20. *guṇān etān atītya trīn dehī deha-samudbhavān*
janma-mṛtyu-jarā-duḥkhair vimukto 'mṛtam aśnute.

Transcending these three constituents which give the body its existence, from the sufferings of birth, death, and old age delivered, the embodied [self] wins immortality.

-samudbhavān, 'which give the body its existence': so Ś., 'which are the seed that gives rise to the body'. The compound more naturally reads, 'which arise from the body', but it is the constituents that give existence to the body not vice versa.

'The sufferings of birth, death, and old age': most commentators starting with Ś. translate 'birth, death, old age, and suffering', but surely this is a reflection of the current Buddhist view that birth, old age, and death are the outward and visible signs that show that all phenomenal existence is 'suffering, pain, or ill' (*dukkha*): 'What is the noble truth about suffering?' the Buddha asks. 'Birth is suffering, old age is suffering, death is suffering . . .' (S. v. 421, and throughout the Pāli canon).

Arjuna uvāca:

21. *kair liṅgais trīn guṇān etān atīto bhavati, prabho,*
kim-ācāraḥ kathaṁ c'aitāṁs trīn guṇān ativartate ?

Arjuna said:

What signs, Lord, mark him out,—[this man] who has transcended these three constituents? How does he behave? And how does he step out beyond these three constituents?

The Man who has transcended the Constituents

Śrī-bhagavān uvāca:

22. *prakāśaṁ ca pravṛttiṁ ca moham eva ca, Pāṇḍava,*
na dveṣṭi saṁpravṛttāni, na nivṛttāni kāṅkṣati.

The Blessed Lord said:

Radiance—activity—yes, delusion too,—when these arise he hates them not; and when [in turn] they cease he pines not after them.

23. *udāsīnavad āsīno guṇair yo na vicālyate*
guṇā vartanta ity eva yo 'vatiṣṭhati n'eṅgate.

As one indifferent he sits, by the constituents unruffled: 'So the constituents are busy': thus he thinks. Firm-based is he, unquavering.

'As one indifferent he sits': cf. 9. 9 where the phrase is used of Krishna who 'sits as one indifferent' though He is active all the while. 'Indifference' is a permanent characteristic of the Sāṁkhya spiritual monad: 'Though agency belongs to the constituents, the [spiritual monad who is] indifferent appears to become an agent' (*Sāṁkhya-kārikā*, 20). So long as he is in the grasp of the three constituents, to all intents and purposes he *is* the agent, but from the absolute point of view he is only an onlooker.

'So the constituents are busy': cf. 3. 28: '"Constituents on constituents act", [thus thinking] he remains unattached.'

yo 'vatiṣṭhati, 'firm-based is he': var. *yo jñas tiṣṭhati*, 'who [thus] knowing abides'; *yo 'nutiṣṭhati*, 'who acts [so thinking]'.

24. *sama-duḥkha-sukhaḥ svasthaḥ sama-loṣṭ'āśma-kāñcanaḥ*
tulya-priy'āpriyo dhīras tulya-nind'ātma-saṁstutiḥ.

The same in pleasure as in pain and self-assured, the same when faced with clods of earth or stones or gold; for him, wise man, are friend and foe of equal weight, equal the praise or blame [with which men cover him].

This and the following verse say in much the same words what has already been said of the 'man of steady wisdom' in 2. 56–7, the 'self-subdued' of 6. 7–9, and the 'man God loves' of 12. 13–19. As in 12. 13–19 the love of God and devotion to Him are added to the standard ascetic virtues.

25. *mān'āpamānayos tulyas, tulyo mitr'āri-pakṣayoḥ*
sarv'ārambha-parityāgī guṇ'ātītaḥ sa ucyate.

Equal [his mind] in honour and disgrace, equal to ally and to enemy, he renounces every [busy] enterprise: 'He has transcended the constituents': so must men say.

26. *māṁ ca yo 'vyabhicāreṇa bhakti-yogena sevate,*
sa guṇān samitīty'aitān brahma-bhūyāya kalpate.

And as to those who do Me honour with spiritual exercise, in loyalty-and-love undeviating, passed [clean] beyond these constituents, to becoming Brahman they are conformed.

The first line is almost identical with 13. 10. As we approach the end of the poem Krishna's insistence on the indispensability of *bhakti*, the love and adoration of Him as personal God, both before and after liberation, becomes the more urgent and imperious. Formerly He had spoken of the activation of love *after* liberation had been won (see 9. 34 n.): now He urges that it is necessary too before one is fit to 'become Brahman'.

27. *brahmaṇo hi pratiṣṭhā 'ham amṛtasy' āvyayasya ca,*
śāśvatasya ca dharmasya sukhasy' aikāntikasya ca.

For I am the base supporting Brahman,—immortal [Brahman] which knows no change,—[supporting] too the eternal law of righteousness and absolute beatitude.

'For I am the base supporting Brahman': no other translation is possible as H. ('ground)', E., Barnett ('foundation'), D. ('Fundament'), and S. ('support') recognize. Rk., who oscillates alarmingly between theism, pantheism, and qualified monism because of his essentially indifferentist attitude to religion, compromises on 'abode' which *pratiṣṭhā* does not happen to mean.

This unqualified claim of the personal God, Krishna, to be the 'base supporting Brahman' confirms everything He has been saying in more guarded terms before. In this chapter Brahman starts off by being no more than the 'womb' of creation, the material Nature of the Sāṁkhya system. It ends, however, in the form in which we have repeatedly met It since 2. 72 where It is the 'fixed still state of Brahman' and 'Nirvāna that is Brahman too', a Hindu adaptation of the Buddhist terms *nirvāṇa* and *brahma-bhūta*. In 13. 13–17 Brahman was the fullest combination of the two and as being 'without' and 'standing afar off' It is in that passage indistinguishable from God. Krishna's present statement, then, coming where it does, can only mean that He, as personal God, transcends even the absolutely transcendent. He is 'what IS and what is not and what surpasses both' (11. 37) as Arjuna, more percipient than most of the commentators on this magnificently subtle poem, intuitively saw. In addition He is the fount of righteousness (*dharma*) and of absolute beatitude.

CHAPTER XV

THIS chapter starts with a description of the Cosmic Fig-tree which is a figure of *saṁsāra*, the endless round of birth and death, of rebirth and redeath. Cut it down, Krishna says, and then fly for refuge to the Primeval Person that you may reach that state of being from which there is no return and which is his own 'highest home' (1–6).

The process of transmigration is then described. Minute particles of God equip themselves with senses and mind, using them while yet they are active in the world. Only those 'possessed of wisdom's eye' can see them as they really are (7–11). This is a special form of the divine immanence. More generally God indwells and gives their being to the heavens and the earth, to plants and animals. More especially again He dwells in the heart of man (12–15).

Here, once again, there is abrupt change of subject. There are two forms of 'person' we are told, the Perishable and the Imperishable, but beyond them there is the 'Person [All-]Sublime', the 'All-Highest Self', who should be known and loved. The chapter is traditionally called the 'Yoga of the Person [All-]Sublime'.

The Eternal Fig-tree

Śrī-bhagavān uvāca:

1. *ūrdhva-mūlam adhaḥ-śākham aśvatthaṁ prāhur avyayam*
chandāṁsi yasya parṇāni: yas taṁ veda, sa veda-vit.

The Blessed Lord said:

With roots above and boughs beneath, they say, the undying fig-tree [stands]: its leaves are the Vedic hymns: who knows it knows the Veda.

The first reference to the Cosmic Tree appears in RV. 1. 24. 7:

> In the bottomless [abyss] king Varuna
> By the power of his pure will upholds aloft
> The [cosmic] tree's high crown. There stand below
> [The branches], and above the roots. Within us
> May the banners of his light be firmly set!

Here, however, the first line is directly borrowed from KaU. 6. 1. As the development of the idea is very different in the Upanishads from what it is in the Gītā, we will leave further comment until the Gītā has come to its own drastic conclusion in verse 4. The tree is, of course, *saṁsāra*, the whole universe of transience.

2. *adhaś c'ordhvaṁ prasṛtās tasya śākhā*
guṇa-pravṛddhā viṣaya-pravālāḥ,
adhaś ca mūlāny anusaṁtatāni
karm'ānubandhīni manuṣya-loke.

Below, above, its branches straggle out, well nourished by the constituents; sense-objects are the twigs. Below its roots proliferate inseparably linked with works in the world of men.

3. *na rūpam asy'eha tath'opalabhyate*
n'ānto na c'ādir na ca saṁpratiṣṭhā:
aśvattham enaṁ suvirūḍha-mūlam
asaṅga-śastreṇa dṛḍhena chittvā,

No form of it can here be comprehended, no end and no beginning, no sure abiding-place: this fig-tree with its roots so fatly nourished—[take] the stout axe of detachment and cut it down!

'No end and no beginning': in 13. 12 Brahman has no beginning, no more have *puruṣa* and *prakṛti* in 13. 19. The Tree, like the Brahman of 13. 12, represents the whole process of *saṁsāra* which includes individual selves or spiritual monads, those 'minute parts' of God (15. 7) which are caught up and enmeshed in the cosmic process.

'No sure abiding-place': this does not mean that it is not 'rooted' or 'grounded' in anything since in 14. 27 we learnt that Krishna was the 'base supporting' even Brahman, its 'ground' and 'foundation'. All the Gītā says is that 'no sure abiding-place of it *can be comprehended*'. There is nothing new in this, for this is the 'Imperishable Unmanifest' which is 'indeterminate' and 'unthinkable' (12. 3), for this is God's 'creative power—his *māyā*—composed of the constituents, divine, hard to transcend' (7. 14). And, Krishna adds as He will add again in the next verse here, 'Whoso shall put his trust in Me alone, shall pass beyond this [my] uncanny power (*māyā*).'

dṛḍhena, 'stout': var. *śitena*, 'sharp'.

chittvā, 'cut it down': or, 'hack at it', since the tree can never be destroyed, it can only be transcended. The author of the Gītā, however, is more impatient of and certainly less awed by this indeterminate and incomprehensible tree than are the authors of the parallel passages we shall be looking at in the note on the next section. Perhaps he has in mind the celebrated passage of the *Chāndogya* Upanishad (6. 11) where we meet with just such a tree, but the moral of the story there is that even if you destroy the tree utterly, life will yet remain:

[Look at] this great tree, my dear. If you were to strike at its root, it would bleed but live on; if you were to strike it in the middle, it would bleed but live on; if you were to strike it at the top, it would bleed but live on. Strengthened by the living Self, it still stands, drinking in the moisture and exulting.

If life leaves one of its branches, it dries up; if it leaves a second, that too dries up; if it leaves a third, that too dries up. If it leaves the whole [tree], the whole [tree] dries up. This, my dear boy, is how you ought to understand it. . . .

When the life has gone out of it, this [body] dies; [but] the life does not die.

This finest essence—the whole universe has it as its Self: That is the Real: That is the Self. That *you* are.

This joyous exultation in eternal *life* belonged to a stage of Indian religion which as yet knew nothing of the Buddha and his teachings. To him the sap of life was hateful, and his use of this same simile of the tree and its destruction must surely have had its effect on the author of the Gītā who, though he borrows his first line from the *Kaṭha* Upanishad, develops the theme on lines that are more Buddhistic than Upanishadic. This is the Buddhist version of the Tree (S. iv. 160, 161):

'Take a fig-tree . . . full of sap, young, tender, and comely. Were a man to hack at it on every side with a sharp axe, would sap flow out?'

'Certainly, sir.'

'Why?'

'Because there is sap in it.'

The sap for the Buddhist is passion, hatred, and delusion, the three deadly sins. Once the tree is dry, sapless, and past its season, then it can be cut down. This changed outlook, which never made up its mind whether Nirvāna should be regarded as eternal life or as eternal death (since both are inseparable from this transient, painful, and unsubstantial world), must surely have affected the Gītā's refashioning of the *Kaṭha* simile.

4. *tataḥ padaṁ tat parimārgitavyaṁ*
yasmin gatā na nivartanti bhūyaḥ:
tam eva c'ādyaṁ puruṣaṁ prapadye
yataḥ pravṛttiḥ prasṛtā purāṇī.

And then search out that [high] estate to which, when once men go, they come not back again. 'I fly for succour to that primeval Person from whom flowed forth primordial creativity.'

tataḥ padaṁ, 'And then . . . estate': var. *tataḥ paraṁ*, '[search out] what is beyond that', perhaps the more satisfactory reading.

'That primeval Person': this is the 'Mighty Lord [who], surveying and approving, supports and [Himself] experiences [the constituents of Nature]: "Highest Self" some call Him, the "Highest Person"' (13. 22).

prapadye, 'I fly for succour': var. *prapadyed*, 'let a man fly for succour'. If we accept the better attested reading, Krishna must be putting the words into the mouth of the devotee.

It is strange but typical of the tension between the Sāṁkhya dualism and Upanishadic pantheism which no one can help noticing in the Gītā and which is only reconciled in and under the One God, Vishnu–Krishna, that the disciple is first asked to cut down the Tree of primordial creativity (*pravṛtti*) and then asked to take refuge in the very author of that Tree 'from whom all things proceed (*pravartate*)' (10. 8). This is, however, utterly typical of mystical religion, and the Muslim mystic, for instance, takes refuge in God's mercy against his wrath. In Hinduism it is not the divine wrath that hides the Eternal from the eyes of his worshipper but his 'divine *māyā*' (7. 14), his creative activity which conceals the timeless peace which is his 'changeless, [all-]highest' mode of being (7. 24).

The original version of the simile of the Cosmic Tree is almost certainly KaU. 6. 1–4:

With roots above and boughs beneath
The immortal fig-tree [stands];
This is the Pure, this Brahman,
This is the Immortal, so men say:
In it all the worlds are stablished;
Beyond it none can pass.
This in truth is That.

This whole moving world, whatever is,
Stirs in the breath of life, deriving from it:
The great fear [this], the upraised thunderbolt;
Whoso shall know it [thus], becomes immortal.

For fear of It the fire burns bright,
For fear [of It] the sun gives forth its heat,
For fear [of It] the gods of storm and wind,
And death, the fifth, [hither and thither] fly.

Could one but know It here [and now]
Before the body's breaking up . . .!
[Falling] from such [a state] a man is doomed
To bodily existence in the created worlds.

Here there is no dichotomy between the Cosmic Tree and the immortal Being which is its source. It may paralyse through fear, yet it is none the less the ladder by which and through which the immortal can be found. In ŚU. 3. 7–9 it is God Himself who is the Tree:

Higher than this, than Brahman higher, the mighty [God],
Hidden in all beings, each according to his kind,
The One, all things encompassing, the Lord—
By knowing Him a man becomes immortal.

I know that mighty Person,
Sun-coloured beyond the darkness:
By knowing Him indeed a man surpasses death;
No other path is there on which to go.

Beyond Him is nothing whatsoever, no other thing;
No one is more minute than He, no one more vast:
Like a sturdy tree firm-fixed in heaven He stands,
The One, the Person, this whole universe full filling!

In the *Anugītā* (MBh. 14. 47. 12–14) the version of the Bhagavad-Gītā is further elaborated:

From the seed of the Unmanifest it grows up, the Tree of Brahman—mighty, primordial—its trunk the soul (*buddhi*), its shoots the great ego, its inmost recesses the senses, its boughs the gross elements and the boughs that tally with them their several parts. Always in leaf, always in flower, producing fair fruits and foul, the means of life of all contingent beings [the primordial Tree of Brahman stands]. Cut it down, chop it up with wisdom, best of swords! Cast it aside, win deathlessness, be done with death and being born [again]. The man who has no truck with 'I' or 'mine' will be liberated, there is no doubt of that.

The *Anugītā* is considerably later than the Bhagavad-Gītā and Buddhist influence has made an even greater inroad.

5. *nirmāna-mohā jita-saṅga-doṣā*
adhyātma-nityā vinivṛtta-kāmāḥ
dvandvair vimuktāḥ sukha-duḥkha-saṁjñair
gacchanty amūḍhāḥ padam avyayaṁ tat.

Not proud, not fooled, [all] taint of attachment crushed, ever abiding in what appertains to self, desire suppressed, released from [all] dualities made known in pleasure as in pain, the undeluded march ahead to that state which knows no change.

'What appertains to self': see 8. 3, 4, nn. Ś., 'ever intent on contemplating the form of the highest Self'.

6. *na tad bhāsayate sūryo, na śaśāṅko, na pāvakaḥ,*
yad gatvā na nivartante: tad dhāma paramaṁ mama.

That [state] is not illumined by sun or moon or fire: once men go thither, they come not back again, for that is my highest home.

'This [state] is not illumined . . .': this line is borrowed with a slight modification from KaU. 5. 15 = MuU. 2. 2. 11: cf. ŚU. 6. 14.

'Highest home': that is, the 'Imperishable Unmanifest' Brahman which is Krishna's 'highest home' (*dhāma*) in 8. 21 (cf. 10. 12).

The Transmigrating Self

7. *mam' aiv' āṁśo jīva-loke jīva-bhūtaḥ sanātanaḥ*
manaḥ-ṣaṣṭhānī'ndriyāṇi prakṛti-sthāni karṣati.

In a world of living things a minute part of Me, eternal [still], becomes a living [self], drawing to itself the five senses and the mind which have their roots in Nature.

jīva-bhūtaḥ, 'becomes a living [self]': *jīva* in the later language is the technical term for the individual, transmigrating self. At the time the Gītā was composed the word seems to have been more loosely applied. The *jīva* is a particle of the divine substance imprisoned in material Nature which, when thus ensouled by these living particles, is called *jīva-bhūtā prakṛtiḥ*, 'living Nature': this is Krishna's 'higher Nature' (7. 5). How, Śankara asks, can the Absolute which is by definition partless, have a 'minute part' divided out from itself? It is, he says, like the reflection of the sun in water: remove the water and the reflection disappears into the sun which alone is real. Or it is like space or ether in a jar: remove the jar, and the continuity of space is again restored. Philosophically, of course, the problem is insoluble; but then even in India religion is not philosophy, and it is as futile to try to confine it to philosophical categories as all the ancient commentators do as it is for a Christian to pretend that the dogma of the Holy Trinity is anything but a mystery. It should be enough for us to note that for the Gītā God, though by definition infinite and indivisible, is none the less capable of assuming a finite and separate form. 'Time am I, wreaker of the world's destruction', Krishna had declared (11. 32), and Time itself, like God, is both infinite and indivisible from one point of view and finite and divisible from another. This is a mystery and can only be stated in terms of paradox. The *Maitrī* Upanishad does its best (6. 15):

> There are certainly two forms of Brahman—time and the timeless. That which existed before the sun is the timeless; it cannot be divided into parts. That which begins with the sun, however, is time. And the form of this [time] which has parts is the year. From the year [all] these creatures are born; through the year, once born, they grow, in the year they find their home [in death]. . . . For thus too did [Maitri] say:
>
> All beings Time digests
> In the Great Self.
> In whom or what is Time digested?
> Who knows this, knows the Veda.

So too particles of God descend into matter and adopt the senses and mind with which, so long as they remain in matter, they are indissolubly identified. This stanza and the following ones make this abundantly clear.

8. *śarīraṁ yad avāpnoti yac c'āpy utkrāmatī'śvaraḥ,*
gṛhītv' aitāni saṁyāti vāyur gandhān iv' āśayāt.

When [this] sovereign [self] takes on a body and when he rises up therefrom, he takes them [with him] and moves on as the wind [wafts] scents away from their proper home.

[ī]*śvaraḥ*, 'sovereign': the usual word for God, the 'Lord'. Here, however, it can only mean the individual self as Ś. himself recognizes.

9. *śrotraṁ cakṣuḥ sparśanaṁ ca rasanaṁ ghrāṇam eva ca*
adhiṣṭhaya manaś c'āyaṁ viṣayān upasevate.

Ear, eye, touch, taste, and smell he turns to due account,—so too the mind; [with these] he moves along the objects of sense.

10. *utkrāmantaṁ sthitaṁ vā 'pi bhuñjānaṁ vā guṇ'ānvitam*
vimūḍhā n'ānupaśyanti, paśyanti jñāna-cakṣuṣaḥ.

Whether he rise up [from the body] or remain [therein], or whether, through contact with the constituents, he tastes experience, fools do not perceive him, but whoso possesses wisdom's eye sees him [indeed].

11. *yatanto yoginaś c'ainaṁ paśyanty ātmany avasthitam,*
yatanto 'py akṛt'ātmāno n'ainaṁ paśyanty acetasaḥ.

And athletes of the spirit, fighting the good fight, see him established in [them]selves; not so the men whose self is unperfected, however much they strive, witless, they see him not.

paśyanty, 'see him': the object of vision is, then, the individual self, the 'minute part', not the 'whole' of God. This should presumably also be understood in the parallel passages (2. 29, 59: 6. 20: 13. 24).

The Immanent God

12. *yad āditya-gataṁ tejo jagad bhāsayate 'khilam*
yac candramasi yac c'āgnau, tat tejo viddhi māmakam.

The splendour centred in the sun which bathes the whole world in light, [the splendour] in the moon and fire,—know that it [all] is mine.

13. *gām āviśya ca bhūtāni dhārayāmy aham ojasā,*
puṣṇāmi c'auṣadhīḥ sarvāḥ somo bhūtvā ras'ātmakaḥ.

[Thus] too I penetrate the earth and so sustain [all] beings with my strength; becoming [the moon-plant] Soma, I, the very sap [of life], cause all healing herbs to grow.

14. *ahaṁ vaiśvānaro bhūtvā prāṇināṁ deham āśritaḥ*
prāṇ'āpāna-samāyuktaḥ pacāmy annaṁ catur-vidham.

Becoming the [digestive] fire in [the bodies of] all men I dwell in the body of all that breathes; conjoined with the inward and outward breaths I digest the fourfold food.

15. *sarvasya c'ahaṁ hṛdi saṁniviṣṭo;*
mattaḥ smṛtir jñānam apohanaṁ ca:
vedaiś ca sarvair aham eva vedyo,
vedānta-kṛd veda-vid eva c'āham.

I make my dwelling in the hearts of all: from Me stem memory, wisdom, the dispelling [of doubt]. Through all the Vedas it is I who should be known, for the maker of the Vedas' end am I, and I the Vedas know.

apohanaṁ, 'the dispelling [of doubt]': translation uncertain. One MS. reads *amohanaṁ*, 'freedom from delusion'.

vedānta-, 'Vedas' end': i.e. the Upanishads.

The Two Persons and the Transcendent God

16. *dvāv imau puruṣau loke kṣaraś c'ākṣara eva ca:*
kṣaraḥ sarvāṇi bhūtāni, kūṭa-stho 'kṣara ucyate.

In the world there are these two persons,—perishable the one, Imperishable the other: the 'perishable' is all contingent beings, the 'Imperishable' they call the 'sublime, aloof'.

puruṣau, 'two persons': H. assumes that the 'two persons' must be the same as the two 'Natures' of Krishna in 7. 4–5 and presumably, though he does not say so, with the two unmanifests of 8. 18–21. This seems most unlikely given the fact that Sāṁkhya terminology is built into the Gītā, and that in the Sāṁkhya system it is just not possible to confuse *puruṣa*, a spiritual substance with material Nature. The total incompatibility of the two is the basis of the whole system. It is of course true that the Gītā mixes Sāṁkhya ideas with the pantheistic monism characteristic of much of the Upanishadic writings, but even so it would be most surprising if it did use *puruṣa* in any sense other than 'spirit' in some form or another.

With the 'Imperishable' we are already fully familiar: it is the 'highest Brahman' (8. 3), the 'Unmanifest beyond the Unmanifest' (8. 21), and the 'sublime, aloof, unmoving, firm' (12. 3), and hence identical with the 'firm-set, unmoved, unmanifest' self of 2. 24–5. In other words, the 'Imperishable Person' is, as Rāmānuja points out, the sum-total of liberated selves, 'each subsisting in its own form and separated from all union with unconscious matter'. Whether or not one wishes to treat Brahman as absolutely One or as the totality of the 'stuff' which is common to all individual selves, is here beside the point: the 'Imperishable' is a timeless mode of existence, it is eternity.

From this it should follow that the 'perishable' is material Nature since it is here defined as 'all contingent beings' and in 8. 4 as '[Brahman] so far as it appertains to contingent beings'. If we accept, as I think we must, that *adhibhūtam* does not mean 'over-being' (E.), or 'essential Being' (H., which makes nonsense of the context), or 'the basis of all created things' (Rk.), but is used as it is invariably used in the Upanishads to mean simply 'with reference to contingent beings in general', then the 'perishable' *person* can only mean selves as they are while still in bondage to material Nature, or, as R. puts it, 'spirit qualified only by its being attached to unconscious matter', in other words, precisely what Krishna has been talking about in this chapter (7–11). This is the *bhūt'ātman* ('self in a contingent being') of MaiU. 3. 2 ff. and the later texts. The 'Imperishable' is Brahman without parts, the 'perishable' is Brahman with parts, the undivided and the seemingly divided (13. 16). And just as the Lord stands above and surveys his two 'Natures' and his two 'Unmanifests', so does He stand above and support the two 'persons'. Again there is nothing new in this since Krishna is simply claiming that superiority to the spiritual world in eternity as well as to the world of time which Rudra-Śiva claims in the *Śvetāśvatara* Upanishad (5. 1: cf. 1. 10):

> In the imperishable, infinite city of Brahman
> Two things there are—
> Wisdom and unwisdom, hidden, established there:
> Perishable is unwisdom, but wisdom is immortal:
> Who over wisdom and unwisdom rules, He is Another.

To sum up: the relationship between the two 'persons', the two 'Unmanifests', and the two 'Natures' of Krishna in the Gītā would seem to be as follows:

Higher Person =	liberated selves =	Higher Unmanifest	= higher Nature
Lower Person =	selves in bondage		
	primal matter =	lower Unmanifest	= lower Nature

17. *uttamaḥ puruṣas tv anyaḥ param'ātm'ety udāhṛtaḥ*
yo loka-trayam āviśya bibharty avyaya īśvaraḥ.

But there is [yet] another Person, the [All-]Sublime, surnamed 'All-Highest Self': the three worlds He enters-and-pervades, sustaining them,—the Lord who passes not away.

'Another Person, the [All-]Sublime': in arrogating this title exclusively to Himself Krishna denies it to the liberated individual self which, though it may have 'become the [very] self of every contingent being' (5. 7) in that the timeless mode of existence it has found within itself is identical and the same throughout the whole universe, is not for that reason the 'Highest Person'. This title was in fact bestowed on the liberated self by the author of ChU. 8. 12. 3, but he emphatically distinguished it from the Supreme Spirit in that he speaks of it as 'revealing itself in its *own form* (*svena svena rūpeṇa*)': hence in that passage I have translated the word as 'superman' which in the context is precisely what it means. The word, of course, is used in a totally different sense here.

18. *yasmāt kṣaram atīto 'ham akṣarād api c'ottamaḥ,*
ato 'smi loke vede ca prathitaḥ puruṣ'ottamaḥ.

Since I transcend the perishable and am more exalted than the Imperishable itself, so am I extolled in Vedic as in common speech as the 'Person [All-]Sublime'.

19. *yo mām evam asaṁmūḍho jānāti puruṣ'ottamam,*
sa sarva-vid bhajati māṁ sarva-bhāvena, Bhārata.

Whoever thus knows Me, unconfused, as the Person [All-] Sublime, knows all and [knowing all] communes with Me with all his being, all his love.

'All his being, all his love': *bhāva* means both, and both meanings are presumably intended. Communion with God, here as elsewhere, results from and follows on the intuitive knowledge of the Absolute (see 9. 34 n.).

20. *iti guhyatamaṁ śāstram idam uktaṁ mayā'nagha:*
etad buddhvā buddhimān syāt kṛta-kṛtyaś ca, Bhārata.

And so have I [at last] revealed this most mysterious doctrine: let a man but understand it, for then he will be a man who [truly] understands, his [life's] work done.

'His [life's] work done': because 'all works without exception in wisdom find their consummation' (4. 33).

CHAPTER XVI

THIS chapter is concerned with morality. In 1–7 Krishna lists the virtues appropriate to the man who is born to inherit a godly destiny. The rest of the chapter is devoted to describing the man who inherits a 'devilish' destiny: he is essentially an atheist, a libertine, a braggart, a murderer, and a hypocrite. Birth after birth he is condemned to lower and lower incarnations. The chapter ends with a description of the 'triple gate of hell' over which the three deadly sins of Desire, Anger, and Greed preside. The chapter is traditionally known as the 'Yoga of the Distinction between a Godly and a Devilish Destiny'.

The Cardinal Virtues and the Deadly Sins

Śrī-bhagavān uvāca:

1. *abhayaṁ sattva-saṁśuddhir jñāna-yoga-vyavasthitiḥ*
dānaṁ damaś ca yajñaś ca svādhyāyas tapa ārjavam,

The Blessed Lord said:

Fearless and pure in heart, steadfast in the exercise of wisdom, open-handed and restrained, performing sacrifice, intent on studying Holy Writ, ascetic and upright,

sattva-, 'heart': the word also means the constituent 'Goodness'. R. says it is not to be taken in this sense, and, with Ś., glosses 'mind'.

jñāna-yoga-, 'exercise of wisdom': this is the sense in which the word is used in 3. 3. Ś. prefers to treat it as a *dvandva* meaning scriptural knowledge and Yogic practice.

2. *ahiṁsā satyam akrodhas tyāgaḥ śāntir apaiśunam*
dayā bhūteṣv aloluptvaṁ mārdavaṁ hrīr acāpalam,

None hurting, truthful, from anger free, renouncing [all], at peace, averse to calumny, compassionate to [all] beings, free from nagging greed, gentle, modest, never fickle,

śāntir, '[at] peace': var. [*a*]*saktir*, 'detachment'.

3. *tejaḥ kṣamā dhṛtiḥ śaucam adroho n'ātimānitā*
bhavanti saṁpadaṁ daivīm abhijātasya, Bhārata.

Ardent, patient, enduring, pure, not treacherous nor arrogant—such is the man who is born to [inherit] a godly destiny.

śaucam, 'purity': var. *tuṣṭir*, 'contentment'.

4. *dambho darpo 'timānaś ca, krodhaḥ pāruṣyam eva ca,*
ajñānaṁ c'ābhijātasya, Pārtha, saṁpadam āsurīm.

A hypocrite, proud of himself and arrogant, angry, harsh and ignorant is the man who is born to [inherit] a devilish destiny.

dambho, 'hypocrisy': Ś., 'making a display of virtue'.

5. *daivī saṁpad vimokṣāya, nibandhāy'āsurī matā:*
mā śucaḥ, saṁpadaṁ daivīm abhijāto 'si, Pāṇḍava.

A godly destiny means deliverance, a devilish one enslavement; this is the usual view. [But] do not worry, Arjuna, [for] you are born to a godly destiny.

'Deliverance': from *saṁsāra*, the phenomenal world.

'Enslavement': bondage to the same.

6. *dvau bhūta-sargau loke 'smin, daiva āsura eva ca:*
daivo vistaraśaḥ prokta, āsuraṁ, Pārtha, me śṛṇu.

There are two orders of beings in this world,—the godly and the devilish. Of the godly I have discoursed at length; now listen to [my words about] the devilish.

Of Human Devils

7. *pravṛttiṁ ca nivṛttiṁ ca janā na vidur āsurāḥ;*
na śaucaṁ n'āpi c'ācāro na satyaṁ teṣu vidyate.

Of creative action and its return to rest the devilish folk know nothing; in them there is no purity, no morality, no truth.

pravṛttiṁ ca nivṛttiṁ ca, 'creative action and its return to rest': this is what the words mean on the cosmic scale. On the personal level they mean activity and the renunciation of activity, or, as R. puts it, the achievement of prosperity on the one hand and liberation on the other. Ś., surprisingly, interprets these words as meaning actions one should perform for the good of man and those one should abstain from in order to avoid evil.

8. *asatyam apratiṣṭhaṁ te jagad āhur anīśvaram*
aparaspara-saṁbhūtaṁ: kim anyat? kāma-haitukam.

'The world is devoid of truth,' they say, 'it has no ground, no ruling Lord; it has not come to be by mutual causal law; desire alone has caused it, nothing else.'

asatyam, 'devoid of truth or reality': Ś., 'devoid of right and wrong'.

aparaspara-saṁbhūtaṁ, 'it has not come to be by mutual causal law': Ś., 'its sole origin is the union of the sexes'. This seems to be an interpretation of *paraspara-saṁbhūtam* rather than of *a-paraspara-saṁbhūtam.*

kim anyat?, 'what else?': var. *akiṁcit*, 'it is nothing'.

kāma-haitukam, 'desire alone has caused it': or, 'caused at random', cf. *kāma-cārin*, 'roving at random'.

9. *etāṁ dṛṣṭim avaṣṭabhya naṣṭ'ātmāno 'lpa-buddhayaḥ*
prabhavanty ugra-karmāṇaḥ kṣayāya jagato 'hitāḥ.

Holding fast to these views, lost souls with feeble minds, they embark on cruel-and-violent deeds, malignant [in their lust] for the destruction of the world.

10. *kāmam āśritya duṣpūraṁ dambha-māna-mad'ānvitāḥ*
mohād gṛhītvā 'sad-grāhān pravartante 'śuci-vratāḥ.

Insatiate desire is their starting-point,—maddened are they by hypocrisy and pride, clutching at false conceptions, deluded as they are: impure are their resolves.

-māna-, 'pride': var. *-lobha-*, 'greed'.

'Maddened by hypocrisy and pride': or, 'possessed of hypocrisy, pride, and frenzy'.

mohād gṛhītvā 'sad-grāhān, 'clutching at false conceptions, deluded as they are': var. *asad-grah'āśritāḥ krūrāḥ*, 'resorting to false conceptions, cruel'.

11. *cintām aparimeyāṁ ca pralay'āntām upāśritāḥ*
kām'opabhoga-paramā, etāvad iti niścitāḥ.

Unmeasured care is theirs right up to the time of death, [for] they have no other aim than to satisfy their lusts, convinced that this is all.

12. *āśā-pāśa-śatair baddhāḥ kāma-krodha-parāyaṇāḥ*
īhante kāma-bhog'ārtham anyāyen'ārtha-saṁcayān.

Bound by hundreds of fetters forged by hope, obsessed by anger and desire, they seek to build up wealth unjustly to satisfy their lusts.

13. *idam adya mayā labdham, imaṁ prāpsye manoratham,*
idam ast'īdam api me bhaviṣyati punar dhanam.

'This have I gained today, this whim I'll satisfy; this wealth is mine and much more too will be mine as time goes on.

14. *asau mayā hataḥ śatrur, haniṣye c'āparān api,*
īśvaro 'ham, ahaṁ bhogī, siddho 'haṁ balavān sukhī.

'He was an enemy of mine, I've killed him, and many another too I'll kill. I'm master [here]. I take my pleasure [as I will]; I'm strong and happy and successful.

15. *āḍhyo 'bhijanavān asmi, ko 'nyo 'sti sadṛśo mayā ?*
yakṣye, dāsyāmi, modiṣya ity ajñāna-vimohitāḥ.

'I'm rich and of good family. Who else can match himself with me? I'll sacrifice and I'll give alms: [why not?] I'll have a marvellous time!' So speak [fools] deluded in their ignorance.

16. *aneka-citta-vibhrāntā, moha-jāla-samāvṛtāḥ,*
prasaktāḥ kāma-bhogeṣu patanti narake 'śucau.

[Their minds] unhinged by many a [foolish] fancy, caught up in delusion's net, obsessed by the satisfaction of their lusts, into foul hell they fall.

17. *ātma-saṁbhāvitāḥ stabdhā dhana-māna-mad'ānvitāḥ*
yajante nāma-yajñais te dambhen'āvidhipūrvakam.

Puffed up with self-conceit, unbending, maddened by their pride in wealth, they offer sacrifices that are but sacrifice in name and not in the way prescribed,—the hypocrites!

'Maddened by their pride in wealth': or, 'filled with the madness and pride of wealth'. One MS. reads *-samanvitāḥ*, 'filled with', for *-mad'ānvitāḥ*, 'filled with the madness'.

nāma-yajñais, 'sacrifice in name': var. *kāma-yajñais*, 'sacrifice of desire'; *māna-yajñais*, 'sacrifice of pride'.

18. *ahaṁkāraṁ balaṁ darpaṁ kāmaṁ krodhaṁ ca saṁśritāḥ*
mām ātma-para-deheṣu pradviṣanto 'bhyasūyakāḥ.

Selfishness, force and pride, desire and anger, [these do] they rely on, envying and hating Me who dwell in their bodies as I dwell in all.

'Who dwell in their bodies as I dwell in all': God dwells in the heart of everyone (15. 15: 18. 61).

19. *tān ahaṁ dviṣataḥ krūrān saṁsāreṣu nar'ādhamān*
kṣipāmy ajasram aśubhān āsurīṣv eva yoniṣu.

Birth after birth in this revolving round, these vilest among men, strangers to [all] good, obsessed with hate and cruel, I ever hurl into devilish wombs.

'Devilish wombs': Ś., 'like those of lions and tigers': R., 'that militate against any fellow-feeling (*ānukūlya*) with Me'.

20. *āsurīṁ yonim āpannā, mūḍhā janmani janmani*
mām aprāpy'aiva, Kaunteya, tato yānty adhamāṁ gatim.

Caught up in devilish wombs, birth after birth deluded, they never attain to Me: and so they tread the lowest way.

'The lowest way': the opposite of the 'highest way' which is a synonym for liberation. It is often asserted that the Hindus (except Madhva and his school) do not believe in eternal damnation. If, however, by damnation we mean eternal separation from God, then the Gītā, in these verses, seems to accept precisely this. These 'vilest among men' have no excuse, not even that of ignorance, for they hate the God 'who dwells in their bodies'; and God, being thus deliberately rejected, so far from helping them, 'hurls them' ever again 'into devilish wombs' so that in the end they 'tread the lowest way'. If, then, the blessed find in the 'highest way' their final release from phenomenal existence, does it not follow that those who 'tread the lowest way' are similarly 'released' into a timeless inferno of self-destruction? The lowest forms of incarnate life, according to Manu (12. 42), are inanimate objects, insects, fish, snakes, and so on. Once one has reached this level, it is difficult to see what hope there is—so, according to the Gītā, there is no alternative but to 'tread the lowest way': the gates of hell are now wide open to receive him. There seems to be absolutely nothing in this passage to justify Rk.'s comment: 'Even the greatest sinner, if he turns to God, can achieve freedom.' But how can a man whose attitude to God is set in hatred to Him bring himself to turn to Him?

It may be argued that Duryodhana, the arch-villain of the MBh., went to heaven despite the fact that he hated Krishna although he knew that He was God. In Krishna's eyes, however, Duryodhana, because he performed his caste-duty as a warrior, fought fairly, and never turned his back to the enemy, was ultimately justified for this if for no other reason. He hated Krishna all right but only because he did not understand Him as He really is. The 'vilest of men' mentioned here hate God because He constantly stands in the way of their own self-centredness, and of the lust, anger, and greed which are the natural fruit of that self-centredness.

The Triple Gate of Hell

21. *tri-vidhaṁ narakasy'edaṁ dvāraṁ nāśanam ātmanaḥ,*
kāmaḥ krodhas tathā lobhas: tasmād etat trayaṁ tyajet.

Desire—Anger—Greed: this is the triple gate of hell, destruction of the self: therefore avoid these three.

nāśanam ātmanaḥ, 'destruction of the self': this can scarcely be taken literally since the self, being a 'minute part' of God (15. 7), is indestructible (2. 18). The self, however, is so intimately connected with *buddhi*, the 'soul' (pp. 143, 269), that the separation of the two means the loss of the self by the soul. This means that the human personality loses its centre and collapses in chaos back into material Nature (cf. 2. 62–3).

22. *etair vimuktaḥ, Kaunteya, tamo-dvārais tribhir naraḥ*
ācaraty ātmanaḥ śreyas, tato yāti parāṁ gatim.

When once a man is freed from these three gates of darkness, then can he work for [his] self's salvation, thence tread the highest way.

'Darkness': probably not the constituent of that name since the three deadly sins mentioned are born of 'Passion' rather than 'Darkness' (3. 37: 14. 7, 12, 17).

23. *yaḥ śāstra-vidhim utsṛjya vartate kāma-kārataḥ,*
na sa siddhim avāpnoti, na sukhaṁ, na parāṁ gatim.

Whoso forsakes the ordinance of Scripture and lives at the whim of his own desires, wins not perfection, [finds] no comfort, [treads] not the highest way.

śāstra-, 'Scripture': the *śāstras* are not the canon of the Veda but later compilations like the *Laws of Manu* which codify the Hindu customary law (*dharma*). This *dharma* Vishnu's incarnations are intended to revive (4. 7). It is, then, significant that Krishna describes Himself as the '*maker* of the Vedas' end' (the Upanishads), but the Vedas themselves He only 'knows' (15. 15). Moreover, He shows more impatience with the Vedic ritualists than with any other class of people (2. 42–6, 52–3). He revives above all the four-class system of which He claims to be the author (4. 13) and this He regards as the principal purpose of his incarnation.

24. *tasmāc chāstraṁ pramāṇaṁ te kāry-ākārya-vyavasthitau:*
jñātvā śāstra-vidhān'oktaṁ karma kartum ih'ārhasi.

Therefore let Scripture be your norm, determining what is right and wrong. Once you know what the ordinance of Scripture bids you do, you should perform down here the works [therein prescribed].

CHAPTER XVII

THE chapter opens with Arjuna asking Krishna what happens to believers who are not orthodox. Krishna does not give a direct answer but says that men are conditioned by faith as they are by the constituents of Nature, and this will determine the type of the deities they worship (1–4). This is followed by a spirited attack on exaggerated asceticism (5–6).

From 7 to 22 we are brought back to a consideration of the three constituents of Nature and how they operate in the domains of food, sacrifice, asceticism, and alms-giving.

The concluding section of the chapter extols the formula *OṀ TAT SAT*,—OṀ, THAT, IT IS,—as representing the quintessence of Reality which is at the same time the Good and the True. The chapter is traditionally known as the 'Yoga of the Distinction of the three Kinds of Faith'.

The Unorthodox

Arjuna uvāca:

1. *ye śāstra vidhim utsṛjya yajante śraddhaya 'nvitāḥ,*
teṣāṁ niṣṭhā tu kā, Kṛṣṇa, sattvam āho rajas tamaḥ ?

Arjuna said:

[And yet there are some] who forsake the ordinance of Scripture and offer sacrifice full filled with faith, where do they stand? On Goodness, Passion, or Darkness?

Śrī-bhagavān uvāca:

2. *tri-vidhā bhavati śraddhā dehināṁ, sā svabhāva-jā;*
sāttvikī rājasī c'aiva tāmasī c'eti, tāṁ śṛṇu.

The Blessed Lord said:

Threefold is the faith of embodied [selves]; each [of the three] springs from [a man's] own nature. [The first is] of Goodness, [the second] of Passion, of Darkness [is the third]. Listen to this.

śraddhā, 'faith': Ś. (on 17. 1), 'belief in a supreme Principle (*āstikya*)': R., 'eagerness to put into practice what one already has confidence in'. According to both Ś. and R. one's type of faith depends on past *karma* which determines one's present character.

3. *sattv'ānurūpā sarvasya śraddhā bhavati, Bhārata,*
śraddhāmayo 'yaṁ puruṣo: yo yac-chraddhaḥ, sa eva saḥ.

Faith is connatural to the soul of every man: man is instinct with faith: as is his faith, so too must he be.

sattv[a]-, 'soul': Ś., R., 'mind' (*antaḥkaraṇa*)—as conditioned by specific tendencies (Ś.).

4. *yajante sāttvikā devān, yakṣa-rakṣāṁsi rājasāḥ,*
pretān bhūta-gaṇāṁś c'ānye yajante tāmasā janāḥ.

To the gods do men of Goodness offer sacrifice, to sprites and monsters men of Passion, to disembodied spirits and the assembled spirits of the dead the others,—men of Darkness,—offer sacrifice.

For the worship of other gods and spirits cf. 7. 20–3: 9. 20–5.

Exaggerated Asceticism

5–6. *aśāstra-vihitaṁ ghoraṁ tapyante ye tapo janāḥ*
dambh'āhaṁkāra-saṁyuktāḥ, kāma-rāga-bal'ānvitāḥ,
karṣayantaḥ śarīra-sthaṁ bhūta-grāmam acetasaḥ
māṁ c'aiv'āntaḥ-śarīra-sthaṁ, tān viddhy āsura-niścayān.

And this know too. Some men there are who, without regard to Scripture's ordinance, savagely mortify [their flesh], buoyed up by hypocrisy and self-regard, yielding to the violence of passion and desire, and so torment the mass of [living] beings whose home their body is, the witless fools,—and [with them] Me Myself within [that same] body abiding: how devilish their intentions!

'The violence of passion and desire': so Ś.: or, 'desire, passion, and violence'.

'Me Myself within [that same] body abiding': as a particle of God (15. 7, so R.): Ś., 'as the witness in their soul (*buddhi*) of what they do': they torment God by not obeying his commands. God is doubly present in the human body, in a general sense as the universal fire which digests food (15. 14) and thereby sustains individual life, and as witness (*Sāṁkhya-kārikā*, 19: cf. 18. 61),—as conscience, which makes Him odious to the evil man (16. 18).

One MS. puts these two verses after verse 17.

The Three Constituents of Nature

(*a*) *In Food*

7 *āhāras tv api sarvasya tri-vidho bhavati priyaḥ,*
yajñas tapas tathā dānaṁ: teṣāṁ bhedam imaṁ śṛṇu.

Threefold again is food,—[food] that agrees with each [different type of] man: [so too] sacrifice, ascetic practice, and the gift of alms. Listen to the difference between them.

8. *āyuḥ-sattva-bal'ārogya-sukha-prīti-vivardhanāḥ*
rasyāḥ snigdhāḥ sthirā hṛdyā āhārāḥ sāttvika-priyāḥ.

Foods that promote a fuller life, vitality, strength, health, pleasure, and good-feeling, [foods that are] savoury, rich in oil and firm, heart-gladdening,—[these] are agreeable to the man of Goodness.

9. *kaṭv-amla-lavaṇ'ātyuṣṇa-tīkṣṇa-rūkṣa-vidāhinaḥ*
āhārā rājasasy'eṣṭā duḥkha-śok'āmaya-pradāḥ.

Foods that are pungent, sour, salty, stinging hot, sharp, rough, and burning,—[these] are what the man of Passion loves. They bring pain, misery, and sickness.

10. *yātayamaṁ gata-rasaṁ pūti paryuṣitaṁ ca yat,*
ucchiṣṭam api c'āmedhyaṁ bhojanaṁ tāmasa-priyam.

What is stale and tasteless, rotten and decayed,—leavings, what is unfit for sacrifice, is food agreeable to the man of Darkness.

yātayāmaṁ, 'stale': Ś., 'cooked too slowly': R., 'that has stood around for a long time'.

(*b*) *In Sacrifice*

11. *aphal'ākāṅkṣibhir yajño vidhi-dṛṣṭo ya ijyate,*
yaṣṭavyam ev'eti manaḥ samādhāya, sa sāttvikaḥ.

The sacrifice approved by [sacred] ordinance and offered up by men who would not taste its fruits, who concentrate their minds on this [alone]: 'In sacrifice lies duty': [such sacrifice] belongs to Goodness.

12. *abhisaṁdhāya tu phalaṁ dambh'ārtham api c'aiva yat*
ijyate, Bharata-śreṣtha, taṁ yajñaṁ viddhi rājasam.

But the sacrifice that is offered up by men who bear its fruits in mind or simply for vain display,—know that [such sacrifice] belongs to Passion.

13. *vidhi-hīnam asṛṣṭ'ānnaṁ mantra-hīnam adakṣiṇam*
śraddhā-virahitaṁ yajñaṁ tāmasaṁ paricakṣate.

The sacrifice in which no proper rite is followed, no food distributed, no sacred words recited, no Brāhmans' fees paid up, no faith enshrined,—[such sacrifice] men say belongs to Darkness.

(*c*) *In Ascetic Practice*

14. *deva-dvija-guru-prājña-pūjanaṁ śaucam ārjavam,*
brahmacaryam ahiṁsā ca śārīraṁ tapa ucyate.

[Due] reverence of gods and Brāhmans, teachers and wise men, purity, uprightness, chastity, refusal to do harm,—[this] is [true] penance of the body.

15. *anudvega-karaṁ vākyaṁ satyaṁ priya-hitaṁ ca yat,*
svādhyāy'ābhyasanaṁ c'aiva vāṅmayaṁ tapa ucyate.

Words that do not cause disquiet, [words] truthful, kind, and pleasing, the constant practice too of sacred recitation,—[this] is the penance of the tongue.

16. *manaḥ-prasādaḥ saumyatvaṁ maunam ātma-vinigrahaḥ,*
bhāva-saṁśuddhir ity etat tapo mānasam ucyate.

Serenity of mind and friendliness, silence and self-restraint, and the cleansing of one's affections,—this is called the penance of the mind.

17. *śraddhayā parayā taptaṁ tapas tat trividhaṁ naraiḥ*
aphal'ākāṅkṣibhir yuktaiḥ sāttvikaṁ paricakṣate.

When men possessed of highest faith, integrated and indifferent to the fruits [of what they do], do penance in this threefold wise, men speak of [penance] in Goodness' way.

yuktaiḥ, 'integrated': var. *muktaiḥ*, 'liberated'.

18. *satkāra-māna-pūj'ārthaṁ tapo dambhena c'aiva yat*
kriyate, tad iha proktaṁ rājasaṁ calam adhruvam.

Some mortify themselves to win respect, honour, and reverence, or from sheer hypocrisy: here [on earth] this must be called [penance] in Passion's way,—fickle and unsure.

19. *mūḍha-grāheṇ'ātmano yat pīḍayā kriyate tapaḥ*
parasy'otsādan'ārthaṁ vā, tat tāmasam udāhṛtam.

Some mortify themselves following perverted theories, torturing themselves, or to destroy another: this is called [penance] in Darkness' way.

(*d*) *In Alms-giving*

20. *dātavyam iti yad dānaṁ dīyate 'nupakāriṇe*
deśe kāle ca pātre ca, tad dānaṁ sāttvikaṁ smṛtam.

Alms given because to give alms is a [sacred] duty to one from whom no favour is expected in return at the [right] place and time and to a [fit] recipient,—this is called alms [given] in Goodness' way.

21. *yat tu pratyupakār'ārthaṁ phalam uddiśya vā punaḥ*
dīyate ca parikliṣṭaṁ, tad dānaṁ rājasaṁ smṛtam.

But [alms] given in expectation of favours in return, or for the sake of fruits [to be reaped] hereafter, [alms given] too against the grain,—this is called alms [given] in Passion's way.

22. *adeśa-kāle yad dānam apātrebhyaś ca dīyate,*
asatkṛtam avajñātaṁ, tat tamasam udāhṛtam.

Alms given at the wrong place and time to an unworthy recipient without respect, contemptuously,—this is called [alms given] in Darkness' way.

OṀ — THAT — IT IS

23. *oṁ tat sad iti nirdeśo brahmaṇas tri-vidhaḥ smṛtaḥ,*
brāhmaṇās tena vedāś ca yajñāś ca vihitāḥ purā.

OṀ — THAT — IT IS: This has been handed down, a threefold pointer to Brahman: by this were allotted their proper place of old Brāhmans, Veda, and sacrifice.

'OṀ': the sacred syllable *par excellence*, the *akṣara*, the 'Imperishable Brahman' (8. 13), for the word *akṣara* means both 'imperishable' and 'syllable'. The importance attached by the Hindus to this most perfect of all *mantras* cannot be exaggerated. Leaving aside for the moment the fascinating speculation on the occult significance of this syllable which runs throughout the Upanishads but which must appear tedious to the modern mind, it is as well to state at once that the meaning of the word in ordinary speech is 'Yes' (BU. 3. 9. 1 ff., etc.): it is the syllable of total affirmation and is therefore aptly associated with the more explicit 'IT IS'. It is 'Brahman as sound' (MaiU. 6. 22), the Word spoken by the Absolute by and through which men can reach the soundless, silent Brahman which is its crown and apex:

There are two Brahmans to be meditated on,—[that which is] sound and the soundless. Now, the soundless one can be revealed by [the one that is] sound. In this case the sound is Oṁ. Ascending by this one ends up in the soundless. . . . This is the Way, this the Immortal, this is union (*sāyujatva*), this is the cessation [of becoming]. . . (23) . . . [Brahman as] sound is the syllable Oṁ. Its summit is silent, soundless, free from fear and sorrow, blissful, well content, stable, motionless, immortal, unfailing, enduring: Vishnu is its name, meaning that It is above and beyond everything. . . .

The higher and the lower God
Whose name is Oṁ,
Soundless and void of contingency,
Fix Him firmly in thy head!

So too KaU. 2. 15–17:

The single word announced by all the Vedas,
Proclaimed by all ascetic practices,
[The word] in search of which men practise chastity,
This word I tell [thee now] in brief.
Oṁ—this is it.

The Imperishable Brahman this,
This the Imperishable Beyond:
Whoso this Imperishable comes to know—
What he desires is his.

Depend on This, the best,
Depend on This, the ultimate:
Who knows that on This [alone all things] depend,
In the Brahman-world is magnified.

This is not a comparative study, but we can scarcely help being reminded of the first words of St. John's Gospel: 'In the beginning was the Word, and the Word was with God, and the Word was God.' For the Hindus the Word is 'Oṁ, Yes': and the Word, though One, is yet three:

The syllable Oṁ ($A+U+M$) is Brahman, both the higher and the lower. Therefore a man who knows can attain to either, if he makes this [syllable] his home.

If he meditates on one element [only], enlightened by that alone, he will come [back] to earth soon enough. The Rig-Vedic verses bring him down to the world of men, and there, naturally endowed with a bent for self-mortification, chastity, and faith, he will experience a great [spiritual] expansion.

But if he meditates with two elements, the Yajur-Vedic formulas will lead him up to the atmosphere, to the world of the moon. In the world of the moon he will experience some enlightenment, but will return again.

Again, he who meditates on the highest Person with this syllable Oṁ in [all] its three elements, will be suffused with glory in the sun.

As a snake sloughs off its skin, so is he set free from evil. The Sāma-Vedic chants lead him up to the Brahman-world. From out of the mass of living beings he beholds that Person who is higher than the highest and [yet] dwells within the city [of the body]. On this there are the following two verses:

> Deadly are the three elements when used in rites
> External, internal, or in between,
> If wholly merged together or wholly separate.
> The wise man, using them in proportion due, is not dismayed.
>
> With Rig-Vedic verses [one gains] this world,
> With Yajur-Vedic formulas the atmosphere,
> With Sāma-Vedic chants that which the sages know:
> With the syllable Oṁ as his firm base, the wise
> Attains to the All-Highest,
> Tranquil, ageless, immortal, free from fear! (PU. 5. 2–7)

So too the *Māṇḍūkya* Upanishad begins with the bald statement:

This syllable Oṁ is the whole universe. And the interpretation thereof is this:

> What was and is and is yet to be—
> All of it is Oṁ;
> And whatever else the three times transcends—
> That too is Oṁ.

Oṁ, then, is the representation in sound of the total Brahman; it is threefold in that it is the three Vedas (Brahman in sound), the three times (past, present, and future), and what is beyond. The three letters A, U, and M again represent the three states of consciousness in man—being awake, dream, and dreamless sleep. The total undivided syllable represents and indeed is the fourth state of pure unity which, for the *Māṇḍūkya* Upanishad, is the One Reality, the real Brahman and the real Self. This 'fourth is beyond [all] letters: there can be no commerce with it; it brings [all] development to an end; it is mild and devoid of duality. Such is Oṁ, the very Self indeed' (MāU. 12).

Hence this august syllable begins and ends every ritual utterance (ChU. 1. 4. 1, 4), for it is the beginning and the end, Alpha and Omega.

tat, 'THAT': that is, Reality as object which is yet the same as Reality as subject as we learn from the all too famous refrain of ChU. 6. 8–16, *tat tvam asi*, 'That *you* are', and the equally laconic *etad vai tat*, 'This indeed is That', of KaU. 4. 3–13: 5. 1–8.

sad, 'IT IS': here there is no question of 'what IS and what is not', 'Being or Not-Being' as in 13. 12, nor even of 'what is beyond both' (11. 37). The whole of Reality is expressed in this one word, as the following stanzas explain.

24. *tasmād om ity udāhṛtya yajña-dāna-tapaḥ-kriyāḥ*
pravartante vidhān'oktāḥ satataṁ brahmavādinām.

And so [all] acts of sacrifice, the giving of alms, and penance enjoined by [sacred] ordinances and ever again [enacted] by Brahman's devotees begin with the utterance of [the one word] Oṁ.

25. *tad ity anabhisaṁdhāya phalaṁ yajña-tapaḥ-kriyāḥ*
dāna-kriyāś ca vividhāḥ kriyante mokṣa-kāṅkṣibhiḥ.

THAT: [so saying] do men who hanker for deliverance perform the various acts of sacrifice, penance, and the gift of alms, having no thought for the fruits [they bring].

Whatever they do, they do it in the context of That Brahman which is pure Being beyond change, because sacrifice, penance or ascetic practices, and the gift of alms are the threefold support of the whole of *dharma*, the whole religious life; and God is 'the base supporting Brahman,—immortal [Brahman] which knows no change,—[supporting] too the eternal law of righteousness (*dharma*) and absolute beatitude' (14. 27).

26. *sad-bhāve sādhu-bhāve ca sad ity etat prayujyate;*
praśaste karmaṇi tathā sac-chabdaḥ, Pārtha, yujyate.

IT IS: in this the meanings are conjoined of 'Being' and of 'Good'; so too the [same] word *sat* is appropriately used for works that call forth praise.

The Real and the Good are interchangeable words. It is somehow gratifying to find the Gītā making this thoroughly Thomistic statement some two thousand years before the appearance of Aquinas.

27. *yajñe tapasi dāne ca sthitiḥ sad iti c'ocyate*
karma c'aiva tad-arthīyaṁ sad ity ev'ābhidhīyate.

In sacrifice, in penance, in the gift of alms [the same word] *sat* is used, meaning 'steadfastness': and works performed with these purposes [in mind], [these] too are surnamed *sat.*

sthitiḥ, 'steadfastness': perhaps the author also had in mind the *brāhmī sthitiḥ*, the 'fixed, still state of Brahman' of 2. 72. Sacrifice, penance, and the gift of alms and the perseverance in them reflect on earth the 'Imperishable Brahman' which itself meets the perishable pre-eminently in the sacrifice (4. 24 n.).

28. *aśraddhayā hutaṁ dattaṁ tapas taptaṁ kṛtaṁ ca yat,*
asad ity ucyate, Pārtha, na ca tat pretya no iha.

Whatever offering is made in unbelief, whatever given, whatever act of penance undertaken, whatever done,—of that is said *asat*, 'It is not': for naught it is in this world or the next.

Everything done must be done with reference to eternity, for eternity alone is real. In Sanskrit *sat* and *satya* mean both 'reality' and 'truth'—truth in every sense of the word, not just 'absolute' truth, but truthfulness in general. By telling a lie you deny that 'You are That', and you thereby destroy the reality, the truth, that is within you: you simply cease to exist. Hence the famous sequence in ChU. 6. 8–16, the refrain of which is 'That *you* are', after explaining in parables how this is to be understood, finishes up by a devastating application of the doctrine to practical life:

Again, my dear boy, people bring in a man handcuffed [to face the ordeal], crying out, 'He has committed a robbery, he has stolen, heat the axe for him!' If he is guilty, he makes himself out to be what he is not, speaks untruly, clothes [him]self in untruth. He takes hold of the red-hot axe and is burnt. Then he is killed.

If, however, he is innocent, he shows himself to be what he is, speaks the truth, clothes [him]self in truth. He takes hold of the red-hot axe and is not burnt. Then he is released.

So, just as such a man is not burnt [because he embodies Truth], so does this whole universe have this [Truth] as its Self. That is the Truth: [That is the Real:] That is the Self: That *you* are.

CHAPTER XVIII

THE eighteenth and last chapter falls into two distinct parts. Verses 1–40 continue Chapter XVII in that they are still concerned with the three constituents of Nature as they effect man's behaviour and character on earth. Verses 41–5 deal with the duties of the four classes of society, while 46–8 are transitional, leading the reader back from the sphere of 'action' to that of 'wisdom'. Then from 49 to 66 Krishna repeats and summarizes his whole doctrine of salvation culminating in the love of man for God and God's answering love for man.

The chapter is opened by Arjuna who asks about renunciation and self-surrender and Krishna reiterates what He had already said earlier, namely, that certain works must be done but in a spirit of complete detachment (1–6). Even so the spirit in which a man renounces will itself be conditioned by whichever of the constituents of Nature predominates in his character (7–12).

Every action has five causes, and it is a great mistake to think that the self alone acts (13–17).

At 18 we return to the constituents again and the effect they have on metaphysical theory, action, the agent, the intellect, constancy, and pleasure (18–40). Here follows a consideration of caste-duty and how essential the performance of it is as a preliminary to liberation (41–8).

From 49 to 66 Krishna describes for the last time the successive stages that lead a man to liberation. Detachment leads to the purity of the 'soul', and this in time leads to the conquest of all passion, to the loss of all sense of individual identity as an ego, and this in turn fits one to 'become Brahman'. Once this state of timeless peace has been attained, the athlete of the spirit receives the highest love and devotion to God; and this bears him up as he continues, though now liberated from the 'bonds' of works, to do the work for which he was destined. Should he kick against the pricks, it will make no difference, for Nature will compel him. In his final 'highest and most mysterious' message Krishna tells Arjuna that just as He expects his loyal devotees to love Him, so does He love them in return. This, as the attentive reader will have recognized, is the supreme message to which the Gītā has slowly but surely been leading him.

There now follows the epilogue which brings us firmly back from the metaphysical heights of Krishna's new theology to the field of Kurukshetra where Arjuna, now fully reassured, will make short work of the enemy and where Krishna, once more reverting to the humble role of a charioteer, will, as man, show Himself strangely impervious to some of the teachings He had himself proclaimed as God.

Renunciation and Self-Surrender

Arjuna uvāca:

1. *saṁnyāsasya, mahā-bāho, tattvam icchāmi veditum*
tyāgasya ca, Hṛṣīkeśa, pṛthak, Keśi-niṣūdana.

Arjuna said:

Krishna, fain would I know the truth concerning renunciation and apart from this [the truth] of self-surrender.

Śrī-bhagavān uvāca:

2. *kāmyānāṁ karmaṇāṁ nyāsaṁ saṁnyāsaṁ kavayo viduḥ,*
sarva-karma-phala-tyāgaṁ prāhus tyāgaṁ vicakṣaṇāḥ.

The Blessed Lord said:

To give up works dictated by desire, wise men allow [this] to be renunciation; surrender of all the fruits that [accrue] to works discerning men call self-surrender.

'Dictated by desire': Ś. takes this to include religious sacrifices like the horse-sacrifice. This is quite unwarrantable since in fact Arjuna does perform the horse-sacrifice traditionally offered by all conquerors when a war has been won. In this he has Krishna's full approval.

'Surrender of all the fruits that [accrue] to works': Krishna here picks up his first great doctrinal theme which He had announced in 2. 47: 'Let not your motive be the fruit of works . . . .'

3. *tyājyaṁ doṣavad ity eke karma prāhur manīṣiṇaḥ;*
yajña-dāna-tapaḥ-karma na tyājyam iti c'āpare.

'[All] works must be surrendered, for [works themselves] are tainted with defect': so say some of the wise; but others say that [works of] sacrifice, the gift of alms, and works of penance are not to be surrendered.

'[Works] are tainted with defect': everyone admits this, but this is no reason for doing nothing (18. 48). In any case all works should be seen as sacrifice (3. 9).

4. *niścayaṁ śṛṇu me tatra tyāge, Bharata-sattama;*
tyāgo hi, puruṣa-vyāghra, tri-vidhaḥ saṁprakīrtitaḥ.

Hear [then] my own decision in this matter of surrender: for threefold is self-surrender; so has it been declared.

'Threefold': in accordance with the three constituents of Nature (18. 7–10). R., 'that is, surrender of fruits, of action itself, and of agency'.

5. *yajña-dāna-tapaḥ-karma na tyājyaṁ, kāryam eva tat;*
yajño dānaṁ tapaś c'aiva pāvanāni manīṣiṇām.

[Works of] sacrifice, the gift of alms, and works of penance are not to be surrendered; these must most certainly be done: it is sacrifice, alms-giving, and ascetic practice that purify the wise.

6. *etāny api tu karmāṇi saṅgaṁ tyaktvā phalāni ca*
kartavyānī'ti me, Pārtha, niścitaṁ matam uttamam.

But even these works should be done [in a spirit of self-surrender], for [all] attachment [to what you do] and [all] the fruits [of what you do] must be surrendered. This is my last decisive word.

7. *niyatasya tu saṁnyāsaḥ karmaṇo n'opapadyate;*
mohāt tasya parityāgas tāmasaḥ parikīrtitaḥ.

For to renounce a work enjoined [by Scripture] is inappropriate; deludedly to give this up is [the way] of Darkness. This [too] has been declared.

8. *duḥkham ity eva yat karma kāya-kleśa-bhayāt tyajet,*
sa kṛtvā rājasaṁ tyāgaṁ n'aiva tyāga-phalaṁ labhet.

The man who gives up a deed simply because it causes pain or because he shrinks from bodily distress, commits an act of self-surrender that accords with Passion['s way]; assuredly he will not reap the fruit of self-surrender.

'The fruit of self-surrender': that is, liberation (Ś.).

9. *kāryam ity eva yat karma niyataṁ kriyate, 'rjuna,*
saṅgaṁ tyaktvā phalaṁ c'aiva, sa tyāgaḥ sāttviko mataḥ.

But if a work is done simply because it should be done and is enjoined [by Scripture], and if [all] attachment, [all thought of] fruit is given up, then that is surrender in Goodness[' way], I deem.

Cf. 3. 8: 'Do the work that is prescribed [for you]': 3. 19, 'Therefore detached, perform unceasingly the works that must be done.'

10. *na dveṣṭy akuśalaṁ karma, kuśale n'ānuṣajjate*
tyāgī sattva-samāviṣṭo medhāvī chinna-saṁśayaḥ.

The self-surrendered man, suffused with Goodness, wise, whose [every] doubt is cut away, hates not his uncongenial work nor cleaves to the congenial.

kuśale, 'congenial': the word also has the sense of 'expert, profitable': hence Ś. glosses, 'productive of liberation'. It will be remembered that *yoga* itself was defined as 'skill (*kauśalam*) in [performing] works' (2. 50).

11. *na hi deha-bhṛtā śakyaṁ tyaktuṁ karmāṇy aśeṣataḥ;*
yas tu karma-phala-tyāgī, sa tyāgī'ty abhidhīyate.

For one still in the body it is not possible to surrender up all works without exception; rather it is he who surrenders up the *fruit* of works who deserves the name, 'A self-surrendered man'.

Cf. 3. 5: 'Not for a moment can a man stand still and do no work, for every man is powerless and made to work by the constituents born of Nature'; 'for without working you will not succeed even in keeping your body in good repair' (3. 8).

12. *aniṣṭam iṣṭaṁ miśraṁ ca tri-vidhaṁ karmaṇaḥ phalam*
bhavaty atyāgināṁ pretya, na tu saṁnyāsināṁ kvacit.

Unwanted—wanted—mixed: threefold is the fruit of work,—[this they experience] at death who have not surrendered [self], but not at all such men as have renounced.

'Unwanted': R., 'hell': Ś., 'hell or an animal incarnation'.

'Wanted': R., 'heaven': Ś., 'incarnation as a god'.

The Five Causes

13. *pañc'aitāni, mahā-bāho, kāraṇāni nibodha me*
sāṁkhye kṛtānte proktāni siddhaye sarva-karmaṇām.

In the system of the Sāṁkhyas these five causes are laid down; by these all works attain fruition. Learn them from Me.

14. *adhiṣṭhānaṁ tathā kartā karaṇaṁ ca pṛthag-vidham*
vividhāś ca pṛthak-ceṣṭā daivaṁ c'aiv'ātra pañcamam.

Material basis, agent, material causes of various kinds, the vast variety of motions, and fate, the fifth and last.

'Material basis': this is usually taken to mean the body.

'Material causes': usually taken to mean the sense-organs.

daivaṁ, 'fate': *daivam* is the ordinary word for 'fate' in the MBh. There is no difficulty about this word as H. supposed.

15. *śarīra-vāṅ-manobhir yat karma prārabhate naraḥ,*
nyāyyaṁ vā viparītaṁ vā, pañc'aite tasya hetavaḥ.

These are the five causes of whatever work a man may undertake,—of body, speech, or mind,—no matter whether right or wrong.

16. *tatr'aivaṁ sati kartāram ātmānaṁ kevalaṁ tu yaḥ*
paśyaty, akṛta-buddhitvān na sa paśyati durmatiḥ.

This being so, the man who sees self isolated [in itself] as the agent, does not see [at all]. Untrained is his intelligence and evil are his thoughts.

'Isolated [in itself]': rather than 'alone' (E., D.), 'merely' (H.), 'sole' (Rk.). Ś. rightly glosses *śuddham*, 'pure', meaning the self as it is when uncontaminated by material Nature. *Kevalam* is the technical Sāṁkhya expression used to represent the liberated spiritual monad or 'self' (in Vedānta terminology): hence S. translates 'indépendant'.

17. *yasya n'āhaṁkṛto bhāvo, buddhir yasya na lipyate,*
hatvā 'pi sa imāṁl lokān, na hanti, na nibadhyate.

A man who has reached a state where there is no sense of 'I', whose soul is undefiled,—were he to slaughter [all] these worlds,—slays nothing. He is not bound.

'Who has reached a state where there is no sense of "I"': Ś., 'who thinks, "I am the agent" '.

'Whose soul is undefiled': Ś., 'who has no remorse at having done something [evil] which would land him in hell'. Killing only takes place on the phenomenal plane, not on that of the Absolute. This disturbing doctrine had already been proclaimed in 2. 18–19 (see note ad loc.) as it had been in the Upanishads: here it is reaffirmed with a vengeance. As the dialogue draws to its end Krishna's thoughts become ever more concentrated on the immediate matter in hand—the successful prosecution of the war.

The Three Constituents again

(*a*) *In Metaphysical Doctrine*

18. *jñānaṁ jñeyaṁ parijñātā tri-vidhā karma-codanā:*
karaṇaṁ karma kart'eti tri-vidhaḥ karma-saṁgrahaḥ.

Knowledge—its object—knower: [these form] the threefold instrumental cause of action. Instrument—action—agent: [such is] action's threefold nexus.

karaṇaṁ, 'instrument': var. *kāraṇaṁ*, 'cause'.

19. *jñānaṁ karma ca kartā ca tridh'aiva guṇa-bhedataḥ*
procyate guṇa-saṁkhyāne, yathāvac chṛṇu tāny api.

Knowledge—action—agent: [these too are] three in kind, distinguished by 'constituent'. The theory of constituents contains it [all]: listen to the manner of these [three].

20. *sarva-bhūteṣu yen'aikaṁ bhāvam avyayam īkṣate*
avibhaktaṁ vibhakteṣu, taj jñānaṁ viddhi sāttvikam.

That [kind of] knowledge by which one sees one mode of being, changeless, undivided in all contingent beings, divided [as they are], is Goodness' [knowledge]. Be sure of this.

avyayam, 'changeless': one MS. has *avyaktam*, 'unmanifest'.
This is the Gītā's consistent metaphysical doctrine: cf. 9. 15: 11. 13: 13. 16, 30.

21. *pṛthaktvena tu yaj jñānaṁ nānā-bhāvān pṛthag-vidhān*
vetti sarveṣu bhūteṣu, taj jñānaṁ viddhi rājasam.

But that [kind of] knowledge which in all contingent beings discerns in separation all manner of modes of being, different and distinct,—this, you must know, is knowledge born of Passion.

22. *yat tu kṛtsnavad ekasmin kārye saktam ahetukam*
atattv'ārthavad alpaṁ ca, tat tāmasam udāhṛtam.

But that [kind of knowledge] which sticks to one effect as if it were all,—irrational, not bothering about the Real as the [true] object [of all knowledge, thinking of it as] finite,—this [knowledge] belongs to Darkness. So is it laid down.

alpaṁ, 'finite': lit. 'small'. For the use of the word meaning 'finite' cf. ChU. 7. 23 where it is contrasted with *bhūman*, the 'plenum or infinite'.

(*b*) *In Works*

23. *niyataṁ saṅga-rahitam arāga-dveṣataḥ kṛtam*
aphala-prepsunā karma yat, tat sāttvikam ucyate.

The work prescribed [by Scripture] from [all] attachment free, performed without passion, without hate, by one who hankers not for fruits, is called [the work] of Goodness.

24. *yat tu kām'epsunā karma s'āhaṁkāreṇa vā punaḥ*
kriyate bahul'āyāsaṁ, tad rājasam udāhṛtam.

But the work in which much effort is expended by one who seeks his own pleasure-and-desire or again thinks, 'It is I who do it', such [work] is assigned to Passion.

'"It is I who do it"': the self or spiritual monad, as we know, is never the agent (13. 29: cf. 3. 27–8: 14. 23).

25. *anubandhaṁ kṣayaṁ hiṁsām anapekṣya ca pauruṣam*
mohād ārabhyate karma yat, tat tāmasam ucyate.

The work embarked on by a man deluded who has no thought of consequence, nor [cares at all] for the loss and hurt [he causes others] or for the human part [he plays himself], is called [a work] of Darkness.

(*c*) *In the Agent*

26. *mukta-saṅgo 'nahaṁ-vādī dhṛty-utsāha-samanvitaḥ*
siddhy-asiddhyor nirvikāraḥ kartā sāttvika ucyate.

The agent who, from attachment freed, steadfast and resolute, remains unchanged in failure and success and never speaks of 'I', is called [an agent] in Goodness' way.

'Unchanged in failure and success': cf. 2. 48: 4. 22.

27. *rāgī karma-phala-prepsur lubdho hiṁs'ātmako 'śuciḥ*
harṣa-śok'ānvitaḥ kartā rājasaḥ parikīrtitaḥ.

The agent who pursues the fruit of works, passionate, greedy, intent on doing harm, impure, a prey to exaltation as to grief, is widely known [to act] in Passion's way.

28. *ayuktaḥ prākṛtaḥ stabdhaḥ śaṭho naikṛtiko 'lasaḥ*
viṣādī dīrgha-sūtrī ca kartā tāmasa ucyate.

The agent, inept and vulgar, stiff-and-proud, a cheat, low-spoken, slothful, who is subject to depression, who procrastinates, is called [an agent] in Darkness' way.

naikṛtiko, 'low-spoken': or, 'dishonest' (R.): Ś. 'intent on breaking up the relationships of others'.

(*d*) *In the Intellect*

29. *buddher bhedaṁ dhṛteś c'aiva guṇatas tri-vidhaṁ śṛṇu*
procyamānam aśeṣeṇa pṛthaktvena, dhanaṁjaya.

Divided threefold too are intellect and constancy according to the constituents. Listen [to Me, for I shall] tell it forth in all its many forms, omitting nothing.

30. *pravṛttiṁ ca nivṛttiṁ ca kāry'ākārye bhay'ābhaye*
bandhaṁ mokṣaṁ ca yā vetti, buddhiḥ sā, Pārtha, sāttvikī.

The intellect that distinguishes between activity and its cessation, between what should be done and what should not, between danger and security, bondage and release, is [an intellect] in Goodness' way.

31. *yayā dharmam adharmaṁ ca kāryaṁ c'ākāryam eva ca*
ayathāvat prajānāti, buddhiḥ sā, Pārtha, rājasī.

The intellect by which lawful-right and lawless wrong, what should be done and what should not, are untruly understood, is [an intellect] in Passion's way.

32. *adharmaṁ dharmam iti yā manyate tamasā 'vṛtā*
sarv'ārthān viparītāṁś ca buddhiḥ, sā, Pārtha, tāmasī.

The intellect which, by Darkness overcast, thinks right is wrong, law lawlessness, all things their opposite, is [an intellect] in Darkness' way.

'All things their opposite': or, 'all things contrary [to truth]'.

(*e*) *In Constancy*

33. *dhṛtyā yayā dhārayate manaḥ-prāṇ'endriya-kriyāḥ*
yogen'āvyabhicāriṇyā, dhṛtiḥ sā, Pārtha, sāttvikī.

The constancy by which a man holds fast in check the works of mind and breath and sense, unswerving in spiritual exercise, is constancy in Goodness' way.

34. *yayā tu dharma-kām'ārthān dhṛtyā dhārayate, 'rjuna,*
prasaṅgena phal'ākāṅkṣī, dhṛtiḥ sā, Pārtha, rājasī.

But the constancy by which a man holds fast [in balance] pleasure, self-interest, and righteousness, yet clings to them, desirous of their fruits, is constancy in Passion's way.

35. *yayā svapnaṁ bhayaṁ śokaṁ viṣādaṁ madam eva ca*
na vimuñcati durmedhā, dhṛtiḥ sā, Pārtha, tāmasī.

[The constancy] by which a fool will not let go sleep, fear, or grief, depression or exaltation, is constancy in Darkness' way.

śokaṁ, 'grief': one MS. has *krodhaṁ*, 'anger'.

madam, 'exaltation, intoxication': one MS. has *moham*, 'delusion'.

(*f*) *In Pleasure*

36. *sukhaṁ tv idānīṁ tri-vidhaṁ śṛṇu me, Bharata'rṣabha,*
abhyāsād ramate yatra duḥkh'āntaṁ ca nigacchati,

Threefold too is pleasure: Arjuna, hear this now from Me. [That pleasure] which a man enjoys after much effort [spent], making an end thereby of suffering,

37. *yat tad agre viṣam iva pariṇāme 'mṛt'opamam*
tat sukhaṁ sāttvikaṁ proktam ātma-buddhi-prasāda-jam.

Which at first seems like poison but in time transmutes itself into what seems to be ambrosia, is called pleasure in Goodness' way, for it springs from that serenity which comes from apperception of the self.

ātma-buddhi-, 'apperception of the self' (so S.): or, 'self (soul) and soul (intellect)', so E.: H., 'his own reason': D., 'der Seele und des Bewußtseins': Ś., 'intellect directed towards self or dependent on self'.

38. *viṣay'endriya-saṁyogād yat tad agre 'mṛt'opamam*
pariṇāme viṣam iva, tat sukhaṁ rājasaṁ smṛtam.

[That pleasure] which at first seems like ambrosia, arising when the senses meet the objects of sense, but in time transmutes itself into what seems to be poison,—that pleasure, so it is said, is in Passion's way.

39. *yad agre c'ānubandhe ca sukhaṁ mohanam ātmanaḥ*
nidr'ālasya-pramād'otthaṁ, tat tāmasam udāhṛtam.

That pleasure which at first and in the sequel leads the self astray, which derives from sleep and sloth and fecklessness, has been declared as [pleasure] in Darkness' way.

40. *na tad asti pṛthivyāṁ vā divi deveṣu vā punaḥ*
sattvaṁ prakṛti-jair muktaṁ yad ebhiḥ syāt tribhir guṇaiḥ.

There is no existent thing in heaven or earth or yet among the gods which is or ever could be free from these three constituents from Nature sprung.

The Four Great Classes of Society

41. *brāhmaṇa-kṣatriya-viśāṁ śūdrāṇāṁ ca, paraṁtapa,*
karmāṇi pravibhaktāni svabhāva-prabhavair guṇaiḥ.

To Brāhmans, princes, peasants-and-artisans, and serfs works have been variously assigned by [these] constituents, and they arise from the nature of things as they are.

According to Ś. Brāhmans originate from Goodness, princes (and warriors) from Passion mixed with Goodness, peasants and artisans from Passion mixed with Darkness, serfs from Darkness with a small admixture of Passion. One's caste is preconditioned by former lives (R.).

42. *śamo damas tapaḥ śaucaṁ kṣāntir ārjavam eva ca*
jñānaṁ vijñānam āstikyaṁ brahma-karma svabhāva-jam.

Calm, self-restraint, ascetic practice, purity, long-suffering and uprightness, wisdom in theory as in practice, religious faith,—[these] are the works of Brāhmans, inhering in their nature.

jñānaṁ vijñānam, 'wisdom in theory as in practice': see 7. 2 n.

43. *śauryaṁ tejo dhṛtir dākṣyaṁ yuddhe c'āpy apalāyanam*
dānam īśvara-bhāvaś ca kṣātraṁ karma svabhāva-jam.

High courage, ardour, endurance, skill, in battle unwillingness to flee, an open hand, a lordly mien,—[these] are the works of princes, inhering in their nature [too].

44. *kṛṣi-gaurakṣya-vāṇijyaṁ vaiśya-karma svabhāva-jam,*
paricary'ātmakaṁ karma śūdrasy'āpi svabhāva-jam.

To till the fields, protect the kine, and engage in trade, [these] are the works of peasants-and-artisans, inhering in their nature; but works whose very soul is service inhere in the very nature of the serf.

45. *sve sve karmaṇy abhirataḥ saṁsiddhiṁ labhate naraḥ:*
sva-karma-nirataḥ siddhiṁ yathā vindati tac chṛṇu.

By [doing] the work that is proper to him [and] rejoicing [in the doing], a man succeeds, perfects himself. [Now] hear just how a man perfects himself by [doing and] rejoicing in his proper work.

46. *yataḥ pravṛttir bhūtānāṁ, yena sarvam idaṁ tatam,*
sva-karmaṇā tam abhyarcya siddhiṁ vindati mānavaḥ.

By dedicating the work that is proper [to his caste] to Him who is the source of the activity of all beings, by whom this whole universe was spun, a man attains perfection-and-success.

'By dedicating . . .': cf. 3. 30: 'Cast all your works on Me, your thoughts [withdrawn] in what appertains to self; have neither hope nor thought that "this is mine".' The same command is repeated in 12. 6 as being both an easier and a more fruitful way of attaining liberation than revering 'the indeterminate Imperishable Unmanifest . . . sublime, aloof, unmoving, firm'. In 5. 10 Brahman, there meaning material Nature as in 14. 3, takes the place of the personal God.

'By whom this whole universe was spun (or pervaded)': the phrase first occurred in 2. 17 where it was applied to the neuter principle, Brahman. It is repeated in 8. 22 where it is used of 'that highest Person' who 'is to be won by love-and-worship directed to none other' and 'in [whom] all beings subsist'. In 9. 4 this 'highest Person', 'Unmanifest in form', is identified with Krishna himself, and Arjuna confesses this when he is privileged to see Krishna in his universal form (11. 38). Hence, once again, Krishna repeats his claim to be the author of all phenomenal existence and as such the only real agent. What is new, however, is that He picks out the performance of caste duty as being perhaps the only perfectly acceptable worship of Himself because He is the author of the ancient social system which divides men into the four classes of Brāhmans, princely warriors, peasants and artisans, and serfs (4. 13). To do one's duty in accordance with the state into which one is born is to conform to the will of God: hence Arjuna must go to war.

47. *śreyān sva-dharmo viguṇaḥ para-dharmāt svanuṣṭhitāt:*
svabhāva-niyataṁ karma kurvan n'āpnoti kilbiṣam.

Better [to do] one's own [caste-] duty, though devoid of merit, than [to do] another's, however well performed. By doing the work prescribed by his own nature a man meets with no defilement.

The duty to remain within the state of life into which one was born had been laid down at a very early stage in the Gītā (3. 35): 'Better one's own duty [to perform], though void of merit, than to do another's well: better to die within [the sphere of] one's own duty: perilous is the duty of other men.' As we saw in the last stanza, to do one's duty in the social station to which one is born is equivalent to worshipping God.

48. *sahajaṁ karma, Kaunteya, sadoṣam api na tyajet,*
sarv'ārambhā hi doṣeṇa dhūmen'āgnir iv'āvṛtāḥ.

Never should a man give up the work to which he is born, defective though it be: for every enterprise is choked by defects, as fire by smoke.

This sums up Krishna's whole teaching on action last clearly enunciated in 18. 6. It had already formed the main teaching of Chapters III and IV.

'Becoming Brahman'

49. *asakta-buddhiḥ sarvatra jit'ātmā vigata-spṛhaḥ*
naiṣkarmya-siddhiṁ paramāṁ saṁnyāsen'ādhigacchati.

With soul detached from everything, with self subdued, [all] longing gone, renounce: and so you will find complete success, perfection, works transcended.

'With soul detached from everything': that is, from all outside objects. Cf. 5. 21: '[His] self detached from contacts with the outside world, in [him]self he finds his joy, [his] self in Brahman integrated by spiritual exercise, he finds unfailing joy.'

'With self subdued': cf. 6. 7: 'The higher self of the self-subdued, quietened, is rapt in enstasy—in cold as in heat, in pleasure as in pain, likewise in honour and disgrace.' The 'self' that is subdued is, of course, the 'carnal' self which 'for the man bereft of self will act as an enemy indeed' (6. 6).

naiṣkarmya-siddhiṁ, 'complete success, perfection, works transcended': *naiṣkarmya*, as we have seen, is the Buddhist *nekkhamma*, 'passionlessness' (3. 4 n.). This Buddhist 'perfection' is not yet even to 'become Brahman', let alone to enter God (18. 55).

50. *siddhiṁ prāpto yathā brahma tath'āpnoti nibodha me*
samāsen'aiva, Kaunteya, niṣṭhā jñānasya yā parā.

Perfection found, now learn from Me how you may reach Brahman too: [this I will tell you] briefly; it is wisdom's highest bourne.

jñānasya, 'wisdom's': var. *dhyānasya*, 'meditation's'. The highest bourne of wisdom is the 'fixed, still state of Brahman' (2. 72): supplemented by the 'highest love-and-loyalty' (*bhakti*) it leads to the personal God himself.

51. *buddhyā viśuddhayā yukto dhṛtyā 'tmānaṁ niyamya ca*
śabdādīn viṣayāṁs tyaktvā rāga-dveṣau vyudasya ca,

Let a man be integrated by his soul [now] cleansed, let him restrain [him]self with constancy, abandon objects of sense,—sound and all the rest,—passion and hate let him cast out;

buddhyā . . . yukto, 'integrated by his soul': this was Krishna's very first practical teaching developed in 2. 39–72: it brings release from the 'bondage of works'.

viśuddhayā, '[with soul now] cleansed': the soul or contemplative intellect is not easily distinguished from the 'higher self' in the Gītā. So in 5. 7 it is the self that must be cleansed in order that it may become 'the [very] self of every contingent being'. So too in 5. 11 attachment is renounced 'for the cleansing of the self' and in 6. 12 the spiritual exercise of integration is performed to obtain the same result.

'Passion and hate': these have their seat in the senses and are 'brigands on the road' (3. 34).

52. *vivikta-sevī laghv'-āśī yata-vāk-kāya-mānasaḥ*
dhyāna-yoga-paro nityaṁ vairāgyaṁ samupāśritaḥ,

Let him live apart, eat lightly, restrain speech, body, and mind; let him practise meditation constantly, let him cultivate dispassion;

'Let him live apart': cf. 6. 10: 'Let the athlete of the spirit ever integrate [him]self standing in a place apart, alone'.

'Eat lightly': cf. 6. 16–17: '[This] spiritual exercise is not for him who eats too much, nor yet for him who does not eat at all . . . [Rather] it is . . . for him who knows-the-mean in food.'

'Restrain speech, body, and mind': cf. 6. 12: 'Let him restrain the operations of his thought and senses.'

dhyāna-yoga-, 'practice of meditation': Ś. takes this compound to mean 'meditation *and* Yoga' and interprets the latter term as meaning 'one-pointed meditation on the self'.

vairāgyaṁ, 'dispassion': for the Buddhists 'dispassion' was synonymous with Nirvāna.

53. *ahaṁkāraṁ balaṁ darpaṁ kāmaṁ krodhaṁ parigraham*
vimucya nirmamaḥ śānto brahma-bhūyāya kalpate.

Let him give up all thought of 'I', force, pride, desire and anger and possessiveness, let him not think of anything as 'mine', at peace;—[if he does this,] to becoming Brahman is he conformed.

'Let him give up . . . anger': this is taken from 16. 18 where these qualities are said to characterize the 'vilest among men' (16. 19) who are destined to go to hell.

'Let him give up all thought of "I" . . ., let him not think of anything as "mine" ': taken from 2. 71 (repeated 12. 13).

'Desire and anger': the basic sins. Cf. 3. 37: 'Desire it is: Anger it is—arising from the constituent of Passion—all devouring, mightily wicked, know that this is [your] enemy on earth.' Together with greed they are the 'triple gate of hell' (16. 21).

'To becoming Brahman is he conformed': cf. 14. 26.

From Brahman to God

54. *brahma-bhūtaḥ prasann'ātmā na śocati, na kāṅkṣati,*
samaḥ sarveṣu bhūteṣu mad-bhaktiṁ labhate parām.

Brahman become, with self serene, he grieves not nor desires; the same to all contingent beings he gains the highest love-and-loyalty to Me.

'Brahman become': this is the same as to achieve the 'fixed, still state of Brahman' and the 'Nirvāna that is Brahman too' (2. 72), which 'fares around' such men who have 'become Brahman' (5. 24–6) and which 'subsists in' God (6. 15). To achieve such a state does not mean to lose sight of the personal God: 'For him I am not lost, nor is he lost to Me' (6. 30), for Krishna is the 'base supporting Brahman' both as it manifests itself in the outside world and as the still centre of the liberated self (14. 27).

na kāṅkṣati, 'nor desires': var. *na hṛṣyati*, 'nor rejoices'.

'The same to all contingent beings': or, 'the same in all contingent beings' as God is (13. 27: 9. 29), since, now that he has 'become Brahman', he has 'become the [very] self of every contingent being' (5. 7), like Brahman 'ever the same' (5. 19). In practical living this means that he will show partiality to none, he will be 'the same to friend and foe, [the same] whether he be respected or despised, the same in heat and cold, in pleasure as in pain' (12. 18: cf. 2. 38, 48: 4. 22), and he will see the selfsame thing 'in a Brāhman wise and courteous as in a cow or in an elephant, nay, as in a dog or outcaste' (5. 18).

'He gains the highest love-and-loyalty to Me': this highest *bhakti* is, then, only bestowed *after* the man has 'become Brahman'. *Bhakti* is, of course, possible at all stages and, at the lower level, helps towards the winning of liberation (9. 26–8). On the highest level, however, it perfects liberation itself. The man who has reached this stage, according to R., counts all things as straw except God.

55. *bhaktyā mām abhijānāti yāvān yaś c'āsmi tattvataḥ;*
tato māṁ tattvato jñātvā viśate tad-anantaram.

By love-and-loyalty he comes to know Me as I really am, how great I am and who; and once he knows Me as I am, he enters [Me] forthwith.

'Forthwith': this, as R. reasonably points out, shows that this 'knowledge' of God is subsequent to the knowledge of self as Brahman. To 'enter' God means to possess Him in his fullness.

56. *sarva-karmāṇy api sadā kurvāṇo mad-vyapāśrayaḥ*
mat-prasādād avāpnoti śāśvataṁ padam avyayam.

Let him then do all manner of works continually, putting his trust in Me; for by my grace he will attain to an eternal, changeless state.

'An eternal, changeless state': this, according to R., means God. What the Gītā appears to mean, however, is that the man who has 'become Brahman' and entered God now enjoys his timeless eternity in union with God by means of love (cf. 18. 64). At this point Krishna finishes his general teaching and from verse 57 to 66 He applies this general teaching to the particular, personal case of Arjuna.

Arjuna's Personal Case

57. *cetasā sarva-karmāṇi mayi saṁnyasya mat-paraḥ*
buddhi-yogam upāśritya mac-cittaḥ satataṁ bhava.

Give up in thought to Me all that you do, make Me your goal: relying on the integration of the soul, think on Me constantly.

'Give up in thought to Me all that you do': cf. 3. 30: 'Cast all your works on Me, your thoughts [withdrawn] in what appertains to self.' The difference between the two passages is obvious: in the earlier the object of meditation is the sphere of the self because that self had not yet 'become Brahman'; here the object of contemplation can only be God who is the 'base supporting Brahman' (14. 27).

'Integration of the soul': since the soul has now been purified of all earthly taint (18. 51). One MS. has *śuddhi-yogam*, 'integration in purity'.

58. *mac-cittaḥ sarva-durgāṇi mat-prasādāt tariṣyasi;*
atha cet tvam ahaṁkārān na śroṣyasi vinaṅkṣyasi.

Thinking on Me you will surmount all dangers by my grace; but if through selfishness you will not listen, then will you [surely] perish.

-durgāṇi, 'dangers': var. *-duḥkhāni*, 'sorrows'; *karmāṇi*, 'works'.

ahaṁkārān, 'through selfishness': the 'selfishness' in question is the illusion that it is the ego and not the constituents of Nature which acts. So 3. 27: 'It is material Nature's [three] constituents that do all works wherever [works are done]; [but] he whose self is by the ego fooled thinks, "It is I who do".' The highest love and loyalty to God means not only a union at the ontological level, to 'become Brahman', but also the willing and joyous conforming of one's own will to the will of God. Failure to do this will, in any case, make no difference to the outcome as the following stanzas show.

na śroṣyasi, 'you will not listen': var. *na mokṣyasi*, 'you will not achieve liberation'.

59. *yad ahaṁkāram āśritya na yotsya iti manyase,*
mithy' aiṣa vyavasāyas te, prakṛtis tvāṁ niyokṣyati.

[But if,] relying on your ego, you should think, 'I will not fight', vain is your resolve, [for] Nature will constrain you.

'Nature': either in general operating through the constituents (3. 27: 14. 23, etc.), or Arjuna's nature as it has developed in past lives (18. 41–4 and the stanza that immediately follows here).

60. *svabhāva-jena, Kaunteya, nibaddhaḥ svena karmaṇā*
kartuṁ n'ecchasi yan mohāt, kariṣyasy avaśo 'pi tat.

You are bound by your own works which spring from your own nature; [for] what, deluded, you would not do you will do perforce.

61. *īśvaraḥ sarva-bhūtānāṁ hṛd-deśe, 'rjuna, tiṣṭhati*
bhrāmayan sarva-bhūtāni yantr' ārūḍhāni māyayā.

In the region of the heart of all contingent beings dwells the Lord, twirling them hither and thither by his uncanny power [like puppets] mounted on a machine.

'In the region of the heart . . .': cf. 15. 15. God indwells human beings both as the 'fixed, still state of Brahman' and as the principle of all activity (*māyā*). He is the cause of damnation as much as of salvation (cf. 16. 19). Moreover, his creative activity distracts from the contemplation of his eternal Being: '[All] this is my creative power (*māyā*) composed of the constituents, divine, hard to transcend. Whoso shall put his trust in Me alone, shall pass beyond this [my] uncanny power (*māyā*)' (7. 14).

62. *tam eva śaraṇaṁ gaccha sarva-bhāvena, Bhārata;*
tat-prasādāt parāṁ śāntiṁ sthānaṁ prāpsyasi śāśvatam.

In Him alone seek refuge with all your being, all your love; and by his grace you will attain an eternal state, the highest peace.

sarva-bhāvena, 'with all your being, all your love': *bhāva* means both 'being' and 'love'. Both senses are implied.

śāntiṁ, 'peace': var. *siddhiṁ*, 'success, perfection'.

63. *iti te jñānam ākhyātaṁ guhyād guhyataraṁ mayā:*
vimṛśy' aitad aśeṣeṇa yath' ecchasi tathā kuru.

Of all the mysteries the most mysterious, this wisdom have I told you; ponder it in all its amplitude, then do whatever you will.

jñānam, 'wisdom': var. *dhyānam*, 'meditation'.

'I love you Well'

64. *sarva-guhyatamaṁ bhūyaḥ śṛṇu me paramaṁ vacaḥ:*
iṣṭo 'si me dṛḍham iti, tato vakṣyāmi te hitam.

And now again give ear to this my highest Word, of all the most mysterious: 'I love you well.' Therefore will I tell you your salvation.

iṣṭo 'si, 'I love you well': one MS. has *dṛṣṭo 'si*, 'I see you'.

65. *man-manā bhava mad-bhakto mad-yājī, māṁ namas-kuru:*
mām ev' aiṣyasi, satyaṁ te pratijāne, priyo 'si me.

Bear Me in mind, love Me and worship Me, sacrifice, prostrate yourself to Me: so will you come to Me, I promise you truly, for you are dear to Me.

'Dear to Me': the man whom God loves was described in 12. 13–20: he is totally detached from worldly things and totally devoted to God.

66. *sarva-dharmān parityajya mām ekaṁ śaraṇaṁ vraja:*
ahaṁ tvā sarva-pāpebhyo mokṣayiṣyāmi, mā śucaḥ.

Give up all things of law, turn to Me, your only refuge, [for] I will deliver you from all evils; have no care.

-dharmān, 'things of law': according to Ś. this refers both to what is lawful and to what is unlawful. The liberated man is emancipated from

'the bonds of both law and lawlessness'. R. says that this means that one should concentrate on God alone as creator, the worshipful, the goal, and the means by which the goal is achieved.

The Supreme Value of the Teaching of the Gītā

67. *idaṁ te n'ātapaskāya n'ābhaktāya kadācana*
na c'āśuśrūṣave vācyaṁ na ca māṁ yo 'bhyasūyati.

Never must you tell this word to one whose life is not austere, to one devoid of love-and-loyalty, to one who refuses to obey, or to one who envies Me.

68. *ya idaṁ paramaṁ guhyaṁ mad-bhakteṣv abhidhāsyati*
bhaktiṁ mayi parāṁ kṛtvā, mām ev'aiṣyaty asaṁśayaḥ.

[But] whoever shall proclaim this highest mystery to my loving devotees, showing the while the highest love-and-loyalty to Me, shall, nothing doubting, come to Me indeed.

asaṁśayaḥ, 'nothing doubting': var. *asaṁśayam*, 'without doubt'.

69. *na ca tasmān manuṣyeṣu kaścin me priya-kṛttamaḥ*
bhavitā na ca me tasmād anyaḥ priyataro bhuvi.

No one among men can render Me more pleasing service than a man like this; nor shall any other man on earth be more beloved by Me than he.

70. *adhyeṣyate ca ya imaṁ dharmyaṁ saṁvādam āvayoḥ*
jñāna-yajñena ten'āham iṣṭaḥ syām iti me matiḥ.

And whoso should read this dialogue which you and I have held concerning what is right, it will be as if he had offered Me a sacrifice of wisdom: so do I believe.

71. *śraddhāvān anasūyaś ca śṛṇuyād api yo naraḥ,*
so 'pi muktaḥ śubhāṁl lokān prāpnuyāt puṇya-karmaṇām.

And the man of faith, not cavilling, who listens [to this my Word], he too shall win deliverance, and attain to the goodly worlds of those whose works are pure.

muktaḥ, 'shall win deliverance': scarcely 'liberation' in the technical sense of the final release from *saṁsāra*, freedom from the round of birth and death, since the 'goodly worlds' or heavens themselves belong to the world of *saṁsāra*. Ś. interprets the word as meaning deliverance from evil, R. as deliverance from the 'evils that obstruct loving devotion'.

72. *kaccid etac chrutaṁ, Pārtha, tvay' aik' āgreṇa cetasā,*
kaccid ajñāna-saṁmohaḥ praṇaṣṭas te, dhanaṁjaya ?

Have you listened, Arjuna, [to these my words] with a mind intent on them alone? And has the confusion [of your mind] that stemmed from ignorance been dispelled?

Arjuna uvāca:

73. *naṣṭo mohaḥ, smṛtir labdhā tvat-prasādān mayā, 'cyuta:*
sthito 'smi gata-saṁdehaḥ, kariṣye vacanaṁ tava.

Arjuna said:

Destroyed is the confusion; and through your grace I have regained a proper way of thinking: with doubts dispelled I stand ready to do your bidding.

Epilogue

Saṁjaya uvāca:

74. *ity ahaṁ Vāsudevasya Pārthasya ca mah' ātmanaḥ*
saṁvādam imam aśrauṣam adbhutaṁ roma-harṣaṇam.

Sanjaya said:

So did I hear this wondrous dialogue of [Krishna,] Vasudeva's son, and the high-souled Arjuna, [and as I listened] I shuddered with delight.

75. *Vyāsa-prasādāc chrutavān etad guhyam ahaṁ param*
yogaṁ yog' eśvarāt Kṛṣṇāt sākṣāt kathayataḥ svayam.

By Vyāsa's favour have I heard this highest mystery, this spiritual exercise from Krishna, the Lord of spiritual exercise himself as He in person told it.

'Vyāsa': the sage, reputedly the author of the MBh., who had given Sanjaya the divine power to hear the Gītā and see the transfigured Krishna.

76. *rājan, saṁsmṛtya saṁsmṛtya saṁvādam imam adbhutam*
Keśav' ārjunayoḥ puṇyaṁ hṛṣyāmi ca muhur muhuḥ.

O King, as often as I recall this marvellous, holy dialogue of Arjuna and Krishna, I thrill with joy, and thrill with joy again.

77. *tac ca saṁsmṛtya saṁsmṛtya rūpam atyadbhutaṁ Hareḥ*
vismayo me mahān, rājan, hṛṣyāmi ca punaḥ punaḥ.

And as often as I recall that form of Vishnu,—so utterly marvellous,—how great is my amazement! I thrill with joy, and thrill with joy again.

78. *yatra yog'eśvaraḥ Kṛṣṇo, yatra Pārtho dhanur-dharaḥ,*
tatra śrīr vijayo bhūtir dhruvā nītir, matir mama.

Wherever Krishna is, the Lord of spiritual exercise, wherever Arjuna, holder of the bow, there is good fortune, victory, success, sound policy assured. This do I believe.

APPENDIX

I. *The Individual Self*

(*a*) *Self as it is in itself*

2. 16–25: Of what is not there is no becoming; of what is there is no ceasing to be: for the boundary-line between the two is seen by men who see things as they really are. (17) Yes, indestructible [alone] is That, —know this,—by which this whole universe was spun. . . . (18) Finite, they say, are these [our] bodies [indwelt] by an eternal embodied [self], —[for this self is] indestructible, incommensurable. . . . (19) Who thinks this [self] can be a slayer, who thinks that it can be slain, both these have no [right] knowledge: it does not slay nor is it slain. (20) Never is it born nor dies; never did it come to be nor will it ever come to be again: unborn, eternal, everlasting is this [self],—primeval. It is not slain when the body is slain. (21) If a man knows it as indestructible, eternal, unborn, never to pass away, how and whom can it cause to be slain or slay? . . . (23) Weapons do not cut it nor does fire burn it, the waters do not wet it nor does the wind dry it. (24) Uncuttable, unburnable, unwettable, undryable it is,—eternal, roving everywhere, firm-set, unmoved, primeval. (25) Unmanifest, unthinkable, immutable is it called: then realize it thus and do not grieve [about it].

2. 29–30: By a rare privilege may someone behold it, and by a rare privilege indeed may another tell of it, and by a rare privilege may such another hear it, yet even having heard there is none that knows it. (30) Never can this embodied [self] be slain in the body by anyone [at all]: and so you have no need to grieve for any contingent being.

2. 55: When a man puts from him all desires that prey upon the mind, himself contented in self alone, then is he called a man of steady wisdom.

2. 64: But he who roves among the objects of sense, his senses subdued to self and disjoined from passion and hate, and who is self-possessed [himself], draws nigh to calm serenity.

3. 17–18: Nay, let a man take pleasure in self alone, in self his satisfaction find, in self alone content: [for then] there is naught he needs to do. (18) In works done and works undone on earth he has no interest,—no [interest] in all contingent beings: on such interest he does not depend.

3. 42–3: Exalted are the senses, or so they say; higher than the senses is the mind; yet higher than the mind the soul: what is beyond the soul is he (the self). (43) So know him who is yet higher than the soul, and make firm [this] self yourself. . . .

4. 35: . . . By [knowing] this you will behold [all] beings in [your]self,—every one of them,—and then in Me.

5. 7: Wellversed in spiritual exercise, his self made pure, his self and senses quelled, his self become the [very] self of every contingent being, though working still, he is not defiled.

5. 13–17. All works renouncing with the mind, quietly he sits in full control,—the embodied [self] within the city with nine gates: he neither works nor makes another work. (14) Neither agency nor worldly works does [the body's] lord engender, nor yet the bond that work to fruit conjoins: it is inherent Nature that initiates the action. (15) He takes not on the good and evil works of anyone at all,—[that] all-pervading lord. . . . (16) But some there are whose ignorance of self by wisdom is destroyed. Their wisdom, like the sun, illumines that [all-]highest. (17) Souls [bent on] that, selves [bent on] that, with that their aim and that their aspiration, they stride [along the path] from which there is no return, [all] taints by wisdom washed away.

5. 21: [His] self detached from contacts with the outside world, in [him]self he finds his joy, [his] self in Brahman integrated by spiritual exercise, he finds unfailing joy.

5. 25–6: Nirvāna that is Brahman too win seers in whom [all] taint-of-imperfection is destroyed; their doubts dispelled, with self controlled, they take their pleasure in the weal of all contingent beings. (26) Around these holy men whose thoughts are [fast] controlled, estranged from anger and desire, knowing [at last] the self, fares Nirvāna that is Brahman too.

6. 5–6: (The two selves, see I (*b*)).

6. 7–9: The higher self of the self-subdued, quietened, is rapt in enstasy,—in cold as in heat, in pleasure as in pain, likewise in honour and disgrace. (8) With self content in wisdom learnt from holy books and wisdom learnt from life, with sense subdued, sublime, aloof, [this] athlete of the spirit [stands]: 'Integrated', so is he called; the same to him are clods of earth, stones, gold. (9) Outstanding is he whose soul views in the selfsame way friends, comrades, enemies, those indifferent, neutrals, men who are hateful and those who are his kin,—the good and the evil too.

6. 18–29: When thought, held well in check, is stilled in self alone, then is a man from longing freed though all desires assail him: then do men

call him 'integrated'. (19) As a lamp might stand in a windless place, unflickering,—this likeness has been heard of such athletes of the spirit who control their thought and practise integration of the self. (20) When thought by {the practice of integration / spiritual exercise} is checked and comes to rest, and when of [one]self one sees the self in self and finds content therein, (21) that is the utmost joy which transcends [all things of] sense and which soul [alone] can grasp. When he knows this and [knowing it] stands still, moving not an inch from the reality [he sees], (22) he wins a prize beyond all others,—or so he thinks. Therein he [firmly] stands, unmoved by any suffering, however grievous it may be. . . . (25) By soul held fast in steadfastness he must make the mind [too] subsist in the self; then little by little will he come to rest; he must think of nothing at all. (26) Wherever the fickle mind unsteady roves around, from thence [the soul] will bring it back and subject it to the self. . . . (28) [And] thus [all] flaws transcending, the athlete of the spirit, constant in integrating [him]self, with ease attains unbounded joy, Brahman's [saving] touch. (29) With self integrated by spiritual exercise [now] he sees the self in all beings standing, all beings in the self: the same in everything he sees.

13. 19–21: 'Nature' and 'Person': know that these two are both beginningless: and know that change and quality arise from Nature. (20) Material Nature, they say, is [itself] the cause of cause, effect, and agency, while 'person' is said to be the cause in the experience of pleasure and of pain. (21) For 'person' is lodged in material Nature, experiencing the 'constituents' that arise from it; because he attaches himself to these he comes to birth in good and evil wombs.

13. 24: By meditation some themselves see self in self, others by putting sound reason into practice, yet others by the exercise of works.

13. 29: Nature it is which in every way does-work-and-acts; no agent is the self.

14. 5: Goodness—Passion—Darkness: these are the [three] constituents from Nature sprung that bind the embodied [self] in the body though [the self itself] is changeless.

14. 20: Transcending these three constituents which give the body its existence, from the sufferings of birth, death, and old age delivered, the embodied [self] wins immortality.

15. 7: In the world of living things a minute part of Me, eternal [still], becomes a living [self], drawing to itself the five senses and the mind which have their roots in Nature.

15. 10–11: Whether [the self] rise up [from the body] or remain [therein], or whether, through contact with the constituents, he tastes experience, fools do not perceive him, but whoso possesses wisdom's eye sees him [indeed]. (11) And athletes of the spirit, fighting the good fight, see him established in [them]selves; not so the men whose self is unperfected, however much they strive, witless, they see him not.

18. 16–17: . . . The man who sees self isolated [in itself] as the agent, does not see [at all]. Untrained is his intelligence and evil are his thoughts. (17) A man who has reached a state where there is no sense of 'I', whose soul is undefiled,—were he to slaughter [all] these worlds,—slays nothing. He is not bound.

18. 36–7: . . . [That pleasure] which a man enjoys after much effort [spent], making an end thereby of suffering, (37) which at first seems like poison but in time transmutes itself into what seems to be ambrosia, is called pleasure in Goodness' way, for it springs from that serenity which comes from apperception of the self.

18. 49–54: With soul detached from everything, with self subdued, [all] longing gone, renounce. . . . (53) . . . [if he does this,] to becoming Brahman is he conformed. (54) Brahman become, with self serene, he grieves not nor desires; the same to all contingent beings he gains the highest love-and-loyalty to Me.

(*b*) *The Transmigrating Self*

2. 12–14: Never was there a time when I was not, nor you, nor yet these princes, nor will there be a time when we shall cease to be,—all of us hereafter. (13) Just as in this body the embodied [self] must pass through childhood, youth, and old age, so too [at death] will it assume another body: in this a thoughtful man is not perplexed. (14) But contacts with the objects of sense give rise to heat and cold, pleasure and pain: they come and go, impermanent. Put up with them [then], Arjuna.

2. 22: As a man casts off his worn-out clothes and takes on other new ones, so does the embodied [self] cast off its worn-out bodies and enters other new ones.

2. 26–8: And even if you think that it is constantly [re-]born and constantly [re-]dies, even so you grieve for it in vain. (27) For sure is the death of all that is born, sure is the birth of all that dies: so in a matter that no one can prevent you have no cause to grieve. (28) Unmanifest are the beginnings of contingent beings, manifest their middle course, unmanifest again their ends: what cause for mourning here?

3. 40: Sense, mind, and soul, they say, are the places where lurks [desire]; through these it smothers wisdom, fooling the embodied [self].

4. 5: Many a birth have I passed through, and [many a birth] have you: I know them all but you do not.

4. 40: The man, unwise, devoid of faith, of doubting self, must perish: this world is not for the man of doubting self, nor the next [world] nor yet happiness.

5. 7: Well-versed in spiritual exercise, his self made pure, his self and senses quelled, his self become the [very] self of every contingent being, though working still, he is not defiled.

5. 11: With body, mind, soul, and senses alone-and-isolated [from the self] do men engaged in spiritual exercise engage in action renouncing attachment for the cleansing of the self.

5. 25: Nirvāna that is Brahman too win seers in whom [all] taint-of-imperfection is destroyed; their doubts dispelled, with self controlled, they take their pleasure in the weal of all contingent beings.

6. 5–6: (The two selves): Raise self by self, let not the self droop down; for self's friend is self indeed, so too is self self's enemy. (6) Self is the friend to the self of him whose self is by the self subdued; but for the man bereft of self self will act as an enemy indeed.

6. 10: Let the athlete of the spirit ever integrate [him]self . . . his thoughts and self restrained.

6. 12: . . . Let him restrain the operations of his thought and senses and practise integration to purify the self.

6. 14–15: Let him sit, [his] self all stilled, his fear all gone, . . . his mind controlled, his thoughts on Me, integrated, [yet] intent on Me. (15) Thus let the athlete of the spirit be constant in integrating [him]self, his mind restrained; then will he approach that peace which has Nirvāna as its end and which subsists in Me.

6. 37–45: (Arjuna:) [Suppose] a man of faith should strive in vain, his restless mind shying away from spiritual exercise: he fails to win the perfect prize of integration,—what path does he tread [then? . . . (40) (The Blessed Lord:) Not in this world nor in the next is such a man destroyed-or-lost: for no doer of fair works will tread an evil path, my friend, no, none whatever. (41) The worlds of doers of good works he'll win and dwell there countless years: and then will he be born again, this man who failed in spiritual exercise, in the house of holy men by fortune blest. (42) Or else he will be born in a family of men well-advanced-in-spiritual-exercise, possessed of insight; but such a birth as this on earth is yet harder to obtain. (43) There is he united with the soul as it had matured in his former body; and once again he strives to win perfection's prize. (44) By [the force of] that same struggle he had waged in former times he is carried away though helpless [of himself]; for even he who only wants to know what integration is, transcends that 'Brahman' which is [no more than] wordy rites. (45) But cleansed of taint [that] athlete of the spirit strives on with utmost zeal, through many, many births [at last] perfected; and then the highest path he treads.

14. 5–8: Goodness—Passion—Darkness: these are the [three] constituents from Nature sprung that bind the embodied [self] in the body though [the self itself] is changeless. (6) Among these Goodness, being immaculate, knowing no sickness, dispenses light, [and yet] it binds by [causing the self] to cling to wisdom and to joy. (7) Passion is instinct with desire, [this] know. From craving and attachment it wells up. It binds the embodied [self] by [causing it] to cling to works. (8) But from ignorance is Darkness born: mark [this] well. All embodied [selves] it leads astray. With fecklessness and sloth and sleepiness it binds.

15. 7–10: In the world of living things a minute part of Me, eternal [still], becomes a living [self], drawing to itself the five senses and the mind which have their roots in Nature. (8) When [this] sovereign [self] takes on a body and when he rises up therefrom, he takes them [with him] and moves on as the wind [wafts] scents away from their proper home. (9) Ear, eye, touch, taste, and smell he turns to due account,—so too the mind; [with these] he moves along the objects of sense. (10) Whether he rise up [from the body] or remain [therein], or whether, through contact with the constituents, he tastes experience, fools do not perceive him, but whoso possesses wisdom's eye sees him [indeed].

II. (*a*) *Material Nature*

(i) *Cosmic*

4. 6: . . . By my creative energy (*māyā*) I consort with Nature—which is mine—and come to be [in time].

7. 4–6: Eightfold divided is my Nature,—thus: earth, water, fire and air, space, mind, and also soul,—and the ego. (5) This is the lower: but other than this I have a higher Nature; this too must you know. [And this is Nature] developed into life by which this world is kept in being. (6) To all beings these [two Natures] are [as] a womb; be very sure of this. Of this whole universe the origin and the dissolution too am I.

7. 14–15: For [all] this [Nature] is my creative power (*māyā*), composed of the constituents, divine, hard to transcend. Whoso shall put his trust in Me alone, shall pass beyond this [my] uncanny power (*māyā*). (15) Doers of evil, deluded, base, put not their trust in Me; their wisdom swept away by [this] uncanny power, they cleave to a devilish mode of existence.

8. 15–16: . . . [Rebirth is] the abode of suffering, knows nothing that abides. . . . (16) The worlds right up to Brahmā's realm [dissolve and] evolve again.

8. 17–19: For a thousand ages lasts [one] day of Brahmā, and for a thousand ages [one such] night. . . . (18) At the day's dawning all things manifest spring forth from the Unmanifest; and then at nightfall they dissolve [again] in that same thing called 'Unmanifest'. (19) Yes, this whole host of beings comes ever anew to be; at the fall of night it dissolves away all helpless; at dawn of day it rises up again.

9. 8: Subduing my own material Nature ever again I emanate this whole host of beings,—powerless [themselves], from Nature comes the power.

9. 10: [A world of] moving and unmoving things material Nature brings to birth while I look-on-and-supervise: this is the cause [and this the means] by which the world revolves.

9. 33: . . . This world, impermanent and joyless, . . .

13. 1. The body is called the 'field'. . . .

13. 5–6: Gross elements, the ego, intellect, the Unmanifest, the eleven senses, and the five [sense-objects] on which the senses thrive, (6) desire, hate, pleasure, pain, *sensus communis*, thought and constancy,—these, in briefest span, are called the field together with their changes.

13. 19–21: 'Nature' and 'Person': know that these two are both beginningless: and know that change and quality arise from Nature. (20) Material Nature, they say, is [itself] the cause of cause, effect, and agency, while 'person' is said to be the cause in the experience of pleasure and of pain. (21) For 'person' is lodged in material Nature, experiencing the 'constituents' that arise from it; because he attaches himself to these he comes to birth in good and evil wombs.

13. 26: Whatever being comes to be, be it motionless or moving, [derives its being] from the union of 'field' and 'knower of the field'.

13. 29: Nature it is which in every way does-work-and-acts; no agent is the self.

13. 34: Whoso . . . knows deliverance from material Nature to which [all] contingent beings are subject goes to the further [shore].

15. 1–3: With roots above and boughs beneath, they say, the undying fig-tree [stands]: its leaves are the Vedic hymns: who knows it knows the Veda. (2) Below, above, its branches straggle out, well nourished by the constituents; sense-objects are the twigs. Below its roots proliferate inseparably linked with works in the world of men. (3) No form of it can here be comprehended, no end and no beginning, no sure abiding-place: this fig-tree with its roots so fatly nourished—[take] the stout axe of detachment and cut it down!

(ii) *Individual*

2. 18: Finite, they say, are these [our] bodies [indwelt] by an eternal embodied [self].

5. 14: Neither agency nor worldly works does [the body's] lord engender, nor yet the bond that work to fruit conjoins: it is inherent Nature that initiates the action.

7. 20: [All] wisdom swept away by manifold desires, men put their trust in other gods . . .: for their own nature forces them thereto.

8. 3: . . . [Brahman] is called 'inherent nature' in so far as it appertains to [an individual] self,—as the creative force known as 'works' which gives rise to the [separate] natures of contingent beings.

9. 11–13: For that a human form I have assumed fools scorn Me, . . . (12) . . . a monstrous devilish nature they embrace which leads [them far] astray. (13) But great-souled men take up their stand in a nature that is divine.

10. 4–5: Intellect, wisdom, freedom from delusion, long-suffering, truth, restraint, tranquillity, pleasure and pain, coming to be and passing away, fear and fearlessness as well, (5) refusal to do harm, equanimity, content, austerity, open-handedness, fame and infamy,—[such are] the dispositions of contingent beings, and from Me in all their diversity they arise.

18. 59–60: [If,] relying on your ego, you should think, 'I will not fight', vain is your resolve, [for] Nature will constrain you. (60) You are bound by your own works which spring from your own nature; [for] what, deluded, you would not do you will do perforce.

II. (*b*) *The Three Constituents of Nature*

2. 45: [All Nature is made up of] the three 'constituents': these are the Veda's goal.

3. 5: . . . Every man is powerless and made to work by the constituents born of Nature.

3. 27–9: It is material Nature's [three] constituents that do all works wherever [works are done]; [but] he whose self is by the ego fooled thinks, 'It is I who do'. (28) But he who knows how constituents and works are parcelled out in categories, seeing things as they are, thinks thus: 'Constituents on constituents act', [and thus thinking] remains unattached. (29) By the constituents of Nature fooled are men attached to the constituents' works. Such men, dull-witted, only know in part. Let not the knower of the whole upset [the knower of the part].

3. 37: Desire it is: Anger it is,—arising from the constituent of Passion,—all devouring, mightily wicked, know that this is [your] enemy on earth.

7. 12–14: Know too that [all] states of being whether they be of [Nature's constituent] Goodness, Passion, or Darkness proceed from Me; but I am not in them, they are in Me. (13) By these three states of being inhering in the constituents this whole universe is led astray . . .. (14) For [all] this is my creative power (*māyā*) composed of the constituents.

14. 5–19: Goodness—Passion—Darkness: these are the [three] constituents from Nature sprung that bind the embodied [self] in the body though [the self itself] is changeless. (6) Among these Goodness, being immaculate, knowing no sickness, dispenses light, [and yet] it binds by [causing the self] to cling to wisdom and to joy. (7) Passion is instinct with desire, [this] know. From craving and attachment it wells up. It binds the embodied [self] by [causing it] to cling to works. (8) But from ignorance is Darkness born: mark [this] well. All embodied [selves] it leads astray. With fecklessness and sloth and sleepiness it binds. (9) Goodness causes [a man] to cling to joy, Passion to works; but Darkness, stifling wisdom, attaches to fecklessness. . . . (11) When at all the body's gates wisdom's light arises, then must you know that Goodness has increased. (12) When Passion is waxing strong, these [states] arise: greed, [purposeful] activity, committing oneself to works, disquiet, and ambition. (13) When Darkness is surging up, these [states] arise: unlighted [darkness], unwillingness to act, fecklessness, delusion. (14) But when an embodied [self] comes face to face with [the body's] dissolution and Goodness prevails, then will he reach the spotless worlds of those who know the highest. (15) [Another] goes to his demise when Passion [predominates]; he will be born among such men as cling to works: and as to him who dies when Darkness [has the upper hand], he will be born in the wombs of deluded fools. (16) Of works well done, they say, the fruits belong to Goodness, being without spot:

but pain is the fruit of Passion, ignorance the fruit of Darkness. (17) From Goodness wisdom springs, from Passion greed, from Darkness fecklessness, delusion, and ignorance—how not? (18) Upward is the path of those who abide in Goodness, in the middle stand the men of Passion. Stuck in the modes of the vilest constituent the men of Darkness go below. (19) When the watching [self] sees there is no agent other than [these] constituents and knows what is beyond them, then will he come to [share in] that mode of being which is mine.

17. 1–4: (The constituents as manifested in faith).

17. 7–22: (The constituents as manifested in food, sacrifice, ascetic practice, and alms-giving).

18. 7–39: (The constituents as manifested in works, the agent, knowledge, the intellect, constancy, and pleasure).

18. 40: There is no existent thing in heaven or earth or yet among the gods which is or ever could be free from these three constituents from Nature sprung.

18. 41–4: (Their operation in the four great classes of society).

II. (*c*) (i) Karma—*Works—Action*

2. 39: . . . If you are controlled (integrated) by the soul, you will put away the bondage that is inherent in [all] works.

2. 47–51: Work alone is *your* proper business, never the fruits [it may produce]; let not your motive be the fruit of works nor your attachment to [mere] worklessness. (48) Stand fast in Yoga, surrendering attachment; in success and failure be the same and then get busy with your works. Yoga means 'sameness-and-indifference'. (49) For lower far is [the path of] active work [for its own sake] than the spiritual exercise (*yoga*) of the soul. Seek refuge in the soul! How pitiful are they whose motive is the fruit [of works]! (50) Whoso performs spiritual exercise with the soul (is integrated by the soul) discards here [and now] both good and evil works: brace yourself then for [this] spiritual exercise (*yoga*); for Yoga is [also] skill in [performing] works. (51) For those wise men who are integrated by the soul, who have renounced the fruit that is born of works, these will be freed from the bondage of [re-]birth and fare to that region that knows no ill.

3. 4–9: Not by leaving works undone does a man win freedom from [the bond of] works, nor by renunciation alone can he win perfection's prize. (5) For not for a moment can a man stand still and do no work, for every man is powerless and made to work by the constituents born of Nature. (6) Whoso controls his limbs through which he acts but sits remembering in his mind sense-objects, deludes [him]self: he is called a hypocrite. (7) But more excellent is he who with the mind controls those limbs and through these limbs [themselves] by which he acts embarks on the spiritual exercise of works, remaining detached the while. (8) Do the work that is prescribed [for you], for to work is better than to do no work at all; for without working you will not succeed even in keeping your body in good repair. (9) This world is bound by bonds of work save where that work is done for sacrifice. Work to this end then, Arjuna, from [all] attachment freed.

3. 14–33: From food do [all] contingent beings derive and food derives from rain; rain derives from sacrifice and sacrifice from works. (15) From Brahman work arises, know this, and Brahman is born from the Imperishable; therefore is Brahman, penetrating everywhere, forever based on sacrifice. (16) So was the wheel in motion set: and whoso here fails to match his turning [with the turning of the wheel], living an evil life, the senses his pleasure-ground, lives out his life in vain.

(17) Nay, let a man take pleasure in self alone, in self his satisfaction find, in self alone content: [for then] there is naught he needs to do. (18) In works done and works undone on earth he has no interest,—no [interest] in all contingent beings: on such interest he does not depend.

(19) Therefore detached, perform unceasingly the works that must be done, for the man detached who labours on to the highest must win through. (20) For only by working on did Janaka and his like attain perfection's prize. Or if again you consider the welfare [and coherence] of the world, then you should work [and act].

(21) Whatever the noblest does, that too will others do: the standard that he sets all the world will follow. (22) In the three worlds there is nothing that I need do, nor anything unattained that I need to gain, yet work [is the element] in which I move. (23) For if I were not tirelessly to busy Myself with works, then would men everywhere follow in my footsteps. (24) If I were not to do my work, these worlds would fall to ruin, and I should be a worker of confusion, destroying these [my] creatures.

(25) As witless [fools] perform their works attached to the work [they do], so, unattached, should the wise man do, longing to bring about the welfare of the world. (26) Let not a wise man split the soul of witless men attached to work: let him encourage all [manner of] works, himself though busy, acting as an integrated man.

(27) It is material Nature's [three] constituents that do all works wherever [works are done]; [but] he whose self is by the ego fooled thinks,

'It is I who do.' (28) But he who knows how constituents and works are parcelled out in categories, seeing things as they are, thinks thus: 'Constituents on constituents act', [and thus thinking] remains unattached. (29) By the constituents of Nature fooled are men attached to the constituents' works. Such men, dull-witted, only know in part. Let not the knower of the whole upset [the knower of the part].

(30) Cast all your works on Me, your thoughts [withdrawn] in what appertains to self; have neither hope nor thought that 'This is mine': cast off this fever! Fight!

(31) Whatever men shall practise constantly this my doctrine, firm in faith, not envying, [not cavilling,] they too will find release from works. . . . (33) As is a man's own nature, so must he act, however wise he be. [All] creatures follow Nature: what will repression do?

4. 12–23: Desiring success in their (ritual) acts men worship here the gods; for swiftly in the world of men comes success engendered by the act [itself].

(13) The four-caste system did I generate with categories of 'constituents' and works; of this I am the doer, [the agent,]—this know,—[and yet I am] the Changeless One who does not do [or act]. (14) Works can never affect Me. I have no yearning for their fruits. Whoso should know that this is how I am will never be bound by works. (15) Knowing this the ancients too did work though seeking [all the while] release [from temporal life]: so do you work [and act] as the ancients did in days of old.

(16) What is work? What worklessness? Herein even sages are perplexed. So shall I preach to you concerning work; and once you have understood my words, you will find release from ill. (17) For a man must understand [the nature] of work, of work ill done, and worklessness [all three]: profound [indeed] are the ways of work.

(18) The man who sees worklessness in work [itself], and work in worklessness, is wise among his fellows, integrated, performing every work. (19) When all a man's emprises are free from desire [for fruit] and motive, his works burnt up in wisdom's fire, then wise men call him learned. (20) When he has cast off [all] attachment to the fruits of works, ever content, on none dependent, though he embarks on work [himself], in fact he does no work at all. (21) Nothing hoping, his thought and self controlled, giving up all possessions, he only does such work as is needed for his body's maintenance, and so he avoids defilement. (22) Content to take whatever chance may bring his way, surmounting [all] dualities, knowing no envy, the same in success and failure, though working [still] he is not bound. (23) Attachment gone, deliverance won, his thoughts are fixed on wisdom: he works for sacrifice [alone], and all the work [he ever did] entirely melts away.

4. 32–3: So, many and various are the sacrifices spread out athwart the mouth of Brahman. They spring from work, all of them: . . . (33) . . . All works without exception in wisdom find their consummation.

4. 37: As a kindled fire reduces its fuel to ashes, so does the fire of wisdom reduce all works to ashes.

4. 41–2: Let a man in spiritual exercise [all] works renounce, let him by wisdom [all] doubts dispel, let him be himself, and then [whatever] his works [may be, they] will never bind him [more]. (42) And so [take up] the sword of wisdom and with it cut this doubt of yours, unwisdom's child, still lurking in your heart: prepare for action now. Stand up!

5. 2–12: Renouncing works,—performing them [as spiritual exercise],—both lead to the highest goal; but of the two to engage in works is more excellent than to renounce them. . . . (4) 'There must be a difference between theory and practice', so say the simple-minded, not the wise. Apply yourself to only one whole-heartedly and win the fruit of both. (5) [True,] the men of [contemplative] theory attain a [high] estate, but that [same estate] achieve the men of practice (*yoga*) too; for theory and practice are all one: who sees [that this is true], he sees [indeed]. (6) But hard to attain is [true] renunciation without [the practice of some] spiritual exercise: the sage well versed in spiritual exercise right soon to Brahman comes. (7) Well versed in spiritual exercise, his self made pure, his self and senses quelled, his self become the [very] self of every contingent being, though working still, he is not defiled.

(8) 'Lo, nothing do I do': so thinks the integrated man who knows things as they really are . . .. (9) . . . 'The senses are busied with their proper objects: [what has that to do with me?' This is the way] he thinks.

(10) And on he works though he has [long] renounced attachment, ascribing his works to Brahman; [yet] is he not stained by evil as a lotus-petal [is not stained] by water. (11) With body, mind, soul, and senses alone-and-isolated [from the self] do men engaged in spiritual exercise engage in action renouncing attachment for the cleansing of the self. (12) The integrated man, renouncing the fruit of works, gains an abiding peace: the man not integrated whose works are prompted by desire, being attached to fruits, is bound.

6. 1–4: The man who does the work that is his to do, yet covets not its fruits, he it is who at once renounces and yet works on (*yogin*), not the man who builds no sacrificial fire and does not work. (2) What men call renunciation is also spiritual exercise (*yoga*): you must know this. For without renouncing [all set] purpose no one can engage in spiritual exercise. (3) For the silent sage who would climb [the ladder of] spiritual exercise works are said to be the means; but for that same [sage] who has reached the state of integration (*yoga*) they say quiescence is the means. (4) For when a man knows no attachment to objects of sense or to the deeds [he does], when he has renounced all purpose, then has he reached the state of integration, or so they say.

8. 3: . . . [Brahman] is called 'inherent nature' in so far as it appertains to [an individual] self,—as the creative force known as 'works' which gives rise to the [separate] natures of contingent beings.

9. 28: So from [those] bonds which works [of their very nature forge], whose fruits are fair and foul, you will be freed.

12. 6–7: Those who cast off all their works on Me . . . (7) these will I lift up on high out of the ocean of recurring death.

12. 10–11: . . . Work-and-act for Me . . .; for even if you work only for my sake, you will receive the prize. (11) And then again if even this exceeds your powers, gird up your loins, renounce the fruit of all your works with self restrained.

14. 7: Passion is instinct with desire, [this] know. From craving and attachment it wells up. It binds the embodied [self] by [causing it] to cling to works.

14. 12: When Passion is waxing strong, these [states] arise: greed, [purposeful] activity, committing oneself to works, disquiet, and ambition.

14. 16: Of works well done, they say, the fruits belong to Goodness, being without spot: but pain is the fruit of passion, ignorance the fruit of Darkness.

18. 5–12: [Works of] sacrifice, the gift of alms, and works of penance are not to be surrendered; these must most certainly be done: it is sacrifice, alms-giving, and ascetic practice that purify the wise. (6) But even these works should be done [in a spirit of self-surrender], for [all] attachment [to what you do] and [all] the fruits [of what you do] must be surrendered. This is my last decisive word.

(7) For to renounce a work enjoined [by Scripture] is inappropriate; deludedly to give this up is [the way] of Darkness. This [too] has been declared. (8) The man who gives up a deed simply because it causes pain or because he shrinks from bodily distress, commits an act of self-surrender that accords with Passion['s way]: assuredly he will not reap the fruit of self-surrender. (9) But if a work is done simply because it should be done and is enjoined [by Scripture], and if [all]

attachment, [all thought of] fruit is given up, then that is surrender in Goodness[' way], I deem.

(10) The self-surrendered man, suffused with Goodness, wise, whose [every] doubt is cut away, hates not his uncongenial work nor cleaves to the congenial. (11) For one still in the body it is not possible to surrender up all works without exception; rather it is he who surrenders up the *fruit* of works who deserves the name, 'A self-surrendered man'.

(12) Unwanted—wanted—mixed: threefold is the fruit of work,—[this they experience] at death who have not surrendered [self], but not at all such men who have renounced.

18. 17: A man who has reached a state where there is no sense of 'I', whose soul is undefiled,—were he to slaughter [all] these worlds,—slays nothing. He is not bound.

18. 23–8: The work prescribed [by Scripture] from [all] attachment free, performed without passion, without hate, by one who hankers not for fruits, is called [the work] of Goodness. (24) But the work in which much effort is expended by one who seeks his own pleasure-and-desire or again thinks, 'It is I who do it', such [work] is assigned to Passion. (25) The work embarked on by a man deluded who has no thought of consequence, nor [care at all] for the loss and hurt [he causes others] or for the human part [he plays himself], is called [a work] of Darkness.

(26) The agent who, from attachment freed, steadfast and resolute, remains unchanged in failure and success and never speaks of 'I', is called [an agent] in Goodness' way. (27) The agent who pursues the fruit of works, passionate, greedy, intent on doing harm, impure, a prey to exaltation as to grief, is widely known [to act] in Passion's way. (28) The agent, inept and vulgar, stiff-and-proud, a cheat, low-spoken, slothful, who is subject to depression, who procrastinates, is called [an agent] in Darkness' way.

18. 46: By dedicating the work that is proper [to his caste] to Him who is the source of the activity of all beings, by whom this whole universe was spun, a man attains perfection-and-success.

18. 49: With soul detached from everything, with self subdued, [all] longing gone, renounce: and so you will find complete success, perfection, works transcended.

18. 57: Give up in thought to Me all that you do. . . .

18. 60: You are bound by your own works which spring from your own nature; [for] what, deluded, you would not do you will do perforce.

II. (*c*) (ii) *Sacrifice*

3. 10–16: Of old the Lord of Creatures said, emitting creatures and with them sacrifice: 'By this shall ye prolong your lineage, let this be to you the cow that yields the milk of all that ye desire. (11) With this shall ye sustain the gods so that the gods may sustain you [in return]. Sustaining one another [thus] ye shall achieve the highest good. (12) For, [so] sustained by sacrifice the gods will give you the food of your desire. Whoso enjoys their gift yet gives them nothing [in return] is a thief, no more nor less.'

(13) Good men who eat the leavings of the sacrifice are freed from every taint, but evil are they and evil do they eat who cook [only] for their own sakes.

(14) From food do [all] contingent beings derive and food derives from rain; rain derives from sacrifice and sacrifice from works. (15) From Brahman work arises, know this, and Brahman is born from the Imperishable; therefore is Brahman, penetrating everywhere, forever based on sacrifice. (16) So was the wheel in motion set: and whoso here fails to match his turning [with the turning of the wheel], living an evil life, the senses his pleasure-ground, lives out his life in vain.

4. 23–33: Attachment gone, deliverance won, his thoughts are fixed on wisdom: he works for sacrifice [alone], and all the work [he ever did] entirely melts away.

(24) The offering is Brahman, Brahman the [sacrificial] ghee offered by Brahman in Brahman's fire: who sinks himself in this [sacrificial] act which is Brahman, to Brahman must he thereby go. (25) Some adepts offer sacrifice to the gods as their sole object; in the fire of Brahman others offer sacrifice as sacrifice [which has merit in itself]. (26) Yet others offer the senses,—hearing and the rest,—in the fires of self-restraint; others the senses' proper objects,—sounds and the like,—in the fires of the senses. (27) Others offer up all works of sense and works of vital breath in the fire of the spiritual exercise of self-control kindled by wisdom. (28) Some offer up their wealth, some their hard penances, some spiritual exercise, and some again make study and knowledge [of scripture] their sacrifice,—religious men whose vows are strict. (29) Some offer the in-breath in the out-breath, likewise the out-breath in the in-breath, checking the flow of both, on breath-control intent. (30) Others restrict their food and offer up breaths in breaths. All these know the [meaning of] sacrifice, and by sacrifice [all] their defilements are made away. (31) Eating of the leavings of the sacrifice, the food of immortality, they come to primeval Brahman. This world is not for him who performs no sacrifice,—much less the other [world].

(32) So, many and various are the sacrifices spread out athwart the mouth of Brahman. They spring from work, all of them: be sure of this; for once you know this, you will win release. (33) Better than the sacrifice of wealth is the sacrifice of wisdom. All works without exception in wisdom find their consummation.

8. 4: . . . In so far as [Brahman] appertains to sacrifice [it is] I here in this body.

9. 16–17: I am the rite, the sacrifice, the offering for the dead, the healing herb; I am the sacred formula, the sacred butter am I: I am the fire and I the oblation offered [in the fire]. (17) I am . . . [the sacred syllable] Om, and the Rig-, Sāma-, and Yajur-Vedas too.

9. 24: For it is I who of all sacrifices am recipient and Lord. . . .

17. 11–13: The sacrifice approved by [sacred] ordinance and offered up by men who would not taste its fruits, who concentrate their minds on this [alone]: 'In sacrifice lies duty': [such sacrifice] belongs to Goodness. (12) But the sacrifice that is offered up by men who bear its fruits in mind or simply for vain display,—know that [such sacrifice] belongs to Passion. (13) The sacrifice in which no proper rite is followed, no food distributed, no sacred words recited, no Brāhmans' fees paid up, no faith enshrined,—[such sacrifice] men say belongs to Darkness.

II. (*c*) (iii) *The Three Great Duties: Sacrifice, Penance, and Alms-giving*

8. 28: For knowledge of the Veda, for sacrifice, for grim austerities, for gifts of alms a meed of merit is laid down. . . .

17. 11–22: (Goodness, Passion, and Darkness as exhibited in these).

17. 23–8: (All three must be prefaced by the syllable, Oṁ: they must be performed with no thought of 'fruits' and in a spirit of belief).

Ascetic Practices

4. 10: . . . Made pure by wisdom and hard penances, they come to [share in] my own mode of being.

7. 9: In ascetics [their] fierce austerity [am I].

17. 5–6: . . . Some men there are who, without regard to Scripture's ordinance, savagely mortify [their flesh], buoyed up by hypocrisy and self-regard, yielding to the violence of passion and desire, and so torment the mass of [living] beings whose home their body is, the witless fools,—and [with them] Me Myself within [that same] body abiding: how devilish their intentions!

17. 14–19: [Due] reverence to gods and Brāhmans, teachers and wise men, purity, uprightness, chastity, refusal to do harm,—[this] is [true] penance of the body. (15) Words that do not cause disquiet, [words] truthful, kind, and pleasing, the constant practice too of sacred recitation,—[this] is the penance of the tongue. (16) Serenity of mind and friendlessness, silence and self-restraint, and the cleansing of one's affections,—this is called the penance of the mind.

(17) When men possessed of highest faith, integrated and indifferent to the fruits [of what they do], do penance in this threefold wise, men speak of [penance] in Goodness' way. (18) Some mortify themselves to win respect, honour, and reverence, or from sheer hypocrisy: here [on earth] this must be called [penance] in Passion's way,—fickle and unsure. (19) Some mortify themselves following perverted theories, torturing themselves, or to destroy another: this is called [penance] in Darkness' way.

11. (*c*) (iv) *Caste Duty*

2. 31-7: Likewise consider your own [caste-]duty, then too you have no cause to quail; for better than a fight prescribed by law is nothing for a man of the princely class. (32) Happy the warriors indeed who become involved in such a war as this, presented by pure chance and opening the doors of paradise. (33) But if you will not wage this war prescribed by [your caste-]duty, then, by casting off both duty and honour, you will bring evil on yourself. . . . (37) If you are slain, paradise is yours, and if you gain the victory, yours is the earth to enjoy.

3. 35: Better one's own duty [to perform], though void of merit, than to do another's well: better to die within [the sphere of] one's own duty: perilous is the duty of other men.

4. 13: The four-caste system did I generate with categories of 'constituents' and works. . . .

18. 41–8: To Brāhmans, princes, peasants-and-artisans, and serfs works have been variously assigned by [these] constituents, and they arise from the nature of things as they are.

(42) Calm, self-restraint, ascetic practice, purity, long-suffering and uprightness, wisdom in theory as in practice, religious faith,—[these] are the works of Brāhmans, inhering in their nature. (43) High courage, ardour, endurance, skill, in battle unwillingness to flee, an open hand, a lordly mien,—[these] are the works of princes, inhering in their nature [too]. (44) To till the fields, protect the kine, and engage in trade, [these] are the works of peasants-and-artisans, inhering in their nature; but works whose very soul is service inhere in the very nature of the serf.

(45) By [doing] the work that is proper to him [and] rejoicing [in the doing], a man succeeds, perfects himself. [Now] hear just how a man perfects himself by [doing and] rejoicing in his proper work. (46) By dedicating the work that is proper [to his caste] to Him who is the source of the activity of all beings, by whom this whole universe was spun, a man attains perfection-and-success. (47) Better [to do] one's

own [caste-]duty, though devoid of merit, than [to do] another's, however well performed. By doing the work prescribed by his own nature a man meets with no defilement. (48) Never should a man give up the work to which he is born, defective though it be: for every enterprise is choked by defects, as fire by smoke.

11. (*d*) *The Human Psyche*

(i) *Mind and Senses*

2. 60–8: And yet however much a wise man strive, the senses' tearing violence may seduce his mind by force. (61) Let him sit, curbing them all, integrated, intent on Me: for firmly established is that man's wisdom whose senses are subdued.

(62) Let a man [but] think of the objects of sense,—attachment to them is born: from attachment springs desire, from desire is anger born. (63) From anger comes bewilderment, from bewilderment wandering of the mind, from wandering of the mind destruction of the soul: once the soul is destroyed the man is lost.

(64) But he who roves among the objects of sense, his senses subdued to self and disjoined from passion and hate, and who is self-possessed [himself], draws near to calm serenity. . . . (67) Hither and thither the senses rove, and when the mind is attuned to them, it sweeps away [whatever of] wisdom a man may possess, as the wind [sweeps away] a ship on the water. (68) And so whose senses are withheld from the objects proper to them, wherever he may be, firm-stablished is the wisdom of such a man.

3. 6–7: Whoso controls his limbs through which he acts but sits remembering in his mind sense-objects, deludes [him]self: he is called a hypocrite. (7) But more excellent is he who with the mind controls those limbs (or senses) and through these limbs [themselves] by which he acts embarks on the spiritual exercise of works, remaining detached the while.

3. 16: . . . Whoso here fails to match his turning [with the turning of the wheel], living an evil life, the senses his pleasure-ground, lives out his life in vain.

3. 34: In [all] the senses passion and hate are seated, [turned] to their proper objects: let none fall victim to their power, for these are brigands on the road.

3. 40–2: Sense, mind, and soul, they say, are the places where lurks [desire]; through these it smothers wisdom, fooling the embodied [self]. (41) Therefore restrain the senses first: . . .

(42) Exalted are the senses, or so they say; higher than the senses is the mind; yet higher than the mind the soul: what is beyond the soul is he (the self).

4. 39: A man of faith, intent on wisdom, his senses [all] restrained, wins wisdom. (Cf. 5. 7: 6. 8, 12.)

5. 8–9: 'Lo, nothing do I do': so thinks the integrated man . . . (9) . . . 'The senses are busied with their proper objects: [what has that to do with me?' This is the way] he thinks.

5. 11: With body, mind, soul, and senses alone-and-isolated [from the self] do men engaged in spiritual exercise engage in action renouncing attachment for the cleansing of the self.

5. 13: All works renouncing with the mind, quietly he sits in full control,—the embodied [self]. . . .

5. 19: While yet in this world they have overcome [the process of] emanation [and decay], for their minds are stilled in that-which-is-ever-the-same.

5. 28: With senses, mind, and soul restrained, the silent sage, on deliverance intent, . . . is truly liberated.

6. 12: There let him sit and make his mind a single point, let him restrain the operations of his thought and senses and practise integration to purify the self.

6. 14–15: Let him sit, [his] self all stilled, . . . his mind controlled, his thoughts on Me, integrated, . . . (15) . . . his mind restrained.

6. 24–7: Let him renounce all desires whose origin lies in the will,—all of them without remainder; let him restrain in every way by mind alone the senses' busy throng. (25) By soul held fast in steadfastness he must make the mind [too] subsist in the self; then little by little will he come to rest; he must think of nothing at all. (26) Wherever the fickle mind unsteady roves around, from thence [the soul] will bring it back and subject it to the self. (27) For upon this athlete of the spirit whose mind is stilled the highest joy descends: [all] passion laid to rest, free from [all] stain, Brahman he becomes.

6. 34–5: (Arjuna:) Fickle is the mind, impetuous, exceeding strong: how difficult to curb it! As difficult as to curb the wind, I would say. (35) (The Blessed Lord:) Herein there is no doubt, hard is the mind to curb and fickle, but by untiring effort and by transcending passion it can be held in check.

7. 1: Attach your mind to Me. . . .

7. 4: (The mind is part of Krishna's lower Nature).

8. 10: With mind unmoving at the time of passing on, . . . [a man] will draw nigh to that divine exalted Person.

18. 52–3: Let him . . . restrain speech, body, and mind, . . . (53) . . . [if he does this,] to becoming Brahman is he conformed.

11. (*d*) (ii) *The Soul* (Buddhi)

2. 39–52: This wisdom (*buddhi*) has [now] been revealed to you in theory; listen now to how it should be practised. If you are controlled (integrated) by the soul, you will put away the bondage that is inherent in [all] works. . . . (41) The essence of the soul is will and it is really single, but many-branched and infinite are the souls of men devoid of will. (42) The essence of the soul is will,—[but the souls] of men who cling to pleasure and to power, their minds seduced by flowery words, are not attuned to enstasy. . . . (49) . . . Lower far is [the path of] active work [for its own sake] than {integration through the soul / spiritual exercise of the soul}. Seek refuge in the soul! How pitiful are they whose motive is the fruit [of works]! (50) Whoso {is integrated by the soul / performs the spiritual exercise of the soul} discards here [and now] both good and evil works: brace yourself then for [this] spiritual exercise. . . . (52) When your soul passes beyond delusion's turbid quicksands, then will you learn disgust for what has been heard [ere now] and for what may yet be heard.

2. 63: . . . From wandering of the mind [comes] destruction of the soul: once the soul is destroyed the man is lost.

2. 65–6: From [a man] thus becalmed all sorrows flee away: for once his thoughts are calmed, his soul stands firmly [in its ground]. (66) The man who is not integrated has no soul, in him there is no development: for the man who does not develop there is no peace. Whence should there be joy to a peaceless man?

3. 40: Sense, mind, and soul, they say, are the places where lurks [desire]; through these it smothers wisdom, fooling the embodied [self].

3. 42: Exalted are the senses, or so they say; higher than the senses is the mind; yet higher than the mind the soul: what is beyond the soul is he (the self).

5. 11: With body, mind, soul, and senses alone-and-isolated [from the self] do men engaged in spiritual exercise engage in action renouncing attachment for the cleansing of the self.

5. 17: Souls [bent on] (wisdom), selves [bent on] that, . . . they stride [along the path] from which there is no return.

5. 20: . . . Steadfast-and-still his soul, [all] unconfused, he will know Brahman, in Brahman [stilled] he'll stand.

5. 28: With senses, mind, and soul restrained, the silent sage, on deliverance intent, . . . is truly liberated.

6. 20–1: When thought by spiritual exercise is checked and comes to rest, and when of [one]self one sees the self in self and finds content therein, (21) that is the utmost joy which transcends [all things of] sense and which soul [alone] can grasp.

6. 25–6: By soul held fast in steadfastness he must make the mind [too] subsist in the self; then little by little will he come to rest; he must think of nothing at all. (26) Wherever the fickle mind unsteady roves around, from thence [the soul] will bring it back and subject it to the self.

6. 43: There is [the reincarnated self] united with the soul as it had matured in his former body; and once again he strives to win perfection's prize.

7. 4: (Is part of God's lower Nature).

7. 10: [I am] *buddhi* in those possessed of *buddhi*.

18. 17: A man who has reached a state where there is no sense of 'I', whose soul is undefiled,—were he to slaughter [all] these worlds,—slays nothing. He is not bound.

18. 30–2: The intellect (*buddhi*) that distinguishes between activity and its cessation, between what should be done and what should not, between danger and security, bondage and release, is [an intellect] in Goodness' way. (31) The intellect by which lawful-right and lawless-wrong, what should be done and what should not, are untruly understood, is [an intellect] in Passion's way. (32) The intellect which, by Darkness overcast, thinks right is wrong, law lawlessness, all things their opposite, is [an intellect] in Darkness' way.

18. 49–53: With soul detached from everything, with self subdued, [all] longing gone, renounce: and so you will find complete success, perfection, works transcended. . . . (51) Let a man be integrated by his soul [now] cleansed, let him restrain [him]self with constancy, abandon objects of sense,—sound and all the rest,—passion and hate let him cast out, . . . (53) . . . [if he does this,] to becoming Brahman is he conformed.

18. 57: Give up in thought to Me all that you do, make Me your goal: relying on the integration of the soul, think on Me constantly.

11. (*e*) *Heaven*

2. 32: Happy the warriors indeed who become involved in such a war as this, presented by pure chance and opening the doors of paradise.

2. 37: If you are slain, paradise is yours.

2. 43: Such men give vent to flowery words, lacking discernment, delighting in the Veda's lore, saying there is naught else. Desire is their essence, paradise their goal.

6. 41: [The doer of fair works] will win the worlds of the doers of good works and dwell there countless years: and then will he be born again . . . in the house of holy men by fortune blest.

9. 20–1: Trusting in the three Vedas the Soma-drinkers, purged of [ritual] fault, worship Me with sacrifice, seeking to go to paradise: these win through to the pure world of the lord of the gods and taste in heaven the gods' celestial joys. (21) [But] once they have [to the full] enjoyed the broad expanse of paradise, their merit exhausted, they come [back] to the world of men. And so it is that those who stick fast to the three Vedas receive [a reward] that comes and goes; for it is desire that they desire.

11. (*f*) (i) *Perdition and Hell*

2. 63: . . . From wandering of mind [comes] destruction of the soul: once the soul is destroyed the man is lost.

2. 66: The man who is not integrated has no soul, in him there is no development: for the man who does not develop there is no peace. Whence should there be joy to a peaceless man?

3. 32: Whoso refuses to perform this my doctrine, envious [yet and cavilling], of every [form of] wisdom fooled, is lost, the witless [dunce]!

4. 40: The man, unwise, devoid of faith, of doubting self, must perish: this world is not for the man of doubting self, nor the next [world] nor yet happiness.

9. 11–12: For that a human form I have assumed fools scorn Me, knowing nothing of my higher state,—great Lord of contingent beings. (12) Vain their hopes and vain their deeds, vain their 'gnosis', vain their wit; a monstrous devilish nature they embrace which leads [them far] astray.

16. 19–21: Birth after birth in this revolving round, these vilest among men, strangers to [all] good, obsessed with hate and cruel, I ever hurl into devilish wombs. (20) Caught up in devilish wombs, birth after birth deluded, they never attain to Me: and so they tread the lowest way. (21) Desire—Anger—Greed: this is the triple gate of hell, destruction of the self: therefore avoid these three.

II. (*f*) (ii) *Sin and Evil*

2. 62–3: Let a man [but] think of the objects of sense,—attachment to them is born: from attachment springs desire, from desire is anger born. (63) From anger comes bewilderment, from bewilderment wandering of the mind, from wandering of the mind destruction of the soul: once the soul is destroyed the man is lost.

3. 34: In [all] the senses passion and hate are seated, [turned] to their proper objects: let none fall victim to their power, for these are brigands on the road.

3. 36–43: (Arjuna:) Then by what impelled does [mortal] man do evil unwilling though he be? He is driven to it by force, or so it seems to me.

(The Blessed Lord:) (37) Desire it is: Anger it is,—arising from the constituent of Passion,—all devouring, mightily wicked, know that this is [your] enemy on earth. (38) As fire is swathed in smoke, as a mirror is [fouled] by grime, as an embryo is all covered up by the membrane envelope, so is this [world] obscured by that. (39) This is the wise man's eternal foe; by this is wisdom overcast, whatever form it takes, a fire insatiable. (40) Senses, mind, and soul, they say, are the places where it lurks; through these it smothers wisdom, fooling the embodied [self]. (41) Therefore restrain the senses first: strike down this evil thing!—destroyer alike of what we learn from holy books and what we learn from life. . . . (43) . . . Vanquish [this] enemy, Arjuna! [Swift is he] to change his form, and hard is he to conquer. (Cf. 4. 10: 5. 23, 26, 28 (desire and anger).)

7. 15: Doers of evil, deluded, base, put not their trust in Me; their wisdom swept away by [this] uncanny power (*māyā*), they cleave to a devilish mode of existence.

7. 27: By dualities are men confused, and these arise from desire and hate; thereby are all contingent beings bewildered the moment they are born.

16. 4–20: A hypocrite, proud of himself and arrogant, angry, harsh, and ignorant is the man who is born to [inherit] a devilish destiny. (5) . . . A devilish [destiny means] enslavement. . . . (7) Of creative action and its return to rest the devilish folk know nothing; in them there is no purity, no morality, no truth. (8) 'The world is devoid of truth,' they say, 'it has no ground, no ruling Lord; it has not come to be by mutual causal law; desire alone has caused it, nothing else.' (9) Holding fast to these views, lost souls with feeble minds, they embark on cruel-and-violent deeds, malignant [in their lust] for the destruction of the world. (10) Insatiate desire is their starting-point,—maddened are they by hypocrisy and pride, clutching at false conceptions, deluded as they are: impure are their resolves. (11) Unmeasured care is theirs right up to the time of death, [for] they have no other aim than to satisfy their lusts, convinced that this is all. (12) Bound by hundreds of fetters forged by hope, obsessed by anger and desire, they seek to build up wealth unjustly to satisfy their lusts.

(13) 'This have I gained today, this whim I'll satisfy; this wealth is mine and much more too will be mine as time goes on. (14) He was an enemy of mine, I've killed him, and many another too I'll kill. I'm master [here]. I take my pleasure [as I will]; I'm strong and happy and successful. (15) I'm rich and of good family. Who else can match himself with me? I'll sacrifice and I'll give alms: [why not?] I'll have a marvellous time!' So speak [fools] deluded in their ignorance.

(16) [Their minds] unhinged by many a [foolish] fancy, caught up in delusion's net, obsessed by the satisfaction of their lusts, into foul hell they fall. (17) Puffed up with self-conceit, unbending, maddened by their pride in wealth, they offer sacrifices that are but sacrifice in name and not in the way prescribed,—the hypocrites! (18) Selfishness, force and pride, desire and anger, [these do] they rely on, envying and hating Me who dwell in their bodies as I dwell in all.

(19) Birth after birth in this revolving round, these vilest among men, strangers to [all] good, obsessed with hate and cruel, I ever hurl into devilish wombs. (20) Caught up in devilish wombs, birth after birth deluded, they never attain to Me: and so they tread the lowest way.

III. *Liberation, Spiritual Freedom, and How to Win it*

(*a*) Yoga: *Integration, Spiritual Exercise, the Athlete of the Spirit*

2. 39–40: . . . If you are controlled (integrated) by the soul, you will put away the bondage that is inherent in [all] works. (40) Herein no effort goes to seed nor is there any slipping back: even a very little of this discipline will protect [you] from great peril.

2. 48–51: Stand fast in {integration by the soul / Yoga}, surrendering attachment; in success and failure be the same and then get busy with your works. Yoga means 'sameness-and-indifference'. (49) For lower far is [the path of] active work [for its own sake] than {integration through the soul / spiritual exercise of the soul}.

Seek refuge in the soul! How pitiful are they whose motive is the fruit [of works]! (50) Whoso is integrated by the soul discards here [and now] both good and evil works: brace yourself then for [this] {Yoga / spiritual exercise}; for Yoga is [also] skill in [performing] works. (51) For those wise men who are integrated by the soul, who have renounced the fruit that is born of works, these will be freed from the bondage of [re-]birth and fare to that region that knows no ill.

2. 53: When your soul, by scripture once bewildered, stands motionless and still, immovable in enstasy, then will you attain to {Yoga / integration}.

2. 58: When a man draws in on every side his senses from their proper objects as a tortoise [might draw in] its limbs,—firm-stablished is the wisdom of such a man.

2. 61: Let him sit curbing all [the senses], integrated, intent on Me: for firmly established is that man's wisdom whose senses are subdued.

2. 66: The man who is not integrated has no soul, in him there is no development: for the man who does not develop there is no peace. Whence should there be joy to a peaceless man?

2. 70: As the waters flow into the sea, full filled, whose ground remains unmoved, so too do all desires flow into [the heart of] man: and such a man wins peace,—not the desirer of desires.

3. 26: Let not a wise man split the soul of witless men attached to work: let him encourage all [manner of] works, himself though busy, acting as an integrated man.

4. 18: The man who sees worklessness in work [itself], and work in worklessness, is wise among his fellows, integrated, performing every work.

4. 38: Nothing on earth resembles wisdom in its power to purify; and this in time a man himself may find within [him]self,—a man perfected in spiritual exercise.

5. 6–12: Hard to attain is [true] renunciation without [the practice of some] spiritual exercise: the sage well versed in spiritual exercise right soon to Brahman comes. (7) Well versed in spiritual exercise, his self made pure, his self and senses quelled, his self become the [very] self of every contingent being, though working still, he is not defiled.

(8) 'Lo, nothing do I do': so thinks the integrated man who knows things as they really are, . . . (9) . . . 'The senses are busied with their

proper objects: [what has that to do with me?' This is the way] he thinks. . . . (11) With body, mind, soul, and senses alone-and-isolated [from the self] do men {who are integrated / engaged in spiritual exercise} engage in action renouncing attachment for the cleansing of the self. (12) The integrated man, renouncing the fruit of works, gains an abiding peace: the man not integrated, whose works are prompted by desire, being attached to fruits, is bound.

5. 21: [His] self detached from contacts with the outside world, in [him]self he finds his joy, [his] self in Brahman integrated by spiritual exercise, he finds unfailing joy.

5. 23–4: Only the man who [remains] in this world and, before he is released from the body, can stand fast against the onset of desire and anger, is [truly] integrated, [truly] happy. (24) His joy within, his bliss within, his light within, the man who-is-integrated-in-spiritual-exercise becomes Brahman and draws nigh to Nirvāna that is Brahman too.

6. 3–4: For the silent sage who would climb [the ladder of] spiritual exercise (*yoga*) works are said to be the means; but for that same [sage] who has reached the state of integration (*yoga*) they say quiescence is the means. (4) For when a man knows no attachment to objects of sense or to the deeds [he does], when he has renounced all purpose, then has he reached the state of integration, or so they say.

6. 8: With self content in wisdom learnt from holy books and wisdom learnt from life, with sense subdued, sublime, aloof, [this] athlete of the spirit (*yogin*) [stands]: 'Integrated (*yukta*)', so is he called; the same to him are clods of earth, stones, gold.

6. 10–29: Let the athlete of the spirit ever integrate [him]self standing in a place apart, alone, his thoughts and self restrained, devoid of [earthly] hope, possessing nothing (11–13: see III (*b*)). (14) Let him sit, [his] self all stilled, his fear all gone, firm in his vow of chastity, his mind controlled, his thoughts on Me, integrated, [yet] intent on Me. (15) Thus let the athlete of the spirit be constant in integrating [him]self, his mind restrained; then will he approach that peace which has Nirvāna as its end and which subsists in Me (16–17: see III (*b*)).

(18) When thought, held well in check, is stilled in self alone, then is a man from longing freed though all desires assail him: then do men call him 'integrated'. (19) As a lamp might stand in a windless place, unflickering,—this likeness has been heard of such athletes of the spirit who control their thought and practise integration of the self.

(20) When thought by spiritual exercise is checked and comes to rest,

and when of [one]self one sees the self in self and finds content therein, (21) that is the utmost joy which transcends [all things of] sense and which soul [alone] can grasp. When he knows this and [knowing it] stands still, moving not an inch from the reality [he sees], (22) he wins a prize beyond all others,—or so he thinks. Therein he [firmly] stands, unmoved by any suffering, however grievous it may be. (23) This he should know is what is meant by 'spiritual exercise' (*yoga*),—the unlinking of the link with suffering-and-pain. This is the act-of-integration (*yoga*) that must be brought about with [firm] resolve and mind all undismayed. (24–6: see III (*f*).) (27) For upon this athlete of the spirit whose mind is stilled the highest joy descends: [all] passion laid to rest, free from [all] stain, Brahman he becomes. (28) [And] thus [all] flaws transcending, the athlete of the spirit, constant in integrating [him]self, with ease attains unbounded joy, Brahman's [saving] touch. (29) With self integrated by spiritual exercise [now] he sees the self in all beings standing, all beings in the self: the same in everything he sees.

6. 46–7: Higher than the [mere] ascetic is the athlete of the spirit held to be, yes, higher than the man of wisdom, higher than the man of works: be, then, a spiritual athlete, Arjuna! (47) But of all athletes of the spirit the man of faith who loves-and-honours Me, his inmost self absorbed in Me,—he is the most fully integrated: this do I believe.

7. 1: . . . Engaging [still] in spiritual exercise (*yoga*) put your trust in Me. . . .

7. 16–18: (The integrated man who has wisdom and loves God): see III (*g*).

8. 8: Let a man's thoughts be integrated by spiritual exercise and constant striving: let him not stray to anything else at all; so by meditating on the divine exalted Person, [that man to that Person] goes.

8. 10: With mind unmoving at the time of passing on, by love-and-devotion integrated and by the power of spiritual exercise too . . . a man will draw nigh to that divine exalted Person.

8. 14: How easily am I won by him who bears Me in mind unceasingly, thinking of nothing else at all,—an athlete of the spirit ever integrated [in himself].

8. 28: . . . All [meeds of merit] the athlete of the spirit leaves behind who knows this [secret teaching; and knowing it] he draws nigh to the exalted primal state.

9. 14: . . . Integrated ever [in themselves] they pay Me worship.

9. 28: . . . [Your]self [now] integrated by renunciation and spiritual exercise, set free, you will draw nigh to Me.

9. 34: . . . Now that you have integrated self, your striving bent on Me, to Me you will [surely] come.

10. 7: Whoso should know this my far-flung power and how I use it, [whoso should know these] as they really are, is [truly] integrated; and this his integration can never be undone. Herein there is no doubt.

10. 10: To these men who are ever integrated and commune with Me in love I give that integration of the soul by which they may draw nigh to Me.

12. 2: Those I deem to be most integrated who fix their thoughts on Me and serve Me, ever integrated [in themselves], filled with the highest faith.

18. 51–3: Let a man be integrated by his soul [now] cleansed . . . (53) . . . [if he does this,] to becoming Brahman is he conformed.

18. 57: . . . Relying on the integration of the soul, think on Me constantly.

III. (*b*) *Yogic Techniques*

5. 27–8: [All] contact with things outside he puts away, fixing his gaze between the eyebrows; inward and outward breaths he makes the same as they pass up and down the nostrils. (28) With senses, mind, and soul restrained, the silent sage, on deliverance intent, who has forever banished fear, anger, and desire, is truly liberated.

6. 11–17: Let him set up for [him]self a steady seat in a clean place, neither too high nor yet too low, bestrewn with cloth or hide or grass. (12) There let him sit and make his mind a single point, let him restrain the operations of his thought and senses and practise integration to purify the self. (13) [Remaining] still, let him keep body, head, and neck in a straight line, unmoving; let him fix his eye on the tip of his nose, not looking round about him. (14) [There] let him sit, [his] self all stilled, his fear all gone, firm in his vow of chastity, his mind controlled, his thoughts on Me, integrated, [yet] intent on Me. (15) Thus let the athlete of the spirit (*yogin*) be constant in integrating [him]self, his mind restrained; then will he approach that peace which has Nirvāna as its end and which subsists in Me.

(16) But [this] spiritual exercise is not for him who eats too much, nor yet for him who does not eat at all, nor for him who is all too prone to sleep, nor yet for him who [always] stays awake. (17) [Rather] is [this]

way of integration (*yoga*) for him who knows-the-mean (*yukta*) in food and recreation, who knows-the-mean in his deeds-and-gestures, who knows-the-mean in sleeping as in waking; [this] practice-of-the-mean [it is] that slaughters pain.

8. 10: . . . Forcing the breath between the eyebrows duly, so will that man draw nigh to that divine exalted Person.

8. 12–13: Let a man close up all [the body's] gates, stem his mind within the heart, fix his breath within the head, engrossed in Yogic concentration, (13) let him utter [the word] Oṁ, Brahman in one syllable, keeping Me in mind; then, when he departs, leaving aside the body, he will tread the highest way.

III. (*c*) *Renunciation*

5. 2–6: Renouncing works,—performing them [as spiritual exercise],—both lead to the highest goal; but of the two to engage in works is more excellent than to renounce them. (3) This is the mark of the man whose renunciation is abiding: he hates not nor desires, for, devoid of all dualities, how easily is he released from bondage. (4) 'There must be a difference between theory and practice', so say the simple-minded, not the wise. Apply yourself to only one whole-heartedly and win the fruit of both. (5) [True,] the men of [contemplative] theory attain a [high] estate, but that [same estate] achieve the men of practice (*yoga*) too; for theory and practice are all one: who sees [that this is true], he sees [indeed]. (6) But hard to attain is [true] renunciation without [the practice of some] spiritual exercise: the sage well versed in spiritual exercise right soon to Brahman comes.

12. 12: . . . Better than meditation is to renounce the fruits of works: renunciation leads straightway to peace.

18. 2–6: To give up works dictated by desire, wise men allow [this] to be renunciation; surrender of all the fruits [that accrue] to works discerning men call self-surrender. (3) '[All] works must be surrendered, for [works themselves] are tainted with defect': so say some of the wise; but others say that [works of] sacrifice, the gift of alms, and works of penance are not to be surrendered. (4) Hear [then] my own decision in this matter of surrender: . . . (5) [Works of] sacrifice, the gift of alms, and works of penance are not to be surrendered; these must most certainly be done: it is sacrifice, alms-giving, and ascetic practice that purify the wise. (6) But even these works should be done [in a spirit of self-surrender], for [all] attachment [to what you do] and [all] the fruits [of what you do] must be surrendered. This is my last decisive word. (For 7–11 see II (*c*) (i).)

18. 12: Unwanted—wanted—mixed: threefold is the fruit of work,—[this they experience] at death who have not surrendered [self], but not at all such men as have renounced.

III. (*d*) *Sameness-and-Indifference—Beyond Duality and Ego*

2. 15: For wise men there are, the same in pleasure as in pain, whom these [contacts] leave undaunted: such are conformed to immortality.

2. 38: Hold pleasure and pain, profit and loss, victory and defeat to be the same.

2. 45: . . . Have done with [all] dualities, stand ever firm on Goodness. . . .

2. 48: Stand fast in Yoga, surrendering attachment; in success and failure be the same and then get busy with your works. Yoga means 'sameness-and-indifference'.

2. 50: Whoso is integrated by the soul discards here [and now] both good and evil works: brace yourself then for [this] Yoga; for Yoga is [also] skill in [performing] works.

2. 53: When your soul . . . stands motionless and still, . . . then will you attain to Yoga (sameness-and-indifference).

2. 56–7: Whose mind is undismayed [though beset] by many a sorrow, who for pleasures has no further longing, from whom all passion, fear, and wrath have fled, such a man is called a man of steadied thought, a silent sage. (57) Who has no love for any thing, who rejoices not at whatever good befalls him nor hates the bad that comes his way,—firm-stablished is the wisdom of such a man.

2. 64: But he who roves among the objects of sense, his senses subdued to self and disjoined from passion and hate, and who is self-possessed [himself], draws nigh to calm serenity.

2. 71: The man who puts away all desires and roams around from longing freed, who does not think, 'This I am', or 'This is mine', draws near to peace.

3. 18: In works done and works undone on earth he has no interest,—no [interest] in all contingent beings: on such interest he does not depend.

3. 30: . . . Have neither hope nor thought that 'This is mine'. . . .

4. 22: Content to take whatever chance may bring his way, surmounting [all] dualities, knowing no envy, the same in success and failure, though working [still] he is not bound.

5. 3: This is the mark of the man whose renunciation is abiding: he hates not nor desires, for, devoid of all dualities, how easily is he released from bondage.

5. 18–20: [These] wise ones see the selfsame thing in a Brāhman wise and courteous as in a cow or an elephant, nay, as in a dog or outcaste. (19) While yet in this world they have overcome [the process of] emanation [and decay], for their minds are stilled in that-which-is-ever-the-same: for devoid of imperfection and ever-the-same is Brahman: therefore in Brahman [stilled] they stand. (20) Winning some pleasant thing [the sage] will not rejoice, nor shrink disquietened when the unpleasant comes his way: steadfast-and-still his soul, [all] unconfused, he will know Brahman, in Brahman [stilled] he'll stand.

6. 7–9: The higher self of the self-subdued, quietened, is rapt in enstasy,—in cold as in heat, in pleasure as in pain, likewise in honour and disgrace. (8) With self content in wisdom learnt from holy books and wisdom learnt from life, with sense subdued, sublime, aloof, [this] athlete of the spirit (*yogin*) [stands]: 'Integrated', so is he called; the same to him are clods of earth, stones, gold. (9) Outstanding is he whose soul views in the selfsame way friends, comrades, enemies, those indifferent, neutrals, men who are hateful and those who are his kin,—the good and the evil too.

6. 29: With self integrated by spiritual exercise [now] he sees the self in all beings standing, all beings in the self: the same in everything he sees.

6. 32: By analogy with self who sees the same [Brahman] everywhere, be it as pleasure or as pain, he is the highest athlete of the spirit, or so men think.

9. 29: In all contingent beings the same am I; none do I hate and none do I fondly love. . . .

12. 3–4: But those who revere the indeterminate Imperishable Unmanifest, unthinkable though coursing everywhere, sublime, aloof, unmoving, firm, (4) who hold in check the complex of the senses, in all things equal-minded, taking pleasure in the weal of all contingent beings, these too attain to Me.

12. 13: Let a man feel hatred for no contingent being, let him be friendly, compassionate; let him be done with thoughts of 'I' and 'mine', the same in pleasure as in pain, long-suffering.

12. 18–19: I love the man who is the same to friend and foe, [the same] whether he be respected or despised, the same in heat and cold, in pleasure as in pain, who has put away attachment and remains unmoved by praise or blame, who is taciturn, contented with whatever comes his way, having no home, of steady mind, [but] loyal-devoted-and-devout.

13. 27–8: The same in all contingent beings, abiding [without change], the Highest Lord, when all things fall to ruin, [Himself] is not destroyed: who sees Him sees [indeed]. (28) For seeing Him, the same, the Lord, established everywhere, he cannot of himself to [him]self do hurt, hence he treads the highest way.

14. 24–5: The same in pleasure as in pain and self-assured, the same when faced with clods of earth or stones or gold; for him, wise man, are friend and foe of equal weight, equal the praise or blame [with which men cover him]. (25) Equal [his mind] in honour and disgrace, equal to ally and to enemy, he renounces every [busy] enterprise: 'He has transcended the constituents': so must men say.

18. 53–4: Let him give up all thought of 'I', . . . let him not think of anything as 'mine', at peace;—[if he does this,] to becoming Brahman is he conformed. (54) Brahman become, with self serene, he grieves not nor desires; the same to all contingent beings he gains the highest love-and-loyalty to Me.

III. (*e*) Bhakti (*the Love of God*) *as Means*

2. 61: Let him sit, curbing all [the senses], integrated, intent on Me: for firmly established is that man's wisdom whose senses are subdued.

4. 3: This is the same primeval mode of life that I preach to you today; for you are loyal, devoted, and my comrade, and this is the highest mystery.

6. 14–15: Let him sit, [his] self all stilled, . . . his thoughts on Me, integrated, [yet] intent on Me. (15) Thus let the athlete of the spirit (*yogin*) be constant in integrating [him]self . . .; then will he approach that peace which has Nirvāna as its end and which subsists in Me.

7. 16: Fourfold are the doers of good who love-and-worship Me,—the afflicted, the man who seeks wisdom, the man who strives for gain, and the man who wisdom knows.

7. 23: . . . Whoso worships the gods, to the gods will [surely] go, but whoso loves-and-worships Me, to Me will come indeed.

7. 29–30: Whoso shall strive to win release from old age and death, putting his trust in Me, will come to know that Brahman in its wholeness,—as it appertains to self, the whole [mystery] of works, (30) as it appertains to contingent beings, and to the divine,—and Me [too] as I appertain to sacrifice. And whoso shall know Me [thus] even at the time of passing on, will know [Me] with an integrated mind.

8. 5–7: Whoso at the hour of death . . . bears Me in mind and passes on, accedes to my own mode of being. . . . (7) Then muse upon Me always . . .; for if you fix your mind and soul on Me, you will, nothing doubting, come to Me.

8. 22: But that highest Person is to be won by love-and-worship directed to none other. In Him do all beings subsist; by Him this universe was spun.

9. 22: For those men who meditate on Me, no other [thought in mind], who do Me honour, ever persevere, I bring attainment and possession of what has been attained.

9. 25: To the gods go the gods' devotees, to the ancestors their votaries, to disembodied spirits go the worshippers of these, but those who worship Me shall come to Me.

9. 26–34: Be it a leaf or flower or fruit or water that a zealous soul may offer Me with love's devotion, that do I [willingly] accept, for it was love that made the offering. (27) Whatever you do, whatever you eat, whatever you offer in sacrifice or give away in alms, whatever penance you may perform, offer it up to Me. (28) So from [those] bonds which works [of their very nature forge], whose fruits are fair and foul, you will be freed: [your]self [now] integrated by renunciation and spiritual exercise, set free, you will draw nigh to Me. (29) In all contingent beings the same am I; none do I hate and none do I fondly love; but those who commune with Me in love's devotion [abide] in Me, and I in them.

(30) However evil a man's livelihood may be, let him but worship Me with love and serve no other, then shall he be reckoned among the good indeed, for his resolve is right. (31) Right soon will his self be justified and win eternal rest. Arjuna, be sure of this: none who worships Me with loyalty-and-love is lost to Me. (32) For whosoever makes Me his haven, base-born though he may be, yes, women too and artisans, even serfs, theirs it is to tread the highest way. (33) How much more, then, Brāhmans pure-and-good, and royal seers who know devoted love. Since your lot has fallen in this world, impermanent and joyless, commune with Me in love. (34) On Me your mind, on Me your loving-service, for Me your sacrifice, to Me be your prostrations: now that you have thus integrated self, your striving bent on Me, to Me you will [surely] come.

11. 54–5: By worship-of-love addressed to [Me,] none other . . . can I be known and seen in such a form and as I really am: [so can my lovers] enter into Me. (55) Do works for Me, make Me your highest goal, be loyal-in-love to Me, cut off all [other] attachments, have no hatred for any being at all: for all who do thus shall come to Me.

12. 6–8: But those who cast off all their works on Me, solely intent on Me, and meditate on Me in spiritual exercise, leaving no room for others, [and so really] do Me honour, (7) these will I lift up on high out of the ocean of recurring death, and that right soon, for their thoughts are fixed on Me. (8) On Me alone let your mind dwell, stir up your soul to enter Me; thenceforth in very truth in Me you will find your home.

12. 13–20: (13–19, 'The man God loves', see IV). (20) But as for those who reverence these deathless [words] of righteousness which I have just now spoken, putting their faith [in them], making Me their goal, my loving-devotees,—these do I love exceedingly.

13. 18: . . . The man who loves-and-worships Me . . . becomes fit to [share in] my own mode of being.

III. (*f*) Moksha: *Liberation or Spiritual Freedom*

2. 15: Wise men there are, the same in pleasure as in pain, whom these [contacts] leave undaunted: such are conformed to immortality.

2. 51: Those wise men who are integrated by the soul, who have renounced the fruit that is born of works, these will be freed from the bondage of [re-]birth and fare to that region that knows no ill.

2. 59: For the embodied [self] who eats no more, objects of sense must disappear,—save only the [recollected] flavour,—and that too must vanish at the vision of the highest.

2. 64: He who roves among the objects of sense, his senses subdued to self and disjoined from passion and hate, and who is self-possessed [himself], draws nigh to calm serenity.

2. 69–72: In what for all [other] folk is night, therein is the man of self-restraint [wide-]awake. When all [other] folk are awake, that is night for the sage who sees. (70) As the waters flow into the sea, full filled, whose ground remains unmoved, so too do all desires flow into [the heart of] man: and such a man wins peace,—not the desirer of desires. (71) The man who puts away all desires and roams around from longing freed, who does not think, 'This I am', or 'This is mine', draws near to peace. (72) This is the fixed, still state of Brahman; he who wins through to this is nevermore perplexed. Standing therein at the time of death, to Nirvāna that is Brahman too he goes.

3. 31: Whatever men shall practise constantly this my doctrine, firm in faith, not envying, [not cavilling,] they too will find release from works.

4. 9–10: Who knows my godly birth and mode of operation (*karma*) thus as they really are, he, his body left behind, is never born again: he comes to Me. (10) Many are they who, passion, fear, and anger spent, inhere in Me, making Me their sanctuary; made pure by wisdom and hard penances, they come to [share in] my own mode of being.

4. 15: Knowing this the ancients too did work though seeking [all the while] release [from temporal life]. . . .

4. 23–4: Attachment gone, deliverance won, his thoughts are fixed on wisdom: he works for sacrifice [alone], and all the work [he ever did] entirely melts away. (24) The offering is Brahman, Brahman the [sacrificial] ghee offered by Brahman in Brahman's fire: who sinks himself in this [sacrificial] act which is Brahman, to Brahman must he thereby go.

4. 31–2: Eating of the leavings of the sacrifice, the food of immortality, they come to primeval Brahman. This world is not for him who performs no sacrifice,—much less the other [world]. (32) So, many and various are the sacrifices spread out athwart the mouth of Brahman. They spring from work, all of them: be sure of this; for once you know this, you will win release.

4. 35: . . . By [knowing] this you will behold [all] beings in [your]self,—every one of them,—and then in Me.

4. 39: A man of faith, intent on wisdom, his senses [all] restrained, wins wisdom; and, wisdom won, he will come right soon to perfect peace.

5. 6: . . . The sage well versed in spiritual exercise (*yoga-yukta*) right soon to Brahman comes.

5. 12: The integrated man, renouncing the fruit of works, gains an abiding peace.

5. 17: Souls [bent on] that, selves [bent on] that, with that their aim and that their aspiration, they stride [along the path] from which there is no return. . . .

5. 19–28: . . . Their minds are stilled in that-which-is-ever-the-same: for devoid of imperfection and ever-the-same is Brahman: therefore in Brahman stilled they stand. (20) . . . Steadfast-and-still his soul, [all] unconfused, he will know Brahman, in Brahman [stilled] he'll stand. (21) [His] self detached from contacts with the outside world, in

[him]self he finds his joy, [his] self in Brahman integrated by spiritual exercise, he finds unfailing joy. . . . (24) His joy within, his bliss within, his light within, the man who-is-integrated-in-spiritual-exercise (*yogin*) becomes Brahman and draws nigh to Nirvāna that is Brahman too. (25) Nirvāna that is Brahman too win seers in whom [all] taint-of-imperfection is destroyed; their doubts dispelled, with self controlled, they take their pleasure in the weal of all contingent beings. (26) Around these holy men whose thoughts are [fast] controlled, estranged from anger and desire, knowing [at last] the self, fares Nirvāna that is Brahman too. . . . (28) With senses, mind, and soul restrained, the silent sage, on deliverance intent, who has forever banished fear, anger, and desire, is truly liberated.

5. 29: Knowing Me to be the proper object of sacrifice and mortification, great Lord of all the worlds, friend of all contingent beings, he reaches peace.

6. 14–15: Let him sit, [his] self all stilled, his fear all gone, firm in his vow of chastity, his mind controlled, his thoughts on Me, integrated, [yet] intent on Me. (15) Thus let the athlete of the spirit (*yogin*) be constant in integrating [him]self, his mind restrained; then will he approach that peace which has Nirvāna as its end and which subsists in Me.

6. 18–22: (For 18–19 see III (*a*)). (20) When thought by spiritual exercise is checked, and when of [one]self one sees the self in self and finds content therein, (21) that is the utmost joy which transcends [all things of] sense and which soul [alone] can grasp. When he knows this and [knowing it] stands still, moving not an inch from the reality [he sees], (22) he wins a prize beyond all others,—or so he thinks. Therein he [firmly] stands, unmoved by any suffering, however grievous it may be.

6. 24–9: Let him renounce all desires whose origin lies in the will,—all of them without remainder; let him restrain in every way by mind alone the senses' busy throng. (25) By soul held fast in steadfastness he must make the mind [too] subsist in the self; then little by little will he come to rest; he must think of nothing at all. (26) Wherever the fickle mind unsteady roves around, from thence [the soul] will bring it back and subject it to the self. (27) For upon this athlete of the spirit whose mind is stilled the highest joy descends: [all] passion laid to rest, free from [all] stain, Brahman he becomes. (28) [And] thus [all] flaws transcending, the athlete of the spirit, constant in integrating [him]self, with ease attains unbounded joy, Brahman's [saving] touch. (29) With self integrated by spiritual exercise [now] he sees the self in all beings standing, all beings in the self: the same in everything he sees.

7. 16–19: (The 'man of wisdom' who confesses and loves God), see III (*g*).

7. 28: (The liberated man who loves God), see III (*h*).

7. 29–30: Whoso shall strive to win release from old age and death, putting his trust in Me, will come to know that Brahman in its wholeness,—as it appertains to self, the whole [mystery] of works, (30) as it appertains to contingent beings, and to the divine,—and Me [too] as I appertain to sacrifice.

8. 28: . . . The athlete of the spirit . . . draws right nigh to the exalted primal state.

9. 28: So from [those] bonds which works [of their very nature forge], whose fruits are fair and foul, you will be freed: [your]self [now] integrated by renunciation and spiritual exercise, set free, you will draw nigh to Me.

10. 3: Whoso shall know Me as unborn, beginningless, great Lord of [all] the worlds, shall never know delusion among men, from every evil freed.

13. 34: Whoso with wisdom's eye discerns the difference between 'field' and 'knower of the field', and knows deliverance from material Nature to which [all] contingent beings are subject, goes to the further [shore].

14. 19–20: When the watching [self] sees there is no agent other than [these] constituents and knows what is beyond them, then will he come to [share in] that mode of being which is mine. (20) Transcending these three constituents which give the body its existence, from the sufferings of birth, death, and old age delivered, the embodied [self] wins immortality.

16. 22: When once a man is freed from these three gates of darkness, then can he work for [his] self's salvation, thence tread the highest way.

18. 51–4: Let a man be integrated by his soul [now] cleansed, . . . (53) . . . [if he does this,] to becoming Brahman is he conformed. (54) Brahman become, with self serene, he grieves not nor desires; the same to all contingent beings he gains the highest love-and-loyalty to Me.

III. (*g*) *Wisdom*

2. 55–68: When a man puts from him all desires that prey upon the mind, himself contented in self alone, then is he called a man of steady wisdom. (56) Whose mind is undismayed [though beset] by many a sorrow, who for pleasures has no further longing, from whom all passion, fear, and wrath have fled, such a man is called a man of steadied thought, a silent sage. (57) Who has no love for any thing, who rejoices not at whatever good befalls him nor hates the bad that comes his way,—firm-stablished is the wisdom of such a man. (58) And when he draws in on every side his senses from their proper objects as a tortoise [might draw in] its limbs,—firm-stablished is the wisdom of such a man. . . . (61) Let him sit curbing all [the senses], integrated (*yukta*), intent on Me: for firmly established is that man's wisdom whose senses are subdued. . . . (68) And so whose senses are withheld from the objects proper to them, wherever he may be, firm-stablished is the wisdom of such a man.

3. 39–40: [Desire] is the wise man's eternal foe; by this is wisdom overcast, whatever form it takes, a fire insatiable. (40) Sense, mind, and soul, they say, are the places where it lurks; through these it smothers wisdom, fooling the embodied [self].

4. 10: . . . Made pure by wisdom and hard penances, they come to [share in] my own mode of being.

4. 19: When all a man's emprises are free from desire [for fruit] and motive, his works burnt up in wisdom's fire, then wise men call him learned.

4. 23: Attachment gone, deliverance won, his thoughts are fixed on wisdom: he works for sacrifice [alone], and all the work [he ever did] entirely melts away.

4. 27: Others offer up all works of sense and works of vital breath in the fire of the spiritual exercise of self-control kindled by wisdom.

4. 33–42: Better than the sacrifice of wealth is the sacrifice of wisdom. All works without exception in wisdom find their consummation. (34) Learn to know this by humble reverence [of the wise], by questioning, by service, [for] the wise who see things as they really are will teach you wisdom. (35) Once you have known this you will never again be perplexed as you are now: by [knowing] this you will behold [all] beings in [your]self,—every one of them,—and then in Me. (36) Even though you were the very worst among all evil-doers, [yet once you have boarded] wisdom's bark, you will surmount all [this] tortuous [stream of life]. (37) As a kindled fire reduces its fuel to ashes, so does the fire of wisdom reduce all works to ashes. (38) For nothing on earth resembles wisdom in its power to purify; and this in time a man himself may find within [him]self,—a man perfected in spiritual exercise. (39) A man of faith, intent on wisdom, his senses [all] restrained, wins wisdom; and, wisdom won, he will come right soon to perfect peace. . . . (41) Let a man in spiritual exercise [all] works renounce, let him by wisdom [all] doubts dispel, let him be himself, and then [whatever] his works [may be, they] will never bind him [more]. (42) And so [take up] the sword of wisdom and with it cut this doubt of yours, unwisdom's child, still lurking in your heart: prepare for action now, stand up!

5. 15–17: . . . By ignorance is wisdom overspread; thereby are creatures fooled. (16) But some there are whose ignorance of self by wisdom is destroyed. Their wisdom, like the sun, illumines that [all-]highest. (17) Souls [bent on] that, selves [bent on] that, with that their aim and that their aspiration, they stride [along the path] from which there is no return, [all] taints by wisdom washed away.

7. 15: Doers of evil, deluded, base, put not their trust in Me; their wisdom swept away by [this] my uncanny power (*māyā*), they cleave to a devilish mode of existence.

7. 16–19: Fourfold are the doers of good who love-and-worship Me,—the afflicted, the man who seeks wisdom, the man who strives for gain, and the man who wisdom knows. (17) Of these the man of wisdom, ever integrated, who loves-and-worships One alone excels: for to the man of wisdom I am exceeding dear and he is dear to Me. (18) All these are noble-and-exalted, but the man of wisdom is [my] very self, so do I hold, for with self [already] integrated he puts his trust in Me, the one all-highest Way. (19) At the end of many a birth the man of wisdom gives himself up to Me, [knowing that Krishna,] Vasudeva's son, is All: so great a self is exceeding hard to find. (20) [All] wisdom swept away by manifold desires, men put their trust in other gods. . . .

7. 29–30: Whoso shall strive to win release from old age and death, putting his trust in Me, will come to know that Brahman in its wholeness,—as it appertains to self, the whole [mystery] of works, (30) as it appertains to contingent beings, and to the divine,—and Me [too] as I appertain to sacrifice. And whoso shall know Me [thus] even at the time of passing on, will know [Me] with an integrated mind.

9. 15: Others again with wisdom's sacrifice make sacrifice to Me and worship Me as One and yet as Manifold, in many a guise with face turned every way.

10. 11: Out of compassion for those same men [all] darkness born of ignorance I dispel with wisdom's shining lamp, abiding [ever] in my own [true] nature.

11. 18: You [Krishna] are wisdom's highest goal.

13. 2: . . . Knowledge of the 'field' and the 'knower of the field' I deem to be [true] knowledge.

13. 7–11: To shun conceit and tricky ways, to wish none harm, to be long-suffering and upright, to reverence one's teacher, purity, steadfastness, self-restraint, (8) detachment from the senses' objects and no sense of 'I' most certainly, insight into birth, death, old age, disease, and pain, and what constitutes their worthlessness, (9) to be detached and not to cling to sons, wives, houses, and the like, a constant equal-mindedness whatever happens, pleasing or unpleasing, (10) unswerving loyalty-and-love for Me with spiritual exercise on no other bent, to dwell apart in desert places, to take no pleasure in the company of men, (11) constant attention to the wisdom that appertains to self, to see where knowledge of reality must lead, [all] this is 'knowledge' (wisdom).

13. 12: I will tell you that which should be known: . . . The highest Brahman It is called. . . . (See V (*d*).)

13. 17: Light of lights, 'Beyond the Darkness' It is called: [true] knowledge, what should be known, accessible to knowledge, established in the heart of all.

14. 6: Among these Goodness, being immaculate, knowing no sickness, dispenses light, [and yet] it binds by [causing the self] to cling to wisdom and to joy.

14. 11: When at all the body's gates wisdom's light arises, then must you know that Goodness has increased.

15. 10: . . . Whoso possesses wisdom's eye sees [the self indeed].

15. 19: Whoever thus knows Me, unconfused, as the Person [All-] Sublime, knows all and [knowing all] communes with Me with all his being, all his love.

18. 20–2: That [kind of] knowledge by which one sees one mode of being, changeless, undivided in all contingent beings, divided [as they are], is Goodness' [knowledge]. . . . (21) But that [kind of] knowledge which in all contingent beings discerns in separation all manner of modes of being, different and distinct,—this, you must know, is knowledge born of Passion. (22) But that [kind of knowledge] which sticks to one effect as if it were all,—irrational, not bothering about the Real as the [true] object [of all knowledge, thinking of it as] finite,—this [knowledge] belongs to Darkness.

18. 50: Perfection found, now learn from Me how you may reach Brahman too: . . . it is wisdom's highest bourne.

18. 70: Whoso shall read this dialogue which you and I have held concerning what is right, it will be as if he had offered Me a sacrifice of wisdom.

III. (*h*) Parā bhakti (*the Love of God*) *as End*

4. 9–11: Who knows my godly birth and mode of operation (*karma*) thus as they really are, he, his body left behind, is never born again: he comes to Me. (10) Many are they who, passion, fear, and anger spent, inhere in Me, making Me their sanctuary; made pure by wisdom and hard penances, they come to [share in] my own mode of being. (11) In whatsoever way [devoted] men approach Me, in that same way do I return their love. [Whatever their occupation and] wherever they may be, men follow in my footsteps.

6. 30–2: Who sees Me everywhere, who sees the All in Me, for him I am not lost, nor is he lost to Me. (31) Who standing firm on unity communes-in-love with Me as abiding in all beings, in whatever state he be, that athlete of the spirit abides in Me. (32) By analogy with self who sees the same [Brahman] everywhere, be it as pleasure or as pain, he is the highest athlete of the spirit, or so men think.

6. 46–7: Higher than the [mere] ascetic is the athlete of the spirit (*yogin*) held to be, yes, higher than the man of wisdom, higher than the man of works. . . . (47) But of all athletes of the spirit the man of faith who loves-and-honours Me, his inmost self absorbed in Me,—he is the most fully integrated: this do I believe.

7. 1: Attach your mind to Me.

7. 3: Among thousands of men but one, maybe, will strive for [self-] perfection, and even among [these] athletes who have won perfection['s crown] but one, maybe, will come to know Me as I really am.

7. 17–18: Of [my devotees] the man of wisdom, ever integrated, who loves-and-worships One alone excels: for to the man of wisdom I am exceeding dear and he is dear to Me. (18) All these are noble-and-exalted, but the man of wisdom is [my] very self . . ., for with self [already] integrated he puts his trust in Me, the one all-highest Way.

7. 28: But some there are for whom [all] ill is ended, doers of what is good-and-pure: released [at last] from the confusion of duality, steady in their vows, they love-and-worship Me.

8. 8–16: Let a man's thoughts be integrated by spiritual exercise and constant striving: let them not stray to anything else at all; so by meditating on the divine exalted Person, [that man to that Person] goes. . . . (10) With mind unmoving at the time of passing on, by love-

and-devotion integrated and by the power of spiritual exercise, . . . so will that man draw nigh to that divine exalted Person. . . . (13) Let him utter [the word] Oṁ, Brahman in one syllable, keeping Me in mind; then, when he departs, leaving aside the body, he will tread the highest way. (14) How easily am I won by him who bears Me in mind unceasingly, thinking of nothing else at all,—an athlete of the spirit ever integrated [in himself]. (15) Coming right nigh to Me these great of self are never born again, . . . they attain the highest prize. (16). . . . He who comes right nigh to Me shall never be born again.

9. 13–15: Great-souled men take up their stand in a nature that is divine; and so with minds intent on naught but [Me], they love-and-worship Me, knowing [Me to be] the beginning of [all] contingent beings, as Him who passes not away. (14) Me do they ever glorify, [for Me] they strive, full firm their vows; to Me do they bow down, devoted-in-their-love, and integrated ever [in themselves] they pay Me worship. (15) Others again with wisdom's sacrifice make sacrifice to Me and worship Me as One and yet as Manifold, in many a guise with face turned every way.

10. 8–11: The source of all am I; from Me all things proceed: this knowing, wise men commune with Me in love, full filled with warm affection. (9) On Me their thoughts, their life they would sacrifice for Me; [and so] enlightening one another and telling my story constantly they take their pleasure and delight. (10) To these men who are ever integrated and commune with Me in love I give that integration of the soul by which they may draw nigh to Me. (11) Out of compassion for those same men [all] darkness born of ignorance I dispel with wisdom's shining lamp, abiding [ever] in my own [true] nature.

12. 2: Those do I deem to be most integrated who fix their thoughts on Me and serve Me, ever integrated [in themselves], filled with the highest faith.

15. 19: Whoever thus knows Me, unconfused, as the Person [All-] Sublime, knows all and [knowing all] communes with Me with all his being, all his love.

18. 54–70: Brahman become, with self serene, he grieves not nor desires; the same to all contingent beings he gains the highest love-and-loyalty to Me. (55) By love-and-loyalty he comes to know Me as I really am, how great I am and who: and once he knows Me as I am, he enters [Me] forthwith. (56) Let him then do all manner of works continually, putting his trust in Me; for by my grace he will attain to an eternal, changeless state.

(57) Give up in thought to Me all that you do, make Me your goal:

relying on the integration of the soul, think on Me constantly. (58) Thinking on Me you will surmount all dangers by my grace; but if through selfishness you will not listen, then you will [surely] perish. (59) [But if,] relying on your ego, you should think, 'I will not fight', vain is your resolve, [for] Nature will constrain you. (60) You are bound by your own works which spring from your own nature; [for] what, deluded, you would not do you will do perforce. (61) In the region of the heart of all contingent beings dwells the Lord, twirling them hither and thither by his uncanny power (*māyā*) [like puppets] mounted on a machine.

(62) In Him alone seek refuge with all your being, all your love; and by his grace you will attain an eternal state, the highest peace. (63) Of all the mysteries the most mysterious, this wisdom have I told you; ponder it in all its amplitude, then do whatever you will. (64) And now again give ear to this my highest Word, of all the most mysterious: 'I love you well.' Therefore will I tell you your salvation. (65) Bear Me in mind, love Me and worship Me, sacrifice, prostrate yourself to Me: so will you come to Me, I promise you truly, for you are dear to Me. (66) Give up all things of law, turn to Me, your only refuge, [for] I will deliver you from all evils; have no care.

(67) Never must you tell this word to one whose life is not austere, to one devoid of love-and-loyalty, to one who refuses to obey, or to one who envies Me. (68) [But] whoever shall proclaim this highest mystery to my loving devotees, showing the while the highest love-and-loyalty to Me, shall, nothing doubting, come to Me indeed. (69) No one among men can render Me more pleasing service than a man like this; nor shall any other man on earth be more beloved by Me than he. (70) And whoso shall read this dialogue which you and I have held concerning what is right, it will be as if he had offered Me a sacrifice of wisdom: so do I believe.

IV. *The Perfect Man*

12. 13–20: Let a man feel hatred for no contingent being, let him be friendly, compassionate; let him be done with thoughts of 'I' and 'mine', the same in pleasure as in pain, long-suffering, (14) content and ever integrated, his self restrained, his purpose firm, let his mind and soul be steeped in Me, let him worship Me with love: then will I love him [in return].

(15) That man I love from whom the people do not shrink and who does not shrink from them, who is free from exaltation, fear, impatience, and excitement. (16) I love the man who has no expectation, is pure and skilled, indifferent, who has no worries and who gives up all [selfish] enterprise, loyal-and-devoted to Me. (17) I love the man who hates not nor exults, who mourns not nor desires, who puts away both

pleasant and unpleasant things, who is loyal-devoted-and-devout. (18–19) I love the man who is the same to friend and foe, [the same] whether he be respected or despised, the same in heat and cold, in pleasure as in pain, who has put away attachment and remains unmoved by praise or blame, who is taciturn, contented with whatever comes his way, having no home, of steady mind, [but] loyal-devoted-and-devout. (20) But as for those who reverence these deathless [words] of righteousness which I have just now spoken, putting their faith [in them], making Me their goal, my loving-devotees,—these do I love exceedingly.

14. 22–6: Radiance—activity—yes, delusion too,—when these arise he hates them not; and when [in turn] they cease he pines not after them. (23) As one indifferent he sits, by the constituents unruffled: 'So the constituents are busy': thus he thinks. Firm-based is he, unquavering. (24) The same in pleasure as in pain and self-assured, the same when faced with clods of earth or stones or gold; for him, wise man, are friend and foe of equal weight, equal the praise and blame [with which men cover him]. (25) Equal [his mind] in honour and disgrace, equal to ally and to enemy, he renounces every [busy] enterprise: 'He has transcended the constituents': so must men say. (26) And as to those who do me honour with spiritual exercise, in loyalty-and-love undeviating, passed [clean] beyond these constituents, to becoming Brahman they are conformed.

16. 1–5: Fearless and pure in heart, steadfast in the exercise of wisdom, open-handed and restrained, performing sacrifice, intent on studying Holy Writ, ascetic and upright, (2) none hurting, truthful, from anger free, renouncing [all], at peace, averse to calumny, compassionate to [all] beings, free from nagging greed, gentle, modest, never fickle, (3) ardent, patient, enduring, pure, not treacherous nor arrogant,—such is the man who is born to [inherit] a godly destiny. . . . (5) A godly destiny means deliverance.

17. 14–16: [Due] reverence to gods and Brāhmans, teachers and wise men, purity, uprightness, chastity, refusal to do harm,—[this] is [true] penance of the body. (15) Words that do not cause disquiet, [words] truthful, kind, and pleasing, the constant practice too of sacred recitation,—[this] is the penance of the tongue. (16) Serenity of mind and friendliness, silence and self-restraint, and the cleansing of one's affections,—this is called the penance of the mind.

V. *Brahman*

(*a*) *The Source of Material Nature*

5. 10: And on he works though he has [long] renounced attachment, ascribing his works to Brahman. . . .

14. 3–4: Great Brahman is to Me a womb, in it I plant the seed: from this derives the origin of all contingent beings. (4) In whatever womb whatever form arises-and-grows-together, of [all] those [forms] Great Brahman is the womb, I the father, giver of the seed.

(*b*) *The Sacrifice*

3. 14–16: From food do [all] contingent beings derive and food derives from rain; rain derives from sacrifice and sacrifice from works. (15) From Brahman work arises . . . and Brahman is born from the Imperishable; therefore is Brahman, penetrating everywhere, forever based on sacrifice. (16) So was the wheel in motion set: and whoso here fails to match his turning [with the turning of the wheel], living an evil life, the senses his pleasure-ground, lives out his life in vain.

4. 23–4: Attachment gone, deliverance won, his thoughts are fixed on wisdom: he works for sacrifice [alone], and all the work [he ever did] entirely melts away. (24) The offering is Brahman, Brahman the [sacrificial] ghee offered by Brahman in Brahman's fire: who sinks himself in this [sacrificial] act which is Brahman, to Brahman must he thereby go.

4. 31–2: Eating of the leavings of the sacrifice, the food of immortality, they come to primeval Brahman. This world is not for him who performs no sacrifice,—much less the other [world]. (32) So, many and various are the sacrifices spread out athwart the mouth of Brahman. They spring from work, all of them: . . . once you know this, you will win release.

(*c*) *Nirvāna*

2. 71–2: The man who puts away all desires and roams around from longing freed, who does not think, 'This I am', or 'This is mine', draws near to peace. (72) This is the fixed, still state of Brahman; he who wins through to this is nevermore perplexed. Standing therein at the time of death, to Nirvāna that is Brahman too he goes.

5. 6: . . . The sage who is integrated in spiritual exercise right soon to Brahman comes.

5. 19–21: . . . Devoid of imperfection and ever-the-same is Brahman: therefore in Brahman [stilled] (the wise) stand. (20) . . . Steadfast-and-still his soul, [all] unconfused, [the sage] will know Brahman, in Brahman [stilled] he'll stand. (21) . . . [His] self in Brahman integrated by spiritual exercise, he finds unfailing joy.

5. 24–6: His joy within, his bliss within, his light within, the man who-is-integrated-in-spiritual-exercise (*yogin*) becomes Brahman and draws nigh to Nirvāna that is Brahman too. (25) Nirvāna that is Brahman too win seers in whom [all] taint-of-imperfection is destroyed. . . . (26) Around these holy men whose thoughts are [fast] controlled, . . . knowing [at last] the self, fares Nirvāna that is Brahman too.

6. 14–15: Let him sit, [his] self all stilled, . . . integrated, [yet] intent on Me. (15) Thus let the athlete of the spirit be constant in integrating [him]self, his mind restrained; then will he approach that peace which has Nirvāna as its end and which subsists in Me.

6. 27–8: Upon this athlete of the spirit whose mind is stilled the highest joy descends: [all] passion laid to rest, free from [all] stain, Brahman he becomes. (28) [And] thus [all] flaws transcending, the athlete of the spirit, constant in integrating [him]self, with ease attains unbounded joy, Brahman's [saving] touch.

14. 26–7: And as to those who do Me honour with spiritual exercise, in loyalty-and-love undeviating, passed [clean] beyond these constituents, to becoming Brahman they are conformed. (27) For I am the base supporting Brahman,—immortal [Brahman] which knows no change. . . .

18. 50–4: Perfection found, now learn from Me how you may reach Brahman too: . . . it is wisdom's highest bourne. . . . (53) Let a man give up all thought of 'I', . . . let him not think of anything as 'mine', at peace;—[if he does this,] to becoming Brahman is he conformed. (54) Brahman become, with self serene, he grieves not nor desires; the same to all contingent beings he gains the highest love-and-loyalty to Me.

(*d*) *The Imperishable*

2. 17: Indestructible [alone] is That . . . by which this whole universe was spun: no one can bring destruction on That which does not pass away.

7. 29–30: Whoso shall strive to win release from old age and death, putting his trust in Me, will come to know that Brahman in its wholeness,—as it appertains to self, the whole [mystery] of works, (30) as it appertains to contingent beings, and to the divine. . . .

8. 3–4: The Imperishable is the highest Brahman; it is called 'inherent nature' in so far as it appertains to [an individual] self,—as the creative force known as 'works' which gives rise to the [separate] natures of contingent beings. (4) In so far as it appertains to [all] contingent beings, it is [their] perishable nature, and in so far as it appertains to the gods, [it is] 'person (spirit)'. In so far as it appertains to sacrifice [it is] I here in this body.

8. 13: . . . Oṁ, Brahman {in one syllable / the One Imperishable} . . . .

8. 20–1: Beyond [the Unmanifest] there is [yet] another mode of being,—beyond the Unmanifest [another] Unmanifest (*masc.*), primeval: this is he who does not fall to ruin when all contingent beings are destroyed. (21) Unmanifest [is he], surnamed 'Imperishable': this, men say, is the highest way and, this once won, there is no more returning: this is my highest home.

8. 24: . . . To Brahman do they go, the men who Brahman know.

12. 3–5: Those who revere the indeterminate Imperishable Unmanifest, unthinkable though coursing everywhere, sublime, aloof, unmoving, firm, (4) who hold in check the complex of the senses, in all things equal-minded, taking pleasure in the weal of all contingent beings, these too attain to Me. (5) [But] greater is the toil of those whose thinking clings to the Unmanifest; for difficult [indeed] it is for embodied men to reach-and-tread the unmanifested way.

13. 12–17: I will tell you that which should be known: once a man knows it, he attains to immortality. The highest Brahman It is called,—beginningless,—It is not Being nor is It Not-Being. (13) Hands and feet It has on every side, on every side eyes, heads, mouths, and ears; in the world all things encompassing [changeless] It abides. (14) Devoid of all the senses, It yet sheds light on all their qualities, [from all] detached, and yet supporting all; free from Nature's constituents, It yet experiences them. (15) Within all beings, yet without them; unmoved, It yet moves indeed; so subtle is It you cannot comprehend It; far off It stands, and yet how near It is! (16) Undivided in beings It abides, seeming divided: this is That which should be known,—[the one] who sustains, devours, and generates [all] beings. (17) Light of lights, 'Beyond the Darkness' It is called: [true] knowledge, what should be known, accessible to knowledge, established in the heart of all.

13. 30: When once a man can see [all] the diversity of contingent beings as abiding in One [alone] and their radiation out of It, then to Brahman he attains.

15. 16: In the world there are these two persons,—perishable the one, Imperishable the other: the 'perishable' is all contingent beings, the 'Imperishable' they call the 'sublime, aloof (*kūṭastha*)'.

17. 23–8: OṀ — THAT — IT IS: This has been handed down, a threefold pointer to Brahman: by this were allotted their proper place of old Brāhmans, Veda, and sacrifice. (24) And so [all] acts of sacrifice, the giving of alms, and penance enjoined by [sacred] ordinances and ever again [enacted] by Brahman's devotees begin with the utterance of [the word] Oṁ.

(25) THAT: [so saying] do men who hanker for deliverance perform the various acts of sacrifice, penance, and the gift of alms, having no thought for the fruits [they bring].

(26) IT IS: in this the meanings are conjoined of 'Being' and of 'Good'; so too the [same] word *sat* is appropriately used for works that call forth praise. (27) In sacrifice, in penance, in the gift of alms [the same word] *sat* is used, meaning 'steadfastness': and works performed with these purposes [in mind], [these] too are surnamed *sat*. (28) Whatever offering is made in unbelief, whatever given, whatever act of penance undertaken, whatever done,—of that is said *asat*, 'It is not': for naught it is in this world or the next.

VI. *God*

(*a*) *His Creative Power and Activity*

3. 21–4: Whatever the noblest does, that too will others do: the standard that he sets all the world will follow. (22) In the three worlds there is nothing that I need do, nor anything unattained that I need to gain, yet work [is the element] in which I move. (23) For if I were not tirelessly to busy Myself with works, then would men everywhere follow in my footsteps. (24) If I were not to do my work, these worlds would fall to ruin, and I should be a worker of confusion, destroying these [my] creatures.

4. 6: . . . By my creative energy (*māyā*) I consort with Nature—which is mine—and come to be [in time].

4. 13–14: The four-caste system did I generate with categories of 'constituents' and works; of this I am the doer, [the agent,]— . . . [and yet I am] the Changeless One who does not do [or act]. (14) Works can never affect Me. I have no yearning for their fruits. Whoso should know that this is how I am will never be bound by works.

7. 4–6: (God's two Natures), see II (*a*) (i).

7. 10: Know that I am the primeval seed of all contingent beings. . . .

7. 12–15: Know too that [all] states of being, whether they be of [Nature's constituent] Goodness, Passion, or Darkness proceed from Me; but I am not in them, they are in Me. (13) By these three states of being inhering in the constituents this whole universe is led astray and does not understand that I am far beyond them and that I neither change-nor-pass-away. (14) For [all] this is my creative power (*māyā*), composed of the constituents, divine, hard to transcend. Whoso shall put his trust in Me alone, shall pass beyond this [my] uncanny power (*māyā*). (15) Doers of evil, deluded, base, put not their trust in Me; their wisdom swept away by [this] uncanny power, they cleave to a devilish mode of existence.

7. 25: Since [my] creative power (*māyā*) and the way I use it (*yoga*) conceal Me, I am not revealed to all. . . .

9. 4–5: By Me, Unmanifest in form, all this universe was spun: . . . (5) . . . Behold my sovereign skill-in-works (*yoga*).

9. 8–10: Subduing my own material Nature ever again I emanate this whole host of beings,—powerless [themselves], from Nature comes the power. (9) These works [of mine] neither bind-nor-limit Me: as one indifferent I sit among these works, detached. (10) [A world of] moving and unmoving things material Nature brings to birth while I look-on-and-supervise: this is the cause [and this the means] by which the world revolves.

9. 17–19: I am the father of this world, mother, ordainer, grandsire, . . . (18) . . . the seed that passes not away. (19) It is I who pour out heat, hold back the rain and send it forth. . . .

10. 7–8: Whoso should know this my far-flung power a d how I use it (*yoga*), [whoso should know these] as they really are, is [truly] integrated; . . . (8) The source of all am I; from Me all things proceed. . . .

10. 34: I am death that snatches all away, and the origin of creatures yet to be.

10. 39–41: What is the seed of all contingent beings, that too am I. No being is there, whether moving or unmoving, that exists or could exist apart from Me. (40) Of [these] my far-flung powers divine there is no end; as much as I have said concerning them must serve as an example. (41) Whatever being shows wide power, prosperity, or strength, be sure that this derives from [but] a fragment of my glory.

11. 33: . . . Long since have these men in truth been slain by Me: yours it is to be the mere occasion.

11. 43: You are the father of the world of moving and unmoving things, You their venerable teacher, most highly prized; none is there like You,—how could there be another greater?—in the three worlds. . . .

12. 6–8: (God's saving activity), see III (*e*).

14. 3–4: Great Brahman is to Me a womb, in it I plant the seed: from this derives the origin of all contingent beings. (4) In whatever womb whatever form arises-and-grows-together, of [all] those [forms] Great Brahman is the womb, I the father, giver of the seed.

16. 19: Birth after birth in this revolving round, these vilest among men, strangers to [all] good, obsessed with hate and cruel, I ever hurl into devilish wombs.

18. 61: In the region of the heart of all contingent beings dwells the Lord, twirling them hither and thither by his uncanny power (*māyā*) [like puppets] mounted on a machine.

(*b*) *His Incarnations*

4. 6–8: Unborn am I, changeless is my Self, of [all] contingent beings I am the Lord! Yet by my creative power (*māyā*) I consort with Nature —which is mine—and come to be [in time]. (7) For whenever the law of righteousness withers away and lawlessness arises, then do I generate myself [on earth]. (8) For the protection of the good, for the destruction of evil-doers, for the setting up of the law of righteousness I come into being age after age.

7. 24: Fools think of Me as one unmanifest [before] who has reached [the stage of] manifestation: they know nothing of my higher state, the Changeless, All-Highest.

9. 11: For that a human form I have assumed fools scorn Me, knowing nothing of my higher state,—great Lord of contingent beings.

(*c*) *His Attributes*

5. 29: Knowing Me to be the proper object of sacrifice and mortification, great Lord of all the worlds, friend of all contingent beings, he reaches peace.

7. 26: [All] beings past and present and yet to come I know. . . .

8. 4: . . . In so far as [Brahman] appertains to sacrifice [it is] I here in this body.

8. 9: The Ancient Seer, Governor [of all things, yet] smaller than the small, Ordainer of all, in form unthinkable, sun-coloured beyond the darkness,—let a man meditate on Him [as such].

9. 11: . . . My higher state,—great Lord of contingent beings.

9. 16–18: I am the rite, the sacrifice, the offering for the dead, the healing herb; I am the sacred formula, the sacred butter am I: I am the fire and the oblation offered [in the fire]. (17) I am the father of this world, mother, ordainer, grandsire, [all] that need be known; vessel of purity [am I, the sacred syllable] Oṁ, and the Rig-, Sāma-, and

Yajur-Vedas too. (18) [I am] the Way, sustainer, Lord, and witness, [true] home and refuge, friend,—origin and dissolution and the stable state [between],—a treasure-house, the seed that passes not away.

9. 24: It is I who of all sacrifices am recipient and Lord. . . .

10. 15: By [your] Self You Yourself do know [your] Self, O You all-highest Person, You who bestow being on contingent beings, Lord of [all] beings, God of gods, and Lord of [all] the world.

10. 21–38: (God is the best in every category of being), see Translation.

10. 30: . . . Among those who reckon I am Time. . . .

10. 32: Among emanations the beginning and the end and the middle too am I; among sciences I am the science concerned with Self. . . .

10. 33–4: . . . Truly I am imperishable Time, I, the Ordainer, with face turned every way. (34) And I am Death that snatches all away, and the origin of creatures yet to be.

11. 9–45: (The great Theophany), see Translation.

11. 16: . . . End, middle, or beginning I cannot see in You, O Monarch Universal, [manifest] in every form!

11. 19: Beginning, middle, or end You do not know,—how infinite your strength!

11. 32: Time am I, wreaker of the world's destruction, matured,—[grimly] resolved here to swallow up the worlds.

11. 40: All hail [to You], . . . the All! How infinite your strength, how limitless your prowess! All things You bring to their consummation: hence You are All.

11. 43: You are the father of the world of moving and unmoving things, You their venerable teacher, most highly prized; none is there like You,—how could there be another greater?—in the three worlds. Oh, matchless is your power.

13. 2: Know that I am the 'knower of the field' in every field.

(*d*) *The Changeless Source of Change*

4. 6: Unborn am I, changeless is my Self.

4. 13: . . . [I am] the Changeless One who does not do [or act].

7. 7: Higher than I there is nothing whatsoever: on Me this universe is strung like clustered pearls upon a thread.

7. 13: . . . I am far beyond [the constituents] and I neither-change-nor-pass-away.

7. 18: . . . [The man of wisdom] puts his trust in Me, the one all-highest Way.

7. 19: . . . [Krishna,] Vasudeva's son, is All.

7. 24: Fools think of Me as one unmanifest [before] who has reached [the stage of] manifestation: they know nothing of my higher state, the Changeless, All-Highest.

8. 21: Unmanifest [is he], surnamed 'Imperishable': this, men say, is the highest way and, this once won, there is no more returning: this is my highest home.

9. 4–6: By Me, Unmanifest in form, all this universe was spun: in Me subsist all beings, I do not subsist in them. (5) And [yet] contingent beings do not subsist in Me,—behold my sovereign skill-in-works (*yoga*): my Self sustains [all] beings, It does not subsist in them; It causes them to be-and-grow. (6) As in [wide] space subsists the mighty wind blowing [at will] ever and everywhere, so do all contingent beings subsist in Me.

9. 9–10: . . . As one indifferent I sit among these works, detached. (10) [A world of] moving and unmoving things material Nature brings to birth while I look-on-and-supervise.

9. 13: . . . [Me] the beginning of [all] contingent beings, as Him who passes not away.

9. 19: . . . Deathlessness am I and death, what IS and what is not.

9. 29: In all contingent beings the same am I. . . .

10. 2–3: None knows from whence I came,—not the gods' celestial host nor yet the mighty seers: for I am the beginning of the gods [themselves] as of the mighty seers and all in every way. (3) Whoso shall know Me as unborn, beginningless, great Lord of [all] the worlds, shall never know delusion among men, from every evil freed.

11. 18: You are the Imperishable, [You] wisdom's highest goal; You, of this universe the last prop-and-resting-place, You the changeless, [You] the guardian of eternal law, You the primeval Person.

13. 27: The same in all contingent beings, abiding [without change], the Highest Lord, when all things fall to ruin, [Himself] is not destroyed.

(e) The One in the Many

9. 15: Others again . . . worship Me as One and yet as Manifold, in many a guise with face turned every way.

11. 7: Do you today the whole universe behold centred here in One, with all that it contains of moving and unmoving things; [behold it] in my body.

11. 13: Then did the son of Pāndu see the whole [wide] universe in One converged, there in the body of the God of gods, yet divided out in multiplicity.

13. 30–3: When once a man can see [all] the diversity of contingent beings as abiding in One [alone] and their radiation out of It, then to Brahman he attains. (31) Because this Highest Self (= the Mighty Lord (13. 22)) knows no beginning, no constituents, it does not pass away: though abiding in [many] a body, it does not act nor is it defiled. (32) Just as the ether, roving everywhere, knows no defilement, so subtle [is its essence], so does [this] Self, though everywhere abiding embodied, know no defilement. (33) As the one sun lights up this whole universe, so does the 'owner of the field' illumine the whole field.

(f) His Transcendence

6. 15: . . . that peace which has Nirvāna as its end and which subsists in Me.

8. 22: But that highest Person (sc. beyond the Imperishable Unmanifest) is to be won by love-and-worship directed to no other. In Him do all beings subsist; by Him this universe is spun.

10. 12–13: [All-]Highest Brahman, highest home, [all-]highest vessel of purity are You. All seers agree that You are the Person eternal and divine, primeval God, unborn and all-pervading Lord.

10. 42: . . . This whole universe I hold apart [supporting it] with [but] one fragment [of Myself], yet I abide [unchanging.]

11. 37–8: And why should they not revere You, great [as is your] Self, more to be prized even than Brahman, first Creator, Infinite, Lord of the gods, home of the universe? You are the Imperishable, what IS and what is not and what surpasses both. (38) You are the Primal God, Primeval Person, You of this universe the last prop-and-resting-place, You the knower and what is to be known, [You our] highest home, O You whose forms are infinite, by You the whole universe was spun.

13. 22: [And yet another One there is who,] surveying and approving, supports and [Himself] experiences [the constituents of Nature], the

Mighty Lord: 'Highest Self' some call Him, the 'Highest Person' in this body.

14. 27: I am the base supporting Brahman,—immortal [Brahman] which knows no change,—[supporting] too the eternal law of righteousness and absolute beatitude.

15. 17–18: But there is [yet] another Person, the [All-]Sublime, surnamed 'All-Highest Self': the three worlds He enters-and-pervades, sustaining them,—the Lord who passes not away. (18) Since I transcend the perishable and am more exalted than the Imperishable itself, so am I extolled in Vedic as in common speech as the 'Person [All-]Sublime'.

(*g*) *His Immanence*

7. 8–11: In water I am the flavour, in sun and moon the light, in all the Vedas [the sacred syllable] Oṁ, in space [I am] sound, in men [their] manliness am I. (9) Pure fragrance in the earth am I, flame's onset in the fire: [and] life am I in all contingent beings, in ascetics [their] fierce austerity. (10) Know that I am the primeval seed of all contingent beings: insight in men of insight, glory in the glorious am I. (11) Power in the powerful am I,—[such power] as knows neither desire nor passion: desire am I in contingent beings, [but such desire as] does not conflict with righteousness. (Cf. 10. 19–39.)

10. 20: I am the Self established in the heart of all contingent beings.

15. 12–15: The splendour centred in the sun which bathes the whole world in light, [the splendour] in the moon and fire,—know that it [all] is mine. (13) [Thus] too I penetrate the earth and so sustain [all] beings with my strength; becoming [the moon-plant] Soma, I, the very sap [of life], cause all healing herbs to grow. (14) Becoming the [digestive] fire in [the bodies of] all men I dwell in the body of all that breathes; conjoined with the inward and outward breaths I digest the fourfold food. (15) I make my dwelling in the hearts of all: from Me stem memory, wisdom, the dispelling [of doubt]. Through all the Vedas it is I who should be known, for the maker of the Vedas' end am I, and I the Vedas know.

16. 18: . . . [These vilest among men] envying and hating Me who dwell in their bodies as I dwell in all.

17. 5–6: . . . Some men there are who . . . savagely mortify [their flesh] . . . and so torment the mass of [living] beings whose home their body is . . . and [with them] Me Myself within [that same] body abiding.

18. 61: In the region of the heart of all contingent beings dwells the Lord, twirling them hither and thither by his uncanny power (*māyā*) [like puppets] mounted on a machine.

(*h*) *Knowing the Unknown God*

7. 3: Among thousands of men but one, maybe, will strive for [self-] perfection, and even among [these] athletes of the spirit who have won perfection['s crown] but one, maybe, will come to know Me as I really am.

7. 26: . . . There is no one at all that knows Me.

7. 29–30: Whoso shall strive to win release from old age and death, putting his trust in Me, will come to know that Brahman in its wholeness,—as it appertains to self, the whole [mystery] of works, (30) as it appertains to contingent beings, and to the divine,—and Me [too] as I appertain to sacrifice. And whoso shall know Me [thus] even at the time of passing on, will know [Me] with an integrated mind.

9. 17: I am . . . [all] that need be known.

10. 2: None knows from whence I came.

11. 38: You are . . . the knower and what is to be known.

18. 55: By love-and-loyalty he comes to know Me as I really am, how great I am and who.

VII. *Life after Death*

8. 5–6: Whoso at the hour of death . . . bears Me in mind and passes on, accedes to my own mode of being. . . . (6) Whatever state a man may bear in mind when in the end he casts his mortal frame aside, even to that state does he accede, for ever does that state make him grow into itself.

8. 8: . . . By meditating on the divine exalted Person, [that man to that Person] goes.

8. 10: . . . At the time of passing on, by love-and-devotion integrated and by the power of spiritual exercise too . . . that man will draw nigh to that divine exalted Person.

8. 13: Let a man utter [the word] Oṁ, Brahman in one syllable, keeping Me in mind; then, when he departs, leaving aside the body, he will tread the highest way.

8. 23–7: Some to return, some never to return, athletes of the spirit set forth when they pass on; the times [and seasons] of them all I shall [now] declare. (24) Fire, light, day, [the moon's] light [fortnight], the six months of the [sun's] northern course,—dying in these to Brahman do they go, the men who Brahman know. (25) Smoke, night, [the moon's] dark [fortnight], the six months of the [sun's] southern course,—[dying] in these an athlete of the spirit wins the light of the moon, and back he comes again. (26) For these two courses,—light and dark,—are deemed to be primeval [laws] on earth. One leads to [the place of] no return, by the other one returns again. (27) Knowing these two courses no athlete of the spirit whatever is perplexed.

14. 14–18: When an embodied [self] comes face to face with [the body's] dissolution and Goodness prevails, then will he reach the spotless worlds of those who know the highest. (15) [Another] goes to his demise when Passion [predominates]; he will be born among such men as cling to works: and as to him who dies when Darkness [has the upper hand], he will be born in the wombs of deluded fools. . . . (18) Upward is the path of those who abide in Goodness, in the middle stand the men of Passion. Stuck in the modes of the vilest constituent the men of Darkness go below.

18. 12: Unwanted—wanted—mixed: threefold is the fruit of work,—[this they experience] at death who have not surrendered [self], but not at all such men as have renounced.

VIII. *Traditional Religion*

2. 42–6: . . . [The souls] of men who cling to pleasure and to power, their minds seduced by flowery words, are not attuned to enstasy. Such men give vent to flowery words, lacking discernment, delighting in the Veda's lore, saying there is naught else. Desire is their essence, paradise their goal,—their words preach [re-]birth as the fruit of works and expatiate about the niceties of ritual by which pleasure and power can be achieved. (45) [All Nature is made up of] the three 'constituents': these are the Veda's goal. . . . (46) As much use as there is in a water-tank flooded with water on every side, so much is there in all the Vedas for the Brāhman who discerns.

2. 52–3: When your soul passes beyond delusion's turbid quicksands, then will you learn disgust for what has been heard [ere now] and for what may yet be heard. (53) When your soul, by scripture once bewildered, stands motionless and still, immovable in enstasy, then will you attain to {integration / sameness-and-indifference} (*yoga*).

6. 44: . . . Even he who only wants to know what integration is, transcends that 'Brahman' which is [no more than] wordy rites.

8. 28: For knowledge of the Veda, for sacrifice, for grim austerities, for gifts of alms a meed of merit is laid down: all this the athlete of the spirit leaves behind who knows this [secret teaching; and knowing it] he draws right nigh to the exalted primal state.

9. 17: I am . . . the Rig-, Sāma-, and Yajur-Vedas too.

9. 20–1: Trusting in the three Vedas the Soma-drinkers, purged of [ritual] fault, worship Me with sacrifice, seeking to go to paradise: these win through to the pure world of the lord of the gods and taste in heaven the gods' celestial joys. (21) [But] once they have [to the full] enjoyed the broad expanse of paradise, their merit exhausted, they come [back] to the world of men. And so it is that those who stick fast to the three Vedas receive [a reward] that comes and goes; for it desire that they desire.

13. 25: But some, not knowing thus, hear it from others and revere it; and even these, taking their stand on what they hear, overcome death indeed.

15. 1–3: With roots above and boughs beneath, they say, the undying fig-tree [stands]: its leaves are the Vedic hymns: who knows it knows the Veda. . . . (3) . . . this fig-tree with its roots so fatly nourished,—[take] the stout axe of detachment and cut it down!

15. 15: . . . Through all the Vedas it is I who should be known, for the maker of the Vedas' end am I, and I the Vedas know.

16. 23–4: Whoso forsakes the ordinance of Scripture (*śāstra*) and lives at the whim of his own desires, wins not perfection, [finds] no comfort, [treads] not the highest Way. (24) Therefore let Scripture (*śāstra*) be your norm, determining what is right and wrong. Once you know what the ordinance of Scripture bids you do, you should perform down here the works [therein prescribed].

17. 23: OṀ — THAT — IT IS: This has been handed down, a threefold pointer to Brahman: by this were allotted their proper place of old Brāhmans, Veda, and sacrifice.

18. 66: Give up all things of law, turn to Me, your only refuge, [for] I will deliver you from all evils; have no care.

IX. *Worship of other Gods*

3. 11–12: With [sacrifice] shall ye sustain the gods so that the gods may sustain you [in return]. Sustaining one another [thus] ye shall achieve the highest good. (12) For, [so] sustained by sacrifice the gods will give you the food of your desire. Whoso enjoys their gift yet gives them nothing [in return] is a thief, no more nor less.

4. 12: Desiring success in their (ritual) acts men worship here the gods; for swiftly in the world of men comes success engendered by the act [itself].

7. 20–3: [All] wisdom swept away by manifold desires, men put their trust in other gods, relying on diverse rules-and-precepts: for their own nature forces them thereto. (21) Whatever form, [whatever god,] a devotee with faith desires to honour, that very faith do I confirm in him [making it] unswerving-and-secure. (22) Firm-stablished in that faith he seeks to reverence that [god] and thence he gains his desires, though it is I who am the true dispenser. (23) But finite is the reward of such men of little wit: whoso worships the gods, to the gods will [surely] go, but whoso loves-and-worships Me, to Me will come indeed.

9. 23–5: Even those who lovingly devote themselves to other gods and sacrifice to them, full filled with faith, do really worship Me though the rite may differ from the norm. (24) For it is I who of all sacrifices am recipient and Lord, but they do not know Me as I really am, and so they fall [back into the world of men]. (25) To the gods go the gods' devotees, to the ancestors their votaries, to disembodied spirits go the worshippers of these, but those who worship Me shall come to Me.

17. 2–4: Threefold is the faith of embodied [selves]; each [of the three] springs from [a man's] own nature. [The first is] of Goodness, [the second] of Passion, of Darkness [is the third]. Listen to this. (3) Faith is connatural to the soul of every man: man is instinct with faith: as is his faith, so too must he be. (4) To the gods do men of Goodness offer sacrifice, to sprites and monsters men of Passion, to disembodied spirits and the assembled spirits of the dead the others,—men of Darkness,—offer sacrifice.

x. *Faith*

7. 14: . . . Whoso shall put his trust in Me alone, shall pass beyond this [my] uncanny power (*māyā*).

7. 21–2: Whatever form, [whatever god,] a devotee with faith desires to honour, that very faith do I confirm in him [making it] unswerving-and-secure. (22) Firm-stablished in that faith he seeks to reverence that [god] and thence he gains his desires, though it is I who am the true dispenser.

17. 3: Faith is connatural to the soul of every man: man is instinct with faith: as is his faith, so too must he be.

18. 71: The man of faith, not cavilling, who listens [to this my Word], he too shall win deliverance, and attain to the goodly worlds of those whose works are pure.

XI. '*Person*'

8. 4: [Brahman] in so far as it appertains to the gods is 'person' (spirit).

8. 8: Let a man's thoughts be integrated by spiritual exercise and constant striving: let them not stray to anything else at all; so by meditating on the divine exalted Person, [that man to that Person] goes.

10. 12: . . . You are the Person, eternal and divine. . . .

10. 15: . . . O You all-highest Person, . . .

11. 18: . . . You are the primeval Person . . . (= 11. 38).

13. 19–23: 'Nature' and 'Person': know that these two are both beginningless: and know that change and quality arise from Nature. (20) Material Nature, they say, is [itself] the cause of cause, effect, and agency, while 'person' is said to be the cause in the experience of pleasure and pain. (21) For 'person' is lodged in material Nature, experiencing the 'constituents' that arise from it; because he attaches himself to these he comes to birth in good and evil wombs. (22) [And yet another One there is who,] surveying and approving, supports and [Himself] experiences [the constituents of Nature], the Mighty Lord: 'Highest Self' some call Him, the 'Highest Person' in this body. (23) Whoever knows 'person', material Nature, and its constituents to be such, in whatever state he be, he is not born again.

13. 26: Whatever being comes to be, be it motionless or moving, [derives its being] from the union of 'field' and 'knower of the field'.

15. 4: Search out that [high] estate to which, when once men go, they come not back again. 'I fly for succour to that primeval Person from whom flowed forth primordial creativity.'

15. 16–17: In the world there are these two persons,—perishable the one, Imperishable the other: the 'perishable' is all contingent beings, the 'Imperishable' they call the 'sublime, aloof'. (17) But there is [yet] another Person, the [All-]Sublime, surnamed 'All-Highest Self': the three worlds He enters-and-pervades, sustaining them,—the Lord who passes not away.

INDEX OF PASSAGES CITED

[N.B. *Italic type* indicates that the passage is translated wholly or in part, or fully paraphrased. **Bold type** indicates that the passage is commented on.]

(i) VEDA

(ii) THE EPICS
(a) Mahābhārata (critical edition unless otherwise stated)

(b) Rāmāyana

(iii) OTHER HINDU TEXTS
(a) *Brahma-sūtras*

GENERAL INDEX

[N.B. There are no references to the Translation or the Appendix since these merely reduplicate Part III (Transliteration, translation, and commentary).]

abhāva, **128**, 206.

Absolute, the, (*see also* Brahman), 129, 134, 135, 142, 146, 159, 167, 183, 187, 190, 228, 234, 335, 364, 380, 388; and God, 8, 27, 153, 275, **321–7**.

action (see also *karma*, works), **160**, 198, 207, 384, 389; and contemplation, 18; and inactivity, 18, 188–9, 201, 206.

adhibhūta, 255, **259–60**, 367.

adhidaivata, 255, **259–60**.

adhyātma, **173**, 255, 256, **259–60**, 303, 337, 363.

Ādityas, 297, 304, 308.

agape, 285.

Agni, Krishna as, 315.

Agnihotra ('Fire-sacrifice'), 193.

ahaṁkāra (*see* ego), 140.

Airāvata, Krishna as, 299.

All, the, 9, 37, 126, 134; in God, 33, 34, 35.

alms-giving, 20, 248, 271, 272, 283, 318, 319, 372, 375, 377, 382, 385, 386; and the three 'constituents', 379.

Ananta, Krishna as, 299.

ancestors, 282.

anger, 150, 154, 160, 175, 176, 185, 212, 216, 221, 227, 369, 372, 374, 397.

Anselm, St., 258.

Anugītā, 7, 363.

Aquinas, St. Thomas, 148, 382.

Aristotle, 129.

Arjuna, 6, 7, 10, 21 and *passim*; his confusion, 161, 402; his despondency, 117, 122 ff; his relationship to Krishna, 301; refuses to fight, 124.

Arnold, Sir Edwin, 1.

Aryaman, Krishna as, 299.

asat, 'Not-being' q.v. **128–9**; is matter, 281.

asceticism (*see also* austerity, mortification, penance) 264, 318, 319, 375, 377, 380; and the three 'constituents', 378–9; exaggerated, 376.

Aśvins, 304, 308.

'athlete of the spirit' (*see also* Yogin), 25, 33, 222, 224–6, 230–3, 235, 237, 244, 265, 269, 271, 272, 294, 296, 324, 326, 365, 384; highest type of ascetic, 34, 219, **241–2**, 250.

ātman (*see* self), **150**, 152, 163, 171, 177, 190, 224, 245.

Ātman-Brahman, 128, 129, 131.

attachment, 18, 146, 152, 154, 165, 200, 201, 206, 207, **210**, 330, 363; to God, 35, 162, **244**, 320, 353; to objects of sense, 220; to worklessness, 145; to works, 20, 122, 172, 189, 353, 386, 387, 390.

austerity (*see also* asceticism, mortification, penance), 247, 272.

Bādarāyana, 335.

Being (*see also* sat), **128–9**, 159, 189, 191, 253, 256, 267, 281, 314, 339–40, 381, 382; equals 'good', 148, 382; unity of, 228.

Bhakti (*see also* love of God), 2, **26–28**, 33, 136, 185, 186, 235, 237, 242, 243, 254–5, 263–4, 269, 270, 273, 274, 279, **294**, 320, 321–2, 326, **327–8**, **329–31**, 332, 337, 351, 357–358, 368, 396, 401; as means, 27; classes of devotees, **250–1**, **281–2**; higher, **27–28**, **30–36**, 251, **265–6**, **279**, 285, **286–90**, **397–8**, 399; lower, 27, **283–6**, 398; meanings of, 26–27, 28, **181**.

bhakti-yoga, 146.

bhāva, **127–8**, 262, 294, 368, 400.

bhāvanā, **155**, 262 (*bhāvita*), 275.

Bhave, Vinoba, 1 n. 2.